INTERNATIONAL POLITICS

INTERNATIONAL POLITICS

Enduring Concepts and Contemporary Issues

SEVENTH EDITION

ROBERT J. ART
Brandeis University

ROBERT JERVIS
Columbia University

PEARSON
Longman

New York • San Francisco • Boston
London • Toronto • Sydney • Tokyo • Singapore • Madrid
Mexico City • Munich • Paris • Cape Town • Hong Kong • Montreal

Vice President and Publisher: Priscilla McGeehon
Executive Editor: Eric Stano
Acquisitions Editor: Edward Costello
Senior Marketing Manager: Elizabeth Fogarty
Production Manager: Denise Phillip
Project Coordination, Text Design, and Electronic Page Makeup: WestWords, Inc.
Cover Designer/Manager: John Callahan
Cover Illustration/Photo: Courtesy of PhotoDisc
Senior Manufacturing Buyer: Alfred C. Dorsey
Printer and Binder: R. R. Donnelley and Sons
Cover Printer: The Lehigh Press, Inc.

Library of Congress Cataloging-in-Publication Data

International politics : enduring concepts and contemporary issues / [edited by] Robert J. Art, Robert Jervis. — 7th ed.
   p. cm.
  ISBN 0-321-20947-8 (pbk.)
  1. International relations. 2. World politics — 1989– 3. Globalization. I. Art, Robert J. II. Jervis, Robert, 1940–

  JZ1242.I574 2005
  327.1—dc22

          2004006652

Please visit our website at *http://www.ablongman.com*

ISBN 0-321-20947-8

3 4 5 6 7 8 9 10—DOC—07   06   05   04

BRIEF CONTENTS

■ DETAILED CONTENTS

▬▬ PREFACE

The first edition of *International Politics* appeared in 1973. Since then, the field of international relations has experienced a dramatic enrichment in the subjects studied and the quality of works published. Political economy came into its own as an important subfield in the 1970s. New and important works in the field of security studies appeared. The literature on cooperation among states flourished in the early 1980s, and important studies about the environment began to appear in the mid-1980s. Feminist, postmodernist, and constructivist critiques of the mainstream made their appearance also. With the end of the Cold War, these new issues came to the fore: human rights, the tension between state sovereignty and the obligations of the international community, the global environment, civil wars, failed states, and nation-building. The growing diversity of the field has closely mirrored the actual developments in international relations.

As for the previous editions, in fashioning the seventh, we have kept in mind both the new developments in world politics and the literature that has accompanied them. Central to this edition, though, as for the other six, is our belief that the realm of international politics differs fundamentally from that of domestic politics. Therefore, we have continued to put both the developments and the literature in the context of the patterns that still remain valid for understanding the differences between politics in an anarchic environment and politics that takes place under a government. The theme for this edition continues to revolve around enduring concepts and contemporary issues in world politics.

The seventh edition retains the four major subdivisions of the sixth edition. We have left Part One as it appears in the sixth edition, but have added new selections by Hans J. Morgenthau, John J. Mearsheimer, and Robert O. Keohane. Part Two retains the first two subsections of the sixth edition, but with two new selections by Robert Art and Robert Pape. In addition, a new subsection on the spread of nuclear weapons has been added with articles by Scott Sagan and Kenneth Waltz. We have consolidated the discussion of globalization in Part Three, and added two new selections by Jeffrey Frankel and William Finnegan. Finally, in Part Four, we have added two new subsections—one on the uses of American power; the other on failed states, civil war, and nation-building—and added eleven new selections by Jessica Stern, Robert Jervis, John Ikenberry, Charles Krauthammer, Joseph Nye, Robert Rotberg, Paul Collier, James Dobbins, Thomas Schelling, Moisés Naím, and Jack Rakove.

The seventh edition of *International Politics* is 40 percent new, but it continues to follow the four principles that have guided us throughout all previous editions:

1. A selection of subjects that, even though they do not exhaustively cover the field of international politics, nevertheless encompasses most of the essential topics that we teach in our introductory courses.
2. Individual readings that are mainly analytical in content, that take issue with one another, and that thereby introduce the student to the fundamental debates and points of view in the field.
3. Editors' introductions to each part that summarize the central concepts the student must master, that organize the central themes of each part, and that relate the readings to one another.
4. A reader that can be used either as the core around which to design an introductory course or as the primary supplement to enrich an assigned text.

Finally, in putting together the fourth, fifth, sixth, and seventh editions, we received excellent advice from the following colleagues, whom we would like to thank for the time and care they took: Andrew Bennett, Georgetown University; Timothy McKeown, University of North Carolina at Chapel Hill; Roslin Simowitz, University of Texas at Arlington; Robert J. Griffiths, University of North Carolina at Greensboro; Linda S. Adams, Baylor University; Timothy M. Cole, University of Maine; Robert C. Gray, Franklin & Marshall College; James A. Mitchell, California State University, Northridge; Margaret E. Scranton, University of Arkansas at Little Rock; David G. Becker, Dartmouth College; James A. Caporaso, University of Washington; Ken Wise, Creighton University; Sonia Gardenas, Trinity College; Philip Schrodt, University of Kansas; and Jane Cramer, University of Oregon.

Robert J. Art

Robert Jervis

PART 1
Anarchy and Its Consequences

Unlike domestic politics, international politics takes place in an arena that has no central governing body. From this central fact flow important consequences for the behavior of states. In Part One, we explore three of them: the role that principles and morality can and should play in statecraft; the effects that anarchy has on how states view and relate to one another; and the ways that the harsher edges of anarchy can be mitigated, even if not wholly removed.

POWER AND PRINCIPLE IN STATECRAFT

Citizens, students, and scholars alike often take up the study of international politics because they want their country to behave in as principled a way as possible. But they soon discover that principle and power, morality and statecraft do not easily mix. Why should this be? Is it inevitable? Can and should states seek to do good in the world? Will they endanger themselves and harm others if they try?

These are timeless questions, having been asked by observers of international politics in nearly every previous era. They therefore make a good starting point for thinking about the nature of international politics and the choices states face in our era. Hans J. Morgenthau, one of the leading proponents of the approach known as Realism (also known as power politics), takes the classic Realist position: universal standards of morality cannot be an invariable guide to statecraft because there is an "ineluctable tension between the moral command and the requirements of successful political action." Rather than base statecraft on morality, Morgenthau argues that state actors must think and act in terms of power and must do whatever it takes to defend the national interests of their state. J. Ann Tickner, commenting on the primacy of power in Morgenthau's writings, explains that what he considers to be a realistic description of international politics is only a picture of the past and therefore not a prediction about the future, and proposes what she considers to be a feminist alternative. A world in which state actors think of power in terms of collective empowerment, not in terms of leverage over one another, could produce more cooperative outcomes and pose fewer conflicts between the dictates of morality and the power of self-interest.

THE CONSEQUENCES OF ANARCHY

Even those who argue that morality should play a large role in statecraft acknowledge that international politics is not like domestic politics. In the latter, there is government; in the former, there is none. As a consequence, no agency exists above the individual states with authority and power to make laws and settle disputes. States can make commitments and treaties, but no sovereign power ensures compliance and punishes deviations. This—the absence of a supreme power—is what is meant by the anarchic environment of international politics. Anarchy is therefore said to constitute a *state of war:* when all else fails, force is the *ultima ratio*—the final and legitimate arbiter of disputes among states.

The state of war does not mean that every nation is constantly at the brink of war or actually at war with other nations. Most countries, though, do feel threatened by some states at some time, and every state has experienced periods of intense insecurity. No two contiguous states, moreover, have had a history of close, friendly relations uninterrupted by severe tension if not outright war. Because a nation cannot look to a supreme body to enforce laws, nor count on other nations for constant aid and support, it must rely on its own efforts, particularly for defense against attack. Coexistence in an anarchic environment thus requires *self-help*. The psychological outlook that self-help breeds is best described by a saying common among British statesmen since Palmerston: "Great Britain has no permanent enemies or permanent friends, she has only permanent interests."

Although states must provide the wherewithal to achieve their own ends, they do not always reach their foreign policy goals. The goals may be grandiose; the means available, meager. The goals may be attainable; the means selected, inappropriate. But even if the goals are realistic and the means both available and appropriate, a state can be frustrated in pursuit of its ends. The reason is simple, but fundamental to an understanding of international politics: what one state does will inevitably impinge on some other states—on some beneficially, but on others adversely. What one state desires another may covet. What one thinks its just due another may find threatening. Steps that a state takes to achieve its goals may be rendered useless by the countersteps others take. No state, therefore, can afford to disregard the effects its actions will have on other nations' behavior. In this sense state behavior is contingent: what one state does is dependent in part upon what others do. Mutual dependence means that each must take the others into account.

Mutual dependence affects nothing more powerfully than it does security—the measures states take to protect their territory. Like other foreign-policy goals, the security of one state is contingent upon the behavior of other states. Herein lies the *security dilemma* to which each state is subject: In its efforts to preserve or enhance its own security, one state can take measures that decrease the security of other states and cause them to take countermeasures that neutralize the actions of the first state and that may even menace it. The first state may feel impelled to take additional actions that will provoke additional countermeasures . . . and so forth. The security dilemma means that an action-reaction spiral can occur between two states or among several of them so that each is forced to spend ever larger sums on arms and be no more secure than before. All will run faster merely to stay where they were.

At the heart of the security dilemma are these two constraints: the inherent difficulty in distinguishing between offensive and defensive postures, and the inability of one state to bank on the fact that another state's present pacific intentions will remain so. The capability to defend can also provide the capability to attack. In adding to its arms, state A may know that its aim is defensive, that its intentions are peaceful, and therefore that it has no aggressive designs on state B. In a world where states must look to themselves for protection, however, B will examine A's actions carefully and suspiciously. B may think that A will attack him when A's arms become powerful enough and that A's protestations of friendship are designed to lull him into lowering his guard. But even if B believes A's actions are not directed against him, B cannot assume that A's intentions will remain peaceful. Anarchy makes it impossible for A to bind itself to continuing to respect B's interests in the future. B must allow for the possibility that what A can do to him, A sometime might do. The need to assess capabilities along with intentions, or, the equivalent, to allow for a change in intentions, makes state actors profoundly conservative. They prefer to err on the side of safety, to have too much rather than too little. Because security is the basis of existence and the prerequisite for the achievement of all other goals, state actors must be acutely sensitive to the security actions of others. The security dilemma thus means that state actors cannot risk *not* reacting to the security actions of other states, but that in so reacting they can produce circumstances that leave them worse off than before.

The anarchic environment of international politics, then, allows every state to be the final judge of its own interests, but requires that each provide the means to attain them. Because the absence of a central authority permits wars to occur, security considerations become paramount. Because of the effects of the security dilemma, efforts of state leaders to protect their peoples can lead to severe tension and war even when all parties sincerely desire peace. Two states, or two groups of states, each satisfied with the status quo and seeking only security, may not be able to achieve it. Conflicts and wars with no economic or ideological basis can occur. The outbreak of war, therefore, does not necessarily mean that some or all states seek expansion, or that humans have an innate drive for power. That states go to war when none of them wants to, however, does not imply that they never seek war. The security dilemma may explain some wars; it does not explain all wars. States often do experience conflicts of interest over trade, real estate, ideology, and prestige. For example, when someone asked Francis I what differences led to his constant wars with Charles V, he replied: "None whatever. We agree perfectly. We both want control of Italy!" (Cited in Frederick L. Schuman, *International Politics*, 7th ed., New York, 1953, p. 283.) If states cannot obtain what they want by blackmail, bribery, or threats, they may resort to war. Wars can occur when no one wants them; wars usually do occur when someone wants them.

Even under propitious circumstances, international cooperation is difficult to achieve, Realists argue, because in anarchy, states are often more concerned with relative advantages than with absolute gains. That is, because international politics is a self-help system in which each state must be prepared to rely on its own resources and strength to further its interests, national leaders often seek to become more powerful than their potential adversaries. Cooperation is then made difficult not only by the fear that others will cheat and fail to live up to their agreements, but also by the felt need to gain a superior position. The reason is not that state actors are concerned with status, but that they fear that arrangements which benefit all, but provide greater benefits to others than to them, will render their country vulnerable to pressure and coercion in the future.

Kenneth N. Waltz develops the above points more fully by analyzing the differences between hierarchic (domestic) and anarchic (international) political systems. He shows why the distribution of capabilities (the relative power positions of states) in anarchic systems is so important and lays out the ways in which political behavior differs in hierarchic and anarchic systems.

There is broad agreement among Realists on the consequences of anarchy for states behavior, but not total agreement. One brand of Realists, who are called the "offensive Realists," argue that the consequences of anarchy go far beyond producing security dilemmas and making cooperation hard to come by. They assert that anarchy forces states, and especially the great powers, to become "power maximizers" because the only way to assure the state's security is to be the most powerful state in the system. Offensive realism envisions a "dog-eat-dog" world of international politics in which power and fear dominate great power interactions and in which war, or the threat of war, among the great powers or among their proxies is a constant feature of international relations. John J. Mearsheimer lays out the tenets of this brand of Realism.

In an anarchic condition, however, the better question to ask may well be, not "Why does war occur?" but rather "Why does war not occur more frequently than it does?" Instead of asking "Why do states not cooperate more to achieve common interests?" we should ask "Given anarchy and the security dilemma, how is it that states are able to cooperate at all?" Anarchy and the security dilemma do not produce their effects automatically, and it is not self evident that states are power maximizers. Thus Alexander Wendt argues that Waltz and other Realists have missed the extent to which the unpleasant patterns they describe are "socially constructed"—i.e., stem from the actors' beliefs, perceptions, and interpretations of others' behavior. If national leaders believe that anarchy requires an assertive stance that endangers others, conflict will be generated. But if they think they have more freedom of action and do not take the hostility of others for granted, they may be able to create more peaceful relationships. In this view, structure (anarchy) does not determine state action; agency (human decision) does.

THE MITIGATION OF ANARCHY

Even Realists note that conflict and warfare is not a constant characteristic of international politics. Most states remain at peace with most others most of the time. State actors have developed a number of ways of coping with anarchy, of gaining more than a modicum of security, of regulating their competition with other states, and of developing patterns that contain, although not eliminate, the dangers of aggression. Kenneth A. Oye shows that even if anarchy and the security dilemma inhibit cooperation, they do not prevent it. A number of conditions and national strategies can make it easier for states to achieve common ends. Cooperation is usually easier if there are a small number of actors. Not only can each more carefully observe the others, but all actors know that their impact on the system is great enough so that if they fail to cooperate with others, joint enterprises are likely to fail. Furthermore, when the number of actors is large, there may be mechanisms and institutions that group them together, thereby reproducing some of the advantages of small numbers. The conditions actors face also influence their fates. The barriers of anarchy are more likely to be overcome when actors have long time horizons, when even successfully exploiting others produces an outcome that is only a little better than mutual cooperation, when being exploited by others is only slightly worse than mutual noncooperation, and when mutual cooperation is much better than unrestricted competition. Under such circumstances, states are particularly likely to undertake contingent strategies such as tit-for-tat. That is, they will cooperate with others if others do likewise and refuse to cooperate if others have refused to cooperate with them.

Most strikingly, it appears that democracies may never have gone to war against each other. This is not to say, as Woodrow Wilson did, that democracies are inherently peaceful. They seem to fight as many wars as do dictatorships. But, as Michael W. Doyle shows, they do not fight each other. If this is correct—and, of course, both the evidence and the reasons are open to dispute—it implies that anarchy and the security dilemma do not prevent peaceful and even harmonious relations among states that share certain common values and beliefs.

Democracies are relatively recent developments. For a longer period of time, two specific devices—international law and diplomacy—have proven useful in resolving conflicts among states. Although not enforced by a world government, international law can provide norms for behavior and mechanisms for settling disputes. The effectiveness of international law derives from the willingness of states to observe it. Its power extends no further than the disposition of states "to agree to agree." Where less than vital interests are at stake, states actors may accept settlements that are not entirely satisfactory because they think the precedents or principles justify the compromises made. Much of international law reflects a consensus among states on what is of equal benefit to all, as, for example, the rules regulating international communications. Diplomacy, too, can facilitate cooperation and resolve disputes. Particularly if diplomacy is skillful, that is, if the legitimate interests of the parties in dispute are taken into account, understandings can often be reached on issues that might otherwise lead to war. These points and others are explored more fully by Stanley Hoffmann and Hans J. Morgenthau.

National leaders use these two traditional tools within a balance-of-power system. Much maligned by President Wilson and his followers and often misunderstood by many others, balance of power refers to the manner in which stability can be the outcome of the efforts of individual states, whether or not any or all of them deliberately pursue that goal. Just as Adam Smith argued that if every individual pursued his or her own self-interest, the interaction of individual egoisms would enhance national wealth, so international relations theorists have argued that even if every state seeks power at the expense of the others, no one state will likely dominate. In both cases a general good can be the unintended product of selfish individual actions. Moreover, even if most states desire only to keep what they have, their own interests dictate that they band together in order to resist any state or coalition of states that threatens to dominate them.

The balance-of-power system is likely to prevent any one state's acquiring hegemony. It will not, however, benefit all states equally nor maintain the peace permanently. Rewards will be unequal because of inequalities in power and expertise. Wars will occur because they are one of the means by which states can preserve what they have or acquire what they covet. Small states may even be eliminated by their more powerful neighbors. The international system will be unstable, however, only if states flock to what they think is the strongest side. What is called *bandwagoning* or the *domino theory* argues that the international system is precarious because successful aggression will attract many followers, either out of fear or out of a desire to share the spoils of victory. Stephen M. Walt disagrees, drawing on balance-of-power theory and historical evidence to argue that rather than bandwagoning, under most conditions states balance against emerging threats. They do not throw in their lot with the stronger side. Instead, they join with others to prevent any state from becoming so strong that it could dominate the system.

Power balancing is a strategy followed by individual states acting on their own. Other ways of coping with anarchy, which may supplement or exist alongside this impulse, are more explicitly collective. Regimes and institutions can help overcome anarchy and facilitate cooperation. When states agree on the principles, rules, and norms that should govern behavior, they can often ameliorate the security dilemma and increase the scope for cooperation. Institutions may not only embody common understandings but, as Robert O. Keohane argues, they can also help states work toward mutually desired outcomes by providing a framework for long-run agreements, making it easier for each state to see whether others are living up to their promises, and increasing the costs the state will pay if it cheats.

In the security area, the United Nations has the potential to be an especially important institution. As Adam Roberts discusses, the end of the Cold War opens up new possibilities for the United Nations and its peacekeeping missions. Over the past decade such missions have proliferated. Success is not automatic, however, and Roberts notes the formidable obstacles that have to be overcome if the UN is to fulfill the hopes that so many state leaders and citizens have for it.

POWER AND PRINCIPLE
IN STATECRAFT

Six Principles of Political Realism

HANS J. MORGENTHAU

1. Political realism believes that politics, like society in general, is governed by objective laws that have their roots in human nature. In order to improve society it is first necessary to understand the laws by which society lives. The operation of these laws being impervious to our preferences, men will challenge them only at the risk of failure.

Realism, believing as it does in the objectivity of the laws of politics, must also believe in the possibility of developing a rational theory that reflects, however imperfectly and one-sidedly, these objective laws. It believes also, then, in the possibility of distinguishing in politics between truth and opinion—between what is true objectively and rationally, supported by evidence and illuminated by reason, and what is only a subjective judgment, divorced from the facts as they are and informed by prejudice and wishful thinking.

Human nature, in which the laws of politics have their roots, has not changed since the classical philosophies of China, India, and Greece endeavored to discover these laws. Hence, novelty is not necessarily a virtue in political theory, nor is old age a defect. The fact that a theory of politics, if there be such a theory, has never been heard of before tends to create a presumption against, rather than in favor of, its soundness. Conversely, the fact that a theory of politics was developed hundreds or even thousands of years ago—as was the theory of the balance of power—does not create a presumption that it must be outmoded and obsolete. . . .

For realism, theory consists in ascertaining facts and giving them meaning through reason. It assumes that the character of a foreign policy can be ascertained only through the examination of the political acts performed and of the foreseeable consequences of these acts. Thus we can find out what statesmen have actually done, and from the foreseeable consequences of their acts we can surmise what their objectives might have been.

Yet examination of the facts is not enough. To give meaning to the factual raw material of foreign policy, we must approach political reality with a kind of rational outline, a map that suggests to us the possible meanings of foreign policy. In other words, we put ourselves in the position of a statesman who must meet a certain problem of foreign policy under certain circumstances, and we ask ourselves what the rational alternatives are from which a statesman may choose who must meet this problem under these circumstances (presuming always that he acts in a rational manner), and which of these rational alternatives this particular statesman, acting under these circumstances, is likely to choose. It is the testing of this rational hypothesis against the actual facts and their consequences that gives theoretical meaning to the facts of international politics.

2. The main signpost that helps political realism to find its way through the landscape of international politics is the concept of interest defined in terms of power. This concept provides the link between reason trying to understand international politics and the facts to be understood. It sets politics as an autonomous sphere of action and understanding apart from other spheres, such as economics (understood in terms of interest defined as wealth), ethics, aesthetics, or religion. Without such a concept a theory of politics, international or domestic, would be altogether impossible, for without it we could not distinguish between political and nonpolitical facts, nor could we bring at least a measure of systematic order to the political sphere.

We assume that statesmen think and act in terms of interest defined as power, and the evidence of history bears that assumption out. That assumption allows us to retrace and anticipate, as it were, the steps a statesman—past, present, or future—has taken or will take on the political scene. We look over his shoulder when he writes his dispatches; we listen in on his conversation with other statesmen; we read and anticipate his very thoughts. Thinking in terms of interest defined as power, we think as he does, and as disinterested observers we understand his thoughts and actions perhaps better than he, the actor on the political scene, does himself.

The concept of interest defined as power imposes intellectual discipline upon the observer, infuses rational order into the subject matter of politics, and thus makes the theoretical understanding of politics possible. On the side of the actor, it provides for rational discipline in action and creates that astounding continuity in foreign policy which makes American, British, or Russian foreign policy appear as an intelligible, rational continuum, by and large consistent within itself, regardless of the different motives, preferences, and intellectual and moral qualities of successive statesmen. A realist theory of international politics, then, will guard against two popular fallacies: the concern with motives and the concern with ideological preferences.

To search for the clue to foreign policy exclusively in the motives of statesmen is both futile and deceptive. It is futile because motives are the most illusive of psychological data, distorted as they are, frequently beyond recognition, by the interests and emotions of actor and observer alike. Do we really know what our own motives are? And what do we know of the motives of others?

Yet even if we had access to the real motives of statesmen, that knowledge would help us little in understanding foreign policies, and might well lead us astray. It is true that the knowledge of the statesman's motives may give us one among many clues as to what the direction of his foreign policy might be. It cannot give us, however, the one clue by which to predict his foreign policies. History shows no exact and necessary correlation between the quality of motives and the quality of foreign policy. This is true in both moral and political terms.

We cannot conclude from the good intentions of a statesman that his foreign policies will be either morally praiseworthy or politically successful. Judging his motives, we can say that he will not intentionally pursue policies that are morally wrong, but we can say nothing about the probability of their success. If we want to know the moral and political qualities of his actions, we must know them, not his motives. How often have statesmen been motivated by the desire to improve the world, and ended by making it worse? And how often have they sought one goal, and ended by achieving something they neither expected nor desired? . . .

A realist theory of international politics will also avoid the other popular fallacy of equating the foreign policies of a statesman with his philosophic or political sympathies, and of deducing the former from the latter. Statesmen, especially under contemporary conditions, may well make a habit of presenting their foreign policies in terms of their philosophic and political sympathies in order to gain popular support for them. Yet they will distinguish with Lincoln between their *"official duty,"* which is to think and act in terms of the national interest, and their *"personal wish,"* which is to see their own moral values and political principles realized throughout the world. Political realism does not require, nor does it condone, indifference to political ideals and moral principles, but it requires indeed a sharp distinction between the desirable and the possible—between what is desirable everywhere and at all times and what is possible under the concrete circumstances of time and place.

It stands to reason that not all foreign policies have always followed so rational, objective, and unemotional a course. The contingent elements of personality, prejudice, and subjective preference, and of all the weaknesses of intellect and will which flesh is heir to, are bound to deflect foreign policies from their rational course. Especially where foreign policy is conducted under the conditions of democratic control, the need to marshal popular emotions to the support of foreign policy cannot fail to impair the rationality of foreign policy itself. Yet a theory of foreign policy which aims at rationality must for the time being, as it were, abstract from these irrational elements and seek to paint a picture of foreign policy which presents the rational essence to be found in experience, without the contingent deviations from rationality which are also found in experience. . . .

The difference between international politics as it actually is and a rational theory derived from it is like the difference between a photograph and a painted portrait. The photograph shows everything that can be seen by the naked eye; the painted portrait does not show everything that can be seen by the naked eye, but it shows, or at least seeks to show, one thing that the naked eye cannot see: the human essence of the person portrayed.

Political realism contains not only a theoretical but also a normative element. It knows that political reality is replete with contingencies and systemic irrationalities and points to the typical influences they exert upon foreign policy. Yet it shares with all social theory the need, for the sake of theoretical understanding, to stress the rational elements of political reality; for it is these rational elements that make reality intelligible for theory. Political realism presents the theoretical construct of a rational foreign policy which experience can never completely achieve.

At the same time political realism considers a rational foreign policy to be good foreign policy; for only a rational foreign policy minimizes risks and maximizes benefits and, hence, complies both with the moral precept of prudence and the political requirement of success. Political realism wants the photographic picture of the political world to resemble as much as possible its painted portrait. Aware of the inevitable gap between good—that is, rational—foreign policy and foreign policy as it actually is, political realism maintains not only that theory must focus upon the rational elements of political reality, but also that foreign policy ought to be rational in view of its own moral and practical purposes.

Hence, it is no argument against the theory here presented that actual foreign policy does not or cannot live up to it. That argument misunderstands the intention of this book, which is to present not an indiscriminate description of political reality, but a rational theory of international politics. Far from being invalidated by the fact that, for instance, a perfect balance of power policy will scarcely be found in reality, it assumes that reality, being deficient in this respect, must be understood and evaluated as an approximation to an ideal system of balance of power.

3. Realism assumes that its key concept of interest defined as power is an objective category which is universally valid, but it does not endow that concept with a meaning that is fixed once and for all. The idea of interest is indeed of the essence of politics and is unaffected by the circumstances of time and place. Thucydides' statement, born of the experiences of ancient Greece, that "identity of interests is the surest of bonds whether between states or individuals" was taken up in the nineteenth century by Lord Salisbury's remark that "the only bond of union that endures" among nations is "the absence of all clashing interests." It was erected into a general principle of government by George Washington:

> A small knowledge of human nature will convince us, that, with far the greatest part of mankind, interest is the governing principle; and that almost every man is more or less, under its influence. Motives of public virtue may for a time, or in particular instances, actuate men to the observance of a conduct purely disinterested; but they are not of themselves sufficient to produce persevering conformity to the refined dictates and obligations of social duty. Few men are capable of making a continual sacrifice of all views of private interest, or advantage, to the common good. It is vain to exclaim against the depravity of human nature on this account; the fact is so, the experience of every age and nation has proved it and we must in a great measure, change the constitution of man, before we can make it otherwise. No institution, not built on the presumptive truth of these maxims can succeed.[1]

It was echoed and enlarged upon in our century by Max Weber's observation:

Interests (material and ideal), not ideas, dominate directly the actions of men. Yet the "images of the world" created by these ideas have very often served as switches determining the tracks on which the dynamism of interests kept actions moving.[2]

Yet the kind of interest determining political action in a particular period of history depends upon the political and cultural context within which foreign policy is formulated. The goals that might be pursued by nations in their foreign policy can run the whole gamut of objectives any nation has ever pursued or might possibly pursue.

The same observations apply to the concept of power. Its content and the manner of its use are determined by the political and cultural environment. Power may comprise anything that establishes and maintains the control of man over man. Thus power covers all social relationships which serve that end, from physical violence to the most subtle psychological ties by which one mind controls another. Power covers the domination of man by man, both when it is disciplined by moral ends and controlled by constitutional safeguards, as in Western democracies, and when it is that untamed and barbaric force which finds its laws in nothing but its own strength and its sole justification in its aggrandizement.

Political realism does not assume that the contemporary conditions under which foreign policy operates, with their extreme instability and the ever present threat of large-scale violence, cannot be changed. The balance of power, for instance, is indeed a perennial element of all pluralistic societies, as the authors of *The Federalist* papers well knew; yet it is capable of operating, as it does in the United States, under the conditions of relative stability and peaceful conflict. If the factors that have given rise to these conditions can be duplicated on the international scene, similar conditions of stability and peace will then prevail there, as they have over long stretches of history among certain nations.

What is true of the general character of international relations is also true of the nation state as the ultimate point of reference of contemporary foreign policy. While the realist indeed believes that interest is the perennial standard by which political action must be judged and directed, the contemporary connection between interest and the nation state is a product of history, and is therefore bound to disappear in the course of history. Nothing in the realist position militates against the assumption that the present division of the political world into nation states will be replaced by larger units of a quite different character, more in keeping with the technical potentialities and the moral requirements of the contemporary world.

The realist parts company with other schools of thought before the all-important question of how the contemporary world is to be transformed. The realist is persuaded that this transformation can be achieved only through the workmanlike manipulation of the perennial forces that have shaped the past as they will the future. The realist cannot be persuaded that we can bring about that transformation by confronting a political reality that has its own laws with an abstract ideal that refuses to take those laws into account.

4. Political realism is aware of the moral significance of political action. It is also aware of the ineluctable tension between the moral command and the

requirements of successful political action. And it is unwilling to gloss over and obliterate that tension and thus to obfuscate both the moral and the political issue by making it appear as though the stark facts of politics were morally more satisfying than they actually are, and the moral law less exacting than it actually is.

Realism maintains that universal moral principles cannot be applied to the actions of states in their abstract universal formulation, but that they must be filtered through the concrete circumstances of time and place. The individual may say for himself: "*Fiat justitia, pereat mundus* (Let justice be done, even if the world perish)," but the state has no right to say so in the name of those who are in its care. Both individual and state must judge political action by universal moral principles, such as that of liberty. Yet while the individual has a moral right to sacrifice himself in defense of such a moral principle, the state has no right to let its moral disapprobation of the infringement of liberty get in the way of successful political action, itself inspired by the moral principle of national survival. There can be no political morality without prudence; that is, without consideration of the political consequences of seemingly moral action. Realism, then, considers prudence—the weighing of the consequences of alternative political actions—to be the supreme virtue in politics. Ethics in the abstract judges action by its conformity with the moral law; political ethics judges action by its political consequences. Classical and medieval philosophy knew this, and so did Lincoln when he said:

> I do the very best I know how, the very best I can, and I mean to keep doing so until the end. If the end brings me out all right, what is said against me won't amount to anything. If the end brings me out wrong, ten angels swearing I was right would make no difference.

5. Political realism refuses to identify the moral aspirations of a particular nation with the moral laws that govern the universe. As it distinguishes between truth and opinion, so it distinguishes between truth and idolatry. All nations are tempted—and few have been able to resist the temptation for long—to clothe their own particular aspirations and actions in the moral purposes of the universe. To know that nations are subject to the moral law is one thing, while to pretend to know with certainty what is good and evil in the relations among nations is quite another. There is a world of difference between the belief that all nations stand under the judgment of God, inscrutable to the human mind, and the blasphemous conviction that God is always on one's side and that what one wills oneself cannot fail to be willed by God also.

The lighthearted equation between a particular nationalism and the counsels of Providence is morally indefensible, for it is that very sin of pride against which the Greek tragedians and the Biblical prophets have warned rulers and ruled. That equation is also politically pernicious, for it is liable to engender the distortion in judgement which, in the blindness of crusading frenzy, destroys nations and civilizations—in the name of moral principle, ideal, or God himself.

On the other hand, it is exactly the concept of interest defined in terms of power that saves us from both that moral excess and that political folly. For if we look at all nations, our own included, as political entities pursuing their respective interests defined in terms of power, we are able to do justice to all of them. And we are able to do justice to all of them in a dual sense: We are able to judge other nations as we judge our own and, having judged them in this fashion, we are then capable of pursuing policies that respect the interests of other nations, while protecting and promoting those of our own. Moderation in policy cannot fail to reflect the moderation of moral judgment.

6. The difference, then, between political realism and other schools of thought is real, and it is profound. However much the theory of political realism may have been misunderstood and misinterpreted, there is no gainsaying its distinctive intellectual and moral attitude to matters political.

Intellectually, the political realist maintains the autonomy of the political sphere, as the economist, the lawyer, the moralist maintain theirs. He thinks in terms of interest defined as power, as the economist thinks in terms of interest defined as wealth; the lawyer, of the conformity of action with legal rules; the moralist, of the conformity of action with moral principles. The economist asks: "How does this policy affect the wealth of society, or a segment of it?" The lawyer asks: "Is this policy in accord with the rules of law?" The moralist asks: "Is this policy in accord with moral principles?" And the political realist asks: "How does this policy affect the power of the nation?" (Or of the federal government, of Congress, of the party, of agriculture, as the case may be.)

The political realist is not unaware of the existence and relevance of standards of thought other than political ones. As political realist, he cannot but subordinate these other standards to those of politics. And he parts company with other schools when they impose standards of thought appropriate to other spheres upon the political sphere. . . .

This realist defense of the autonomy of the political sphere against its subversion by other modes of thought does not imply disregard for the existence and importance of these other modes of thought. It rather implies that each should be assigned its proper sphere and function. Political realism is based upon a pluralistic conception of human nature. Real man is a composite of "economic man," "political man," "moral man," "religious man," etc. A man who was nothing but "political man" would be a beast, for he would be completely lacking in moral restraints. A man who was nothing but "moral man" would be a fool, for he would be completely lacking in prudence. A man who was nothing but "religious man" would be a saint, for he would be completely lacking in worldly desires.

Recognizing that these different facets of human nature exist, political realism also recognizes that in order to understand one of them one has to deal with it on its own terms. That is to say, if I want to understand "religious man," I must for the time being abstract from the other aspects of human nature and deal with its religious aspect as if it were the only one. Furthermore, I must apply to the religious sphere the standards of thought appropriate to it, always remaining aware of the existence of other standards and their actual influence upon the religious qualities of man. What is true of this facet of human nature is true of all the others. No modern economist, for instance, would conceive of his science and its relations to other sciences of man in any other way. It is exactly through such a process of emancipation from other standards of thought, and the development of one appropriate to its subject matter, that economics has developed as an autonomous theory of the economic activities of man. To contribute to a similar development in the field of politics is indeed the purpose of political realism.

It is in the nature of things that a theory of politics which is based upon such principles will not meet with unanimous approval—nor does, for that matter, such a foreign policy. For theory and policy alike run counter to two trends in our culture which are not able to reconcile themselves to the assumptions and results of a rational, objective theory of politics. One of these trends disparages the role of power in society on grounds that stem from the experience and philosophy of the nineteenth century; we shall address ourselves to this tendency later in greater detail. The other trend, opposed to the realist theory and practice of politics, stems from the very relationship that exists, and must exist, between the human mind and the political sphere. . . . The human mind in its day-by-day operations cannot bear to look the truth of politics straight in the face. It must disguise, distort, belittle, and embellish the truth—the more so, the more the individual is actively involved in the processes of politics, and particularly in those of international politics. For only by deceiving himself about the nature of politics and the role he plays on the political scene is man able to live contentedly as a political animal with himself and his fellow men.

Thus it is inevitable that a theory which tries to understand international politics as it actually is and as it ought to be in view of its intrinsic nature, rather than as people would like to see it, must overcome a psychological resistance that most other branches of learning need not face.

NOTES

1. *The Writings of George Washington*, edited by John C. Fitzpatrick (Washington: United States Printing Office, 1931–44), Vol. X, p. 363.
2. Marianne Weber, *Max Weber* (Tuebingen: J. C. B. Mohr, 1926), pp. 347–8. See also Max Weber, *Gesammelte Aufsätze zur Religionssociology* (Tuebingen: J. C. B. Mohr, 1920), p. 252.

A Critique of Morgenthau's Principles of Political Realism

███████ J. ANN TICKNER

It is not in giving life but in risking life that man is raised above the animal: that is why superiority has been accorded in humanity not to the sex that brings forth but to that which kills.

SIMONE DE BEAUVOIR[1]

International politics is a man's world, a world of power and conflict in which warfare is a privileged activity. Traditionally, diplomacy, military service and the science of international politics have been largely male domains. In the past women have rarely been included in the ranks of professional diplomats or the military; of the relatively few women who specialize in the academic discipline of international relations, few are security specialists. Women political scientists who do study international relations tend to focus on areas such as international political economy, North–South relations and matters of distributive justice.

Today, in the United States, where women are entering the military and the foreign service in greater numbers than ever before, they are rarely to be found in positions of military leadership or at the top of the foreign policy establishment.[2] One notable exception, Jeane Kirkpatrick, who was U.S. ambassador to the United Nations in the early 1980s, has described herself as "a mouse in a man's world"; for, in spite of her authoritative and forceful public style and strong conservative credentials, Kirkpatrick maintains that she failed to win the respect or attention of her male colleagues on matters of foreign policy.[3]

Kirkpatrick's story could serve to illustrate the discrimination that women often encounter when they rise to high political office. However, the doubts as to whether a woman would be strong enough to press the nuclear button (an issue raised when a tearful Patricia Schroeder was pictured sobbing on her husband's shoulder as she bowed out of the 1988 U.S. presidential race), suggest that there may be an even more fundamental barrier to women's entry into the highest ranks of the military or of foreign policy making. Nuclear strategy, with its vocabulary of power, threat, force and deterrence, has a distinctly masculine ring;[4] moreover, women are stereotypically judged to be lacking in qualities which these terms

From J. Ann Tickner, "A Critique Of Morgenthau's Principles of Political Realism" in *Gender and International Relations,* eds. Rebecca Grant and Kathleen Newland. Published by Indiana University Press. Reprinted by permission of Kathleen Newland. Portions of the text and some footnotes have been omitted.

evoke. It has also been suggested that, although more women are entering the world of public policy, they are more comfortable dealing with domestic issues such as social welfare that are more compatible with their nurturing skills. Yet the large number of women in the ranks of the peace movement suggests that women are not uninterested in issues of war and peace, although their frequent dissent from national security policy has often branded them as naive, uninformed or even unpatriotic.

In this chapter I propose to explore the question of why international politics is perceived as a man's world and why women remain so underrepresented in the higher echelons of the foreign policy establishment, the military and the academic discipline of international relations. Since I believe that there is something about this field that renders it particularly inhospitable and unattractive to women, I intend to focus on the nature of the discipline itself rather than on possible strategies to remove barriers to women's access to high policy positions. As I have already suggested, the issues that are given priority in foreign policy are issues with which men have had a special affinity. Moreover, if it is primarily men who are describing these issues and constructing theories to explain the workings of the international system, might we not expect to find a masculine perspective in the academic discipline also? If this were so then it could be argued that the exclusion of women has operated not only at the level of discrimination but also through a process of self-selection which begins with the way in which we are taught about international relations.

In order to investigate this claim that the discipline of international relations, as it has traditionally been defined by realism, is based on a masculine world view, I propose to examine the six principles of political realism formulated by Hans J. Morgenthau in his classic work *Politics Among Nations*. I shall use some ideas from feminist theory to show that the way in which Morgenthau describes and explains international politics, and the prescriptions that ensue are embedded in a masculine perspective. Then I shall suggest some ways in which feminist theory might help us begin to conceptualize a world view from a feminine perspective and to formulate a feminist epistemology of international relations. Drawing on these observations I shall conclude with a reformulation of Morgenthau's six principles. Male critics of contemporary realism have already raised many of the same questions about realism that I shall address. However, in undertaking this exercise, I hope to make a link between a growing critical perspective on international relations theory and feminist writers interested in global issues. Adding a feminist perspective to its discourse could also help to make the field of international relations more accessible to women scholars and practitioners.

HANS J. MORGENTHAU'S PRINCIPLES OF POLITICAL REALISM: A MASCULINE PERSPECTIVE?

I have chosen to focus on Hans J. Morgenthau's six principles of political realism because they represent one of the most important statements of contemporary realism from which several generations of scholars and practitioners of international relations in the United States have been nourished. Although Morgenthau has frequently been criticized for his lack of scientific rigour and ambiguous use of language, these six principles have significantly framed the way in which the majority of international relations scholars and practitioners in the West have thought about international politics since 1945.[5]

Morgenthau's principles of political realism can be summarized as follows:

1. Politics, like society in general, is governed by objective laws that have their roots in human nature, which is unchanging: therefore it is possible to develop a rational theory that reflects these objective laws.

2. The main signpost of political realism is the concept of interest defined in terms of power which infuses rational order into the subject matter of politics, and thus makes the theoretical understanding of politics possible. Political realism stresses the rational, objective and unemotional.

3. Realism assumes that interest defined as power is an objective category which is universally valid but not with a meaning that is fixed once and for all. Power is the control of man over man.

4. Political realism is aware of the moral significance of political action. It is also aware of the tension between the moral command and the requirements of successful political action.

5. Political realism refuses to identify the moral aspirations of a particular nation with the moral laws that govern the universe. It is the concept of interest defined in terms of power that saves us from moral excess and political folly.

6. The political realist maintains the autonomy of the political sphere; he asks "How does this policy affect the power of the nation?" Political realism is based on a pluralistic conception of human nature. A man who was nothing but "political man" would be a beast, for he would be completely lacking in moral restraints. But, in order to develop an autonomous theory of political behaviour, "political man" must be abstracted from other aspects of human nature.[6]

I am not going to argue that Morgenthau is incorrect in his portrayal of the international system. I do believe, however, that it is a partial description of international politics because it is based on assumptions about human nature that are partial and that privilege masculinity. First, it is necessary to define masculinity and femininity. According to almost all feminist theorists, masculinity and femininity refer to a set of socially constructed categories, which vary in time and place, rather than to biological determinants. In the West, conceptual dichotomies such as objectivity vs. subjectivity, reason vs. emotion, mind vs. body, culture vs. nature, self vs. other or autonomy vs. relatedness, knowing vs. being and public vs. private have typically been used to describe male/female differences by feminists and non-feminists alike.[7] In the United States, psychological tests conducted across different socioeconomic groups confirm that individuals perceive these dichotomies as masculine and feminine and also that the characteristics associated with masculinity are more highly valued by men and women alike.[8] It is important to stress, however, that these characteristics are stereotypical; they do not necessarily describe individual men or women, who can exhibit characteristics and modes of thought associated with the opposite sex.

Using a vocabulary that contains many of the words associated with masculinity as I have identified it, Morgenthau asserts that it is possible to develop a rational (and unemotional) theory of international politics based on objective laws that have their roots in human nature. Since Morgenthau wrote the first edition of *Politics Among Nations* in 1948, this search for an objective science of international politics based on the model of the natural sciences has been an important part of the realist and neorealist agenda. In her feminist critique of the natural sciences, Evelyn Fox Keller points out that most scientific communities share the "assumption that the universe they study is directly accessible, represented by concepts and shaped not by language but only by the demands of logic and experiment."[9] The laws of nature, according to this view of science, are "beyond the relativity of language." Like most feminists, Keller rejects this view of science which, she asserts, imposes a coercive, hierarchical and conformist pattern on scientific inquiry. Feminists in general are sceptical about the possibility of finding a universal and objective foundation for knowledge, which Morgenthau claims is possible. Most share the belief that knowledge is socially constructed: since it is language that transmits knowledge, the use of language and its claims to objectivity must continually be questioned.

Keller argues that objectivity, as it is usually defined in our culture, is associated with masculinity. She identifies it as "a network of interactions between gender development, a belief system that equates objectivity with masculinity, and a set of cultural values that simultaneously (and cojointly) elevates what is defined as scientific and what is defined as masculine."[10] Keller links the separation of self from other, an important stage of masculine gender development, with this notion of objectivity. Translated into scientific inquiry this becomes the striving for the separation of subject and object, an important goal of modern science and one which, Keller asserts, is based on the need for control; hence objectivity becomes associated with power and domination.

The need for control has been an important motivating force for modern realism. To begin his search for an objective, rational theory of international politics, which could impose order on a chaotic and conflictual world, Morgenthau constructs an abstraction which he calls political man, a beast completely lacking in moral restraints. Morgenthau is deeply aware that real men, like real states, are both moral and bestial but, because states do not live up to the universal moral laws that govern the universe, those who behave morally in international politics are doomed to failure because of the immoral actions of others. To solve this tension Morgenthau postulates a realm of international politics in which the amoral behaviour of political man is not only permissible but prudent. It is a Hobbesian world, separate and distinct from the world of domestic order. In it, states may act like beasts, for survival depends on a maximization of power and a willingness to fight.

Having long argued that the personal is political, most feminist theory would reject the validity of constructing an autonomous political sphere around which boundaries of permissible modes of conduct have been drawn. As Keller maintains, "the demarcation between public and private not only defines and defends the boundaries of the political but also helps form its content and style."[11] Morgenthau's political man is a social construct based on a partial representation of human nature. One might well ask where the women were in Hobbes's state of nature;

presumably they must have been involved in reproduction and childrearing, rather than warfare, if life was to go on for more than one generation.[12] Morgenthau's emphasis on the conflictual aspects of the international system contributes to a tendency, shared by other realists, to de-emphasize elements of cooperation and regeneration which are also aspects of international relations.[13]

Morgenthau's construction of an amoral realm of international power politics is an attempt to resolve what he sees as a fundamental tension between the moral laws that govern the universe and the requirements of successful political action in a world where states use morality as a cloak to justify the pursuit of their own national interests. Morgenthau's universalistic morality postulates the highest form of morality as an abstract ideal, similar to the Golden Rule, to which states seldom adhere: the morality of states, by contrast, is an instrumental morality guided by self-interest.

Morgenthau's hierarchical ordering of morality contains parallels with the work of psychologist Lawrence Kohlberg. Based on a study of the moral development of 84 American boys, Kohlberg concludes that the highest stage of human moral development (which he calls stage 6) is the ability to recognize abstract universal principles of justice; lower on the scale (stage 2) is an instrumental morality concerned with serving one's own interests while recognizing that others have interests too. Between these two is an interpersonal morality which is contextual and characterized by sensitivity to the needs of others (stage 3).[14]

In her critique of Kohlberg's stages of moral development, Carol Gilligan argues that they are based on a masculine conception of morality. On Kohlberg's scale women rarely rise above the third or contextual stage. Gilligan claims that this is not a sign of inferiority but of difference. Since women are socialized into a mode of thinking which is contextual and narrative, rather than formal and abstract, they tend to see issues in contextual rather than in abstract terms.[15] In international relations the tendency to think about morality either in terms of abstract, universal and unattainable standards or as purely instrumental, as Morgenthau does, detracts from our ability to tolerate cultural differences and to seek potential for building community in spite of these differences.

Using examples from feminist literature I have suggested that Morgenthau's attempt to construct an objective, universal theory of international politics is rooted in assumptions about human nature and morality that, in modern Western culture, are associated with masculinity. Further evidence that Morgenthau's principles are not the basis for a universalistic and objective theory is contained in his frequent references to the failure of what he calls the "legalistic–moralistic" or idealist approach to world politics which he claims was largely responsible for both the world wars. Having laid the blame for the Second World War on the misguided morality of appeasement, Morgenthau's *realpolitik* prescriptions for successful political action appear as prescriptions for avoiding the mistakes of the 1930s rather than as prescriptions with timeless applicability.

If Morgenthau's world view is embedded in the traumas of the Second World War, are his prescriptions still valid as we move further away from this event? I share with other critics of realism the view that, in a rapidly changing world, we must begin to search for modes of behaviour different from those prescribed by Morgenthau. Given that any war between the major powers is likely to be nuclear, increasing security by increasing power could be suicidal.[16] Moreover, the nation state, the primary constitutive element of the international system for Morgenthau and other realists, is no longer able to deal with an increasingly pluralistic array of problems ranging from economic interdependence to environmental degradation. Could feminist theory make a contribution to international relations theory by constructing an alternative, feminist perspective on international politics that might help us to search for more appropriate solutions?

A FEMINIST PERSPECTIVE ON INTERNATIONAL RELATIONS?

If the way in which we describe reality has an effect on the ways we perceive and act upon our environment, new perspectives might lead us to consider alternative courses of action. With this in mind I shall first examine two important concepts in international relations, power and security, from a feminist perspective and then discuss some feminist approaches to conflict resolution.

Morgenthau's definition of power, the control of man over man, is typical of the way power is usually defined in international relations. Nancy Hartsock argues that this type of power-as-domination has always been associated with masculinity, since the exercise of power has generally been a masculine activity: rarely have women exercised legitimized power in the public domain. When women write about power they stress energy, capacity and potential, says Hartsock. She notes that women theorists, even when they have little else in common, offer similar definitions of power which differ substantially from the understanding of power as domination.[17]

Hannah Arendt, frequently cited by feminists writing about power, defines power as the human ability to act in concert, or to take action in connection with others who share similar concerns.[18] This definition of power is similar to that of psychologist David McClelland's portrayal of female power, which he describes as shared rather than assertive.[19] Jane Jaquette argues that, since women have had less access to the instruments of coercion, they have been more apt to rely on power as persuasion; she compares women's domestic activities to coalition building.[20]

All of these writers are portraying power as a relationship of mutual enablement. Tying her definition of female power to international relations, Jaquette sees similarities between female strategies of persuasion and strategies of small states operating from a position of weakness in the international system. There are also examples of states' behaviour that contain elements of the female strategy of coalition building. One such example is the Southern African Development Coordination Conference (SADCC), which is designed to build regional infrastructure based on mutual cooperation and collective self-reliance in order to decrease dependence on the South African economy. Another is the European Community, which has had considerable success in building mutual cooperation in an area of the world whose history would not predict such a course of events.[21] It is rare, however, that cooperative outcomes in international relations are described in these terms, although Karl Deutsch's notion of pluralistic security communities might be one such example where power is associated with building community.[22] I am not denying that power as domination is a pervasive reality in international relations. However, there are also instances of cooperation in interstate relations, which tend to be obscured when power is seen solely as domination. Thinking about power in this multidimensional sense may help us to think constructively about the potential for cooperation as well as conflict, an aspect of international relations generally played down by realism.

Redefining national security is another way in which feminist theory could contribute to new thinking about international relations.[23] Traditionally in the West, the concept of national security has been tied to military strength and its role in the physical protection of the nation state from external threats. Morgenthau's notion of defending the national interest in terms of power is consistent with this definition. But this traditional definition of national security is partial at best in today's world.[24] The technologically advanced states are highly interdependent, and rely on weapons whose effects would be equally devastating to winners and losers alike. For them to defend national security by relying on war as the last resort no longer appears very useful. Moreover, if one thinks of security in North–South rather than East–West terms, for a large portion of the world's population security has as much to do with the satisfaction of basic material needs as with military threats. According to Johan Galtung's notion of structural violence, to suffer a lower life expectancy by virtue of one's place of birth is a form of violence whose effects can be as devastating as war.[25]

Basic needs satisfaction has a great deal to do with women, but only recently have women's roles as providers of basic needs, and in development more generally, become visible as important components in development strategies.[26] Traditionally the development literature has focused on aspects of the development process that are in the public sphere, are technologically complex and are usually undertaken by men. Thinking about the role of women in development and the way in which we can define development and basic needs satisfaction to be inclusive of women's roles and needs are topics that deserve higher priority on the international agenda. Typically, however, this is an area about which traditional international relations theory, with the priority it gives to order over justice, has had very little to say.

A further threat to national security, more broadly defined, which has also been missing from the agenda of traditional international relations, concerns the environment. Carolyn Merchant argues that a mechanistic view of nature, contained in modern science, has helped to guide an industrial and technological development which has resulted in environmental damage that has now become a matter of global concern. In the introduction to her book *The Death of Nature,* Merchant suggests that, "Women and nature have an age-old association—an affiliation that has persisted throughout culture, language, and history."[27] Hence she maintains that the ecology movement, which is growing up in response to environmental threats, and the women's movement are deeply interconnected. Both stress living in equilibrium with nature rather than dominating it, both see nature as a living non-hierarchical entity in which each part is mutually dependent on the whole. Ecologists, as well as many feminists, are now suggesting that only such a fundamental change of world view will allow the human species to survive the damage it is inflicting on the environment.

Thinking about military, economic and environmental security in interdependent terms suggests the need for new methods of conflict resolution that seek to achieve mutually beneficial, rather than zero sum, outcomes. One such method comes from Sara Ruddick's work on "maternal thinking."[28] Ruddick describes maternal thinking as focused on the preservation of life and the growth of children. To foster a domestic environment conducive to these goals, tranquility must be preserved by avoiding conflict where possible, engaging in it non-violently and restoring community when it is over. In such an environment the ends for which disputes are fought are subordinate to the means by which they are resolved. This method of conflict resolution involves making contextual judgements rather than appealing to absolute standards and thus has much in common with Gilligan's definition of female morality.

While non-violent resolution of conflict in the domestic sphere is a widely accepted norm, passive resistance in the public realm is regarded as deviant. But, as Ruddick argues, the peaceful resolution of conflict by mothers does not usually extend to the children of one's enemies, an important reason why women have been ready to support men's wars.[29] The question for Ruddick then becomes how to get maternal thinking, a mode of thinking which she believes can be found in men as well as women, out into the public realm. Ruddick believes that finding a common humanity among one's opponents has become a condition of survival in the nuclear age when the notion of winners and losers has become questionable.[30] Portraying the adversary as less than human has all too often been a technique of the nation state to command loyalty and to increase its legitimacy in the eyes of its citizens. Such behaviour in an age of weapons of mass destruction may be self-defeating.

We might also look to Gilligan's work for a feminist perspective on conflict resolution. Reporting on a study of playground behaviour of American boys and girls, Gilligan argues that girls are less able to tolerate high levels of conflict, and more likely than boys to play games that involve taking turns and in which the success of one does not depend on the failure of another.[31] While Gilligan's study does not take into account attitudes toward other groups (racial, ethnic, economic or national), it does suggest the validity of investigating whether girls are socialized to use different modes of problem solving when dealing with conflict, and whether such behaviour might be useful in thinking about international conflict resolution.

TOWARD A FEMINIST EPISTEMOLOGY OF INTERNATIONAL RELATIONS

I am deeply aware that there is no *one* feminist approach but many, which come out of various disciplines and intellectual traditions. Yet there are common themes in the different feminist literatures that I have reviewed which could help us to begin to formulate a feminist epistemology of international relations. Morgenthau encourages us to try to stand back from the world and to think about theory building in terms of constructing a rational outline or map that has universal applications. In contrast, the feminist literature reviewed here emphasizes connection and contingency. Keller argues for a form of knowledge, which she calls "dynamic objectivity," "that grants to the world around us its independent integrity, but does so in a way that remains cognizant of, indeed relies on, our connectivity with that world."[32] Keller illustrates this mode of thinking in her study of Barbara McClintock, whose work on genetic transposition won her a Nobel prize after many years of marginalization by the scientific community.[33] McClintock, Keller argues, was a scientist with a respect for complexity, diversity and individual difference whose methodology allowed her data to speak rather than imposing explanations on it.

Keller's portrayal of McClintock's science contains parallels with what Sandra Harding calls an African world view.[34] Harding tells us that the Western liberal notion of rational economic man, an individualist and a welfare maximizer, similar to the image of rational political man on which realism has based its theoretical investigations, does not make any sense in the African world view where the individual is seen as part of the social order acting within that order rather than upon it. Harding believes that this view of human behaviour has much in common with a feminist perspective. If we combine this view of human behaviour with Merchant's holistic perspective which stresses the interconnectedness of all things, including nature, it may help us to begin to think from a more global perspective. Such a perspective appreciates cultural diversity but at the same time recognizes a growing interdependence, which makes anachronistic the exclusionary thinking fostered by the nation state system.

Keller's dynamic objectivity, Harding's African world view and Merchant's ecological thinking all point us in the direction of an appreciation of the "other" as a subject whose views are as legitimate as our own, a way of thinking that has been sadly lacking in the history of international relations. Just as Keller cautions us against the construction of a feminist science which could perpetuate similar exclusionary attitudes, Harding warns us against schema that contrast people by race, gender or class and that originate within projects of social domination. Feminist thinkers generally dislike dichotomization and the distancing of subject from object that goes with abstract thinking, both of which, they believe, encourage a we/they attitude characteristic of international relations. Instead, feminist literature urges us to construct epistemologies that value ambiguity and difference. These qualities could stand us in good stead as we begin to build a human or ungendered theory of international relations which contains elements of both masculine and feminine modes of thought.

MORGENTHAU'S PRINCIPLES OF POLITICAL REALISM: A FEMINIST REFORMULATION

The first part of this paper used feminist theory to develop a critique of Morgenthau's principles of political realism in order to demonstrate how the theory and practice of international relations may exhibit a masculine bias. The second part suggested some contributions that feminist theory might make to reconceptualizing some important elements in international relations and to thinking about a feminist epistemology. Drawing on these observations, this conclusion will present

a feminist reformulation of Morgenthau's six principles of political realism, outlined earlier in this paper, which might help us to begin to think differently about
international relations. I shall not use the term realism since feminists believe that
there are multiple realities: a truly realistic picture of international politics must
recognize elements of cooperation as well as conflict, morality as well as *realpolitik,*
and the strivings for justice as well as order.[35] This reformulation may help us to
think in these multidimensional terms.

1. A feminist perspective believes that objectivity, as it is culturally defined, is
   associated with masculinity. Therefore, supposedly "objective" laws of
   human nature are based on a partial, masculine view of human nature.
   Human nature is both masculine and feminine; it contains elements of
   social reproduction and development as well as political domination.
   Dynamic objectivity offers us a more connected view of objectivity with less
   potential for domination.

2. A feminist perspective believes that the national interest is multidimensional and contextually contingent. Therefore, it cannot be defined solely in
   terms of power. In the contemporary world the national interest demands
   cooperative rather than zero sum solutions to a set of interdependent global
   problems which include nuclear war, economic well-being and environmental degradation.

3. Power cannot be infused with meaning that is universally valid. Power as
   domination and control privileges masculinity and ignores the possibility of
   collective empowerment, another aspect of power often associated with
   femininity.

4. A feminist perspective rejects the possibility of separating moral command
   from political action. All political action has moral significance. The realist
   agenda for maximizing order through power and control gives priority to
   the moral command of order over those of justice and the satisfaction of
   basic needs necessary to ensure social reproduction.

5. While recognizing that the moral aspirations of particular nations cannot be
   equated with universal moral principles, a feminist perspective seeks to
   find common moral elements in human aspirations which could become
   the basis for de-escalating international conflict and building international
   community.

6. A feminist perspective denies the autonomy of the political. Since autonomy is associated with masculinity in Western culture, disciplinary efforts
   to construct a world view which does not rest on a pluralistic conception of
   human nature are partial and masculine. Building boundaries around a narrowly defined political realm defines political in a way that excludes the
   concerns and contributions of women.

To construct this feminist alternative is not to deny the validity of Morgenthau's work. But adding a feminist perspective to the epistemology of international
relations is a stage through which we must pass if we are to think about constructing an ungendered or human science of international politics which is sensitive to,
but goes beyond, both masculine and feminine perspectives. Such inclusionary

thinking, as Simone de Beauvoir tells us, values the bringing forth of life as much as the risking of life; it is becoming imperative in a world in which the technology of war and a fragile natural environment threaten human existence. An ungendered, or human, discourse becomes possible only when women are adequately represented in the discipline and when there is equal respect for the contributions of women and men alike.

NOTES

An earlier version of this paper was presented at a symposium on Gender and International Relations at the London School of Economics in June 1988. I would like to thank the editors of *Millennium,* who organized this symposium, for encouraging me to undertake this rewriting. I am also grateful to Hayward Alker Jr. and Susan Okin for their careful reading of the manuscript and helpful suggestions.

1. Quoted in Sandra Harding, *The Science Question in Feminism* (Ithaca, N.Y.: Cornell University Press, 1986), p. 148.
2. In 1987 only 4.8 per cent of the top career Foreign Service employees were women. Statement of Patricia Schroeder before the Committee on Foreign Affairs, U.S. House of Representatives, p. 4; *Women's Perspectives on U.S. Foreign Policy: A Compilation of Views* (Washington, D.C.: U.S. Government Printing Office, 1988). For an analysis of women's roles in the American military, see Cynthia Enloe, *Does Khaki Become You? The Militarisation of Women's Lives* (London: Pluto Press, 1983).
3. Edward P. Crapol (ed.), *Women and American Foreign Policy* (Westport, Conn.: Greenwood Press, 1987), p. 167.
4. For an analysis of the role of masculine language in shaping strategic thinking see Carol Cohn, "Sex and Death in the Rational World of Defense Intellectuals," *Signs: Journal of Women in Culture and Society* (Vol. 12, No. 4, Summer 1987).
5. The claim for the dominance of the realist paradigm is supported by John A. Vasquez, "Colouring It Morgenthau: New Evidence for an Old Thesis on Quantitative International Studies," *British Journal of International Studies* (Vol. 3, No. 5, October 1979), pp. 210–28. For a critique of Morgenthau's ambiguous use of language see Inis L. Claude Jr., *Power and International Relations* (New York: Random House, 1962), especially pp. 25–37.
6. These are drawn from Hans Morgenthau, *Politics Among Nations: The Struggle for Power and Peace,* 5th revised edition (New York: Alfred Knopf, 1973), pp. 4–15. I am aware that these principles embody only a partial statement of Morgenthau's very rich study of international politics, a study which deserves a much more detailed analysis than I can give here.
7. This list is a composite of the male/female dichotomies which appear in Evelyn Fox Keller's *Reflections on Gender and Science* (New Haven, Conn.: Yale University Press, 1985) and Harding, *op. cit.*
8. Inge K. Broverman, Susan R. Vogel, Donald M. Broverman, Frank E. Clarkson and Paul S. Rosenkranz, "Sex-role Stereotypes: A Current Appraisal," *Journal of Social Issues* (Vol. 28, No. 2, 1972), pp. 59–78. Replication of this research in the 1980s confirms that these perceptions still hold.
9. Keller, *op. cit.,* p. 130.
10. *Ibid.,* p. 89.

11. *Ibid.*, p. 9.

12. Sara Ann Ketchum, "Female Culture, Woman Culture and Conceptual Change: Toward a Philosophy of Women's Studies," *Social Theory and Practice* (Vol. 6, No. 2, Summer 1980).

13. Others have questioned whether Hobbes's state of nature provides an accurate description of the international system. See for example Charles Beitz, *Political Theory and International Relations* (Princeton, N.J.: Princeton University Press, 1979), pp. 35–50 and Stanley Hoffmann, *Duties Beyond Borders* (Syracuse, N.Y.: Syracuse University Press, 1981), chap. 1.

14. Kohlberg's stages of moral development are described and discussed in Robert Kegan, *The Evolving Self: Problem and Process in Human Development* (Cambridge, Mass.: Harvard University Press, 1982), chap. 2.

15. Carol Gilligan, *In a Different Voice: Psychological Theory and Women's Development* (Cambridge, Mass.: Harvard University Press, 1982). See chap. 1 for Gilligan's critique of Kohlberg.

16. There is evidence that, toward the end of his life, Morgenthau himself was aware that his own prescriptions were becoming anachronistic. In a seminar presentation in 1978 he suggested that power politics as the guiding principle for the conduct of international relations had become fatally defective. For a description of this seminar presentation see Francis Anthony Boyle, *World Politics and International Law* (Durham, N.C.: Duke University Press, 1985), pp. 70–4.

17. Nancy C. M. Hartsock, *Money, Sex and Power: Toward a Feminist Historical Materialism* (Boston: Northeastern University Press, 1983), p. 210.

18. Hannah Arendt, *On Violence* (New York: Harcourt, Brace and World, 1969), p. 44. Arendt's definition of power, as it relates to international relations, is discussed more extensively in Jean Bethke Elshtain's "Reflections on War and Political Discourse: Realism, Just War, and Feminism in a Nuclear Age," *Political Theory* (Vol. 13, No. 1, February 1985), pp. 39–57.

19. David McClelland, "Power and the Feminine Role," in David McClelland, *Power: The Inner Experience* (New York: Wiley, 1975).

20. Jane S. Jaquette, "Power as Ideology: A Feminist Analysis," in Judith H. Stiehm (ed.), *Women's Views of the Political World of Men* (Dobbs Ferry, N.Y.: Transnational Publishers, 1984).

21. These examples are cited by Christine Sylvester, "The Emperor's Theories and Transformations: Looking at the Field through Feminist Lenses," in Dennis Pirages and Christine Sylvester (eds.), *Transformations in the Global Political Economy* (Basingstoke: Macmillan, 1989).

22. Karl W. Deutsch et al., *Political Community and the North Atlantic Area* (Princeton, N.J.: Princeton University Press, 1957).

23. New thinking is a term that is also being used in the Soviet Union to describe foreign policy reformulations under Gorbachev. There are indications that the Soviets are beginning to conceptualize security in the multidimensional terms described here. See Margot Light, *The Soviet Theory of International Relations* (New York: St. Martin's Press, 1988), chap. 10.

24. This is the argument made by Edward Azar and Chung-in Moon, "Third World National Security: Toward a New Conceptual Framework," *International Interactions* (Vol. 11, No. 2, 1984), pp. 103–35.

25. Johan Galtung, "Violence, Peace, and Peace Research," in Galtung, *Essays in Peace Research*, Vol. I (Copenhagen: Christian Ejlers, 1975).

26. See, for example, Gita Sen and Caren Grown, *Development, Crises and Alternative Visions: Third World Women's Perspectives* (New York: Monthly Review Press, 1987).

This is an example of a growing literature on women and development which deserves more attention from the international relations community.

27. Carolyn Merchant, *The Death of Nature: Women, Ecology and the Scientific Revolution* (New York: Harper and Row, 1982), p. xv.

28. Sara Ruddick, "Maternal Thinking" and "Preservative Love and Military Destruction: Some Reflections on Mothering and Peace," in Joyce Treblicot, *Mothering: Essays in Feminist Theory* (Totowa, N.J.: Rowman and Allenhead, 1984).

29. For a more extensive analysis of this issue see Jean Bethke Elshtain, *Women and War* (New York: Basic Books, 1987).

30. This type of conflict resolution contains similarities with the problem solving approach of Edward Azar, John Burton and Herbert Kelman. See, for example, Edward E. Azar and John W. Burton, *International Conflict Resolution: Theory and Practice* (Brighton: Wheatsheaf, 1986) and Herbert C. Kelman, "Interactive Problem Solving: A Social-Psychological Approach to Conflict Resolution," in W. Klassen (ed.), *Dialogue Toward Inter-Faith Understanding* (Tantur/Jerusalem: Ecumenical Institute for Theoretical Research, 1986), pp. 293–314.

31. Gilligan, *op. cit.*, pp. 9–10.

32. Keller, *op. cit.*, p. 117.

33. Evelyn Fox Keller, *A Feeling for the Organism: The Life and Work of Barbara McClintock* (New York: Freeman, 1983).

34. Harding, *op. cit.*, chap. 7.

35. "Utopia and reality are . . . the two facets of political science. Sound political thought and sound political life will be found only where both have their place": E. H. Carr, *The Twenty Years Crisis: 1919–1939* (New York: Harper and Row, 1964), p. 10.

THE CONSEQUENCES
■ OF ANARCHY

The Anarchic Structure
of World Politics
■■■■■ KENNETH N. WALTZ

POLITICAL STRUCTURES

Only through some sort of systems theory can international politics be understood. To be a success, such a theory has to show how international politics can be conceived of as a domain distinct from the economic, social, and other international domains that one may conceive of. To mark international-political systems off from other international systems, and to distinguish systems-level from unit-level forces, requires showing how political structures are generated and how they affect, and are affected by, the units of the system. How can we conceive of international politics as a distinct system? What is it that intervenes between interacting units and the results that their acts and interactions produce? To answer these questions, this chapter first examines the concept of social structure and then defines structure as a concept appropriate for national and for international politics.

A system is composed of a structure and of interacting units. The structure is the system-wide component that makes it possible to think of the system as a whole. The problem is . . . to contrive a definition of structure free of the attributes and the interactions of units. Definitions of structure must leave aside, or abstract from, the characteristics of units, their behavior, and their interactions. Why must those obviously important matters be omitted? They must be omitted so that we can distinguish between variables at the level of the units and variables at the level of the system. The problem is to develop theoretically useful concepts to replace the vague and varying systemic notions that are customarily employed—notions such as environment, situation, context, and milieu. Structure is a useful concept if it gives clear and fixed meaning to such vague and varying terms.

From Kenneth N. Waltz, *Theory of International Politics* © 1979 by McGraw-Hill, pp. 79–106. Reprinted with permission of The McGraw-Hill Companies.

We know what we have to omit from any definition of structure if the definition is to be useful theoretically. Abstracting from the attributes of units means leaving aside questions about the kinds of political leaders, social and economic institutions, and ideological commitments states may have. Abstracting from relations means leaving aside questions about the cultural, economic, political, and military interactions of states. To say what is to be left out does not indicate what is to be put in. The negative point is important nevertheless because the instruction to omit attributes is often violated and the instruction to omit interactions almost always goes unobserved. But if attributes and interactions are omitted, what is left? The question is answered by considering the double meaning of the term "relation." As S. F. Nadel points out, ordinary language obscures a distinction that is important in theory. "Relation" is used to mean both the interaction of units and the positions they occupy vis-à-vis each other.[1] To define a structure requires ignoring how units relate with one another (how they interact) and concentrating on how they stand in relation to one another (how they are arranged or positioned). Interactions, as I have insisted, take place at the level of the units. How units stand in relation to one another, the way they are arranged or positioned, is not a property of the units. The arrangement of units is a property of the system.

By leaving aside the personality of actors, their behavior, and their interactions, one arrives at a purely positional picture of society. Three propositions follow from this. First, structures may endure while personality, behavior, and interactions vary widely. Structure is sharply distinguished from actions and interactions. Second, a structural definition applies to realms of widely different substance so long as the arrangement of parts is similar.[2] Third, because this is so, theories developed for one realm may with some modification be applicable to other realms as well. . . .

The concept of structure is based on the fact that units differently juxtaposed and combined behave differently and in interacting produce different outcomes. I first want to show how internal political structure can be defined. In a book on international-political theory, domestic political structure has to be examined in order to draw a distinction between expectations about behavior and outcomes in the internal and external realms. Moreover, considering domestic political structure now will make the elusive international-political structure easier to catch later on.

Structure defines the arrangement, or the ordering, of the parts of a system. Structure is not a collection of political institutions but rather the arrangement of them. How is the arrangement defined? The constitution of a state describes some parts of the arrangement, but political structures as they develop are not identical with formal constitutions. In defining structures, the first question to answer is this: What is the principle by which the parts are arranged?

Domestic politics is hierarchically ordered. The units—institutions and agencies—stand vis-à-vis each other in relations of super- and subordination. The ordering principle of a system gives the first, and basic, bit of information about how the parts of a realm are related to each other. In a polity the hierarchy of offices is by no means completely articulated, nor are all ambiguities about relations of super- and subordination removed. Nevertheless, political actors are formally differentiated according to the degrees of their authority, and their distinct functions are specified. By "specified" I do not mean that the law of the land fully describes the duties that different agencies perform, but only that broad agreement prevails on the tasks that various parts of a government are to undertake and on the extent of the power they legitimately wield. Thus Congress supplies the military forces; the President commands them. Congress makes the laws; the executive branch enforces them; agencies administer laws; judges interpret them. Such specification of roles and differentiation of functions is found in any state, the more fully so as the state is more highly developed. The specification of functions of formally differentiated parts gives the second bit of structural information. This second part of the definition adds some content to the structure, but only enough to say more fully how the units stand in relation to one another. The roles and the functions of the British Prime Minister and Parliament, for example, differ from those of the American President and Congress. When offices are juxtaposed and functions are combined in different ways, different behaviors and outcomes result, as I shall shortly show.

The placement of units in relation to one another is not fully defined by a system's ordering principle and by the formal differentiation of its parts. The standing of the units also changes with changes in their relative capabilities. In the performance of their functions, agencies may gain capabilities or lose them. The relation of Prime Minister to Parliament and of President to Congress depends on, and varies with, their relative capabilities. The third part of the definition of structure acknowledges that even while specified functions remain unchanged, units come to stand in different relation to each other through changes in relative capability.

A domestic political structure is thus defined: first, according to the principle by which it is ordered; second, by specification of the functions of formally differentiated units; and third, by the distribution of capabilities across those units. Structure is a highly abstract notion, but the definition of structure does not abstract from everything. To do so would be to leave everything aside and to include nothing at all. The three-part definition of structure includes only what is required to show how the units of the system are positioned or arranged. Everything else is omitted. Concern for tradition and culture, analysis of the character and personality of political actors, consideration of the conflictive and accommodative processes of politics, description of the making and execution of policy—all such matters are left aside. Their omission does not imply their unimportance. They are omitted because we want to figure out the expected effects of structure on process and of process on structure. That can be done only if structure and process are distinctly defined.

I defined domestic political structures first by the principle according to which they are organized or ordered, second by the differentiation of units and the specification of their functions, and third by the distribution of capabilities across units. Let us see how the three terms of the definition apply to international politics.

1. Ordering Principles

Structural questions are questions about the arrangement of the parts of a system. The parts of domestic political systems stand in relations of super- and subordination. Some are entitled to command; others are required to obey. Domestic systems are centralized and hierarchic. The parts of international-political systems stand in relations of coordination. Formally, each is the equal of all the others. None is entitled to command; none is required to obey. International systems are decentralized and anarchic. The ordering principles of the two structures are distinctly different, indeed, contrary to each other. Domestic political structures have governmental institutions and offices as their concrete counterparts. International politics, in contrast, has been called "politics in the absence of government."[3] International organizations do exist, and in ever-growing numbers. Supranational agents able to act effectively, however, either themselves acquire some of the attributes and capabilities of states, as did the medieval papacy in the era of Innocent III, or they soon reveal their inability to act in important ways except with the support, or at least the acquiescence, of the principal states concerned with the matters at hand. Whatever elements of authority emerge internationally are barely once removed from the capability that provides the foundation for the appearance of those elements. Authority quickly reduces to a particular expression of capability. In the absence of agents with system-wide authority, formal relations of super- and subordination fail to develop.

The first term of a structural definition states the principle by which the system is ordered. Structure is an organizational concept. The prominent characteristic of international politics, however, seems to be the lack of order and of organization. How can one think of international politics as being any kind of an order at all? The anarchy of politics internationally is often referred to. If structure is an organizational concept, the terms "structure" and "anarchy" seem to be in contradiction. If international politics is "politics in the absence of government," what are we in the presence of? In looking for international structure, one is brought face to face with the invisible, an uncomfortable position to be in.

The problem is this: how to conceive of an order without an orderer and of organizational effects where formal organization is lacking. Because these are difficult questions, I shall answer them through analogy with microeconomic theory. Reasoning by analogy is helpful where one can move from a domain for which theory is well developed to one where it is not. Reasoning by analogy is permissible where different domains are structurally similar.

Classical economic theory, developed by Adam Smith and his followers, is microtheory. Political scientists tend to think that microtheory is theory about small-scale matters, a usage that ill accords with its established meaning. The term "micro" in economic theory indicates the way in which the theory is constructed rather than the scope of the matters it pertains to. Microeconomic theory describes how an order is spontaneously formed from the self-interested acts and interactions of individual units—in this case, persons and firms. The theory then turns upon the two central concepts of the economic units and of the market. Economic units and economic markets are concepts, not descriptive realities or concrete entities. This must be emphasized since from the early eighteenth century to the present, from the sociologist Auguste Comte to the psychologist George Katona, economic theory has been faulted because its assumptions fail to correspond with realities.[4] Unrealistically, economic theorists conceive of an economy operating in isolation from its society and polity. Unrealistically, economists assume that the economic world is the world of the world. Unrealistically, economists think of the acting unit, the famous "economic man," as a single-minded profit maximizer.

They single out one aspect of man and leave aside the wondrous variety of human life. As any moderately sensible economist knows, "economic man" does not exist. Anyone who asks businessmen how they make their decisions will find that the assumption that men are economic maximizers grossly distorts their characters. The assumption that men behave as economic men, which is known to be false as a descriptive statement, turns out to be useful in the construction of theory.

Markets are the second major concept invented by microeconomic theorists. Two general questions must be asked about markets: How are they formed? How do they work? The answer to the first question is this: The market of a decentralized economy is individualist in origin, spontaneously generated, and unintended. The market arises out of the activities of separate units—persons and firms—whose aims and efforts are directed not toward creating an order but rather toward fulfilling their own internally defined interests by whatever means they can muster. The individual unit acts for itself. From the coaction of like units emerges a structure that affects and constrains all of them. Once formed, a market becomes a force in itself, and a force that the constitutive units acting singly or in small numbers cannot control. Instead, in lesser or greater degree as market conditions vary, the creators become the creatures of the market that their activity gave rise to. Adam Smith's great achievement was to show how self-interested, greed-driven actions may produce good social outcomes if only political and social conditions permit free competition. If a laissez-faire economy is harmonious, it is so because the intentions of actors do not correspond with the outcomes their actions produce. What intervenes between the actors and the objects of their action in order to thwart their purposes? To account for the unexpectedly favorable outcomes of selfish acts, the concept of a market is brought into play. Each unit seeks its own good; the result of a number of units simultaneously doing so transcends the motives and the aims of the separate units. Each would like to work less hard and price his product higher. Taken together, all have to work harder and price their products lower. Each firm seeks to increase its profit; the result of many firms doing so drives the profit rate downward. Each man seeks his own end, and, in doing so, produces a result that was no part of his intention. Out of the mean ambition of its members, the greater good of society is produced.

The market is a cause interposed between the economic actors and the results they produce. It conditions their calculations, their behaviors, and their interactions. It is not an agent in the sense of A being the agent that produces outcome X. Rather it is a structural cause. A market constrains the units that comprise it from taking certain actions and disposes them toward taking others. The market, created by self-directed interacting economic units, selects behaviors according to their consequences. The market rewards some with high profits and assigns others to bankruptcy. Since a market is not an institution or an agent in any concrete or palpable sense, such statements become impressive only if they can be reliably inferred from a theory as part of a set of more elaborate expectations. They can be. Microeconomic theory explains how an economy operates and why certain effects are to be expected. . . .

International-political systems, like economic markets, are formed by the coaction of self-regarding units. International structures are defined in terms of the primary political units of an era, be they city states, empires, or nations. Structures emerge from the coexistence of states. No state intends to participate in the formation of a structure by which it and others will be constrained. International-political systems, like economic markets, are individualist in origin, spontaneously generated, and unintended. In both systems, structures are formed by the coaction of their units. Whether those units live, prosper, or die depends on their own efforts. Both systems are formed and maintained on a principle of self-help that applies to the units. . . .

In a microtheory, whether of international politics or of economics, the motivation of the actors is assumed rather than realistically described. I assume that states seek to ensure their survival. The assumption is a radical simplification made for the sake of constructing theory. The question to ask of the assumption, as ever, is not whether it is true but whether it is the most sensible and useful one that can be made. Whether it is a useful assumption depends on whether a theory based on the assumption can be contrived, a theory from which important consequences not otherwise obvious can be inferred. Whether it is a sensible assumption can be directly discussed.

Beyond the survival motive, the aims of states may be endlessly varied; they may range from the ambition to conquer the world to the desire merely to be left alone. Survival is a prerequisite to achieving any goals that states may have, other than the goal of promoting their own disappearance as political entities. The survival motive is taken as the ground of action in a world where the security of states is not assured, rather than as a realistic description of the impulse that lies behind every act of state. The assumption allows for the fact that no state always acts exclusively to ensure its survival. It allows for the fact that some states may persistently seek goals that they value more highly than survival; they may, for example, prefer amalgamation with other states to their own survival in form. It allows for the fact that in pursuit of its security no state will act with perfect knowledge and wisdom—if indeed we could know what those terms might mean. . . .

Actors may perceive the structure that constrains them and understand how it serves to reward some kinds of behavior and to penalize others. But then again they either may not see it or, seeing it, may for any of many reasons fail to conform their actions to the patterns that are most often rewarded and least often punished. To say that "the structure selects" means simply that those who conform to accepted and successful practices more often rise to the top and are likelier to stay there. The game one has to win is defined by the structure that determines the kind of player who is likely to prosper. . . .

2. The Character of the Units

The second term in the definition of domestic political structure specifies the functions performed by differentiated units. Hierarchy entails relations of super- and subordination among a system's parts, and that implies their differentiation. In defining domestic political structure the second term, like the first and third, is needed because each term points to a possible source of structural variation. The states that are the units of international-political systems are not formally differentiated by the functions they perform. Anarchy entails relations of coordination among a system's units, and that implies their sameness. The second term is not needed in defining international-political structure, because, so long as anarchy endures, states remain like units. International structures vary only through a change of organizing principle or, failing that, through variations in the capabilities of units. Nevertheless I shall discuss these like units here, because it is by their interactions that international-politics structures are generated.

Two questions arise: Why should states be taken as the units of the system? Given a wide variety of states, how can one call them "like units"? Questioning the choice of states as the primary units of international-political systems became popular in the 1960s and 1970s as it was at the turn of the century. Once one understands what is logically involved, the issue is easily resolved. Those who question the state-centric view do so for two main reasons. First, states are not the only actors of importance on the international scene. Second, states are declining in importance, and other actors are gaining, or so it is said. Neither reason is cogent, as the following discussion shows.

States are not and never have been the only international actors. But then structures are defined not by all of the actors that flourish within them but by the major ones. In defining a system's structure one chooses one or some of the infinitely many objects comprising the system and defines its structure in terms of them. For international-political systems, as for any system, one must first decide which units to take as being the parts of the system. Here the economic analogy will help again. The structure of a market is defined by the number of firms competing. If many roughly equal firms contend, a condition of perfect competition is approximated. If a few firms dominate the market, competition is said to be oligopolistic even though many smaller firms may also be in the field. But we are told that definitions of this sort cannot be applied to international politics because of the interpenetration of states, because of their inability to control the environment of their action, and because rising multinational corporations and other nonstate actors are difficult to regulate and may rival some states in influence. The importance of nonstate actors and the extent of transnational activities are obvious. The conclusion that the state-centric conception of international politics is made obsolete by them does not follow. That economists and economically minded politics scientists have thought that it does is ironic. The irony lies in the fact that all of the reasons given for scrapping the state-centric concept can be related more strongly and applied to firms. Firms competing with numerous others have no hope of controlling their market, and oligopolistic firms constantly struggle with imperfect success to do so. Firms interpenetrate, merge, and buy each up at a merry pace. Moreover, firms are constantly threatened and regulated by, shall we say, "nonfirm" actors. Some governments encourage concentration; others work to prevent it. The market structure of parts of an economy may move from a wider to a narrower competition or may move in the opposite direction, but whatever the extent and the frequency of change, market structures, generated by the interaction of firms, are defined in terms of them.

Just as economists define markets in terms of firms, so I define international-political structures in terms of states. If Charles P. Kindleberger were right in saying that "the nation-state is just about through as an economic unit,"[5] then the structure of international politics would have to be redefined. That would be necessary because economic capabilities cannot be separated from the other capabilities of states. The distinction frequently drawn between matters of high and low politics is misplaced. States use economic means for military and political ends; and military and political means for the achievement of economic interests.

An amended version of Kindleberger's statement may hold: Some states may be nearly washed up as economic entities, and others not. That poses no problem for international-political theory since international politics is mostly about inequalities anyway. So long as the major states are the major actors, the structure of international politics is defined in terms of them. That theoretical statement is of course borne out in practice. States set the scene in which they, along with non-state actors, state their dramas or carry on their humdrum affairs. Though they may choose to interfere little in the affairs of nonstate actors for long periods of time, states nevertheless set the terms of intercourse, whether by passively permitting informal rules to develop or by actively intervening to change rules that no longer suit them. When the crunch comes, states remake the rules by which other actors operate. Indeed, one may be struck by the ability of weak states to impede the operation of strong international corporations and by the attention the latter pay to the wishes of the former. . . .

States are the units whose interactions form the structure of international-political systems. They will long remain so. The death rate among states is remarkably low. Few states die; many firms do. . . . To call states "like units" is to say that each state is like all other states in being an autonomous political unit. It is another way of saying that states are sovereign. But sovereignty is also a bothersome concept. Many believe, as the anthropologist M. G. Smith has said, that "in a system of sovereign states no state is sovereign."[6] The error lies in identifying the sovereignty of states with their ability to do as they wish. To say that states are sovereign is not to say that they can do as they please, that they are free of others' influence, that they are able to get what they want. Sovereign states may be hardpressed all around, constrained to act in ways they would like to avoid, and able to do hardly anything just as they would like to. The sovereignty of states has never entailed their insulation from the effects of other states' actions. To be sovereign and to be dependent are not contradictory conditions. Sovereign states have seldom led free and easy lives. What then is sovereignty? To say that a state is sovereign means that it decides for itself how it will cope with its internal and external problems, including whether or not to seek assistance from others and in doing so to limit its freedom by making commitments to them. States develop their own strategies, chart their own courses, make their own decisions about how to meet whatever needs they experience and whatever desires they develop. It is no more contradictory to say that sovereign states are always constrained and often tightly so than it is to say that free individuals often make decisions under the heavy pressure of events.

Each state, like every other state, is a sovereign political entity. And yet the differences across states, from Costa Rica to the Soviet Union, from Gambia to the United States, are immense. States are alike, and they are also different. So are corporations, apples, universities, and people. Whenever we put two or more objects in the same category, we are saying that they are alike not in all respects but in some. No two objects in this world are identical, yet they can often be usefully compared and combined. "You can't add apples and oranges" is an old saying that seems to be especially popular among salesmen who do not want you to compare their wares with others. But we all know that the trick of adding dissimilar objects is to express the result in terms of a category that comprises them. Three apples plus four oranges equals seven pieces of fruit. The only interesting question is whether the category that classifies objects according to their common qualities is useful. One can add up a large number of widely varied objects and say that one has eight million things, but seldom need one do that.

States vary widely in size, wealth, power, and form. And yet variations in these and in other respects are variations among like units. In what way are they like units? How can they be placed in a single category? States are alike in the tasks that they face, though not in their abilities to perform them. The differences are of capability, not of function. States perform or try to perform tasks, most of which are common to all of them; the ends they aspire to are similar. Each state duplicates the activities of other states at least to a considerable extent. Each state has its agencies for making, executing, and interpreting laws and regulations, for raising revenues, and for defending itself. Each state supplies out of its own resources and by its own means most of the food, clothing, housing, transportation, and amenities consumed and used by its citizens. All states, except the smallest ones, do much more of their business at home than abroad. One has to be impressed with the functional similarity of states and, now more than ever before, with the similar lines their development follows. From the rich to the poor states, from the old to the new ones, nearly all of them take a larger hand in matters of economic regulation, of education, health, and housing, of culture and the arts, and so on almost endlessly. The increase of the activities of states is a strong and strikingly uniform international trend. The functions of states are similar, and distinctions among them arise principally from their varied capabilities. International politics consists of like units duplicating one another's activities.

3. The Distribution of Capabilities

The parts of a hierarchic system are related to one another in ways that are determined both by their functional differentiation and by the extent of their capabilities. The units of an anarchic system are functionally undifferentiated. The units of such an order are then distinguished primarily by their greater or lesser capabilities for performing similar tasks. This states formally what students of international politics have long noticed. The great powers of an era have always been marked off from others by practitioners and theorists alike. Students of national government make such distinctions as that between parliamentary and presidential systems; governmental systems differ in form. Students of international politics make distinctions between international-political systems only according to the number of their great powers. The structure of a system changes with changes in the distribution of capabilities across the system's units. And changes in structure change expectations about how the units of the system will behave and about the outcomes their interactions will produce. Domestically, the differentiated parts of a system may perform similar tasks. We know from observing the American government that executives sometimes legislate and legislatures sometimes execute. Internationally, like units sometimes perform different tasks . . . but two problems should be considered.

The first problem is this: Capability tells us something about units. Defining structure partly in terms of the distribution of capabilities seems to violate my instruction to keep unit attributes out of structural definitions. As I remarked earlier, structure is a highly but not entirely abstract concept. The maximum of abstraction allows a minimum of content, and that minimum is what is needed to enable one to say how the units stand in relation to one another. States are differently placed by their power. And yet one may wonder why only *capability* is included in the third part of the definition, and not such characteristics as ideology, form of government, peacefulness, bellicosity, or whatever. The answer is this: Power is estimated by comparing the capabilities of a number of units. Although capabilities are attributes of units, the distribution of capabilities across units is not. The distribution of capabilities is not a unit attribute, but rather a system-wide concept. . . .

The second problem is this: Though relations defined in terms of interactions must be excluded from structural definitions, relations defined in terms of grouping of states do seem to tell us something about how states are placed in the system. Why not specify how states stand in relation to one another by considering the alliances they form? Would doing so not be comparable to defining national political structures partly in terms of how presidents and prime ministers are related to other political agents? It would not be. Nationally as internationally, structural definitions deal with the relation of agents and agencies in terms of the organization of realms and not in terms of the accommodations and conflicts that may occur within them or the groupings that may now and then form. Parts of a government may draw together or pull apart, may oppose each other or cooperate in greater or lesser degree. These are the relations that form and dissolve within a system rather than structural alterations that mark a change from one system to another. This is made clear by the example that runs nicely parallel to the case of alliances. Distinguishing systems of political parties according to their number is common. A multiparty system changes if, say, eight parties become two, but not if two groupings of the eight form merely for the occasion of fighting an election. By the same logic, an international-political system in which three or more great powers have split into two alliances remains a multipolar system—structurally distinct from a bipolar system, a system in which no third power is able to challenge the top two. . . .

In defining international-political structures we take states with whatever traditions, habits, objectives, desires, and forms of government they may have. We do not ask whether states are revolutionary or legitimate, authoritarian or democratic, ideological or pragmatic. We abstract from every attribute of states except their capabilities. Nor in thinking about structure do we ask about the relations of states—their feelings of friendship and hostility, their diplomatic exchanges, the alliances they form, and the extent of the contacts and exchanges among them. We ask what range of expectations arises merely from looking at the type of order that prevails among them and at the distribution of capabilities within that order. We abstract from any particular qualities of states and from all of their concrete connections. What emerges is a positional picture, a general description of the ordered overall arrangement of a society written in terms of the placement of units rather than in terms of their qualities. . . .

ANARCHIC STRUCTURES AND BALANCES OF POWER

[We must now] examine the characteristics of anarchy and the expectations about outcomes associated with anarchic realms. . . . [This] is best accomplished by drawing some comparisons between behavior and outcomes in anarchic and hierarchic realms.

4. Violence at Home and Abroad

The state among states, it is often said, conducts its affairs in the brooding shadow of violence. Because some states may at any time use force, all states must be prepared to do so—or live at the mercy of their militarily more vigorous neighbors. Among states, the state of nature is a state of war. This is meant not in the sense that war constantly occurs but in the sense that, with each state deciding for itself whether or not to use force, war may at any time break out. Whether in the family, the community, or the world at large, contact without at least occasional conflict is inconceivable; and the hope that in the absence of an agent to manage or to manipulate conflicting parties the use of force will always be avoided cannot be realistically entertained. Among men as among states, anarchy, or the absence of government, is associated with the occurrence of violence.

The threat of violence and the recurrent use of force are said to distinguish international from national affairs. But in the history of the world surely most rulers have had to bear in mind that their subjects might use force to resist or overthrow them. If the absence of government is associated with the threat of violence, so also is its presence. A haphazard list of national tragedies illustrates the point all too well. The most destructive wars of the hundred years following the defeat of Napoleon took place not among states but *within* them. Estimates of deaths in China's Taiping Rebellion, which began in 1851 and lasted 13 years, range as high as 20 million. In the American Civil War some 600 thousand people lost their lives. In more recent history, forced collectivation and Stalin's purges eliminated 5 million Russians, and Hitler exterminated 6 million Jews. In some Latin American countries, coups d'états and rebellions have been normal features of national life. Between 1948 and 1957, for example, 200 thousand Colombians were killed in civil strife. In the middle 1970s most inhabitants of Idi Amin's Uganda must have felt their lives becoming nasty, brutish, and short, quite as in Thomas Hobbes's state of nature. If such cases constitute aberrations, they are uncomfortably common ones. We easily lose sight of the fact that struggles to achieve and maintain power, to establish order, and to contrive a kind of justice within states may be bloodier than wars among them.

If anarchy is identified with chaos, destruction, and death, then the distinction between anarchy and government does not tell us much. Which is more precarious: the life of a state among states, or of a government in relation to its subjects?

The answer varies with time and place. Among some states at some times, the actual or expected occurrence of violence is low. Within some states at some times, the actual or expected occurrence of violence is high. The use of force, or the constant fear of its use, are not sufficient grounds for distinguishing international from domestic affairs. If the possible and the actual use of force mark both national and international orders, then no durable distinction between the two realms can be drawn in terms of the use or the nonuse of force. No human order is proof against violence.

To discover qualitative differences between internal and external affairs one must look for a criterion other than the occurrence of violence. The distinction between international and national realms of politics is not found in the use or the nonuse of force but in their different structures. But if the dangers of being violently attacked are greater, say, in taking an evening stroll through downtown Detroit than they are in picnicking along the French and German border, what practical difference does the difference of structure make? Nationally as internationally, contact generates conflict and at times issues in violence. The difference between national and international politics lies not in the use of force but in the different modes of organization for doing something about it. A government, ruling by some standard of legitimacy, arrogates to itself the right to use force—that is, to apply a variety of sanctions to control the use of force by its subjects. If some use private force, others may appeal to the government. A government has no monopoly on the use of force, as is all too evident. An effective government, however, has a monopoly on the *legitimate* use of force, and legitimate here means that public agents are organized to prevent and to counter the private use of force. Citizens need not prepare to defend themselves. Public agencies do that. A national system is not one of self-help. The international system is.

5. Interdependence and Integration

The political significance of interdependence varies depending on whether a realm is organized, with relations of authority specified and established, or remains formally unorganized. Insofar as a realm is formally organized, its units are free to specialize, to pursue their own interests without concern for developing the means of maintaining their identity and preserving their security in the presence of others. They are free to specialize because they have no reason to fear the increased interdependence that goes with specialization. If those who specialize most benefit most, then competition in specialization ensues. Goods are manufactured, grain is produced, law and order are maintained, commerce is conducted, and financial services are provided by people who ever more narrowly specialize. In simple economic terms, the cobbler depends on the tailor for his pants and the tailor on the cobbler for his shoes, and each would be ill-clad without the services of the other. In simple political terms, Kansas depends on Washington for protection and regulation and Washington depends on Kansas for beef and wheat. In saying that in such situations interdependence is close, one need not maintain that the one part could not learn to live without the other. One need only say that the cost of breaking the interdependent relation would be high. Persons and institutions depend

heavily on one another because of the different tasks they perform and the different goods they produce and exchange. The parts of a polity bind themselves
together by their differences.[7]

Differences between national and international structures are reflected in the
ways the units of each system define their ends and develop the means for reaching them. In anarchic realms, like units coact. In hierarchic realms, unlike units
interact. In an anarchic realm, the units are functionally similar and tend to remain
so. Like units work to maintain a measure of independence and may even strive for
autarchy. In a hierarchic realm, the units are differentiated, and they tend to
increase the extent of their specialization. Differentiated units become closely
interdependent, the more closely so as their specialization proceeds. Because of
the difference of structure, interdependence within and interdependence among
nations are two distinct concepts. So as to follow the logicians' admonition to keep
a single meaning for a given term throughout one's discourse, I shall use "integration" to describe the condition within nations and "interdependence" to describe
the condition among them.

Although states are like units functionally, they differ vastly in their capabilities. Out of such differences something of a division of labor develops. The division
of labor across nations, however, is slight in comparison with the highly articulated
division of labor within them. Integration draws the parts of a nation closely
together. Interdependence among nations leaves them loosely connected.
Although the integration of nations is often talked about, it seldom takes place.
Nations could mutually enrich themselves by further dividing not just the labor
that goes into the production of goods but also some of the other tasks they perform, such as political management and military defense. Why does their integration not take place? The structure of international politics limits the cooperation of
states in two ways.

In a self-help system each of the units spends a portion of its effort, not in for-
warding its own good, but in providing the means of protecting itself against others. Specialization in a system of divided labor works to everyone's advantage,
though not equally so. Inequality in the expected distribution of the increased
product works strongly against extension of the division of labor internationally.
When faced with the possibility of cooperating for mutual gain, states that feel
insecure must ask how the gain will be divided. They are compelled to ask not
"Will both of us gain?" but "Who will gain more?" If an expected gain is to be
divided, say, in the ratio of two to one, one state may use its disproportionate gain
to implement a policy intended to damage or destroy the other. Even the
prospect of large absolute gains for both parties does not elicit their cooperation
so long as each fears how the other will use its increased capabilities. Notice that
the impediments to collaboration may not lie in the character and the immediate
intention of either party. Instead, the condition of insecurity—at the least, the
uncertainty of each about the other's future intentions and actions—works against
their cooperation. . . .

A state worries about a division of possible gains that may favor others more
than itself. That is the first way in which the structure of international politics limits
the cooperation of states. A state also worries lest it become dependent on others

through cooperative endeavors and exchanges of goods and services. That is the second way in which the structure of international politics limits the cooperation of states. The more a state specializes, the more it relies on others to supply the materials and goods that it is not producing. The larger a state's imports and exports, the more it depends on others. The world's well-being would be increased if an ever more elaborate division of labor were developed, but states would thereby place themselves in situations of ever closer interdependence. Some states may not resist that. For small and ill-endowed states the costs of doing so are excessively high. But states that can resist becoming ever more enmeshed with others ordinarily do so in either or both of two ways. States that are heavily dependent, or closely interdependent, worry about securing that which they depend on. The high interdependence of states means that the states in question experience, or are subject to, the common vulnerability that high interdependence entails. Like other organizations, states seek to control what they depend on or to lessen the extent of their dependency. This simple thought explains quite a bit of the behavior of states: their imperial thrusts to widen the scope of their control and their autarchic strivings toward greater self-sufficiency.

Structures encourage certain behaviors and penalize those who do not respond to the encouragement. Nationally, many lament the extreme development of the division of labor, a development that results in the allocation of ever narrower tasks to individuals. And yet specialization proceeds, and its extent is a measure of the development of societies. In a formally organized realm a premium is put on each unit's being able to specialize in order to increase its value to others in a system of divided labor. The domestic imperative is "specialize"! Internationally, many lament the resources states spend unproductively for their own defense and the opportunities they miss to enhance the welfare of their people through cooperation with other states. And yet the ways of states change little. In an unorganized realm each unit's incentive is to put itself in a position to be able to take care of itself since no one else can be counted on to do so. The international imperative is "take care of yourself"! Some leaders of nations may understand that the wellbeing of all of them would increase through their participation in a fuller division of labor. But to act on the idea would be to act on a domestic imperative, an imperative that does not run internationally. What one might want to do in the absence of structural constraints is different from what one is encouraged to do in their presence. States do not willingly place themselves in situations of increased dependence. In a self-help system, considerations of security subordinate economic gain to political interest. . . .

6. Structures and Strategies

That motives and outcomes may well be disjoined should now be easily seen. Structures cause nations to have consequences they were not intended to have. Surely most of the actors will notice that, and at least some of them will be able to figure out why. They may develop a pretty good sense of just how structures work their effects. Will they not then be able to achieve their original ends by appropriately adjusting their strategies? Unfortunately, they often cannot. To show why this is so I shall give only a few examples; once the point is made, the reader will easily think of others.

If shortage of a commodity is expected, all are collectively better off if they buy less of it in order to moderate price increases and to distribute shortages equitably. But because some will be better off if they lay in extra supplies quickly, all have a strong incentive to do so. If one expects others to make a run on a bank, one's prudent course is to run faster then they do even while knowing that if few others run, the bank will remain solvent, and if many run, it will fail. In such cases, pursuit of individual interest produces collective results that nobody wants, yet individuals by behaving differently will hurt themselves without altering outcomes. These two much used examples establish the main point. Some courses of action I cannot sensibly follow unless we are pretty sure that many others will as well. . . .

We may well notice that our behavior produces unwanted outcomes, but we are also likely to see that such instances as these are examples of what Alfred E. Kahn describes as "large" changes that are brought about by the accumulation of "small" decisions. In such situations people are victims of the "tyranny of small decisions," a phrase suggesting that "if one hundred consumers choose option x, and this causes the market to make decision X (where X equals $100x$), it is not necessarily true that those same consumers would have voted for that outcome if that large decision had ever been presented for their explicit consideration."[8] If the market does not present the large question for decision, then individuals are doomed to making decisions that are sensible within their narrow contexts even though they know all the while that in making such decisions they are bringing about a result that most of them do not want. Either that or they organize to overcome some of the effects of the market by changing its structure—for example, by bringing consumer units roughly up to the size of the units that are making producers' decisions. This nicely makes the point: So long as one leaves the structure unaffected it is not possible for changes in the intentions and the actions of particular actors to produce desirable outcomes or to avoid undesirable ones. . . . The only remedies for strong structural effects are structural changes.

Structural constraints cannot be wished away, although many fail to understand this. In every age and place, the units of self-help systems—nations, corporations, or whatever—are told that the greater good, along with their own, requires them to act for the sake of the system and not for their own narrowly defined advantage. In the 1950s, as fear of the world's destruction in nuclear war grew, some concluded that the alternative to world destruction was world disarmament. In the 1970s, with the rapid growth of population, poverty, and pollution, some concluded, as one political scientist put it, that "states must meet the needs of the political ecosystem in its global dimensions or court annihilation."[9] The international interest must be served; and if that means anything at all, it means that national interests are subordinate to it. The problems are found at the global level. Solutions to the problems continue to depend on national policies. What are the conditions that would make nations more or less willing to obey the injunctions that are so often laid on them? How can they resolve the tension between pursuing their own interests and acting for the sake of the system? No one has shown how that can be done, although many wring their hands and plead for rational behavior. The very problem, however, is that rational behavior, given structural constraints, does not lead to the wanted results. With each country constrained to take care of itself, no one can take care of the system.[10]

A strong sense of peril and doom may lead to a clear definition of ends that must be achieved. Their achievement is not thereby made possible. The possibility of effective action depends on the ability to provide necessary means. It depends even more so on the existence of conditions that permit nations and other organizations to follow appropriate policies and strategies. World-shaking problems cry for global solutions, but there is no global agency to provide them. Necessities do not create possibilities. Wishing that final causes were efficient ones does not make them so.

Great tasks can be accomplished only by agents of great capability. That is why states, and especially the major ones, are called on to do what is necessary for the world's survival. But states have to do whatever they think necessary for their own preservation, since no one can be relied on to do it for them. Why the advice to place the international interest above national interests is meaningless can be explained precisely in terms of the distinction between micro- and macrotheories. . . .

Some have hoped that changes in the awareness and purpose, in the organization and ideology of states would change the quality of international life. Over the centuries states have changed in many ways, but the quality of international life has remained much the same. States may seek reasonable and worthy ends, but they cannot figure out how to reach them. The problem is not in their stupidity or ill will, although one does not want to claim that those qualities are lacking. The depth of the difficulty is not understood until one realizes that intelligence and goodwill cannot discover and act on adequate programs. Early in this century Winston Churchill observed that the British-German naval race promised disaster *and* that Britain had no realistic choice other than to run it. States facing global problems are like individual consumers trapped by the "tyranny of small decisions." States, like consumers, can get out of the trap only by changing the structure of their field of activity. The message bears repeating: The only remedy for a strong structural effect is a structural change.

7. The Virtues of Anarchy

To achieve their objectives and maintain their security, units in a condition of anarchy—be they people, corporations, states, or whatever—must rely on the means they can generate and the arrangements they can make for themselves. Self-help is necessarily the principle of action in an anarchic order. A self-help situation is one of high risk—of bankruptcy in the economic realm and of war in a world of free states. It is also one in which organizational costs are low. Within an economy or within an international order, risks may be avoided or lessened by moving from a situation of coordinate action to one of super- and subordination, that is, by erecting agencies with effective authority and extending a system of rules. Government emerges where the functions of regulation and management themselves become distinct and specialized tasks. The costs of maintaining a hierarchic order are frequently ignored by those who deplore its absence. Organizations have at least two aims: to get something done and to maintain themselves as organizations. Many of their activities are directed toward the second purpose. The leaders of organizations, and political leaders preeminently, are not masters of the matters their organizations deal with. They have become leaders not by being experts on one thing or another but by excelling in the organizational arts—in maintaining control of a group's members, in eliciting predictable and satisfactory efforts from them, in holding a group together. In making political decisions, the first and most important concern is not to achieve the aims the members of an organization may have but to secure the continuity and health of the organization itself.[11]

Along with the advantages of hierarchic orders go the costs. In hierarchic orders, moreover, the means of control become an object of struggle. Substantive issues become entwined with efforts to influence or control the controllers. The hierarchic ordering of politics adds one to the already numerous objects of struggle, and the object added is at a new order of magnitude.

If the risks of war are unbearably high, can they be reduced by organizing to manage the affairs of nations? At a minimum, management requires controlling the military forces that are at the disposal of states. Within nations, organizations have to work to maintain themselves. As organizations, nations, in working to maintain themselves, sometimes have to use force against dissident elements and areas. As hierarchical systems, governments nationally or globally are disrupted by the defection of major parts. In a society of states with little coherence, attempts at world government would founder on the inability of an emerging central authority to mobilize the resources needed to create and maintain the unity of the system by regulating and managing its parts. The prospect of world government would be an invitation to prepare for world civil war. . . . States cannot entrust managerial powers to a central agency unless that agency is able to protect its client states. The more powerful the clients and the more the power of each of them appears as a threat to the others, the greater the power lodged in the center must be. The greater the power of the center, the stronger the incentive for states to engage in a struggle to control it.

States, like people, are insecure in proportion to the extent of their freedom. If freedom is wanted, insecurity must be accepted. Organizations that establish relations of authority and control may increase insecurity as they decrease freedom. If might does not make right, whether among people or states, then some institution or agency has intervened to lift them out of nature's realm. The more influential the agency, the stronger the desire to control it becomes. In contrast, units in an anarchic order act for their own sakes and not for the sake of preserving an organization and furthering their fortunes within it. Force is used for one's own interest. In the absence of organization, people or states are free to leave one another alone. Even when they do not do so, they are better able, in the absence of the politics of the organization, to concentrate on the politics of the problem and to aim for a minimum agreement that will permit their separate existence rather than a maximum agreement for the sake of maintaining unity. If might decides, then bloody struggles over right can more easily be avoided.

Nationally, the force of a government is exercised in the name of right and justice. Internationally, the force of a state is employed for the sake of its own protection and advantage. Rebels challenge a government's claim to authority; they question the rightfulness of its rule. Wars among states cannot settle questions of authority and right; they can only determine the allocation of gains and losses among contenders and settle for a time the question of who is the stronger. Nationally, relations of authority are established. Internationally, only relations of strength result. Nationally, private force used against a government threatens the political system. Force used by a state—a public body—is, from the international perspective, the private use of force; but there is no government to overthrow and no governmental apparatus to capture. Short of a drive toward world hegemony, the private use of force does not threaten the system of international politics, only some of its members. War pits some states against others in a struggle among similarly constituted entities. The power of the strong may deter the weak from asserting their claims, not because the weak recognize a kind of rightfulness of rule on the part of the strong, but simply because it is not sensible to tangle with them. Conversely, the weak may enjoy considerable freedom of action if they are so far removed in their capabilities from the strong that the latter are not much bothered by their actions or much concerned by marginal increases in their capabilities.

National politics is the realm of authority, of administration, and of law. International politics is the realm of power, of struggle, and of accommodation. The international realm is preeminently a political one. The national realm is variously described as being hierarchic, vertical, centralized, heterogeneous, directed, and contrived; the international realm, as being anarchic, horizontal, decentralized, homogeneous, undirected, and mutually adaptive. The more centralized the order, the nearer to the top the locus of decisions ascends. Internationally, decisions are made at the bottom level, there being scarcely any other. In the vertical–horizontal dichotomy, international structures assume the prone position. Adjustments are made internationally, but they are made without a formal or authoritative adjuster. Adjustment and accommodation proceed by mutual adaptation.[12] Action and reaction, and reaction to the reaction, proceed by a piecemeal process. The parties feel each other out, so to speak, and define a situation simultaneously with its development. Among coordinate units, adjustment is achieved and accommodations arrived at by the exchange of "considerations," in a condition, as Chester Barnard put it, "in which the duty of command and the desire to obey are essentially absent."[13] Where the contest is over considerations, the parties seek to maintain or improve their positions by maneuvering, by bargaining, or by fighting. The manner and intensity of the competition is determined by the desires and the abilities of parties that are at once separate and interacting.

Whether or not by force, each state plots the course it thinks will best serve its interests. If force is used by one state or its use is expected, the recourse of other states is to use force or be prepared to use it singly or in combination. No appeal can be made to a higher entity clothed with the authority and equipped with the ability to act on its own initiative. Under such conditions the possibility that force will be used by one or another of the parties looms always as a threat in the background. In politics force is said to be the *ultima ratio*. In international politics force serves, not only as the *ultima ratio*, but indeed as the first and constant one. To limit force to being the *ultima ratio* of politics implies, in the words of Ortega y Gasset, "the previous submission of force to methods of reason."[14] The constant possibility that force will be used limits manipulations, moderates demands, and serves as an incentive for the settlement of disputes. One who knows that pressing too hard may lead to war has strong reason to consider whether possible gains are worth the risks entailed. The threat of force internationally is comparable to the role of the strike in labor and management bargaining. "The few strikes that take place are in a sense," as Livernash has said, "the cost of the strike option which produces settlements in the large mass of negotiations."[15] Even if workers seldom strike, their doing so is always a possibility. The possibility of industrial disputes leading to long and costly strikes encourages labor and management to face difficult issues, to try to understand each other's problems, and to work hard to find accommodations. The possibility that conflicts among nations may lead to long and costly wars has similarly sobering effects.

8. Anarchy and Hierarchy

I have described anarchies and hierarchies as though every political order were of one type or the other. Many, and I suppose most, political scientists who write of structures allow for a greater, and sometimes for a bewildering, variety of types. Anarchy is seen as one end of a continuum whose other end is marked by the presence of a legitimate and competent government. International politics is then described as being flecked with particles of government and alloyed with elements of community—supranational organizations whether universal or regional, alliances, multinational corporations, networks of trade, and whatnot. International-political systems are thought of as being more or less anarchic.

Those who view the world as a modified anarchy do so, it seems, for two reasons. First, anarchy is taken to mean not just the absence of government but also the presence of disorder and chaos. Since world politics, although not reliably peaceful, falls short of unrelieved chaos, students are inclined to see a lessening of anarchy in each outbreak of peace. Since world politics, although not formally organized, is not entirely without institutions and orderly procedures, students are inclined to see a lessening of anarchy when alliances form, when transactions across national borders increase, and when international agencies multiply. Such views confuse structure with process, and I have drawn attention to that error often enough.

Second, the two simple categories of anarchy and hierarchy do not seem to accommodate the infinite social variety our senses record. Why insist on reducing the types of structure to two instead of allowing for a greater variety? Anarchies are ordered by the juxtaposition of similar units, but those similar units are not identical. Some specialization by function develops among them. Hierarchies are ordered by the social division of labor among units specializing in different tasks, but the resemblance of units does not vanish. Much duplication of effort continues. All societies are organized segmentally or hierarchically in greater or lesser degree. Why not, then, define additional social types according to the mixture of organizing principles they embody? One might conceive of some societies approaching the purely anarchic, of others approaching the purely hierarchic, and of still others reflecting specified mixes of the two organizational types. In anarchies the exact likeness of units and the determination of relations by capability alone would describe a realm wholly of politics and power with none of the interaction of units guided by administration and conditioned by authority. In hierarchies the complete differentiation of parts and the full specification of their functions would produce a realm wholly of authority and administration with none of the interaction of parts affected by politics and power. Although such pure orders do not exist, to distinguish realms by their organizing principles is nevertheless proper and important.

Increasing the number of categories would bring the classification of societies closer to reality. But that would be to move away from a theory claiming explanatory power to a less theoretical system promising greater descriptive accuracy. One who wishes to explain rather than to describe should resist moving in that direction if resistance is reasonable. Is it? What does one gain by insisting on two types when admitting three or four would still be to simplify boldly? One gains clarity and economy of concepts. A new concept should be introduced only to cover matters that existing concepts do not reach. If some societies are neither anarchic or hierarchic, if their structures are defined by some third ordering principle, then we would have to define a third system.[16] All societies are mixed. Elements in them represent both of the ordering principles. That does not mean that some societies are ordered according to a third principle. Usually one can easily identify the principle by which a society is ordered. The appearance of anarchic sectors within hierarchies does not alter and should not obscure the ordering principle of the larger system, for those sectors are anarchic only within limits. The attributes and behavior of the units populating those sectors within the larger system differ, moreover, from what they should be and how they would behave outside of it. Firms in oligopolistic markets again are perfect examples of this. They struggle against one another, but because they need not prepare to defend themselves physically, they can afford to specialize and to participate more fully in the division of economic labor than states can. Nor do the states that populate an anarchic world find it impossible to work with one another, to make agreements limiting their arms, and to cooperate in establishing organizations. Hierarchic elements within international structures limit and restrain the exercise of sovereignty but only in ways strongly conditioned by the anarchy of the larger system. The anarchy of that order strongly affects the likelihood of cooperation, the extent of arms agreements, and the jurisdiction of international organizations. . . .

NOTES

1. S. F. Nadel, *The Theory of Social Structure* (Glencoe, Ill.: Free Press, 1957), pp. 8–11.
2. Ibid., pp. 104–9.
3. William T. R. Fox, "The Uses of International Relations Theory," in William T. R. Fox, ed., *Theoretical Aspects of International Relations* (Notre Dame, Ind.: University of Notre Dame Press, 1959), p. 35.
4. Marriet Martineau, *The Positive Philosophy of Auguste Comte: Freely Translated and Condensed*, 3rd ed. (London: Kegan Paul, Trench, Trubner, 1983), vol. 2, pp. 51–53;

George Katona, "Rational Behavior and Economic Behavior," *Psychological Review* 60 (September 1953).

5. Charles P. Kindleberger, *American Business Abroad* (New Haven, Ct.: Yale University Press, 1969), p. 207.

6. Smith should know better. Translated into terms that he has himself so effectively used, to say that states are sovereign is to say that they are segments of a plural society. See his "A Structural Approach to Comparative Politics" in David Easton, ed., *Varieties of Politics Theories* (Englewood Cliffs, N.J.: Prentice Hall, 1966), p. 122; cf. his "On Segmentary Lineage Systems," *Journal of the Royal Anthropological Society of Great Britain and Ireland* 86 (July–December 1956).

7. Émile Durkheim, *The Division of Labor in Society,* trans. George Simpson (New York: Free Press, 1964), p. 212.

8. Alfred E. Kahn, "The Tyranny of Small Decision: Market Failure, Imperfections and Limits of Econometrics," in Bruce M. Russett, ed., *Economic Theories of International Relations* (Chicago, Ill.: Markham, 1966), p. 23.

9. Richard W. Sterling, *Macropolitics: International Relations in a Global Society* (New York: Knopf, 1974), p. 336.

10. Put differently, states face a "prisoners' dilemma." If each of two parties follows his own interest, both end up worse off than if each acted to achieve joint interests. For thorough examination of the logic of such situations, see Glenn H. Snyder and Paul Diesing, *Conflict among Nations* (Princeton, N.J.: Princeton University Press, 1977); for brief and suggestive international applications, see Robert Jervis, "Cooperation under the Security Dilemma," *World Politics* 30 (January 1978).

11. Cf. Paul Diesing, *Reason in Society* (Urbana, Ill.: University of Illinois Press, 1962), pp. 198–204; Anthony Downs, *Inside Bureaucracy* (Boston: Little, Brown, 1967), pp. 262–70.

12. Cf. Chester I. Barnard, "On Planning for World Government," in Chester I. Barnard, ed., *Organization and Management* (Cambridge, Mass.: Harvard University Press, 1948), pp. 148–52; Michael Polanyi, "The Growth of Thought in Society," *Economica* 8 (November 1941), pp. 428–56.

13. Barnard, "On Planning," pp. 150–51.

14. Quoted in Chalmers A. Johnson, *Revolutionary Change* (Boston: Little, Brown, 1966), p. 13.

15. E. R. Livernash, "The Relation of Power to the Structure and Process of Collective Bargaining," in Bruce M. Russett, ed., *Economic Theories of International Politics* (Chicago, Ill.: Markham, 1963), p. 430.

16. Émile Durkheim's depiction of solidary and mechanical societies still provides the best explication of the two ordering principles, and his logic in limiting the types of society to two continues to be compelling despite the efforts of his many critics to overthrow it (see esp. *The Division of Labor in Society*).

Anarchy and the Struggle for Power

JOHN J. MEARSHEIMER

Great powers, I argue, are always searching for opportunities to gain power over their rivals, with hegemony as their final goal. This perspective does not allow for status quo powers, except for the unusual state that achieves preponderance. Instead, the system is populated with great powers that have revisionist intentions at their core. This chapter presents a theory that explains this competition for power. Specifically, I attempt to show that there is a compelling logic behind my claim that great powers seek to maximize their share of world power. . . .

WHY STATES PURSUE POWER

My explanation for why great powers vie with each other for power and strive for hegemony is derived from five assumptions about the international system. None of these assumptions alone mandates that states behave competitively. Taken together, however, they depict a world in which states have considerable reason to think and sometimes behave aggressively. In particular, the system encourages states to look for opportunities to maximize their power vis-à-vis other states. . . .

The first assumption is that the international system is anarchic, which does not mean that it is chaotic or riven by disorder. It is easy to draw that conclusion, since realism depicts a world characterized by security competition and war. By itself, however, the realist notion of anarchy has nothing to do with conflict; it is an ordering principle, which says that the system comprises independent states that have no central authority above them. Sovereignty, in other words, inheres in states because there is no higher ruling body in the international system. There is no "government over governments."

The second assumption is that great powers inherently possess some offensive military capability, which gives them the wherewithal to hurt and possibly destroy each other. States are potentially dangerous to each other, although some states have more military might than others and are therefore more dangerous. A state's military power is usually identified with the particular weaponry at its disposal, although even if there were no weapons, the individuals in those states could still use their feet and hands to attack the population of another state. After all, for every neck, there are two hands to choke it.

The third assumption is that states can never be certain about other states' intentions. Specifically, no state can be sure that another state will not use its offensive military capability to attack the first state. This is not to say that states necessarily have hostile intentions. Indeed, all of the states in the system may be reliably benign, but it is impossible to be sure of that judgment because intentions are impossible to divine with 100 percent certainty. There are many possible causes of aggression, and no state can be sure that another state is not motivated by one of them. Furthermore, intentions can change quickly, so a state's intentions can be benign one day and hostile the next. Uncertainty about intentions is unavoidable, which means that states can never be sure that other states do not have offensive intentions to go along with their offensive capabilities.

The fourth assumption is that survival is the primary goal of great powers. Specifically, states seek to maintain their territorial integrity and the autonomy of their domestic political order. Survival dominates other motives because, once a state is conquered, it is unlikely to be in a position to pursue other aims. . . . States can and do pursue other goals, of course, but security is their most important objective.

The fifth assumption is that great powers are rational actors. They are aware of their external environment and they think strategically about how to survive in it. In particular, they consider the preferences of other states and how their own behavior is likely to affect the behavior of those other states, and how the behavior of those other states is likely to affect their own strategy for survival. Moreover, states pay attention to the long term as well as the immediate consequences of their actions.

As emphasized, none of these assumptions alone dictates that great powers as a general rule *should* behave aggressively toward each other. There is surely the possibility that some state might have hostile intentions, but the only assumption dealing with a specific motive that is common to all states says that their principal objective is to survive, which by itself is a rather harmless goal. Nevertheless, when the five assumptions are married together, they create powerful incentives for great powers to think and act offensively with regard to each other. In particular, three general patterns of behavior result: fear, self-help, and power maximization.

STATE BEHAVIOR

Great powers fear each other. They regard each other with suspicion, and they worry that war might be in the offing. They anticipate danger. There is little room for trust among states. For sure, the level of fear varies across time and space, but it cannot be reduced to a trivial level. From the perspective of any one great power, all other great powers are potential enemies. This point is illustrated by the reaction of the United Kingdom and France to German reunification at the end of the Cold War. Despite the fact that these three states had been close allies for almost forty-five years, both the United Kingdom and France immediately began worrying about the potential dangers of a united Germany.

The basis of this fear is that in a world where great powers have the capability to attack each other and might have the motive to do so, any state bent on survival must be at least suspicious of other states and reluctant to trust them. Add to this the "911" problem—the absence of a central authority to which a threatened state can turn for help—and states have even greater incentive to fear each other. Moreover, there is no mechanism, other than the possible self-interest of third parties, for punishing an aggressor. Because it is sometimes difficult to deter potential aggressors, states have ample reason not to trust other states and to be prepared for war with them.

The possible consequences of falling victim to aggression further amplify the importance of fear as a motivating force in world politics. Great powers do not compete with each other as if international politics were merely an economic marketplace. Political competition among states is a much more dangerous business than mere economic intercourse; the former can lead to war, and war often means mass killing on the battlefield as well as mass murder of civilians. In extreme cases, war can even lead to the destruction of states. The horrible consequences of war sometimes cause states to view each other not just as competitors, but as potentially deadly enemies. Political antagonism, in short, tends to be intense, because the stakes are great.

States in the international system also aim to guarantee their own survival. Because other states are potential threats, and because there is no higher authority to come to their rescue when they dial 911, states cannot depend on others for their own security. Each state tends to see itself as vulnerable and alone, and therefore it aims to provide for its own survival. In international politics, God helps those who help themselves. This emphasis on self-help does not preclude states from forming alliances. But alliances are only temporary marriages of convenience: today's alliance partner might be tomorrow's enemy, and today's enemy might be tomorrow's alliance partner. For example, the United States fought with China and the Soviet Union against Germany and Japan in World War II, but soon thereafter flip-flopped enemies and partners and allied with West Germany and Japan against China and the Soviet Union during the Cold War.

States operating in a self-help world almost always act according to their own self-interest and do not subordinate their interests to the interests of other states, or to the interests of the so-called international community. The reason is simple: it pays to be selfish in a self-help world. This is true in the short term as well as in the long term, because if a state loses in the short run, it might not be around for the long haul.

Apprehensive about the ultimate intentions of other states, and aware that they operate in a self-help system, states quickly understand that the best way to ensure their survival is to be the most powerful state in the system. The stronger a state is relative to its potential rivals, the less likely it is that any of those rivals will attack it and threaten its survival. Weaker states will be reluctant to pick fights with more powerful states because the weaker states are likely to suffer military defeat. Indeed, the bigger the gap in power between any two states, the less likely it is that the weaker will attack the stronger. Neither Canada nor Mexico, for example, would countenance attacking the United States, which is far more powerful than its neighbors. The ideal situation is to be the hegemon in the system. . . . Survival would then be almost guaranteed.

Consequently, states pay close attention to how power is distributed among them, and they make a special effort to maximize their share of world power. Specifically, they look for opportunities to alter the balance of power by acquiring additional increments of power at the expense of potential rivals. States employ a variety of means—economic, diplomatic, and military—to shift the balance of power in their favor, even if doing so makes other states suspicious or even hostile. Because one state's gain in power is another state's loss, great powers tend to have a zero-sum mentality when dealing with each other. The trick, of course, is to be the winner in this competition and to dominate the other states in the system. Thus, the claim that states maximize relative power is tantamount to arguing that states are disposed to think offensively toward other states, even though their ultimate motive is simply to survive. In short, great powers have aggressive intentions.

Even when a great power achieves a distinct military advantage over its rivals, it continues looking for chances to gain more power. The pursuit of power stops only when hegemony is achieved. The idea that a great power might feel secure without dominating the system, provided it has an "appropriate amount" of power, is not persuasive, for two reasons. First, it is difficult to assess how much relative power one state must have over its rivals before it is secure. Is twice as much power an appropriate threshold? Or is three times as much power the magic number? The root of the problem is that power calculations alone do not determine which side wins a war. Clever strategies, for example, sometimes allow less powerful states to defeat more powerful foes.

Second, determining how much power is enough becomes even more complicated when great powers contemplate how power will be distributed among them ten or twenty years down the road. The capabilities of individual states vary over time, sometimes markedly, and it is often difficult to predict the direction and scope of change in the balance of power. Remember, few in the West anticipated the collapse of the Soviet Union before it happened. In fact, during the first half of the Cold War, many in the West feared that the Soviet economy would eventually generate greater wealth than the American economy, which would cause a marked power shift against the United States and its allies. What the future holds for China and Russia and what the balance of power will look like in 2020 is difficult to foresee.

Given the difficulty of determining how much power is enough for today and tomorrow, great powers recognize that the best way to ensure their security is to achieve hegemony now, thus eliminating any possibility of a challenge by another great power. Only a misguided state would pass up an opportunity to be the hegemon in the system because it thought it already had sufficient power to survive. But even if a great power does not have the wherewithal to achieve hegemony (and that is usually the case), it will still act offensively to amass as much power as it can, because states are almost always better off with more rather than less power. In short, states do not become status quo powers until they completely dominate the system.

All states are influenced by this logic, which means that not only do they look for opportunities to take advantage of one another, they also work to ensure that other states do not take advantage of them. After all, rival states are driven by the same logic, and most states are likely to recognize their own motives at play in the actions of other states. In short, states ultimately pay attention to defense as well as offense. They think about conquest themselves, and they work to check aggressor states from gaining power at their expense. This inexorably leads to a world of constant security competition, where states are willing to lie, cheat, and use brute force if it helps them gain advantage over their rivals. Peace, if one defines that concept as a state of tranquility or mutual concord, is not likely to break out in this world. . . .

It should be apparent from this discussion that saying that states are power maximizers is tantamount to saying that they care about relative power, not absolute power. There is an important distinction here, because states concerned about relative power behave differently than do states interested in absolute power. States that maximize relative power are concerned primarily with the distribution of material capabilities. In particular, they try to gain as large a power advantage as possible over potential rivals, because power is the best means to survival in a dangerous world. Thus, states motivated by relative power concerns are likely to forgo large gains in their own power, if such gains give rival states even greater power, for smaller national gains that nevertheless provide them with a power advantage over their rivals. States that maximize absolute power, on the other hand, care only about the size of their own gains, not those of other states. They are not motivated by balance-of-power logic but instead are concerned with amassing power without regard to how much power other states control. They would jump at the opportunity for large gains, even if a rival gained more in the deal. Power, according to this logic, is not a means to an end (survival), but an end in itself.

CALCULATED AGGRESSION

There is obviously little room for status quo powers in a world where states are inclined to look for opportunities to gain more power. Nevertheless, great powers cannot always act on their offensive intentions, because behavior is influenced not only by what states want, but also by their capacity to realize these desires. Every state might want to be king of the hill, but not every state has the wherewithal to compete for that lofty position, much less achieve it. Much depends on how military might is distributed among the great powers. A great power that has a marked power advantage over its rivals is likely to behave more aggressively, because it has the capability as well as the incentive to do so.

By contrast, great powers facing powerful opponents will be less inclined to consider offensive action and more concerned with defending the existing balance of power from threats by their more powerful opponents. Let there be an opportunity for those weaker states to revise the balance in their own favor, however, and they will take advantage of it.

In short, great powers are not mindless aggressors so bent on gaining power that they charge headlong into losing wars or pursue Pyrrhic victories. On the contrary, before great powers take offensive actions, they think carefully about the balance of power and about how other states will react to their moves. They weigh the costs and risks of offense against the likely benefits. If the benefits do not outweigh the risks, they sit tight and wait for a more propitious moment. Nor do states start arms races that are unlikely to improve their overall position. . . . States sometimes limit defense spending either because spending more would bring no strategic advantage or because spending more would weaken the economy and undermine the state's power in the long run. To paraphrase Clint Eastwood, a state has to know its limitations to survive in the international system.

Nevertheless, great powers miscalculate from time to time because they invariably make important decisions on the basis of imperfect information. States hardly ever have complete information about any situation they confront. There are two dimensions to this problem. Potential adversaries have incentives to misrepresent their own strength or weakness, and to conceal their true aims. For example, a weaker state trying to deter a stronger state is likely to exaggerate its own power to discourage the potential aggressor from attacking. On the other hand, a state bent on aggression is likely to emphasize its peaceful goals while exaggerating its military weakness, so that the potential victim does not build up its own arms and thus leaves itself vulnerable to attack. Probably no national leader was better at practicing this kind of deception than Adolf Hitler.

But even if disinformation was not a problem, great powers are often unsure about how their own military forces, as well as the adversary's, will perform on the battlefield. For example, it is sometimes difficult to determine in advance how new weapons and untested combat units will perform in the face of enemy fire. Peacetime maneuvers and war games are helpful but imperfect indicators of what is likely to happen in actual combat. Fighting wars is a complicated business in which it is often difficult to predict outcomes. . . .

Great powers are also sometimes unsure about the resolve of opposing states as well as allies. For example, Germany believed that if it went to war against France and Russia in the summer of 1914, the United Kingdom would probably stay out of the fight. Saddam Hussein expected the United States to stand aside when he invaded Kuwait in August 1990. Both aggressors guessed wrong, but each had good reason to think that its initial judgment was correct. In the 1930s, Adolf Hitler believed that his great-power rivals would be easy to exploit and isolate because each had little interest in fighting Germany and instead was determined to get someone else to assume that burden. He guessed right. In short, great powers constantly find themselves confronting situations in which they have to make important decisions with incomplete information. Not surprisingly, they sometimes make faulty judgments and end up doing themselves serious harm.

Some defensive realists go so far as to suggest that the constraints of the international system are so powerful that offense rarely succeeds, and that aggressive great powers invariably end up being punished. . . . They emphasize that 1) threatened states balance against aggressors and ultimately crush them, and 2) there is an offense-defense balance that is usually heavily tilted toward the defense, thus making conquest especially difficult. Great powers, therefore, should be content with the existing balance of power and not try to change it by force. . . .

There is no question that systemic factors constrain aggression, especially balancing by threatened states. But defensive realists exaggerate those restraining forces. Indeed, the historical record provides little support for their claim that offense rarely succeeds. One study estimates that there were 63 wars between 1815 and 1980, and the initiator won 39 times, which translates into about a 60 percent success rate. . . . In short, the historical record shows that offense sometimes succeeds and sometimes does not. The trick for a sophisticated power maximizer is to figure out when to raise and when to fold.

HEGEMONY'S LIMITS

Great powers, as I have emphasized, strive to gain power over their rivals and hopefully become hegemons. Once a state achieves that exalted position, it becomes a status quo power. More needs to be said, however, about the meaning of hegemony.

A hegemon is a state that is so powerful that it dominates all the other states in the system. No other state has the military wherewithal to put up a serious fight against it. In essence, a hegemon is the only great power in the system. A state that is substantially more powerful than the other great powers in the system is not a hegemon, because it faces, by definition, other great powers. The United Kingdom in the mid-nineteenth century, for example, is sometimes called a hegemon. But it was not a hegemon, because there were four other great powers in Europe at the time—Austria, France, Prussia, and Russia—and the United Kingdom did not dominate them in any meaningful way. In fact, during that period, the United Kingdom considered France to be a serious threat to the balance of power. Europe in the nineteenth century was multipolar, not unipolar.

Hegemony means domination of the system, which is usually interpreted to mean the entire world. It is possible, however, to apply the concept of a system more narrowly and use it to describe particular regions, such as Europe, Northeast Asia, and the Western Hemisphere. Thus, one can distinguish between *global hegemons*, which dominate the world, and *regional hegemons*, which dominate distinct geographical areas. The United States has been a regional hegemon in the Western Hemisphere for at least the past one hundred years. No other state in the Americas has sufficient military might to challenge it, which is why the United States is widely recognized as the only great power in its region. . . .

POWER AND FEAR

That great powers fear each other is a central aspect of life in the international system. But as noted, the level of fear varies from case to case. For example, the Soviet Union worried much less about Germany in 1930 than it did in 1939. How much states fear each other matters greatly, because the amount of fear between them largely determines the severity of their security competition, as well as the probability that they will fight a war. The more profound the fear is, the more intense is the security competition, and the more likely is war. The logic is straight-forward: a scared state will look especially hard for ways to enhance its security, and it will be disposed to pursue risky policies to achieve that end. Therefore, it is important to understand what causes states to fear each other more or less intensely.

Fear among great powers derives from the fact that they invariably have some offensive military capability that they can use against each other, and the fact that one can never be certain that other states do not intend to use that power against oneself. Moreover, because states operate in an anarchic system, there is no night watchman to whom they can turn for help if another great power attacks them. Although anarchy and uncertainty about other states' intentions create an irre-ducible level of fear among states that leads to power-maximizing behavior, they cannot account for why sometimes that level of fear is greater than at other times. The reason is that anarchy and the difficulty of discerning state intentions are con-stant facts of life, and constants cannot explain variation. The capability that states have to threaten each other, however, varies from case to case, and it is the key fac-tor that drives fear levels up and down. Specifically, the more power a state pos-sesses, the more fear it generates among its rivals. Germany, for example, was much more powerful at the end of the 1930s than it was at the decade's beginning, which is why the Soviets became increasingly fearful of Germany over the course of that decade. . . .

THE HIERARCHY OF STATE GOALS

Survival is the number one goal of great powers, according to my theory. In prac-tice, however, states pursue non-security goals as well. For example, great powers invariably seek greater economic prosperity to enhance the welfare of their citi-zenry. They sometimes seek to promote a particular ideology abroad, as happened during the Cold War when the United States tried to spread democracy around the world and the Soviet Union tried to sell communism. National unification is another goal that sometimes motivates states, as it did with Prussia and Italy in the nineteenth century and Germany after the Cold War. Great powers also occasion-ally try to foster human rights around the globe. States might pursue any of these, as well as a number of other non-security goals.

Offensive realism certainly recognizes that great powers might pursue these non-security goals, but it has little to say about them, save for one important point: states can pursue them as long as the requisite behavior does not conflict with balance-of-power logic, which is often the case. Indeed, the pursuit of these non-security goals sometimes complements the hunt for relative power. For exam-ple, Nazi Germany expanded into eastern Europe for both ideological and realist reasons, and the superpowers competed with each other during the Cold War for similar reasons. Furthermore, greater economic prosperity invariably means greater wealth, which has significant implications for security, because wealth is the foundation of military power. Wealthy states can afford powerful military forces, which enhance a state's prospects for survival. . . .

Sometimes the pursuit of non-security goals has hardly any effect on the balance of power, one way or the other. Human rights interventions usually fit this description, because they tend to be small-scale operations that cost little and do not detract from a great power's prospects for survival. For better or for worse, states are rarely willing to expend blood and treasure to protect foreign populations from gross abuses, including genocide. For instance, despite claims that American foreign policy is infused with moralism, Somalia (1992–93) is the only instance during the past one hundred years in which U.S. soldiers were killed in action on a humanitarian mission. And in that case, the loss of a mere eighteen soldiers in an infamous firefight in October 1993 so traumatized American policymakers that they immediately pulled all U.S. troops out of Somalia and then refused to intervene in Rwanda in the spring of 1994, when ethnic Hutu went on a genocidal rampage against their Tutsi neighbors. Stopping that genocide would have been relatively easy and it would have had virtually no effect on the position of the United States in the balance of power. Yet nothing was done. In short, although realism does not prescribe human rights interventions, it does not necessarily proscribe them.

But sometimes the pursuit of non-security goals conflicts with balance-of-power logic, in which case states usually act according to the dictates of realism. For example, despite the U.S. commitment to spreading democracy across the globe, it helped overthrow democratically elected governments and embraced a number of authoritarian regimes during the Cold War, when American policymakers felt that these actions would help contain the Soviet Union. In World War II, the liberal democracies put aside their antipathy for communism and formed an alliance with the Soviet Union against Nazi Germany. "I can't take communism," Franklin Roosevelt emphasized, but to defeat Hitler "I would hold hands with the Devil." In the same way, Stalin repeatedly demonstrated that when his ideological preferences clashed with power considerations, the latter won out. To take the most blatant example of his realism, the Soviet Union formed a non-aggression pact with Nazi Germany in August 1939—the infamous Molotov-Ribbentrop Pact—in hopes that the agreement would at least temporarily satisfy Hitler's territorial ambitions in eastern Europe and turn the Wehrmacht toward France and the United Kingdom. When great powers confront a serious threat, in short, they pay little attention to ideology as they search for alliance partners.

Security also trumps wealth when those two goals conflict, because "defence," as Adam Smith wrote in *The Wealth of Nations*, "is of much more importance than opulence." Smith provides a good illustration of how states behave when forced to choose between wealth and relative power. In 1651, England put into effect the famous Navigation Act, protectionist legislation designed to damage Holland's commerce and ultimately cripple the Dutch economy. The legislation mandated that all goods imported into England be carried either in English ships or ships owned by the country that originally produced the goods. Since the Dutch produced few goods themselves, this measure would badly damage their shipping, the central ingredient in their economic success. Of course, the Navigation Act would hurt England's economy as well, mainly because it would rob England of the benefits of free trade. "The act of navigation," Smith wrote, "is not favorable to foreign commerce, or to the growth of that opulence that can arise from it." Nevertheless, Smith considered the legislation "the wisest of all the commercial regulations of England" because it did more damage to the Dutch economy than to the English economy, and in the mid-seventeenth century Holland was "the only naval power which could endanger the security of England." . . .

COOPERATION AMONG STATES

One might conclude from the preceding discussion that my theory does not allow for any cooperation among the great powers. But this conclusion would be wrong. States can cooperate, although cooperation is sometimes difficult to achieve and always difficult to sustain. Two factors inhibit cooperation: considerations about relative gains and concern about cheating. Ultimately, great powers live in a fundamentally competitive world where they view each other as real, or at least potential, enemies, and they therefore look to gain power at each other's expense.

Any two states contemplating cooperation must consider how profits or gains will be distributed between them. They can think about the division in terms of either absolute or relative gains (recall the distinction made earlier between pursuing either absolute power or relative power; the concept here is the same). With absolute gains, each side is concerned with maximizing its own profits and cares little about how much the other side gains or loses in the deal. Each side cares about the other only to the extent that the other side's behavior affects its own prospects for achieving maximum profits. With relative gains, on the other hand, each side considers not only its own individual gain, but also how well it fares compared to the other side.

Because great powers care deeply about the balance of power, their thinking focuses on relative gains when they consider cooperating with other states. For sure, each state tries to maximize its absolute gains; still, it is more important for a state to make sure that it does no worse, and perhaps better, than the other state in any agreement. Cooperation is more difficult to achieve, however, when states are attuned to relative gains rather than absolute gains. This is because states concerned about absolute gains have to make sure that if the pie is expanding, they are getting at least some portion of the increase, whereas states that worry about relative gains must pay careful attention to how the pie is divided, which complicates cooperative efforts.

Concerns about cheating also hinder cooperation. Great powers are often reluctant to enter into cooperative agreements for fear that the other side will cheat on the agreement and gain a significant advantage. This concern is especially acute in the military realm, causing a "special peril of defection," because the nature of military weaponry allows for rapid shifts in the balance of power. Such a development could create a window of opportunity for the state that cheats to inflict a decisive defeat on its victim.

These barriers to cooperation notwithstanding, great powers do cooperate in a realist world. Balance-of-power logic often causes great powers to form alliances and cooperate against common enemies. The United Kingdom, France, and Russia, for example, were allies against Germany before and during World War I. States sometimes cooperate to gang up on a third state, as Germany and the Soviet Union did against Poland in 1939. More recently, Serbia and Croatia agreed to conquer and divide Bosnia between them, although the United States and its European allies prevented them from executing their agreement. Rivals as well as allies cooperate. After all, deals can be struck that roughly reflect the distribution of power and satisfy concerns about cheating. The various arms control agreements signed by the superpowers during the Cold War illustrate this point.

The bottom line, however, is that cooperation takes place in a world that is competitive at its core—one where states have powerful incentives to take advantage of other states. This point is graphically highlighted by the state of European politics in the forty years before World War I. The great powers cooperated frequently during this period, but that did not stop them from going to war on August 1, 1914. The United States and the Soviet Union also cooperated considerably during World War II, but that cooperation did not prevent the outbreak of the Cold War shortly after Germany and Japan were defeated. Perhaps most amazingly, there was significant economic and military cooperation between Nazi Germany and the Soviet Union during the two years before the Wehrmacht attacked the Red Army. No amount of cooperation can eliminate the dominating logic of security competition. Genuine peace, or a world in which states do not compete for power, is not likely as long as the state system remains anarchic.

Anarchy Is What States Make of It

ALEXANDER WENDT

Classical realists such as Thomas Hobbes, Reinhold Niebuhr, and Hans J. Morgenthau attributed egoism and power politics primarily to human nature, whereas structural realists or neorealists emphasize anarchy. The difference stems in part from different interpretations of anarchy's causal powers. Kenneth Waltz's work is important for both. In *Man, the State, and War,* he defines anarchy as a condition of possibility for or "permissive" cause of war, arguing that "wars occur because there is nothing to prevent them."[1] It is the human nature or domestic politics of predator states, however, that provide the initial impetus or "efficient" cause of conflict which forces other states to respond in kind. . . . But . . . In Waltz's *Theory of International Politics* . . . the logic of anarchy seems by itself to constitute self-help and power politics as necessary features of world politics.[2] . . .

Waltz defines political structure in three dimensions: ordering principles (in this case, anarchy), principles of differentiation (which here drop out), and the distribution of capabilities.[3] By itself, this definition predicts little about state behavior. It does not predict whether two states will be friends or foes, will recognize each other's sovereignty, will have dynastic ties, will be revisionist or status quo powers, and so on. These factors, which are fundamentally intersubjective, affect states' security interests and thus the character of their interaction under anarchy. . . . Put more generally, without assumptions about the structure of identities and interests in the system, Waltz's definition of structure cannot predict the content or dynamics of anarchy. Self-help is one such intersubjective structure and, as such, does the decisive explanatory work in the theory. The question is whether self-help is a logical or contingent feature of anarchy. In this section, I develop the concept of a "structure of identity and interest" and show that no particular one follows logically from anarchy.

A fundamental principle of constructivist social theory is that people act toward objects, including other actors, on the basis of the meanings that the objects have for them. States act differently toward enemies than they do toward friends because enemies are threatening and friends are not. Anarchy and the distribution of power are insufficient to tell us which is which. U.S. military power has a different significance for Canada than for Cuba, despite their similar "structural"

Excerpted/abridged from "Anarchy Is What States Make of It: The Social Construction of Power Politics," by Alexander Wendt from *International Organization,* Vol. 46, No. 2 (Spring 1992), pp. 395–410. Copyright © 1992 by the World Peace Foundation and the Massachusetts Institute of Technology. Portions of the text and some footnotes have been omitted.

positions, just as British missiles have a different significance for the United States than do Soviet missiles. The distribution of power may always affect states' calculations, but how it does so depends on the intersubjective understandings and expectations, on the "distribution of knowledge," that constitute their conceptions of self and other.[4] If society "forgets" what a university is, the powers and practices of professor and student cease to exist; if the United States and Soviet Union decide that they are no longer enemies, "the Cold War is over." It is collective meanings that constitute the structures which organize our actions.

Actors acquire identities—relatively stable, role-specific understandings and expectations about self—by participating in such collective meanings. Identities are inherently relational: "Identity, with its appropriate attachments of psychological reality, is always identity within a specific, socially constructed world," Peter Berger argues.[5] Each person has many identities linked to institutional roles, such as brother, son, teacher, and citizen. Similarly, a state may have multiple identities as "sovereign," "leader of the free world," "imperial power," and so on. The commitment to and the salience of particular identities vary, but each identity is an inherently social definition of the actor grounded in the theories which actors collectively hold about themselves and one another and which constitute the structure of the social world.

Identities are the basis of interests. Actors do not have a "portfolio" of interests that they carry around independent of social context; instead, they define their interests on the process of defining situations. . . . Sometimes situations are unprecedented in our experience, and in these cases we have to construct their meaning, and thus our interests, by analogy or invent them de novo. More often they have routine qualities in which we assign meanings on the basis of institutionally defined roles. When we say that professors have an "interest" in teaching, research, or going on leave, we are saying that to function in the role identity of "professor," they have to define certain situations as calling for certain actions. This does not mean that they will necessarily do so (expectations and competence do not equal performance), but if they do not, they will not get tenure. The absence or failure of roles makes defining situations and interests more difficult, and identity confusion may result. This seems to be happening today in the United States and the former Soviet Union: Without the cold war's mutual attributions of threat and hostility to define their identities, these states seem unsure of what their "interests" should be.

An institution is a relatively stable set or "structure" of identities and interests. Such structures are often codified in formal rules and norms, but these have motivational force only in virtue of actors' socialization to and participation in collective knowledge. Institutions are fundamentally cognitive entities that do not exist apart from actors' ideas about how the world works. This does not mean that institutions are not real or objective, that they are "nothing but" beliefs. As collective knowledge, they are experienced as having an existence "over and above the individuals who happen to embody them at the moment."[6] In this way, institutions come to confront individuals as more or less coercive social facts, but they are still a function of what actors collectively "know." Identities and such collective cognitions do not exist apart from each other; they are "mutually constitutive." On this view, institutionalization is a process of internalizing new identities and interests, not something occurring outside them and affecting only behavior; socialization is a cognitive process, not just a behavioral one. Conceived in this way, institutions may be cooperative or conflictual, a point sometimes lost in scholarship on international regimes, which tends to equate institutions with cooperation. There are important differences between conflictual and cooperative institutions to be sure, but all relatively stable self-other relations—even those of "enemies"—are defined intersubjectively.

Self-help is an institution, one of various structures of identity and interest that may exist under anarchy. Processes of identity formation under anarchy are concerned first and foremost with preservation or "security" of the self. Concepts of security therefore differ in the extent to which and the manner in which the self is identified cognitively with the other, and, I want to suggest, it is upon this cognitive variation that the meaning of anarchy and the distribution of power depends. Let me illustrate with a standard continuum of security systems.

At one end is the "competitive" security system, in which states identify negatively with each other's security so that ego's gain is seen as alter's loss. Negative identification under anarchy constitutes systems of "realist" power politics: risk-averse actors that infer intentions from capabilities and worry about relative gains and losses. At the limit—in the Hobbesian war of all against all—collective action is nearly impossible in such a system because each actor must constantly fear being stabbed in the back.

In the middle is the "individualistic" security system, in which states are indifferent to the relationship between their own and others' security. This constitutes "neoliberal" systems: States are still self-regarding about their security but are concerned primarily with absolute gains rather than relative gains. One's position in the distribution of power is less important, and collective action is more possible (though still subject to free riding because states continue to be "egoists").

Competitive and individualistic systems are both "self-help" forms of anarchy in the sense that states do not positively identify the security of self with that of others but instead treat security as the individual responsibility of each. Given the lack of a positive cognitive identification on the basis of which to build security regimes, power politics within such systems will necessarily consist of efforts to manipulate others to satisfy self-regarding interests.

This contrasts with the "cooperative" security system, in which states identify positively with one another so that the security of each is perceived as the responsibility of all. This is not self-help in any interesting sense, since the "self" in terms of which interests are defined is the community; national interests are international interests. In practice, of course, the extent to which states identify with the community varies from the limited form found in "concerts" to the full-blown form seen in "collective security" arrangements. Depending on how well developed the collective self is, it will produce security practices that are in varying degrees altruistic or prosocial. This makes collective action less dependent on the presence of active threats and less prone to free riding. Moreover, it restructures efforts to advance one's objectives, or "power politics," in terms of shared norms rather than relative power.

On this view, the tendency in international relations scholarship to view power and institutions as two opposing explanations of foreign policy is therefore misleading, since anarchy and the distribution of power only have meaning for state action in virtue of the understandings and expectations that constitute institutional identities and interests. Self-help is one such institution, constituting one kind of anarchy but not the only kind. Waltz's three-part definition of structure therefore seems underspecified. In order to go from structure to action, we need to add a fourth: the intersubjectively constituted structure of identities and interests in the system.

This has an important implication for the way in which we conceive of states in the state of nature before their first encounter with each other. Because states do not have conceptions of self and other, and thus security interests, apart from or prior to interaction, we assume too much about the state of nature if we concur with Waltz that, in virtue of anarchy, "international political systems, like economic markets, are formed by the coaction of self-regarding units."[7] We also assume too much if we argue that, in virtue of anarchy, states in the state of nature necessarily face a "stag hunt" or "security dilemma."[8] These claims presuppose a history of interaction in which actors have acquired "selfish" identities and interests; before interaction (and still in abstraction from first- and second-image factors) they would have no experience upon which to base such definitions of self and other. To assume otherwise is to attribute to states in the state of nature qualities that they can only possess in society. Self-help is an institution, not a constitutive feature of anarchy.

What, then, *is* a constitutive feature of the state of nature before interaction? Two things are left if we strip away those properties of the self which presuppose interaction with others. The first is the material substrate of agency, including its intrinsic capabilities. For human beings, this is the body; for states, it is an organizational apparatus of governance. In effect, I am suggesting for rhetorical purposes that the raw material out of which members of the state system are constituted is created by domestic society before states enter the constitutive process of international society, although this process implies neither stable territoriality nor sovereignty, which are internationally negotiated terms of individuality (as discussed further below). The second is a desire to preserve this material substrate, to survive. This does not entail "self-regardingness," however, since actors do not have a self prior to interaction with another; how they view the meaning and requirements of this survival therefore depends on the processes by which conceptions of self evolve.

This may all seem very arcane, but there is an important issue at stake: Are the foreign policy identities and interests of states exogenous or endogenous to the state system? The former is the answer of an individualistic or undersocialized systemic theory for which rationalism is appropriate; the latter is the answer of a fully socialized systemic theory. Waltz seems to offer the latter and proposes two mechanisms, competition and socialization, by which structure conditions state action.[9] The content of his argument about this conditioning, however, presupposes a self-help system that is not itself a constitutive feature of anarchy. As James Morrow points out, Waltz's two mechanisms condition behavior, not identity and interest. . . . [10]

If self-help is not a constitutive feature of anarchy, it must emerge causally from processes in which anarchy plays only a permissive role. This reflects a second principle of constructivism: that the meanings in terms of which action is organized arise out of interaction. . . .

Consider two actors—ego and alter—encountering each other for the first time.[11] Each wants to survive and has certain material capabilities, but neither actor has biological or domestic imperatives for power, glory, or conquest . . . and there is no history of security or insecurity between the two. What should they do? Realists would probably argue that each should act on the basis of worst-case assumptions about the other's intentions, justifying such an attitude as prudent in view of the possibility of death from making a mistake. Such a possibility always exists, even in civil society; however, society would be impossible if people made decisions purely on the basis of worst-case possibilities. Instead, most decisions are and should be made on the basis of probabilities, and these are produced by interaction, by what actors *do*.

In the beginning is ego's gesture, which may consist, for example, of an advance, a retreat, a brandishing of arms, a laying down of arms, or an attack. For ego, this gesture represents the basis on which it is prepared to respond to alter. This basis is unknown to alter, however, and so it must make an inference or "attribution" about ego's intentions and, in particular, given that this is anarchy, about whether ego is a threat. The content of this inference will largely depend on two considerations. The first is the gesture's and ego's physical qualities, which are in part contrived by ego and which include the direction of movement, noise, numbers, and immediate consequences of the gesture. The second consideration concerns what alter would intend by such qualities were it to make such a gesture itself. Alter may make an attributional "error" in its inference about ego's intent, but there is also no reason for it to assume a priori—before the gesture—that ego is threatening, since it is only through a process of signaling and interpreting that the costs and probabilities of being wrong can be determined. Social threats are constructed, not natural.

Consider an example. Would we assume, a priori, that we were about to be attacked if we are ever contacted by members of an alien civilization? I think not. We would be highly alert, of course, but whether we placed our military forces on alert or launched an attack would depend on how we interpreted the import of their first gesture for our security—if only to avoid making an immediate enemy out of what may be a dangerous adversary. The possibility of error, in other words, does not force us to act on the assumption that the aliens are threatening: Action depends on the probabilities we assign, and these are in key part a function of what the aliens do; prior to their gesture, we have no systemic basis for assigning probabilities. If their first gesture is to appear with a thousand spaceships and destroy New York, we will define the situation as threatening and respond accordingly. But if they appear with one spaceship, saying what seems to be "we come in peace," we will feel "reassured" and will probably respond with a gesture intended to reassure them, even if this gesture is not necessarily interpreted by them as such.

This process of signaling, interpreting, and responding completes a "social act" and begins the process of creating intersubjective meanings. It advances the same way. The first social act creates expectations on both sides about each other's future behavior: potentially mistaken and certainly tentative, but expectations nonetheless. Based on this tentative knowledge, ego makes a new gesture, again signifying the basis on which it will respond to alter, and again alter responds, adding to the pool of knowledge each has about the other, and so on over time. The mechanism here is reinforcement; interaction rewards actors for holding certain ideas about each other and discourages them from holding others. If repeated long enough, these "reciprocal typifications" will create relatively stable concepts of self and other regarding the issue at stake in the interaction.[12]

Competitive systems of interaction are prone to security "dilemmas," in which the efforts of actors to enhance their security unilaterally threatens the security of the others, perpetuating distrust and alienation. The forms of identity and interest that constitute such dilemmas, however, are themselves ongoing effects of, not exogenous to, the interaction; identities are produced in and through "situated activity."[13] We do not *begin* our relationship with the aliens in a security dilemma; security dilemmas are not given by anarchy or nature. . . .

The mirror theory of identity formation is a crude account of how the process of creating identities and interests might work, but it does not tell us why a system of states—such as, arguably, our own—would have ended up with self-regarding and not collective identities. In this section, I examine an efficient cause, predation, which, in conjunction with anarchy as a permissive cause, may generate a self-help system. In so doing, however, I show the key role that the structure of identities and interests plays in mediating anarchy's explanatory role.

The predator argument is straightforward and compelling. For whatever reasons—biology, domestic politics, or systemic victimization—some states may become predisposed toward aggression. The aggressive behavior of these predators or "bad apples" forces other states to engage in competitive power politics, to meet fire with fire, since failure to do so may degrade or destroy them. One predator will best a hundred pacifists because anarchy provides no guarantees. This argument is powerful in part because it is so weak: Rather than making the strong assumption that all states are inherently power-seeking (a purely reductionist theory of power politics), it assumes that just one is power-seeking and that the others have to follow suit because anarchy permits the one to exploit them.

In making this argument, it is important to reiterate that the possibility of predation does not in itself force states to anticipate it a priori with competitive power politics of their own. The possibility of predation does not mean that "war may at any moment occur"; it may in fact be extremely unlikely. Once a predator emerges, however, it may condition identity and interest formation in the following manner.

In an anarchy of two, if ego is predatory, alter must either define its security in self-help terms or pay the price. . . . The timing of the emergence of predation relative to the history of identity formation in the community is therefore crucial to anarchy's explanatory role as a permissive cause. Predation will always lead victims to defend themselves, but whether defense will be collective or not depends on the history of interaction within the potential collective as much as on the ambitions of the predator. Will the disappearance of the Soviet threat renew old insecurities among the members of the North Atlantic Treaty Organization? Perhaps, but not if they have reasons independent of that threat for identifying their security with one another. Identities and interests are relationship-specific, not intrinsic attributes of a "portfolio"; states may be competitive in some relationships and solidary in others. . . .

The source of predation also matters. If it stems from unit-level causes that are immune to systemic impacts (causes such as human nature or domestic politics taken in isolation), then it functions in a manner analogous to a "genetic trait" in the constructed world of the state system. Even if successful, this trait does not select for other predators in an evolutionary sense so much as it teaches other states to respond in kind, but since traits cannot be unlearned, the other states will continue competitive behavior until the predator is either destroyed or transformed from within. However, in the more likely event that predation stems at least in part from prior systemic interaction—perhaps as a result of being victimized in the past (one thinks here of Nazi Germany or the Soviet Union)—then it is more a response to a learned identity and, as such, might be transformed by future social interaction in the form of appeasement, reassurances that security needs will be met, systemic effects on domestic politics, and so on. In this case, in other words, there is more hope that process can transform a bad apple into a good one. . . .

This raises anew the question of exactly how much and what kind of role human nature and domestic politics play in world politics. The greater and more destructive this role, the more significant predation will be, and the less amenable anarchy will be to formation of collective identities. Classical realists, of course, assumed that human nature was possessed by an inherent lust for power or glory. My argument suggests that assumptions such as this were made for a reason: An unchanging Hobbesian man provides the powerful efficient cause necessary for a relentless pessimism about world politics that anarchic structure alone, or even structure plus intermittent predation, cannot supply. . . .

Assuming for now that systemic theories of identity formation in world politics are worth pursuing, let me conclude by suggesting that the realist-rationalist alliance "reifies" self-help in the sense of treating it as something separate from the practices by which it is produced and sustained. Peter Berger and Thomas Luckmann define reification as follows: "[It] is the apprehension of the products of human activity *as if* they were something else than human products—such as facts of nature, results of cosmic laws, or manifestations of divine will. Reification implies that man is capable of forgetting his own authorship of the human world, and further, that the dialectic between man, the producer, and his products is lost to consciousness. The reified world is . . . experienced by man as a strange facticity, an *opus alienum* over which he has no control rather than as the *opus proprium* of his own productive activity."[14] By denying or bracketing states' collective authorship of their identities and interests, in other words, the realist-rationalist alliance denies or brackets the fact that competitive power politics help create a very "problem of order" they are supposed to solve—that realism is a self-fulfilling prophecy. Far from being exogenously given, the intersubjective knowledge that constitutes competitive identities and interests is constructed every day by processes of "social will formation."[15] It is what states have made of themselves.

NOTES

1. Kenneth Waltz, *Man, the State, and War* (New York: Columbia University Press, 1959), p. 232.
2. Kenneth Waltz, *Theory of International Politics* (Boston: Addison-Wesley, 1979).
3. Waltz, *Theory of International Politics*, pp. 79–101.
4. The phrase "distribution of knowledge" is Barry Barnes's, as discussed in his work *The Nature of Power* (Cambridge: Polity Press, 1988); see also Peter Berger and Thomas Luckmann, *The Social Construction of Reality* (New York: Anchor Books, 1966).
5. Berger, "Identity as a Problem in the Sociology of Knowledge," *European Journal of Sociology*, 7, 1 (1966), 111.
6. Berger and Luckmann, p. 58.
7. Waltz, *Theory of International Politics*, p. 91.
8. See Waltz, *Man, the State, and War;* and Robert Jervis, "Cooperation Under the Security Dilemma," *World Politics* 30 (January 1978), 167–214.
9. Waltz, *Theory of International Politics*, pp. 74–77.
10. See James Morrow, "Social Choice and System Structure in World Politics," *World Politics* 41 (October 1988), 89.
11. This situation is not entirely metaphorical in world politics, since throughout history states have "discovered" each other, generating an instant anarchy as it were. A systematic empirical study of first contacts would be interesting.
12. On "reciprocal typifications," see Berger and Luckmann, pp. 54–58.
13. See C. Norman Alexander and Mary Glenn Wiley, "Situated Activity and Identity Formation," in Morris Rosenberg and Ralph Turner, eds., *Social Psychology: Sociological Perspectives* (New York: Basic Books, 1981), pp. 269–89.
14. See Berger and Luckmann, p. 89.
15. See Richard Ashley, "Social Will and International Anarchy," in Hayward Alker and Richard Ashley, eds., *After Realism*, work in progress, Massachusetts Institute of Technology, Cambridge, and Arizona State University, Tempe, 1992.

THE MITIGATION
█ OF ANARCHY

The Conditions for Cooperation in World Politics

█ KENNETH A. OYE

I. INTRODUCTION

Nations dwell in perpetual anarchy, for no central authority imposes limits on the
pursuit of sovereign interests. This common condition gives rise to diverse outcomes. Relations among states are marked by war and concert, arms races and
arms control, trade wars and tariff truces, financial panics and rescues, competitive
devaluation and monetary stabilization. At times, the absence of centralized international authority precludes attainment of common goals. Because, as states, they
cannot cede ultimate control over their conduct to a supranational sovereign, they
cannot guarantee that they will adhere to their promises. The possibility of a breach
of promise can impede cooperation even when cooperation would leave all better
off. Yet, at other times, states do realize common goals through cooperation under
anarchy. Despite the absence of any ultimate international authority, governments
often bind themselves to mutually advantageous courses of action. And, though no
international sovereign stands ready to enforce the terms of agreement, states can
realize common interests through tacit cooperation, formal bilateral and multilateral negotiation, and the creation of international regimes. The question is: if
international relations can approximate both a Hobbesian state of nature and a
Lockean evil society, why does cooperation emerge in some cases and not in others?

[Scholars] address both explanatory and prescriptive aspects of this perennial
question. *First, what circumstances favor the emergence of cooperation under
anarchy?* Given the lack of a central authority to guarantee adherence to agreements, what features of situations encourage or permit states to bind themselves
to mutually beneficial courses of action? What features of situations preclude

From "Explaining Cooperation under Anarchy: Hypothesis and Strategies" by Kenneth A. Oye from
World Politics, pp. 1–22. Reprinted by permission of Johns Hopkins University Press. Portions of the
text and some footnotes have been omitted.

cooperation? *Second, what strategies can states adopt to foster the emergence of cooperation by altering the circumstances they confront?* Governments need not necessarily accept circumstances as given. To what extent are situational impediments to cooperation subject to willful modification? Through what higher order strategies can states create the preconditions for cooperation?. . .

I submit that three circumstantial dimensions serve both as proximate explanations of cooperation and as targets of longer-term strategies to promote cooperation. Each of the three major sections of this piece defines a dimension, explains how that dimension accounts for the incidence of cooperation and conflict in the absence of centralized authority, and examines associated strategies for enhancing the prospects for cooperation.

In the section entitled "Payoff Structure: Mutual and Conflicting Preferences," I discuss how payoffs affect the prospects for cooperation and present strategies to improve the prospects for cooperation by altering payoffs. Orthodox game theorists identify optimal strategies *given* ordinally defined classes of games, and their familiar insights provide the starting point for the discussion. Recent works in security studies, institutional microeconomics, and international political economy suggest strategies to *alter* payoff structures and thereby improve the prospects for cooperation.[1]

In the next section, entitled "Shadow of the Future: Single-play and Iterated Games," I discuss how the prospect of continuing interaction affects the likelihood of cooperation; examine how strategies of reciprocity can provide direct paths to cooperative outcomes under iterated conditions; and suggest strategies to lengthen the shadow of the future.[2] In addition, this section shows that recognition and control capabilities—the ability to distinguish between cooperation and defection by others and to respond in kind—can affect the power of reciprocity, and suggests strategies to improve recognition capabilities.

In the third section, "Number of Players: Two-Person and N-Person Games," I explain why cooperation becomes more difficult as the number of actors increases; present strategies for promoting cooperation in N-actor situations; and offer strategies for promoting cooperation by reducing the number of actors necessary to the realization of common interests. Game theorists and oligopoly theorists have long noted that cooperation becomes more difficult as numbers increase, and their insights provide a starting point for discussion. Recent work in political economy focuses on two strategies for promoting cooperation in thorny N-person situations: functionalist analysts of regimes suggest strategies for increasing the likelihood and robustness of cooperation *given* large numbers of actors,[3] analysts of *ad hoc* bargaining in international political economy suggest strategies of bilateral and regional decomposition to *reduce* the number of actors necessary to the realization of some mutual interests, at the expense of the magnitude of gains from cooperation. . . . [4]

II. PAYOFF STRUCTURE: MUTUAL AND CONFLICTING PREFERENCES

The structure of payoffs in a given round of play—the benefits of mutual cooperation (CC) relative to mutual defection (DD) and the benefits of unilateral defection (DC) relative to unrequited cooperation (CD)—is fundamental to the analysis of cooperation. The argument proceeds in three stages. First, how does payoff structure affect the significance of cooperation? More narrowly, when is cooperation, defined in terms of conscious policy coordination, necessary to the realization of mutual interests? Second, how does payoff structure affect the likelihood and robustness of cooperation? Third, through what strategies can states increase the long-term prospects for cooperation by altering payoff structures?

Before turning to these questions, consider briefly some tangible and intangible determinants of payoff structures. The security and political economy literatures examine the effects of military force structure and doctrine, economic ideology, the size of currency reserves, macroeconomic circumstance, and a host of other factors on national assessments of national interests. In "Cooperation under the Security Dilemma," Robert Jervis has explained how the diffusion of offensive military technology and strategies can increase rewards from defection and thereby reduce the prospects for cooperation. In "International Regimes, Transactions, and Chance: Embedded Liberalism in the Postwar Economic Order," John Ruggie has demonstrated how the diffusion of liberal economic ideas increased the perceived benefits of mutual economic openness over mutual closure (CC-DD), and diminished the perceived rewards from asymmetric defection relative to asymmetric cooperation (DC-CD). In "Firms and Tariff Regime Change," Timothy McKeown has shown how downturns in the business cycle alter national tastes for protection and thereby decrease the perceived benefits of mutual openness relative to mutual closure and increase the perceived rewards of asymmetric defection. . . . [5]

A. Payoff Structure and Cooperation

How does payoff structure determine the significance of cooperation? More narrowly, when is *cooperation,* defined in terms of conscious policy coordination, *necessary* to the realization of *mutual benefits?* For a *mutual benefit* to exist, actors must prefer mutual cooperation (CC) to mutual defection (DD). For coordination to be *necessary* to the realization of the mutual benefit, actors must prefer unilateral defection (DC) to unrequited cooperation (CD). These preference orderings are consistent with the familiar games of Prisoners' Dilemma, Stag Hunt, and Chicken. Indeed, these games have attracted a disproportionate share of scholarly attention precisely because cooperation is desirable but not automatic. In these cases, the capacity of states to cooperate under anarchy, to bind themselves to mutually beneficial courses of action without resort to any ultimate central authority, is vital to the realization of a common good. . . .

In the class of games—including Prisoners' Dilemma, Stag Hunt, and Chicken—where cooperation is necessary to the realization of mutual benefits, how does payoff structure affect the likelihood and robustness of cooperation in these situations? Cooperation will be less likely in Prisoners' Dilemma than in Stag Hunt or Chicken. To understand why, consider each of these games in conjunction with the illustrative stories from which they derive their names.

Prisoners' Dilemma: Two prisoners are suspected of a major crime. The authorities possess evidence to secure conviction on only a minor charge. If neither prisoner squeals, both will draw a light sentence on the minor charge (CC). If one prisoner squeals and the other stonewalls, the rat will go free (DC) and the sucker will draw a very heavy sentence (CD). If both squeal, both will draw a moderate sentence (DD). Each prisoner's preference ordering is: DC > CC > DD > CD. If the prisoners expect to "play" only one time, each prisoner will be better off squealing than stonewalling, no matter what his partner chooses to do (DC > CC and DD > CD). The temptation of the rat payoff and fear of the sucker payoff will drive single-play Prisoners' Dilemmas toward mutual defection. Unfortunately, if both prisoners act on this reasoning, they will draw a moderate sentence on the major charge, while cooperation could have led to a light sentence on the minor charge (CC > DD). In single-play Prisoners' Dilemmas, individually rational actions produce a collectively suboptimal outcome.

Stag Hunt: A group of hunters surround a stag. If all cooperate to trap the stag, all will eat well (CC). If one person defects to chase a passing rabbit, the stag will escape. The defector will eat lightly (DC) and none of the others will eat at all (CD). If all chase rabbits, all will have some chance of catching a rabbit and eating lightly (DD). Each hunter's preference ordering is: CC > DC > DD > CD. The mutual interest in plentiful venison (CC) relative to all other outcomes militates strongly against defection. However, because a rabbit in the hand (DC) is better than a stag in the bush (CD), cooperation will be assured only if each hunter believes that all hunters will cooperate. In single-play Stag Hunt, the temptation to defect to protect against the defection of others is balanced by the strong universal preference for stag over rabbit.

Chicken: Two drivers race down the center of a road from opposite directions. If one swerves and the other does not, then the first will suffer the stigma of being known as a chicken (CD) while the second will enjoy being known as a hero (DC). If neither swerves, both will suffer grievously in the ensuing collision (DD). If both swerve, damage to the reputation of each will be limited (CC). Each driver's preference ordering is: DC > CC > CD > DD. If each believes that the other will swerve, then each will be tempted to defect by continuing down the center of the road. Better to be a live hero than a live chicken. If both succumb to this temptation, however, defection will result in collision. The fear that the other driver may not swerve decreases the appeal of continuing down the center of the road. In single-play Chicken, the temptations of unilateral defection are balanced by fear of mutual defection.

In games that are not repeated, only ordinally defined preferences matter. Under single-play conditions, interval-level payoffs in ordinally defined categories of games cannot (in theory) affect the likelihood of cooperation. In the illustrations above, discussions of dominant strategies do not hinge on the magnitude of differences among the payoffs. Yet the magnitude of differences between CC and DD and between DC and CD can be large or small, if not precisely measurable, and can increase or decrease. Changes in the magnitude of differences in the value placed on outcomes can influence the prospects for cooperation through two paths.

First, changes in the value attached to outcomes can transform situations from one ordinally defined class of game into another. For example, in "Cooperation under the Security Dilemma," Robert Jervis described how difficult Prisoners'

Dilemmas may evolve into less challenging Stag Hunts if the gains from mutual cooperation (CC) increase relative to the gains from exploitation (DC). He related the structure of payoffs to traditional concepts of offensive and defensive dominance, and offensive and defensive dominance to technological and doctrinal shifts. Ernst Haas, Mary Pat Williams, and Don Babai have emphasized the importance of cognitive congruence as a determinant of technological cooperation. The diffusion of common conceptions of the nature and effects of technology enhanced perceived gains from cooperation and diminished perceived gains from defection, and may have transformed some Prisoners' Dilemmas into Harmony.[6]

Second, under iterated conditions, the magnitude of differences among payoffs *within* a given class of games can be an important determinant of cooperation. The more substantial the gains from mutual cooperation (CC-DD) and the less substantial the gains from unilateral defection (DC-CD), the greater the likelihood of cooperation. In iterated situations, the magnitude of the difference between CC and DD and between DC and CD in present and future rounds of play affects the likelihood of cooperation in the present. This point is developed at length in the section on the shadow of the future.

B. Strategies to Alter Payoff Structure

If payoff structure affects the likelihood of cooperation, to what extent can states alter situations by modifying payoff structures, and thereby increase the long-term likelihood of cooperation? Many of the tangible and intangible determinants of payoff structure, discussed at the outset of this section, are subject to willful modification through unilateral, bilateral, and multilateral strategies. In "Cooperation under the Security Dilemma," Robert Jervis has offered specific suggestions for altering payoff structures through unilateral strategies. Procurement policy can affect the prospects for cooperation. If one superpower favors procurement of defensive over offensive weapons, it can reduce its own gains from exploitation through surprise attack (DC) and reduce its adversary's fear of exploitation (CD). Members of alliances have often resorted to the device of deploying troops on troubled frontiers to increase the likelihood of cooperation. A state's use of troops as hostages is designed to diminish the payoff from its own defection—to reduce its gains from exploitation (DC)—and thereby render defensive defection by its partner less likely. Publicizing an agreement diminishes payoffs associated with defection from the agreement, and thereby lessens gains from exploitation. These observations in international relations are paralleled by recent developments in microeconomics. Oliver Williamson has identified unilateral and bilateral techniques used by firms to facilitate interfirm cooperation by diminishing gains from exploitation. He distinguishes between specific and nonspecific costs associated with adherence to agreements. Specific costs, such as specialized training, machine tools, and construction, cannot be recovered in the event of the breakdown of an agreement. When parties to an agreement incur high specific costs, repudiation of commitments will entail substantial losses. Firms can thus reduce their gains from exploitation through the technique of acquiring dedicated assets that serve as hostages to continuing cooperation. Nonspecific assets, such as general-purpose trucks and airplanes, are salvageable if agreements break down; firms can reduce their fear of being exploited by maximizing the use of nonspecific assets, but such assets cannot diminish gains from exploitation by serving as hostages.[7] Unilateral strategies can improve the prospects of cooperation by reducing both the costs of being exploited (CD) and the gains from exploitation (DC). The new literature on interfirm cooperation indirectly raises an old question on the costs of unilateral strategies to promote cooperation in international relations.

In many instances, unilateral actions that limit one's gains from exploitation may have the effect of increasing one's vulnerability to exploitation by others. For example, a state could limit gains from defection from liberal international economic norms by permitting the expansion of sectors of comparative advantage and by permitting liquidation of inefficient sectors. Because a specialized economy is a hostage to international economic cooperation, this strategy would unquestionably increase the credibility of the nation's commitment to liberalism. It also has the effect, however, of increasing the nation's vulnerability to protection by others. In the troops-as-hostage example, the government that stations troops may promote cooperation by diminishing an ally's fear of abandonment, but in so doing it raises its own fears of exploitation by the ally. . . .

Unilateral strategies do not exhaust the range of options that states may use to alter payoff structures. Bilateral strategies—most significantly strategies of issue linkage—can be used to alter payoff structures by combining dissimilar games. Because resort to issue linkage generally assumes iteration, analysis of how issue linkage can be used to alter payoffs is presented in the section on the shadow of the future. Furthermore, bilateral "instructional" strategies can aim at altering another country's understanding of cause-and-effect relationships, and result in altered perceptions of interest. For example, American negotiators in SALT I sought to instruct their Soviet counterparts on the logic of mutual assured destruction.[8]

Multilateral strategies, centering on the formation of international regimes, can be used to alter payoff structures in two ways. First, norms generated by regimes may be internalized by states, and thereby alter payoff structure. Second, information generated by regimes may alter states' understanding of their interests. As Ernst Haas argues, new regimes may gather and distribute information that can highlight cause-and-effect relationships not previously understood. Changing perceptions of means-ends hierarchies can, in turn, result in changing perceptions of interest.[9]

III. THE SHADOW OF THE FUTURE: SINGLE-PLAY AND ITERATED GAMES

The distinction between cases in which similar transactions among parties are unlikely to be repeated and cases in which the expectation of future interaction can influence decisions in the present is fundamental to the emergence of cooperation among egoists. As the previous section suggests, states confronting strategic situations that resemble single-play Prisoners' Dilemma and, to a lesser extent, single-play Stag Hunt and Chicken, are constantly tempted by immediate gains from unilateral defection, and fearful of immediate losses from unrequited cooperation. How does continuing interaction affect prospects for cooperation? The argument proceeds in four stages. First, why do iterated conditions improve the prospects for cooperation in Prisoners' Dilemma and Stag Hunt while diminishing the prospects for cooperation in Chicken? Second, how do strategies of reciprocity improve the prospects for cooperation under iterated conditions? Third, why does the effectiveness of reciprocity hinge on conditions of play—the ability of actors to distinguish reliably between cooperation and defection by others and to respond in kind? Fourth, through what strategies can states improve conditions of play and lengthen the shadow of the future?

Before turning to these questions, consider the attributes of iterated situations. First, states must expect to continue dealing with each other. This condition is, in practice, not particularly restrictive. With the possible exception of global thermonuclear war, international politics is characterized by the expectation of future interaction. Second, payoff structures must not change substantially over time. In other words, each round of play should not alter the structure of the game in the future. This condition is, in practice, quite restrictive. For example, states considering surprise attack when offense is dominant are in a situation that has many of the characteristics of a single-play game: Attack alters options and payoffs in future rounds of interaction. Conversely, nations considering increases or decreases in their military budgets are in a situation that has many of the characteristics of an iterated game: Spending options and associated marginal increases or decreases in military strength are likely to remain fairly stable over future rounds of interaction. In international monetary affairs, governments considering or fearing devaluation under a gold-exchange standard are in a situation that has many of the characteristics of a single-play game: Devaluation may diminish the value of another state's foreign currency reserves on a one-time basis, while reductions in holdings of reserves would diminish possible losses on a one-time basis. Conversely, governments considering intervention under a floating system with minimal reserves are in a situation that has many of the characteristics of an iterated game: Depreciation or appreciation of a currency would not produce substantial one-time losses or gains. Third, the size of the discount rate applied to the future affects the iterativeness of games. If a government places little value on future payoffs, its situation has many of the characteristics of a single-play game. If it places a high value on future payoffs, its situation may have many of the characteristics of an iterated game. For example, political leaders in their final term are likely to discount the future more substantially than political leaders running for, or certain of, reelection.

A. The Shadow of the Future and Cooperation

How does the shadow of the future affect the likelihood of cooperation? Under single-play conditions without a sovereign, adherence to agreements is often irrational. Consider the single-play Prisoners' Dilemma. Each prisoner is better off squealing, whether or not his partner decides to squeal. In the absence of continuing interaction, defection would emerge as the dominant strategy. Because the prisoners can neither turn to a central authority for enforcement of an agreement to cooperate nor rely on the anticipation of retaliation to deter present defection, cooperation will be unlikely under single-play conditions. If the prisoners expect to be placed in similar situations in the future, the prospects for cooperation improve. Experimental evidence suggests that under iterated Prisoners' Dilemma the incidence of cooperation rises substantially.[10] Even in the absence of centralized authority, tacit agreements to cooperate through mutual stonewalling are frequently reached and maintained. Under iterated Prisoners' Dilemma, a potential defector compares the immediate gain from squealing with the possible sacrifice of future gains that may result from squealing. In single-play Stag Hunt, each hunter is tempted to defect in order to defend himself against the possibility of defection by others. A reputation for reliability, for resisting temptation, reduces the likelihood of defection. If the hunters are a permanent group, and expect to hunt together again, the immediate gains from unilateral defection relative to unrequited cooperation must be balanced against the cost of diminished cooperation in the future. In both Prisoners' Dilemma and Stag Hunt, defection in the present *decreases* the likelihood of cooperation in the future. In both, therefore, iteration improves the prospects for cooperation. In Chicken, iteration may decrease the prospects for cooperation. Under single-play conditions, the temptation of unilateral defection is balanced by the fear of the collision that follows from mutual defection. How does iteration affect this balance? If the game is repeated indefinitely, then each driver may refrain from swerving in the present to coerce the other driver into swerving in the future. Each driver may seek to acquire a reputation for not swerving to cause the other driver to swerve. In iterated Chicken, one driver's defection in the present may decrease the likelihood of the other driver's defection in the future.

B. Strategies of Reciprocity and Conditions of Play

It is at this juncture that strategy enters the explanation. Although the expectation of continuing interaction has varying effects on the likelihood of cooperation in the illustrations above, an iterated environment permits resort to strategies of reciprocity that may improve the prospects of cooperation in Chicken as well as in Prisoners' Dilemma and Stag Hunt. Robert Axelrod argues that strategies of reciprocity have the effect of promoting cooperation by establishing a direct connection between an actor's present behavior and anticipated future benefits. Tit-for-tat, or conditional cooperation, can increase the likelihood of joint cooperation by shaping the future consequences of present cooperation or defection.

   In iterated Prisoners' Dilemma and Stag Hunt, reciprocity underscores the future consequences of present cooperation and defection. The argument presented above—that iteration enhances the prospects for cooperation in these games—rests on the assumption that defection in the present will decrease the likelihood of cooperation in the future. Adoption of an implicit or explicit strategy of matching stonewalling with stonewalling, squealing with squealing, rabbit chasing with rabbit chasing, and cooperative hunting with cooperative hunting validates the assumption. In iterated Chicken, a strategy of reciprocity can offset the perverse effects of reputational considerations on the prospects for cooperation. Recall that in iterated Chicken, each driver may refrain from swerving in the present to coerce the other driver into swerving in the future. Adoption of an implicit or explicit strategy of tit-for-tat in iterated games of Chicken alters the failure stream of benefits associated with present defection. If a strategy of reciprocity is credible, then the mutual losses associated with future collisions can encourage present swerving. In all three games, a promise to respond to present cooperation with future cooperation and a threat to respond to present defection with future defection can improve the prospects for cooperation.

The effectiveness of strategies of reciprocity hinges on conditions of play—the ability of actors to distinguish reliably between cooperation and defection by others and to respond in kind. In the illustrations provided above, the meaning of "defect" and "cooperate" is unambiguous. Dichotomous choices—between squeal and stonewall, chase the rabbit or capture the stag, continue down the road or swerve—limit the likelihood of misperception. Further, the actions of all are transparent. Given the definitions of the situations, prisoners, hunters, and drivers can reliably detect defection and cooperation by other actors. Finally, the definition of the actors eliminates the possibility of control problems. Unitary prisoners, hunters, and drivers do not suffer from factional, organizational, or bureaucratic dysfunctions that might hinder implementation of strategies of reciprocity.

In international relations, conditions of play can limit the effectiveness of reciprocity. The definition of cooperation and defection may be ambiguous. For example, the Soviet Union and the United States hold to markedly different definitions of "defection" from the terms of détente as presented in the Basic Principles Agreement;[11] the European Community and the United States differ over whether domestic sectoral policies comprise indirect export subsidies. Further, actions may not be transparent. For example, governments may not be able to detect one another's violations of arms control agreements or indirect export subsidies. If defection cannot be reliably detected, the effect of present cooperation on possible future reprisals will erode. Together, ambiguous definitions and a lack of transparency can limit the ability of states to recognize cooperation and defection by others.

Because reciprocity requires flexibility, control is as important as recognition. Internal factional, organizational, and bureaucratic dysfunctions may limit the ability of nations to implement tit-for-tat strategies. It may be easier to sell one unvarying line of policy than to sell a strategy of shifting between lines of policy in response to the actions of others. For example, arms suppliers and defense planners tend to resist the cancellation of weapons systems even if the cancellation is a response to the actions of a rival. Import-competing industries tend to resist the removal of barriers to imports, even if trade liberalization is in response to liberalization by another state. At times, national decision makers may be unable to implement strategies of reciprocity. On other occasions, they must invest heavily in selling reciprocity. For these reasons, national decision makers may display a bias against conditional strategies: The domestic costs of pursuing such strategies may partially offset the value of the discounted stream of future benefits that conditional policies are expected to yield. . . .

C. Strategies to Improve Recognition and Lengthen the Shadow of the Future

To what extent can governments promote cooperation by creating favorable conditions of play and by lengthening the shadow of the future? The literature on international regimes offers several techniques for creating favorable conditions of play. Explicit codification of norms can limit definitional ambiguity. The very act of clarifying standards of conduct, of defining cooperative and uncooperative behavior, can permit more effective resort to strategies of reciprocity. Further, provisions for surveillance—for example, mechanisms for verification in arms control agreements or for sharing information on the nature and effects of domestic sectoral policies—can increase transparency. In practice, the goal of enhancing recognition capabilities is often central to negotiations under anarchy.

The game-theoretic and institutional microeconomic literatures offer several approaches to increasing the iterative character of situations. Thomas Schelling and Robert Axelrod suggest tactics of decomposition over time to lengthen the shadow of the future.[12] For example, the temptation to defect in a deal promising thirty billion dollars for a billion barrels of oil may be reduced if the deal is sliced up into a series of payments and deliveries. Cooperation in arms reduction or in territorial disengagement may be difficult if the reduction or disengagement must be achieved in one jump. If a reduction or disengagement can be sliced up into increments, the problem of cooperation may be rendered more tractable. Finally, strategies of issue linkage can be used to alter payoff structures and to interject elements of iterativeness into single-play situations. Relations among states are rarely limited to one single-play issue of overriding importance. When nations confront a single-play game on one issue, present defection may be deterred by threats of retaliation on other iterated issues. In international monetary affairs, for instance, a government fearing one-time reserve losses if another state devalues its currency may link devaluation to an iterated trade game. By establishing a direct connection between present behavior in a single-play game and future benefits in an iterated game, tacit or explicit cross-issue linkage can lengthen the shadow of the future. . . .

IV. NUMBER OF PLAYERS: TWO-PERSON AND N-PERSON GAMES

Up to now, I have discussed the effects of payoff structure and the shadow of the future on the prospects of cooperation in terms of two-person situations. What happens to the prospects for cooperation as the number of significant actors rises? In this section, I explain why the prospects for cooperation diminish as the number of players increases; examine the function of international regimes as a response to the problems created by large numbers; and offer strategies to improve the prospects for cooperation by altering situations to diminish the number of significant players.

The numbers problem is central to many areas of the social sciences. Mancur Olson's theory of collective action focuses on N-person versions of Prisoners'

Dilemma. The optimism of our earlier discussions of cooperation under iterated Prisoners' Dilemma gives way to the pessimism of analyses of cooperation in the provision of public goods. Applications of Olsonian theory to problems ranging from cartelization to the provision of public goods in alliances underscore the significance of "free-riding" as an impediment to cooperation.[13] In international relations, the numbers problem has been central to two debates. The longstanding controversy over the stability of bipolar versus multipolar systems reduces to a debate over the impact of the number of significant actors on international conflict.[14] A more recent controversy, between proponents of the theory of hegemonic stability and advocates of international regimes, reduces to a debate over the effects of large numbers on the robustness of cooperation.[15]

A. Number of Players and Cooperation

How do numbers affect the likelihood of cooperation? There are at least three important channels of influence.[16] First, cooperation requires recognition of opportunities for the advancement of mutual interests, as well as policy coordination once these opportunities have been identified. As the number of players increases, transactions and information costs rise. In simple terms, the complexity of N-person situations militates against identification and realization of common interests. Avoiding nuclear war during the Cuban missile crisis called for cooperation by the Soviet Union and the United States. The transaction and information costs in this particularly harrowing crisis, though substantial, did not preclude cooperation. By contrast, the problem of identifying significant actors, defining interests, and negotiating agreements that embodied mutual interests in the N-actor case of 1914 was far more difficult. These secondary costs associated with attaining cooperative outcomes in N-actor cases erode the difference between CC and DD. More significantly, the intrinsic difficulty of anticipating the behavior of other players and of weighing the value of the future goes up with the number of players. The complexity of solving N-person games, even in the purely deductive sense, has stunted the development of formal work on the problem. This complexity is even greater in real situations, and operates against multilateral cooperation.

Second, as the number of players increases, the likelihood of autonomous defection and of recognition and control problems increases. Cooperative behavior rests on calculations of expected utility—merging discount rates, payoff structures, and anticipated behavior of other players. Discount rates and approaches to calculation are likely to vary across actors, and the prospects for mutual cooperation may decline as the number of players and probable heterogeneity of actors increases. The chances of including a state that discounts the future heavily, that is too weak (domestically) to detect, react, or implement a strategy of reciprocity, that cannot distinguish reliably between cooperation and defection by other states, or that departs from even minimal standards of rationality increase with the number of states in a game. For example, many pessimistic analyses of the consequences of nuclear proliferation focus on how breakdowns of deterrence may become more likely as the number of countries with nuclear weapons increases.

Third, as the number of players increases, the feasibility of sanctioning defectors diminishes. Strategies of reciprocity become more difficult to implement without triggering a collapse of cooperation. In two-person games, tit-for-tat works well because the costs of defection are focused on only one other party. If defection imposes costs on all parties in an N-person game, however, the power of strategies of reciprocity is underminded. The infeasibility of sanctioning defectors creates the possibility of free-riding. What happens if we increase the number of actors in the iterated Prisoners' Dilemma from 2 to 20? Confession by any one of them could lead to the conviction of all on the major charge; therefore, the threat to retaliate against defection in the present with defection in the future will impose costs on all prisoners, and could lead to wholesale defection in subsequent rounds. For example, under the 1914 system of alliances, retaliation against one member of the alliance was the equivalent of retaliation against all. In N-person games, a strategy of conditional defection can have the effect of spreading, rather than containing, defection.

B. Strategies of Institutionalization and Decomposition

Given a large number of players, what strategies can states use to increase the likelihood of cooperation? Regime creation can increase the likelihood of cooperation in N-person games. First, conventions provide rules of thumb that can diminish transaction and information costs. Second, collective enforcement mechanisms both decrease the likelihood of autonomous defection and permit selective punishment of violators of norms. These two functions of international regimes directly address problems created by large numbers of players. For example, Japan and the members of NATO profess a mutual interest in limiting flows of militarily useful goods and technology to the Soviet Union. Obviously, all suppliers of militarily useful goods and technology must cooperate to deny the Soviet Union access to such items. Although governments differ in their assessment of the military value of some goods and technologies, there is consensus on a rather lengthy list of prohibited items. By facilitating agreement of the prohibited list, the Coordinating Committee on the Consultative Group of NATO (CoCom) provides a relatively clear definition of what exports would constitute defection. By defining the scope of defection, the CoCom list forestalls the necessity of retaliation against nations that ship technology or goods that do not fall within the consensual definition of defection. Generally, cooperation is a prerequisite of regime creation. The creation of rules of thumb and mechanisms of collective enforcement and the maintenance and administration of regimes can demand an extraordinary degree of cooperation. This problem may limit the range of situations susceptible to modification through regimist strategies.

What strategies can reduce the number of significant players in a game and thereby render cooperation more likely? When governments are unable to cooperate on a global scale, they often turn to discriminatory strategies to encourage bilateral or regional cooperation. Tactics of decomposition across actors can, at times, improve the prospects for cooperation. Both the possibilities and the limits of strategies to reduce the number of players are evident in the discussions that follow. First, reductions in the number of actors can usually be purchased at the expense of the magnitude of gains from cooperation. The benefits of regional openness are smaller than the gains from global openness. A bilateral clearing arrangement is less economically efficient than a multilateral clearing arrangement. Strategies to reduce the number of players in a game generally diminish the gains from cooperation while they increase the likelihood and robustness of cooperation. Second, strategies to reduce the number of players generally impose substantial costs on third parties. These externalities may motivate third parties to undermine the limited area of cooperation or may serve as an impetus for a third party to enlarge the zone of cooperation. In the 1930s, for example, wholesale resort to discriminatory trading policies facilitated creation of exclusive zones of commercial openness. When confronted by a shrinking market share, Great Britain adopted a less liberal and more discriminatory commercial policy in order to secure preferential access to its empire and to undermine preferential agreements between other countries. As the American market share diminished, the United States adopted a more liberal and more discriminatory commercial policy to increase its access to export markets. It is not possible, however, to reduce the number of players in all situations. For example, compare the example of limited commercial openness with the example of a limited strategic embargo. To reduce the number of actors in a trade war, market access can simply be offered to only one country and withheld from others. By contrast, defection by only one supplier can permit the target of a strategic embargo to obtain a critical technology. These problems may limit the range of situations susceptible to modification through strategies that reduce the number of players in games.

NOTES

1. For examples, see Robert Jervis, "Cooperation under the Security Dilemma," *World Politics* 30 (January 1978), pp. 167–214; Oliver E. Williamson, "Credible Commitments: Using Hostages to Support Exchange," *American Economic Review* (September 1983), pp. 519–40; John Gerard Ruggie, "International Regimes, Transactions, and Change: Embedded Liberalism in the Postwar Economic Order," in Stephen D. Krasner, ed., *International Regimes* (Ithaca, N.Y.: Cornell University Press, 1983).

2. For orthodox game-theoretic analyses of the importance of iteration, see R. Duncan Luce and Howard Raiffa, *Games and Decisions* (New York: Wiley, 1957), Appendix 8, and David M. Kreps, Paul Milgrom, John Roberts, and Robert Wilson, "Rational Cooperation in Finitely-Repeated Prisoner's Dilemma," *Journal of Economic Theory* 27 (August 1982), pp. 245–52. For the results of laboratory experiments, see Robert Radlow, "An Experimental Study of Cooperation in the Prisoners' Dilemma Game," *Journal of Conflict Resolution* 9 (June 1965), pp. 221–27. On the importance of indefinite iteration to the emergence of cooperation in business transactions, see Robert Telsor, "A Theory of Self-Enforcing Agreements," *Journal of Business* 53 (January 1980), pp. 27–44.

3. See Robert O. Keohane, *After Hegemony: Cooperation and Discord in the World Political Economy* (Princeton, N.J.: Princeton University Press, 1984), and Krasner (fn. 1).

4. See John A. C. Conybeare, "International Organization and the Theory of Property Rights," *International Organization* 34 (Summer 1980), pp. 307–34, and Kenneth A. Oye, "Belief Systems, Bargaining, and Breakdown: International Political Economy 1929–1936," Ph.D. diss. (Harvard University, 1983), chap. 3.

5. See Jervis (fn. 1); Ruggie (fn. 1); Timothy J. McKeown, "Firms and Tariff Regime Change: Explaining the Demand for Protection," *World Politics* 36 (January 1984), pp. 215–33. On the effects of *ambiguity* of preferences on the prospects of cooperation, see the concluding sections of Jervis (fn. 1).

6. Haas, Williams, and Babai, *Scientists and World Order: The Uses of Technical Knowledge in International Organizations* (Berkeley: University of California Press, 1977).

7. Williamson (fn. 1).

8. See John Newhouse, *Cold Dawn: The Story of SALT I* (New York: Holt, Rinehart & Winston, 1973).

9. See Haas, "Words Can Hurt You; Or Who Said What to Whom About Regimes," in Krasner (fn. 1).

10. See Anatol Rapoport and Albert Chammah, *Prisoners' Dilemma* (Ann Arbor: University of Michigan Press, 1965), and subsequent essays in *Journal of Conflict Resolution.*

11. See Alexander L. George, *Managing U.S.–Soviet Rivalry: Problems of Crisis Prevention* (Boulder, Colo.: Westview, 1983).

12. Schelling, *Strategy of Conflict* (Cambridge, Mass.: Harvard University Press, 1960), pp. 43–46.

13. See Mancur Olson, Jr., *The Logic of Collective Action: Public Goods and the Theory of Groups* (Cambridge, Mass.: Harvard University Press, 1965), and Mancur Olson and Richard Zeckhauser, "An Economic Theory of Alliances," *Review of Economics and Statistics* 48 (August 1966), pp. 266–79. For a recent elegant summary and extension of the large literature on dilemmas of collective action, see Russell Hardin, *Collective Action* (Baltimore: Johns Hopkins University Press, 1982).

14. See Kenneth N. Waltz, "The Stability of a Bipolar World," *Daedalus* 93 (Summer 1964), and Richard N. Rosecrance, "Bipolarity, Multipolarity, and the Future," *Journal of Conflict Resolution* (September 1966), pp. 314–27.

15. On hegemony, see Robert Gilpin, *U.S. Power and the Multinational Corporation* (New York: Basic Books, 1975), pp. 258–59. On duopoly, see Timothy McKeown, "Hegemonic Stability Theory and 19th-Century Tariff Levels in Europe," *International Organization* 37 (Winter 1983), pp. 73–91.

16. See Keohane (fn. 3), chap. 6, for extensions of these points.

Kant, Liberal Legacies, and Foreign Affairs

■■■■■■■ MICHAEL W. DOYLE

I

What difference do liberal principles and institutions make to the conduct of the foreign affairs of liberal states? A thicket of conflicting judgments suggests that the legacies of liberalism have not been clearly appreciated. For many citizens of liberal states, liberal principles and institutions have so fully absorbed domestic politics that their influence on foreign affairs tends to be either overlooked altogether or, when perceived, exaggerated. Liberalism becomes either unselfconsciously patriotic or inherently "peace-loving." For many scholars and diplomats, the relations among independent states appear to differ so significantly from domestic politics that influences of liberal principles and domestic liberal institutions are denied or denigrated. They judge that international relations are governed by perceptions of national security and the balance of power; liberal principles and institutions, when they do intrude, confuse and disrupt the pursuit of balance-of-power politics.

Although liberalism is misinterpreted from both these points of view, a crucial aspect of the liberal legacy is captured by each. Liberalism is a distinct ideology and set of institutions that has shaped the perceptions of and capacities for foreign relations of political societies that range from social welfare or social democratic to laissez faire. It defines much of the content of the liberal patriot's nationalism. Liberalism does appear to disrupt the pursuit of balance-of-power politics. Thus its foreign relations cannot be adequately explained (or prescribed) by a sole reliance on the balance of power. But liberalism is not inherently "peace-loving"; nor is it consistently restrained or peaceful in intent. Furthermore, liberal practice may reduce the probability that states will successfully exercise the consistent restraint and peaceful intentions that a world peace may well require in the nuclear age. Yet the peaceful intent and restraint that liberalism does manifest in limited aspects of its foreign affairs announces the possibility of a world peace this side of the grave or of world conquest. It has strengthened the prospects for a world peace established by the steady expansion of a separate peace among liberal societies. . . .

"Kant, Liberal Legacies, and Foreign Affairs, Part 2," by Michael W. Doyle from *Philosophy and Public Affairs*, Vol. 12, No. 4 (Fall 1983). Copyright © 1983. Reprinted by permission of Blackwell Publishing.

II

Liberalism has been identified with an essential principle—the importance of the freedom of the individual. Above all, this is a belief in the importance of moral freedom, of the right to be treated and a duty to treat others as ethical subjects, and not as objects or means only. This principle has generated rights and institutions.

A commitment to a threefold set of rights forms the foundation of liberalism. Liberalism calls for freedom from arbitrary authority, often called "negative freedom," which includes freedom of conscience, a free press and free speech, equality under the law, and the right to hold, and therefore to exchange, property without fear of arbitrary seizure. Liberalism also calls for those rights necessary to protect and promote the capacity and opportunity for freedom, the "positive freedoms." Such social and economic rights as equality of opportunity in education and rights to health care and employment, necessary for effective self-expression and participation, are thus among liberal rights. A third liberal right, democratic participation or representation, is necessary to guarantee the other two. To ensure that morally autonomous individuals remain free in those areas of social action where public authority is needed, public legislation has to express the will of the citizens making laws for their own community.

These three sets of rights, taken together, seem to meet the challenge that Kant identified:

> To organize a group of rational beings who demand general laws for their survival, but of whom each inclines toward exempting himself, and to establish their constitution in such a way that, in spite of the fact their private attitudes are opposed, these private attitudes mutually impede each other in such a manner that [their] public behavior is the same as if they did not have such evil attitudes.[1]

But the dilemma within liberalism is how to reconcile the three sets of liberal rights. The right to private property, for example, can conflict with equality of opportunity and both rights can be violated by democratic legislation. During the 180 years since Kant wrote, the liberal tradition has evolved two high roads to individual freedom and social order; one is laissez-faire, or "conservative," liberalism and the other is social welfare, or social democratic, or "liberal," liberalism. Both reconcile these conflicting rights (though in differing ways) by successfully organizing free individuals into a political order.

The political order of laissez-faire and social welfare liberals is marked by a shared commitment to four essential institutions. First, citizens possess juridical equality and other fundamental civil rights such as freedom of religion and the press. Second, the effective sovereigns of the state are representative legislatures deriving their authority from the consent of the electorate and exercising their authority free from all restraint apart from the requirement that basic civic rights be preserved. Most pertinently for the impact of liberalism on foreign affairs, the state is subject to neither the external authority of other states nor to the internal authority of special prerogatives held, for example, by monarchs or military castes over foreign policy. Third, the economy rests on a recognition of the rights of private property including the ownership of means of production. Property is justified by individual acquisition (for example, by labor) or by social agreement or social utility. This excludes state socialism or state capitalism, but it need not exclude market socialism or various forms of the mixed economy. Fourth, economic decisions are predominantly shaped by the forces of supply and demand, domestically and internationally, and are free from strict control by bureaucracies. . . .

III

In foreign affairs liberalism has shown, as it has in the domestic realm, serious weaknesses. But unlike liberalism's domestic realm, its foreign affairs have experienced startling but less than fully appreciated successes. Together they shape an unrecognized dilemma, for both these successes and weaknesses in large part spring from the same cause: the international implications of liberal principles and institutions.

The basic postulate of liberal international theory holds that states have the right to be free from foreign intervention. Since morally autonomous citizens hold rights to liberty, the states that democratically represent them have the right to exercise political independence. Mutual respect for these rights then becomes the touchstone of international liberal theory. When states respect each other's rights, individuals are free to establish private international ties without state interference. Profitable exchange between merchants and educational exchanges among scholars then create a web of mutual advantages and commitments that bolsters sentiments of public respect.

These conventions of mutual respect have formed a cooperative foundation for relations among liberal democracies of a remarkably effective kind. *Even though liberal states have become involved in numerous wars with nonliberal states, constitutionally secure liberal states have yet to engage in war with one another.*[2] No one should argue that such wars are impossible; but preliminary evidence does appear to indicate that there exists a significant predisposition against warfare between liberal states. Indeed, threats of war also have been regarded as illegitimate. A liberal zone of peace, a pacific union, has been maintained and has expanded despite numerous particular conflicts of economic and strategic interest. . . .

Statistically, war between any two states (in any single year or other short period of time) is a low probability event. War between any two adjacent states, considered over a long period of time, may be somewhat more probable. The apparent absence of war among the more clearly liberal states, whether adjacent or not, for almost two hundred years thus has some significance. Politically more significant, perhaps, is that, when states are forced to decide, by the pressure of an impinging world war, on which side of a world contest they will fight, liberal states wind up all on the same side, despite the real complexity of the historical, economic, and political factors that affect their foreign policies. And historically, we should recall that medieval and early modern Europe were the warring cockpits of states, wherein France and England and the Low Countries engaged in near constant strife. Then in the late eighteenth century there began to emerge liberal regimes. At first hesitant and confused, and later clear and confident as liberal regimes gained deeper domestic foundations and longer international experience, a pacific union of these liberal states became established.

The realist model of international relations, which provides a plausible explanation of the general insecurity of states, offers little guidance in explaining the pacification of the liberal world. Realism, in its classical formation, holds that the state is and should be formally sovereign, effectively unbounded by individual rights nationally and thus capable of determining its own scope of authority. (This determination can be made democratically, oligarchically, or autocratically.) Internationally, the sovereign state exists in an anarchical society in which it is radically independent, neither bounded nor protected by international "law" or treaties or duties, and hence, insecure. Hobbes, one of the seventeenth-century founders of the realist approach, drew the international implications of realism when he argued that the existence of international anarchy, the very independence of states, best accounts for the competition, the fear, and the temptation toward preventive war that characterize international relations. Politics among nations is not a continuous combat, but it is in this view a "state of war . . . a tract of time, wherein the will to contend by battle is sufficiently known."[3] . . .

Finding that all states, including liberal states, do engage in war, the realist concludes that the effects of differing domestic regimes (whether liberal or not) are overridden by the international anarchy under which all states live.[4] . . . But the ends that shape the international state of war are decreed for the realist by the anarchy of the international order and the fundamental quest for power that directs the policy of all states, irrespective of differences in their domestic regimes. As Rousseau argued, international peace therefore depends on the abolition of international relations either by the achievement of a world state or by a radical isolationism (Corsica). Realists judge neither to be possible.

Recent additions to game theory specify some of the circumstances under which prudence could lead to peace. Experience; geography; expectations of cooperation and belief patterns; and the differing payoffs to cooperation (peace) or conflict associated with various types of military technology all appear to influence the calculus.[5] But when it comes to acquiring the techniques of peaceable interaction, nations appear to be slow, or at least erratic, learners. The balance of power (more below) is regarded as a primary lesson in the realist primer, but centuries of experience did not prevent either France (Louis XIV, Napoleon I) or Germany (Wilhelm II, Hitler) from attempting to conquer Europe, twice each. Yet some, very new, black African states appear to have achieved a twenty-year-old system of impressively effective standards of mutual toleration. These standards are not completely effective (as in Tanzania's invasion of Uganda); but they have confounded expectations of a scramble to redivide Africa.[6] Geography—"insular security" and "continental insecurity"—may affect foreign policy attitudes; but it does not appear to determine behavior, as the bellicose records of England and Japan suggest. Beliefs, expectations, and attitudes of leaders and masses should influence strategic behavior. . . . Nevertheless, it would be difficult to determine if liberal leaders have had more peaceable attitudes than leaders who lead nonliberal states.

But even if one did make that discovery, he also would have to account for why these peaceable attitudes only appear to be effective in relations with other liberals (since wars with nonliberals have not been uniformly defensive). . . .

Second, at the level of social determinants, some might argue that relations among any group of states with similar social structures or with compatible values would be peaceful. But again, the evidence for feudal societies, communist societies, fascist societies, or socialist societies does not support this conclusion. Feudal warfare was frequent and very much a sport of the monarchs and nobility. There have not been enough truly totalitarian, fascist powers (nor have they lasted long enough) to test fairly their pacific compatibility; but fascist powers in the wider sense of nationalist, capitalist, military dictatorships fought each other in the 1930s. Communist powers have engaged in wars more recently in East Asia. And we have not had enough socialist societies to consider the relevance of socialist pacification. The more abstract category of pluralism does not suffice. Certainly Germany was pluralist when it engaged in war with liberal states in 1914; Japan as well in 1941. But they were not liberal.

And third, at the level of interstate relations, neither specific regional attributes nor historic alliances or friendships can account for the wide reach of the liberal peace. The peace extends as far as, and no further than, the relations among liberal states, not including nonliberal states in an otherwise liberal region (such as the north Atlantic in the 1930s) nor excluding liberal states in a nonliberal region (such as Central America or Africa).

At this level, Raymond Aron has identified three types of interstate peace: empire, hegemony, and equilibrium.[7] An empire generally succeeds in creating an internal peace, but this is not an explanation of peace among independent liberal states. Hegemony can create peace by over-awing potential rivals. Although far from perfect and certainly precarious, United States hegemony, as Aron notes, might account for the interstate peace in South America in the postwar period during the height of the Cold War conflict. However, the liberal peace cannot be attributed merely to effective international policing by a predominant hegemon— Britain in the nineteenth century, the United States in the postwar period. Even though a hegemon might well have an interest in enforcing a peace for the sake of commerce or investments or as a means of enhancing its prestige or security, hegemons such as seventeenth-century France were not peace-enforcing police, and the liberal peace persisted in the interwar period when international society lacked a predominant hegemonic power. Moreover, this explanation overestimates hegemonic control in both periods. Neither England nor the United States was able to prevent direct challenges to its interests (colonial competition in the nineteenth century, Middle East diplomacy and conflicts over trading with the enemy in the postwar period). Where then was the capacity to prevent all armed conflicts between liberal regimes, many of which were remote and others strategically or economically insignificant? Liberal hegemony and leadership are important, but they are not sufficient to explain a liberal peace. . . .

Finally, some realists might suggest that the liberal peace simply reflects the absence of deep conflicts of interest among liberal states. Wars occur outside the liberal zone because conflicts of interest are deeper there. But this argument does nothing more than raise the question of why liberal states have fewer or less fundamental conflicts of interest with other liberal states than liberal states have with nonliberal, or nonliberal states have with other nonliberals. We must therefore examine the workings of liberalism among its own kind—a special pacification of the "state of war" resting on liberalism and nothing either more specific or more general.

IV

Most liberal theorists have offered inadequate guidance in understanding the exceptional nature of liberal pacification. Some have argued that democratic states would be inherently peaceful simply and solely because in these states citizens rule the polity and bear the costs of wars. Unlike monarchs, citizens are not able to indulge their aggressive passions and have the consequences suffered by someone else. Other liberals have argued that laissez-faire capitalism contains an inherent tendency toward rationalism, and that, since war is irrational, liberal capitalisms will be pacifistic. Others still, such as Montesquieu, claim that "commerce is the cure for the most destructive prejudices," and "Peace is the natural effect of trade."[8] While these developments can help account for the liberal peace, they do not explain the fact that liberal states are peaceful only in relations with other liberal states. France and England fought expansionist, colonial wars throughout the nineteenth century (in the 1830s and 1840s against Algeria and China); the United States fought a similar war with Mexico in 1848 and intervened again in 1914 under president Wilson. Liberal states are as aggressive and war prone as any other form of government or society in their relations with nonliberal states.

Immanuel Kant offers the best guidance. "Perpetual Peace," written in 1795, predicts the ever-widening pacification of the liberal pacific union, explains that pacification, and at the same time suggests why liberal states are not pacific in their relations with nonliberal states. . . .

Kant shows how republics, once established, lead to peaceful relations. He argues that once the aggressive interests of absolutist monarchies are tamed and once the habit of respect for individual rights is engrained by republican government, wars would appear as the disaster to the people's welfare that he and the other liberals thought them to be. The fundamental reason is this:

> If the consent of the citizens is required in order to decide that war should be declared (and in this constitution it cannot but be the case), nothing is more natural than that they would be very cautious in commencing such a poor game, decreeing for themselves all the calamities of war. Among the latter would be: having to fight, having to pay the costs of war from their own resources, having painfully to repair the devastation war leaves behind, and, to fill up the measure of evils, load themselves with a heavy national debt that would embitter peace itself and that can never be liquidated on account of constant wars in the future. But, on the other hand, in a constitution which is not republican, and under which the subjects are not citizens, a declaration of war is the easiest thing in the world to decide upon, because war does not require of the ruler, who is the proprietor and not a member of the state, the least sacrifice of the pleasure

of his table, the chase, his country houses, his court functions, and the like. He may, therefore, resolve on war as on a pleasure party for the most trivial reasons, and with perfect indifference leave the justification which decency requires to the diplomatic corps who are ever ready to provide it.[9]

One could add to Kant's list another source of pacification specific to liberal constitutions. The regular rotation of office in liberal democratic polities is a nontrivial device that helps ensure that personal animosities among heads of government provide no lasting, escalating source of tension.

These domestic republican restraints do not end war. If they did, liberal states would not be warlike, which is far from the case. They do introduce Kant's "caution" in place of monarchical caprice. Liberal wars are only fought for popular, liberal purposes. To see how this removes the occasion of wars among liberal states and not wars between liberal and nonliberal states, we need to shift our attention from constitutional law to international law, Kant's second source.

Complementing the constitutional guarantee of caution, *international law* adds a second source—a guarantee of respect. The separation of nations that asocial sociability encourages is reinforced by the development of separate languages and religions. These further guarantee a world of separate states—an essential condition needed to avoid a "global, soul-less despotism." Yet, at the same time, they also morally integrate liberal states "as culture progresses and men gradually come closer together toward a greater agreement on principles for peace and understanding."[10] As republics emerge (the first source) and as culture progresses, an understanding of the legitimate rights of all citizens and of all republics comes into play; and this, now that caution characterizes policy, sets up the moral foundations for the liberal peace. Correspondingly, international law highlights the importance of Kantian publicity. Domestically, publicity helps ensure that the officials of republics act according to the principles they profess to hold just and according to the interests of the electors they claim to represent. Internationally, free speech and the effective communication of accurate conceptions of the political life of foreign peoples is essential to establish and preserve the understanding on which the guarantee of respect depends. In short, domestically just republics, which rest on consent, presume foreign republics to be also consensual, just, and therefore deserving of accommodation. The experience of cooperation helps engender further cooperative behavior when the consequences of state policy are unclear but (potentially) mutually beneficial.[11]

Lastly, *cosmopolitan law* adds material incentives to moral commitments. The cosmopolitan right to hospitality permits the "spirit of commerce" sooner or later to take hold of every nation, thus impelling states to promote peace and to try to avert war.

Liberal economic theory holds that these cosmopolitan ties derive from a cooperative international division of labor and free trade according to comparative advantage. Each economy is said to be better off than it would have been under autarky; each thus acquires an incentive to avoid policies that would lead the other to break these economic ties. Since keeping open markets rests upon the assumption that the next set of transactions will also be determined by prices rather than coercion, a sense of mutual security is vital to avoid security-motivated searches for economic autarky. Thus, avoiding a challenge to another liberal state's security or even enhancing each other's security by means of alliance naturally follows economic interdependence.

A further cosmopolitan source of liberal peace is that the international market removes difficult decisions of production and distribution from the direct sphere of state policy. A foreign state thus does not appear directly responsible for these outcomes; states can stand aside from, and to some degree above, these contentious market rivalries and be ready to step in to resolve crises. Furthermore, the interdependence of commerce and the connections of state officials help create crosscutting transnational ties that serve as lobbies for mutual accommodation. According to modern liberal scholars, international financiers and transnational, bureaucratic, and domestic organizations create interests in favor of accommodation and have ensured by their variety that no single conflict sours an entire relationship.[12]

No one of these constitutional, international or cosmopolitan sources is alone sufficient, but together (and only where together) they plausibly connect the characteristics of liberal politics and economies with sustained liberal peace. Liberal states have not escaped from the realists' "security dilemma," the insecurity caused by anarchy in the world political system considered as a whole. But the effects of international anarchy have been tamed in the relations among states of a similarly liberal character. Alliances of purely mutual strategic interest among liberal and nonliberal states have been broken, economic ties between liberal and nonliberal states have proven fragile, but the political bond of liberal rights and interests has proven a remarkably firm foundation for mutual nonaggression. A separate peace exists among liberal states.

NOTES

1. Immanuel Kant, "Perpetual Peace" (1795), in *The Philosophy of Kant*, ed. Carl J. Friedrich (New York: Modern Library, 1949), p. 453.
2. There appear to be some exceptions to the tendency for liberal states not to engage in a war with each other. Peru and Ecuador, for example, entered into conflict. But for each, the war came within one to three years after the establishment of a liberal regime, that is, before the pacifying effects of liberalism could become deeply ingrained. The Palestinians and the Israelis clashed frequently along the Lebanese border, which Lebanon could not hold secure from either belligerent. But at the beginning of the 1967 War, Lebanon seems to have sent a flight of its own jets into Israel. The jets were repulsed. Alone among Israel's Arab neighbors, Lebanon engaged in no further hostilities with Israel. Israel's recent attack on the territory of Lebanon was an attack on a country that had already been occupied by Syria (and the P.L.O.). Whether Israel actually will withdraw (if Syria withdraws) and restore an independent Lebanon is yet to be determined.
3. Thomas Hobbes, *Leviathan* (New York: Penguin, 1980), I, chap. 13, 62, p. 186.
4. Kenneth N. Waltz, *Man, the State, and War* (New York: Columbia University Press, 1954, 1959), pp. 120–23; and see his *Theory of International Politics* (Reading, Mass.: Addison-Wesley, 1979). The classic sources of this form of Realism are Hobbes and, more particularly, Rousseau's "Essay on St. Pierre's Peace Project" and his "State of

War" in *A Lasting Peace* (London: Constable, 1917), E. H. Carr's *The Twenty Year's Crisis: 1919–1939* (London: Macmillan & Co., 1951), and the works of Hans Morgenthau.

5. Jervis, "Cooperation under the Security Dilemma," *World Politics* 30, no. 1 (January 1978), pp. 172–86.

6. Robert H. Jackson and Carl G. Rosberg, "Why West Africa's Weak States Persist," *World Politics* 35, no. 1 (October 1962).

7. Raymond Aron, *Peace and War* (New York: Praeger, 1968), pp. 151–54.

8. The incompatibility of democracy and war is forcefully asserted by Paine in *The Rights of Man*. The connection between liberal capitalism, democracy, and peace is argued by, among others, Joseph Schumpeter in *Imperialism and Social Classes* (New York: Meridian, 1955); and Montesquieu, *Spirit of the Laws* I, bk. 20, chap. 1. This literature is surveyed and analyzed by Albert Hirschman, "Rival Interpretations of Market Society: Civilizing, Destructive, or Feeble?" *Journal of Economic Literature* 20 (December 1982).

9. Immanuel Kant, "Perpetual Peace," in *The Enlightenment*, ed. Peter Gay (New York: Simon & Schuster, 1974), pp. 790–92.

10. Kant, *The Philosophy of Kant*, p. 454. These factors also have a bearing on Karl Deutsch's "compatibility of values" and "predictability of behavior."

11. A highly stylized version of this effect can be found in the realist's "Prisoners' Dilemma" game. There, a failure of mutual trust and the incentives to enhance one's own position produce a noncooperative solution that makes both parties worse off. Contrarily, cooperation, a commitment to avoid exploiting the other party, produces joint gains. The significance of the game in this context is the character of its participants. The "prisoners" are presumed to be felonious, unrelated apart from their partnership in crime, and lacking in mutual trust—competitive nation-states in an anarchic world. A similar game between fraternal or sororal twins—Kant's republics—would be likely to lead to different results. See Robert Jervis, "Hypotheses on Misperception," *World Politics* 20, no. 3 (April 1968), for an exposition of the role of presumptions; and "Cooperation under the Security Dilemma," *World Politics* 30, no. 2 (January 1978), for the factors realists see as mitigating the security dilemma caused by anarchy.

  Also, expectations (including theory and history) can influence behavior, making liberal states expect (and fulfill) pacific policies toward each other. These effects are explored at a theoretical level in R. Dacey, "Some Implications of 'Theory Absorption' for Economic Theory and the Economics Information," in *Philosophical Dimensions of Economics,* ed. J Pitt (Dordrecht, Holland: D. Reidel, 1980).

12. Karl Polanyi, *The Great Transformation* (Boston: Beacon Press, 1944), chaps. 1–2 and Samuel Huntington and Z. Brzezinski, *Political Power: USA/USSR* (New York: Viking Press, 1963, 1964), chap. 9. And see Richard Neustadt, *Alliance Politics* (New York: Columbia University Press, 1970) for a detailed case study of interliberal politics.

TABLE 1 ■ WARS INVOLVING LIBERAL REGIMES

Period	Liberal regimes and the pacific union (by date "liberal")[a]	Total number
18th century	Swiss Cantons[b] French Republic 1790–1795 the United States[b] 1776–	3
1800–1850	Swiss Confederation, the United States France 1830–1849 Belgium 1830– Great Britain 1832– Netherlands 1848– Piedmont 1848– Denmark 1849–	8
1850–1900	Switzerland, the United States, Belgium, Great Britain, Netherlands Piedmont 1861, Italy 1861– Denmark 1866 Sweden 1864– Greece 1864– Canada 1867– France 1871– Argentina 1880– Chile 1891–	13
1900–1945	Switzerland, the United States, Great Britain, Sweden, Canada Greece 1911, 1928–1936 Italy 1922 Belgium 1940 Netherlands 1940 Argentina 1943 France 1940 Chile 1924, 1932 Australia 1901– Norway 1905–1940 New Zealand 1907– Colombia 1910–1949 Denmark 1914–1940 Poland 1917–1935 Latvia 1922–1934 Germany 1918–1932 Austria 1918–1934 Estonia 1919–1934 Finland 1919– Uruguay 1919– Costa Rica 1919– Czechoslovakia 1920–1939	29

TABLE 1 ■ (Continued)

Period	Liberal regimes and the pacific union (by date "liberal")[a]	Total number
	Ireland 1920–	
	Mexico 1928–	
	Lebanon 1944–	
1945[c]	Switzerland, the United States, Great Britain, Sweden, Canada, Australia, New Zealand, Finland, Ireland, Mexico	49
	Uruguay 1973	
	Chile 1973	
	Lebanon 1975	
	Costa Rica 1948, 1953–	
	Iceland 1944–	
	France 1945–	
	Denmark 1945–	
	Norway 1945–	
	Austria 1945–	
	Brazil 1945–1954, 1955–1964	
	Belgium 1946–	
	Luxemburg 1946–	
	Netherlands 1946–	
	Italy 1946–	
	Philippines 1946–1972	
	India 1947–1975, 1977–	
	Sri Lanka 1948–1961, 1963–1977, 1978–	
	Ecuador 1948–1963, 1979–	
	Israel 1949–	
	West Germany 1949–	
	Peru 1950–1962, 1963–1968, 1980–	
	El Salvador 1950–1961	
	Turkey 1950–1960, 1966–1971	
	Japan 1951–	
	Bolivia 1956–1969	
	Colombia 1958–	
	Venezuela 1959–	
	Nigeria 1961–1964, 1979–	
	Jamaica 1962–	
	Trinidad 1962–	
	Senegal 1963–	
	Malaysia 1963–	
	South Korea 1963–1972	
	Botswana 1966–	
	Singapore 1965–	
	Greece 1975–	

(continued)

TABLE 1 ■ (Continued)

Period	Liberal regimes and the pacific union (by date "liberal")[a]	Total number
	Portugal 1976– Spain 1978– Dominican Republic 1978–	

[a]I have drawn up this approximate list of "Liberal Regimes" according to the four institutions described as essential: market and private property economies; politics that are extremely sovereign; citizens who possess juridical rights; and "republican" (whether republican or monarchical), representative, government. This latter includes the requirement that the legislative branch have an effective role in public policy and be formally and competitively, either potentially or actually, elected. Furthermore, I have taken into account whether male suffrage is wide (that is, 30 percent) or open to "achievement" by inhabitants (for example, to poll-tax payers or householders) of the national or metropolitan territory. Female suffrage is granted within a generation of its being demanded; and representative government is internally sovereign (for example, including and especially over military and foreign affairs) as well as stable (in existence for at least three years).

[b]There are domestic variations within these liberal regimes. For example, Switzerland was liberal only in certain cantons; the United States was liberal only north of the Mason-Dixon line until 1865, when it became liberal throughout. These lists also exclude ancient "republics," since none appear to fit Kant's criteria. See Stephen Holmes, "Aristippus in and out of Athens," *American Political Science Review* 73, no. 1 (March 1979).

[c]Selected list, excludes liberal regimes with populations less than one million.

Sources: Arthur Banks and W. Overstreet, eds., *The Political Handbook of the World,* 1980 (New York: McGraw-Hill, 1980; Foreign and Commonwealth Office. *A Year Book of the Commonwealth* 1980 (London: HMSO, 1980); *Europa Yearbook* 1981 (London: Europe, 1981); W. L. Langer, *An Encyclopedia of World History* (Boston: Houghton-Mifflin, 1968); Department of State, *Country Reports on Human Rights Practices* (Washington, D.C.: U.S. Government Printing Office, 1981); and *Freedom at Issue,* no. 54 (January–February 1980).

TABLE 2 ■ INTERNATIONAL WARS LISTED CHRONOLOGICALLY

British-Maharattan (1817–1818)	Roman Republic (1849)
Greek (1821–1828)	La Plata (1851–1852)
Franco-Spanish (1823)	First Turco-Montenegran (1852–1853)
First Anglo-Burmese (1823–1826)	Crimean (1853–1856)
Japanese (1825–1830)	Russo-Japanese (1904–1905)
Russo-Persian (1826–1828)	Sepoy (1857–1859)
Russo-Turkish (1828–1829)	Second Turco-Montenegran (1858–1859)
First Polish (1831)	Italian Unification (1859)
First Syrian (1831–1832)	Spanish-Moroccan (1859–1860)
Texan (1835–1836)	Italo-Roman (1860)
First British-Afghan (1838–1842)	Italo-Sicilian (1860–1861)
Second Syrian (1839–1840)	Franco-Mexican (1862–1867)
Franco-Algerian (1839–1847)	Ecuadorian-Colombian (1863)
Peruvian-Bolivian (1841)	Second Polish (1863–1864)
First British-Sikh (1845–1846)	Spanish-Santo Dominican (1863–1865)
Mexican-American (1846–1848)	Second Schleswig-Holstein (1864)
Austro-Sardinian (1848–1849)	Lopez (1864–1870)
First Schleswig-Holstein (1848–1849)	Spanish-Chilean (1865–1866)
Hungarian (1848–1849)	Seven Weeks (1866)
Second British-Sikh (1848–1849)	Ten Years (1868–1878)

TABLE 2 ■ (Continued)

Franco-Prussian (1870–1871)	Manchurian (1931–1933)
Dutch-Achinese (1873–1878)	Chaco (1932–1935)
Balkan (1875–1877)	Italo-Ethiopian (1935–1936)
Russo-Turkish (1877–1878)	Sino-Japanese (1937–1941)
Bosnian (1878)	Changkufeng (1938)
Second British-Afghan (1878–1880)	Nomohan (1939)
Pacific (1879–1880)	World War II (1939–1945)
British-Zulu (1879)	Russo-Finnish (1939–1940)
Franco-Indochinese (1882–1884)	Franco-Thai (1940–1941)
Mahdist (1882–1885)	Indonesian (1945–1946)
Sino-French (1884–1885)	Indochinese (1945–1954)
Central American (1885)	Palestine (1948–1949)
Serbo-Bulgarian (1885)	Hyderabad (1948)
Sino-Japanese (1894–1895)	Madagascan (1947–1948)
Franco-Madagascan (1894–1895)	First Kashmir (1947–1949)
Cuban (1895–1896)	Korean (1950–1953)
Italo-Ethiopian (1895–1896)	Algerian (1954–1962)
First Philippine (1896–1898)	Russo-Hungarian (1956)
Greco-Turkish (1897)	Sinai (1956)
Spanish-American (1898)	Tibetan (1956–1959)
Second Philippine (1899–1902)	Sino-Indian (1962)
Boer (1899–1902)	Vietnamese (1965–1975)
Boxer Rebellion (1900)	Second Kashmir (1965)
Ilinden (1903)	Six Day (1967)
Russo-Japanese (1904–1905)	Israeli-Egyptian (1969–1970)
Central American (1906)	Football (1969)
Central American (1907)	Bangladesh (1971)
Spanish-Moroccan (1909–1910)	Philippine-MNLF (1972–)
Italo-Turkish (1911–1912)	Yom Kippur (1973)
First Balkan (1912–1913)	Turco-Cypriot (1974)
Second Balkan (1913)	Ethiopian-Eritrean (1974–)
World War I (1914–1918)	Vietnamese-Cambodian (1975–)
Russian Nationalities (1917–1921)	Timor (1975–)
Russo-Polish (1919–1920)	Saharan (1975–)
Hungarian-Allies (1919)	Ogaden (1976–)
Greco-Turkish (1919–1922)	Ugandan-Tanzanian (1978–1979)
Riffian (1921–1926)	Sino-Vietnamese (1979)
Druze (1925–1927)	Russo-Afghan (1979–1989)
Sino-Soviet (1929)	Irani-Iraqi (1980–1988)

*The table is reprinted by permission from Melvin Small and J. David Singer from *Resort to Arms* (Beverly Hills, Calif.: Sage Publications, 1962), pp. 79–80. This is a partial list of international wars fought between 1816 and 1980. In Appendices A and B of *Resort to Arms,* Small and Singer identify a total of 575 wars in this period, but approximately 159 of them appear to be largely domestic or civil wars.

   This definition of war excludes covert interventions, some of which have been directed by liberal regimes against other liberal regimes. One example is the United States' effort to destabilize the Chilean election and Allende's government. Nonetheless, it is significant . . . that such interventions are not pursued publicly as acknowledged policy. The covert destabilization campaign against Chile is recounted in U.S. Congress, Senate, Select Committee to Study Governmental Operations with Respect to Intelligence Activities, *Covert Action in Chile,* 1963–73, 94th Congress, 1st Session (Washington, D.C.: U.S. Government Printing Office, 1975).

Alliances: Balancing and Bandwagoning

STEPHEN M. WALT

When confronted by a significant external threat, states may either balance or bandwagon. *Balancing* is defined as allying with others against the prevailing threat; *bandwagoning* refers to alignment with the source of danger. Thus two distinct hypotheses about how states will select their alliance partners can be identified on the basis of whether the states ally against or with the principal external threat.[1]

These two hypotheses depict very different worlds. If balancing is more common than bandwagoning, then states are more secure, because aggressors will face combined opposition. But if bandwagoning is the dominant tendency, then security is scarce, because successful aggressors will attract additional allies, enhancing their power while reducing that of their opponents. . . .

BALANCING BEHAVIOR

The belief that states form alliances in order to prevent stronger powers from dominating them lies at the heart of traditional balance-of-power theory. According to this view, states join alliances to protect themselves from states or coalitions whose superior resources could pose a threat. States choose to balance for two main reasons.

First, they place their survival at risk if they fail to curb a potential hegemon before it becomes too strong. To ally with the dominant power means placing one's trust in its continued benevolence. The safer strategy is to join with those who cannot readily dominate their allies, in order to avoid being dominated by those who can. As Winston Churchill explained Britain's traditional alliance policy: "For four hundred years the foreign policy of England has been to oppose the strongest, most aggressive, most dominating power on the Continent. . . . [I]t would have been easy . . . and tempting to join with the stronger and share the fruits of his conquest. However, we always took the harder course, joined with the less strong powers, . . . and thus defeated the Continental military tyrant whoever he was."[2] More recently,

Henry Kissinger advocated a rapprochement with China, because he believed that in a triangular relationship, it was better to align with the weaker side.

Second, joining the weaker side increases the new member's influence within the alliance, because the weaker side has greater need for assistance. Allying with the strong side, by contrast, gives the new member little influence (because it adds relatively less to the coalition) and leaves it vulnerable to the whims of its partners. Joining the weaker side should be the preferred choice.

BANDWAGONING BEHAVIOR

The belief that states will balance is unsurprising, given the many familiar examples of states joining together to resist a threatening state or coalition. Yet, despite the powerful evidence that history provides in support of the balancing hypothesis, the belief that the opposite response is more likely is widespread. According to one scholar: "In international politics, nothing succeeds like success. Momentum accrues to the gainer and accelerates his movement. The appearance of irreversibility in his gains enfeebles one side and stimulates the other all the more. The bandwagon collects those on the sidelines."[3]

The bandwagoning hypothesis is especially popular with statesmen seeking to justify overseas involvements or increased military budgets. For example, German admiral Alfred von Tirpitz's famous risk theory rested on this type of logic. By building a great battle fleet, Tirpitz argued, Germany could force England into neutrality or alliance with her by posing a threat to England's vital maritime supremacy.

Bandwagoning beliefs have also been a recurring theme throughout the Cold War. Soviet efforts to intimidate both Norway and Turkey into not joining NATO reveal the Soviet conviction that states will accommodate readily to threats, although these moves merely encouraged Norway and Turkey to align more closely with the West.[4] Soviet officials made a similar error in believing that the growth of Soviet military power in the 1960s and 1970s would lead to a permanent shift in the correlation of forces against the West. Instead, it contributed to a Sino-American rapprochement in the 1970s and the largest peacetime increase in U.S. military power in the 1980s.

American officials have been equally fond of bandwagoning notions. According to NSC–68, the classified study that helped justify a major U.S. military buildup in the 1950s: "In the absence of an affirmative decision [to increase U.S. military capabilities] . . . our friends will become more than a liability to us, they will become a positive increment to Soviet power."[5] President John F. Kennedy once claimed that "if the United States were to falter, the whole world . . . would inevitably begin to move toward the Communist bloc."[6] And though Henry Kissinger often argued that the United States should form balancing alliances to contain the Soviet Union, he apparently believed that U.S. allies were likely to bandwagon. As he put it, "If leaders around the world . . . assume that the U.S. lacked either the forces or the will . . . they will accommodate themselves to what they will regard as the dominant trend."[7] Ronald Reagan's claim, "If we cannot defend ourselves [in Central America] . . . then we cannot expect to prevail else-where. . . . [O]ur credibility will collapse and our alliances will crumble," reveals the same logic in a familiar role—that of justifying overseas intervention.[8]

Balancing and bandwagoning are usually framed solely in terms of capabili-ties. Balancing is alignment with the weaker side, bandwagoning with the stronger. This conception should be revised, however, to account for the other factors that statesmen consider when deciding with whom to ally. Although power is an important part of the equation, it is not the only one. It is more accu-rate to say that states tend to ally with or against the foreign power that poses the greatest threat. For example, states may balance by allying with other strong states if a weaker power is more dangerous for other reasons. Thus the coalitions that defeated Germany in World War I and World War II were vastly superior in total resources, but they came together when it became clear that the aggressive aims of the Wilhelmines and Nazis posed the greater danger. Because balancing and bandwagoning are more accurately viewed as a response to threats, it is important to consider other factors that will affect the level of threat that states may pose: aggregate power, geographic proximity, offensive power, and aggres-sive intentions. . . .

By defining the basic hypotheses in terms of threats rather than power alone, we gain a more complete picture of the factors that statesmen will consider when making alliance choices. One cannot determine a priori, however, which sources of threat will be most important in any given case; one can say only that all of them are likely to play a role. And the greater the threat, the greater the probability that the vulnerable state will seek an alliance.

THE IMPLICATIONS OF BALANCING AND BANDWAGONING

The two general hypotheses of balancing and bandwagoning paint starkly contrast-ing pictures of international politics. Resolving the question of which hypothesis is more accurate is especially important, because each implies very different policy prescriptions. What sort of world does each depict, and what policies are implied?

If balancing is the dominant tendency, then threatening states will provoke others to align against them. Because those who seek to dominate others will attract widespread opposition, status quo states can take a relatively sanguine view of threats. Credibility is less important in a balancing world, because one's allies will resist threatening states out of their own self-interest, not because they expect others to do it for them. Thus the fear of allies defecting will decline. Moreover, if balancing is the norm and if statesmen understand this tendency, aggression will be discouraged because those who contemplate it will anticipate resistance.

In a balancing world, policies that convey restraint and benevolence are best. Strong states may be valued as allies because they have much to offer their part-ners, but they must take particular care to avoid appearing aggressive. Foreign and defense policies that minimize the threat one poses to others make the most sense in such a world.

A bandwagoning world, by contrast, is much more competitive. If states tend to ally with those who seem most dangerous, then great powers will be rewarded if they appear both strong and potentially aggressive. International rivalries will be more intense, because a single defeat may signal the decline of one side and the ascendancy of the other. This situation is especially alarming in a bandwagoning world, because additional defections and a further decline in position are to be expected. Moreover, if statesmen believe that bandwagoning is widespread, they will be more inclined to use force. This tendency is true for both aggressors and status quo powers. The former will use force because they will assume that others will be unlikely to balance against them and because they can attract more allies through belligerence or brinkmanship. The latter will follow suit because they will fear the gains their opponents will make by appearing powerful and resolute.[9]

Finally, misperceiving the relative propensity to balance or bandwagon is dangerous, because the policies that are appropriate for one situation will backfire in the other. If statesmen follow the balancing prescription in a bandwagoning world, their moderate responses and relaxed view of threats will encourage their allies to defect, leaving them isolated against an overwhelming coalition. Conversely, following the bandwagoning prescription in a world of balancers (employing power and threats frequently) will lead others to oppose you more and more vigorously.[10]

These concerns are not merely theoretical. In the 1930s, France failed to recognize that her allies in the Little Entente were prone to bandwagon, a tendency that French military and diplomatic policies reinforced. As noted earlier, Soviet attempts to intimidate Turkey and Norway after World War II reveal the opposite error; they merely provoked a greater U.S. commitment to these regions and cemented their entry into NATO. Likewise, the self-encircling bellicosity of Wilhelmine Germany and Imperial Japan reflected the assumption, prevalent in both states, that bandwagoning was the dominant tendency in international affairs.

WHEN DO STATES BALANCE? WHEN DO THEY BANDWAGON?

These examples highlight the importance of identifying whether states are more likely to balance or bandwagon and which sources of threat have the greatest impact on the decision. . . . In general, we should expect balancing behavior to be much more common than bandwagoning, and we should expect bandwagoning to occur only under certain identifiable conditions.

Although many statesmen fear that potential allies will align with the strongest side, this fear receives little support from most of international history. For example, every attempt to achieve hegemony in Europe since the Thirty Years' War has been thwarted by a defensive coalition formed precisely for the purpose of defeating the potential hegemon. Other examples are equally telling. Although isolated cases of bandwagoning do occur, the great powers have shown a remarkable tendency to ignore other temptations and follow the balancing prescription when necessary.

This tendency should not surprise us. Balancing should be preferred for the simple reason that no statesman can be completely sure of what another will do. Bandwagoning is dangerous because it increases the resources available to a threatening power and requires placing trust in its continued forbearance. Because perceptions are unreliable and intentions can change, it is safer to balance against potential threats than to rely on the hope that a state will remain benevolently disposed.

But if balancing is to be expected, bandwagoning remains a possibility. Several factors may affect the relative propensity for states to select this course.

Strong versus Weak States

In general, the weaker the state, the more likely it is to bandwagon rather than balance. This situation occurs because weak states add little to the strength of a defensive coalition but incur the wrath of the more threatening states nonetheless. Because weak states can do little to affect the outcome (and may suffer grievously in the process), they must choose the winning side. Only when their decision can affect the outcome is it rational for them to join the weaker alliance. By contrast, strong states can turn a losing coalition into a winning one. And because their decision may mean the difference between victory and defeat, they are likely to be amply rewarded for their contribution.

Weak states are also likely to be especially sensitive to proximate power. Where great powers have both global interests and global capabilities, weak states will be concerned primarily with events in their immediate vicinity. Moreover, weak states can be expected to balance when threatened by states with roughly equal capabilities but they will be tempted to bandwagon when threatened by a great power. Obviously, when the great power is capable of rapid and effective action (i.e., when its offensive capabilities are especially strong), this temptation will be even greater.

The Availability of Allies

States will also be tempted to bandwagon when allies are simply unavailable. This statement is not simply tautological, because states may balance by mobilizing their own resources instead of relying on allied support. They are more likely to do so, however, when they are confident that allied assistance will be available. Thus a further prerequisite for balancing behavior is an effective system of diplomatic communication. The ability to communicate enables potential allies to recognize their shared interests and coordinate their responses. If weak states see no possibility of outside assistance, however, they may be forced to accommodate the most imminent threat. Thus the first Shah of Iran saw the British withdrawal from Kandahar in 1881 as a signal to bandwagon with Russia. As he told the British representative, all he had received from Great Britain was "good advice and honeyed words—nothing else."[11] Finland's policy of partial alignment with the Soviet Union suggests the same lesson. When Finland joined forces with Nazi Germany during World War II, it alienated the potential allies (the United States and Great Britain) that might otherwise have helped protect it from Soviet pressure after the war.

Of course, excessive confidence in allied support will encourage weak states to free-ride, relying on the efforts of others to provide security. Free-riding is the optimal policy for a weak state, because its efforts will contribute little in any case. Among the great powers, the belief that allies are readily available encourages buck-passing; states that are threatened strive to pass to others the burdens of standing up to the aggressor. Neither response is a form of bandwagoning, but both suggest that effective balancing behavior is more likely to occur when members of an alliance are not convinced that their partners are unconditionally loyal.

Taken together, these factors help explain the formation of spheres of influence surrounding the great powers. Although strong neighbors of strong states are likely to balance, small and weak neighbors of the great powers may be more inclined to bandwagon. Because they will be the first victims of expansion, because they lack the capabilities to stand alone, and because a defensive alliance may operate too slowly to do them much good, accommodating a threatening great power may be tempting.

Peace and War

Finally, the context in which alliance choices are made will affect decisions to balance or bandwagon. States are more likely to balance in peacetime or in the early stages of a war, as they seek to deter or defeat the powers posing the greatest threat. But once the outcome appears certain, some will be tempted to defect from the losing side at an opportune moment. Thus both Rumania and Bulgaria allied with Nazi Germany initially and then abandoned Germany for the Allies, as the tides of war ebbed and flowed across Europe in World War II.

The restoration of peace, however, restores the incentive to balance. As many observers have noted, victorious coalitions are likely to disintegrate with the conclusion of peace. Prominent examples include Austria and Prussia after their war with Denmark in 1864, Britain and France after World War I, the Soviet Union and the United States after World War II, and China and Vietnam after the U.S. withdrawal from Vietnam. This recurring pattern provides further support for the proposition that balancing is the dominant tendency in international politics and that bandwagoning is the opportunistic exception.

SUMMARY OF HYPOTHESES ON BALANCING AND BANDWAGONING

Hypotheses on Balancing

1. *General form:* States facing an external threat will align with others to oppose the states posing the threat.
2. The greater the threatening state's aggregate power, the greater the tendency for others to align against it.
3. The nearer a powerful state, the greater the tendency for those nearby to align against it. Therefore, neighboring states are less likely to be allies than are states separated by at least one other power.
4. The greater a state's offensive capabilities, the greater the tendency for others to align against it. Therefore, states with offensively oriented military capabilities are likely to provoke other states to form defensive coalitions.
5. The more aggressive a state's perceived intentions, the more likely others are to align against that state.

6. Alliances formed during wartime will disintegrate when the enemy is defeated.

Hypotheses on Bandwagoning

The hypotheses on bandwagoning are the opposite of those on balancing.

1. *General form:* States facing an external threat will ally with the most threatening power.
2. The greater a state's aggregate capabilities, the greater the tendency for others to align with it.
3. The nearer a powerful state, the greater the tendency for those nearby to align with it.
4. The greater a state's offensive capabilities, the greater the tendency for others to align with it.
5. The more aggressive a state's perceived intentions, the less likely other states are to align against it.
6. Alliances formed to oppose a threat will disintegrate when the threat becomes serious.

Hypotheses on the Conditions Favoring Balancing or Bandwagoning

1. Balancing is more common than bandwagoning.
2. The stronger the state, the greater its tendency to balance. Weak states will balance against other weak states but may bandwagon when threatened by great powers.
3. The greater the probability of allied support, the greater the tendency to balance. When adequate allied support is certain, however, the tendency for free-riding or buck-passing increases.
4. The more unalterably aggressive a state is perceived to be, the greater the tendency for others to balance against it.
5. In wartime, the closer one side is to victory, the greater the tendency for others to bandwagon with it.

NOTES

1. My use of the terms *balancing* and *bandwagoning* follows that of Kenneth Waltz (who credits it to Stephen Van Evera) in his *Theory of International Politics* (Reading, Mass., 1979). Arnold Wolfers uses a similar terminology in his essay "The Balance of Power in Theory and Practice," in *Discord and Collaboration: Essays on International Politics* (Baltimore, Md., 1962), pp. 122–24.
2. Winston S. Churchill, *The Second World War*, vol. 1: *The Gathering Storm* (Boston, 1948), pp. 207–8.
3. W. Scott Thompson, "The Communist International System," *Orbis* 20, no. 4 (1977).
4. For the effects of the Soviet pressure on Turkey, see George Lenczowski, *The Middle East in World Affairs*, 4th ed. (Ithaca, 1980), pp. 134–38; and Bruce R. Kuniholm,

The Origins of the Cold War in the Near East (Princeton, N.J., 1980), pp. 355–78. For the Norwegian response to Soviet pressure, see Herbert Feis, *From Trust to Terror: The Onset of the Cold War, 1945–50* (New York, 1970), p. 381; and Geir Lundestad, *America, Scandinavia, and the Cold War: 1945–1949* (New York, 1980), pp. 308–9.

5. NSC–68 ("United States Objectives and Programs for National Security"), reprinted in Gaddis and Etzold, *Containment*, p. 404. Similar passages can be found on pp. 389, 414, and 434.

6. Quoted in Seyom Brown, *The Faces of Power: Constancy and Change in United States Foreign Policy from Truman to Johnson* (New York, 1968), p. 217.

7. Quoted in U.S. House Committee on Foreign Affairs, *The Soviet Union and the Third World: Watershed in Great Power Policy?* 97th Cong., 1st sess., 1977, pp. 157–58.

8. *New York Times*, April 28, 1983, p. A12. In the same speech, Reagan also said: "If Central America were to fall, what would the consequences be for our position in Asia and Europe and for alliances such as NATO? . . . Which ally, which friend would trust us then?"

9. It is worth noting that Napoleon and Hitler underestimated the costs of aggression by assuming that their potential enemies would bandwagon. After Munich, for example, Hitler dismissed the possibility of opposition by claiming that British and French statesmen were "little worms." Napoleon apparently believed that England could not "reasonably make war on us unaided" and assumed that the Peace of Amiens guaranteed that England had abandoned its opposition to France. Because Hitler and Napoleon believed in a bandwagoning world, they were excessively eager to go to war.

10. This situation is analogous to Robert Jervis's distinction between the deterrence model and the spiral model. The former calls for opposition to a suspected aggressor, the latter for appeasement. Balancing and bandwagoning are the alliance equivalents of deterring and appeasing. See Robert Jervis, *Perception and Misperception in International Politics* (Princeton, N.J., 1976), chap. 3.

11. Quoted in C. J. Lowe, *The Reluctant Imperialists* (New York, 1967), p. 85.

The Future of Diplomacy

HANS J. MORGENTHAU

FOUR TASKS OF DIPLOMACY

. . . Diplomacy [is] an element of national power. The importance of diplomacy for the preservation of international peace is but a particular aspect of that general function. For a diplomacy that ends in war has failed in its primary objective: the promotion of the national interest by peaceful means. This has always been so and is particularly so in view of the destructive potentialities of total war.

Taken in its widest meaning, comprising the whole range of foreign policy, the task of diplomacy is fourfold: (1) Diplomacy must determine its objectives in the light of the power actually and potentially available for the pursuit of these objectives. (2) Diplomacy must assess the objectives of other nations and the power actually and potentially available for the pursuit of these objectives. (3) Diplomacy must determine to what extent these different objectives are compatible with each other. (4) Diplomacy must employ the means suited to the pursuit of its objectives. Failure in any one of these tasks may jeopardize the success of foreign policy and with it the peace of the world.

A nation that sets itself goals which it has not the power to attain may have to face the risk of war on two counts. Such a nation is likely to dissipate its strength and not to be strong enough at all points of friction to deter a hostile nation from challenging it beyond endurance. The failure of its foreign policy may force the nation to retrace its steps and to redefine its objectives in view of its actual strength. Yet it is more likely that, under the pressure of an inflamed public opinion, such a nation will go forward on the road toward an unattainable goal, strain all its resources to achieve it, and finally, confounding the national interest with that goal, seek in war the solution to a problem that cannot be solved by peaceful means.

A nation will also invite war if its diplomacy wrongly assesses the objectives of other nations and the power at their disposal. . . . A nation that mistakes a policy of imperialism for a policy of the status quo will be unprepared to meet the threat to its own existence which the other nation's policy entails. Its weakness will invite attack and may make war inevitable. A nation that mistakes a policy of the status quo for a policy of imperialism will evoke through its disproportionate reaction the very danger of war which it is trying to avoid. For as A mistakes B's policy for imperialism, so B might mistake A's defensive reaction for imperialism. Thus both nations, each intent upon forestalling imaginary aggression from the other side, will rush to arms. Similarly, the confusion of one type of imperialism with another may call for disproportionate reaction and thus evoke the risk of war.

As for the assessment of the power of other nations, either to overrate or to underrate it may be equally fatal to the cause of peace. By overrating the power of B, A may prefer to yield to B's demands until, finally, A is forced to fight for its very existence under the most unfavorable conditions. By underrating the power of B, A may become overconfident in its assumed superiority. A may advance demands and impose conditions upon B which the latter is supposedly too weak to resist. Unsuspecting B's actual power of resistance, A may be faced with the alternative of either retreating and conceding defeat or of advancing and risking war.

A nation that seeks to pursue an intelligent and peaceful foreign policy cannot cease comparing its own objectives and the objectives of other nations in the light of their compatibility. If they are compatible, no problem arises. If they are not compatible, nation A must determine whether its objectives are so vital to itself that they must be pursued despite that incompatibility with the objectives of B. If it is found that A's vital interests can be safeguarded without the attainment of these objectives, they ought to be abandoned. On the other hand, if A finds that these objectives are essential for its vital interests, A must then ask itself whether B's objectives, incompatible with its own, are essential for B's vital interests. If the answer seems to be in the negative, A must try to induce B to abandon its objectives, offering B equivalents not vital to A. In other words, through diplomatic bargaining, the give and take of compromise, a way must be sought by which the interests of A and B can be reconciled.

Finally, if the incompatible objectives of A and B should prove to be vital to either side, a way might still be sought in which the vital interests of A and B might be redefined, reconciled, and their objectives thus made compatible with each other. Here, however—even provided that both sides pursue intelligent and peaceful policies—A and B are moving dangerously close to the brink of war.

It is the final task of an intelligent diplomacy, intent upon preserving peace, to choose the appropriate means for pursuing its objectives. The means at the disposal of diplomacy are three: persuasion, compromise, and threat of force. No diplomacy relying only upon the threat of force can claim to be both intelligent and peaceful. No diplomacy that would stake everything on persuasion and compromise deserves to be called intelligent. Rarely, if ever, in the conduct of the foreign policy of a great power is there justification for using only one method to the exclusion of the others. Generally, the diplomatic representative of a great power, in order to be able to serve both the interests of his country and the interests of peace, must at the same time use persuasion, hold out the advantages of a compromise, and impress the other side with the military strength of his country.

The art of diplomacy consists in putting the right emphasis at any particular moment on each of these three means at its disposal. A diplomacy that has been successfully discharged in its other functions may well fail in advancing the national interest and preserving peace if it stresses persuasion when the give and take of compromise is primarily required by the circumstances of the case. A diplomacy that puts most of its eggs in the basket of compromise when the military might of the nation should be predominantly displayed, or stresses military might when the political situation calls for persuasion and compromise, will like-wise fail. . . .

The Promise of Diplomacy: Its Nine Rules[1]

Diplomacy could revive if it would part with [the] vices, which in recent years have well-nigh destroyed its usefulness, and if it would restore the techniques which have controlled the mutual relations of nations since time immemorial. By doing so, however, diplomacy would realize only one of the preconditions for the preservation of peace. The contribution of a revived diplomacy to the cause of peace would depend upon the methods and purposes of its use. . . .

We have already formulated the four main tasks with which a foreign policy must cope successfully in order to be able to promote the national interest and preserve peace. It remains for us now to reformulate those tasks in the light of the special problems with which contemporary world politics confront diplomacy. . . .

The main reason for [the] threatening aspect of contemporary world politics [lies] in the character of modern war, which has changed profoundly under the impact of nationalistic universalism* and modern technology. The effects of modern technology cannot be undone. The only variable that remains subject to deliberate manipulation is the new moral force of nationalistic universalism. The attempt to reverse the trend toward war through the techniques of a revived diplomacy must start with this phenomenon. That means, in negative terms, that a revived diplomacy will have a chance to preserve peace only when it is not used as the instrument of a political religion aiming at universal dominion.

Four Fundamental Rules

Diplomacy Must Be Divested of the Crusading Spirit   This is the first of the rules that diplomacy can neglect only at the risk of war. In the words of William Graham Sumner:

> If you want war, nourish a doctrine. Doctrines are the most frightful tyrants to which men ever are subject, because doctrines get inside of a man's own reason and betray him against himself. Civilised men have done their fiercest fighting for doctrines. The reconquest of the Holy Sepulcher, "the balance of power," "no universal dominion," "trade follows the flag," "he who holds the land will hold the sea," "the throne and the altar," the revolution, the faith—these are the things for which men have given their lives. . . . Now when any doctrine arrives at that degree of authority, the name of it is a club which any demagogue may swing over you at any time and apropos of anything. In order to describe a doctrine, we must have recourse to theological language. A doctrine is an article of faith. It is something which you are bound to believe, not because you have some rational grounds for believing it is true, but because you belong to such and such a church or denomination. . . . A policy in a state we can understand; for instance, it was the policy of the United States at the end of the eighteenth century to get the

---

*[Editors' Note: By this term Professor Morgenthau refers to the injection of ideology into international politics and to each nation's claim that its own ethical code would serve as the basis of international conduct for all nations.]

free navigation of the Mississippi to its mouth, even at the expense of war with Spain. That policy had reason and justice in it; it was founded in our interests; it had positive form and definite scope. A doctrine is an abstract principle; it is necessarily absolute in its scope and abstruse in its terms; it is metaphysical assertion. It is never true, because it is absolute, and the affairs of men are all conditioned and relative. . . . Now to turn back to politics, just think what an abomination in statecraft an abstract doctrine must be. Any politician or editor can, at any moment, put a new extension on it. The people acquiesce in the doctrine and applaud it because they hear the politicians and editors repeat it, and the politicians and editors repeat it because they think it is popular. So it grows. . . . It may mean anything or nothing, at any moment, and no one knows how it will be. You accede to it now, within the vague limits of what you suppose it to be; therefore, you will have to accede to it tomorrow when the same name is made to cover something which you never have heard or thought of. If you allow a political catchword to go on and grow, you will awaken some day to find it standing over you, the arbiter of your destiny, against which you are powerless, as men are powerless against delusions. . . . What can be more contrary to sound statesmanship and common sense than to put forth an abstract assertion which has no definite relation to any interest of ours now at stake, but which has in it any number of possibilities of producing complications which we cannot foresee, but which are sure to be embarrassing when they arise![2]

The Wars of Religion have shown that the attempt to impose one's own religion as the only true one upon the rest of the world is as futile as it is costly. A century of almost unprecedented bloodshed, devastation, and barbarization was needed to convince the contestants that the two religions could live together in mutual toleration. The two political religions of our time have taken the place of the two great Christian denominations of the sixteenth and seventeenth centuries. Will the political religions of our time need the lesson of the Thirty Years' War, or will they rid themselves in time of the universalistic aspirations that inevitably issue in inconclusive war?

Upon the answer to that question depends the cause of peace. For only if it is answered in the affirmative can a moral consensus, emerging from shared convictions and common values, develop—a moral consensus within which a peace-preserving diplomacy will have a chance to grow. Only then will diplomacy have a chance to face the concrete political problems that require peaceful solution. If the objectives of foreign policy are not to be defined in terms of a world-embracing political religion, how are they to be defined? This is a fundamental problem to be solved once the crusading aspirations of nationalistic universalism have been discarded.

The Objectives of Foreign Policy Must Be Defined in Terms of the National Interest and Must Be Supported with Adequate Power   This is the second rule of a peace-preserving diplomacy. The national interest of a peace-loving nation can only be defined in terms of national security, and national security must be defined as integrity of the national territory and of its institutions. National security, then, is the irreducible minimum that diplomacy must defend with adequate power without compromise. But diplomacy must ever be alive to the radical transformation that national security has undergone under the impact of the nuclear age. Until the advent of that age, a nation could use its diplomacy to purchase its security at the expense of another nation. Today, short of a radical change in the atomic balance of power in favor of a particular nation, diplomacy, in order to make one nation secure from nuclear destruction, must make them all secure. With the national interest defined in such restrictive and transcendent terms, diplomacy must observe the third of its rules.

Diplomacy Must Look at the Political Scene from the Point of View of Other Nations   "Nothing is so fatal to a nation as an extreme of self-partiality, and the total want of consideration of what others will naturally hope or fear."[3] What are the national interests of other nations in terms of national security and are they compatible with one's own? The definition of the national interest in terms of national security is easier, and the interests of the two opposing nations are more likely to be compatible in a bipolar system than in any other system of the balance of power. The bipolar system, as we have seen, is more unsafe from the point of view of peace than any other, when both blocs are in competitive contact throughout the world and the ambition of both is fired by the crusading zeal of a universal mission. ". . . Vicinity, or nearness of situation, constitutes nations natural enemies."[4]

Yet once they have defined their national interests in terms of national security, they can draw back from their outlying positions, located close to, or within, the sphere of national security of the other side, and retreat into their respective spheres, each self-contained within its orbit. Those outlying positions add nothing to national security; they are but liabilities, positions that cannot be held in case of war. Each bloc will be the more secure the wider it makes the distance that separates both spheres of national security. Each side can draw a line far distant from each other, making it understood that to touch or even to approach it means war. What then about the interjacent spaces, stretching between the two lines of demarcation? Here the fourth rule of diplomacy applies.

Nations Must Be Willing to Compromise on All Issues that Are Not Vital to Them

> All government, indeed every human benefit and enjoyment, every virtue and every prudent act, is founded on compromise and barter. We balance inconveniences; we give and take; we remit some rights, that we may enjoy others; and we choose rather to be happy citizens than subtle disputants. As we must give away some natural liberties, for the advantages to be derived from the communion and fellowship of a great empire. But, in all fair dealings, the thing bought must bear some proportion to the purchase paid. None will barter away the immediate jewel of his soul.[5]

Here diplomacy meets its most difficult task. For minds not beclouded by the crusading zeal of a political religion and capable of viewing the national interests of both sides with objectivity, the delimitation of these vital interests should not prove too difficult. Compromise on secondary issues is a different matter. Here the task is not to separate and define interests that by their very nature already tend toward separation and definition, but to keep in balance interests that touch each other at many points and may be intertwined beyond the possibility of separation. It is an immense task to allow the other side a certain influence in those interjacent spaces without allowing them to be absorbed into the orbit of the other side. It is hardly a less immense task to keep the other side's influence as small as possible in the regions close to one's own security zone without absorbing those regions into one's own orbit. For the performance of these tasks, no formula stands ready for automatic application. It is only through a continuous process of adaptation, supported both by firmness and self-restraint, that compromise on secondary issues can be made to work. It is, however, possible to indicate a priori what approaches will facilitate or hamper the success of policies of compromise.

First of all, it is worth noting to what extent the success of compromise—that is, compliance with the fourth rule—depends upon compliance with the other three rules, which in turn are similarly interdependent. As the compliance with the second rule depends upon the realization of the first, so the third rule must await its realization from compliance with the second. A nation can only take a rational view of its national interests after it has parted company with the crusading spirit of a political creed. A nation is able to consider the national interests of the other side with objectivity only after it has become secure in what it considers its own national interests. Compromise on any issue, however minor, is impossible so long as both sides are not secure in their national interests. Thus nations cannot hope to comply with the fourth rule if they are not willing to comply with the other three. Both morality and expediency require compliance with these four fundamental rules.

Compliance makes compromise possible, but it does not assure its success. To give compromise, made possible through compliance with the first three rules, a chance to succeed, five other rules must be observed.

Five Prerequisites of Compromise

Give up the Shadow of Worthless Rights for the Substance of Real Advantage A diplomacy that thinks in legalistic and propagandistic terms is particularly tempted to insist upon the letter of the law, as it interprets the law, and to lose sight of the consequences such insistence may have for its own nation and for humanity. Since there are rights to be defended, this kind of diplomacy thinks that the issue cannot be compromised. Yet the choice that confronts the diplomat is not between legality and illegality, but between political wisdom and political folly. "The question with me," said Edmund Burke, "is not whether you have a right to render your people miserable, but whether it is not your interest to make them happy. It is not what a lawyer tells me I *may* do, but what humanity, reason and justice tell me I ought to do."[6]

Never Put Yourself in a Position from Which You Cannot Retreat Without Losing Face and from Which You Cannot Advance Without Grave Risks The violation of this rule often results from disregard for the preceding one. A diplomacy that confounds the shadow of legal right with the actuality of political advantage is likely to find itself in a position where it may have a legal right, but no political business, to be. In other words, a nation may identify itself with a position, which it may or may not have a right to hold, regardless of the political consequences. And again compromise becomes a difficult matter. A nation cannot retreat from that position without incurring a serious loss of prestige. It cannot advance from that position without exposing itself to political risks, perhaps even the risk of war. That heedless rush into untenable positions and, more particularly, the stubborn refusal to extricate oneself from them in time is the earmark of incompetent diplomacy. Its classic examples are the policy of Napoleon III on the eve of the Franco-Prussian War of 1870 and the policies of Austria and Germany on the eve of the First World War. These examples also show how closely the risk of war is allied with the violation of this rule.

Never Allow a Weak Ally to Make Decisions for You   Strong nations that are oblivious to the preceding rules are particularly susceptible to violating this one. They lose their freedom of action by identifying their own national interests completely with those of the weak ally. Secure in the support of its powerful friend, the weak ally can choose the objectives and methods of its foreign policy to suit itself. The powerful nation then finds that it must support interests not its own and that it is unable to compromise on issues that are vital not to itself, but only to its ally.

The classic example of the violation of this rule is to be found in the way in which Turkey forced the hand of Great Britain and France on the eve of the Crimean War in 1853. The Concert of Europe had virtually agreed upon a compromise settling the conflict between Russia and Turkey, when Turkey, knowing that the Western powers would support it in a war with Russia, did its best to provoke that war and thus involved Great Britain and France in it against their will. Thus Turkey went far in deciding the issue of war and peace for Great Britain and France according to its own national interests. Great Britain and France had to accept that decision even though their national interests did not require war with Russia and they had almost succeeded in preventing its outbreak. They had surrendered their freedom of action to a weak ally, which used its control over their policies for its own purposes.

The Armed Forces Are the Instrument of Foreign Policy, Not Its Master No successful and no peaceful foreign policy is possible without observance of this rule. No nation can pursue a policy of compromise with the military determining the ends and means of foreign policy. The armed forces are instruments of war; foreign policy is an instrument of peace. It is true that the ultimate objectives of the conduct of war and of the conduct of foreign policy are identical: Both serve the national interest. Both, however, differ fundamentally in their immediate objective, in the means they employ, and in the modes of thought they bring to bear upon their respective tasks.

The objective of war is simple and unconditional: to break the will of the enemy. Its methods are equally simple and unconditional: to bring the greatest amount of violence to bear upon the most vulnerable spot in the enemy's armor. Consequently, the military leader must think in absolute terms. He lives in the present and in the immediate future. The sole question before him is how to win victories as cheaply and quickly as possible and how to avoid defeat.

The objective of foreign policy is relative and conditional: to bend, not to break, the will of the other side as far as necessary in order to safeguard one's own vital interests without hurting those of the other side. The methods of foreign policy are relative and conditional: not to advance by destroying the obstacles in one's way, but to retreat before them, to circumvent them, to maneuver around them, to soften and dissolve them slowly by means of persuasion, negotiation, and pressure. In consequence, the mind of the diplomat is complicated and subtle. It sees the issue in hand as a moment in history, and beyond the victory of tomorrow it anticipates the incalculable possibilities of the future. In the words of Bolingbroke:

> Here let me only say, that the glory of taking towns, and winning battles, is to be measured by the utility that results from those victories. Victories that bring honour to the arms, may bring shame to the councils, of a nation. To win a battle, to take a town, is the glory of a general, and of an army. . . . But the glow of a nation is to proportion the ends she proposes, to her interest and her strength; the means she employs to the ends she proposes, and the vigour she exerts to both.[7]

To surrender the conduct of foreign affairs to the military, then, is to destroy the possibility of compromise and thus surrender the cause of peace. The military mind knows how to operate between the absolutes of victory and defeat. It knows nothing of that patient intricate and subtle maneuvering of diplomacy, whose main purpose is to avoid the absolutes of victory and defeat and meet the other side on the middle ground of negotiated compromise. A foreign policy conducted by military men according to the rules of the military art can only end in war, for "what we prepare for is what we shall get."[8]

For nations conscious of the potentialities of modern war, peace must be the goal of their foreign policies. Foreign policy must be conducted in such a way as to make the preservation of peace possible and not make the outbreak of war inevitable. In a society of sovereign nations, military force is a necessary instrument of foreign policy. Yet the instrument of foreign policy should not become the master of foreign policy. As war is fought in order to make peace possible, foreign policy should be conducted in order to make peace permanent. For the performance of both tasks, the subordination of the military under the civilian authorities which are constitutionally responsible for the conduct of foreign affairs is an indispensable prerequisite.

The Government Is the Leader of Public Opinion, Not Its Slave   Those responsible for the conduct of foreign policy will not be able to comply with the foregoing principles of diplomacy if they do not keep this principle constantly in mind. As has been pointed out above in greater detail, the rational requirements of good foreign policy cannot from the outset count upon the support of a public opinion whose preferences are emotional rather than rational. This is bound to be particularly true of a foreign policy whose goal is compromise, and which, therefore, must concede some of the objectives of the other side and give up some of its own. Especially when foreign policy is conducted under conditions of democratic control and is inspired by the crusading zeal of a political religion, statesmen are always tempted to sacrifice the requirements of good foreign policy to the applause of the masses. On the other hand, the statesmen who would defend the integrity of these requirements against even the slightest contamination with popular passion would seal his own doom as a political leader and, with it, the doom of his foreign policy, for he would lose the popular support which put and keeps him in power.

The statesman, then, is allowed neither to surrender to popular passions nor disregard them. He must strike a prudent balance between adapting himself to them and marshaling them to the support of his policies. In one word, he must lead. He must perform that highest feat of statesmanship: trimming his sails to the winds of popular passion while using them to carry the ship to the port of good foreign policy, on however roundabout and zigzag a course.

CONCLUSION

The road to international peace which we have outlined cannot compete in inspirational qualities with the simple and fascinating formulae that for a century and a half have fired the imagination of a war-weary world. There is something spectacular in the radial simplicity of a formula that with one sweep seems to dispose of the problem of war once and for all. This has been the promise of such solutions as free trade, arbitration, disarmament, collective security, universal socialism, international government, and the world state. There is nothing spectacular, fascinating, or inspiring, at least for the people at large, in the business of diplomacy.

We have made the point, however, that these solutions, insofar as they deal with the real problem and not merely with some of its symptoms, presuppose the existence of an integrated international society, which actually does not exist. To bring into existence such an international society and keep it in being, the accommodating techniques of diplomacy are required. As the integration of domestic society and its peace develop from the unspectacular and almost unnoticed day-by-day operations of the techniques of accommodation and change, so the ultimate ideal of international life—that is, to transcend itself in a supranational society—must await its realization from the techniques of persuasion, negotiation, and pressure, which are the traditional instruments of diplomacy.

The reader who has followed us to this point may well ask: But has not diplomacy failed in preventing war in the past? To that legitimate question two answers can be given.

Diplomacy has failed many times, and it has succeeded many times, in its peace-preserving task. It has failed sometimes because nobody wanted it to succeed. We have seen how different in their objectives and methods the limited wars of the past have been from the total war of our time. When war was the normal activity of kings, the task of diplomacy was not to prevent it, but to bring it about at the most propitious moment.

On the other hand, when nations have used diplomacy for the purpose of preventing war, they have often succeeded. The outstanding example of a successful war-preventing diplomacy in modern times is the Congress of Berlin of 1878. By the peaceful means of an accommodating diplomacy, that Congress settled, or at least made susceptible of settlement, the issues that had separated Great Britain and Russia since the end of the Napoleonic Wars. During the better part of the nineteenth century, the conflict between Great Britain and Russia over the Balkans, the Dardanelles, and the Eastern Mediterranean hung like a suspended sword over the peace of the world. Yet, during the fifty years following the Crimean War, though hostilities between Great Britain and Russia threatened to break out time and again, they never actually did break out. The main credit for the preservation of peace must go to the techniques of an accommodating diplomacy which culminated in the Congress of Berlin. When British Prime Minister Disraeli returned from that Congress to London, he declared with pride that he was bringing home "peace . . . with honor." In fact, he had brought peace for later generations, too; for a century there has been no war between Great Britain and Russia.

We have, however, recognized the precariousness of peace in a society of sovereign nations. The continuing success of diplomacy in preserving peace depends, as we have seen, upon extraordinary moral and intellectual qualities that all the leading participants must possess. A mistake in the evaluation of one of the elements of national power, made by one or the other of the leading statesmen, may spell the difference between peace and war. So may an accident spoiling a plan or a power calculation.

Diplomacy is the best means of preserving peace which a society of sovereign nations has to offer, but, especially under the conditions of contemporary world politics and of contemporary war, it is not good enough. It is only when nations have surrendered to a higher authority the means of destruction which modern technology has put in their hands—when they have given up their sovereignty—that international peace can be made as secure as domestic peace. Diplomacy can make peace more secure than it is today, and the world state can make peace more secure than it would be if nations were to abide by the rules of diplomacy. Yet, as there can be no permanent peace without a world state, there can be no world state without the peace-preserving and community-building processes of diplomacy. For the world state to be more than a dim vision, the accommodating processes of diplomacy, mitigating and minimizing conflicts, must be revived. Whatever one's conception of the ultimate state of international affairs may be, in the recognition of that need and in the demand that it be met all men of good will can join.

NOTES

1. We by no means intend to give here an exhaustive account of rules of diplomacy. We propose to discuss only those which seem to have a special bearing upon the contemporary situation.
2. "War." *Essays of William Graham Sumner* (New Haven, Conn.: Yale University Press, 1934), vol. I, pp. 169 ff.
3. Edmund Burke, "Remarks on the Policy of the Allies with Respect to France" (1793), *Works*, vol. IV (Boston: Little, Brown and Company, 1889), p. 447.
4. *The Federalist,* no. 6.
5. Edmund Burke, "Speech on the Conciliation with America," *loc. cit.*, vol. II, p. 169.
6. "Speech on Conciliation with the Colonies" (1775), *The Works of Edmund Burke,* vol. II (Boston: Little, Brown and Company, 1865), p. 140.
7. *Bolingbroke's Defense of the Treaty of Utrecht* (Cambridge: Cambridge University Press, 1932), p. 95.
8. William Graham Sumner, *op. cit.*, p. 173.

The Uses and Limits of International Law

STANLEY HOFFMANN

The student of international law who examines its functions in the present international system and in the foreign policy of states will, unless he takes refuge in the comforting seclusion from reality that the pure theory of law once provided, be reduced to one of three attitudes. He will become a cynic, if he chooses to stress, like Giraudoux in *Tiger at the Gates,* the way in which legal claims are shaped to support any position a state deems useful or necessary on nonlegal grounds, or if he gets fascinated by the combination of cacophony and silence that characterizes international law as a system of world public order. He will become a hypocrite, if he chooses to rationalize either the conflicting interpretations and uses of law by states as a somehow converging effort destined to lead to some such system endowed with sufficient stability and solidity, or else if he endorses one particular construction (that of his own statesmen) as a privileged and enlightened contribution to the achievement of such a system, he will be overcome by consternation, if he reflects upon the gap between, on the one hand, the ideal of a world in which traditional self-help will be at least moderated by procedures and rules made even more indispensable by the proliferation both of states and of lethal weapons, and, on the other hand, the realities of inexpiable conflicts, sacred egoisms, and mutual recriminations. . . .

1. Some of the functions of international law constitute *assets both for the policy maker and from the viewpoint of world order,* i.e., of providing the international milieu with a framework of predictability and with procedures for the transaction of interstate business.

    (a) International law is an instrument of *communication.* To present one's claims in legal terms means, 1, to signal to one's partner or opponent which "basic conduct norms" (to use Professor Scheinman's expression) one considers relevant or essential, and 2, to indicate which procedures one intends to follow and would like the other side to follow. At a time when both the size of a highly heterogeneous international milieu and the imperatives of prudence in the resort to force make communication essential and often turn international relations into a psychological contest, international law provides a kind of common language that does not amount to a common code of legitimacy yet can serve as a joint frame of reference. (One must however remember, 1, that communication is no guarantee against misperception, and 2, that what is being communicated may well determine the other side's response to the message: If "we" communicate to "them" an understanding of the situation that threatens their basic values or goals—like our interpretation of the war in South Vietnam as a case of aggression—there will be no joint frame of reference at all, and in fact the competition may become fiercer.)

(b) International law affords means of *channeling conflict*—of diverting inevitable tensions and clashes from the resort to force. Whenever there have been strong independent reasons for avoiding armed conflict—in an international system in which the superpowers in particular have excellent reasons for "managing" their confrontations, either by keeping them nonviolent, or by using proxies—international law has provided statesmen both with alibis for shunning force and with alternatives to violence. . . . In Berlin, both the Soviets and the West shaped their moves in such a way as to leave to the other side full responsibility for a first use of force, and to avoid the kind of frontal collision with the other side's legal claim that could have obliged the opponent to resort to force in order not to lose power or face. Thus, today as in earlier periods, law can indeed . . . serve as an alternative to confrontation whenever states are eager or forced to look for an alternative.

2. International law also plays various useful roles in the policy process, which however do not ipso facto contribute to world order. Here, we are concerned with *law as a tool of policy* in the competition of state visions, objectives, and tactics.

(a) The establishment of a network of rights and obligations, or the resort to legal arguments can be useful for the *protection or enhancement of a position:* if one wants to give oneself a full range of means with which to buttress a threatened status quo (cf. the present position of the West in Berlin; this is also what treaties of alliance frequently are for); if one wants to enhance one's power in a way that is demonstrably authorized by principles in international law (cf. Nasser's claim when he nationalized the Suez Canal, and Sukarno's invocation of the principle of self-determination against Malaysia); if one wants to restore a political position badly battered by an adversary's move, so that the resort to legal arguments becomes part of a strategy of restoring the status quo ante (Western position during the Berlin blockade; Kennedy's strategy during the Cuban missile crisis; Western powers' attempts during the first phase of the Suez crisis; Soviet tactics in the U.N. General Assembly debates on the financing of peace-keeping operations).

(b) In all those instances, policy makers use law as a way of putting pressure on an opponent by *mobilizing international support* behind the legal rules invoked: law serves as a focal point, as the tool for "internationalizing" a national interest and as the cement of a political coalition. States that may have political misgivings about pledging direct support to a certain power whose interests only partly coincide with theirs, or because they do not want to antagonize another power thereby, may find it both easier and useful to rally to the defense of a legal principle in whose maintenance or promotion they may have a stake.

(c) A policy maker who ignores international law leaves the field of political-competition-through-legal-manipulation open to his opponents or rivals. International law provides one of the numerous *chessboards* on which state contests occur.

3. Obviously, this indicates not only that to the statesmen international law provides an instrument rather than a guide for action, but also that this tool is often *not used,* when resort to it would hamper the state's interest as defined by the policy maker.

(a) One of the reasons why international law often serves as a technique of political mobilization is the appeal of reciprocity: "You must support my invocation of the rule against him, because if you let the rule be violated at my expense, someday it may be breached at yours; and we both have an interest in its preservation." But *reciprocity cuts both ways:* My using a certain legal argument to buttress my case against him may encourage him, now or later, to resort to the same argument against me; I may therefore be unwise to play on a chessboard in which, given the solemn and abstract nature of legal rights and obligations, I may not be able to make the kind of distinction between my (good) case and your (bad) one that can best be made by resort to ad hoc, political and circumstantial evidence that is irrelevant or ruled out in legal argumentation. Thus . . . during the Cuban crisis, when the United States tried to distinguish between Soviet missiles in Cuba and American ones in Turkey in order to build its case and get support, America's use of the OAS [Organization of American States] Charter as the legal basis for its "quarantine" established a dangerous precedent which the Soviets could use some day, against the U.S. or its allies, on behalf of the Warsaw Pact. And in the tragicomedy of the battle over Article 19 of the U.N. Charter, one reason why the U.S. finally climbed down from its high legal horse and gave up the attempt to deprive the Soviets of their right to vote, unless they paid their share, was the growing awareness of the peril which the principle of the exercise of the U.N. taxing power by the General Assembly could constitute some day for the United States if it lost control of the Assembly.

(b) One of the things that international law "communicates" is the solemnity of a commitment: a treaty, or a provision of the Charter, serves as a kind of tripwire or burglar alarm. When it fails to deter, the victim and third parties have a fateful choice between upholding the legal principle by all means, at the cost of a possible escalation in violence, and choosing to settle the dispute more peacefully, at the cost of *fuzzing the legal issue.* For excellent political reasons, the latter course is frequently adopted . . . in the form of dropping any reference to the legal principle at stake. . . .

(c) The very *ambiguity* of international law, which in many essential areas displays either gaping holes or conflicting principles, allows policy makers in an emergency to act as if international law were irrelevant—as if it were neither a restraint nor a guide. . . .

However, precisely because there is a legal chessboard for state competition, the fact that international law does not, in a crisis, really restrict one's freedom of action, does not mean that one will forgo legal rationalizations of the moves selected. Here we come to the last set of considerations about the role of law:

4. The resort to legal arguments by policy makers may be *detrimental to world order and thereby counterproductive for the state* that used such arguments.

(a) In the legal vacuum or confusion which prevails in areas as vital to states as internal war or the use of force, each state tries to justify its conduct with legal rationalizations. The result is a kind of *escalation of claims and counterclaims*, whose consequence, in turn, is both a further devaluation of international law and a "credibility gap" at the expense of those states who have debased the currency. America's rather indiscriminate resort to highly debatable legal arguments to support its Vietnam policy is a case in point. The unsubtle reduction of international law to a mere storehouse of convenient *ex post* justifications (as in the case of British intervention at Suez, or American interventions in Santo Domingo and Vietnam) undermines the very pretense of contributing to world order with which these states have tried to justify their unilateral acts.

(b) Much of contemporary international law authorizes states to *increase their power.* In this connection, Nasser's nationalization of the Suez Canal Company was probably quite legal, and those who accept the rather tortured argument put forth by the State Department legal advisers to justify the Cuban "quarantine" have concluded that this partial blockade was authorized by the OAS Charter and not in contradiction with the U.N. Charter. Yet it is obvious that a full exploitation by all states of all permissions granted by international law would be a perfect recipe for chaos.

(c) *Attempts to enforce or to strengthen international law,* far from consolidating a system of desirable restraints on state (mis)behavior, may actually *backfire* if the political conditions are not ripe. This is the central lesson of the long story of the financing of U.N. peace-keeping operations. American self-intoxication with the importance of the rule of law, fed by misleading analogies between the U.N. Charter and the U.S. Constitution, resulted ultimately in a weakening of the influence of the World Court (which largely followed America's line of reasoning), and in an overplaying of America's hand during the "non-session" of the General Assembly in the fall of 1964 and winter of 1965.

These are sobering considerations. But what they tell us is not, as so many political scientists seem to believe, that international law is, at best, a farce, and, at worst, even a potential danger; what they tell us is that *the nature of the international system condemns international law to all the weaknesses and perversions that it is so easy to deride.* International law is merely a magnifying mirror that reflects faithfully and cruelly the essence and the logic of international politics. In a fragmented world, there is no "global perspective" from which anyone can authoritatively assess, endorse, or reject the separate national efforts at making international law serve national interests above all. Like the somber universe of Albert Camus' Caligula, this is a judgeless world where no one is innocent. . . .

The permanent plight of international law is that, now as before, it shows on its body of rules all the scars inflicted by the international state of war. The tragedy of contemporary international law is that of a double divorce: first, between the old liberal dream of a world rule of law, and the realities of an international system of multiple minidramas that always threaten to become major catastrophes; second, between the old dream and the new requirements of moderation which in the circumstances of the present system suggest a *down-playing* of formal law in the realm of peace-and-war issues, and an *upgrading* of more flexible techniques, until the system has become less fierce. The interest of international law for the political scientist is that there is no better way of grasping the continuing differences between order within a national society and the fragile order of international affairs than to study how and when states use legal language, symbols, and documents, and with what results. . . .

International Institutions: Can Interdependence Work?

ROBERT O. KEOHANE

To analyze world politics in the [current era] is to discuss international institutions: the rules that govern elements of world politics and the organizations that help implement those rules. . . . Under what conditions should China be admitted to the World Trade Organization (WTO)? How many billions of dollars does the International Monetary Fund (IMF) need at its disposal to remain an effective "lender of last resort" for countries such as Indonesia, Korea, and Thailand that were threatened in 1997 with financial collapse? Will the tentative Kyoto Protocol on Climate Change be renegotiated, ratified, and implemented effectively? Can future United Nations peacekeeping practices—in contrast to the UN fiascoes in Bosnia and Somalia—be made more effective?

These questions help illustrate the growing importance of international institutions for maintaining world order. . . . Superpowers need general rules because they seek to influence events around the world. Even an unchallenged superpower such as the United States would be unable to achieve its goals through the bilateral exercise of influence: the costs of such massive "arm-twisting" would be too great.

International institutions are increasingly important, but they are not always successful. Ineffective institutions such as the United Nations Industrial Development Organization or the Organization of African Unity exist alongside effectual ones such as the Montreal Protocol on Substances that Deplete the Ozone Layer and the European Union. In recent years, we have gained insight into what makes some institutions more capable than others—how such institutions best promote cooperation among states and what mechanics of bargaining they use. But our knowledge is incomplete, and as the world moves toward new forms of global regulation and governance, the increasing impact of international institutions has raised new questions about how these institutions themselves are governed.

THEORY AND REALITY, 1919–89

Academic "scribblers" did not always have to pay much attention to international institutions. The 1919 Versailles Treaty constituted an attempt to construct an institution for multilateral diplomacy—the League of Nations. But the rejection of the

League Covenant by the U.S. Senate ensured that until World War II the most important negotiations in world politics—from the secret German-Russian deals of the 1920s to the 1938 Munich conference—took place on an ad hoc basis. Only after the United Nations was founded in 1945, with strong support from the United States and a multiplicity of specialized agencies performing different tasks, did international institutions begin to command substantial international attention. . . .

[After 1945], however, even the most powerful states [came to] rely increasingly on international institutions. . . . From the late 1960s onward, the Treaty on the Non-Proliferation of Nuclear Weapons was the chief vehicle for efforts to prevent the dangerous spread of nuclear weapons. NATO was not only the most successful multilateral alliance in history but also the most highly institutionalized, with a secretary-general, a permanent staff, and elaborate rules governing relations among members. From its founding in 1947 through the Uruguay Round that concluded in 1993, the General Agreement on Tariffs and Trade (GATT) presided over a series of trade rounds that have reduced import tariffs among industrialized countries by up to 90 percent, boosting international trade. After a shaky start in the 1940s, the IMF had—by the 1960s—become the centerpiece of efforts by the major capitalist democracies to regulate their monetary affairs. When that function atrophied with the onset of flexible exchange rates in the 1970s, it became their leading agent for financing and promoting economic development in Africa, Asia, and Latin America. The sheer number of inter-governmental organizations also rose dramatically—from about 30 in 1910 to 70 in 1940 to more than 1,000 by 1981.

The exchange rate and oil crises of the early 1970s helped bring perceptions in line with reality. Suddenly, both top policymakers and academic observers in the United States realized that global issues required systematic policy coordination and that such coordination required institutions. In 1974, then secretary of state Henry Kissinger, who had paid little attention to international institutions, helped establish the International Energy Agency to enable Western countries to deal cooperatively with the threat of future oil embargoes like the 1973 OPEC embargo of the Netherlands and United States. And the Ford administration sought to construct a new international monetary regime based on flexible rather than pegged exchange rates. Confronted with complex interdependence and the efforts of states to manage it, political scientists began to redefine the study of international institutions, broadening it to encompass what they called "international regimes"—structures of rules and norms that could be more or less informal. The international trade regime, for example, did not have strong formal rules or integrated, centralized management; rather, it provided a set of interlocking institutions, including regular meetings of the GATT contracting parties, formal dispute settlement arrangements, and delegation of technical tasks to a secretariat, which gradually developed a body of case law and practice. . . .

In the 1980s, research on international regimes moved from attempts to describe the phenomena of interdependence and international regimes to closer analysis of the conditions under which countries cooperate. How does cooperation occur among sovereign states and how do international institutions affect it? From the standpoint of political realism, both the reliance placed by states on certain international institutions and the explosion in their numbers were puzzling. Why should international institutions exist at all in a world dominated by sovereign states? This question seemed unanswerable if institutions were seen as opposed to, or above, the state but not if they were viewed as devices to help states accomplish their objectives.

The new research on international institutions broke decisively with legalism—the view that law can be effective regardless of political conditions—as well as with the idealism associated with the field's origins. Instead, scholars adopted the assumptions of realism, accepting that relative state power and competing interests were key factors in world politics, but at the same time drawing new conclusions about the influence of institutions on the process. Institutions create the capability for states to cooperate in mutually beneficial ways by reducing the costs of making and enforcing agreements—what economists refer to as "transaction costs." They rarely engage in centralized enforcement of agreements, but they do reinforce practices of reciprocity, which provide incentives for governments to keep their own commitments to ensure that others do so as well. Even powerful states have an interest, most of the time, in following the rules of well-established international institutions, since general conformity to rules makes the behavior of other states more predictable.

This scholarship drew heavily on the twin concepts of uncertainty and credibility. Theorists increasingly recognized that the preferences of states amount to "private information"—that absent full transparency, states are uncertain about what their partners and rivals value at any given time. They naturally respond to uncertainty by being less willing to enter into agreements, since they are unsure how their partners will later interpret the terms of such agreements. International institutions can reduce this uncertainty by promoting negotiations in which transparency is encouraged; by dealing with a series of issues over many years and under similar rules, thus encouraging honesty in order to preserve future reputation; and by systematically monitoring the compliance of governments with their commitments.

Even if a government genuinely desires an international agreement, it may be unable to persuade its partners that it will, in the future, be willing and able to implement it. Successful international negotiations may therefore require changes in domestic institutions. For instance, without "fast-track" authority on trade, the United States' negotiating partners have no assurance that Congress will refrain from adding new provisions to trade agreements as a condition for their ratification. Hence, other states are reluctant to enter into trade negotiations with the United States since they may be confronted, at the end of tortuous negotiations, with a redesigned agreement less favorable to them than the draft they initialed. By the same token, without fast-track authority, no promise by the U.S. government to abide by negotiated terms has much credibility, due to the president's lack of control over Congress.

In short, this new school of thought argued that, rather than imposing themselves on states, international institutions should respond to the demand by states for cooperative ways to fulfill their own purposes. By reducing uncertainty and the costs of making and enforcing agreements, international institutions help states achieve collective gains.

YESTERDAY'S CONTROVERSIES: 1989–95

This new institutionalism was not without its critics, who focused their attacks on three perceived shortcomings: First, they claimed that international institutions are fundamentally insignificant since states wield the only real power in world politics. They emphasized the weakness of efforts by the UN or League of Nations to achieve collective security against aggression by great powers, and they pointed to the dominant role of major contributors in international economic organizations. Hence, any effects of these international institutions were attributed more to the efforts of their great power backers than to the institutions themselves.

This argument was overstated. Of course, great powers such as the United States exercise enormous influence within international institutions. But the policies that emerge from these institutions are different from those that the United States would have adopted unilaterally. . . . Where agreement by many states is necessary for policy to be effective, even the United States finds it useful to compromise on substance to obtain the institutional seal of approval. Therefore, the decision-making procedures and general rules of international institutions matter. They affect both the substance of policy and the degree to which other states accept it.

The second counterargument focused on "anarchy": the absence of a world government or effective international legal system to which victims of injustice can appeal. As a result of anarchy, critics argued, states prefer relative gains (i.e., doing better than other states) to absolute gains. They seek to protect their power and status and will resist even mutually beneficial cooperation if their partners are likely to benefit more than they are. For instance, throughout the American-Soviet arms race, both sides focused on their relative positions—who was ahead or threatening to gain a decisive advantage—rather than on their own levels of armaments. Similar dynamics appear on certain economic issues, such as the fierce Euro-American competition (i.e., Airbus Industrie versus Boeing) in the production of large passenger jets.

Scholarly disputes about the "relative gains question" were intense but short-lived. It turned out that the question needed to be reframed: not, "do states seek relative or absolute gains?" but "under what conditions do they forego even mutually beneficial cooperation to preserve their relative power and status?" When there are only two major players, and one side's gains may decisively change power relationships, relative gains loom large: in arms races, for example, or monopolistic competition (as between Airbus and Boeing). Most issues of potential cooperation, however, from trade liberalization to climate change, involve multilateral negotiations that make relative gains hard to calculate and entail little risk of decisive power shifts for one side over another. Therefore, states can be expected most of the time to seek to enhance their own welfare without being worried that others will also make advances. So the relative gains argument merely highlights the difficulties of cooperation where there is tough bilateral competition; it does not by any means undermine prospects for cooperation in general.

The third objection to theories of cooperation was less radical but more enduring. Theorists of cooperation had recognized that cooperation is not harmonious: it emerges out of discord and takes place through tough bargaining. Nevertheless, they claimed that the potential joint gains from such cooperation explained the dramatic increases in the number and scope of cooperative multilateral institutions. Critics pointed out, however, that bargaining problems could produce obstacles to achieving joint gains. For instance, whether the Kyoto Protocol will lead to a global agreement is questionable in part because developing countries refused to accept binding limits on their emissions and the U.S. Senate declared its unwillingness to ratify any agreement not containing such commitments by developing countries. Both sides staked out tough bargaining positions, hindering efforts at credible compromise. As a result of these bargaining problems, the fact that possible deals could produce joint gains does not assure that cooperative solutions will be reached. The tactics of political actors and the information they have available about one another are both key aspects of a process that does not necessarily lead to cooperation. Institutions may help provide "focal points," on which competing actors may agree, but new issues often lack such institutions. In this case, both the pace and the extent of cooperation become more problematic.

TODAY'S DEBATES

The general problem of bargaining raises specific issues about how institutions affect international negotiations, which always involve a mixture of discord and potential cooperation. Thinking about bargaining leads to concerns about subjectivity, since bargaining depends so heavily on the beliefs of the parties involved. And the most fundamental question scholars wish to answer concerns effectiveness: What structures, processes, and practices make international institutions more or less capable of affecting policies—and outcomes—in desired ways?

The impact of institutional arrangements on bargaining remains puzzling. We understand from observation, from game theory, and from explorations of bargaining in a variety of contexts that outcomes depend on more than the resources available to the actors or the pay-offs they receive. Institutions affect bargaining patterns in complex and nuanced ways. Who, for example, has authority over the agenda? In the 1980s, Jacques Delors used his authority as head of the European Commission to structure the agenda of the European Community, thus leading to the Single European Act and the Maastricht Treaty. What voting or consensus arrangements are used and who interprets ambiguities? At the Kyoto Conference, agreement on a rule of "consensus" did not prevent the conference chair from ignoring objections as he gaveled through provision after provision in the final session. Can disgruntled participants block implementation of formally ratified agreements? In the GATT, until 1993, losers could prevent the findings of dispute resolution panels from being implemented; but in the WTO, panel recommendations take effect unless there is a consensus not to implement them. Asking such questions systematically about international institutions may well yield significant new insights in future years.

Institutional maneuvers take place within a larger ideological context that helps define which purposes such institutions pursue and which practices they find acceptable. The Mandates System of the League of Nations depended in part on specific institutional arrangements, but more fundamental was the shared understanding that continued European rule over non-European peoples was acceptable. No system of rule by Europeans over non-Europeans could remain legitimate after the collapse of that consensus during the 15 years following World War II. . . .

The procedures and rules of international institutions create informational structures. They determine what principles are acceptable as the basis for reducing conflicts and whether governmental actions are legitimate or illegitimate. Consequently, they help shape actors' expectations. For instance, trade conflicts are increasingly ritualized in a process of protesting in the WTO—promising tough action on behalf of one's own industries, engaging in quasi-judicial dispute resolution procedures, claiming victory if possible, or complaining about defeat when necessary. There is much sound and fury, but regularly institutionalized processes usually relegate conflict to the realm of dramatic expression. Institutions thereby create differentiated information. "Insiders" can interpret the language directed toward "outsiders" and use their own understandings to interpret, or manipulate, others' beliefs.

Finally, students of international institutions continue to try to understand why some institutions are so much more effective than others. Variation in the coherence of institutional policy or members' conformity with institutional rules is partially accounted for by the degree of common interests and the distribution of power among members. Institutions whose members share social values and have similar political systems—such as NATO or the European Union—are likely to be stronger than those such as the Organization for Security and Cooperation in Europe or the Association of South East Asian Nations, whose more diverse membership does not necessarily have the same kind of deep common interests. Additionally, the character of domestic politics, . . . has a substantial impact on international institutions. The distribution of power is also important. Institutions dominated by a small number of members—for example, the IMF, with its weighted voting system—can typically take more decisive action than those where influence is more widely diffused, such as the UN General Assembly.

OVERCOMING THE DEMOCRATIC DEFICIT

Even as scholars pursue these areas of inquiry, they are in danger of overlooking a major normative issue: the "democratic deficit" that exists in many of the world's most important international institutions. As illustrated most recently by the far-reaching interventions of the IMF in East Asia, the globalization of the world economy and the expanding role of international institutions are creating a powerful form of global regulation. Major international institutions are increasingly laying down rules and guidelines that governments, if they wish to attract foreign investment and generate growth, must follow. But these international institutions are managed by technocrats and supervised by high governmental officials. That is, they are run by élites. Only in the most attenuated sense is democratic control exercised over major international organizations. Key negotiations in the WTO are made in closed sessions. The IMF negotiates in secret with potential borrowers, and it has only begun in the last few months to provide the conditions it imposes on recipients. . . .

Admittedly, democracy does not always work well. American politicians regularly engage in diatribes against international institutions, playing on the dismay of a vocal segment of their electorates at the excessive number of foreigners in the United Nations. More seriously, an argument can be made that the IMF, like central banks, can only be effective if it is insulated from direct democratic control. Ever since 1787, however, practitioners and theorists have explored how authoritative decision making can be combined with accountability to publics and indirect democratic control. The U.S. Constitution is based on such a theory—the idea that popular sovereignty, though essential, is best exercised indirectly, through rather elaborate institutions. An issue that scholars should now explore is how to devise international institutions that are not only competent and effective but also accountable, at least ultimately, to democratic publics.

One possible response is to say that all is well, since international institutions are responsible to governments—which, in turn, are accountable in democracies to their own people. International regulation simply adds another link to the chain of delegation. But long chains of delegation, in which the public affects action only at several removes, reduce actual public authority. If the terms of multilateral cooperation are to reflect the interests of broader democratic publics rather than just those of narrow élites, traditional patterns of delegation will have to be supplemented by other means of ensuring greater accountability to public opinion.

One promising approach would be to seek to invigorate transnational society in the form of networks among individuals and nongovernmental organizations. The growth of such networks—of scientists, professionals in various fields, and human rights and environmental activists—has been aided greatly by the fax machine and the Internet and by institutional arrangements that incorporate these networks into decision making. For example, natural and social scientists developed the scientific consensus underlying the Kyoto Protocol through the Intergovernmental Panel on Climate Change (IPCC) whose scientific work was organized by scientists who did not have to answer to any governments. The Kyoto Protocol was negotiated, but governments opposed to effective action on climate change could not hope to renegotiate the scientific guidelines set by the IPCC. . . .

Therefore, the future accountability of international institutions to their publics may rest only partly on delegation through formal democratic institutions. Its other pillar may be voluntary pluralism under conditions of maximum transparency. International policies may increasingly be monitored by loose groupings of scientists or other professionals, or by issue advocacy networks such as Amnesty International and Greenpeace, whose members, scattered around the world, will be linked even more closely by modern information technology. Accountability will be enhanced not only by chains of official responsibility, but by the requirement of transparency. Official actions, negotiated among state representatives in international organizations, will be subjected to scrutiny by transnational networks.

Such transparency, however, represents nongovernmental organizations and networks more than ordinary people, who may be as excluded from élite networks as they are from government circles. That is, transnational civil society may be a necessary but insufficient condition for democratic accountability. Democracies should insist that, wherever feasible, international organizations maintain sufficient transparency for transnational networks of advocacy groups, domestic legislators, and democratic publics to evaluate their actions. But proponents of democratic accountability should also seek counterparts to the mechanisms of control embedded in national democratic institutions. Governors of the Federal Reserve Board are, after all, nominated by the president and confirmed by the Senate, even if they exercise great authority during their terms of office. If Madison, Hamilton, and Jay could invent indirect mechanisms of popular control in the *Federalist Papers* two centuries ago, it should not be beyond our competence to devise comparable mechanisms at the global level in the twenty-first century.

The United Nations and International Security

ADAM ROBERTS

In recent years, there has been a remarkable growth in demands for the services of the United Nations (UN) in the field of international security. The 1991 authorized action in Iraq was quickly followed in 1992 by a fivefold increase in the numbers of troops deployed in UN peace-keeping activities and by an increase in the types of roles they perform. At long last, the United Nations seemed to offer the prospect of moving decisively away from the anarchic reliance on force, largely on a unilateral basis, by individual sovereign states. The United Nations has, and will probably continue to have, a far more central role in security issues than it did during the Cold War.

However, the United Nations' multifaceted role in the security field faces a huge array of problems. Almost every difficulty connected with the preparation, deployment, and use of force has re-emerged in a UN context and does not appear to be any easier to address. Excessive demands have been placed on the United Nations, which has been asked to pour the oil of peace-keeping on the troubled waters of a huge number of conflicts, to develop its role in preventing breaches of the peace, and to play a central part in defeating aggression and tackling the after-effects of war. Arms control, too, is embroiled in controversy, with various states—Iraq and North Korea being the clearest examples—challenging what they see as a discriminatory non-proliferation regime. Above all, the increasing role of the United Nations in international security raises two central questions: First, is there a real coherence in the vast array of security activities undertaken by the United Nations? Second, is there a danger that the elemental force of ethnic conflict could defeat the United Nations' efforts? . . .

This article advances the following propositions about the United Nations' post–Cold War role in the field of international security:

1. The United Nations has become seriously overloaded with security issues, for good and enduring reasons. The extent to which it can transfer these responsibilities to regional organizations is debatable.
2. Most conflicts in the contemporary world involve an element of civil war or inter-ethnic struggle. They are different in character from those conflicts, essentially interstate, that the United Nations was established to tackle.

Excerpted from Adam Roberts, "The United Nations and International Security," *Survival: The IISS Quarterly*, Vol. 35, No. 2 (Summer 1993), pp. 3–30.

3. There is only limited agreement among the major powers about the basis of international security and only a limited shared interest in ensuring that international norms are effectively implemented.
4. The structure of the Security Council, including the system of five veto-wielding permanent members, is in danger of losing its legitimacy. Although a formal change of membership or powers will be very hard to achieve, changes in the Council's procedures and practices may be both desirable and possible.
5. There are some advantages in the practice whereby enforcement has taken the form of authorized military action by groups of states, rather than coming under direct UN command as a literal reading of the UN Charter would suggest. . . .
6. Although the United Nations' role is increasing, basic questions about collective security remain. There is no prospect of a general system of collective security supplanting existing strategic arrangements.

These propositions . . . are in no way intended as criticism of the increased emphasis given to the United Nations and its role in the foreign policies of many states. Rather, they constitute a plea for the sober assessment of both the merits and defects of an increased role, as well as for constructive thinking about some of the difficult issues it poses, and a caution against the hasty abandonment of some still-valuable aspects of traditional approaches to international relations.

THE OVERLOAD PROBLEM

. . . Reasons for such a heavy demand to deal with wars, civil strife, and other crises are numerous and persuasive. Whatever difficulties the United Nations may face in the coming years, these reasons will not suddenly disappear. Three stand out. First, the impressive record of the United Nations in the years 1987–92 has raised expectations. The United Nations has contributed to the settlement of numerous regional conflicts, including the Iran–Iraq War, the South African presence in Namibia, the Soviet presence in Afghanistan, and the Vietnamese presence in Cambodia. It provided a framework for the expulsion of Iraq from Kuwait. Second, given a choice, states contemplating the use of force beyond their borders often prefer to do it in a multilateral, especially UN, context. A multilateral approach helps neutralize domestic political opposition, increases the opportunity that operations have limited and legitimate goals, and reduces the risk of large-scale force being used by adversaries or rival powers. Third, the United Nations has some notable advantages over regional organizations in tackling security problems: It is universal; it has a reputation, even if it is now under threat, for impartiality; and it has a more clear set of arrangements for making decisions on security issues than do most regional organizations, including even the North Atlantic Treaty Organization (NATO). . . .

Recognizing that the United Nations is seriously overloaded, much thought has been given to the question of cooperation with regional security organizations.

. . . The idea that the United Nations and regional institutions could share responsibility for security seems to be emerging, albeit hesitantly, in Europe. The proliferation of European bodies with responsibilities in the security field is notorious: The Conference on Security and Cooperation in Europe (CSCE), NATO, the European Community (EC), the Western European Union (WEU), and the North Atlantic Cooperation Council (NACC) all play roles of varying importance. . . . Despite such developments, enlarging the international security role of regional organizations is easier said than done. These organizations have a bewildering variety of purposes and memberships, and they often have great difficulty in reaching decisions and in taking action. Many regional bodies are seen as too partial to one side. Moreover, it is often far from self-evident which regional body should have the principal role in addressing a given problem. The United Nations has often encouraged regional bodies to handle crises only to find that important aspects of the problems remained within its own domain.

THE CHANGING CHARACTER OF CONFLICT

Many of the conflicts in the contemporary world have a very different character from those that the United Nations was designed to address. Above all, those who framed the UN Charter had in mind the problem of international war, waged by well-organized states. This reflected the view, still common today, that aggression and international war constitute the supreme problem of international relations. Although the problem of interstate war has by no means disappeared, for many, civil war—whether internationalized or not—has always represented the deadlier threat. Some of the twentieth century's principal political philosophies have underestimated the significance of ethnicity, however defined, as a powerful political force and source of conflict; this is now changing through the pressure of events. . . .

In the overwhelming majority of UN Security Council operations today, there is a strong element of civil war and communal conflict. For the United Nations, involvement in such a conflict is hardly new, as the long-standing and continuing problems of Palestine/Israel and Cyprus bear witness. The collapse of large multinational states and empires almost always causes severe dislocations, including the emergence or re-emergence of ethnic, religious, regional, and other animosities. The absence of fully legitimate political systems, traditions, regimes, and state frontiers all increase the likelihood that a narrowly ethnic definition of "nations" prevails. These difficulties are compounded by the fact that, for the most part, the geographical distribution of populations is so messy that the harmonious realization of national self-determination is impossible. Conflict-ridden parts of the former Yugoslavia and the former Soviet Union are merely the two most conspicuous contemporary examples of imperial collapse leading to inter-ethnic war. In both cases, the taboo against changing old "colonial" frontiers has been undermined much more quickly and seriously than occurred in post-colonial states in Africa and elsewhere in the decades following European decolonization. . . . It is by no means impossible that internal conflicts could drag the United Nations down; its inability to prevent a resumption of war in Angola following the September 1992 elections is an ominous indicator of this type of hazard.

Internal conflicts, especially those with a communal or ethnic dimension, present special risks for international engagement, whether in the form of mediation, peace-keeping, or forceful military intervention. First, internal conflicts tend to be "nasty, brutish, and long," and they leave communities with deep and enduring mutual suspicions based on traumatic experiences and continuing proximity. Intervention requires a willingness to stay what may be a very long course. Second, internal conflicts are typically conducted under the leadership of non-governmental or semi-governmental entities, which may see great advantages in the degree of recognition involved in negotiating with UN representatives and yet be unwilling or unable to carry out the terms of agreements. Third, internal conflicts typically involve the use of force directed against the civilian populations, thus becoming especially bitter and posing difficult problems related to the protection of dispersed and vulnerable civilians. Fourth, internal conflicts are often conducted with small weapons: rifles, knives and the arsonist's match. It is very difficult to control the use of such weaponry by bombing, arms embargoes, or formal methods of arms control. Finally, in cases such as these, there is frequently no territorial *status quo ante* to which to return. Cease-fires and other agreements are vulnerable to the charge that they legitimize the use of force and that they create impossibly complicated "leopard-spot" territorial arrangements, based on ethnic territorial units that are small and separated and, thus, difficult to defend. . . .

Communal and ethnic conflicts raise awkward issues about the criteria used in recognizing political entities as states and in favoring their admission to the United Nations. When the United Nations admits member-states, it is in fact conferring a particularly important form of recognition, and it is also implicitly underwriting the inviolability of their frontiers. Yet, the United Nations does not appear to be taking sufficient account of traditional criteria for recognition, which include careful consideration of whether a state really exists and coheres as a political and social entity. Many European states also forgot these traditional criteria in some of their recent acts of recognition, many of which did not involve setting up diplomatic missions. If the results of recognition are risky security commitments to purported states that never really attained internal cohesion, public support for UN action may be weakened.

Such conflicts also raise issues about the appropriateness of certain principles derived from interstate relations, including the principle that changing frontiers by force can never be accepted. This principle, which is very important in contemporary international relations, has been frequently reiterated by the international community in connection with the Yugoslav crisis. A successful armed grab for territory on largely ethnic grounds would indeed set a deeply worrying precedent. Yet, it must be asked whether it is wise to express this legal principle so forcefully in circumstances in which existing "frontiers" have no physical existence, in which they lack both logic and legitimacy, in which there are such deep-seated ethnic problems, and in which almost any imaginable outcome will involve recognition of the consequences of frontier violations.

LIMITED HARMONY AMONG THE MAJOR POWERS

. . . It is undeniable, and very welcome, that there is more agreement among states about international security issues now than there was during the Cold War. However, there remain fundamental differences of both interest and perception. These may not be enough to prevent the Security Council from reaching decisions on key issues, but they can frustrate efforts to turn decisions into actions in fast-changing situations. . . .

Differences of interest amongst states are complemented by differences in perceptions about the fundamental nature of world politics. Depending largely on their different historical experiences, some states view colonial domination and imperialism as the most serious problems in international relations; others see civil war as the most dangerous threat to international security; yet others view aggressive conquest and international war as the central problems.

Such serious differences of perception and interest are, of course, reflected in the proceedings of the UN Security Council. One should not necessarily expect relations among major powers to be good, and there may be perfectly valid reasons why countries perceive major security problems differently. [For example,] China's world-view, although undergoing important changes, retains distinctive elements—including a fear of foreign subversion, a strong belief in state sovereignty, and some identification with developing states—which could set it against other Security Council members.

THE PROBLEMATIC STRUCTURE OF THE SECURITY COUNCIL

. . . If the United Nations is indeed to have an enlarged role in security affairs, its system of decision-making must be seen to be legitimate.

The powers of the Security Council are, in theory, very extensive: "The Members of the United Nations agree to accept and carry out the decisions of the Security Council in accordance with the present Charter." In practice, the Security Council cannot impose its will on the membership in the way this statement implies and, despite the absence of any system of formal constitutional challenge, there is no sign of the emergence of a doctrine even hinting at the infallibility of UN Security Council pronouncements. However, these limitations on the power of the Security Council do not mean that states, having successfully retained considerable sovereign powers in security matters, see the existing arrangements as satisfactory.

The criticisms of the composition of the Security Council involve several elements: doubt about preserving unaltered, half a century later, the special position of those countries that were allies in the Second World War; concern that three of those powers—France, Britain, and the United States—make most of the agenda-setting decisions in running the Security Council; irritation, especially on the part of Germany and Japan, about "taxation without representation," and frustration that the views of the non-permanent members of the Security Council, and indeed of the great majority of the 181-strong General Assembly, count for little. These criticisms could become much more serious if events take such a turn that they coincide with a perception that the Security Council has made serious misjudgments on central issues. . . .

In the history of the United Nations, much more has been achieved by changes in practice, rather than Charter revision. More thought will have to be given to how the Security Council might develop its procedures and practices: for example, by strengthening the selection of non-permanent members to reflect their contributions to the United Nations' work and developing more regular Security Council consultation with major states and interested parties. Such changes, although difficult to implement, might go at least some way towards meeting the strong concerns of certain states about being left out of decisions that affect them vitally.

THE PROBLEM OF ORGANIZING ENFORCEMENT ACTIONS

The issue of organizing enforcement actions is central to almost every discussion of the United Nations' future role. It brings out the conflict between "Charter fundamentalists," who would like such actions to be organized precisely in accord with the UN Charter, and those with a "common law" approach, who believe the most important guide is UN practice.

Three times in the UN era, major military action authorized by the United Nations has been under US, not UN, command: in Korea in 1950–53, Iraq in 1990–91, and Somalia in 1992–93. These episodes suggest the emergence of a system in which the United Nations authorizes military actions, which are then placed under the control of a state or group of states. There are important advantages to such an arrangement. First, it reflects the reality that not all states feel equally involved in every enforcement action. Moreover, military actions require extremely close coordination between intelligence-gathering and operations, a smoothly functioning decision-making machine, and forces with some experience of working together to perform dangerous and complex tasks. These things are more likely to be achieved through existing national armed forces, alliances, and military relationships, than they are within the structure of a UN command. As habits of cooperation between armed forces develop, and as the United Nations itself grows, the scope for action under direct UN command may increase, but this will inevitably be a slow process. . . .

Experience seems to show that mobilizing for collective security only works when one power takes the lead. However, as a result of the effort, that same power may be reluctant to continue assuming the entire burden of collective security. After the Korean War, the United States tried to set up regional alliances to reduce its direct military obligation. After the 1991 Gulf War, the United States was manifestly reluctant to get entangled in Iraq and to underwrite all security arrangements in the area. . . . The issue of UN versus authorized national command arises in non-enforcement connections as well. As UN-controlled peace-keeping forces become involved in more complex missions, in which neat distinctions between peace-keeping and enforcement are eroded, the adequacy of the United Nations' existing machinery for controlling complex operations in distant countries is increasingly called into question. . . .

PROSPECTS FOR COLLECTIVE SECURITY

Is it possible to say that out of the rubble of the Cold War a system of collective security is emerging? . . . The term "collective security" normally refers to a system in which each state in the system accepts that the security of one is the concern of all and agrees to join in a collective response to aggression. In this sense, it is distinct from collective defense or alliance systems, in which groups of states ally with each other, principally against possible external threats.

"Collective security" proposals have been in circulation since the beginning of the modern states system and were indeed aired at the negotiations that led to the 1648 Peace of Westphalia. The attractive theory of collective security, when tested against some basic questions, often reveals some fundamental flaws.

Whose collective security? There is always a risk that a collective security system will be seen as protecting only certain countries or interests or as privileging certain principles at the expense of others. Some countries may, for whatever reason, feel excluded from its benefits or threatened by it. The anxieties expressed by some countries in the developing world regarding the concept of the "New World Order," while they have not yet crystallized into definite opposition to any specific UN action, are evidence of concern on this point.

Can there be consistent responses to security problems? Although the UN system is the first truly global international system and although it involves the subscription of virtually all countries in the world to a common set of principles, it is not yet evident that the same principles and practices could or should be applied consistently to different problems, countries, and regions. Difficulties can arise both from the consistent application of principles to situations that are fundamentally different and from the inconsistent application of principles. It is also not yet apparent that collective security can operate as effectively for East Timor or Tibet as for Kuwait. The widespread perception that Israel has successfully defied UN Security Council resolutions while other states have not, although arguably facile in certain respects, illustrates the explosiveness of emerging accusations of "double standards" at the United Nations. The political price of apparent inconsistency could be high.

Against which types of threat is a system of collective security intended to operate? There is no agreement that collective security should apply equally to the following: massive aggression and annexation; cross-border incursions; environmental despoliation; acts of terrorism; human rights violations within a state; communal and ethnic conflict; and the collapse of state structures under assault from internal opposition. In 1990–91, many people argued that it was the particularly flagrant nature of the Iraqi invasion, occupation, and annexation of Kuwait that justified the coalition's response; even then, the international military response was far from unanimous. The fact that this argument was so widely used underlines the point that in cases in which aggression is not so blatant, it might be much harder to secure an international military response; a state caught up in such a conflict might have to look after its own interests. Since 1991, inspired partly by the establishment of "safe havens" in northern Iraq and partly by a trend of opinion, admittedly far from universal, in favor of democracy, there has been some increased advocacy, not least in France and the United States, of a right of intervention in states even in the absence of a formal invitation. This remains a deeply contentious issue and serves as a useful reminder that the ends towards which collective security efforts might be directed are not fixed.

How collective does enforcement have to be? Is complete unanimity impossible to attain, especially in the case of military action? Is there still space for some states to be neutral? In practice, there has never been, on the global level, a truly "collective" case (let alone system) of collective security. In the Gulf crisis of 1990–91, the key UN Security Council resolution avoided the call for all states to take military action. Instead, it merely authorized "member-states co-operating with the Government of Kuwait" to use "all necessary means" to implement relevant UN resolutions. This implied that it was still legitimate for a state to have a status of neutrality or non-belligerency in this conflict. It marked an interesting and realistic interpretation of some optimistic provisions in Chapter VII of the UN Charter.

How can a system of collective security actively deter a particular threat to a particular country? In the wake of the 1991 Gulf War, there was much discussion as to possible means by which, in the future, invasions could be deterred before disaster struck. . . . Following a unanimous Security Council decision of 11 December 1992, the idea was implemented by the United Nations for the first time in Macedonia. Ironically, a state that until April 1993 remained a non-member was thus receiving protection from a state, Yugoslavia, that was still, for most practical purposes, a UN member. Despite remarkable progress, the idea of "preventive deployment" is fraught with difficulty. There is the risk that large numbers of states would request it, that it would be insufficient to discourage aggression, and that it might be used by a government as an alternative to providing for its own defense. It should not, however, be taken for granted that military deployments are absolutely essential. There may also be some residual deterrent value in the lessons of Korea (1950–53) and Kuwait (1990–91); twice, under UN auspices, the United States has led coalitions that have gone to the defense of invaded states to which the United States was not bound by formal alliance commitments and in which it had no troops deployed at the time. This curious fact may not be entirely lost on would-be aggressors. Yet, there are bound to be cases in which some kinds of preventive UN deployments, of which Macedonia is a harbinger, are considered necessary.

Who pays for collective security? The question of burden-sharing in international security matters is notoriously complex, as shown by the experience of NATO, of UN peace-keeping, and of the US-led operations in the 1990–91 Gulf crisis. In 1992, the annual cost of UN peace-keeping activities was the highest ever—about $2.8 billion. Unpaid contributions towards UN peace-keeping operations in September 1992 stood at $844 million, but by the beginning of 1993, this figure was reduced to about $670 million. States have responded well to the increased costs of peace-keeping. However if more UN peace-keeping (or other) operations go badly, there could be added difficulty in securing payment. Even if they do not, there are problems to be addressed. During the US presidential campaign, Bill Clinton, while indicating that he would act on payment of the US debt to the United Nations, repeatedly called for new agreements for sharing the costs of maintaining peace and suggested that the US apportionment of UN peace-keeping costs be reduced from 30.4% to 25%. The extraordinary paradox of the country most deeply involved in military support for an international organization being simultaneously its major (though steadily repaying) defaulter is yet one more illustration of the gulf between the theory of collective security and its practice. However, future payment difficulties may come from states not involved in, or critical of, Security Council decisions.

What is the place of disarmament and arms control in a system of collective security? Most proposals for collective security call for lower levels of armaments, consistent with the needs of internal security and international obligations. . . . However, the United Nations has yet to work out a coherent philosophy to guide its efforts in the field of disarmament and arms control in the post–Cold War era. "Arms control" is still seen by many as a suspect, meliorist concept. Attempts to develop guidelines for conventional arms transfers have many sharp critics, including China. The rationale for arms reductions, for control of arms transfers, and for nuclear non-proliferation efforts, all still need to be carefully examined and refined. This is especially important in view of the common fears that existing arms control arrangements are discriminatory—fears that could be exacerbated if the Security Council assumes a more central role in non-proliferation matters.

2 The Uses of Force

With the end of both the Cold War and the Soviet Union, the nightmare of an all-out nuclear war between the superpowers that so dominated world politics since 1945 ended. It is not likely that a new danger of the same magnitude will arise, at least for the economically developed democracies of North America, Japan, and Western Europe. Indeed, for the first time since the formation of these nation-states, the citizens of these countries may live out their lives without worrying that they or their children will have to die or kill in a major war.

This fact, however, does not mean that we should no longer be concerned with how states use force. Even if the optimistic prediction is correct, we still need to understand previous eras in which warfare played such a large role. To take the recent past, we cannot understand the course of the Cold War without studying the role nuclear weapons played in it. Moreover, an understanding of the role that nuclear weapons played in that era is central for determining the role they will play in this era. This is so for no other reason than that national leaders' views of the present are heavily influenced by their reading of the past. Furthermore, even within the developed rich world, where a great-power war is unlikely, military power still remains useful to the conduct of statecraft. If it were not, these states would have already disarmed. They have not because the use of force must always be available, even if it is not always necessary. For much of the rest of the world, unfortunately, circumstances are different. Threats to the security of states remain real, and war among them has not been abolished. For all states, then—those likely to enjoy peace and those that will have to endure war—what has changed is not the utility of military power so much as how it can be usefully employed.

THE POLITICAL USES OF FORCE

The use of force almost always represents the partial failure of a policy. The exception, of course, is the case in which fighting is valued for its own sake—when it is believed that war brings out heroic values and purifies individuals and cultures, or when fighting is seen as entertainment. Changes in states' values and the increased destructiveness of war, however, have led state actors to view armed conflicts as the last resort. Threats are a second choice to diplomatic maneuvers; actual use of force follows only if the threats fail.

Because of the high costs of violence, its use is tempered by restraints and bargaining. As bloody as most wars are, they could always be bloodier. Brutalities are limited in part by the combatants' shared interests, if not by their scruples. Because two states differ enough to go to war, it does not follow that they have no common interests. Only when everything that is good for one side is bad for the other (a "zero-sum" situation) do the opponents gain nothing by bargaining. In most cases, however, some outcomes are clearly bad for both sides; and therefore, even though they are at war, each side shares an interest in avoiding them.

The shared nature of the interest, as Thomas Schelling points out, stems from the fact that it is easier to destroy than to create. Force can be used to take—or to bargain. If you can take what you want, you do not need your adversary's cooperation and do not have to bargain with him. A country may use force to seize disputed territory just as a robber may kill you to get your wallet. Most of the things people and nations want, however, cannot be taken in this way. A nation not only wants to take territory, it wants to govern and exploit it. A nation may want others to stop menacing it; it may even want others to adopt its values. Brute force alone cannot achieve these goals. A nation that wants to stop others from menacing it may not want to fight them in order to remove the threat. A nation that wants others to adopt its values cannot impose them solely through conquest. Where the cooperation of an adversary is needed, bargaining will ensue. The robber does not need the cooperation of his victim if he kills him to get his wallet. However, the thief who must obtain the combination of a safe from the hostage who carries it only in his head does need such cooperation. The thief may use force to demonstrate that the hostage can lose his life if he does not surrender the combination. But the thief no more wishes to kill the hostage and lose the combination than the hostage wishes to die. The hostage may trade the combination for his life. The bargain may be unequal or unfair, but it is still a bargain.

The mutual avoidance of certain outcomes explains why past wars have not been as bloody as they could have been; but an analysis of why wars were not more destructive should not blind us to the factors that made them as destructive as they were. By 1914, for example, all the statesmen of Europe believed a war inevitable, and all were ready to exploit it. None, however, imagined the staggering losses that their respective nations would inflict and bear in the field, or the extent to which noncombatants would be attacked. Yet by the second year of the war, the same men were accepting the deaths of hundreds or thousands for a few yards' gain in the front lines; and by the end of the war, they were planning large-scale aerial gas attacks on each other's major cities. The German bombing of Guernica in 1937 and Rotterdam in 1940 shocked statesmen and citizens alike, but by the middle of the war both were accepting as routine the total destruction of German and Japanese cities.

Three factors largely account for the increasing destructiveness of the wars of the last two centuries. First was the steady technological improvement in weaponry. Weapons such as machine guns, submarines, poison gas, and aircraft made it feasible to maim or kill large numbers of people quickly. The rapidity of destruction that is possible with nuclear weapons is only the most recent, albeit biggest, advance. Second was the growth in the capacity, and thus the need, of states to field ever larger numbers of forces. As states became more industrialized and centralized, they acquired the wealth and developed the administrative apparatus to move men on a grand scale. Concomitant with the increase in military potential was the necessity to realize the potential. As soon as one state expanded the forces at its disposal, all other states had to follow suit. Thus when Prussia instituted universal conscription and the general-staff system and then demonstrated their advantages by its swift victories over Austria and France, the rest of the continent quickly adopted its methods. An increase in the potential power of states led to an increase in their standing power.

Third was the gradual "democratization" of war: the expansion of the battlefield and hence the indiscriminate mass killing of noncombatants. Everyone, citizens and soldiers alike, began fighting and dying. World War II, with its extensive use of airpower, marked not the debut but the zenith of this mass killing. Once war became the burden of the masses, not the province of the princes, the distinction between combatants and noncombatants increasingly blurred. Most of the wars of the eighteenth century did impinge upon the citizenry, but mainly financially; few civilians died in them. With the widespread use of conscription in the nineteenth and twentieth centuries, however, more citizens became soldiers. With the advent of industrialization and with the increasing division of labor, the citizens who did not fight remained behind to produce weapons. Now a nation not only had to conquer its enemy's armies but also had to destroy the industrial plant that supplied their weapons. Gradually the total energy of a country was diverted into waging wars, and, of course, as the costs of wars increased, so did the justifications given for them and the benefits claimed to derive from them. The greater the sacrifices asked, the larger the victory spoils demanded. Because wars became literally wars of, by, and for the people, governments depended increasingly upon the support of their citizens. As wars became democratized, so too did they become popularized and propagandized.

The readings in the first section explore how force has been and can be used in a changing world. Robert J. Art notes that the threat and use of force has four distinct functions and shows how their relative importance varies from one situation to another. Thomas Schelling examines the differences between the uses of conventional and nuclear weapons and the links between force and foreign policy goals. Robert Art analyzes the concept of coercive diplomacy—the resort to force short of all-out war—and demonstrates why it is difficult to execute. Robert Jervis argues that the extent to which states can make themselves more secure without menacing others depends in large part on whether offensive postures can be distinguished from defensive ones and whether the offense is believed to be more efficacious than the defense.

THE POLITICAL UTILITY OF FORCE TODAY

It is a mistake to examine the possible use of force in a vacuum. As Clausewitz stressed, force is an instrument for reaching political goals. Its utility, as well as the likelihood of its use, depends not only on the costs and perceived benefits of fighting but on the general political context, the values statesmen and citizens hold, the alternative policy instruments available, and the objectives sought.

Robert O. Keohane and Joseph S. Nye contrast the models or "ideal types" of Realism and complex interdependence in dealing with the role of force and military threats. Realism, represented in many of the readings in Part One, stresses the importance of military power. Complex interdependence, by contrast, is designed to capture relations not among military adversaries but among those states with close economic and political ties. In the latter case, so argue Keohane and Nye, military force is likely to play a smaller role; and international organizations, economic issues and resources, and relations among nongovernmental groups, a larger one. They argue that what was true for the relations between America and her major allies during the Cold War is likely to characterize relations among developed democracies in the future.

But military strength is likely to loom larger if this form of power is fairly fungible—that is, it can be used to help reach a number of goals, a proposition that Koehane and Nye reject. To the contrary, Robert Art argues that even for states like the United States that lack strong enemies, force still can serve many purposes. Finally, in this section, Robert Pape provides an analysis of suicide terrorism, a phenomenon unfortunately quite prevalent in our era. He surveys the universe of cases of suicide terrorism from 1980 to 2001 and argues that "it pays" because it has forced liberal democracies to compromise.

THE SPREAD OF NUCLEAR WEAPONS

During the Cold War, nuclear weapons, it was argued, helped make competition between the two superpowers safer than it would otherwise have been. That is, nuclear weapons made the two superpowers run scared, not safe, and this restrained them. Each had to worry that if it pushed the other too far, matters could get out of hand and escalate to nuclear war. Each learned, especially after the Cuban Missile Crisis of 1962, not to push the other to the point where it faced the choice of upping the ante and risk losing control, or backing down and risk being humiliated. Rules of the road between the two superpowers gradually developed, and their subsequent competition proved safer in the last twenty-eight years of the Cold War than it had been in the first fifteen.

How relevant for today is the superpower experience with nuclear weapons? Will states that experience intense political conflicts with one another be deterred from pushing one another too far? Or will they be less restrained than were the superpowers and find themselves in the horror of escalation to the use of nuclear weapons? How valid a model is the US-Soviet experience for dyadic conflicts today?

Scott Sagan and Kenneth Waltz analyze what is today the most dangerous political conflict between two nuclear armed states—the Pakistani-Indian conflict over the state of Kashmir. They look at the 1999 shooting conflict over Kargil and draw opposite conclusions from it. Sagan argues that we should take no comfort from the fact that a large war did not ensue because there were too many near misses and because the next time the two states might not be so lucky. Waltz argues that the limited use of force by both sides in 1999 shows clearly how the mutual possession of nuclear weapons causes states to restrain their ambitions and reign in their military. The Kargil case serves as a good exemplar by which to extrapolate to other possible conflicts between nuclear armed adversaries that the world may experience in the future.

THE POLITICAL USES
■ OF FORCE

The Four Functions of Force
■ ROBERT J. ART

In view of what is likely to be before us, it is vital to think carefully and precisely about the uses and limits of military power. That is the purpose of this essay. It is intended as a backdrop for policy debates, not a prescription of specific policies. It consciously eschews elaborate detail on the requisite military forces for scenarios *a . . . n* and focuses instead on what military power has and has not done, can and cannot do. Every model of how the world works has policy implications. But not every policy is based on a clear view of how the world works. What, then, are the uses to which military power can be put? How have nuclear weapons affected these uses? And what is the future of force in a world of nuclear parity and increasing economic interdependence?

WHAT ARE THE USES OF FORCE?

The goals that states pursue range widely and vary considerably from case to case. Military power is more useful for realizing some goals than others, though it is generally considered of some use by most states for all of the goals that they hold. If we attempt, however, to be descriptively accurate, to enumerate all of the purposes for which states use force, we shall simply end up with a bewildering list. Descriptive accuracy is not a virtue *per se* for analysis. In fact, descriptive accuracy is generally bought at the cost of analytical utility. (A concept that is descriptively accurate is usually analytically useless.) Therefore, rather than compile an exhaustive list of such purposes, I have selected four categories that themselves analytically exhaust the functions that force can serve: defense, deterrence, compellence, and "swaggering."

From "To What Ends Military Power" by Robert J. Art, in *International Security*, Vol. 4 (Spring 1980), pp. 4–35. Portions of the text and the footnotes have been omitted.

Not all four functions are necessarily well or equally served by a given military posture. In fact, usually only the great powers have the wherewithal to develop military forces that can serve more than two functions at once. Even then, this is achieved only vis-á-vis smaller powers, not vis-á-vis the other great ones. The measure of the capabilities of a state's military forces must be made relative to those of another state, not with reference to some absolute scale. A state that can compel another state can also defend against it and usually deter it. A state that can defend against another state cannot thereby automatically deter or compel it. A state can deter another state without having the ability to either defend against or compel it. A state that can swagger vis-á-vis another may or may not be able to perform any of the other three functions relative to it. Where feasible, defense is the goal that all states aim for first. If defense is not possible, deterrence is generally the next priority. Swaggering is the function most difficult to pin down analytically; deterrence, the one whose achievement is the most difficult to demonstrate; compellence, the easiest to demonstrate but among the hardest to achieve. The following discussion develops these points more fully.

The *defensive* use of force is the deployment of military power so as to be able to do two things—to ward off an attack and to minimize damage to oneself if attacked. For defensive purposes, a state will direct its forces against those of a potential or actual attacker, but not against his unarmed population. For defensive purposes, a state can deploy its forces in place prior to an attack, use them after an attack has occurred to repel it, or strike first if it believes that an attack upon it is imminent or inevitable. The defensive use of force can thus involve both peaceful and physical employment and both repellent (second) strikes and offensive (first) strikes. If a state strikes first when it believes an attack upon it is imminent, it is launching a preemptive blow. If it strikes first when it believes an attack is inevitable but not momentary, it is launching a preventive blow. Preemptive and preventive blows are undertaken when a state calculates, first, that others plan to attack it and, second, that to delay in striking offensively is against its interests. A state preempts in order to wrest the advantage of the first strike from an opponent. A state launches a preventive attack because it believes that others will attack it when the balance of forces turns in their favor and therefore attacks while the balance of forces is in its favor. In both cases it is better to strike first than to be struck first. The major distinction between preemption and prevention is the calculation about when an opponent's attack will occur. For preemption, it is a matter of hours, days, or even a few weeks at the most; for prevention, months or even a few years. In the case of preemption, the state has almost no control over the timing of its attack; in the case of prevention, the state can in a more leisurely way contemplate the timing of its attack. For both cases, it is the belief in the certainty of war that governs the offensive, defensive attack. For both cases, the maxim, "the best defense is a good offense," makes good sense.

The *deterrent* use of force is the deployment of military power so as to be able to prevent an adversary from doing something that one does not want him to do and that he might otherwise be tempted to do by threatening him with unacceptable punishment if he does it. Deterrence is thus the threat of retaliation. Its purpose is to prevent something undesirable from happening. The threat of punishment is directed at the adversary's population and/or industrial infrastructure. The effectiveness of the threat depends upon a state's ability to convince a potential adversary that it has both the will and power to punish him severely if he undertakes the undesirable action in question. Deterrence therefore employs force peacefully. It is the threat to resort to force in order to punish that is the essence of deterrence. If the threat has to be carried out, deterrence by definition has failed. A deterrent threat is made precisely with the intent that it will not have to be carried out. Threats are made to prevent actions from being undertaken. If the threat has to be implemented, the action has already been undertaken. Hence deterrence can be judged successful only if the retaliatory threats have not been implemented.

Deterrence and defense are alike in that both are intended to protect the state or its closest allies from physical attacks. The purpose of both is dissuasion—persuading others *not* to undertake actions harmful to oneself. The defensive use of force dissuades by convincing an adversary that he cannot conquer one's military forces. The deterrent use of force dissuades by convincing the adversary that his population and territory will suffer terrible damage if he initiates the undesirable action. Defense dissuades by presenting an unvanquishable military force. Deterrence dissuades by presenting the certainty of retaliatory devastation.

Defense is possible without deterrence, and deterrence is possible without defense. A state can have the military wherewithal to repel an invasion without also being able to threaten devastation to the invader's population or territory. Similarly, a state can have the wherewithal credibly to threaten an adversary with such devastation and yet be unable to repel his invading force. Defense, therefore, does not necessarily buy deterrence, nor deterrence defense. A state that can defend itself from attack, moreover, will have little need to develop the wherewithal to deter. If physical attacks can be repelled or if the damage from them drastically minimized, the incentive to develop a retaliatory capability is low. A state that cannot defend itself, however, will try to develop an effective deterrent if that be possible. No state will leave its population and territory open to attack if it has the means to redress the situation. Whether a given state can defend or deter or do both vis-á-vis another depends upon two factors: (1) the quantitative balance of forces between it and its adversary; and (2) the qualitative balance of forces, that is, whether the extant military technology favors the offense or the defense. These two factors are situation-specific and therefore require careful analysis of the case at hand.

The *compellent* use of force is the deployment of military power so as to be able either to stop an adversary from doing something that he has already undertaken or to get him to do something that he has not yet undertaken. Compellence, in Schelling's words, "involves initiating an action . . . that can cease, or become harmless, only if the opponent responds." Compellence can employ force either physically or peacefully. A state can start actually harming another with physical destruction until the latter abides by the former's wishes. Or, a state can take actions against another that do not cause physical harm but that require the latter to pay some type of significant price until it changes its behavior. America's bombing of North Vietnam in early 1965 was an example of physical compellence; Tirpitz's building of a German fleet aimed against England's in the two decades before World War I, an example of peaceful compellence. In the first case, the

United States started bombing North Vietnam in order to compel it to stop assisting the Vietcong forces in South Vietnam. In the latter case, Germany built a battlefleet that in an engagement threatened to cripple England's in order to compel her to make a general political settlement advantageous to Germany. In both cases, one state initiated some type of action against another precisely so as to be able to stop it, to bargain it away for the appropriate response from the "put upon" state.

The distinction between compellence and deterrence is one between the active and passive use of force. The success of a deterrent threat is measured by its not having to be used. The success of a compellent action is measured by how closely and quickly the adversary conforms to one's stipulated wishes. In the case of successful deterrence, one is trying to demonstrate a negative, to show why something did not happen. It can never be clear whether one's actions were crucial to, or irrelevant to, why another state chose *not* to do something. In the case of successful compellence, the clear sequence of actions and reactions lends a compelling plausibility to the centrality of one's actions. Figure 1 illustrates the distinction. In successful compellence, state B can claim that its pressure deflected state A from its course of action. In successful deterrence, state B has no change in state A's behavior to point to, but instead must resort to claiming that its threats were responsible for the continuity in A's behavior. State A may have changed its behavior for reasons other than state B's compellent action. State A may have continued with its same behavior for reasons other than state B's deterrent threat. "Proving" the importance of B's influence on A for either case is not easy, but it is more plausible to claim that B influenced A when there is a change in A's behavior than when there is not. Explaining why something did not happen is more difficult than explaining why something did.

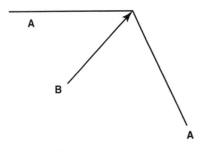

Compellence

(1) A is doing something that B cannot tolerate

(2) B initiates action against A in order to get him to stop his intolerable actions

(3) A stops his intolerable actions and B stops his (or both cease simultaneously)

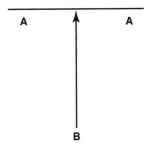

Deterrence

(1) A is presently not doing anything that B finds intolerable

(2) B tells A that if A changes his behavior and does something intolerable, B will punish him

(3) A continues not to do anything B finds intolerable

FIGURE 1

Compellence may be easier to demonstrate than deterrence, but it is harder to achieve. Schelling argues that compellent actions tend to be vaguer in their objectives than deterrent threats and for that reason more difficult to attain. If an adversary has a hard time understanding what it is that one wished him to do, his compliance with one's wishes is made more difficult. There is, however, no inherent reason why a compellent action must be vaguer than a deterrent threat with regard to how clearly the adversary understands what is wanted from him. "Do not attack me" is not any clearer in its ultimate meaning than "stop attacking my friend." A state can be as confused or as clear about what it wishes to prevent as it can be about what it wishes to stop. The clarity, or lack of it, of the objectives of compellent actions and deterrent threats does not vary according to whether the given action is compellent or deterrent in nature, but rather according to a welter of particularities associated with the given action. Some objectives, for example, are inherently clearer and hence easier to perceive than others. Some statesmen communicate more clearly than others. Some states have more power to bring to bear for a given objective than others. It is the specifics of a given situation, not any intrinsic difference between compellence and deterrence, that determines the clarity with which an objective is perceived.

We must, therefore, look elsewhere for the reason as to why compellence is comparatively harder to achieve than deterrence. It lies, not in what one asks another to do, but in *how* one asks. With deterrence, state B asks something of state A in this fashion: "Do not take action *X;* for if you do, I will bash you over the head with this club." With compellence, state B asks something of state A in this fashion: "I am now going to bash you over the head with this club and will continue to do so until you do what I want." In the former case, state A can easily deny with great plausibility any intention of having planned to take action *X.* In the latter case, state A cannot deny either that it is engaged in a given course of action or that it is being subjected to pressure by state B. If they are to be successful, compellent actions require a state to alter its behavior in a manner quite visible to all in response to an equally visible forceful initiative taken by another state. In contrast to compellent actions, deterrent threats are both easier to appear to have ignored or easier to acquiesce to without great loss of face. In contrast to deterrent threats, compellent actions more directly engage the prestige and the passions of the put-upon state. Less prestige is lost in not doing something than in clearly altering behavior due to pressure from another. In the case of compellence, a state has publicly committed its prestige and resources to a given line of conduct that it is now asked to give up. This is not so for deterrence. Thus, compellence is intrinsically harder to attain than deterrence, not because its objectives are vaguer, but because it demands mere humiliation from the compelled state.

The fourth purpose to which military power can be put is the most difficult to be precise about. *Swaggering* is in part a residual category, the deployment of military power for purposes other than defense, deterrence, or compellence. Force is not aimed directly at dissuading another state from attacking, at repelling attacks, nor at compelling it to do something specific. The objectives for swaggering are more diffuse, ill-defined, and problematic than that. Swaggering almost always involves only the peaceful use of force and is expressed usually in one of two ways: displaying one's military might at military exercises and national demonstrations and buying or building the era's most prestigious weapons. The swagger use of force is the most egoistic: It aims to enhance the national pride of a people or to satisfy the personal ambitions of its ruler. A state or statesman swaggers in order to look and feel more powerful and important, to be taken seriously by others in the councils of international decision making, to enhance the nation's image in the eyes of others. If its image is enhanced, the nation's defense, deterrent, and compellent capabilities may also be enhanced; but swaggering is not undertaken solely or even primarily for these specific purposes. Swaggering is pursued because it offers to bring prestige "on the cheap." Swaggering is pursued because of the fundamental yearning of states and statesmen for respect and prestige. Swaggering is more something to be enjoyed for itself than to be employed for a specific, consciously thought-out end.

And yet, the instrumental role of swaggering cannot be totally discounted because of the fundamental relation between force and foreign policy that it obtains in an anarchic environment. Because there is a connection between the military might that a nation is thought to possess and the success that it achieves in attaining its objectives, the enhancement of a state's stature in the eyes of others can always be justified on *realpolitik* lines. If swaggering causes other states to take one's interests more seriously into account, then the general interests of the state will benefit. Even in its instrumental role, however, swaggering is undertaken less for any given end than for all ends. The swaggering function of military power is thus at one and the same time the most comprehensive and the most diffuse, the most versatile in its effects and the least focused in its immediate aims, the most instrumental in the long run and the least instrumental in the short run, easy to justify on hardheaded grounds and often undertaken on emotional grounds. Swaggering mixes the rational and irrational more than the other three functions of military power and, for that reason, remains both pervasive in international relations and elusive to describe.

Defense, deterrence, compellence, and swaggering—these are the four general purposes for which force can be employed. Discriminating among them analytically, however, is easier than applying them in practice. This is due to two factors. First, we need to know the motives behind an act in order to judge its purpose; but the problem is that motives cannot be readily inferred from actions because several motives can be served by the same action. But neither can one readily infer the motives of a state from what it publicly or officially proclaims them to be. Such statements should not necessarily be taken at face value because of the role that bluff and dissimulation play in statecraft. Such statements are also often concocted with domestic political, not foreign audiences in mind, or else are deliberate exercises in studied ambiguity. Motives are important in order to interpret actions, but neither actions nor words always clearly delineate motives.

It is, moreover, especially difficult to distinguish defensive from compellent actions and deterrent from swaggering ones unless we know the reasons for which they were undertaken. Peaceful defensive preparations often look largely the same as peaceful compellent ones. Defensive attacks are nearly indistinguishable from compellent ones. Is he who attacks first the defender or the compeller? Deterrence and swaggering both involve the acquisition and display of an era's prestigious weapons. Are such weapons acquired to enhance prestige or to dissuade an attack?

Second, to make matters worse, consider the following example. Germany launched an attack upon France and Russia at the end of July 1914 and thereby began World War I. There are two schools of thought as to why Germany did this. One holds that its motives were aggressive—territorial aggrandizement, economic gain, and elevation to the status of a world empire. Another holds that her motives were preventive and hence defensive. She struck first because she feared encirclement, slow strangulation, and then inevitable attack by her two powerful neighbors, foes whom she felt were daily increasing their military might faster than she was. She struck while she had the chance to win.

It is not simple to decide which school is the more nearly correct because both can marshall evidence to build a powerful case. Assume for the moment, though, that the second is closer to the truth. There are then two possibilities to consider: (1) Germany launched an attack because it *was* the case that her foes were planning to attack her ultimately, and Germany had the evidence to prove it; or (2) Germany felt she had reasonable evidence of her foes' *intent* to attack her eventually, but in fact her evidence was wrong because she misperceived their intent from their actions. If the first was the case, then we must ask this question: How responsible was Germany's diplomacy in the fifteen years before 1914, aggressive and blundering as it was, in breeding hostility in her neighbors? Germany attacked in the knowledge that they would eventually have struck her, but if her fifteen-year diplomatic record was a significant factor in causing them to lay these plans, must we conclude that Germany in 1914 was merely acting defensively? Must we confine our judgment about the defensive or aggressive nature of the act to the month or even the year in which it occurred? If not, how many years back in history do we go in order to make a judgment? If the second was the case, then we must ask this question: If Germany attacked in the belief, mistakenly as it turns out, that she would be attacked, must we conclude that Germany was acting defensively? Must we confine our judgment about the defensive or aggressive nature of the act simply to Germany's beliefs about others' intent, without reference to their actual intent?

It is not easy to answer these questions. Fortunately, we do not have to. Asking them is enough because it illustrates that an assessment of the *legitimacy* of a state's motives in using force is integral to the task of determining what its motives are. One cannot, that is, specify motives without at the same time making judgments about their legitimacy. The root cause of this need lies in the nature of state action. In anarchy every state is a valid judge of the legitimacy of its goals because there is no supranational authority to enforce agreed upon rules. Because of the lack of universal standards, we are forced to examine each case within its given context and to make individual judgments about the meaning of the particulars. When individual judgment is exercised, individuals may well differ. Definitive answers are more likely to be the exception rather than the rule.

Where does all of this leave us? Our four categories tell us what are the four possible purposes for which states can employ military power. The attributes of each alert us to the types of evidence for which to search. But because the context

TABLE 1 ■ THE PURPOSES OF FORCE

Type	Purpose	Mode	Targets	Characteristics
Defensive	Fend off attacks and/or reduce damage of an attack	Peaceful and physical	Primarily military Secondarily industrial	Defensive preparations can have dissuasion value; Defensive preparations can look aggressive; First strikes can be taken for defense.
Deterrent	Prevent adversary from initiating an action	Peaceful	Primarily civilian Tertiarily military	Threats of retaliation made as not to have to be carried out; Second strike preparations can be viewed as first strike preparations.
Compellent	Get adversary to stop doing something or start doing something	Peaceful and physical	All three with no clear ranking	Easy to recognize but hard to achieve; Competent actions can be justified on defensive grounds
Swaggering	Enhance prestige	Peaceful	None	Difficult to describe because of instrumental and irrational nature; Swaggering can be threatening.

of an action is crucial in order to judge its ultimate purpose, these four categories cannot be applied mindlessly and ahistorically. Each state's purpose in using force in a given instance must fall into one of these four categories. We know *a priori* what the possibilities are. Which one it is, is an exercise in judgment, an exercise that depends as much upon the particulars of the given case as it does upon the general features of the given category . . . (See Table 1).

The Diplomacy of Violence

THOMAS C. SCHELLING

The usual distinction between diplomacy and force is not merely in the instruments, words or bullets, but in the relation between adversaries—in the interplay of motives and the role of communication, understandings, compromise, and restraint. Diplomacy is bargaining; it seeks outcomes that, though not ideal for either party, are better for both than some of the alternatives. In diplomacy each party somewhat controls what the other wants, and can get more by compromise, exchange, or collaboration than by taking things in his own hands and ignoring the other's wishes. The bargaining can be polite or rude, entail threats as well as offers, assume a status quo or ignore all rights and privileges, and assume mistrust rather than trust. But whether polite or impolite, constructive or aggressive, respectful or vicious, whether it occurs among friends or antagonists and whether or not there is a basis for trust and goodwill, there must be some common interest, if only in the avoidance of mutual damage, and an awareness of the need to make the other party prefer an outcome acceptable to oneself.

With enough military force a country may not need to bargain. Some things a country wants it can take, and some things it has it can keep, by sheer strength, skill, and ingenuity. It can do this *forcibly,* accommodating only to opposing strength, skill, and ingenuity and without trying to appeal to an enemy's wishes. Forcibly a country can repel and expel, penetrate and occupy, seize, exterminate, disarm and disable, confine, deny access, and directly frustrate intrusion or attack. It can, that is, if it has enough strength. "Enough" depends on how much an opponent has.

There is something else, though, that force can do. It is less military, less heroic, less impersonal, and less unilateral; it is uglier, and has received less attention in Western military strategy. In addition to seizing and holding, disarming and confining, penetrating and obstructing, and all that, military force can be used to *hurt.* In addition to taking and protecting things of value it can destroy value. In addition to weakening an enemy militarily it can cause an enemy plain suffering. . . .

THE CONTRAST OF BRUTE FORCE WITH COERCION

There is a difference between taking what you want and making someone give it to you, between fending off assault and making someone afraid to assault you, between holding what people are trying to take and making them afraid to take it, between losing what someone can forcibly take and giving it up to avoid risk or damage. It is the difference between defense and deterrence, between brute force and intimidation, between conquest and blackmail, between action and threats. It is the difference between the unilateral, "undiplomatic" recourse to strength, and coercive diplomacy based on the power to hurt.

The contrasts are several. The purely "military" or "undiplomatic" recourse to forcible action is concerned with enemy strength, not enemy interests; the coercive use of the power to hurt, though, is the very exploitation of enemy wants and fears. And brute strength is usually measured relative to enemy strength, the one directly opposing the other, while the power to hurt is typically not reduced by the enemy's power to hurt in return. Opposing strengths may cancel each other, pain and grief do not. The willingness to hurt, the credibility of a threat, and the ability to exploit the power to hurt will indeed depend on how much the adversary can hurt in return but there is little or nothing about an adversary's pain or grief that directly reduces one's own. Two sides cannot both overcome each other with superior strength; they may both be able to hurt each other. With strength they can dispute objects of value; with sheer violence they can destroy them.

And brute force succeeds when it is used, whereas the power to hurt is most successful when held in reserve. It is the *threat* of damage, or of more damage to come, that can make someone yield or comply. It is *latent* violence that can influence someone's choice—violence that can still be withheld or inflicted or that a victim believes can be withheld or inflicted. The threat of pain tries to structure someone's motives, while brute force tries to overcome his strength. Unhappily, the power to hurt is often communicated by some performance of it. Whether it is sheer terroristic violence to induce an irrational response, or cool premeditated violence to persuade somebody that you mean it and may do it again, it is not the pain and damage itself but its influence on somebody's behavior that matters. It is the expectation of *more* violence that gets the wanted behavior, if the power to hurt can get it at all.

To exploit a capacity for hurting and inflicting damage one needs to know what an adversary treasures and what scares him and one needs the adversary to understand what behavior of his will cause the violence to be inflicted and what will cause it to be withheld. The victim has to know what is wanted, and he may have to be assured of what is not wanted. The pain and suffering have to appear *contingent* on his behavior; it is not alone the threat that is effective—the threat of pain or loss if he fails to comply—but the corresponding assurance, possibly an implicit one, that he can avoid the pain or loss if he does comply. The prospect of certain death may stun him, but it gives him no choice.

Coercion by threat of damage also requires that our interests and our opponent's not be absolutely opposed. If his pain were our greatest delight and our satisfaction his great woe, we would just proceed to hurt and to frustrate each other. It is when his pain gives us little or no satisfaction compared with what he can do for us, and the action or inaction that satisfies us costs him less than the pain we can cause, that there is room for coercion. Coercion requires finding a bargain, arranging for him to be better off doing what we want—worse off not . . . doing what we want—when he takes the threatened penalty into account. . . .

This difference between coercion and brute force is as often in the intent as in the instrument. To hunt down Comanches and to exterminate them was brute force; to raid their villages to make them behave was coercive diplomacy, based on the power to hurt. The pain and loss to the Indians might have looked much the same one way as the other; the difference was one of purpose and effect. If Indians were killed because they were in the way, or somebody wanted their land, or the authorities despaired of making them behave and could not confine them and decided to exterminate them, that was pure unilateral force. If *some* Indians were killed to make *other* Indians behave, that was coercive violence—or intended to be, whether or not it was effective. The Germans at Verdun perceived themselves to be chewing up hundreds of thousands of French soldiers in a gruesome "meatgrinder." If the purpose was to eliminate a military obstacle—the French infantryman, viewed as a military "asset" rather than as a warm human being—the offensive at Verdun was a unilateral exercise of military force. If instead the object was to make the loss of young men—not of impersonal "effectives," but of sons, husbands, fathers and the pride of French manhood—so anguishing as to be unendurable, to make surrender a welcome relief and to spoil the foretaste of an Allied victory, then it was an exercise in coercion, in applied violence, intended to offer relief upon accommodation. And of course, since any use of force tends to be brutal, thoughtless, vengeful, or plain obstinate, the motives themselves can be mixed and confused. The fact that heroism and brutality can be either coercive diplomacy or a contest in pure strength does not promise that the distinction will be made, and the strategies enlightened by the distinction, every time some vicious enterprise gets launched. . . .

War appears to be, or threatens to be, not so much a contest of strength as one of endurance, nerve, obstinacy, and pain. It appears to be, and threatens to be, not so much a contest of military strength as a bargaining process—dirty, extortionate, and often quite reluctant bargaining on one side or both—nevertheless a bargaining process.

The difference cannot quite be expressed as one between the *use* of force and the *threat* of force. The actions involved in forcible accomplishment, on the one hand, and in fulfilling a threat, on the other, can be quite different. Sometimes the most effective direct action inflicts enough cost or pain on the enemy to serve as a threat, sometimes not. The United States threatens the Soviet Union with virtual destruction of its society in the event of a surprise attack on the United States; a hundred million deaths are awesome as pure damage, but they are useless in stopping the Soviet attack—especially if the threat is to do it all afterward anyway. So it is worthwhile to keep the concepts distinct—to distinguish forcible action from the threat of pain—recognizing that some actions serve as both a means of forcible accomplishment and a means of inflicting pure damage; some do not. Hostages tend to entail almost pure pain and damage, as do all forms of reprisal after the fact. Some modes of self-defense may exact so little in blood or treasure as to entail negligible violence; and some forcible actions entail so much violence that their threat can be effective by itself.

The power to hurt, though it can usually accomplish nothing directly, is potentially more versatile than a straightforward capacity for forcible accomplishment. By force alone we cannot even lead a horse to water—we have to drag him—much less make him drink. Any affirmative action, any collaboration, almost anything but physical exclusion, expulsion, or extermination, requires that an opponent or a victim do something, even if only to stop or get out. The threat of pain and damage may make him want to do it, and anything he can do is potentially susceptible to inducement. Brute force can only accomplish what requires no collaboration. The principle is illustrated by a technique of unarmed combat: One can disable a man by various stunning, fracturing, or killing blows, but to take him to jail one has to exploit the man's own efforts. "Come-along" holds are those that threaten pain or disablement, giving relief as long as the victim complies, giving him the option of using his own legs to get to jail. . . .

The fact that violence—pure pain and damage—can be used or threatened to coerce and to deter, to intimidate and to blackmail, to demoralize and to paralyze, in a conscious process of dirty bargaining, does not by any means imply that violence is not often wanton and meaningless or, even when purposive, in danger of getting out of hand. Ancient wars were often quite "total" for the loser, the men being put to death, the women sold as slaves, the boys castrated, the cattle slaughtered, and the buildings leveled, for the sake of revenge, justice, personal gain, or merely custom. If an enemy bombs a city, by design or by carelessness, we usually bomb his if we can. In the excitement and fatigue of warfare, revenge is one of the few satisfactions that can be savored. . . . Pure violence, like fire, can be harnessed to a purpose; that does not mean that behind every holocaust is a shrewd intention successfully fulfilled.

But if the occurrence of violence does not always bespeak a shrewd purpose, the absence of pain and destruction is no sign that violence was idle. Violence is most purposive and most successful when it is threatened and not used. Successful threats are those that do not have to be carried out. . . .

THE STRATEGIC ROLE OF PAIN AND DAMAGE

Pure violence, nonmilitary violence, appears most conspicuously in relations between unequal countries, where there is no substantial military challenge and the outcome of military engagement is not in question: Hitler could make his threats contemptuously and brutally against Austria; he could make them, if he wished, in a more refined way against Denmark. It is noteworthy that it was Hitler, not his generals, who used this kind of language; proud military establishments do not like to think of themselves as extortionists. Their favorite job is to deliver victory, to dispose of opposing military force and to leave most of the civilian violence to politics and diplomacy. But if there is no room for doubt how a contest in strength will come out, it may be possible to bypass the military stage altogether and to proceed at once to the coercive bargaining.

A typical confrontation of unequal forces occurs at the *end* of a war, between victor and vanquished. Where Austria was vulnerable before a shot was fired, France was vulnerable after its military shield had collapsed in 1940. Surrender negotiations are the place where the threat of civil violence can come to the fore. Surrender negotiations are often so one-sided, or the potential violence so unmistakable, that bargaining succeeds and the violence remains in reserve. But the fact that most of the actual damage was done during the military stage of the war, prior to victory and defeat, does not mean that violence was idle in the aftermath, only that it was latent and the threat of it successful. . . .

The Russians crushed Budapest in 1956 and cowed Poland and other neighboring countries. There was a lag of ten years between military victory and this show of violence, but the principle was the one [just] explained. . . . Military victory is often the prelude to violence, not the end of it, and the fact that successful violence is usually held in reserve should not deceive us about the role it plays.

What about pure violence during war itself, the infliction of pain and suffering as a military technique? Is the threat of pain involved only in the political use of victory, or is it a decisive technique of war itself?

Evidently between unequal powers it has been part of warfare. Colonial conquest has often been a matter of "punitive expeditions" rather than genuine military engagements. If the tribesmen escape into the brush you can burn their villages without them until they assent to receive what, in strikingly modern language, used to be known as the Queen's "protection.". . .

Pure hurting, as a military tactic, appeared in some of the military actions against the plains Indians. In 1868, during the war with the Cheyennes, General Sheridan decided that his best hope was to attack the Indians in their winter camps. His reasoning was that the Indians could maraud as they pleased during the seasons when their ponies could subsist on grass, and in the winter hide away in remote places. "To disabuse their minds from the idea that they were secure from punishment, and to strike at a period when they were helpless to move their stock and villages, a winter campaign was projected against the large bands hiding away in the Indian territory."[1]

These were not military engagements; they were punitive attacks on people. They were an effort to subdue by the use of violence, without a futile attempt to draw the enemy's military forces into decisive battle. They were "massive retaliation" on a diminutive scale, with local effects not unlike those of Hiroshima. The Indians themselves totally lacked organization and discipline, and typically could not afford enough ammunitions for target practice and were no military match for the calvary; their own rudimentary strategy was at best one of harassment and reprisal. Half a century of Indian fighting in the West left us a legacy of cavalry tactics; but it is hard to find a serious treatise on American strategy against the Indians or Indian strategy against the whites. The twentieth is not the first century in which "retaliation" has been part of our strategy, but it is the first in which we have systematically recognized it. . . .

Making it "terrible beyond endurance" is what we associate with Algeria and Palestine, the crushing of Budapest, and the tribal warfare in Central Africa. But in the great wars of the last hundred years it was usually military victory, not the hurting of the people, that was decisive; General Sherman's attempt to make war hell for the Southern people did not come to epitomize military strategy for the century to follow. To seek out and destroy the enemy's military force, to achieve a crushing victory over enemy armies, was still the avowed purpose and the central aim of American strategy in both world wars. Military action was seen as an *alternative* to bargaining, not a *process* of bargaining.

The reason is not that civilized countries are so averse to hurting people that they prefer "purely military" wars. (Nor were all of the participants in these wars entirely civilized.) The reason is apparently that the technology and geography of warfare, at least for a war between anything like equal powers during the century ending in World War II, kept coercive violence from being decisive before military victory was achieved. Blockade indeed was aimed at the whole enemy nation, not concentrated on its military forces; the German civilians who died of influenza in the First World War were victims directed at the whole country. It has never been quite clear whether blockade—of the South in the Civil War or of the Central Powers in both world wars, or submarine warfare against Britain—was expected to make war unendurable for the people or just to weaken the enemy forces by deny-ing economic support. Both arguments were made, but there was no need to be clear about the purpose as long as either purpose was regarded as legitimate and either might be served. "Strategic bombing" of enemy homelands was also occa-sionally rationalized in terms of the pain and privation it could inflict on people and the civil damage it could do to the nation, as an effort to display either to the pop-ulation or to the enemy leadership that surrender was better than persistence in view of the damage that could be done. It was also rationalized in more "military" terms, as a way of selectively denying war material to the troops or as a way of gen-erally weakening the economy on which the military effort rested.

But terrorism—as violence intended to coerce the enemy rather than to weaken him militarily—blockade and strategic bombing by themselves were not quite up to the job in either world war in Europe. (They might have been sufficient in the war with Japan after straightforward military action had brought American aircraft into range.) Airplanes could not quite make punitive, coercive violence decisive in Europe, at least on a tolerable time schedule, and preclude the need to defeat or to destroy enemy forces as long as they had nothing but conventional explosives and incendiaries to carry. Hitler's V–1 buzz bomb and his V–2 rocket are fairly pure cases of weapons whose purpose was to intimidate, to hurt Britain itself rather than Allied military forces. What the V–2 needed was a punitive payload worth carrying, and the Germans did not have it. Some of the expectations in the 1920s and the 1930s that another major war would be one of pure civilian violence, of shock and terror from the skies, were not borne out by the available technology. The threat of punitive violence kept occupied countries quiescent; but the wars were won in Europe on the basis of brute strength and skill and not by intimida-tion, not by the threat of civilian violence but by the application of military force. Military victory was still the price of admission. Latent violence against people was reserved for the politics of surrender and occupation.

The great exception was the two atomic bombs on Japanese cities. These were weapons of terror and shock. They hurt, and promised more hurt, and that was their purpose. The few "small" weapons we had were undoubtedly of some direct military value but their enormous advantage was in pure violence. In a military sense the United States could gain a little by destruction of two Japanese industrial cities; in a civilian sense, the Japanese could lose much. The bomb that hit Hiroshima was a threat aimed at all of Japan. The political target of the bomb was not the dead of Hiroshima or the factories they worked in, but the survivors of

Tokyo. The two bombs were in the tradition of Sheridan against the Comanches and Sherman in Georgia. Whether in the end those two bombs saved lives or wasted them, Japanese lives or American lives; whether punitive coercive violence is uglier than straightforward military force or more civilized; whether terror is more or less humane than military destruction; we can at least perceive that the bombs on Hiroshima and Nagasaki represented violence against the country itself and not mainly an attack on Japan's material strength. The effect of the bombs, and their purpose, was not mainly the military destruction they accomplished but the pain and the shock and the promise of more.

THE NUCLEAR CONTRIBUTION TO TERROR AND VIOLENCE

Man has, it is said, for the first time in history enough military power to eliminate his species from the earth, weapons against which there is no conceivable defense. War has become, it is said, so destructive and terrible that it ceases to be an instrument of national power. "For the first time in human history," says Max Lerner in a book whose title, *The Age of Overkill,* conveys the point, "men have bottled up a power . . . which they have thus far not dared to use." And Soviet military authorities, whose party dislikes having to accommodate an entire theory of history to a single technological event, have had to re-examine a set of principles that had been given the embarrassing name of "permanently operating factors" in warfare. Indeed, our era is epitomized by words like "the first time in human history," and by the abdication of what was "permanent."

For dramatic impact these statements are splendid. Some of them display a tendency, not at all necessary, to belittle the catastrophe of earlier wars. They may exaggerate the historical novelty of deterrence and the balance of terror.[2] More important, they do not help to identify just what is new about war when so much destructive energy can be packed in warheads at a price that permits advanced countries to have them in large numbers. Nuclear warheads are incomparably more devastating than anything packaged before. What does that imply about war?

It is not true that for the first time in history man has the capability to destroy a large fraction, even the major part, of the human race. Japan was defenseless by August 1945. With a combination of bombing and blockade, eventually invasion, and if necessary the deliberate spread of disease, the United States could probably have exterminated the population of the Japanese islands without nuclear weapons. . . .

It is a grisly thing to talk about. We did not do it and it is not imaginable that we would have done it. We had no reason; if we had had a reason, we would not have the persistence of purpose once the fury of war had been dissipated in victory and we had taken on the task of the executioner. If we and our enemies might do such a thing to each other now, and to others as well, it is not because nuclear weapons have for the first time made it feasible.

Nuclear weapons can do it quickly. . . . To compress a catastrophic war within the span of time that a man can stay awake drastically changes the politics of war, the process of decision, the possibility of central control and restraint, the motivations of people in charge, and the capacity to think and reflect while war is in progress. It *is* imaginable that we might destroy 200,000,000 Russians in a war of the present, though not 80,000,000 Japanese in a war of the past. It is not only imaginable, it is imagined. It is imaginable because it could be done "in a moment, in the twinkling of an eye, at the last trumpet."

This may be why there is so little discussion of how an all-out war might be brought to a close. People do not expect it to be "brought" to a close, but just to come to an end when everything has been spent. It is also why the idea of "limited war" has become so explicit in recent years. Earlier wars, like the World Wars I and II or the Franco-Prussian War, were limited by *termination,* by an ending that occurred before the period of greatest potential violence, by negotiation that brought the *threat* of pain and privation to bear but often precluded the massive *exercise* of civilian violence. With nuclear weapons available, the restraint of violence cannot await the outcome of a contest of military strength; restraint, to occur at all, must occur during war itself.

This is a difference between nuclear weapons and bayonets. It is not in the number of people they can eventually kill but in the speed with which it can be done, in the centralization of decision, in the divorce of the war from political process, and in computerized programs that threaten to take the war out of human hands once it begins.

That nuclear weapons make it *possible* to compress the fury of global war into a few hours does not mean that they make it *inevitable.* We have still to ask whether that is the way a major nuclear war would be fought, or ought to be fought. Nevertheless, that the whole war might go off like one big string of firecrackers makes a critical difference between our conception of nuclear war and the world wars we have experienced. . . .

There is another difference. In the past it has usually been the victors who could do what they pleased to the enemy. War has often been "total war" for the loser. With deadly monotony the Persians, Greeks and Romans "put to death all men of military age, and sold the women and children into slavery," leaving the defeated territory nothing but its name until new settlers arrived sometime later. But the defeated could not do the same to their victors. The boys could be castrated and sold only after the war had been won, and only on the side that lost it. The power to hurt could be brought to bear only after military strength had achieved victory. The same sequence characterized the great wars of this century; for reasons of technology and geography, military force has usually had to penetrate, to exhaust, or to collapse opposing military force—to achieve military victory—before it could be brought to bear on the enemy nation itself. The Allies in World War I could not inflict coercive pain and suffering directly on the Germans in a decisive way until they could defeat the German army; and the Germans could not coerce the French people with bayonets unless they first beat the Allied troops that stood in their way. With two-dimensional warfare, there is a tendency for troops to confront each other, shielding their own lands while attempting to press into each other's. Small penetrations could not do major damage to the people; large penetrations were so destructive of military organization that they usually ended the military phase of the war.

Nuclear weapons make it possible to do monstrous violence to the enemy without first achieving victory. With nuclear weapons and today's means of delivery, one expects to penetrate an enemy homeland without first collapsing his military force. What nuclear weapons have done, or appear to do, is to promote this kind of warfare to first place. Nuclear weapons threaten to make war less military, and are responsible for the lowered status of "military victory" at the present time. *Victory is no longer a prerequisite for hurting the enemy.* And it is no assurance against being terribly hurt. One need not wait until he has won the war before inflicting "unendurable" damages on his enemy. One need not wait until he has lost the war. There was a time when the assurance of victory—false or genuine assurance—could make national leaders not just willing but sometimes enthusiastic about war. Not now.

Not only *can* nuclear weapons hurt the enemy before the war has been won, and perhaps hurt decisively enough to make the military engagement academic, but it is widely assumed that in a major war that is *all* they can do. Major war is often discussed as though it would be only a contest in national destruction. If this is indeed the case—if the destruction of cities and their populations has become, with nuclear weapons, the primary object in an all-out war—the sequence of war has been reversed. Instead of destroying enemy forces as a prelude to imposing one's will on the enemy nation, one would have to destroy the nation as a means or a prelude to destroying the enemy forces. If one cannot disable enemy forces without virtually destroying the country, the victor does not even have the option of sparing the conquered nation. He has already destroyed it. Even with blockade and strategic bombing it could be supposed that a country would be defeated before it was destroyed, or would elect surrender before annihilation had gone far. In the Civil War it could be hoped that the South would become too weak to fight before it became too weak to survive. For "all-out" war, nuclear weapons threaten to reverse this sequence.

So nuclear weapons do make a difference, marking an epoch in warfare. The difference is not just in the amount of destruction that can be accomplished but in the role of destruction and in the decision process. Nuclear weapons can change the speed of events, the control of events, the sequence of events, the relation of victor to vanquished, and the relation of homeland to fighting front. Deterrence rests today on the threat of pain and extinction, not just on the threat of military defeat. We may argue about the wisdom of announcing "unconditional surrender" as an aim in the last major war, but seem to expect "unconditional destruction" as a matter of course in another one.

Something like the same destruction always *could* be done. With nuclear weapons there is an expectation that it would be done. . . . What is new is . . . the idea that major war might be just a contest in the killing of countries, or not even a contest but just two parallel exercises in devastation.

That is the difference nuclear weapons make. At least they *may* make the difference. They also may not. If the weapons themselves are vulnerable to attack, or the machines that carry them, a successful surprise might eliminate the opponent's means of retribution. That an enormous explosion can be packaged in a single bomb does not by itself guarantee that the victor will receive deadly punishment.

Two gunfighters facing each other in a Western town had an unquestioned capacity to kill one another; that did not guarantee that both would die in a gunfight—only the slower of the two. Less deadly weapons, permitting an injured one to shoot back before he died, might have been more conducive to a restraining balance of terror, or of caution. The very efficiency of nuclear weapons could make them ideal for starting war, if they can suddenly eliminate the enemy's capability to shoot back.

And there is a contrary possibility: that nuclear weapons are not vulnerable to attack and prove not to be terribly effective against each other, posing no need to shoot them quickly for fear they will be destroyed before they are launched, and with no task available but the systematic destruction of the enemy country and no necessary reason to do it fast rather than slowly. Imagine that nuclear destruction had to go slowly—that the bombs could be dropped only one per day. The prospect would look very different, something like the most terroristic guerilla warfare on a massive scale. It happens that nuclear war does not have to go slowly; but it may also not have to go speedily. The mere existence of nuclear weapons does not itself determine that everything must go off in a blinding flash, any more than that it must go slowly. Nuclear weapons do not simplify things quite that much. . . .

In World Wars I and II one went to work on enemy military forces, not his people, because until the enemy's military forces had been taken care of there was typically not anything decisive that one could do to the enemy nation itself. The Germans did not, in World War I, refrain from bayoneting French citizens by the millions in the hopes that the Allies would abstain from shooting up the German population. They could not get at the French citizens until they had breached the Allied lines. Hitler tried to terrorize London and did not make it. The Allied air forces took the war straight to Hitler's territory, with at least some thought of doing in Germany what Sherman recognized he was doing in Georgia; but with the bombing technology of World War II one could not afford to bypass the troops and go exclusively for enemy populations—not, anyway, in Germany. With nuclear weapons one has that alternative.

To concentrate on the enemy's military installations while deliberately holding in reserve a massive capacity for destroying his cities, for exterminating his people and eliminating his society, on condition that the enemy observe similar restraint with respect to one's own society is not the "conventional approach." In World Wars I and II the first order of business was to destroy enemy armed forces because that was the only promising way to make him surrender. To fight a purely military engagement "all-out" while holding in reserve a decisive capacity for violence, on condition the enemy do likewise, is not the way military operations have traditionally been approached.

. . . In the present era noncombatants appear to be not only deliberate targets but primary targets. . . . In fact, noncombatants appeared to be primary targets at both ends of the scale of warfare; thermonuclear war threatened to be a contest in the destruction of cities and populations; and, at the other end of the scale, insurgency is almost entirely terroristic. We live in an era of dirty war.

Why is this so? Is war properly a military affair among combatants, and is it a depravity peculiar to the twentieth century that we cannot keep it within decent bounds? Or is war inherently dirty?

To answer this question it is useful to distinguish three stages in the involvement of noncombatants—of plain people and their possessions—in the fury of war. These stages are worth distinguishing; but their sequence is merely descriptive of Western Europe during the past three hundred years, not a historical generalization. The first stage is that in which the people may get hurt by inconsiderate combatants. This is the status that people had during the period of "civilized warfare" that the International Committee had in mind.

From about 1648 to the Napoleonic era, war in much of Western Europe was something superimposed on society. It was a contest engaged in by monarchies for stakes that were measured in territories, and, occasionally, money or dynastic claims. The troops were mostly mercenaries and the motivation for war was confined to the aristocratic elite. Monarchs fought for bits of territory, but the residents of disputed terrain were more concerned with protecting their crops and their daughters from marauding troops than with whom they owed allegiance to. They were, as Quincy Wright remarked in his classic *Study of War*, little concerned that the territory in which they lived had a new sovereign.[3] Furthermore, as far as the King of Prussia and the Emperor of Austria were concerned, the loyalty and enthusiasm of the Bohemian farmer were not decisive considerations. It is an exaggeration to refer to European war during this period as a sport of kings, but not a gross exaggeration. And the military logistics of those days confined military operations to a scale that did not require the enthusiasm of a multitude.

Hurting people was not a decisive instrument in warfare. Hurting people or destroying property only reduced the value of things that were being fought over, to the disadvantage of both sides. Furthermore, the monarchs who conducted wars often did not want to discredit the social institutions they shared with their enemies. Bypassing an enemy monarch and taking the war straight to his people would have had revolutionary implications. Destroying the opposing monarchy was often not in the interest of either side; opposing sovereigns had much more in common with each other than with their own subjects, and to discredit the claims of a monarchy might have produced a disastrous backlash. It is not surprising—or, if it is surprising, not altogether astonishing—that on the European continent in that particular era war was fairly well confined to military activity.

One could still, in those days and in that part of the world, be concerned for the rights of noncombatants and hope to devise rules that both sides in the war might observe. The rules might well be observed because both sides had something to gain from preserving social order and not destroying the enemy. Rules might be a nuisance, but if they restricted both sides the disadvantages might cancel out.

This was changed during the Napoleonic wars. In Napoleon's France, people cared about the outcome. The nation was mobilized. The war was a national effort, not just an activity of the elite. It was both political and military genius on the part of Napoleon and his ministers that an entire nation could be mobilized for war. Propaganda became a tool of warfare, and war became vulgarized.

Many writers deplored this popularization of war, this involvement of the democratic masses. In fact, the horrors we attribute to thermonuclear war were already foreseen by many commentators, some before the First World War and more after it, but the new "weapon" to which these terrors were ascribed was people, millions of people, passionately engaged in national wars, spending themselves in a quest for total victory and desperate to avoid total defeat. Today we are impressed that a small number of highly trained pilots can carry enough energy to blast and burn tens of millions of people and the buildings they live in; two or three generations ago there was concern that tens of millions of people using bayonets and barbed wire, machine guns and shrapnel, could create the same kind of destruction and disorder.

That was the second stage in the relation of people to war, the second in Europe since the middle of the seventeenth century. In the first stage people had been neutral but their welfare might be disregarded; in the second stage people were involved because it was *their* war. Some fought, some produced materials of war, some produced food, and some took care of children; but they were all part of a war-making nation. When Hitler attacked Poland in 1939, the Poles had reason to care about the outcome. When Churchill said the British would fight on the beaches, he spoke for the British and not for a mercenary army. The war was about something that mattered. If people would rather fight a dirty war than lose a clean one, the war will be between nations and not just between governments. If people have an influence on whether the war is continued or on the terms of a truce, making the war hurt people serves a purpose. It is a dirty purpose, but war itself is often about something dirty. The Poles and the Norwegians, the Russians and the British, had reason to believe that if they lost the war the consequences would be dirty. This is so evident in modern civil wars—civil wars that involve popular feelings—that we expect them to be bloody and violent. To hope that they would be fought cleanly with no violence to people would be a little like hoping for a clean race riot.

There is another way to put it that helps to bring out the sequence of events. If a modern war were a clean one, the violence would not be ruled out but merely saved for the postwar period. Once the army has been defeated in the clean war, the victorious enemy can be as brutally coercive as he wishes. A clean war would determine which side gets to use its power to hurt coercively after victory, and it is likely to be worth some violence to avoid being the loser.

"Surrender" is the process following military hostilities in which the power to hurt is brought to bear. If surrender negotiations are successful and not followed by overt violence, it is because the capacity to inflict pain and damage was successfully used in the bargaining process. On the losing side, prospective pain and damage were averted by concessions; on the winning side, the capacity for inflicting further harm was traded for concessions. The same is true in a successful kidnapping. It only reminds us that the purpose of pure pain and damage is extortion; it is *latent* violence that can be used to advantage. A well-behaved occupied country is not one in which violence plays no part; it may be one in which latent violence is used so skillfully that it need not be spent in punishment.

This brings us to the third stage in the relation of civilian violence to warfare. If the pain and damage can be inflicted during war itself, they need not wait for the surrender negotiation that succeeds a military decision. If one can coerce people and their governments while war is going on, one does not need to wait until he has achieved victory or risk losing that coercive power by spending it all in a losing war. General Sherman's march through Georgia might have made as much sense, possibly more, had the North been losing the war, just as the German buzz bombs and V–2 rockets can be thought of as coercive instruments to get the war stopped before suffering military defeat.

In the present era, since at least the major East-West powers are capable of massive civilian violence during war itself beyond anything available during the Second World War, the occasion for restraint does not await the achievement of military victory or truce. The principal restraint during the Second World War was a temporal boundary, the date of surrender. In the present era we find the violence dramatically restrained during war itself. The Korean War was furiously "all-out" in the fighting, not only on the peninsular battlefield but in the resources used by both sides. It was "all-out," though, only within some dramatic restraints; no nuclear weapons, no Russians, no Chinese territory, no Japanese territory, no bombing of ships at sea or even airfields on the United Nations side of the line. It was a contest in military strength circumscribed by the threat of unprecedented civilian violence. Korea may or may not be a good model for speculation on limited war in the age of nuclear violence, but it was dramatic evidence that the capacity for violence can be consciously restrained even under the provocation of war that measures its military dead in tens of thousands and that fully preoccupies two of the largest countries in the world.

A consequence of this third stage is that "victory" inadequately expresses what a nation wants from its military forces. Mostly it wants, in these times, the influence that resides in latent force. It wants the bargaining power that comes from its capacity to hurt, not just the direct consequence of successful military action. Even total victory over an enemy provides at best an opportunity for unopposed violence against the enemy population. How to use that opportunity in the national interest, or in some wider interest, can be just as important as the achievement of victory itself; but traditional military science does not tell us how to use that capacity for inflicting pain. And if a nation, victor or potential loser, is going to use its capacity for pure violence to influence the enemy, there may be no need to await the achievement of total victory.

Actually, this third stage can be analyzed into two quite different variants. In one, sheer pain and damage are primary instruments of coercive warfare and may actually be applied, to intimidate or to deter. In the other, pain and destruction *in* war are expected to serve little or no purpose but *prior threats* of sheer violence, even of automatic and uncontrolled violence, are coupled to military force. The difference is in the all-or-none character of deterrence and intimidation. Two acute dilemmas arise. One is the choice of making prospective violence as frightening as possible or hedging with some capacity for reciprocated restraint. The other is the choice of making retaliation as automatic as possible or keeping deliberate control over the fateful decisions. The choices are determined partly by governments, partly by technology. Both variants are characterized by the coercive role of pain and destruction—of threatened (not inflicted) pain and destruction. But in one the threat either succeeds or fails altogether, and any ensuing violence is gratuitous; in the other, progressive pain and damage may actually be used to threaten more. The present era, for countries possessing nuclear weapons, is a complex and uncertain blend of the two. . . .

The power to hurt is nothing new in warfare, but for the United States modern technology has drastically enhanced the strategic importance of pure, unconstructive, unacquisitive pain and damage, whether used against us or in our own defense. This in turn enhances the importance of war and threats of war as techniques of influence, not of destruction; of coercion and deterrence, not of conquest and defense; of bargaining and intimidation. . . .

War no longer looks like just a contest of strength. War and the brink of war are more a contest of nerve and risk-taking, of pain and endurance. Small wars embody the threat of a larger war; they are not just military engagements but "crisis diplomacy." The threat of war has always been somewhere underneath international diplomacy, but for Americans it is now much nearer the surface. Like the threat of a strike in industrial relations, the threat of divorce in a family dispute, or the threat of bolting the party at a political convention, the threat of violence continuously circumscribes international politics. Neither strength nor goodwill procures immunity.

Military strategy can no longer be thought of, as it could for some countries in some eras, as the science of military victory. It is now equally, if not more, the art of coercion, of intimidation and deterrence. The instruments of war are more punitive than acquisitive. Military strategy, whether we like it or not, has become the diplomacy of violence.

NOTES

1. Paul I. Wellman, *Death on the Prairie* (New York: Macmillan, 1934), p. 82.
2. Winston Churchill is often credited with the term, "balance of terror," and the following quotation succinctly expresses the familiar notion of nuclear mutual deterrence. This, though, is from a speech in Commons in November 1934. "The fact remains that when all is said and done as regards defensive methods, pending some new discovery the only direct measure of defense upon a great scale is the certainty of being able to inflict simultaneously upon the enemy as great damage as he can inflict upon ourselves. Do not let us undervalue the efficiency of this procedure. It may well prove in practice—I admit I cannot prove it in theory—capable of giving complete immunity. If two Powers show themselves equally capable of inflicting damage upon each other by some particular process of war, so that neither gains an advantage from its adoption and both suffer the most hideous reciprocal injuries, it is not only possible but it seems probable that neither will employ that means. . . "
3. (Chicago: University of Chicago Press), 1942, p. 296.

Coercive Diplomacy

ROBERT J. ART

Coercive diplomacy is, in Alexander George's words, "forceful persuasion": the attempt to get a target—a state, a group (or groups) within a state, or a nonstate actor—to change its objectionable behavior through either the threat to use force or the actual use of limited force. It is a strategy that "seeks to *persuade* an opponent to cease his aggression rather than bludgeon him into stopping." Coercive diplomacy can include, but need not include, positive inducements, and these inducements can involve either a transfer of resources to the target or the offer of things that do not involve resource transfer but that are nonetheless of tangible benefit to the target. Coercive diplomacy is intended to be an alternative to war, even though it involves some employment of military power to achieve a state's desired objective. It is a technique for achieving objectives "on the cheap" and has allure because it promises big results with small costs (to the coercer). Next to outright war, however, coercive diplomacy represents the most dangerous way to use a state's military power because, if coercive diplomacy fails, the state that tries it then faces two stark choices: back down or wage war. The first risks loss of face and future bargaining power; the second, loss of life and military defeat. Because both outcomes are possible, a state should never undertake coercive diplomacy lightly . . . we distinguish between coercive diplomacy and coercive attempts. The feature that distinguishes the two is the presence or absence of the employment of force. Coercive diplomacy has as one of its essential features, and often its only feature, the threat or the limited use of force. Coercive attempts utilize levers over a target, but these levers do not involve the threat or use of force. Therefore, we have excluded from our cases of coercive diplomacy those coercive attempts that involve only the use of economic sanctions, only the withholding of benefits to a target, only the cessation of benefits that a target currently enjoys, or more generally any coercive attempt that does not entail some employment of military power. Clearly, all these actions are coercive in nature, but they do not constitute coercive diplomacy as we have defined it. In distinguishing between coercive attempts and coercive diplomacy, we follow the convention set by George: coercive diplomacy must involve the threat or limited use of force, even though it can also include some of these other types of coercive actions.

Because it entails coercion, coercive diplomacy is a form of compellence—a term first coined by Thomas Schelling in order to distinguish it from deterrence. For Schelling, the distinction between compellence and deterrence is the difference between an action "intended to make an adversary do something"—compellence—and an action "intended to keep him from starting something"—deterrence. The change in behavior sought by compellence can be manifested in one of two ways: either the adversary starts doing something it is not now doing, or the adversary stops doing something it is now doing. Either way, the adversary changes its behavior. Deterrence, in contrast, is a strategy designed to prevent an adversary from changing its behavior by dissuading it from initiating an action. Deterrence seeks to get the adversary not to change its behavior—that is, to continue "not doing what it is not doing." Thus, compellence aims to alter an adversary's behavior; deterrence, to keep it the same. Deterrence generally involves only threats to use force, whereas compellence can involve both the threat to use force and the actual use of force. In a deterrent situation, if the threat has to be carried out, then, by definition, the adversary has changed its behavior and deterrence has failed. In contrast, because compellence can entail both threats and actual use of force, compellence has not necessarily failed if the threats are carried out.

Although deterrence and compellence are analytically distinct strategies, they usually become conflated when disputing parties contest the legitimacy of the status quo, which they generally do. The deterrer defends the status quo because of the benefits it confers; the target tries to overthrow the status quo because of the injury it inflicts. The target views the deterrer's attempt to maintain the status quo as compellence: "You are coercing me (the target) to accept a situation that benefits you but not me." If the target attempts to alter the status quo, however, then the deterrer will view that attempt as compellence: "You are attempting to coerce me (the deterrer) to stop defending the status quo and accept a revision in it that is less beneficial to me." In such a situation, deterrence and compellence become intermingled. Similarly, deterrent threats can become transformed into compellent actions in situations where deterrence has failed, for in that case the would-be deterrer must decide whether to carry out its threat. If it does so, not for purposes of revenge but to get the adversary to stop its objectionable behavior, then, by definition, execution of the deterrent threat becomes a compellent action. Finally, the deterrer may calculate that deterrence is weakening, even though it has not totally failed, and may decide to bolster deterrence by engaging in actions that are compellent in nature. In that case, compellence is exercised to deter.

Compellence can come in three doses or forms: (1) diplomatic use—the issuance of threats to use force against an adversary if it does not change its behavior, (2) demonstrative use—the exemplary and limited uses of force, and (3) full-scale use, or war—the use of whatever amount of force it takes to get the adversary to change its behavior. The first form of compellence does not use force physically against the target state but only threatens use. The second form uses "just enough force of an appropriate kind to demonstrate resolution to protect one's interests and to establish the credibility of one's determination to use more force if necessary." The third form is to be understood as war—the large-scale use of military power to make the adversary change its behavior. In this volume we follow Alexander George and define coercive diplomacy to encompass only the first two forms of compellence—the diplomatic and demonstrative uses of force. The third form—war—is coercion but not coercive diplomacy, even though diplomacy is never totally absent from war.

The meanings of threat and war are clear. Threat can involve mobilizing and moving large amounts of military force to make the coercer's seriousness of purpose as credible as possible to the target state, or it can simply mean the issuance of verbal warnings. The one thing threat does not mean is the actual physical use of force against the target. War involves sustained, large-scale combat operations against the target, with the goal of either militarily defeating it or bringing about its surrender short of achieving a complete victory over it. Either way, war involves the use of force that is massive, at least to the target.

The meaning of demonstrative use is more difficult to pin down. Although George argues that demonstrative should mean only the "quite limited" use of force, we have used a somewhat broader meaning of demonstrative use. How much is "just enough force" to demonstrate resolution and establish credibility can vary enormously from one situation to another and depends on the nature of the coercer's goals, on the one hand, and on the military capabilities and intensity of interests of the target, on the other. We have therefore defined demonstrative use to include both exemplary and limited use. Exemplary use serves as both a model and a warning of what can or will come: "You did not believe my threat; here is an example for you to chew on of what I can do to you if you do not change your ways." Exemplary use can encompass a one-time employment of force, or a few instances of use, but the major constraint is that it is at the low end of force employment, close to the boundary between threat and use. Exemplary use means moving just beyond the border of threat to make clear by the actions taken that the coercer is deadly serious about escalating the use of force if the target does not comply. In this volume limited use can mean anything from one to several steps beyond exemplary use. The meaning of limited use is this: "You failed to take both my threat and my exemplary use seriously; you obviously need more persuading; let me now give you a better idea of the consequences that your continued non-compliance will bring." More force is used, but not so much such that the boundary to war has been crossed.

A central point follows when coercive diplomacy is conceived to encompass only threat and demonstrative use, but not full-scale use: coercive diplomacy has failed when full-scale use occurs. Wherever one draws the line between limited and full-scale use, if the coercer has to cross that line to achieve its objectives, then, by definition, coercive diplomacy has failed. In this case, war, not coercive diplomacy, produced the change. Any employment of force beyond threat, exemplary use, or limited use signals the failure of coercive diplomacy, even though the subsequent full-scale use of force may succeed in accomplishing the original objectives. As a consequence, exactly where the boundary between limited and full-scale use is drawn becomes crucial for coding cases in which limited use involves escalatory steps that skirt the boundary. Such cases can be coded as either successes or failures of coercive diplomacy, depending on which side of the boundary it is placed. Categorizing such cases becomes an exercise in qualitative judgment. . . .

WHY IS COERCIVE DIPLOMACY DIFFICULT?

There are good theoretical reasons why coercive diplomacy is difficult. In particular, four factors, which stem from the inherent nature of coercive diplomacy and which therefore operate in every such attempt, explain why this technique is hard to pull off. In addition, depending on the specific situation, two other factors can manifest themselves, and when they are present, they make the successful exercise of coercive diplomacy even more difficult.

Compellence Is Difficult

First, coercive diplomacy is a form of compellence and, as Thomas Schelling observed, compellence is harder to pull off than deterrence. It is intrinsically more difficult to get a target to change its behavior than to keep its behavior as is. Compellent actions require that the target alter its behavior in a manner quite visible to all in response to an equally visible initiative taken by the coercer. In contrast, deterrent threats are easier for the target to appear to have ignored or to acquiesce in without great loss of face. In deterrent situations the target can claim plausible deniability, maintaining that it had no intention of changing its behavior in the first place, or it can simply appear to ignore the deterrent threats while not changing its behavior. The target has no such plausible deniability in the case of compellence because its overt submission is required. Greater face is thus lost when a target, under pressure, reverses a course of action to which it has committed its prestige and devoted resources than when it simply persists in the same behavior. Finally, compellence more directly engages the passions of the target state than does deterrence because of the pain and humiliation inflicted upon it, but passions, once engaged, are dangerous and produce boomerang effects: they cause the government to mobilize domestic opinion against the coercer, and they increase domestic support for the target government. Both effects perversely make the government more popular after it becomes subject to coercive action than it was before, with the ironic result that the target becomes less susceptible to coercive diplomacy. For these reasons, compellence is harder than deterrence.

Denial, Punishment, and Risk Strategies Are Hard with Diplomatic and Demonstrative Uses of Force

Coercive diplomacy is a form of coercion, and coercion, as Robert Pape has argued, can be applied in a denial, punishment, or risk fashion.[1] Denial strategies seek to change an adversary's behavior by thwarting its military strategy. Denial takes aim at the target's military forces in order to undercut their effectiveness, seeking to stalemate these forces rather than bring outright military victory over them. A successful denial strategy is one that prevents the target from achieving its political objectives with its military strategy. Punishment strategies seek to change an adversary's behavior by raising the costs of its continued resistance. Punishment imposes pain, either directly to the target's population or to those assets that are important for the population's or the leadership's quality of life. A successful punishment strategy is one that causes the target to give way, not because its military strategy has been thwarted, but because the costs to its population have become too great. Risk strategies seek to change an adversary's behavior by raising the probability that it will suffer ever-greater punishment in the future if it fails to comply. Risk means escalation, and risk threatens more pain to the population or to its valuable assets. A successful risk strategy is one that causes the target to give way because it becomes convinced that the pain it will suffer from looming punishment is not worth the objectives it seeks.

To the extent that it is applied to produce risk, coercive diplomacy is inherently difficult to pull off because risk strategies, Pape tells us, are inherently difficult. They fail for several reasons. For starters, risk strategies are successful to the extent that they create in the target's mind fear of future punishment sufficiently costly that the target changes its behavior. As Pape points out, however, the pain suffered from damage done in the present is greater than the pain imagined from damage done in the future. This happens because human beings discount the future, which means they value the present more. Risk should be conceived as future punishment, and imagined future pain hurts less than present pain. Moreover, because of political considerations, risk strategies are generally applied incrementally, with the coercer gradually ratcheting up the pain inflicted. This produces more perverse effects: the target has time to adapt its tactics to reduce the damage done, time to get used to the pain being inflicted, and time to mobilize domestic opinion against the foreign intruder—all of which make the target better able to tolerate the pain being doled out by the coercer. Finally, when the pain is only threatened or is severely limited when inflicted, as is the case, by definition, with coercive diplomacy, then a coercive risk strategy becomes all the more difficult.

For similar reasons, punishment and denial strategies are difficult to execute with coercive diplomacy. After all, it is hard to inflict much punishment with coercive diplomacy: the limited use of force produces only limited punishment. Delivering limited punishment is not likely to cause a target that cares a great deal about its objectives to change course. Similarly, the threat to deny is not denial, and the limited use of force can produce only limited denial. Strictly speaking, coercive diplomacy cannot employ denial in the sense that it cannot use enough force to stalemate a target. Instead, to the extent that coercive diplomacy aims at denial, it employs "demonstrative denial." Through limited military action the coercer demonstrates to the target that the coercer can, if it so chooses, undercut the effectiveness of the target's military strategy but without actually undercutting it.

Whether the coercer intends to employ its military power to manipulate risk, inflict punishment, or execute denial, all three are hard to bring off when the employment of military power is severely constricted, as it is with coercive diplomacy. To the coercer, its threats and limited use are intended to signal its firm resolve to escalate the use of force—for risk, punishment, or denial purposes—unless the target knuckles under, but the target, especially a highly motivated one, can just as easily see threats and limited use as signaling weak resolve. After all, if the coercer cares that much about its objective, why pull its punches in the first place? What looks to the coercer as steely determination can appear to the target as an unwillingness or inability to employ large-scale use of force to attain its goal. Threats and limited use are not unequivocal in their meaning; they can be interpreted to signify both firmness and weakness in resolve, depending on the perspective of the viewer.

Some of these dynamics appear to have been at work in the Kosovo War. Before the war, the NATO allies thought that Slobodan Milosevic would cave in after a few days of bombing, because they concluded, incorrectly, that he had done so once before—in September 1995, after a period of short intensive bombing strikes against Serbian forces in Bosnia. In 1999, however, Milosevic proved them wrong. Apparently, he believed that he could ride out a few days of bombing and calculated that the alliance could not hold together if it engaged in a sustained, heavy bombing campaign against him. Believing he could outlast the alliance, he forced NATO to resort to an extensive air campaign and ultimately to threaten a ground campaign in order to win the war.

In sum, neither significant punishment nor significant denial is possible with coercive diplomacy. Therefore, what coercive diplomacy can most easily communicate to the target is the increasing probability of more punishment to come if it fails to comply, which is risk, and also some indication of the denial powers of the coercer.

Estimating Resolve Is Difficult

The third reason that coercive diplomacy is hard to execute lies in the fact that estimating resolve both before and during a coercive diplomatic attempt is a tricky affair and therefore easy to get wrong. Resolve refers to the strength of a party's will to prevail, and the balance of resolve refers to whose will—the target's or the coercer's—is the stronger. Before the fact, the coercer can never know for certain whose resolve is the stronger—its own or the target's. Indeed, this is the function of the crisis produced by the resort to coercive diplomacy: to test the relative strength of the two parties' resolves. Coercive diplomatic attempts are games of chicken that reveal to the target and the coercer which one cares more about something and just how much more. After all, if the relative strength of the parties' resolves were known before coercive diplomacy began, then there would be no reason to begin it. If the target knew, for example, that it cared much less than the coercer and knew that the coercer was intent on getting its way no matter what, and if the coercer also knew that the target cared less than it did, then the target would most likely relent at the first signs of serious intent by the coercer. In serious disputes, however, this does not happen because each party cares intensely about its respective goals. Hence, the resulting crisis serves the function of demonstrating who cares more.

Even if the coercer accurately estimates the relative strength of the two parties' resolves before the crisis gets under way, this is no guarantee that their resolves will remain the same once the crisis begins. Indeed, once it begins, resolves can change and usually do, but generally in the direction of greater firmness by both parties. Each party digs in, in order to see how strongly the other cares. Moreover, when threats are made, and especially when some force is used, both sides are likely to harden their initial positions even more, because the use of force engages passions and almost always causes both the target and the coercer to stiffen their wills. As a consequence, both will bear more sacrifice in order to justify the pain already suffered.

Economists argue that sunk costs should be ignored when making current decisions. Their motto is, "Never throw good money after bad." Statesmen, however, cannot ignore sunk costs because of political considerations: the costs already incurred impel them to pour in even more resources. Their motto is, "Sacrifices already borne justify those currently being made." As a consequence, initial resolves are likely to harden, not weaken, under the impact of a coercive attempt; threats to use force are likely to lead to exemplary use; and exemplary use is likely to lead to full-scale use of force. Therefore, as Glenn Snyder and Paul Diesing have demonstrated, crises that look like games of chicken have an inherent dynamic toward escalation before they are resolved because neither party will give way at the outset.[2] None of this is to argue that coercive diplomacy is inevitably doomed to fail, only that the odds are not in its favor when the resulting crisis hardens the initial resolves of the parties.

Credibility and Power Are at Stake

Fourth, coercive diplomacy is difficult because the target has to worry about the effects of a confrontation not only on its credibility stakes but also on its power stakes. Credibility stakes concern reputation; power stakes, capabilities. Both are involved in the target's calculations about whether to stand firm or give way to the coercer. Credibility considerations make compromise difficult enough for the target because they involve the following sorts of issues: if the target gives way on this matter, will this be the coercer's last demand, or is it only the first in a series of demands? Even if the coercer will not demand more, what will the effects of giving way to this coercer have on other would-be coercers? In this regard a target is in the same situation that British leaders were in when dealing with Hitler in the late 1930s: will appeasement satiate Hitler, or will it only whet his appetite and that of other potential coercers as well? Actions in the present always set precedents for the future, and the target can never ignore how its reactions to pressures from others will affect its reputation.

Power stakes are equally, if not more, important. Giving way to the coercer is usually not cost free for the target's power. For example, when the United Nations began to push for representative councils in Somalia in March 1993, Mohammed Farah Aideed, the most powerful of the Somali warlords, understood that he would lose a lot of territory and hence power if representative councils were to emerge in a reconstructed Somalia. He therefore resisted the establishment of these councils. Similarly, both Iraq and North Korea would have faced a significant weakening in their military power if they had acceded to U.S. demands to give up their programs to acquire weapons of mass destruction. North Korea demanded a great deal in return, and Iraq tried to do everything to thwart UN inspectors. Hence, when giving way means that the target's future capacity to resist is significantly diminished, its incentives to stand firm go up dramatically. In these situations a coercive diplomatic demand looks to the target like unilateral disarmament: actions that are being demanded of the target weaken its future power. Thus, giving way represents a double whammy for the target because both its reputation for resolve and its ability to stand firm are undercut.

The inherent difficulty of both compellent and risk strategies, the formidable task of estimating resolves before and during crises, and the target's concern for its power and credibility stakes—all make every attempt at coercive diplomacy hard, not easy, to bring off. Two other factors can complicate the task even further when they are present.

Multiple Coercers and Multiple Targets Complicate Coercive Diplomacy

Coercive diplomacy becomes even more demanding in situations in which more than a single coercer and a single target are present. If there is a coalition of coercers, it may be united in its overall goal, but more often than not, the coalition will be divided over the means to achieve the goal. Sometimes the coalition will even be divided on the goal itself. If either is the case, then actions are required to keep the members united in their effort. The rub lies here: actions taken to hold the coalition together can degrade the military and diplomatic effectiveness of the coercive attempt. If several targets are present, it becomes more difficult to design actions that coerce them all. Sometimes steps that coerce one of the parties can actually encourage the others to resist. Other times it may be necessary to favor one of the targets in order to induce the others to cooperate. The presence of two or more targets thus requires that the coercer devise actions that ultimately induce all the targets to change their behavior. Neither holding together a coalition while maintaining its military effectiveness nor devising actions to alter the behavior of all the targets is an easy task to accomplish, and success in such situations requires finesse, diplomacy, patience, compromise, and, oftentimes, duplicity. Thus, two or more parties at either the target or the coercer end, or both, complicate what is already an inherently difficult task.

Five of our cases—Bosnia, Kosovo, Iraq, Somalia, and even North Korea—involved more than two parties, and complications ensued as a consequence. Steven Burg and Paul Shoup report that NATO's bombing in late August and early September 1995, which helped end the Bosnian War, was a two-edged sword. It helped bring the Serbs to the negotiating table, but it also encouraged the Muslims and Croats, who were allied at that time, to continue to resist and achieve all their goals through continued battle, using NATO as their air force. As a consequence NATO had to walk a fine line between bombing the Serbs enough to bring them to the negotiating table and bombing them not so much that it pushed the Croatian-Muslim alliance away from the negotiating table.[3] The Kosovo War witnessed serious conflicts among the NATO members over the selection of targets for the bombing campaign. The United States wanted to escalate both the scope and the intensity of the bombing more quickly than did many of its European allies, and these conflicts threatened the cohesiveness of the coalition and probably the efficiency of the bombing campaign, even if they did not ultimately degrade the campaign's military effectiveness. The coalition against Iraq, united during the war, began to fall apart during the 1990s as members became more and more disaffected with the continuing costs of the sanctions. The intervention in Somalia had to deal with dozens of factions vying for power, with two of them, one led by Ali Mahdi Mohammed and the other by Mohammed Farah Aideed, being the most important. Ali Mahdi cooperated more with the United Nations than did Aideed, who viewed the United Nations and the actions it took as hurting his interests and benefiting Ali Mahdi's. This set the stage for the armed confrontation that led to the collapse of the United Nations' mission in Somalia. Finally, even though the United States was the only coercer of North Korea, it could not ignore the views and interests of both South Korea and Japan, its close allies in the region. Their views made U.S. air strikes on North Korea's nuclear facilities difficult because of the fear they would release radioactive material that could disperse over both Japan and South Korea as well as re-ignite the Korean War.

Belief in "Counter-Coercion" Techniques Can Foil Coercive Diplomacy

Finally, if the target believes that it has the ability to counter the coercer's diplomatic and military pressures, then coercive diplomacy becomes so difficult that it will generally fail. The task for the coercer is to convince the target that sufficient pain and suffering will ensue if the target does not cease its actions. If the target believes that it can foil or significantly mitigate the coercer's measures or in turn impose risks on the coercer, through what are called "counter-coercion" techniques, which can be political, economic, or military in nature, then the target is much less likely to give way. Milosevic must have made such calculations when contemplating NATO's air war against him, because in the months before the war, Serbian military figures visited Iraq to see if they could learn how to thwart U.S. airpower. One device the Serbs hit upon was not to fire most of their surface-to-air missiles (SAMs) but instead to hold them back. This forced NATO pilots to fly at high altitudes over Kosovo and impeded their ability to knock out Serbian armor placed there. Thus, believing that he had the means to ride out an air war, Milosevic did not back down under NATO's threats.

Matters become especially vexing in those situations in which the target will not reveal its counter-coercion techniques for fear that doing so will negate their effectiveness. Not all counter-coercion techniques are undermined if the target makes them known beforehand to the coercer. Indeed, there are often strong incentives to make such measures known ahead of time if doing so will deter the coercer from undertaking his actions. For example, before the onset of the Persian Gulf War, Saddam Hussein argued that Americans could not suffer heavy casualties the way that Iraqis could, thereby attempting to make Iraqi willingness to suffer more than the Americans a counter-coercion tool for deterrence. In the Kosovo conflict there is credible evidence that Milosevic believed his threat to expel large numbers of Albanians from Kosovo to surrounding states in order to destabilize them would deter the NATO alliance from launching the air war against him. The counter-coercion measures that the target must conceal are those that the coercer can quickly design around once they become known, thereby enabling it to make the threat of significant punishment once again credible. In these cases the target has no incentive to forewarn the coercer of its counter-coercion techniques because such foreknowledge would degrade the target's defenses against the coercer's attack, not enhance deterrence of it.

The target's failure to reveal its counter-coercion techniques produces a perverse result: not only does it make the coercer's resort to coercive diplomacy more likely; it also raises the probability that the attempt will fail. Ignorant that its initial measures might be thwarted, the coercer will begin its coercive diplomatic maneuver. Confident that it can defend itself, the target then applies its counter-coercion methods to undermine the coercer's gambit once it begins. The coercer then works furiously to devise its own counters to the target's counters; the target responds in kind; both persist in their respective actions, pouring more into their respective efforts. In short, the dynamics of crisis behavior take over, and the confrontation escalates from threats and exemplary use to the third stage of coercion—war. Thus, when a target believes that it possesses effective counter-coercion techniques that cannot be revealed, it will not find the coercer's threats or exemplary use of force credible, and full-scale use of force will be required if the coercer wants to get its way.

In sum, these six factors explain why coercive diplomacy is difficult. The first four are "permanently operating factors" and explain why, even if executed well, coercive diplomacy often fails. The last two are occasional factors, present or absent depending on the exact nature of the coercive diplomatic attempt. The first five factors make coercive diplomacy inherently hard but not impossible. The last factor— the target's belief that it has effective counter-coercion techniques—makes it highly likely, if not guaranteed, that coercive diplomacy will fail.

CONCLUSION: WHAT POLICY GUIDELINES CAN BE OFFERED?

Based on the logic and evidence presented, what guidelines can we give to policymakers who are contemplating resort to coercive diplomacy? Six seem in order.

- *First, coercive diplomacy is difficult and has a relatively low success rate.*
- *Second, it is difficult to estimate the likely outcome of any given coercive diplomatic gambit.*
- *Third, possession of military superiority over the target does not guarantee success at coercive diplomacy.*
- *Fourth, positive inducements seem to enhance the likelihood of success, but only if they are offered after the threatened or actual use of exemplary or limited force.*

- *Fifth, demonstrative denial works better than limited punishment for coercive diplomacy.*
- *Sixth, never resort to coercive diplomacy unless you are prepared to go to war should it fail, or unless you have devised a suitable political escape hatch if war is not acceptable.*

Because the fourth and fifth guidelines have already been discussed at length in the preceding section, I deal here with only the other four.

1. Coercive Diplomacy Is Difficult

As I argued earlier, coercive diplomacy is difficult because coercion in general is difficult and because coercive diplomacy is the most difficult form of coercion. The case studies [examined] . . . show that coercive diplomacy has a success rate of 32 percent. Even that figure may be too high because two of our cases (Bosnia 1995 and Haiti 1994) were borderline successes and because one (Iraq 1993) may not be a success at all. A tougher coding could easily rank all three as failures, driving the success rate down significantly.

Standing alone, this 32 percent figure lacks context, but fortunately we have some statistics on how other instruments and strategies compare—not as much as we would like but enough to provide some context within which to place the record of coercive diplomacy. The evidence concerning economic sanctions provides a useful starting point, because the imposition of sanctions is roughly analogous to what happens in coercive diplomacy: something is done to try to force a change in a target's behavior without going to war against it. Although the primary instrument of each differs (military versus economic), the objectives and general method of procedure of both are roughly the same. The evidence on sanctions is remarkably similar to our coercive diplomacy data. Gary Hufbauer, Jeffrey Schott, and Kimberly Elliot have produced the most comprehensive study to date of economic sanctions, having reviewed 120 cases in the twentieth century when sanctions were imposed. They concluded that sanctions worked 33 percent of the time to produce a modest change in the target's policies and 25 percent of the time to produce a major policy change. These figures are not identical to the upper and lower bounds of the success rate for our coercive diplomacy cases, but they are close enough to support the proposition that coercion short of war through either economic or economic-military means is difficult and fails more than it succeeds.

Still, the data on sanctions do not provide sufficient context because it could be the case that most other types of diplomatic gambits also fail more than they succeed. Fortunately, we have one other evidentiary benchmark that shows this does not have to be the case and that helps put into comparative perspective the success rate of coercion short of war. It concerns extended deterrence—a diplomatic gambit wherein one state (the defender) tries to protect another (the protégé) from attack by a third party (the attacker). Paul Huth and Bruce Russett studied the universe of cases of extended deterrence—fifty-four such instances— from 1900 to 1980. They found that extended deterrence was successful in thirty-one of these cases, for a success rate of 57 percent. The Huth-Russett study not

TABLE 5 ■ COMPARATIVE SUCCESS RATES

Type of Strategy or Instrument	Success Rate
Coercive diplomacy	32%
Economic sanctions	25–33%
Extended deterrence	57%

only shows that some political-military uses of force can succeed more than they fail but also provides empirical support for the proposition that deterrence is easier than compellence.

Table 5 displays the success rates for these three data sets. Taken together, the evidence about economic sanctions, coercive diplomacy, and extended deterrence gives us greater confidence that coercive diplomacy's success rate is not due simply to flawed execution and, therefore, that coercion short of war is indeed an inherently difficult enterprise. . . .

2. Estimating Outcomes Is Difficult

We have seen that positive inducements and denial strategies enhance the likelihood of success at coercive diplomacy, but they alone cannot guarantee success because the size of the disparity in resolve between the coercer and the target plays a significant role in determining the outcome. Therefore, determining before the fact whether any given coercive diplomatic attempt will be successful is also hard, and again the problem derives from the inherent difficulty of estimating relative resolves.

First, before the coercive diplomatic crisis begins, the coercer cannot know the strength of the target's resolve compared with its own, nor can it fully know how strongly the target is attached to the interest it is trying to defend. Oftentimes in such situations, the coercer may not be fully certain about the strength of its own resolve and how firmly it is committed to the interests it is defending. The same may be true for the target. To complicate matters, the coercer will find it difficult to credibly communicate to the target just how strong its resolve is, because only resort to war will reveal the full lengths to which it is prepared to go to prevail. War, however, is generally not desired by the coercer since it has chosen coercive diplomacy in the hope of avoiding war. It is therefore inherently hard for the coercer to persuade the target that it is prepared to wage war if coercive diplomacy fails when the coercer has chosen a step short of war to signify the seriousness of its intent. Furthermore, for its part, the target will, more often than not, believe that it has effective counter-coercion instruments available to it, some of which it will want to hide and some or all of which will cause it to believe that it can persevere and ultimately prevail in the test of wills. If the coercer cannot fully reveal its resolve and if the target believes it can counter the coercer, then accurately predicting the outcome of the encounter is difficult. Finally, under the impact of events, wills can change, standing interests can take on different values, and new interests can be formed.

All these factors make *ex ante* estimation of outcomes extraordinarily difficult. As a consequence, the United States should be wary of putting high confidence in estimates about the likely outcome of any given coercive diplomatic attempt. This also means that it should put little confidence in the notion that the less demanding changes in a target's behavior are easier to bring about than the more demanding ones.

3. Military Superiority Is No Guarantee of Success

In every one of our cases, the United States possessed military capabilities far superior to the target's. If military superiority alone guaranteed success, then the United States should have had a 100 percent success rate. The fact that it had only a 32 percent success rate shows that the militarily stronger adversary does not necessarily prevail at coercive diplomacy.

The reason why is clear. Compare coercive diplomatic gambits to war. In war, if the wills (resolves) and skills of the opponents are equally matched, then the outcome is decided by relative military capabilities, and the party with superior military strength prevails. If the weaker party has the stronger will, it still cannot prevail against a stronger adversary unless that adversary cares so little about what is at stake that it will quit the fight, which is usually not the case once the war begins. After all, states do not wage war over things that one or both care little about; they wage war only over things that they both care a great deal about.

In coercive diplomacy, in contrast, will counts more heavily than capability. Clearly, capability counts to a degree. Both parties do make estimates of each other's power, calculating how much it can hurt the other, how well it can defend itself from the blows of the other, and to what extent it can foil the other's military strategy. These power estimates do affect resolve, especially when the target believes it possesses effective counter-coercion techniques that can thwart or mitigate the coercer's military power. However, military capability still takes second place to will in coercive diplomacy situations because estimates about the efficacy of military power are different from the actual use of military power. In a coercive diplomatic gambit the coercer employs only threats and limited force, not the full panoply of its military capabilities. Its purpose is to signal to the target just how far it is willing to go in its use of force without having to use much force. With military power partly sheathed, it is the value that each party puts on the objectives at stake that largely determines how many risks each will take and how many costs each will bear. True, confidence about its military capability can strengthen a target's resolve, but the target must have a strong resolve to begin with because it can never be certain that its counter-coercion techniques will work as envisioned. It must therefore value the objective highly enough to take the risk that its counter-coercion techniques may well not work. At their core, then, coercive diplomatic crises are akin to games of chicken in which wills more than capabilities are being tested. In such situations the more the target values its objectives, the more pain it is willing to bear to achieve them, and hence the less likely the coercer is to succeed.

In all the cases we studied, the United States faced targets that, although militarily inferior, were initially more highly motivated than the United States. After all, in the bulk of our cases, the issues at stake between the United States and the target were vital for the target, but not for the United States, with the 1994 North Korean, 1990–91 Iraqi, and 2001 Afghanistan cases being the clear exceptions. How much military power the United States is prepared to commit, and therefore how far it is willing to go in signaling its intent to commit its vast resources, depends on how much the United States values the interests at stake. The United States can always militarily overwhelm such a target, but to win at coercive diplomacy, it must convince the target that the United States cares more about winning than does the target, and that the United States will use a sufficient portion of its superior strength to prevail. This is not easy to accomplish in situations in which the target views the issues at stake as vital. As a consequence, targets with strong wills but inferior military capabilities may well believe that their superior determination will offset their capabilities' deficit.

For all these reasons, the United States should never bank on the fact that being militarily stronger automatically brings victory in coercive diplomatic encounters the way it can in wars. Were that the case, the United States could dispense with war and do only coercive diplomacy.

4. Do Not Resort to Coercive Diplomacy Unless, Should It Fail, You Are Prepared to Go Down the Path of War or You Have Prepared a Suitable Political Escape Hatch

This advice does not imply that policymakers should eschew coercive diplomacy. Indeed, it is reasonable for U.S. national security decision makers to use it in order to achieve their objectives because coercion short of war, if it works, is cheaper than waging war. Because the odds are against success, however, the United States should not start down the road of coercive diplomacy unless it is willing to resort to war, or unless it has devised a political strategy that will enable it to back down without too much loss of face, should coercive diplomacy fail. To resort to coercive diplomacy and then to abandon pursuit of the objective when coercive diplomacy fails, if done too much, weakens the technique for future use and may well discredit it. Although it is true that the objectives at hand determine to a great degree how both the target and the coercer view the coercer's determination, repeated use of coercive diplomacy, followed by hasty retreats when strong resistance is encountered, cannot but have a negative effect on the coercer's reputation and, by extension, on its use of this technique. For this reason, if for no other, resort to coercive diplomacy should be undertaken only when the objectives sought are worth going to war for, or can somehow be easily discounted politically to the U.S. public and its external audiences, should coercive diplomacy fail. There is obviously a tension here, however, because if the objective is worth going to war for, it is more difficult to discount politically. Thus, although the temptation to try coercion on the cheap is great, the United States should not try it unless it is prepared to go the expensive route or can find a suitable escape hatch.

NOTES

1. Robert P. Pape, *Bombing to Win: Airpower and Coercion* (Ithaca, N.Y.: Cornell University Press, 1996), pp. 18–19.
2. Glenn Snyder and Paul Diesing, *Conflict among Nations: Bargaining, Decision Making, and System Structure in International Crises* (Princeton, N.J.: Princeton University Press, 1977), pp. 118–122.
3. Steven L. Burg and Paul S. Sharp, *The War in Bosnia-Herzegovina: Ethnic Conflict and International Intervention* (Armonk, N.Y.: M. E. Sharpe, 1991), pp. 354–355.

Offense, Defense, and the Security Dilemma

ROBERT JERVIS

Another approach starts with the central point of the security dilemma—that an increase in one state's security decreases the security of others—and examines the conditions under which this proposition holds. Two crucial variables are involved: whether defensive weapons and policies can be distinguished from offensive ones, and whether the defense or the offense has the advantage. The definitions are not always clear, and many cases are difficult to judge, but these two variables shed a great deal of light on the question of whether status-quo powers will adopt compatible security policies. All the variables discussed so far leave the heart of the problem untouched. But when defensive weapons differ from offensive ones, it is possible for a state to make itself more secure without making others less secure. And when the defense has the advantage over the offense, a large increase in one state's security only slightly decreases the security of the others, and status-quo powers can all enjoy a high level of security and largely escape from the state of nature.

OFFENSE-DEFENSE BALANCE

When we say that the offense has the advantage, we simply mean that it is easier to destroy the other's army and take its territory than it is to defend one's own. When the defense has the advantage, it is easier to protect and to hold than it is to move forward, destroy, and take. If effective defenses can be erected quickly, an attacker may be able to keep territory he has taken in an initial victory. Thus, the dominance of the defense made it very hard for Britain and France to push Germany out of France in World War I. But when superior defenses are difficult for an aggressor to improvise on the battlefield and must be constructed during peacetime, they provide no direct assistance to him.

The security dilemma is at its most vicious when commitments, strategy, or technology dictate that the only route to security lies through expansion. Status-quo powers must then act like aggressors: the fact that they would gladly agree to

From "Cooperation Under the Security Dilemma" from *World Politics*, Vol. 30, No. 2 (January 1978), pp. 186–214 by Robert Jervis. Reprinted with permission of Johns Hopkins University Press. Portions of the text and some footnotes have been omitted.

forego the opportunity for expansion in return for guarantees for their security has no implications for their behavior. Even if expansion is not sought as a goal in itself, there will be quick and drastic changes in the distribution of territory and influence. Conversely, when the defense has the advantage, status-quo states can make themselves more secure without gravely endangering others.[1] Indeed, if the defense has enough of an advantage and if the states are of roughly equal size, not only will the security dilemma cease to inhibit status-quo states from cooperating, but aggression will be next to impossible, thus rendering international anarchy relatively unimportant. If states cannot conquer each other, then the lack of sovereignty, although it presents problems of collective goods in a number of areas, no longer forces states to devote their primary attention to self-preservation. Although, if force were not usable, there would be fewer restraints on the use of nonmilitary instruments, these are rarely powerful enough to threaten the vital interests of a major state.

Two questions of the offense-defense balance can be separated. First, does the state have to spend more or less than one dollar on defensive forces to offset each dollar spent by the other side on forces that could be used to attack? If the state has one dollar to spend on increasing its security, should it put it into offensive or defensive forces? Second, with a given inventory of forces, is it better to attack or to defend? Is there an incentive to strike first or to absorb the other's blow? These two aspects are often linked: If each dollar spent on offense can overcome each dollar spent on defense, and if both sides have the same defense budgets, then both are likely to build offensive forces and find it attractive to attack rather than to wait for the adversary to strike.

These aspects affect the security dilemma in different ways. The first has its greatest impact on arms races. If the defense has the advantage, and if the status-quo powers have reasonable subjective security requirements, they can probably avoid an arms race. Although an increase in one side's arms and security will still decrease the other's security, the former's increase will be larger than the latter's decrease. So if one side increases its arms, the other can bring its security back up to its previous level by adding a smaller amount to its forces. And if the first side reacts to this change, its increase will also be smaller than the stimulus that produced it. Thus a stable equilibrium will be reached. Shifting from dynamics to statics, each side can be quite secure with forces roughly equal to those of the other. Indeed, if the defense is much more potent than the offense, each side can be willing to have forces much smaller than the other's, and can be indifferent to a wide range of the other's defense policies.

The second aspect—whether it is better to attack or to defend—influences short-run stability. When the offense has the advantage, a state's reaction to international tension will increase the chances of war. The incentives for preemption and the "reciprocal fear of surprise attack" in this situation have been made clear by analyses of the dangers that exist when two countries have first-strike capabilities.[2] There is no way for the state to increase its security without menacing, or even attacking, the other. Even Bismarck, who once called preventive war "committing suicide from fear of death," said that "no government, if it regards war as inevitable even if it does not want it, would be so foolish as to leave to the enemy the choice of time and occasion and to wait for the moment which is most convenient for the enemy."[3] In another arena, the same dilemma applies to the policeman in a dark alley confronting a suspected criminal who appears to be holding a weapon. Though racism may indeed be present, the security dilemma can account for many of the tragic shootings of innocent people in the ghettos.

Beliefs about the course of a war in which the offense has the advantage further deepen the security dilemma. When there are incentives to strike first, a successful attack will usually so weaken the other side that victory will be relatively quick, bloodless, and decisive. It is in these periods when conquest is possible and attractive that states consolidate power internally—for instance, by destroying the feudal barons—and expand externally. There are several consequences that decrease the chance of cooperation among status-quo states. First, war will be profitable for the winner. The costs will be low and the benefits high. Of course, losers will suffer; the fear of losing could induce states to try to form stable cooperative arrangements, but the temptation of victory will make this particularly difficult. Second, because wars are expected to be both frequent and short, there will be incentives for high levels of arms, and quick and strong reaction to the other's increases in arms. The state cannot afford to wait until there is unambiguous evidence that the other is building new weapons. Even large states that have faith in their economic strength cannot wait, because the war will be over before their products can reach the army. Third, when wars are quick, states will have to recruit allies in advance.[4] Without the opportunity for bargaining and realignments during the opening stages of hostilities, peacetime diplomacy loses a degree of the fluidity that facilitates balance-of-power policies. Because alliances must be secured during peacetime, the international system is more likely to become bipolar. It is hard to say whether war therefore becomes more or less likely, but this bipolarity increases tension between the two camps and makes it harder for status-quo states to gain the benefits of cooperation. Fourth, if wars are frequent, statesmen's perceptual thresholds will be adjusted accordingly and they will be quick to perceive ambiguous evidence as indicating that others are aggressive. Thus, there will be more cases of status-quo powers arming against each other in the incorrect belief that the other is hostile.

When the defense has the advantage, all the foregoing is reversed. The state that fears attack does not preempt—since that would be a wasteful use of its military resources—but rather prepares to receive an attack. Doing so does not decrease the security of others, and several states can do it simultaneously; the situation will therefore be stable, and status-quo powers will be able to cooperate. When Herman Kahn argues that ultimatums "are vastly too dangerous to give because . . . they are quite likely to touch off a pre-emptive strike,"[5] he incorrectly assumes that it is always advantageous to strike first.

More is involved than short-run dynamics. When the defense is dominant, wars are likely to become stalemates and can be won only at enormous cost. Relatively small and weak states can hold off larger and stronger ones, or can deter attack by raising the costs of conquest to an unacceptable level. States then approach equality in what they can do to each other. Like the .45-caliber pistol in the American West, fortifications were the "great equalizer" in some periods.

Changes in the status quo are less frequent and cooperation is more common wherever the security dilemma is thereby reduced.

Many of these arguments can be illustrated by the major powers' policies in the periods preceding the two world wars. Bismarck's wars surprised statesmen by showing that the offense had the advantage, and by being quick, relatively cheap, and quite decisive. Falling into a common error, observers projected this pattern into the future.[6] The resulting expectations had several effects. First, states sought semi-permanent allies. In the early stages of the Franco-Prussian War, Napoleon III had thought that there would be plenty of time to recruit Austria to his side. Now, others were not going to repeat this mistake. Second, defense budgets were high and reacted quite sharply to increases on the other side. It is not surprising that Richardson's theory of arms races fits this period well. Third, most decision makers thought that the next European war would not cost much blood and treasure.[7] That is one reason why war was generally seen as inevitable and why mass opinion was so bellicose. Fourth, once war seemed likely, there were strong pressures to preempt. Both sides believed that whoever moved first could penetrate the other deep enough to disrupt mobilization and thus gain an insurmountable advantage. (There was no such belief about the use of naval forces. Although Churchill made an ill-advised speech saying that if German ships "do not come out and fight in time of war they will be dug out like rats in a hole,"[8] everyone knew that submarines, mines and coastal fortifications made this impossible. So at the start of the war each navy prepared to defend itself rather than attack, and the short-run destabilizing forces that launched the armies toward each other did not operate.)[9] Furthermore, each side knew that the other saw the situation the same way, thus increasing the perceived danger that the other would attack, and giving each added reasons to precipitate a war if conditions seemed favorable. In the long and the short run, there were thus both offensive and defensive incentives to strike. This situation casts light on the common question about German motives in 1914: "Did Germany unleash the war deliberately to become a world power or did she support Austria merely to defend a weakening ally," thereby protecting her own position?[10] To some extent, this question is misleading. Because of the perceived advantage of the offense, war was seen as the best route both to gaining expansion and to avoiding drastic loss of influence. There seemed to be no way for Germany merely to retain and safeguard her existing position.

Of course the war showed these beliefs to have been wrong on all points. Trenches and machine guns gave the defense an overwhelming advantage. The fighting became deadlocked and produced horrendous casualties. It made no sense for the combatants to bleed themselves to death. If they had known the power of the defense beforehand, they would have rushed for their own trenches rather than for the enemy's territory. Each side could have done this without increasing the other's incentives to strike. War might have broken out anyway; but at least the pressures of time and the fear of allowing the other to get the first blow would not have contributed to this end. And, had both sides known the costs of the war, they would have negotiated much more seriously. The obvious question is why the states did not seek a negotiated settlement as soon as the shape of the war became clear. Schlieffen had said that if his plan failed, peace should be sought.[11]

The answer is complex, uncertain, and largely outside of the scope of our concerns. But part of the reason was the hope and sometimes the expectation that breakthroughs could be made and the dominance of the offensive restored. Without that hope, the political and psychological pressures to fight to a decisive victory might have been overcome.

The politics of the interwar period were shaped by the memories of the previous conflict and the belief that any future war would resemble it. Political and military lessons reinforced each other in ameliorating the security dilemma. Because it was believed that the First World War had been a mistake that could have been avoided by skillful conciliation, both Britain and, to a lesser extent, France were highly sensitive to the possibility that interwar Germany was not a real threat to peace, and alert to the danger that reacting quickly and strongly to her arms could create unnecessary conflict. And because Britain and France expected the defense to continue to dominate, they concluded that it was safe to adopt a more relaxed and nonthreatening military posture.[12] Britain also felt less need to maintain tight alliance bonds. The Allies' military posture then constituted only a slight danger to Germany; had the latter been content with the status quo, it would have been easy for both sides to have felt secure behind their lines of fortifications. Of course the Germans were not content, so it is not surprising that they devoted their money and attention to finding ways out of a defense-dominated stalemate. *Blitzkrieg* tactics were necessary if they were to use force to change the status quo.

The initial stages of the war on the Western Front also contrasted with the First World War. Only with the new air arm were there any incentives to strike first, and these forces were too weak to carry out the grandiose plans that had been both dreamed and feared. The armies, still the main instrument, rushed to defensive positions. Perhaps the allies could have successfully attacked while the Germans were occupied in Poland.[13] But belief in the defense was so great that this was never seriously contemplated. Three months after the start of the war, the French Prime Minister summed up the view held by almost everyone but Hitler: on the Western Front there is "deadlock. Two Forces of equal strength and the one that attacks seeing such enormous casualties that it cannot move without endangering the continuation of the war or of the aftermath."[14] The Allies were caught in a dilemma they never fully recognized, let alone solved. On the one hand, they had very high war aims; although unconditional surrender had not yet been adopted, the British had decided from the start that the removal of Hitler was a necessary condition for peace.[15] On the other hand, there were no realistic plans or instruments for allowing the Allies to impose their will on the other side. The British Chief of the Imperial General Staff noted, "The French have no intention of carrying out an offensive for years, if at all"; the British were only slightly bolder.[16] So the Allies looked to a long war that would wear the Germans down, cause civilian suffering through shortages, and eventually undermine Hitler. There was little analysis to support this view—and indeed it probably was not supportable—but as long as the defense was dominant and the numbers on each side relatively equal, what else could the Allies do?

To summarize, the security dilemma was much less powerful after World War I than it had been before. In the later period, the expected power of the defense allowed status-quo states to pursue compatible security policies and avoid arms races. Furthermore, high tension and fear of war did not set off short-run dynamics by which each state, trying to increase its security, inadvertently acted to make war more likely. The expected high costs of war, however, led the Allies to believe that no sane German leader would run the risks entailed in an attempt to dominate the Continent, and discouraged them from risking war themselves.

Technology and Geography

Technology and geography are the two main factors that determine whether the offense or the defense has the advantage. As Brodie notes, "On the tactical level, as a rule, few physical factors favor the attacker but many favor the defender. The defender usually has the advantage of cover. He characteristically fires from behind some form of shelter while his opponent crosses open ground."[17] Anything that increases the amount of ground the attacker has to cross, or impedes his progress across it, or makes him more vulnerable while crossing, increases the advantage accruing to the defense. When states are separated by barriers that produce these effects, the security dilemma is eased, since both can have forces adequate for defense without being able to attack. Impenetrable barriers would actually prevent war; in reality, decision makers have to settle for a good deal less. Buffer zones slow the attacker's progress; they thereby give the defender time to prepare, increase problems of logistics, and reduce the number of soldiers available for the final assault. At the end of the nineteenth century, Arthur Balfour noted Afghanistan's "non-conducting" qualities. "So long as it possesses few roads, and no railroads, it will be impossible for Russia to make effective use of her great numerical superiority at any point immediately vital to the Empire." The Russians valued buffers for the same reasons; it is not surprising that when Persia was being divided into Russian and British spheres of influence some years later, the Russians sought assurances that the British would refrain from building potentially menacing railroads in their sphere. Indeed, since railroad construction radically altered the abilities of countries to defend themselves and to attack others, many diplomatic notes and much intelligence activity in the late nineteenth century centered on this subject.[18]

Oceans, large rivers, and mountain ranges serve the same function as buffer zones. Being hard to cross, they allow defense against superior numbers. The defender has merely to stay on his side of the barrier and so can utilize all the men he can bring up to it. The attacker's men, however, can cross only a few at a time, and they are very vulnerable when doing so. If all states were self-sufficient islands, anarchy would be much less of a problem. A small investment in shore defenses and a small army would be sufficient to repel invasion. Only very weak states would be vulnerable, and only very large ones could menace others. As noted above, the United States, and to a lesser extent Great Britain, have partly been able to escape from the state of nature because their geographical positions approximated this ideal.

Although geography cannot be changed to conform to borders, borders can and do change to conform to geography. Borders across which an attack is easy tend to be unstable. States living within them are likely to expand or be absorbed. Frequent wars are almost inevitable since attacking will often seem the best way to protect what one has. This process will stop, or at least slow down, when the state's borders reach—by expansion or contraction—a line of natural obstacles. Security without attack will then be possible. Furthermore, these lines constitute salient solutions to bargaining problems and, to the extent that they are barriers to migration, are likely to divide ethnic groups, thereby raising the costs and lowering the incentives for conquest.

Attachment to one's state and its land reinforce one quasi-geographical aid to the defense. Conquest usually becomes more difficult the deeper the attacker pushes into the other's territory. Nationalism spurs the defenders to fight harder; advancing not only lengthens the attacker's supply lines, but takes him through unfamiliar and often devastated lands that require troops for garrison duty. These stabilizing dynamics will not operate, however, if the defender's war matériel is situated near its borders, or if the people do not care about their state, but only about being on the winning side. In such cases, positive feedback will be at work and initial defeats will be insurmountable.[19]

Imitating geography, men have tried to create barriers. Treaties may provide for demilitarized zones on both sides of the border, although such zones will rarely be deep enough to provide more than warning. Even this was not possible in Europe, but the Russians adopted a gauge for their railroads that was broader than that of the neighboring states, thereby complicating the logistics problems of any attacker—including Russia.

Perhaps the most ambitious and at least temporarily successful attempts to construct a system that would aid the defenses of both sides were the interwar naval treaties, as they affected Japanese-American relations. As mentioned earlier, the problem was that the United States could not defend the Philippines without denying Japan the ability to protect her home islands.[20] (In 1941 this dilemma became insoluble when Japan sought to extend her control to Malaya and the Dutch East Indies. If the Philippines had been invulnerable, they could have provided a secure base from which the United States could interdict Japanese shipping between the homeland and the areas she was trying to conquer.) In the 1920s and early 1930s each side would have been willing to grant the other security for its possessions in return for a reciprocal grant, and the Washington Naval Conference agreements were designed to approach this goal. As a Japanese diplomat later put it, their country's "fundamental principle" was to have "a strength insufficient for attack and adequate for defense."[21] Thus Japan agreed in 1922 to accept a navy only three-fifths as large as that of the United States, and the United States agreed not to fortify its Pacific islands.[22] (Japan had earlier been forced to agree not to fortify the islands she had taken from Germany in World War I.) Japan's navy would not be large enough to defeat America's anywhere other than close to the home islands. Although the Japanese could still take the Philippines, not only would they be unable to move farther, but they might be weakened enough by their efforts to be vulnerable to counterattack. Japan, however, gained security. An American attack was rendered more difficult because the American bases were unprotected and because, until 1930, Japan was allowed unlimited numbers of cruisers, destroyers, and submarines that could weaken the American fleet as it made its way across the ocean.[23]

The other major determinant of the offense-defense balance is technology. When weapons are highly vulnerable, they must be employed before they are attacked. Others can remain quite invulnerable in their bases. The former characteristics are embodied in unprotected missiles and many kinds of bombers. (It should be noted that it is not vulnerability *per se* that is crucial, but the location of the vulnerability. Bombers and missiles that are easy to destroy only after having been launched toward their targets do not create destabilizing dynamics.) Incentives to strike first are usually absent for naval forces that are threatened by a naval attack. Like missiles in hardened silos, they are usually well protected when in their bases. Both sides can then simultaneously be prepared to defend themselves successfully.

In ground warfare under some conditions, forts, trenches, and small groups of men in prepared positions can hold off large numbers of attackers. Less frequently, a few attackers can storm the defenses. By and large, it is a contest between fortifications and supporting light weapons on the one hand, and mobility and heavier weapons that clear the way for the attack on the other. As the erroneous views held before the two world wars show, there is no simple way to determine which is dominant. "[T]hese oscillations are not smooth and predictable like those of a swinging pendulum. They are uneven in both extent and time. Some occur in the course of a single battle or campaign, others in the course of a war, still others during a series of wars." Longer-term oscillations can also be detected:

> The early Gothic age, from the twelfth to the late thirteenth century, with its wonderful cathedrals and fortified places, was a period during which the attackers in Europe generally met serious and increasing difficulties, because the improvement in the strength of fortresses outran the advance in the power of destruction. Later, with the spread of firearms at the end of the fifteenth century, old fortresses lost their power to resist. An age ensued during which the offense possessed, apart from short-term setbacks, new advantages. Then, during the seventeenth century, especially after about 1660, and until at least the outbreak of the War of the Austrian Succession in 1740, the defense regained much of the ground it had lost since the great medieval fortresses had proved unable to meet the bombardment of the new and more numerous artillery.[24]

Another scholar has continued the argument: "The offensive gained an advantage with new forms of heavy mobile artillery in the nineteenth century, but the stalemate of World War I created the impression that the defense again had an advantage; the German invasion in World War II, however, indicated the offensive superiority of highly mechanized armies in the field."[25]

The situation today with respect to conventional weapons is unclear. Until recently it was believed that tanks and tactical air power gave the attacker an advantage. The initial analyses of the 1973 Arab-Israeli war indicated that new anti-tank and anti-aircraft weapons have restored the primacy of the defense. These weapons are cheap, easy to use, and can destroy a high proportion of the attacking vehicles and planes that are sighted. It then would make sense for a status-quo power to buy lots of $20,000 missiles rather than buy a few half-million dollar fighter-bombers. Defense would be possible even against a large and well-equipped force; states that care primarily about self-protection would not need to engage in arms races. But further examinations of the new technologies and the history of the October War cast doubt on these optimistic conclusions and leave us unable to render any firm judgment.[26]

Concerning nuclear weapons, it is generally agreed that defense is impossible— a triumph not of the offense, but of deterrence. Attack makes no sense, not because it can be beaten off, but because the attacker will be destroyed in turn. In terms of the questions under consideration here, the result is the equivalent of the primacy of the defense. First, security is relatively cheap. Less than one percent of the G.N.P. is devoted to deterring a direct attack on the United States; most of it is spent on acquiring redundant systems to provide a lot of insurance against the worst conceivable contingencies. Second, both sides can simultaneously gain security in the form of second-strike capability. Third, and related to the foregoing, second-strike capability can be maintained in the face of wide variations in the other side's military posture. There is no purely military reason why each side has to react quickly and strongly to the other's increases in arms. Any spending that the other devotes to trying to achieve first-strike capability can be neutralized by the state's spending much smaller sums on protecting its second-strike capability. Fourth, there are no incentives to strike first in a crisis.

Important problems remain, of course. Both sides have interests that go well beyond defense of the homeland. The protection of these interests creates conflicts even if neither side desires expansion. Furthermore, the shift from defense to deterrence has greatly increased the importance and perceptions of resolve. Security now rests on each side's belief that the other would prefer to run high risks of total destruction rather than sacrifice its vital interests. Aspects of the security dilemma thus appear in a new form. Are weapons procurements used as an index of resolve? Must they be so used? If one side fails to respond to the other's buildup, will it appear weak and thereby invite predation? Can both sides simultaneously have images of high resolve or is there a zero-sum element involved? Although these problems are real, they are not as severe as those in the prenuclear era: There are many indices of resolve, and states do not so much judge images of resolve in the abstract as ask how likely it is that the other will stand firm in a particular dispute. Since states are most likely to stand firm on matters which concern them most, it is quite possible for both to demonstrate their resolve to protect their own security simultaneously.

OFFENSE-DEFENSE DIFFERENTIATION

The other major variable that affects how strongly the security dilemma operates is whether weapons and policies that protect the state also provide the capability for attack. If they do not, the basic postulate of the security dilemma no longer applies. A state can increase its own security without decreasing that of others. The advantage of the defense can only ameliorate the security dilemma. A differentiation between offensive and defensive stances comes close to abolishing it. Such differentiation does not mean, however, that all security problems will be abolished. If the offense has the advantage, conquest and aggression will still be possible. And if the offense's advantage is great enough, status-quo powers may find it too expensive to protect themselves by defensive forces and decide to procure offensive weapons even though this will menace others. Furthermore, states will still have to worry that even if the other's military posture shows that it is peaceful now, it may develop aggressive intentions in the future.

Assuming that the defense is at least as potent as the offense, the differentiation between them allows status-quo states to behave in ways that are clearly different from those of aggressors. Three beneficial consequences follow. First, status-quo powers can identify each other, thus laying the foundations for cooperation. Conflicts growing out of the mistaken belief that the other side is expansionist will be less frequent. Second, status-quo states will obtain advance warning when others plan aggression. Before a state can attack, it has to develop and deploy offensive weapons. If procurement of these weapons cannot be disguised and takes a fair amount of time, as it almost always does, a status-quo state will have the time to take countermeasures. It need not maintain a high level of defensive arms as long as its potential adversaries are adopting a peaceful posture. (Although being so armed should not, with the one important exception noted below, alarm other status-quo powers.) States do, in fact, pay special attention to actions that they believe would not be taken by a status-quo state because they feel that states exhibiting such behavior are aggressive. Thus the seizure or development of transportation facilities will alarm others more if these facilities have no commercial value, and therefore can only be wanted for military reasons. In 1906, the British rejected a Russian protest about their activities in a district of Persia by claiming that this area was "only of [strategic] importance [to the Russians] if they wished to attack the Indian frontier, or to put pressure upon us by making us think that they intend to attack it."[27]

The same inferences are drawn when a state acquires more weapons than observers feel are needed for defense. Thus, the Japanese spokesman at the 1930 London naval conference said that his country was alarmed by the American refusal to give Japan a 70 percent ratio (in place of a 60 percent ratio) in heavy cruisers: "As long as America held that ten percent advantage, it was possible for her to attack. So when America insisted on sixty percent instead of seventy percent, the idea would exist that they were trying to keep that possibility, and the Japanese people could not accept that."[28] Similarly, when Mussolini told Chamberlain in January 1939 that Hitler's arms program was motivated by defensive considerations, the Prime Minister replied that "German military forces were now so strong as to make it impossible for any Power or combination of Powers to attack her successfully. She could not want any further armaments for defensive purposes; what then did she want them for?"[29]

Of course these inferences can be wrong—as they are especially likely to be because states underestimate the degree to which they menace others.[30] And when they are wrong, the security dilemma is deepened. Because the state thinks it has received notice that the other is aggressive, its own arms building will be less restrained and the chances of cooperation will be decreased. But the dangers of incorrect inferences should not obscure the main point: When offensive and defensive postures are different, much of the uncertainty about the other's intentions that contributes to the security dilemma is removed.

The third beneficial consequence of a difference between offensive and defensive weapons is that if all states support the status quo, an obvious arms control agreement is a ban on weapons that are useful for attacking. As President Roosevelt put it in his message to the Geneva Disarmament Conference in 1933: "If all nations will agree wholly to eliminate from possession and use the weapons which make possible a successful attack, defenses automatically will become impregnable, and the frontiers and independence of every nation will become secure."[31] The fact that such treaties have been rare—the Washington naval agreements discussed above and the anti-ABM treaty can be cited as examples—shows either that states are not always willing to guarantee the security of others, or that it is hard to distinguish offensive from defensive weapons.

Is such a distinction possible? Salvador de Madariaga, the Spanish statesman active in the disarmament negotiations of the interwar years, thought not: "A weapon is either offensive or defensive according to which end of it you are looking at." The French Foreign Minister agreed (although French policy did not always follow this view): "Every arm can be employed offensively or defensively in turn. . . . The only way to discover whether arms are intended for purely defensive purposes or are held in a spirit of aggression is in all cases to enquire into the intentions of the country concerned." Some evidence for the validity of this argument is provided by the fact that much time in these unsuccessful negotiations was devoted to separating offensive from defensive weapons. Indeed, no simple and unambiguous definition is possible and in many cases no judgment can be reached. Before the American entry into World War I, Woodrow Wilson wanted to arm merchantmen only with guns in the back of the ship so they could not initiate a fight, but this expedient cannot be applied to more common forms of armaments.[32]

There are several problems. Even when a differentiation is possible, a status-quo power will want offensive arms under any of three conditions: (1) If the offense has a great advantage over the defense, protection through defensive forces will be too expensive. (2) Status-quo states may need offensive weapons to regain territory lost in the opening stages of war. It might be possible, however, for a state to wait to procure these weapons until war seems likely, and they might be needed only in relatively small numbers, unless the aggressor was able to construct strong defenses quickly in the occupied areas. (3) The state may feel that it must be prepared to take the offensive either because the other side will make peace only if it loses territory or because the state has commitments to attack if the other makes war on a third party. As noted above, status-quo states with extensive commitments are often forced to behave like aggressors. Even when they lack such commitments, status-quo states must worry about the possibility that if they are able to hold off an attack, they will still not be able to end the war unless they move into the other's territory to damage its military forces and inflict pain. Many American naval officers after the Civil War, for example, believed that "only by destroying the commerce of the opponent could the United States bring him to terms."[33]

A further complication is introduced by the fact that aggressors as well as status-quo powers require defensive forces as a prelude to acquiring offensive ones, to protect one frontier while attacking another, or for insurance in case the war goes badly. Criminals as well as policemen can use bulletproof vests. Hitler as well as Maginot built a line of forts. Indeed, Churchill reports that in 1936 the German Foreign Minister said: "As soon as our fortifications are constructed [on our western borders] and the countries in Central Europe realize that France cannot enter German territory, all these countries will begin to feel very differently about their foreign policies, and a new constellation will develop."[34] So a state may not necessarily be reassured if its neighbor constructs strong defenses.

More central difficulties are created by the fact that whether a weapon is offensive or defensive often depends on the particular situation—for instance, the geographical setting and the way in which the weapon is used. "Tanks. . . . spearheaded the fateful German thrust through the Ardennes in 1940, but if the French had disposed of a properly concentrated armored reserve, it would have provided the best means for their cutting off the penetration and turning into a disaster for the Germans what became instead an overwhelming victory."[35] Anti-aircraft weapons seem obviously defensive—to be used, they must wait for the other side to come to them. But the Egyptian attack on Israel in 1973 would have been impossible without effective air defenses that covered the battlefield. Nevertheless, some distinctions are possible. Sir John Simon, then the British Foreign Secretary, in response to the views cited earlier, stated that just because a fine line could not be drawn, "that was no reason for saying that there were not stretches of territory on either side which all practical men and women knew to be well on this or that side of the line." Although there are almost no weapons and strategies that are useful only for attacking, there are some that are almost exclusively defensive. Aggressors could want them for protection, but a state that relied mostly on them could not menace others. More frequently, we cannot "determine the absolute character of a weapon, but [we can] make a comparison . . . [and] discover whether or not the offensive potentialities predominate, whether a weapon is more useful in attack or in defense."[36]

The essence of defense is keeping the other side out of your territory. A purely defensive weapon is one that can do this without being able to penetrate the enemy's land. Thus a committee of military experts in an interwar disarmament conference declared that armaments "incapable of mobility by means of self-contained power," or movable only after long delay, were "only capable of being used for the defense of a State's territory."[37] The most obvious examples are fortifications. They can shelter attacking forces, especially when they are built right along the frontier,[38] but they cannot occupy enemy territory. A state with only a strong line of forts, fixed guns, and a small army to man them would not be much of a menace. Anything else that can serve only as a barrier against attacking troops is similarly defensive. In this category are systems that provide warning of an attack, the Russian's adoption of a different railroad gauge, and nuclear land mines that can seal off invasion routes.

If total immobility clearly defines a system that is defensive only, limited mobility is unfortunately ambiguous. As noted above, short-range fighter aircraft and anti-aircraft missiles can be used to cover an attack. And, unlike forts, they can advance with the troops. Still, their inability to reach deep into enemy territory does make them more useful for the defense than for the offense. Thus, the United States and Israel would have been more alarmed in the early 1970s had the

Russians provided the Egyptians with long-range instead of short-range aircraft. Naval forces are particularly difficult to classify in these terms, but those that are very short-legged can be used only for coastal defense.

Any forces that for various reasons fight well only when on their own soil in effect lack mobility and therefore are defensive. The most extreme example would be passive resistance. Noncooperation can thwart an aggressor, but it is very hard for large numbers of people to cross the border and stage a sit-in on another's territory. Morocco's recent march on the Spanish Sahara approached this tactic, but its success depended on special circumstances. Similarly, guerrilla warfare is defensive to the extent to which it requires civilian support that is likely to be forthcoming only in opposition to a foreign invasion. Indeed, if guerrilla warfare were easily exportable and if it took ten defenders to destroy each guerrilla, then this weapon would not only be one which could be used as easily to attack the other's territory as to defend one's own, but one in which the offense had the advantage: so the security dilemma would operate especially strongly.

If guerrillas are unable to fight on foreign soil, other kinds of armies may be unwilling to do so. An army imbued with the idea that only defensive wars were just would fight less effectively, if at all, if the goal were conquest. Citizen militias may lack both the ability and the will for aggression. The weapons employed, the short term of service, the time required for mobilization, and the spirit of repelling attacks on the homeland, all lend themselves much more to defense than to attacks on foreign territory.[39]

Less idealistic motives can produce the same result. A leading student of medieval warfare has described the armies of that period as follows: "Assembled with difficulty, insubordinate, unable to maneuver, ready to melt away from its standard the moment that its short period of service was over, a feudal force presented an assemblage of unsoldierlike qualities such as have seldom been known to coexist. Primarily intended to defend its own borders from the Magyar, the Northman, or the Saracen . . . , the institution was utterly unadapted to take the offensive."[40] Some political groupings can be similarly described. International coalitions are more readily held together by fear than by hope of gain. Thus Castlereagh was not being entirely self-serving when in 1816 he argued that the Quadruple Alliance "could only have owed its origin to a sense of common danger; in its very nature it must be conservative; it cannot threaten either the security or the liberties of other States."[41] It is no accident that most of the major campaigns of expansion have been waged by one dominant nation (for example, Napoleon's France and Hitler's Germany), and that coalitions among relative equals are usually found defending the status quo. Most gains from conquest are too uncertain and raise too many questions of future squabbles among the victors to hold an alliance together for long. Although defensive coalitions are by no means easy to maintain—conflicting national objectives and the free-rider problem partly explain why three of them dissolved before Napoleon was defeated—the common interest of seeing that no state dominates provides a strong incentive for solidarity.

Weapons that are particularly effective in reducing fortifications and barriers are of great value to the offense. This is not to deny that a defensive power will want some of those weapons if the other side has them: Brodie is certainly correct to argue that while their tanks allowed the Germans to conquer France, properly used French tanks could have halted the attack. But France would not have needed these weapons if Germany had not acquired them, whereas even if France had no tanks, Germany could not have foregone them since they provided the only chance of breaking through the French lines. Mobile heavy artillery is, similarly, especially useful in destroying fortifications. The defender, while needing artillery to fight off attacking troops or to counterattack, can usually use lighter guns since they do not need to penetrate such massive obstacles. So it is not surprising that one of the few things that most nations at the interwar disarmament conferences were able to agree on was that heavy tanks and mobile heavy guns were particularly valuable to a state planning an attack.[42]

Weapons and strategies that depend for their effectiveness on surprise are almost always offensive. That fact was recognized by some of the delegates to the interwar disarmament conferences and is the principle behind the common national ban on concealed weapons. An earlier representative of this widespread view was the mid-nineteenth-century Philadelphia newspaper that argued: "As a measure of defense, knives, dirks, and sword canes are entirely useless. They are fit only for attack, and all such attacks are of murderous character. Whoever carries such a weapon has prepared himself for homicide."[43]

It is, of course, not always possible to distinguish between forces that are most effective for holding territory and forces optimally designed for taking it. Such a distinction could not have been made for the strategies and weapons in Europe during most of the period between the Franco-Prussian War and World War I. Neither naval forces nor tactical air forces can be readily classified in these terms. But the point here is that when such a distinction is possible, the central characteristic of the security dilemma no longer holds, and one of the most troublesome consequences of anarchy is removed.

Offense-Defense Differentiation and Strategic Nuclear Weapons

In the interwar period, most statesmen held the reasonable position that weapons that threatened civilians were offensive.[44] But when neither side can protect its civilians, a counter-city posture is defensive because the state can credibly threaten to retaliate only in response to an attack on itself or its closest allies. The costs of this strike are so high that the state could not threaten to use it for the less-than-vital interest of compelling the other to abandon an established position.

In the context of deterrence, offensive weapons are those that provide defense. In the now familiar reversal of common sense, the state that could take its population out of hostage, either by active or passive defense or by destroying the other's strategic weapons on the ground, would be able to alter the status quo. The desire to prevent such a situation was one of the rationales for the anti-ABM agreements; it explains why some arms controllers opposed building ABMs to protect cities, but favored sites that covered ICBM fields. Similarly, many analysts wanted to limit warhead accuracy and favored multiple re-entry vehicles (MRVs), but opposed multiple independently targetable re-entry vehicles (MIRVs). The former are more useful than single warheads for penetrating city defenses, and ensure that the state has a second-strike capability. MIRVs enhance counterforce capabilities. . . .

What is most important for the argument here is that land-based ICBMs are both offensive and defensive, but when both sides rely on Polaris-type systems (SLBMs), offense and defense use different weapons. ICBMs can be used either to destroy the other's cities in retaliation or to initiate hostilities by attacking the other's strategic missiles. Some measures—for instance, hardening of missile sites and warning systems—are purely defensive, since they do not make a first strike easier. Others are predominantly offensive—for instance, passive or active city defenses, and highly accurate warheads. But ICBMs themselves are useful for both purposes. And because states seek a high level of insurance, the desire for protection as well as the contemplation of a counterforce strike can explain the acquisition of extremely large numbers of missiles. So it is very difficult to infer the other's intentions from its military posture. Each side's efforts to increase its own security by procuring more missiles decreases, to an extent determined by the relative efficacy of the offense and the defense, the other side's security. That is not the case when both sides use SLBMs. The point is not that sea-based systems are less vulnerable than land-based ones (this bears on the offense-defense ratio) but that SLBMs are defensive, retaliatory weapons. . . . SLBMs are not the main instrument of attack against other SLBMs. The hardest problem confronting a state that wants to take its cities out of hostage is to locate the other's SLBMs, a job that requires not SLBMs but anti-submarine weapons. A state might use SLBMs to attack the other's submarines (although other weapons would probably be more efficient), but without anti-submarine warfare (ASW) capability the task cannot be performed. A status-quo state that wanted to forego offensive capability could simply forego ASW research and procurement. . . .

When both sides rely on ICBMs, one side's missiles can attack the other's, and so the state cannot be indifferent to the other's building program. But because one side's SLBMs do not menace the other's, each side can build as many as it wants and the other need not respond. Each side's decision on the size of its force depends on technical questions, its judgment about how much destruction is enough to deter, and the amount of insurance it is willing to pay for—and these considerations are independent of the size of the other's strategic force. Thus the crucial nexus in the arms race is severed. . . .

FOUR WORLDS

The two variables we have been discussing—whether the offense or the defense has the advantage, and whether offensive postures can be distinguished from defensive ones—can be combined to yield four possible worlds.

The first world is the worst for status-quo states. These is no way to get security without menacing others, and security through defense is terribly difficult to obtain. Because offensive and defensive postures are the same, status-quo states acquire the same kind of arms that are sought by aggressors. And because the offense has the advantage over the defense, attacking is the best route to protecting what you have; status-quo states will therefore behave like aggressors. The situation will be unstable. Arms races are likely. Incentives to strike first will turn

TABLE 1 ■

	Offense has the advantage	Defense has the advantage
Offensive posture not distinguishable from defensive one	1 Doubly dangerous	2 Security dilemma, but security requirements may be compatible
Offensive posture distinguishable from defensive one	3 No security dilemma, but aggression possible Status-quo states can follow different policy than aggressors Warning given	4 Doubly stable

crises into wars. Decisive victories and conquests will be common. States will grow and shrink rapidly, and it will be hard for any state to maintain its size and influence without trying to increase them. Cooperation among status-quo powers will be extremely hard to achieve.

There are no cases that totally fit this picture, but it bears more than a passing resemblance to Europe before World War I. Britain and Germany, although in many respects natural allies, ended up as enemies. Of course much of the explanation lies in Germany's ill-chosen policy. And from the perspective of our theory, the powers' ability to avoid war in a series of earlier crises cannot be easily explained. Nevertheless, much of the behavior in this period was the product of technology and beliefs that magnified the security dilemma. Decision makers thought that the offense had a big advantage and saw little difference between offensive and defensive military postures. The era was characterized by arms races. And once war seemed likely, mobilization races created powerful incentives to strike first.

In the nuclear era, the first world would be one in which each side relied on vulnerable weapons that were aimed at similar forces and each side understood the situation. In this case, the incentives to strike first would be very high—so high that status-quo powers as well as aggressors would be sorely tempted to preempt. And since the forces could be used to change the status quo as well as to preserve it, there would be no way for both sides to increase their security simultaneously. Now the familiar logic of deterrence leads both sides to see the dangers in this world. Indeed, the new understanding of this situation was one reason why vulnerable bombers and missiles were replaced. Ironically, the 1950s would have been more hazardous if the decision makers had been aware of the dangers of their posture and had therefore felt greater pressure to strike first.

In the second world, the security dilemma operates because offensive and defensive postures cannot be distinguished; but it does not operate as strongly as in the first world because the defense has the advantage, and so an increment in one side's strength increases its security more than it decreases the other's. So, if both sides have reasonable subjective security requirements, are of roughly equal power, and the variables discussed earlier are favorable, it is quite likely that status-quo states can adopt compatible security policies. Although a state will not be able to judge the other's intentions from the kinds of weapons it procures, the level of arms spending will give important evidence. Of course a state that seeks a high level of arms might be not an aggressor but merely an insecure state, which if conciliated will reduce its arms, and if confronted will reply in kind. To assume that the apparently excessive level of arms indicates aggressiveness could therefore lead to a response that would deepen the dilemma and create needless conflict. But empathy and skillful statesmanship can reduce this danger. Furthermore, the advantageous position of the defense means that a status-quo state can often maintain a high degree of security with a level of arms lower than that of its expected adversary. Such a state demonstrates that it lacks the ability or desire to alter the status quo, at least at the present time. The strength of the defense also allows states to react slowly and with restraint when they fear that others are menacing them. So, although status-quo powers will to some extent be threatening to others, that extent will be limited.

This world is the one that comes closest to matching most periods in history. Attacking is usually harder than defending because of the strength of fortifications and obstacles. But purely defensive postures are rarely possible because fortifications are usually supplemented by armies and mobile guns which can support an attack. In the nuclear era, this world would be one in which both sides relied on relatively invulnerable ICBMs and believed that limited nuclear war was impossible. Assuming no MIRVs, it would take more than one attacking missile to destroy one of the adversary's. Preemption is therefore unattractive. If both sides have large inventories, they can ignore all but drastic increases on the other side. A world of either ICBMs or SLBMs in which both sides adopted the policy of limited nuclear war would probably fit in this category too. The means of preserving the status quo would also be the means of changing it, as we discussed earlier. And the defense usually would have the advantage, because compellence is more difficult than deterrence. Although a state might succeed in changing the status quo on issues that matter much more to it than to others, status-quo powers could deter major provocations under most circumstances.

In the third world there may be no security dilemma, but there are security problems. Because states can procure defensive systems that do not threaten others, the dilemma need not operate. But because the offense has the advantage, aggression is possible, and perhaps easy. If the offense has less of an advantage, stability and cooperation are likely because the status-quo states will procure defensive forces. They need not react to others who are similarly armed, but can wait for the warning they would receive if others started to deploy offensive weapons. But each state will have to watch the others carefully, and there is room for false suspicions. The costliness of the defense and the allure of the offense can lead to unnecessary mistrust, hostility, and war, unless some of the variables discussed earlier are operating to restrain defection.

A hypothetical nuclear world that would fit this description would be one in which both sides relied on SLBMs, but in which ASW techniques were very effective. Offense and defense would be different, but the former would have the advantage. This situation is not likely to occur; but if it did, a status-quo state could show its lack of desire to exploit the other by refraining from threatening its submarines. The desire to have more protecting you than merely the other side's fear of retaliation is a strong one, however, and a state that knows that it would not expand even if its cities were safe is likely to believe that the other would not feel threatened by its ASW program. It is easy to see how such a world could become unstable, and how spirals of tensions and conflict could develop.

The fourth world is doubly safe. The differentiation between offensive and defensive systems permits a way out of the security dilemma; the advantage of the defense disposes of the problems discussed in the previous paragraphs. There is no reason for a status-quo power to be tempted to procure offensive forces, and aggressors give notice of their intentions by the posture they adopt. Indeed, if the advantage of the defense is great enough, there are no security problems. The loss of the ultimate form of the power to alter the status quo would allow greater scope for the exercise of nonmilitary means and probably would tend to freeze the distribution of values.

This world would have existed in the first decade of the twentieth century if the decision makers had understood the available technology. In that case, the European powers would have followed different policies both in the long run and in the summer of 1914. Even Germany, facing powerful enemies on both sides, could have made herself secure by developing strong defenses. France could also have made her frontier almost impregnable. Furthermore, when crises arose, no one would have had incentives to strike first. There would have been no competitive mobilization races reducing the time available for negotiations.

In the nuclear era, this world would be one in which the superpowers relied on SLBMs, ASW technology was not up to its task, and limited nuclear options were not taken seriously. . . . Because the problem of violence below the nuclear threshold would remain, on issues other than defense of the homeland, there would still be security dilemmas and security problems. But the world would nevertheless be safer than it has usually been.

NOTES

1. Thus, when Wolfers argues that a status-quo state that settles for rough equality of power with its adversary, rather than seeking preponderance, may be able to convince the other to reciprocate by showing that it wants only to protect itself, not menace the other, he assumes that the defense has an advantage. See Arnold Wolfers, *Discord and Collaboration* (Baltimore: Johns Hopkins Press, 1962), p. 126.
2. Thomas Schelling, *The Strategy of Conflict* (New York: Oxford University Press, 1963), chap. 9.
3. Quoted in Fritz Fischer, *War of Illusions* (New York: Norton, 1975), pp. 377, 461.
4. George Quester, *Offense and Defense in the International System* (New York: John Wiley, 1977), p. 105.
5. Herman Kahn, *On Thermonuclear War* (Princeton, N.J.: Princeton University Press, 1960), p. 211 (also see p. 144).
6. For a general discussion of such mistaken learning from the past, see Jervis, *Perception and Misperception in International Relations* (Princeton, N.J.: Princeton University Press, 1976), chap. 6. The important and still not completely understood question of

why this belief formed and was maintained throughout the war is examined in Bernard Brodie, *War and Politics* (New York: Macmillan, 1973), pp. 262–70; Brodie, "Technological Change, Strategic Doctrine, and Political Outcomes," in Klaus Knorr, ed., *Historical Dimensions of National Security Problems* (Lawrence: University Press of Kansas, 1976), pp. 290–92; and Douglas Porch, "The French Army and the Spirit of the Offensive, 1900–14," in Brian Bond and Ian Roy, eds., *War and Society* (New York: Holmes & Meier, 1975), pp. 117–43.

7. Some were not so optimistic. Grey's remark is well-known: "The lamps are going out all over Europe; we shall not see them lit again in our life-time." The German Prime Minister, Bethmann Hollweg, also feared the consequences of the war. But the controlling view was that it would certainly pay for the winner.

8. Quoted in Martin Gilbert, *Winston S. Churchill*, III, *The Challenge of War, 1914–1916* (Boston: Houghton Mifflin, 1971), p. 84.

9. Quester (fn. 4), pp. 98–99. Robert Art, *The Influence of Foreign Policy on Seapower*, II (Beverly Hills: Sage Professional Papers in International Studies Series, 1973), pp. 14–18, 26–28.

10. Konrad Jarausch, "The Illusion of Limited War: Chancellor Bethmann Hollweg's Calculated Risk, July 1914," *Central European History*, II (March 1969): p. 50.

11. Brodie, *War and Politics* (New York: Macmillan, 1973), p. 58.

12. President Roosevelt and the American delegates to the League of Nations Disarmament Conference maintained that the tank and the mobile heavy artillery had reestablished the dominance of the offensive, thus making disarmament more urgent (Marion Boggs, *Attempts to Define and Limit "Aggressive" Armament in Diplomacy and Strategy* [Columbia: University of Missouri Studies, XVI, no. 1, 1941]: pp. 31, 108), but this was a minority position and may not even have been believed by the Americans. The reduced prestige and influence of the military, and the high pressures to cut government spending throughout this period also contributed to the lowering of defense budgets.

13. Jon Kimche, *The Unfought Battle* (New York: Stein, 1968); Nicholas William Bethell, *The War Hitler Won: The Fall of Poland, September 1939* (New York: Holt, 1972); Alan Alexandroff and Richard Rosecrance, "Deterrence in 1939," *World Politics*, XXIX (April 1977): pp. 404–24.

14. Roderick Macleod and Denis Kelly, eds., *Time Unguarded: The Ironside Diaries, 1937–1940* (New York: McKay, 1962), p. 173.

15. For a short time, as France was falling, the British Cabinet did discuss reaching a negotiated peace with Hitler. The official history downplays this, but it is covered in P. M. H. Bell, *A Certain Eventuality* (Farnborough, England: Saxon House, 1974), pp. 40–48.

16. MacLeod and Kelly (fn. 14), 174. In flat contradiction to common sense and almost everything they believed about modern warfare, the Allies planned an expedition to Scandinavia to cut the supply of iron ore to Germany and to aid Finland against the Russians. But the dominant mood was the one described above.

17. Brodie (fn. 11), p. 179.

18. Arthur Balfour, "Memorandum," Committee on Imperial Defence, April 30, 1903, pp. 2–3; see the telegrams by Sir Arthur Nicolson, in G. P. Gooch and Harold Temperley, eds., *British Documents on the Origins of the War*, vol. 4 (London: H.M.S.O., 1929), pp. 429, 524. These barriers do not prevent the passage of long-range aircraft; but even in the air, distance usually aids the defender.

19. See, for example, the discussion of warfare among Chinese warlords in Hsi-Sheng Chi, "The Chinese Warlord System as an International System," in Morton Kaplan, ed., *New Approaches to International Relations* (New York: St. Martin's, 1968), pp. 405–25.

20. Some American decision makers, including military officers, thought that the best way out of the dilemma was to abandon the Philippines.

21. Quoted in Elting Morrison, *Turmoil and Tradition: A Study of the Life and Times of Henry L. Stimson* (Boston: Houghton Mifflin, 1960), p. 326.

22. The U.S. "refused to consider limitations on Hawaiian defenses, since these works posed no threat to Japan." William Braisted, *The United States Navy in the Pacific, 1909–1922* (Austin: University of Texas Press, 1971), p. 612.

23. That is part of the reason why the Japanese admirals strongly objected when the civilian leaders decided to accept a seven-to-ten ratio in lighter craft in 1930. Stephen Pelz, *Race to Pearl Harbor* (Cambridge, Mass.: Harvard University Press, 1974), p. 3.

24. John Nef, *War and Human Progress* (New York: Norton, 1963), p. 185. Also see *ibid.*, pp. 237, 242–43, and 323; C. W. Oman, *The Art of War in the Middle Ages* (Ithaca, N.Y.: Cornell University Press, 1953), pp. 70–72; John Beeler, *Warfare in Feudal Europe, 730–1200* (Ithaca, N.Y.: Cornell University Press, 1971), pp. 212–14; Michael Howard, *War in European History* (London: Oxford University Press, 1976), pp. 33–37.

25. Quincy Wright, *A Study of War* (abridged ed.; Chicago: University of Chicago Press, 1964), p. 142. Also see pp. 63–70, 74–75. There are important exceptions to these generalizations—the American Civil War, for instance, falls in the middle of the period Wright says is dominated by the offense.

26. Geoffrey Kemp, Robert Pfaltzgraff, and Uri Ra'anan, eds., *The Other Arms Race* (Lexington, Mass.: D.C. Heath, 1975); James Foster, "The Future of Conventional Arms Control," *Policy Sciences*, no. 8 (Spring 1977): pp. 1–19.

27. Richard Challener, *Admirals, Generals, and American Foreign Policy, 1898–1914* (Princeton, N.J.: Princeton University Press, 1973); Grey to Nicolson, in Gooch and Temperley (fn. 18), p. 414.

28. Quoted in James Crowley, *Japan's Quest for Autonomy* (Princeton, N.J.: Princeton University Press, 1966), p. 49. American naval officers agreed with the Japanese that a ten-to-six ratio would endanger Japan's supremacy in her home waters.

29. E. L. Woodward and R. Butler, ed., *Documents on British Foreign Policy, 1919–1939.* 3d ser. III (London: H.M.S.O., 1950), p. 526.

30. Jervis (fn. 6), pp. 69–72, 352–55.

31. Quoted in Merze Tate, *The United States and Armaments* (Cambridge, Mass.: Harvard University Press, 1948), p. 108.

32. Boggs (fn. 12), pp. 15, 40.

33. Kenneth Hagan, *American Gunboat Diplomacy and the Old Navy, 1877–1899* (Westport, Conn.: Greenwood Press, 1973), p. 20.

34. Winston Churchill, *The Gathering Storm* (Boston: Houghton, 1948), p. 206.

35. Brodie, *War and Politics* (fn. 6), p. 325.

36. Boggs (fn. 12), pp. 42, 83. For a good argument about the possible differentiation between offensive and defensive weapons in the 1930s, see Basil Liddell Hart, "Aggression and the Problem of Weapons," *English Review*, 55 (July 1932): pp. 71–78.

37. Quoted in Boggs (fn. 12), p. 39.

38. On these grounds, the Germans claimed in 1932 that the French forts were offensive (*ibid.*, p. 49). Similarly, fortified forward naval bases can be necessary for launching an attack; see Braisted (fn. 22), p. 643.

39. The French made this argument in the interwar period; see Richard Challener, *The French Theory of the Nation in Arms* (New York: Columbia University Press, 1955), pp. 181–82. The Germans disagreed; see Boggs (fn. 12), pp. 44 – 45.

40. Oman (fn. 24), pp. 57–58.

41. Quoted in Charles Webster, *The Foreign Policy of Castlereagh, II, 1815–1822* (London: G. Bell and Sons, 1963), p. 510.

42. Boggs (fn. 12), pp. 14–15, 47– 48, 60.

43. Quoted in Philip Jordan, *Frontier Law and Order* (Lincoln: University of Nebraska Press, 1970), p. 7; also see pp. 16–17.

44. Boggs (fn. 12), pp. 20, 28.

THE POLITICAL UTILITY OF
▇ FORCE TODAY

Complex Interdependence and the Role of Force

▇▇▇▇ ROBERT O. KEOHANE AND JOSEPH S. NYE

We live in an era of interdependence. This vague phrase expressed a poorly understood but widespread feeling that the very nature of world politics is changing. The power of nations—that age-old touchstone of analysts and statesmen—has become more elusive: "calculations of power are even more delicate and deceptive than in previous ages."[1] Henry Kissinger, though deeply rooted in the classical tradition, has stated that "the traditional agenda of international affairs—the balance among major powers, the security of nations—no longer defines our perils or our possibilities. . . . Now we are entering a new era. Old international patterns are crumbling; old slogans are uninstructive; old solutions are unavailing. The world has become interdependent in economics, in communications, in human aspirations."[2]

How profound are the changes? A modernist school sees telecommunications and jet travel as creating a "global village" and believes that burgeoning social and economic transactions are creating a "world without borders."[3] To greater or lesser extent, a number of scholars see our era as one in which the territorial state, which has been dominant in world politics for the four centuries since feudal times ended, is being eclipsed by nonterritorial actors such as multinational corporations, transnational social movements, and international organizations. As one economist put it, "the state is about through as an economic unit."[4]

Traditionalists call these assertions unfounded "globaloney." They point to the continuity in world politics. Military interdependence has always existed, and military power is still important in world politics—witness nuclear deterrence; the Vietnam, Middle East, and Indian-Pakistan wars; and Soviet influence in Eastern

Europe or American influence in the Caribbean. Moreover, as the Soviet Union has shown, authoritarian states can, to a considerable extent, control telecommunications and social transactions that they consider disruptive. Even poor and weak countries have been able to nationalize multinational corporations, and the prevalence of nationalism casts doubt on the proposition that the nation-state is fading away.

Neither the modernists nor the traditionalists have an adequate framework for understanding the politics of global interdependence.[5] Modernists point correctly to the fundamental changes now taking place, but they often assume without sufficient analysis that advances in technology and increases in social and economic transactions will lead to a new world in which states, and their control of force, will no longer be important.[6] Traditionalists are adept at showing flaws in the modernist vision by pointing out how military interdependence continues, but find it very difficult accurately to interpret today's multidimensional economic, social, and ecological interdependence.

Our task . . . is not to argue either the modernist or traditionalist position. Because our era is marked by both continuity and change, this would be fruitless. Rather, our task is to provide a means of distilling and blending the wisdom in both positions by developing a coherent theoretical framework for the political analysis of interdependence. We shall develop several different but potentially complementary models, or intellectual tools, for grasping the reality of interdependence in contemporary world politics. Equally important, we shall attempt to explore the *conditions* under which each model will be most likely to produce accurate predictions and satisfactory explanations. Contemporary world politics is not a seamless web; it is a tapestry of diverse relationships. In such a world, one model cannot explain all situations. The secret of understanding lies in knowing which approach or combination of approaches to use in analyzing a situation. There will never be a substitute for careful analysis of actual situations. . . .

THE NEW RHETORIC OF INTERDEPENDENCE

During the Cold War, "national security" was a slogan American political leaders used to generate support for their policies. The rhetoric of national security justified strategies designed, at considerable cost, to bolster the economic, military, and political structure of the "free world." It also provided a rationale for international cooperation and support for the United Nations, as well as justification for alliances, foreign aid, and extensive military involvements.

National security became the favorite symbol of the internationalists who favored increased American involvement in world affairs. The key foreign policy coordinating unit in the White House was named the National Security Council. The Truman administration used the alleged Soviet threat to American security to push the loan to Britain and then the Marshall Plan through Congress. The Kennedy administration employed the security argument to promote the 1962 Trade Expansion Act. Presidents invoked national security to control certain sectoral economic interests in Congress, particularly those favoring protectionist trade policies. Congressmen who protested adverse economic effects on their districts or increased taxes were assured—and in turn explained to constituents—that the "national security interests" required their sacrifice. At the same time, special interests frequently manipulated the symbolism of national security for their own purposes, as in the case of petroleum import quotas, promoted particularly by domestic oil producers and their political allies.[7]

National security symbolism was largely a product of the Cold War and the severe threat Americans then felt. Its persuasiveness was increased by realist analysis, which insisted that national security is the primary national goal and that in international politics security threats are permanent. National security symbolism, and the realist mode of analysis that supported it, not only epitomized a certain way of reacting to events, but helped to codify a perspective in which some changes, particularly those toward radical regimes in Third World countries, seemed inimical to national security, while fundamental changes in the economic relations among advanced industrialized countries seemed insignificant.

As the Cold War sense of security threat slackened, foreign economic competition and domestic distributional conflict increased. The intellectual ambiguity of "national security" became more pronounced as varied and often contradictory forms of involvement took shelter under a single rhetorical umbrella.[8] In his imagery of a world balance of power among five major centers (the United States, the Soviet Union, China, Europe, Japan), President Nixon tried unsuccessfully to extend traditional realist concepts to apply to the economic challenge posed by America's postwar allies, as well as the political and military actions of the Soviet Union and China.

As the descriptive accuracy of a view of national security dominated by military concerns declined, so did the term's symbolic power. This decline reflected not only the increased ambiguity of the concept, but also American reaction to the Vietnam imbroglio, to the less hostile relationship with Russia and China summed up by the word *détente,* and to misuse of national security rhetoric by President Nixon in the Watergate affair. National security had to share its position as the prime symbol in the internationalists' lexicon with *interdependence.*

Political leaders often use interdependence rhetoric to portray interdependence as a natural necessity, as a fact to which policy (and domestic interest groups) must adjust, rather than as a situation partially created by policy itself. They usually argue that conflicts of interest are reduced by interdependence, and that cooperation alone holds the answer to world problems.

"We are all engaged in a common enterprise. No nation or group of nations can gain by pushing beyond the limits that sustain world economic growth. No one benefits from basing progress on tests of strength."[9] These words clearly belong to a statesman intending to limit demands from the Third World and influence public attitudes at home, rather than to analyze contemporary reality. For those who wish the United States to retain world leadership, interdependence has become part of the new rhetoric, to be used against both economic nationalism at home and assertive challenges abroad. Although the connotations of interdependence rhetoric may seem quite different from those of national security symbolism, each has often been used to legitimize American presidential leadership in world affairs. . . .

Yet interdependence rhetoric and national security symbolism coexist only uneasily. In its extreme formulation, the former suggests that conflicts of interest are passé, whereas the latter argues that they are, and will remain, fundamental, and potentially violent. The confusion in knowing what analytical models to apply to world politics (as we noted earlier) is thus paralleled by confusion about the policies that should be employed by the United States. Neither interdependence rhetoric nor national security symbolism provides reliable guidelines for problems of extensive interdependence.

Rhetoriticians of interdependence often claim that since the survival of the human race is threatened by environmental as well as military dangers, conflicts of interest among states and people no longer exist. This conclusion would only follow if three conditions were met: an international economic system on which everyone depended or our basic life-supporting ecological system were in danger; all countries were significantly vulnerable to such a catastrophe; *and* there were only one solution to the problem (leaving no room for conflict about how to solve it and who should bear the costs). Obviously these conditions are rarely all present.

Yet balance of power theories and national security imagery are also poorly adapted to analyzing problems of economic or ecological interdependence. Security, in traditional terms, is not likely to be the principal issue facing governments. Insofar as military force is ineffective on certain issues, the conventional notion of power lacks precision. In particular, different power resources may be needed to deal with different issues. Finally, in the politics of interdependence, domestic and transnational as well as governmental interests are involved. Domestic and foreign policy become closely linked. The notion of national interest—the traditionalists' lodestar—becomes increasingly difficult to use effectively. Traditional maxims of international politics—that states will act in their national interests or that they will attempt to maximize their power—become ambiguous.

We are not suggesting that international conflict disappears when interdependence prevails. On the contrary, conflict will take new forms, and may even increase. But the traditional approaches to understanding conflict in world politics will not explain interdependence conflict particularly well. Applying the wrong image and the wrong rhetoric to problems will lead to erroneous analysis and bad policy. . . .

Manipulating economic or sociopolitical vulnerabilities, however, also bears risks. Strategies of manipulating interdependence are likely to lead to counterstrategies. It must always be kept in mind, furthermore, that military power dominates economic power in the sense that economic means alone are likely to be ineffective against the serious use of military force. Thus, even effective manipulation of asymmetrical interdependence within a nonmilitary area can create risks of military counteraction. When the United States exploited Japanese vulnerability to economic embargo in 1940–41, Japan countered by attacking Pearl Harbor and the Philippines. Yet military actions are usually very costly; and for many types of actions, these costs have risen steeply during the last thirty years.

Table 1 shows the three types of asymmetrical interdependence that we have been discussing. The dominance ranking column indicates that the power resources provided by military interdependence dominate those provided by nonmilitary vulnerability, which in turn dominate those provided by asymmetries in sensitivity. Yet exercising more dominant forms of power brings higher costs.

TABLE 1 ■ ASYMMETRICAL INTERDEPENDENCE AND ITS USES

Source of interdependence	Dominance ranking	Cost ranking	Contemporary use
Military (costs of using military force)	1	1	Used in extreme situations or against weak foes when costs may be slight.
Nonmilitary vulnerability (costs of pursuing alternative policies)	2	2	Used when normative constraints are low, and international rules are not considered binding (including nonmilitary relations between adversaries, and situations of extremely high conflict between close partners and allies).
Nonmilitary sensitivity (costs of change under existing policies)	3	3	A power resource in the short run or when normative constraints are high and international rules are binding. Limited, since if high costs are imposed, disadvantaged actors may formulate new policies.

Thus, *relative to cost,* there is no guarantee that military means will be more effective than economic ones to achieve a given purpose. We can expect, however, that as the interests at stake become more important, actors will tend to use power resources that rank higher in both dominance and cost. . . .

One's assumptions about world politics profoundly affect what one sees and how one constructs theories to explain events. We believe that the assumptions of political realists, whose theories dominated the postwar period, are often an inadequate basis for analyzing the politics of interdependence. The realist assumptions about world politics can be seen as defining an extreme set of conditions or *ideal type.* One could also imagine very different conditions. In this chapter, we shall construct another ideal type, the opposite of realism. We call it *complex interdependence.* After establishing the differences between realism and complex interdependence, we shall argue that complex interdependence sometimes comes closer to reality than does realism. When it does, traditional explanations of change in international regimes become questionable and the search for new explanatory models becomes more urgent.

For political realists, international politics, like all other politics, is a struggle for power but, unlike domestic politics, a struggle dominated by organized violence. In the words of the most influential postwar textbook, "All history shows that nations active in international politics are continuously preparing for, actively involved in, or recovering from organized violence in the form of war."[10] Three assumptions are integral to the realist vision. First, states as coherent units are the dominant actors in world politics. This is a double assumption: States are predominant; and they act as coherent units. Second, realists assume that force is a usable and effective instrument of policy. Other instruments may also be employed, but using or threatening force is the most effective means of wielding power. Third, partly because of their second assumption, realists assume a hierarchy of issues in world politics, headed by questions of military security: the "high politics" of military security dominates the "low politics" of economic and social affairs.

These realist assumptions define an ideal type of world politics. They allow us to imagine a world in which politics is continually characterized by active or potential conflict among states, with the use of force possible at any time. Each state attempts to defend its territory and interests from real or perceived threats. Political integration among states is slight and lasts only as long as it serves the national interests of the most powerful states. Transitional actors either do not exist or are politically unimportant. Only the adept exercise of force or the threat of force permits states to survive, and only while statesmen succeed in adjusting their interests, as in a well-functioning balance of power, is the system stable.

Each of the realist assumptions can be challenged. If we challenge them all simultaneously, we can imagine a world in which actors other than states participate directly in world politics, in which a clear hierarchy of issues does not exist, and in which force is an ineffective instrument of policy. Under these conditions— which we call the characteristics of complex interdependence—one would expect world politics to be very different than under realist conditions. . . .

We do not argue, however, that complex interdependence faithfully reflects world political reality. Quite the contrary: Both it and the realist portrait are ideal types. Most situations will fall somewhere between these two extremes. Sometimes, realist assumptions will be accurate, or largely accurate, but frequently complex interdependence will provide a better portrayal of reality. Before one decides what explanatory model to apply to a situation or problem, one will need to understand the degree to which realist or complex interdependence assumptions correspond to the situation.

THE CHARACTERISTICS OF COMPLEX INTERDEPENDENCE

Complex interdependence has three main characteristics:

1. *Multiple channels* connect societies, including: informal ties between governmental elites as well as formal foreign office arrangements; informal ties among nongovernmental elites (face-to-face and through telecommunications); and transnational organizations (such as multinational banks or corporations). These channels can be summarized as interstate, transgovernmental, and transnational relations. *Interstate* relations are the normal channels assumed by realists. *Transgovernmental* applies when we relax the realist assumption that states act coherently as units; *transnational* applies when we relax the assumption that states are the only units.
2. The agenda of interstate relationships consists of multiple issues that are not arranged in a clear or consistent hierarchy. This *absence of hierarchy*

among issues means, among other things, that military security does not consistently dominate the agenda. Many issues arise from what used to be considered domestic policy, and the distinction between domestic and foreign issues becomes blurred. These issues are considered in several government departments (not just foreign offices), and at several levels. Inadequate policy coordination on these issues involves significant costs. Different issues generate different coalitions, both within governments and across them, and involve different degrees of conflict. Politics does not stop at the waters' edge.

3. Military force is not used by governments toward other governments within the region, or on the issues, when complex interdependence prevails. It may, however, be important in these governments' relations with governments outside that region, or on other issues. Military force could, for instance, be irrelevant to resolving disagreements on economic issues among members of an alliance, yet at the same time be very important for the alliance's political and military relations with a rival bloc. For the former relationships this condition of complex interdependence would be met; for the latter, it would not.

Traditional theories of international politics implicitly or explicitly deny the accuracy of these three assumptions. Traditionalists are therefore tempted also to deny the relevance of criticisms based on the complex interdependence ideal type. We believe, however, that our three conditions are fairly well approximated on some global issues of economic and ecological interdependence and that they come close to characterizing the entire relationship between some countries. One of our purposes here is to prove that contention. . . .

Multiple Channels

A visit to any major airport is a dramatic way to confirm the existence of multiple channels of contact among advanced industrial countries; there is a voluminous literature to prove it.[11] Bureaucrats from different countries deal directly with one another at meetings and on the telephone as well as in writing. Similarly, nongovernmental elites frequently get together in the normal course of business, in organizations such as the Trilateral Commission, and in conferences sponsored by private foundations.

In addition, multinational firms and banks affect both domestic and interstate relations. The limits on private firms, or the closeness of ties between government and business, vary considerably from one society to another; but the participation of large and dynamic organizations, not controlled entirely by governments, has become a normal part of foreign as well as domestic relations.

These actors are important not only because of their activities in pursuit of their own interests, but also because they act as transmission belts, making government policies in various countries more sensitive to one another. As the scope of governments' domestic activities has broadened, and as corporations, banks, and (to a lesser extent) trade unions have made decisions that transcend national boundaries, the domestic policies of different countries impinge on one another more and more. Transnational communications reinforce these effects. Thus, foreign economic policies touch more domestic economic activity than in the past, blurring the lines between domestic and foreign policy and increasing the number of issues relevant to foreign policy. Parallel developments in issues of environmental regulation and control over technology reinforce this trend.

Absence of Hierarchy Among Issues

Foreign affairs agendas—that is, sets of issues relevant to foreign policy with which governments are concerned—have become larger and more diverse. No longer can all issues be subordinated to military security. As Secretary of State Kissinger described the situation in 1975:

> Progress in dealing with the traditional agenda is no longer enough. A new and unprecedented kind of issue has emerged. The problems of energy, resources, environment, population, the uses of space and the seas now rank with questions of military security, ideology and territorial rivalry which have traditionally made up the diplomatic agenda.[12]

Kissinger's list, which could be expanded, illustrates how governments' policies, even those previously considered merely domestic, impinge on one another. The extensive consultative arrangements developed by the OECD, as well as the GATT, IMF, and the European Community, indicate how characteristic the overlap of domestic and foreign policy is among developed pluralist countries. The organization within nine major departments of the United States government (Agriculture, Commerce, Defense, Health, Education and Welfare, Interior, Justice, Labor, State, and Treasury) and many other agencies reflects their extensive international commitments. The multiple, overlapping issues that result make a nightmare of governmental organization.[13]

When there are multiple issues on the agenda, many of which threaten the interests of domestic groups but do not clearly threaten the nation as a whole, the problems of formulating a coherent and consistent foreign policy increase. In 1975 energy was a foreign policy problem, but specific remedies, such as a tax on gasoline and automobiles, involved domestic legislation opposed by auto workers and companies alike. As one commentator observed, "virtually every time Congress has set a national policy that changed the way people live . . . the action came after a consensus had developed, bit by bit, over the years, that a problem existed and that there was one best way to solve it."[14] Opportunities for delay, for special protection, for inconsistency and incoherence abound when international politics requires aligning the domestic policies of pluralist democratic countries.

Minor Role of Military Force

Political scientists have traditionally emphasized the role of military force in international politics. . . . [F]orce dominates other means of power: *if* there are no constraints on one's choice of instruments (a hypothetical situation that has only been approximated in the two world wars), the state with superior military force will prevail. If the security dilemma for all states were extremely acute, military force, supported by economic and other resources, would clearly be the dominant source of power. Survival is the primary goal of all states, and in the worst situations, force is ultimately necessary to guarantee survival. Thus military force is always a central component of national power.

Yet particularly among industrialized, pluralist countries, the perceived margin of safety has widened: Fears of attack in general have declined, and fears of attacks *by one another* are virtually nonexistent. France has abandoned the *tous azimuts* (defense in all directions) strategy that President de Gaulle advocated (it was not taken entirely seriously even at the time). Canada's last war plans for fighting the United States were abandoned half a century ago. Britain and Germany no longer feel threatened by each other. Intense relationships of mutual influence exist between these countries, but in most of them force is irrelevant or unimportant as an instrument of policy.

Moreover, force is often not an appropriate way of achieving other goals (such as economic and ecological welfare) that are becoming more important. It is not impossible to imagine dramatic conflict or revolutionary change in which the use or threat of military force over an economic issue or among advanced industrial countries might become plausible. Then realist assumptions would again be a reliable guide to events. But in most situations, the effects of military force are both costly and uncertain.[15]

Even when the direct use of force is barred among a group of countries, however, military power can still be used politically. [During the Cold War] each superpower . . . used the threat of force to deter attacks by other superpowers on itself or its allies; its deterrence ability thus served an indirect, protective role, which it [could] use in bargaining on other issues with its allies. . . .

Thus, even for countries whose relations approximate complex interdependence, two serious qualifications remain: (1) drastic social and political change could cause force again to become an important direct instrument of policy; and (2) even when elites' interests are complementary, a country that uses military force to protect another may have significant political influence over the other country. . . .

The recourse to force seems less likely now than at most times during the century before 1945. The destructiveness of nuclear weapons makes any attack against a nuclear power dangerous. Nuclear weapons are mostly used as a deterrent. Threats of nuclear action against much weaker countries may occasionally be efficacious, but they are equally or more likely to solidify relations between one's adversaries. The limited usefulness of conventional force to control socially mobilized populations has been shown by the United States failure in Vietnam as well as by the rapid decline of colonialism in Africa. Furthermore, employing force on one issue against an independent state with which one has a variety of relationships is likely to rupture mutually profitable relations on other issues. In other words, the use of force often has costly effects on nonsecurity goals. And finally, in Western democracies, popular opposition to prolonged military conflicts is very high.[16]

It is clear that these constraints bear unequally on various countries, or on the same countries in different situations. Risks of nuclear escalation affect everyone, but domestic opinion is far less constraining for communist states, or for authoritarian regional powers, than for the United States, Europe, or Japan. Even authoritarian countries may be reluctant to use force to obtain economic objectives when such use might be ineffective and disrupt other relationships. Both the difficulty of controlling socially mobilized populations with foreign troops and the changing technology of weaponry may actually enhance the ability of certain countries, or nonstate groups, to use terrorism as a political weapon without effective fear of reprisal.

The fact that the changing role of force has uneven effects does not make the change less important, but it does make matters more complex. This complexity is compounded by differences in the usability of force among issue areas. When an issue arouses little interest or passion, force may be unthinkable. In such instances, complex interdependence may be a valuable concept for analyzing the political process. But if that issue becomes a matter of life and death—as some people thought oil might become—the use or threat of force could become decisive again. Realist assumptions would then be more relevant.

It is thus important to determine the applicability of realism or of complex interdependence to each situation. Without this determination, further analysis is likely to be confused. Our purpose in developing an alternative to the realist description of world politics is to encourage a differentiated approach that distinguishes among dimensions and areas of world politics—not (as some modernist observers do) to replace one oversimplification with another.

THE POLITICAL PROCESS OF COMPLEX INTERDEPENDENCE

The three main characteristics of complex interdependence give rise to distinctive political processes, which translate power resources into power as control of outcomes. As we argued earlier, something is usually lost or added in the translation. Under conditions of complex interdependence the translation will be different than under realist conditions, and our predictions about outcomes will need to be adjusted accordingly.

In the realist world, military security will be the dominant goal of states. It will even affect issues that are not directly involved with military power or territorial defense. Nonmilitary problems will not only be subordinated to military ones; they will be studied for their politico-military implications. Balance of payments issues, for instance, will be considered at least as much in the light of their implications for world power generally as for their purely financial ramifications. McGeorge Bundy conformed to realist expectations when he argued in 1964 that devaluation of the dollar should be seriously considered if necessary to fight the war in Vietnam.[17] To some extent, so did former Treasury Secretary Henry Fowler when he contended in 1971 that the United States needed a trade surplus of $4 billion to $6 billion in order to lead in Western defense.[18]

In a world of complex interdependence, however, one expects some officials, particularly at lower levels, to emphasize the *variety* of state goals that must be pursued. In the absence of a clear hierarchy of issues, goals will vary by issue, and may not be closely related. Each bureaucracy will pursue its own concerns; and although several agencies may reach compromises on issues that affect them all, they will find that a consistent pattern of policy is difficult to maintain. Moreover, transnational actors will introduce different goals into various groups of issues.

Linkage Strategies

Goals will therefore vary by issue area under complex interdependence, but so will the distribution of power and the typical political processes. Traditional analysis focuses on *the* international system, and leads us to anticipate similar political processes on a variety of issues. Militarily and economically strong states will dominate a variety of organizations and a variety of issues, by linking their own policies on some issues to other states' policies on other issues. By using their overall dominance to prevail on their weak issues, the strongest states will, in the traditional model, ensure a congruence between the overall structure of military and economic power and the pattern of outcomes on any one issue area. Thus world politics can be treated as a seamless web.

Under complex interdependence, such congruence is less likely to occur. As military force is devalued, militarily strong states will find it more difficult to use their overall dominance to control outcomes on issues in which they are weak. And since the distribution of power resources in trade, shipping, or oil, for example, may be quite different, patterns of outcomes and distinctive political processes are likely to vary from one set of issues to another. If force were readily applicable, and military security were the highest foreign policy goal, these variations in the issue structures of power would not matter very much. The linkages drawn from them to military issues would ensure consistent dominance by the overall strongest states. But when military force is largely immobilized, strong states will find that linkage is less effective. They may still attempt such links, but in the absence of hierarchy of issues, their success will be problematic.

Dominant states may try to secure much the same result by using overall economic power to affect results on other issues. If only economic objectives are at stake, they may succeed: Money, after all, is fungible. But economic objectives have political implications, and economic linkage by the strong is limited by domestic, transnational, and transgovernmental actors who resist having their interests traded off. Furthermore, the international actors may be different on different issues, and the international organizations in which negotiations take place are often quite separate. Thus it is difficult, for example, to imagine a military or economically strong state linking concessions on monetary policy to reciprocal concessions in oceans policy. On the other hand, poor weak states are not similarly inhibited from linking unrelated issues, partly because their domestic interests are less complex. Linkage of unrelated issues is often a means of extracting concessions or side payments from rich and powerful states. And unlike powerful states whose instrument for linkage (military force) is often too costly to use, the linkage instrument used by poor, weak states—international organization—is available and inexpensive.

Thus as the utility of force declines, and as issues become more equal in importance, the distribution of power within each issue will become more important. If linkages become less effective on the whole, outcomes of political bargaining will increasingly vary by issue area.

The differentiation among issue areas in complex interdependence means that linkages among issues will become more problematic and will tend to reduce rather than reinforce international hierarchy. Linkage strategies, and defense against them, will pose critical strategic choices for states. Should issues be considered separately or as a package? If linkages are to be drawn, which issues should be linked, and on which of the linked issues should concessions be made? How far can one push a linkage before it becomes counterproductive? For instance, should one seek formal agreements or informal, but less politically sensitive, understandings? The fact that world politics under complex interdependence is not a seamless web leads us to expect that efforts to stitch seams together advantageously, as reflected in linkage strategies, will, very often, determine the shape of the fabric.

The negligible role of force leads us to expect states to rely more on other instruments in order to wield power. For the reasons we have already discussed, less vulnerable states will try to use asymmetrical interdependence in particular groups of issues as a source of power; they will also try to use international organizations and transnational actors and flows. States will approach economic interdependence in terms of power as well as its effects on citizens' welfare, although welfare considerations will limit their attempts to maximize power. Most economic and ecological interdependence involves the possibility of joint gains or joint losses. Mutual awareness of potential gains and losses and the danger of worsening each actor's position through overly rigorous struggles over the distribution of the gains can limit the use of asymmetrical interdependence.

Agenda Setting

Our second assumption of complex interdependence, the lack of clear hierarchy among multiple issues, leads us to expect that the politics of agenda formation and control will become more important. Traditional analyses lead statesmen to focus on politico-military issues and to pay little attention to the broader politics of agenda formation. Statesmen assume that the agenda will be set by shifts in the balance of power, actual or anticipated, and by perceived threats to the security of states. Other issues will only be very important when they seem to affect security and military power. In these cases, agendas will be influenced strongly by considerations of the overall balance of power.

Yet, today, some nonmilitary issues are emphasized in interstate relations at one time, whereas others of seemingly equal importance are neglected or quietly handled at a technical level. International monetary politics, problems of commodity terms of trade, oil, food, and multinational corporations have all been important during the last decade; but not all have been high on interstate agendas throughout that period.

Traditional analysts of international politics have paid little attention to agenda formation: to how issues come to receive sustained attention by high officials. The traditional orientation toward military and security affairs implies that the crucial problems of foreign policy are imposed on states by the actions or threats of other states. These are high politics as opposed to the low politics of economic affairs. Yet, as the complexity of actors and issues in world politics increases, the utility of force declines and the line between domestic policy and foreign policy becomes blurred: As the conditions of complex interdependence are more closely approximated, the politics of agenda formation becomes more subtle and differentiated.

Under complex interdependence we can expect the agenda to be affected by the international and domestic problems created by economic growth and increasing sensitivity interdependence. . . . Discontented domestic groups will politicize issues and force more issues once considered domestic onto the interstate agenda. Shifts in the distribution of power resources within sets of issues will also affect agendas. During the early 1970s the increased power of oil-producing governments over the transnational corporation and the consumer countries dramatically altered the policy agenda. Moreover, agendas for one group of issues may change as a result of linkages from other groups in which power resources are changing; for example, the broader agenda of North-South trade issues changed after the OPEC price rises and the oil embargo of 1973–74. Even if capabilities among states do not change, agendas may be affected by shifts in the importance of transnational actors. The publicity surrounding multinational corporations in the early 1970s, coupled with their rapid growth over the past twenty years, put the regulation of such corporations higher on both the United Nations agenda and national agendas.

Politicization—agitation and controversy over an issue that tend to raise it to the top of the agenda—can have many sources, as we have seen. Governments whose strength is increasing may politicize issues by linking them to other issues. An international regime that is becoming ineffective or is not serving important issues may cause increasing politicization, as dissatisfied governments press for change. Politicization, however, can also come from below. Domestic groups may become upset enough to raise a dormant issue, or to interfere with interstate bargaining at high levels. In 1974 the American secretary of state's tacit linkage of a Soviet-American trade pact with progress in détente was upset by the success of domestic American groups working through Congress to link a trade agreement with Soviet policies on emigration.

The technical characteristics and institutional setting in which issues are raised will strongly affect politicization patterns. In the United States, congressional attention is an effective instrument of politicization. Generally, we expect transnational economic organizations and transgovernmental networks of bureaucrats to seek to avoid politicization. Domestically based groups (such as trade unions) and domestically oriented bureaucracies will tend to use politicization (particularly congressional attention) against their transnationally mobile competitors. At the international level, we expect states and actors to "shop among forums" and struggle to get issues raised in international organizations that will maximize their advantage by broadening or narrowing the agenda.

Transnational and Transgovernmental Relations

Our third condition of complex interdependence, multiple channels of contact among societies, further blurs the distinction between domestic and international politics. The availability of partners in political coalitions is not necessarily limited by national boundaries as traditional analysis assumes. The nearer a situation is to complex interdependence, the more we expect the outcomes of political bargaining to be affected by transnational relations. Multinational corporations may be significant both as independent actors and as instruments manipulated by governments. The attitudes and policy stands of domestic groups are likely to be affected by communications, organized or not, between them and their counterparts abroad.

Thus the existence of multiple channels of contact leads us to expect limits, beyond those normally found in domestic politics, on the ability of statesmen to calculate the manipulation of interdependence or follow a consistent strategy of linkage. Statesmen must consider differential as well as aggregate effects of interdependence strategies and their likely implications for politicization and agenda control. Transactions among societies—economic and social transactions more than security ones—affect groups differently. Opportunities and costs from increased transnational ties may be greater for certain groups—for instance, American workers in the textile or shoe industries—than for others. Some organizations or groups may interact directly with actors in other societies or with other governments to increase their benefits from a network of interaction. Some actors may therefore be less vulnerable as well as less sensitive to changes elsewhere in the network than are others, and this will affect patterns of political action.

The multiple channels of contact found in complex interdependence are not limited to nongovernmental actors. Contacts between governmental bureaucracies charged with similar tasks may not only alter their perspectives but lead to transgovernmental coalitions on particular policy questions. To improve their chances of success, government agencies attempt to bring actors from other governments into their own decision-making processes as allies. Agencies of powerful states such as the United States have used such coalitions to penetrate weaker governments in such countries as Turkey and Chile. They have also been used to help agencies of other governments penetrate the United States bureaucracy.[19]... [T]ransgovernmental politics frequently characterizes Canadian-American relations, often to the advantage of Canadian interests.

The existence of transgovernmental policy networks leads to a different interpretation of one of the standard propositions about international politics—that states act in their own interest. Under complex interdependence, this conventional wisdom begs two important questions: Which self and which interest? A government agency may pursue its own interests under the guise of the national interest; and recurrent interactions can change official perceptions of their interests. As a careful study of the politics of United States trade policy has documented, concentrating only on pressures of various interests for decisions leads to an overly mechanistic view of a continuous process and neglects the important role of communications in slowly changing perceptions of self-interest.[20]

The ambiguity of the national interest raises serious problems for the top political leaders of governments. As bureaucracies contact each other directly across national borders (without going through foreign offices), centralized control becomes more difficult. There is less assurance that the state will be united when dealing with foreign governments or that its components will interpret national interests similarly when negotiating with foreigners. The state may prove to be multifaceted, even schizophrenic. National interest will be defined differently on different issues, at different times, and by different governmental units. States that are better placed to maintain their coherence (because of a centralized political tradition such as France's) will be better able to manipulate uneven interdependence than fragmented states that at first glance seem to have more resources in an issue area.

NOTES

1. Stanley Hoffmann, "Notes on the Elusiveness of Modern Power," *International Journal* 30 (Spring 1975): p. 184.
2. "A New National Partnership," speech by Secretary of State Henry A. Kissinger at Los Angeles, January 24, 1975. News release, Department of State, Bureau of Public Affairs, Office of Media Services, p. 1.
3. See, for example, Lester R. Brown, *World Without Borders: The Interdependence of Nations* (New York: Foreign Policy Association, Headline Series, 1972).
4. Charles Kindleberger, *American Business Abroad* (New Haven, Conn.: Yale University Press, 1969), p. 207.
5. The terms are derived from Stanley Hoffmann, "Choices," *Foreign Policy* 12 (Fall 1973): p. 6.
6. For instance, see Robert Angell, *Peace on the March: Transnational Participation* (New York: Van Nostrand, 1969).
7. See Robert Engler, *The Politics of Oil: Private Power and Democratic Directions* (Chicago: University of Chicago Press, 1962).
8. Arnold Wolfers' "National Security as an Ambiguous Symbol" remains the classic analysis. See his collection of essays, *Discord and Collaboration* (Baltimore: Johns Hopkins University Press, 1962). Daniel Yergin's study of the emergence of the doctrine of national security (in place of the traditional concept of defense) portrays it as a "commanding idea" of the Cold War era. See Daniel Yergin, *The Shattered Peace: The Rise of the National Security State* (Boston: Houghton Mifflin, 1976).
9. Secretary of State Henry A. Kissinger, Address before the Sixth Special Session of the United Nations General Assembly, April 15, 1974. News release, Department of State, Office of Media Services, 2. Reprinted in *International Organization* 28, no. 3 (Summer 1974): pp. 573–83.
10. Hans J. Morgenthau, *Politics Among Nations: The Struggle for Power and Peace*, 4th ed. (New York: Knopf, 1967), p. 36.
11. See Edward L. Morse, "Transnational Economic Processes," in Robert O. Keohane and Joseph S. Nye, Jr., eds., *Transnational Relations and World Politics* (Cambridge, Mass.: Harvard University Press, 1972).

12. Henry A. Kissinger, "A New National Partnership," *Department of State Bulletin,* February 17, 1975, p. 199.

13. See the report of the Commission on the Organization of the Government for the Conduct of Foreign Policy (Murphy Commission) (Washington, D.C.: U.S. Government Printing Office, 1975), and the studies prepared for that report. See also Raymond Hopkins, "The International Role of 'Domestic' Bureaucracy," *International Organization* 30, no. 3 (Summer 1976).

14. *The New York Times,* May 22, 1975.

15. For a valuable discussion, see Klaus Knorr, *The Power of Nations: The Political Economy of International Relations* (New York: Basic Books, 1975).

16. Stanley Hoffmann, "The Acceptability of Military Force," and Laurence Martin, "The Utility of Military Force," in *Force in Modern Societies: Its Place in International Politics* (Adelphi Paper, International Institute for Strategic Studies, 1973). See also Knorr, *The Power of Nations.*

17. Henry Brandon, *The Retreat of American Power* (New York: Doubleday, 1974), p. 218.

18. *International Implications of the New Economic Policy,* U.S. Congress, House of Representatives, Committee on Foreign Affairs, Subcommittee on Foreign Economic Policy, Hearings, September 16, 1971.

19. For a more detailed discussion, see Robert O. Keohane and Joseph S. Nye, Jr., "Transgovernmental Relations and International Organizations," *World Politics* 27, no. 1 (October 1974): pp. 39–62.

20. Raymond Bauer, Ithiel de Sola Pool, and Lewis Dexter, *American Business and Foreign Policy* (New York: Atherton, 1963), chap. 35, esp. pp. 472–75.

The Fungibility of Force

ROBERT J. ART

There are two fundamental reasons why military power remains more essential to statecraft than is commonly thought. First, in an anarchic realm (one without a central government), force is integral to political interaction. Foreign policy cannot be divorced from military power. Second, force is "fungible." It can be used for a wide variety of tasks and across different policy domains; it can be employed for both military and nonmilitary purposes. . . .

POWER ASSETS: COMPARISONS AND CONFUSIONS

. . . I have argued that force is integral to statecraft because international politics is anarchic. By itself, that fact makes force fungible to a degree. Exactly how fungible an instrument is military power, however, and how does it compare in this regard to the other power assets a state wields? In this section, I answer these questions. First, I make a rough comparison as to the fungibility of the main instruments of statecraft. Second, I present a counterargument that force has little fungibility and then critique it.

Comparing Power Assets

Comparing the instruments of statecraft according to their fungibility is a difficult task. We do not have a large body of empirical studies that systematically analyze the comparative fungibility of a state's power assets. The few studies we do have, even though they are carefully done, focus on only one or two instruments and are more concerned with looking at assets within specific issue areas than with comparing assets across issue areas. As a consequence, we lack sufficient evidence to compare power assets according to their fungibility. Through a little logic, however, we can provide some ballpark estimates.

Consider what power assets a state owns. They include population—the size, education level, and skills of its citizenry; geography—the size, location, and natural resource endowment of the state; governance—the effectiveness of its political system; values—the norms a state lives by and stands for, the nature of its ideology,

From "American Foreign Policy and the Fungibility of Force," *Security Studies*, Vol. 5, No. 4 (Summer 1996), pp. 7–42. Copyright © 1996 from Security Studies by Robert Art. Reproduced by permission of Taylor & Francis, Inc., http://www.routledge-ny.com.

and the extent of its appeal to foreigners; wealth—the level, sources, and nature of its productive economy; leadership—the political skill of its leaders and the number of skillful leaders it has; and military power—the nature, size, and composition of its military forces. Of all these assets, wealth and political skill look to be the most versatile, geography and governance the least versatile, because both are more in the nature of givens that set the physical and political context within which the other assets operate; values and population are highly variable, depending, respectively, on the content of the values and on the education and skill of the populace; and military power lies somewhere between wealth and skill on the one hand, and geography and governance on the other hand, but closer to the former than to the latter. In rank order, the three most fungible power assets appear to be wealth, political skill, and military power.

Economic wealth has the highest fungibility. It is the easiest to convert into the most liquid asset of all, namely, money, which in turn can be used to buy many different things—such as a good press, topflight international negotiators, smart lawyers, cutting-edge technology, bargaining power in international organizations, and so on. Wealth is also integral to military power. A rich state can generate more military power than a poor one. A state that is large and rich can, if it so chooses, generate especially large amounts of military power. The old mercantilist insight that wealth generates power (and vice-versa) is still valid.

Political skill is a second power asset that is highly fungible. By definition, skilled political operators are ones who can operate well in different policy realms because they have mastered the techniques of persuasion and influence. They are equally adept at selling free trade agreements, wars, or foreign aid to their citizens. Politically skillful statesmen can roam with ease across different policy realms. Indeed, that is what we commonly mean by a politically skillful leader—one who can lead in many different policy arenas. Thus, wealth and skill are resources that are easily transferable from one policy realm to another and are probably the two most liquid power assets.

Military power is a third fungible asset. It is not as fungible as wealth or skill, but that does not make it illiquid. Military power possesses versatility because force is integral to politics, even when states are at peace. If force is integral to international politics, it must be fungible. It cannot have pervasive effects and yet be severely restricted in its utility. Its pervasive effects, however, can be uniformly strong, uniformly weak, or variable in strength. Which is the case depends on how military power affects the many domains, policy arenas, and disparate issues that come within its field. At the minimum, however, military power is fungible to a degree because its physical use, its threatened use, or simply its mere presence structure expectations and influence the political calculations of actors. The gravitational effects of military power mean that its influence pervades the other policy realms, even if it is not dominant in most of them. Pervasiveness implies fungibility.

In the case of military power, moreover, greater amounts of it increase its fungibility. Up to a reasonable point, more of it is therefore better than less. It is more desirable to be militarily powerful than militarily weak. Militarily powerful states have greater clout in world politics than militarily weak ones. Militarily strong states are less subject to the influence of other states than militarily weak ones.

Militarily powerful states can better offer protection to other states, or more seriously threaten them, in order to influence their behavior than can militarily weak ones. Finally, militarily powerful states are more secure than militarily weak ones. To have more clout, to be less subject to the will of others, to be in a stronger position to offer protection or threaten harm, and to be secure in a world where others are insecure—these are political advantages that can be diplomatically exploited, and they can also strengthen the will, resolve, and bargaining stance of the state that has them. Thus, although military power ranks behind wealth and skill in terms of its versatility, it can be a close third behind those two, at least for those great powers that choose to generate large amounts of it and then to exploit it.

Conflating Sufficiency and Fungibility

The view argued here—that military power possesses a relatively high degree of fungibility—is not the conventional wisdom. Rather, the commonly accepted view is that put forward by David Baldwin, who argues that military power is of restricted utility. Baldwin asserts:

> Two of the most important weaknesses in traditional theorizing about international politics have been the tendency to exaggerate the effectiveness of military power resources and the tendency to treat military power as the ultimate measuring rod to which other forms of power should be compared.[1]

Baldwin's view of military power follows from his more general argument that power assets tend to be situationally specific. By that he means: "What functions as a power resource in one policy-contingency framework may be irrelevant in another." If assets are situationally or domain-specific, then they are not easily transferable from one policy realm to another. In fact, as Baldwin argues: "Political power resources . . . tend to be much less liquid than economic resources"; and although power resources vary in their degree of fungibility, "no political power resource begins to approach the degree of fungibility of money."[2]

For Baldwin, two consequences flow from the domain-specific nature of power resources. First, we cannot rely on a gross assessment of a state's overall power assets in order to determine how well it will do in any specific area. Instead, we must assess the strength of the resources that it wields in that specific domain. Second, the generally low fungibility of political power resources explains what Baldwin calls the "paradox of unrealized power": the fact that a strong state can prevail in one policy area and lose in another. The reason for this, he tells us, is simple: The state at issue has strong assets in the domain where it prevails and weak ones where it does not.

On the face of it, Baldwin's argument is reasonable. It makes intuitive sense to argue, for example, that armies are better at defeating armies than they are at promoting stable exchange rates. It also makes good sense to take the position that the more carefully we assess what specific assets a state can bring to bear on a specific issue, the more fine-tuned our feel will be of what the state can realistically accomplish on that issue. To deny that all power assets are domain-specific to a degree is therefore absurd. Equally absurd, however, are the positions that all assets are domain-specific to the same degree, and that a gross inventory of a state's overall power assets is not a reliable, even if only a rough, guide to how well the state is likely to do in any given domain. Assets are not equal in fungibility, and fine-tuning does not mean dramatically altering assessments.

What does all this mean for the fungibility of military power? Should we accept Baldwin's view about it? I argue that we should not. To see why, let us look in greater detail at what else he has to say.

Baldwin adduces four examples that purport to demonstrate the limited versatility of military power.[3] The examples are hypothetical, but are nonetheless useful to analyze because they are equivalent to thought experiments. These are the examples:

> Possession of nuclear weapons is not just irrelevant to securing the election of a U.S. citizen as UN secretary-general; it is a hindrance.
>
> ... The owner of a political power resource, such as the means to deter atomic attack, is likely to have difficulty converting this resource into another resource that would, for instance, allow his country to become the leader of the Third World.
>
> Planes loaded with nuclear weapons may strengthen a state's ability to deter nuclear attacks but may be irrelevant to rescuing the *Pueblo* [a U.S. destroyer seized by the North Koreans in early 1968] on short notice.
>
> The ability to get other countries to refrain from attacking one's homeland is not the same as the ability to "win the hearts and minds of the people" in a faraway land [the reference is to the Vietnam War].[4]

Seemingly persuasive at first glance, the examples are, in fact, highly misleading. A little reflection about each will show how Baldwin has committed the cardinal error of conflating the insufficiency of an instrument with its low fungibility, and, therefore, how he has made military power look more domain-specific in each example than it really is.

Consider first the United Nations case. Throughout the United Nations' history, the United States never sought, nor did it ever favor, the election of an American as secretary-general. If it had, money and bribes would have been of as little use as a nuclear threat. The Soviet Union would have vetoed it, just as the United States would have vetoed a Soviet national as secretary-general. Neither state would have countenanced the appointment of a citizen from the other, or from one of its client states. The reason is clear: The Cold War polarized the United Nations between East and West, and neither superpower was willing to allow the other to gain undue influence in the institution if they could prevent it. Therefore, because neither superpower would have ever agreed on a national from the other camp, both sought a secretary-general from the ranks of the unaligned, neutral nations. This explains why cold war secretaries-general came from the unaligned Scandinavian or Third World nations (Dag Hammarskjold from Sweden; U Thant from Burma, for example), particularly during the heyday of the Cold War. This arrangement, moreover, served both superpowers' interest. At those rare times when they both agreed that the United Nations could be helpful, UN mediation was made more effective because it had a secretary-general that was neutral, not aligned.

Finally, even if America's military power had nothing to do with electing secretaries-general, we should not conclude that it has nothing to do with America's standing within the institution. America's preeminence within the United

Nations has been clear. So, too, is the fact that this stems from America's position as the world's strongest nation, a position deriving from both its economic and military strength. Thus, although nuclear weapons cannot buy secretary-general elections, great military power brings great influence in an international organization, one of whose main purposes, after all, is to achieve collective security through the threat or use of force.

The Third World example is equally misleading. To see why, let us perform a simple "thought experiment." Although a Third World leader that had armed his state with nuclear weapons might not rise automatically to the top of the Third World pack, he or she would become a mighty important actor nonetheless. Think of how less weighty China and India, which have nuclear weapons, would appear to other states if they did not possess them; and think of how Iraq, Iran, or Libya, which do not have them, would be viewed if they did. For the former set of states, nuclear weapons add to their global political standing; for the latter set, their mere attempts to acquire them have caused their prominence to rise considerably. By themselves, nuclear weapons cannot buy the top slot in the Third World or elsewhere. Neither economic wealth, nor military power, nor any other power asset alone, can buy top dog. That slot is reserved for the state that surpasses the others in all the key categories of power. Although they do not buy the top position, nuclear weapons nevertheless do significantly enhance the international influence of any state that possesses them, if influence is measured by how seriously a state is taken by others. In this particular case, then, Baldwin is correct to argue that nuclear weapons are not readily convertible into another instrument asset. Although true, the point is irrelevant: They add to the ultimate resource for which all the other assets of a state are mustered—political influence.

The *Pueblo* example is the most complex of the cases, and the one, when reexamined, that provides the strongest support for Baldwin's general argument.[5] Even when reexamined, this strong case falls far short of demonstrating that military power has little fungibility.

The facts of the *Pueblo* case are straightforward. On 23 January 1968, North Korea seized the USS *Pueblo*, an intelligence ship that was fitted with sophisticated electronic eavesdropping capabilities and that was listening in on North Korea, and did not release the ship's crew members until 22 December 1968, almost a year after they had been captured. North Korea claimed the ship was patrolling inside its twelve-mile territorial waters limit; the United States denied the claim because its radio "fix" on the *Pueblo* showed that it was patrolling fifteen and a half nautical miles from the nearest North Korean land point. Immediately after the seizure, the United States beefed up its conventional and nuclear forces in East Asia, sending 14,000 Navy and Air Force reservists and 350 additional aircraft to South Korea, as well as moving the aircraft carrier USS *Enterprise* and its task force within a few minutes' flying time of Wonsan, North Korea. Some of the aircraft sent to South Korean bases and those on the *Enterprise* were nuclear capable. According to President Johnson, several military options were considered but ultimately rejected:

> mining Wonsan harbor; mining other North Korean harbors; interdicting coastal shipping; seizing a North Korean ship; striking selected North Korean targets by air and naval gunfire. In each case we decided that the risk was too great and the possible

accomplishment too small. "I do not want to win the argument and lose the sale," I consistently warned my advisers.[6]

The American government's denial, its military measures, and its subsequent diplomatic efforts, were to no avail. North Korea refused to release the crew. In fact, right from the outset of the crisis, the North Korean negotiators made clear that only an American confession that it had spied on North Korea and had intruded into its territorial waters would secure the crew's release. For eleven months the United States continued to insist that the *Pueblo* was not engaged in illegal activity, and that it had not violated North Korea's territorial waters. Only on 22 December, when General Gilbert Woodward, the U.S. representative to the negotiations, signed a statement in which the U.S. government apologized for the espionage and the intrusion, did North Korea release the crew. The American admission of guilt, however, was made under protest: Immediately before signing the statement, the government disavowed what it was about to sign; and immediately after the signing, the government disavowed what it had just admitted.

Although the facts of the *Pueblo* case are straightforward, the interpretation to be put on them is not. This much is clear: Neither nuclear weapons, nor any of America's other military assets, appear to have secured the crew's release. Equally clear, however, is that none of its other assets secured the crew's release either. Should we then conclude from this case that military power, diplomacy, and whatever other assets were employed to secure the crew's release have low fungibility? Clearly, that would be a foolish conclusion to draw. There was only one thing that secured the crew's release: the public humiliation of the United States. If nothing but humiliation worked, it is reasonable to conclude that humiliation either was, or more likely, quickly became North Korea's goal. When an adversary is firmly fixed on humiliation, military posturing, economic bribes, diplomatic pressure, economic threats, or any other tool used in moderation is not likely to succeed. Only extreme measures, such as waging war or economic blockade, are likely to be successful. At that point, the costs of such actions must be weighed against the benefits. One clear lesson we can draw from the *Pueblo* case is that sometimes there are tasks for which none of the traditional tools of statecraft are sufficient. These situations are rare, but they do on occasion occur. The *Pueblo* was one of them.

There is, however, a second and equally important point to be drawn from this example. Although it is true that America's military power did not secure the crew's release, nevertheless, there were other reasons to undertake the military buildup the United States subsequently engaged in. Neither the United States nor South Korea knew why the North had seized the *Pueblo*. President Johnson and his advisors, however, speculated that the seizure was related to the Tet offensive in Vietnam that began eight days after the *Pueblo's* capture. They reasoned that the *Pueblo's* seizure was deliberately timed to distract the United States and to frighten the South Koreans. Adding weight to this reasoning was the fact that the *Pueblo* was not an isolated incident. Two days earlier, thirty-one special North Korean agents infiltrated into Seoul and got within one-half mile of the presidential palace before they were overcome in battle. Their mission was to kill President Park. The United States feared that through these two incidents, and perhaps others to come, North Korea was trying to divert American military resources from

Vietnam to Korea and to make the South Koreans sufficiently nervous that they would bring their two divisions fighting in Vietnam back home.[7]

The *Pueblo*'s seizure thus raised three problems for the United States: how to get its crew and ship back; how to deter the North from engaging in further provocative acts; and how to reassure the South Koreans sufficiently so that they would keep their troops in South Vietnam. A strong case could be made that the last two tasks, not the first, were the primary purposes for the subsequent American military buildup in East Asia. After all, the United States did not need additional forces there to pressure the North militarily to release the crew. There were already about 100,000 American troops in East Asia. A military buildup, however, would be a useful signal for deterrence of further provocations and reassurance of its ally. Until (or if) North Korea's archives are opened up, we cannot know whether deterrence of further provocation worked, because we do not know what additional plans the North had. What we do know is that the reassurance function of the buildup did work: South Korea kept its divisions in South Vietnam. Thus, America's military buildup had three purposes. Of those, one was achieved, another was not, and the third we cannot be certain about. In sum, it is wrong to draw the conclusion that the *Pueblo* case shows that force has little fungibility, even though military posturing appears not to have gotten the crew released.

Baldwin's final example is equally problematic if the point is to show that military power has little fungibility. Yes, it is true that preventing an attack on one's homeland is a different task than winning the hearts and minds of a people in a distant land. Presumably, however, the point of the example is to argue that the latter task is not merely different from the former, but also more difficult. If this is the assertion, it is unexceptionable: Compelling another government to change its behavior has always been an inherently more difficult task than deterring a given government from attacking one's homeland. Not only is interstate compellence more difficult than interstate deterrence, but intrastate compellence is more difficult than interstate compellence. Forcing the adversaries in a civil war to lay down their arms and negotiate an end to their dispute is a notoriously difficult task, as the Chinese civil war in the 1940s, the Vietnamese civil war in the 1960s, and the Bosnian civil war in the 1990s all too tragically show. It is an especially difficult task in a situation like Vietnam, where the outside power's internal ally faces an adversary that has the force of nationalism on its side. (Ho Chi Minh was Vietnam's greatest nationalist figure of the twentieth century and was widely recognized as such within Vietnam.) It is hard to prevail in a civil war when the adversary monopolizes the appeal of nationalism. Equally important, however, it is hard to prevail in a civil war without resort to force. The United States could not have won in Vietnam by force alone, but it would have had no chance at all to win without it.

No thoughtful analyst of military power would therefore disagree with the following propositions that can be teased out of the fourth example: (1) military power works better for defense than for conquest; (2) military power alone cannot guarantee pacification once conquest has taken place; (3) military power alone is not sufficient to compel a populace to accept the legitimacy of its government; and (4) compellence is more difficult than deterrence. These are reasonable statements. There is, however, also a fifth that should be drawn from this example:

(5) when an outside power arrays itself in a civil war on the wrong side of nationalism, not only will force be insufficient to win, but so, too, will nearly all the other
tools of statecraft—money, political skill, propaganda, and so on. In such cases military power suffers from the same insufficiency as the other instruments. That
makes it no more, but no less, fungible than they are.

　　All four of Baldwin's examples demonstrate an important fact about military
power: Used alone, it cannot achieve many things. Surely, this is an important point
to remember, but is it one that is peculiar to military power alone or that proves that
it has little fungibility? Surely not. Indeed, no single instrument of statecraft is ever
sufficient to attain any significant foreign policy objective—a fact I shall term "task
insufficiency."[8] There are two reasons for this. First, a statesman must anticipate the
counteractions that will be undertaken by the states he is trying to influence. They
will attempt to counter his stratagems with those of their own; they will use different
types of instruments to offset the ones he is using; and they will attempt to compensate for their weakness in one area with their strength in another. A well-prepared
influence attempt therefore requires a multi-instrumental approach to deal with the
likely counters to it. Second, any important policy itself has many facets. A multifaceted policy by necessity requires many instruments to implement it. For both reasons, all truly important matters require a statesman to muster several, if not all, the
instruments at his disposal, even though he may rely more heavily on some than on
others. In sum, in statecraft no tool can stand alone.

　　For military power, then, as for the other instruments of statecraft, fungibility
should not be equated with sufficiency, and insufficiency should not be equated
with low fungibility. A given instrument can carry a state part of the way to a given
goal, even though it cannot carry the state all the way there. At one and the same
time, an instrument of statecraft can usefully contribute to attaining many goals
and yet by itself be insufficient to attain any one of them. Thus, careful consideration of Baldwin's examples demonstrates the following: (1) military power was not
sufficient to achieve the defined task; (2) none of the other traditional policy instruments were sufficient either; and (3) military power was of some value, either for
the defined task or for another task closely connected to it. What the examples did
not demonstrate is that states are unable to transfer military power from one policy task to another. Indeed, to the contrary: Each showed that military power can
be used for a variety of tasks, even though it may not be sufficient, by itself, to
achieve any of them.

HOW FORCE ACHIEVES FUNGIBILITY

If military power is a versatile instrument of statecraft, then exactly how does it
achieve its fungibility? What are the paths through which it can influence events in
other domains?

　　There are two paths. The first is through the spill-over effects that military
power has on other policy domains; the second, through the phenomenon of "linkage politics." In the first case, military power encounters military power, but from
this military encounter ensues an outcome with significant consequences for nonmilitary matters. In the second case, military power is deliberately linked to a non-

military issue, with the purpose of strengthening a state's bargaining leverage on that issue. In the first case, force is used against force; in the second, force is linked with another issue. In both cases, military power becomes fungible because it produces effects outside the strictly military domain. I explain how each path works and illustrate both with examples.

Spill-Over Effects

A military encounter, whether peaceful or forceful, yields a result that can be consequential to the interactions and the outcomes that take place in other domains. This result, which I term the "spill-over effect," is too often forgotten.[9] Military-to-military encounters do not produce only military results—cities laid waste, armies defeated, enemies subdued, attacks prevented, allies protected. They also bring about political effects that significantly influence events in other domains. Military power achieves much of its fungibility through this effect: The political shock waves of a military encounter reverberate beyond the military domain and extend into the other policy domains as well. The exercise of successful deterrence, compellence, or defense affects the overall political framework of relations between two states. Because all policy domains are situated within this overarching framework, what happens in the latter affects what happens in these domains. Spill-over effects define with more precision why force acts akin to a gravitational field.

A spill-over effect can be understood either as a prerequisite or a by-product. As a prerequisite, the result produced by the act of force checking force creates something that is deliberate and viewed as essential in order to reach a given outcome in another domain. As a by-product, the encounter produces something in another domain that may be beneficial but is incidental or even unintended. Of course, what is by-product and what is prerequisite hangs on what outcomes are valued in that other domain. Two examples will illustrate how the spill-over effect works and how it manifests itself either as a prerequisite or a by-product.

Examples: Banking and Cold War Interdependence

The first example has to do with banks; the second with recent history. The banking example demonstrates the role force plays in solvency; the historical example, the role that U.S. military power played in creating today's economic interdependence.

First, the banking example. Begin with this question, Why do we deposit our money in a bank? The answer is we put our money in a bank because we think we can take it out whenever we want. We believe the money is there when we want it. In short, we believe the bank to be solvent.

Solvency is usually thought of solely in economic terms: A bank is solvent because it has enough assets to meet its financial liabilities if they are called.[10] Solvency, however, is a function, not simply of finances, but of physical safety. A bank's solvency depends on the fact both that its assets exceed its liabilities (its balance sheet is in the black) and that its assets are physically secure (not easily stolen). Physical security is therefore as important to a bank's solvency as its liquidity, even though we generally take the former for granted when we reside in a stable domestic order. If the banks within a state could be robbed at will, then its citizens would not put their money in them. A state makes banks physically secure by using its military power to deter and defend against would-be robbers and to compel them to give back the funds if a robbery takes place (assuming they are caught and the funds recovered). Through its use of its legitimate monopoly on the use of force, a state seeks to neutralize the threat of forcible seizure. If the state succeeds in establishing the physical security of its banks, it produces one of the two prerequisites required for a bank's solvency.

In sum, in a well-ordered state, public force suppresses private force. The effect of this suppression is to create a generalized stability that sets the context within which all societal interactions take place. This effect spills over into numerous other domains and produces many manifestations, one of which is confidence about the physical security of banks. This confidence can be viewed as a by-product of the public suppression of private force, as a prerequisite to banking solvency, or, more sensibly, as both.

A good historical example of the spill-over effect of military power is the economic interdependence produced among the free world's economies during the Cold War. In a fundamental sense, this is the banking analogy writ large. The bank is the free world economies, the potential robber is the Soviet Union, and the provider of physical safety is the United States.

During the Cold War era, the United States used its military power to deter a Soviet attack on its major allies, the Western Europeans and the Japanese. American military power checked Soviet military power. This military-to-military encounter yielded a high degree of military security for America's allies, but it also produced several by-products, one of the most important of which was the creation of an open and interdependent economic order among the United States, Western Europe, and Japan. Today's era of economic interdependence is in no small part due to the exercise of American military power during the Cold War. A brief discussion will show how American military power helped create the economic interdependence from which much of today's world benefits.

America's forty-year struggle with the Soviets facilitated economic integration within Western Europe and among Western Europe, North America, and Japan. Obviously, American military power was not the sole factor responsible for today's interdependence among the major industrialized nations. Also crucial were the conversion of governments to Keynesian economics; their overwhelming desire to avoid the catastrophic experience of the Great Depression and the global war it brought in its wake; the lesson they learned from the 1930s about how noncooperative, beggar-thy-neighbor policies ultimately redound to the disadvantage of all; the willingness of the United States to underwrite the economic costs of setting up the system and of sustaining it for a time; the acceptance by its allies of the legitimacy of American leadership; the hard work of the peoples involved; and so on. Important as all these factors were, however, we must remember where economic openness first began and where it subsequently flourished most: among the great powers that were allied with the United States against the Soviet Union.

How, then, did the Soviet threat and the measures taken to counter it help produce the modern miracle of economic interdependence among America's industrial allies? And how, exactly, did America's military power and its overseas military presence contribute to it? There were four ways.

First, the security provided by the United States created a political stability that was crucial to the orderly development of trading relations. As I discussed at the outset of this article, markets do not exist in political vacuums; rather, they work best when embedded in political frameworks that yield predictable expectations. American military power deployed in the Far East and on the European continent brought these stable expectations, first, by providing the psychological reassurance that the Europeans and the Japanese needed to rebuild themselves and, second, by continuing to provide them thereafter with a sense of safety that enabled their economic energies to work their will. Indeed, we should remember that the prime reason NATO was formed was psychological, not military: to make the Europeans feel secure enough against the Soviets so that they would have the political will to rebuild themselves economically. The initial purpose of NATO is the key to its (and to the U.S.-Japan defense treaty's) long-lasting function: the creation of a politically stable island amidst a turbulent international sea.

Second, America's provision of security to its allies in Europe and in the Far East dampened their respective concerns about German and Japanese military rearmament. The United States presence protected its allies not only from the Soviets, but also from the Germans and the Japanese. Because German and Japanese military power was contained in alliances that the United States dominated, and especially because American troops were visibly present and literally within each nation, Germany's and Japan's neighbors, while they did not forget the horrors they suffered at the hands of these two during the Second World War, nevertheless, were not paralyzed from cooperating with them. The success of the European Common Market owes as much to the presence of American military power on the continent of Europe as it does to the vision of men like Monnet. The same can be said for the Far East. America's military presence has helped "oil the waters" for Japan's economic dominance there.

Third, America's military presence helped to dampen concerns about disparities in relative economic growth and about vulnerabilities inherent in interdependence, both of which are heightened in an open economic order. Freer trade benefits all nations, but not equally. The most efficient benefit the most; and economic efficiencies can be turned to military effect. Interdependence brings dependencies, all the greater the more states specialize economically. Unequal gains from trade and trade dependencies all too often historically have had adverse political and military effects. Through its provision of military protection to its allies, the United States mitigated the security externalities of interdependence and enabled the Germans and the Japanese to bring their neighbors (America's allies) into their economic orbits without those neighbors fearing that German or Japanese military conquest or political domination would follow. With the security issue dealt with, the economic predominance of the Germans and Japanese was easier for their neighbors to swallow.

Finally, America's military presence fostered a solidarity that came by virtue of being partners against a common enemy. That sense of solidarity, in turn, helped develop the determination and the good will necessary to overcome the inevitable economic disputes that interdependencies bring. The "spill-over" effects of military cooperation against the Soviets on the political will to sustain economic openness should not be underestimated, though they are difficult to pinpoint and quantify. Surely, however, the sense of solidarity and good will that alliance in a common cause bred must have had these spill-over effects. Finally, the need to preserve a united front against the common enemy put limits on how far the allies, and the United States, would permit their economic disputes to go. The need to maintain a united political-military front bounded the inevitable economic disputes and prevented them from escalating into a downward-spiraling economic nationalism. Political stability, protection from potential German and Japanese military resurgence, the dampening of concerns about relative gains and dependencies, and the sense of solidarity—all of these were aided by the American military presence in Europe and the Far East.

Linkage Politics

The second way force exerts influence on other domains of policy is through the power of linkage politics. In politics, whether domestic or foreign, issues are usually linked to one another. The link can be either functional or artificial. If two issues are linked functionally, then there is a causal connection between them: A change in one produces a change in the other. The price of the dollar (its exchange rate value) and the price of oil imports, for example, are functionally linked, because the global oil market is priced in dollars. (Not only that, oil can only be bought with dollars.) A decline in the value of the dollar will increase the cost of a given amount of oil imported to the United States. Similarly, a rise in the value of the dollar will decrease the cost of a given amount of imported oil. As long as oil remains priced in dollars, the functional tie between exchange rates and energy cannot be delinked. Moreover, as the oil-dollar example illustrates, functional linkages generally have corresponding spill-over effects. That is, weakness on one issue (a weaker dollar) produces more weakness on the other (more money spent on energy imports); and strength on one (a stronger dollar) produces greater strength on the other (cheaper energy imports). Thus, functional linkages produce causal effects that either magnify a state's weakness or add to its strength.

When two issues are linked artificially, there is no causal connection between them. A change in one does not automatically produce a change in the other. Instead, the two issues become linked because a statesman has made a connection where none before existed. Usually, but not always, this will be done to gain bargaining leverage. By making a link between two heretofore unconnected issues, statesmen try to bring about politically what is not produced functionally. They make a link in order to compensate for weakness on a given issue. Their method is to tie an issue where they are weak to an issue where they are strong. Their goal is to produce a more desirable outcome in the weak area either by threatening to do something undesirable in the strong area, or by promising to do something beneficial there. If they can make the connection stick, then the result of an artificial linkage is a strengthening of a state's overall position. Unlike a functional linkage, where weakness begets weakness and strength begets strength, in an artificial link-age, strength offsets weakness. Thus, an artificial linkage is a bargaining connection that is made in the head of a statesman, but it is not any less real or any less effec-tive as a result. I provide an example of a bargaining linkage below.

Whether functional or artificial, issue linkages have a crucial consequence for both the analysis and the exercise of state power. We can put the point more strongly: Because issues are connected, domains cannot be wholly delinked from one another. If they cannot be delinked, then we should not view them in isolation from one another. Therefore, any explanation of an outcome in a given domain that is based only on what goes on in that domain will always be incomplete, if not downright wrong. In sum, issue linkages limit the explanatory power of a domain-restricted analysis.

Bargaining linkages in particular make state assets more fungible than they might otherwise be. Linkage politics is a fact of international political life. We should not expect otherwise. Statesmen are out to make the best deals they can by compensating for weakness in one area with strength in others. Powerful states can better engage in these compensatory linkages than can weak ones. They are stronger in more areas than they are weak; consequently, they can more easily uti-lize their leverage in the strong areas to make up for their deficit in the weak ones. Great powers are also better able to shift assets among issue areas in order to build positions of bargaining strength when necessary. They can, for example, more eas-ily generate military power when they need to in order to link it to nonmilitary tasks. Therefore, because powerful states can link issues more easily than can weaker ones, can compensate for deficiencies better, can generate more resources and do so more quickly when needed, and can shift assets around with greater ease, how powerful a state is overall remains an essential determinant to how suc-cessful it is internationally, irrespective of how weak it may be at any given moment on any specific issue in any particular domain. In sum, linkage politics enhances the advantages of being powerful and boosts the fungibility of force by enabling it to cross domains. . . .

Examples: Deficits, Petrodollars, and Oil Prices

Three . . . brief examples show the range of state goals that can be served by con-structing such linkages.

The first involves the relation between America's large and continuing balance of payments deficits and its global alliance system. Throughout most of the Cold War era, the United States ran an annual large balance of payments deficits. His-torically, no nation has been able to buy more abroad than it sells abroad (import more than it exports) in as huge a volume and for as long a period as has the United States. There were many reasons why it was able to, ranging from the liquidity that deficit dollars provided, which enabled world trade to grow, to general confidence in the American economy, which caused foreigners to invest their dollar holdings in the United States. Part of the reason that foreigners continued to take America's continuing flow of dollars, however, was an implicit, if not explicit, tradeoff: In return for their acceptance of American IOU's (deficit dollars), the United States provided the largest holders of them (the Germans, the Japanese, and the Saudis) military protection against their enemies. America's military strength compensated for its lack of fiscal discipline.[11]

A second example involves the recycling of petrodollars.[12] After the oil price hikes of the 1970s, the OPEC producers, especially the Persian Gulf members, were accumulating more dollars than they could profitably invest at home. Where to put those dollars was an important financial decision, especially for the Saudis, who were generating the largest dollar surpluses. There is strong circumstantial evidence that the Saudis agreed to park a sizable portion of their petrodollars in U.S. Treasury bills (T-bills) in part because of an explicit American proposal "to provide a security umbrella for the Gulf."[13] As David Spiro notes: "By the fourth quarter of 1977, Saudi Arabia accounted for twenty percent of all holdings of Treasury notes and bonds by foreign central banks."[14] The Saudis also continued to agree to price oil in dollars rather than peg it to a basket of currencies. Although there were clear financial incentives for both Saudi decisions, the incentives are not sufficient to explain Saudi actions. The Kuwaitis, for example, never put as many of their petrodollars in the United States, nor as many in T-bills, as did the Saudis. Moreover, an internal U.S. Treasury study concluded that the Saudis would have done better if oil had been pegged to a basket of currencies than to dollars. Indeed, OPEC had decided in 1975 to price oil in such a basket, but never followed through.[15] America's provision of security to the Saudis was an important, even if not sufficient, ingredient in persuading them both to price oil in dollars and then to park the dollars in the United States. Both decisions were of considerable economic benefit to the United States. Parking Saudi dollars in T-bills gave the American government "access to a huge pool of foreign capital"; pricing oils in dollars meant that the United States "could print money to buy oil."[16] Military power bought economic benefits.

A third example, again involving the Saudis, concerns the link between American military protection and the price of oil. The Saudis have a long-term economic interest that dictates moderation in oil prices. With a relatively small population and with the world's largest proven oil reserves, their strategy lies in maximizing revenue from oil over the long term. It is therefore to their advantage to keep the price of oil high enough to earn sizable profits, but not so high as to encourage investment in alternative energy sources. Periodically, Saudi Arabia has faced considerable pressure from the price hawks within OPEC to push prices higher than its interest dictates. American military protection has strengthened Saudi willingness to resist the hawks.

A specific instance of this interaction between U.S. protection and Saudi moderation, for example, occurred in the fall of 1980, with the onset of the Iran-Iraq war. Iraq attacked Iran in September, and the two countries proceeded to bomb one another's oil facilities. The initial stages of the war removed about four million barrels of oil per day from world markets and drove the price of oil to its highest level ever ($42 per barrel).[17] As part of their balancing strategy in the Gulf, this time the Saudis had allied themselves with Iraq and, fearing Iranian retaliation against their oil fields, asked for American military intervention to deter Iranian attacks on their oil fields and facilities. The United States responded by sending AWACS aircraft to Saudi Arabia and by setting up a joint Saudi-American naval task force to guard against Iranian attacks on oil tankers in the Gulf.[18] In return, the Saudis increased their oil production from 9.7 million barrels per day (mbd) to 10.3, which was the highest level it could sustain, and kept it there for the next ten months. Saudi actions had a considerable effect on oil prices, as Safran argues:

> Physically, the Saudi increase of 0.5 mbd was hardly enough to make up for the short-fall caused by the war. . . . Psychologically, however, the Saudi action was crucial in preventing the development of the kind of panic that had sent oil prices soaring after the fall of the shah and the Saudis' April 1979 decision to cut production by 1 mbd.[19]

As in the other cases, in this instance, American military power alone was not sufficient to cause Saudi actions to lower oil prices, but it was essential because during this turbulent period Saudi decisions on how much oil they would pump were not determined solely by economic factors. True, the Saudis, against the desires of the price hawks, which included the Iranians, had been pumping more oil since 1978 in order to lower oil prices. The Saudis had also violated their long-term strategy in March 1979, however, when they decided to cut oil production by 1 mbd, primarily to appease Iran, a move that triggered a rapid increase in oil prices. This pumping decision followed a political decision to move diplomatically away from the United States. Only a few months later, however, the conflict within the Saudi ruling family between an American- versus an Arab-oriented strategy was resolved in a compromise that led to a political reconciliation with the United States; and this political decision was followed by another to increase oil production by 1 mbd, starting 1 July 1979.[20] Before the Iran-Iraq war, then, Saudi pumping decisions were affected by political calculations about their security, in which the strategic connection with the Americans played a prominent role. If this was true in peacetime, surely it was so in wartime, too. The military protection announced by the Americans on 30 September 1980 was a necessary condition for the Saudi increase in oil production that followed in October. Again, military power had bought an economic benefit.

In sum, these . . . examples— . . . America's ability to run deficits, petrodollar recycling, and moderate oil prices—all illustrate just how pervasive bargaining linkages are in international politics and specifically how military power can be linked politically to produce them. In all cases, military power was not sufficient. Without it, however, the United States could not have produced the favorable economic outcomes it achieved.

NOTES

1. David Baldwin, *Paradoxes of Power* (New York: Blackwell, 1989), 151–52. Baldwin first developed his argument in his "Power Analysis and World Politics," *World Politics* 31, 1 (January 1979), 161–94, which is reprinted in *Paradoxes of Power.*
2. Quotes from Baldwin, *Paradoxes of Power*, 134–35, 135, and 136, respectively.

3. In fairness to Baldwin, these examples were not fully developed, but consist of only a sentence or two. Nevertheless, they are fair game because Baldwin used them as illustrations of his more general point about the limits to the utility of military power. The fact that he did not develop them further led him astray, in my view. He was trying to show with them that military power is less effective than commonly thought. I reinterpret these examples to show how versatile military power in fact is. Neither Baldwin nor I, however, can put a number on the fungibility of military power, and I certainly agree with him that "no political power resource begins to approach the degree of fungibility of money" (Baldwin, *Paradoxes of Power,* 135).

4. Baldwin, *Paradoxes of Power,* 134, 135, 133.

5. For the facts and interpretation of this case, I have relied on Lyndon Baines Johnson, *The Vantage Point: Perspectives of the Presidency, 1963–1969* (New York: Holt, Rinehart, Winston, 1971), 385, 387, and 532–37; Barry M. Blechman and Stephen S. Kaplan, *Force Without War: U.S. Armed Forces as a Political Instrument* (Washington, D.C.: Brookings, 1978), 48 and 71–72; Richard P. Stebbins and Elaine P. Adam, *Documents on American Foreign Relations, 1968–69* (New York: Simon & Schuster, 1972), 292–302; and the *New York Times Index,* 1968, 732–36.

6. Johnson, 536.

7. Johnson, 535; Blechman and Kaplan, 72.

8. Baldwin, of course, agrees with this point. He has written: "Actually, any technique of statecraft works poorly in isolation from the others." See David A. Baldwin, *Economic Statecraft* (Princeton: Princeton University Press, 1985), 143.

9. I have borrowed this term from Ernst Haas, even though I am using it differently than he does. He used the phrase to describe the effects that cooperation on economic matters among the states of Western Europe could have on their political relations. He argued that cooperation on economic matters would spill over into their political relations, induce greater cooperation there, and lead ultimately to the political integration of Western Europe. See Ernst Haas, *Beyond the Nation State: Functionalism and International Organization* (Stanford: Stanford University Press, 1964), 48. For Haas's later assessment of how effective spill-over effects were, see Ernst Haas, *The Obsolescence of Regional Integration Theory* (Berkeley: Institute of International Studies, University of California, 1974).

10. Solvency is to be distinguished from liquidity. A bank can be solvent but not liquid. Liquidity refers to the ability of a bank to meet all its liabilities upon demand. Most banks are not able to do so if all the demands are called at the same time. The reason is that many assets of any given bank are tied up in investments that cannot be called back on short notice but take time to convert into cash. The function of a central bank is to solve the liquidity problem of a nation's banking system by providing the liquidity in the short term in order to prevent runs on a bank.

11. As Gilpin put it: "Partially for economic reasons, but more importantly for political and strategic ones, Western Europe (primarily West Germany) and Japan agreed to finance the American balance of payments deficit." See Robert Gilpin, *U.S. Power and the Multinational Corporation: The Political Economy of Direct Investment* (New York: Basic Books, 1975), 154.

12. For this example, I have relied exclusively on David Spiro's original and thorough research. See David E. Spiro, *Hegemony Unbound: Petrodollar Recycling and the De-Legitimation of American Power* (Ithaca: Cornell University Press, forthcoming), chap. 4.

13. The quote is from an interview conducted by Spiro in Boston in 1984 with a former American ambassador to the Middle East. See Spiro, 271. (All page references are for the manuscript version.)

14. Spiro, 261.
15. Spiro, 263–66, 281–83.
16. Spiro, 259, 287.
17. Daniel Yergin, *The Prize: The Epic Quest for Oil, Money and Power* (New York: Simon & Schuster, 1992), 711.
18. Nadar Safran, *Saudi Arabia: The Ceaseless Quest for Security* (Ithaca: Cornell University Press, 1988), 322, 410–11.
19. Safran, 411.
20. Safran, 237.

The Strategic Logic of Suicide Terrorism

ROBERT A. PAPE

Terrorist organizations are increasingly relying on suicide attacks to achieve major
political objectives. For example, spectacular suicide terrorist attacks have recently
been employed by Palestinian groups in attempts to force Israel to abandon the
West Bank and Gaza, by the Liberation Tigers of Tamil Eelam to compel the Sri
Lankan government to accept an independent Tamil homeland, and by Al Qaeda
to pressure the United States to withdraw from the Saudi Arabian Peninsula.
Moreover, such attacks are increasing both in tempo and location. Before the early
1980s, suicide terrorism was rare but not unknown. However, since the attack on
the U.S. embassy in Beirut in April 1983, there have been at least 188 separate suicide terrorist attacks worldwide, in Lebanon, Israel, Sri Lanka, India, Pakistan,
Afghanistan, Yemen, Turkey, Russia and the United States. The rate has increased
from 31 in the 1980s, to 104 in the 1990s, to 53 in 2000–2001 alone. The rise of suicide terrorism is especially remarkable, given that the total number of terrorist
incidents worldwide fell during the period, from a peak of 666 in 1987 to a low of
274 in 1998, with 348 in 2001.

What accounts for the rise in suicide terrorism, especially, the sharp escalation
from the 1990s onward? Although terrorism has long been part of international
politics, we do not have good explanations for the growing phenomenon of suicide
terrorism. Traditional studies of terrorism tend to treat suicide attack as one of
many tactics that terrorists use and so do not shed much light on the recent rise of
this type of attack. The small number of studies addressed explicitly to suicide terrorism tend to focus on the irrationality of the act of suicide from the perspective
of the individual attacker. As a result, they focus on individual motives—either
religious indoctrination (especially Islamic Fundamentalism) or psychological predispositions that might drive individual suicide bombers.

The first-wave explanations of suicide terrorism were developed during the
1980s and were consistent with the data from that period. However, as suicide
attacks mounted from the 1990s onward, it has become increasingly evident that

From "The Logic of Suicide Terrorism" by Robert A. Pape from *American Political Science Review*,
Vol. 97, No. 3 (August 2003), pp. 1–13. Reprinted with the permission of Cambridge University Press.

these initial explanations are insufficient to account for which individuals become suicide terrorists and, more importantly, why terrorist organizations are increasingly relying on this form of attack. First, although religious motives may matter, modern suicide terrorism is not limited to Islamic Fundamentalism. Islamic groups receive the most attention in Western media, but the world's leader in suicide terrorism is actually the Liberation Tigers of Tamil Eelam (LTTE), a group who recruits from the predominantly Hindu Tamil population in northern and eastern Sri Lanka and whose ideology has Marxist/Leninist elements. The LTTE alone accounts for 75 of the 186 suicide terrorist attacks from 1980 to 2001. Even among Islamic suicide attacks, groups with secular orientations account for about a third of these attacks.

Second, although study of the personal characteristics of suicide attackers may someday help identify individuals terrorist organizations are likely to recruit for this purpose, the vast spread of suicide terrorism over the last two decades suggests that there may not be a single profile. Until recently, the leading experts in psychological profiles of suicide terrorists characterized them as uneducated, unemployed, socially isolated, single men in their late teens and early 20s. Now we know that suicide terrorists can be college educated or uneducated, married or single, men or women, socially isolated or integrated, from age 13 to age 47. In other words, although only a tiny number of people become suicide terrorists, they come from a broad cross section of lifestyles, and it may be impossible to pick them out in advance.

In contrast to the first-wave explanations, this article shows that suicide terrorism follows a strategic logic. Even if many suicide attackers are irrational or fanatical, the leadership groups that recruit and direct them are not. Viewed from the perspective of the terrorist organization, suicide attacks are designed to achieve specific political purposes: to coerce a target government to change policy, to mobilize additional recruits and financial support, or both. Crenshaw has shown that terrorism is best understood in terms of its strategic function; the same is true for suicide terrorism. In essence, suicide terrorism is an extreme form of what Thomas Schelling calls "the rationality of irrationality," in which an act that is irrational for individual attackers is meant to demonstrate credibility to a democratic audience that still more and greater attacks are sure to come. As such, modern suicide terrorism is analogous to instances of international coercion. For states, air power and economic sanctions are often the preferred coercive tools. For terrorist groups, suicide attacks are becoming the coercive instrument of choice.

To examine the strategic logic of suicide terrorism, this article collects the universe suicide terrorist attacks worldwide from 1980 to 2001, explains how terrorist organizations have assessed the effectiveness of these attacks, and evaluates the limits on their coercive utility.

Five principal findings follow. First, suicide terrorism is strategic. The vast majority of suicide terrorist attacks are not isolated or random acts by individual fanatics but, rather, occur in clusters as part of a larger campaign by an organized group to achieve a specific political goal. Groups using suicide terrorism consistently announce specific political goals and stop suicide attacks when those goals have been fully or partially achieved.

Second, the strategic logic of suicide terrorism is specifically designed to coerce modern democracies to make significant concessions to national self-determination. In general, suicide terrorist campaigns seek to achieve specific territorial goals, most often the withdrawal of the target state's military forces from what the terrorists see as national homeland. From Lebanon to Israel to Sri Lanka to Kashmir to Chechnya, every suicide terrorist campaign from 1980 to 2001 has been waged by terrorist groups whose main goal has been to establish or maintain self-determination for their community's homeland by compelling an enemy to withdraw. Further, every suicide terrorist campaign since 1980 has been targeted against a state that had a democratic form of government.

Third, during the past 20 years, suicide terrorism has been steadily rising because terrorists have learned that it pays. Suicide terrorists sought to compel American and French military forces to abandon Lebanon in 1983, Israeli forces to leave Lebanon in 1985, Israeli forces to quit the Gaza Strip and the West Bank in 1994 and 1995, the Sri Lankan government to create an independent Tamil state from 1990 on, and the Turkish government to grant autonomy to the Kurds in the late 1990s. Terrorist groups did not achieve their full objectives in all these cases. However, in all but the case of Turkey, the terrorist political cause made more gains after the resort to suicide operations than it had before. . . .

Fourth, although moderate suicide terrorism led to moderate concessions, these more ambitious suicide terrorist campaigns are not likely to achieve still greater gains and may well fail completely. In general, suicide terrorism relies on the threat to inflict low to medium levels of punishment on civilians. In other circumstances, this level of punishment has rarely caused modern nation states to surrender significant political goals, partly because modern nation states are often willing to countenance high costs for high interests and partly because modern nation states are often able to mitigate civilian costs by making economic and other adjustments. Suicide terrorism does not change a nation's willingness to trade high interests for high costs, but suicide attacks can overcome a country's efforts to mitigate civilian costs. Accordingly, suicide terrorism may marginally increase the punishment that is inflicted and so make target nations somewhat more likely to surrender modest goals, but it is unlikely to compel states to abandon important interests related to the physical security or national wealth of the state. National governments have in fact responded aggressively to ambitious suicide terrorist campaigns in recent years, events which confirm these expectations.

Finally, the most promising way to contain suicide terrorism is to reduce terrorists' confidence in their ability to carry out such attacks on the target society. States that face persistent suicide terrorism should recognize that neither offensive military action nor concessions alone are likely to do much good and should invest significant resources in border defenses and other means of homeland security.

THE LOGIC OF SUICIDE TERRORISM

Most suicide terrorism is undertaken as a strategic effort directed toward achieving particular political goals; it is not simply the product of irrational individuals or an expression of fanatical hatreds. The main purpose of suicide terrorism is to use the threat of punishment to coerce a target government to change policy, especially to cause democratic states to withdraw forces from territory terrorists view as their homeland. The record of suicide terrorism from 1980 to 2001 exhibits tendencies in the timing, goals, and targets of attack that are consistent with this strategic logic but not with irrational or fanatical behavior: (1) *timing*—nearly all suicide attacks occur in organized, coherent campaigns, not as isolated or randomly timed incidents; (2) *nationalist goals*—suicide terrorist campaigns are directed at gaining control of what the terrorists see as their national homeland territory, specifically at ejecting foreign forces from that territory; and (3) *target selection*—all suicide terrorist campaigns in the last two decades have been aimed at democracies, which make more suitable targets from the terrorists' point of view.

Defining Suicide Terrorism

Terrorism involves the use of violence by an organization other than a national government to cause intimidation or fear among a target audience. Although one could broaden the definition of terrorism so as to include the actions of a national government to cause terror among an opposing population, adopting such a broad definition would distract attention from what policy makers would most like to know: how to combat the threat posed by subnational groups to state security. Further, it could also create analytic confusion. Terrorist organizations and state governments have different levels of resources, face different kinds of incentives, and are susceptible to different types of pressures. Accordingly, the determinants of their behavior are not likely to be the same and, thus, require separate theoretical investigations.

In general, terrorism has two purposes—to gain supporters and to coerce opponents. Most terrorism seeks both goals to some extent, often aiming to affect enemy calculations while simultaneously mobilizing support for the terrorists cause and, in some cases, even gaining an edge over rival groups in the same social movement. However, there are trade-offs between these objectives and terrorists can strike various balances between them. These choices represent different forms of terrorism, the most important of which are demonstrative, destructive, and suicide terrorism.

Demonstrative terrorism is directed mainly at gaining publicity, for any or all of three reasons: to recruit more activists, to gain attention to grievances from softliners on the other side, and to gain attention from third parties who might exert pressure on the other side. Groups that emphasize ordinary, demonstrative terrorism include the Orange Volunteers (Northern Ireland), National Liberation Army (Columbia), and Red Brigades (Italy). Hostage taking, airline hijacking, and explosions announced in advance are generally intended to use the possibility of harm to bring issues to the attention of the target audience. In these cases, terrorists often avoid doing serious harm so as not to undermine sympathy for the political cause. Brian Jenkins captures the essence of demonstrative terrorism with his well-known remark, "Terrorists want a lot of people watching, not a lot of people dead."

Destructive terrorism is more aggressive, seeking to coerce opponents as well as mobilize support for the cause. Destructive terrorists seek to inflict real harm on members of the target audience at the risk of losing sympathy for their cause.

Exactly how groups strike the balance between harm and sympathy depends on the nature of the political goal. For instance, the Baader-Meinhoft group selectively assassinated rich German industrialists, which alienated certain segments of German society but not others. Palestinian terrorists in the 1970s often sought to kill as many Israelis as possible, fully alienating Jewish society but still evoking sympathy from Muslim communities. Other groups that emphasize destructive terrorism include the Irish Republican Army, the Revolutionary Armed Forces of Colombia (FARC), and the nineteenth-century Anarchists.

Suicide terrorism is the most aggressive form of terrorism, pursuing coercion even at the expense of losing support among the terrorists' own community. What distinguishes a suicide terrorist is that the attacker does not expect to survive a mission and often employs a method of attack that requires the attacker's death in order to succeed (such as planting a car bomb, wearing a suicide vest, or ramming an airplane into a building). In essence, a suicide terrorist kills others at the same time that he kills himself. In principle, suicide terrorists could be used for demonstrative purposes or could be limited to targeted assassinations. In practice, however, suicide terrorists often seek simply to kill the largest number of people. Although this maximizes the coercive leverage that can be gained from terrorism, it does so at the greatest cost to the basis of support for the terrorist cause. Maximizing the number of enemy killed alienates those in the target audience who might be sympathetic to the terrorists cause, while the act of suicide creates a debate and often loss of support among moderate segments of the terrorists' community, even if also attracting support among radical elements. Thus, while coercion is an element in all terrorism, coercion is the paramount objective of suicide terrorism.

The Coercive Logic of Suicide Terrorism

At its core, suicide terrorism is a strategy of coercion, a means to compel a target government to change policy. The central logic of this strategy is simple: Suicide terrorism attempts to inflict enough pain on the opposing society to overwhelm their interest in resisting the terrorists demands and, so, to cause either the government to concede or the population to revolt against the government. The common feature of all suicide terrorist campaigns is that they inflict punishment on the opposing society, either directly by killing civilians or indirectly by killing military personnel in circumstances that cannot lead to meaningful battlefield victory. As we shall see, suicide terrorism is rarely a one time event but often occurs in a series of suicide attacks. As such, suicide terrorism generates coercive leverage both from the immediate panic associated with each attack and from the risk of civilian punishment in the future.

Suicide terrorism does not occur in the same circumstances as military coercion used by states, and these structural differences help to explain the logic of the strategy. In virtually all instances of international military coercion, the coercer is the stronger state and the target is the weaker state; otherwise, the coercer would likely be deterred or simply unable to execute the threatened military operations. In these circumstances, coercers have a choice between two main coercive strategies, punishment and denial. Punishment seeks to coerce by raising the costs or risks to the target society to a level that overwhelms the value of the interests in dispute. Denial seeks to coerce by demonstrating to the target state that it simply cannot win the dispute regardless of its level of effort, and therefore fighting to a finish is pointless—for example, because the coercer has the ability to conquer the disputed territory. Hence, although coercers may initially rely on punishment, they often have the resources to create a formidable threat to deny the opponent victory in battle and, if necessary, to achieve a brute force military victory if the target government refuses to change its behavior. The Allied bombing of Germany in World War II, American bombing of North Vietnam in 1972, and Coalition attacks against Iraq in 1991 all fit this pattern.

Suicide terrorism (and terrorism in general) occurs under the reverse structural conditions. In suicide terrorism, the coercer is the weaker actor and the target is the stronger. Although some elements of the situation remain the same, flipping the stronger and weaker sides in a coercive dispute has a dramatic change on the relative feasibility of punishment and denial. In these circumstances, denial is impossible, because military conquest is ruled out by relative weakness. Even though some groups using suicide terrorism have received important support from states and some have been strong enough to wage guerrilla military campaigns as well as terrorism, none have been strong enough to have serious prospects of achieving their political goals by conquest. The suicide terrorist group with the most significant military capacity has been the LTTE, but it has not had a real prospect of controlling the whole of the homeland that it claims, including Eastern and Northern Provinces of Sri Lanka.

As a result, the only coercive strategy available to suicide terrorists is punishment. Although the element of "suicide" is novel and the pain inflicted on civilians is often spectacular and gruesome, the heart of the strategy of suicide terrorism is the same as the coercive logic used by states when they employ air power or economic sanctions to punish an adversary: to cause mounting civilian costs to overwhelm the target state's interest in the issue in dispute and so to cause it to concede the terrorists' political demands. What creates the coercive leverage is not so much actual damage as the expectation of future damage. Targets may be economic or political, military or civilian, but in all cases the main task is less to destroy the specific targets than to convince the opposing society that they are vulnerable to more attacks in the future. These features also make suicide terrorism convenient for retaliation, a tit-for-tat interaction that generally occurs between terrorists and the defending government (Crenshaw 1981). . . .

Suicide terrorists' willingness to die magnifies the coercive effects of punishment in three ways. First, suicide attacks are generally more destructive than other terrorist attacks. An attacker who is willing to die is much more likely to accomplish the mission and to cause maximum damage to the target. Suicide attackers can conceal weapons on their own bodies and make last-minute adjustments more easily than ordinary terrorists. They are also better able to infiltrate heavily guarded targets because they do not need escape plans or rescue teams. Suicide attackers are also able to use certain especially destructive tactics such as wearing "suicide vests" and ramming vehicles into targets. The 188 suicide terrorist attacks from 1980 to

2001 killed an average of 13 people each, not counting the unusually large number of fatalities on September 11 and also not counting the attackers themselves. During the same period, there were about 4,155 total terrorist incidents worldwide, which killed 3,207 people (also excluding September 11), or less than one person per incident. Overall, from 1980 to 2001, suicide attacks amount to 3% of all terrorist attacks but account for 48% of total deaths due to terrorism, again excluding September 11.

Second, suicide attacks are an especially convincing way to signal the likelihood of more pain to come, because suicide itself is a costly signal, one that suggests that the attackers could not have been deterred by a threat of costly retaliation. Organizations that sponsor suicide attacks can also deliberately orchestrate the circumstances around the death of a suicide attacker to increase further expectations of future attacks. This can be called the "art of martyrdom." The more suicide terrorists justify their actions on the basis of religious or ideological motives that match the beliefs of a broader national community, the more the status of terrorist martyrs is elevated, and the more plausible it becomes that others will follow in their footsteps. Suicide terrorist organizations commonly cultivate "sacrificial myths" that include elaborate sets of symbols and rituals to mark an individual attacker's death as a contribution to the nation. Suicide attackers' families also often receive material rewards both from the terrorist organizations and from other supporters. As a result, the art of martyrdom elicits popular support from the terrorists' community, reducing the moral backlash that suicide attacks might otherwise produce, and so establishes the foundation for credible signals of more attacks to come.

Third, suicide terrorist organizations are better positioned than other terrorists to increase expectations about escalating future costs by deliberately violating norms in the use of violence. They can do this by crossing thresholds of damage, by breaching taboos concerning legitimate targets, and by broadening recruitment to confound expectations about limits on the number of possible terrorists. The element of suicide itself helps increase the credibility of future attacks, because it suggests that attackers cannot be deterred. Although the capture and conviction of Timothy McVeigh gave reason for some confidence that others with similar political views might be deterred, the deaths of the September 11 hijackers did not, because Americans would have to expect that future Al Qaeda attackers would be equally willing to die.

The Record of Suicide Terrorism, 1980 to 2001

To characterize the nature of suicide terrorism, this study identified every suicide terrorist attack from 1980 to 2001 that could be found in Lexis Nexis's on-line database of world news media. Examination of the universe shows that suicide terrorism has three properties that are consistent with the above strategic logic but not with irrational or fanatical behavior: (1) *timing*—nearly all suicide attacks occur in organized, coherent campaigns, not as isolated or randomly timed incidents; (2) *nationalist goals*—suicide terrorist campaigns are directed at gaining control of what the terrorists see as their national homeland territory, specifically at ejecting foreign forces from that territory; and (3) *target selection*—all suicide terrorist campaigns in the last two decades have been aimed at democracies, which make more suitable targets from the terrorists' point of view. Nationalist movements that face nondemocratic opponents have not resorted to suicide attack as a means of coercion.

Timing.

As Table 1 indicates, there have been 188 separate suicide terrorist attacks between 1980 and 2001. Of these, 179, or 95%, were parts of organized, coherent campaigns, while only nine were isolated or random events. Seven separate disputes have led to suicide terrorist campaigns: the presence of American and French forces in Lebanon, Israeli occupation of West Bank and Gaza, the independence of the Tamil regions of Sri Lanka, the independence of the Kurdish region of Turkey, Russian occupation of Chechnya, Indian occupation of Kashmir, and the presence of American forces on the Saudi Arabian Peninsula. Overall, however, there have been 16 distinct campaigns, because in certain disputes the terrorists elected to suspend operations one or more times either in response to concessions or for other reasons. Eleven of the campaigns have ended and five were ongoing as of the end of 2001. The attacks comprising each campaign were organized by the same terrorist group (or, sometimes, a set of cooperating groups as in the ongoing "second *intifada*" in Israel/Palestine), clustered in time, publically justified in terms of a specified political goal, and directed against targets related to that goal.

The most important indicator of the strategic orientation of suicide terrorists is the timing of the suspension of campaigns, which most often occurs based on a strategic decision by leaders of the terrorist organizations that further attacks would be counterproductive to their coercive purposes—for instance, in response to full or partial concessions by the target state to the terrorists' political goals. Such suspensions are often accompanied by public explanations that justify the decision to opt for a "cease-fire." Further, the terrorist organizations' discipline is usually fairly good; although there are exceptions, such announced cease-fires usually do stick for a period of months at least, normally until the terrorist leaders take a new strategic decision to resume in pursuit of goals not achieved in the earlier campaign. This pattern indicates that both terrorist leaders and their recruits are sensitive to the coercive value of the attacks.

As an example of a suicide campaign, consider Hamas's suicide attacks in 1995 to compel Israel to withdraw from towns in the West Bank Hamas leaders deliberately withheld attacking during the spring and early summer in order to give PLO negotiations with Israel an opportunity to finalize a withdrawal. However, when in early July, Hamas leaders came to believe that Israel was backsliding and delaying withdrawal, Hamas launched a series of suicide attacks. Israel accelerated the pace of its withdrawal, after which Hamas ended the campaign. . . .

If suicide terrorism were mainly irrational or even disorganized, we would expect a much different pattern in which either political goals were not articulated (e.g., references in news reports to "rogue" attacks) or the stated goals varied considerably even within the same conflict. We would also expect the timing to be

TABLE 1 ■ SUICIDE TERRORIST CAMPAIGNS, 1980–2001

Date	Terrorist Group	Terrorist's Goal	No. of Attacks	No. Killed	Target Behavior
Completed Campaigns					
1. Apr–Dec 1983	Hezbollah	U.S./France out of Lebanon	6	384	Complete withdrawal
2. Nov 1983– Apr 1985	Hezbollah	Israel out of Lebanon	6	96	Partial withdrawal
3. June 1985– June 1986	Hezbollah	Israel out of Lebanon security zone	16	179	No change
4. July 1990– Nov 1994	LTTE	Sri Lanka accept Tamil state	14	164	Negotiations
5. Apr 1995– Oct 2000	LTTE	Sri Lanka accept Tamil state	54	629	No change
6. Apr 1994	Hamas	Israel out of Palestine	2	15	Partial withdrawal from Gaza
7. Oct 1994– Aug 1995	Hamas	Israel out of Palestine	7	65	Partial withdrawal from West Bank
8. Feb–Mar 1996	Hamas	Retaliation for Israeli assassination	4	58	No change
9. Mar–Sept 1997	Hamas	Israel out of Palestine	3	24	Hamas leader released
10. June–Oct 1996	PKK	Turkey accept Kurd autonomy	3	17	No change
11. Mar–Aug 1999	PKK	Turkey release jailed leader	6	0	No change
Ongoing Campaigns, as of December 2001					
12. 1996–	Al Qaeda	U.S. out of Saudi Peninsula	5	3,329	TBD[*]
13. 2000–	Chechnen Rebels	Russia out of Chechnya	4	53	TBD
14. 2000–	Kashmir Rebels	India out of Kashmir	3	45	TBD
15. 2001–	LTTE	Sri Lanka accept Tamil state	6	51	TBD
16. 2000–	Several	Israel out of Palestine	39	177	TBD
Total incidents	188				
No. of campaigns	179				
No. isolated	9				

Source: Robert Pape, "The Universe of Suicide Terrorist Attacks Worldwide, 1980–2001," University of Chicago, Typescript.

[*]To be determined.

TABLE 2 ■ MOTIVATION AND TARGETS OF SUICIDE TERRORIST CAMPAIGNS, 1980–2001

Region Dispute	Homeland Status	Terrorist Goal	Target a Democracy?
Lebanon, 1983–86	U.S./F/IDF military presence	U.S./F/IDF withdrawal	Yes
West Bank/ Gaza, 1994–	IDF military presence	IDF withdrawal	Yes
Tamils in Sri Lanka, 1990–	SL military presence	SL withdrawal	Yes (1950)
Kurds in Turkey, 1990s	Turkey military presence	Turkey withdrawal	Yes (1983)
Chechnya, 2000–	Russia military presence	Russian withdrawal	Yes (1993)
Kashmir, 2000–	Indian military presence	Indian withdrawal	Yes
Saudi Peninsula, 1996–	U.S. military presence	U.S. withdrawal	Yes

either random or, perhaps, event-driven, in response to particularly provocative or infuriating actions by the other side, but little if at all related to the progress of negotiations over issues in dispute that the terrorists want to influence.

Nationalist Goals.

Suicide terrorism is a high-cost strategy, one that would only make strategic sense for a group when high interests are at stake and, even then, as a last resort. The reason is that suicide terrorism maximizes coercive leverage at the expense of support among the terrorists' own community and so can be sustained over time only when there already exists a high degree of commitment among the potential pool of recruits. The most important goal that a community can have is the independence of its homeland (population, property, and way of life) from foreign influence or control. As a result, a strategy of suicide terrorism is most likely to be used to achieve nationalist goals, such as gaining control of what the terrorists see as their national homeland territory and expelling foreign military forces from that territory.

In fact, every suicide campaign from 1980 to 2001 has had as a major objective—or as its central objective—coercing a foreign government that has military forces in what they see as their homeland to take those forces out. Table 2 summarizes the disputes that have engendered suicide terrorist campaigns. Since 1980, there has not been a suicide terrorist campaign directed mainly against domestic opponents or against foreign opponents who did not have military forces in the terrorists homeland. Although attacks against civilians are often the most salient to Western observers, actually every suicide terrorist campaign in the past two decades has included attacks directly against the foreign military forces in the country, and most have been waged by guerrilla organizations that also use more conventional methods of attack against those forces.

Even Al Qaeda fits this pattern. Although Saudi Arabia is not under American military occupation per se and the terrorists have political objectives against the

Saudi regime and others, one major objective of Al Qaeda is the expulsion of U.S. troops from the Saudi Peninsula and there have been attacks by terrorists loyal to Osama Bin Laden against American troops in Saudi Arabia. To be sure, there is a major debate among Islamists over the morality of suicide attacks, but within Saudi Arabia there is little debate over Al Qaeda's objection to American forces in the region and over 95% of Saudi society reportedly agrees with Bin Laden on this matter.

Still, even if suicide terrorism follows a strategic logic, could some suicide terrorist campaigns be irrational in the sense that they are being waged for unrealistic goals? The answer is that some suicide terrorist groups have not been realistic in expecting the full concessions demanded of the target, but this is normal for disputes involving overlapping nationalist claims and even for coercive attempts in general. Rather, the ambitions of terrorist leaders are realistic in two other senses. First, suicide terrorists' political aims, if not their methods, are often more mainstream than observers realize; they generally reflect quite common, straightforward nationalist self-determination claims of their community. Second, these groups often have significant support for their policy goals versus the target state, goals that are typically much the same as those of other nationalists within their community. Differences between the terrorists and more "moderate" leaders usually concern the usefulness of a certain level of violence and—sometimes—the legitimacy of attacking additional targets besides foreign troops in the country, such as attacks in other countries or against third parties and civilians. Thus, it is not that the terrorists pursue radical goals and then seek others' support. Rather, the terrorists are simply the members of their societies who are the most optimistic about the usefulness of violence for achieving goals that many, and often most, support.

The behavior of Hamas illustrates the point. Hamas terrorism has provoked Israeli retaliation that has been costly for Palestinians, while pursuing the—apparently unrealistic—goal of abolishing the state of Israel. Although prospects of establishing an Arab state in all of "historic Palestine" may be poor, most Palestinians agree that it would be desirable if possible. Hamas's terrorist violence was in fact carefully calculated and controlled. In April 1994, as its first suicide campaign was beginning, Hamas leaders explained that "martyrdom operations" would be used to achieve intermediate objectives, such as Israeli withdrawal from the West Bank and Gaza, while the final objective of creating an Islamic state from the Jordan River to the Mediterranean may require other forms of armed resistance.

Democracies as the Targets.

Suicide terrorism is more likely to be employed against states with democratic political systems than authoritarian governments for several reasons. First, democracies are often thought to be especially vulnerable to coercive punishment. Domestic critics and international rivals, as well as terrorists, often view democracies as "soft," usually on the grounds that their publics have low thresholds of cost tolerance and high ability to affect state policy. Even if there is little evidence that democracies are easier to coerce than other regime types, this image of democracy matters. Since terrorists can inflict only moderate damage in comparison to even small interstate wars, terrorism can be expected to coerce only if the target state is viewed as especially vulnerable to punishment. Second, suicide terrorism is a tool of the weak, which means that, regardless of how much punishment the terrorists inflict, the target state almost always has the capacity to retaliate with far more extreme punishment or even by exterminating the terrorists' community. Accordingly, suicide terrorists must not only have high interests at stake, they must also be confident that their opponent will be at least somewhat restrained. While there are infamous exceptions, democracies have generally been more restrained in their use of force against civilians, at least since World War II. Finally, suicide attacks may also be harder to organize or publicize in authoritarian police states, although these possibilities are weakened by the fact that weak authoritarian states are also not targets.

In fact, the target state of every modern suicide campaign has been a democracy. The United States, France, Israel, India, Sri Lanka, Turkey, and Russia were all democracies when they were attacked by suicide terrorist campaigns, even though the last three became democracies more recently than the others. . . .

The Kurds, which straddle Turkey and Iraq, illustrate the point that suicide terrorist campaigns are more likely to be targeted against democracies than authoritarian regimes. Although Iraq has been far more brutal toward its Kurdish population than has Turkey, violent Kurdish groups have used suicide attacks exclusively against democratic Turkey and not against the authoritarian regime in Iraq. There are plenty of national groups living under authoritarian regimes with grievances that could possibly inspire suicide terrorism, but none have. Thus, the fact that rebels have resorted to this strategy only when they face the more suitable type of target counts against arguments that suicide terrorism is a nonstrategic response, motivated mainly by fanaticism or irrational hatreds.

TERRORISTS' ASSESSMENTS OF SUICIDE TERRORISM

The main reason that suicide terrorism is growing is that terrorists have learned that it works. Even more troubling, the encouraging lessons that terrorists have learned from the experience of 1980s and 1990s are not, for the most part, products of wild-eyed interpretations or wishful thinking. They are, rather, quite reasonable assessments of the outcomes of suicide terrorist campaigns during this period.

To understand how terrorists groups have assessed the effectiveness of suicide terrorism requires three tasks: (1) explanation of appropriate standards for evaluating the effectiveness of coercion from the standpoint of coercers; (2) analysis of the 11 suicide terrorist campaigns that have ended as of 2001 to determine how frequently target states made concessions that were, or at least could have been, interpreted as due to suicide attack; and (3) close analysis of terrorists' learning from particular campaigns. Because some analysts see suicide terrorism as fundamentally irrational, it is important to assess whether the lessons that the terrorists drew were reasonable conclusions from the record. The crucial cases are the Hamas and Islamic Jihad campaigns against Israel during the 1990s, because they are most frequently cited as aimed at unrealistic goals and therefore as basically irrational.

Standards of Assessment

Terrorists, like other people, learn from experience. Since the main purpose of suicide terrorism is coercion, the learning that is likely to have the greatest impact on terrorists' future behavior is the lessons that they have drawn from past campaigns about the coercive effectiveness of suicide attack.

Most analyses of coercion focus on the decision making of target states, largely to determine their vulnerability to various coercive pressures. The analysis here, however, seeks to determine why terrorist coercers are increasingly attracted to a specific coercive strategy. For this purpose, we must develop a new set of standards, because assessing the value of coercive pressure for the coercer is not the same problem as assessing its impact on the target.

From the perspective of a target state, the key question is whether the value of the concession that the coercer is demanding is greater than the costs imposed by the coercive pressure, regardless of whether that pressure is in the form of lives at risk, economic hardship, or other types of costs. However, from the perspective of the coercer, the key question is whether a particular coercive strategy promises to be more effective than alternative methods of influence and, so, warrants continued (or increased) effort. This is especially true for terrorists who are highly committed to a particular goal and so willing to exhaust virtually any alternative rather than abandoning it. In this search for an effective strategy, coercers' assessments are likely to be largely a function of estimates of the success of past efforts; for suicide terrorists, this means assessments of whether past suicide campaigns produced significant concessions.

A glance at the behavior of suicide terrorists reveals that such trade-offs between alternative methods are important in their calculations. All of the organizations that have resorted to suicide terrorism began their coercive efforts with more conventional guerrilla operations, nonsuicide terrorism, or both. Hezbollah, Hamas, Islamic Jihad, the PKK, the LTTE, and Al Qaeda all used demonstrative and destructive means of violence long before resorting to suicide attack. Indeed, looking at the trajectory of terrorist groups over time, there is a distinct element of experimentation in the techniques and strategies used by these groups and distinct movement toward those techniques and strategies that produce the most effect. Al Qaeda actually prides itself for a commitment to even tactical learning over time—the infamous "terrorist manual" stresses at numerous points the importance of writing "lessons learned" memoranda that can be shared with other members to improve the effectiveness of future attacks. . . .

The Apparent Success of Suicide Terrorism

Perhaps the most striking aspect of recent suicide terrorist campaigns is that they are associated with gains for the terrorists' political cause about half the time. As Table 1 shows, of the 11 suicide terrorist campaigns that were completed during

1980–2001, six closely correlate with significant policy changes by the target state toward the terrorists' major political goals. In one case, the terrorists' territorial goals were fully achieved (Hezbollah v. US/F, 1983); in three cases, the terrorists territorial aims were partly achieved (Hezbollah v. Israel, 1983–85; Hamas v. Israel, 1994; and Hamas v. Israel, 1994–95); in one case, the target government to entered into sovereignty negotiations with the terrorists (LTTE v. Sri Lanka, 1993–94); and in one case, the terrorist organization's top leader was released from prison (Hamas v. Israel, 1997). Five campaigns did not lead to noticeable concessions (Hezbollah's second effort against Israel in Lebanon, 1985–86; a Hamas campaign in 1996 retaliating for an Israeli assassination; the LTTE v. Sri Lanka, 1995–2002; and both PKK campaigns). Coercive success is so rare that even a 50% success rate is significant, because international military and economic coercion, using the same standards as above, generally works less than a third of the time.

There were limits to what suicide terrorism appeared to gain in the 1980s and 1990s. Most of the gains for the terrorists' cause were modest, not involving interests central to the target countries' security or wealth, and most were potential revocable. For the United States and France, Lebanon was a relatively minor foreign policy interest. Israel's apparent concessions to the Palestinians from 1994 to 1997 were more modest than they might appear. Although Israel withdrew its forces from parts of Gaza and the West Bank and released Sheikh Yassin, during the same period Israeli settlement in the occupied territories almost doubled, and recent events have shown that the Israel is not deterred from sending force back in when necessary. In two disputes, the terrorists achieved initial success but failed to reach greater goals. Although Israel withdrew from much of Lebanon in June 1985, it retained a six-mile security buffer zone along the southern edge of the country for another 15 years from which a second Hezbollah suicide terrorist campaign failed to dislodge it. The Sri Lankan government did conduct apparently serious negotiations with the LTTE from November 1994 to April 1995, but did not concede the Tamil's main demand, for independence, and since 1995, the government has preferred to prosecute the war rather than consider permitting Tamil secession.

Still, these six concessions, or at least apparent concessions, help to explain why suicide terrorism is on the rise. In three of the cases, the target government policy changes are clearly due to coercive pressure from the terrorist group. The American and French withdrawal was perhaps the most clear-cut coercive success for suicide terrorism. In his memoirs, President Ronald Reagan explained the U.S. decision to withdraw from Lebanon:

> The price we had to pay in Beirut was so great, the tragedy at the barracks was so enormous. . . . We had to pull out. . . . We couldn't stay there and run the risk of another suicide attack on the Marines.

The IDF withdrawal from most of southern Lebanon in 1985 and the Sri Lankan government decision to hold negotiations with the LTTE were also widely understood to be a direct result of the coercive punishment imposed by Hezbollah and LTTE respectively. In both cases, the concessions followed periods in which the terrorists had turned more and more to suicide attacks, but since Hezbollah and the LTTE employed a combination of suicide attack and conventional attack on their opponents, one can question the relative weight of suicide attack in coercing these target states. However, there is little question in either case that punishment pressures inflicted by these terrorist organizations were decisive in the outcomes. For instance, as a candidate in the November 9, 1994, presidential election of Sri Lanka, Mrs. Chandrika Kumaratunga explicitly asked for a mandate to redraw boundaries so as to appease the Tamils in their demand for a separate homeland in the island's northeast provinces, often saying, "We definitely hope to begin discussions with the Tamil people, with their representatives—including the Tigers—and offer them political solutions to end the war . . . [involving] extensive devolution." This would, Kumaratunga said, "create an environment in which people could live without fear."

The other three concessions, or arguable concessions, are less clear-cut. All three involve Hamas campaigns against Israel. Not counting the ongoing second intifada, Hamas waged four separate suicide attack campaigns against Israel, in 1994, 1995, 1996, and 1997. One, in 1996, did not correspond with Israeli concessions. This campaign was announced as retaliation for Israel's assassination of a Hamas leader; no particular coercive goal was announced, and it was suspended by Hamas after four attacks in two weeks. The other three all do correspond with Israeli concessions. In April 1994, Hamas begin a series of suicide bombings in relation for the Hebron Massacre. After two attacks, Israel decided to accelerate its withdrawal from Gaza, which was required under the Oslo Agreement but which had been delayed. Hamas then suspended attacks for five months. From October 1994 to August 1995, Hamas (and Islamic Jihad) carried out a total of seven suicide attacks against Israel. In September 1995, Israel agreed to withdraw from certain West Bank towns that December, which it earlier had claimed could not be done before April 1996 at the soonest. Hamas then suspended attacks until its retaliation campaign during the last week of February and first week of March 1996. Finally, in March 1997, Hamas began a suicide attack campaign that included an attack about every two months until September 1997. In response Israeli Prime Minister Netanyahu authorized the assassination of a Hamas leader. The attempt, in Amman, Jordan, failed and the Israeli agents were captured. To get them back Israel agreed to release Sheikh Ahmed Yassin, spiritual leader of Hamas. While this was not a concession to the terrorists' territorial goals, there is no evidence that Hamas interpreted this in anyway different from the standard view that this release was the product of American and Jordanian pressure. . . .

THE LIMITS OF SUICIDE TERRORISM

Despite suicide terrorists' reasons for confidence in the coercive effectiveness of this strategy, there are sharp limits to what suicide terrorism is likely to accomplish in the future. During the 1980s and 1990s, terrorist leaders learned that moderate punishment often leads to moderate concessions and so concluded that more ambitious suicide campaigns would lead to greater political gains. However, today's more ambitious suicide terrorist campaigns are likely to fail. Although suicide terrorism is somewhat more effective than ordinary coercive punishment using air power or economic sanctions, it is not drastically so.

Suicide Terrorism Is Unlikely to Achieve Ambitious Goals

In international military coercion, threats to inflict military defeat often generate more coercive leverage than punishment. Punishment, using anything short of nuclear weapons, is a relatively weak coercive strategy because modern nation states generally will accept high costs rather than abandon important national goals, while modern administrative techniques and economic adjustments over time often allow states to minimize civilian costs. The most punishing air attacks with conventional munitions in history were the American B-29 raids against Japan's 62 largest cities from March to August 1945. Although these raids killed nearly 800,000 Japanese civilians—almost 10% died on the first day, the March 9, 1945, fire-bombing of Tokyo, which killed over 85,000—the conventional bombing did not compel the Japanese to surrender.

Suicide terrorism makes adjustment to reduce damage more difficult than for states faced with military coercion or economic sanctions. However, it does not affect the target state's interests in the issues at stake. As a result, suicide terrorism can coerce states to abandon limited or modest goals, such as withdrawal from territory of low strategic importance or, as in Israel's case in 1994 and 1995, a temporary and partial withdrawal from a more important area. However, suicide terrorism is unlikely to cause targets to abandon goals central to their wealth or security, such as a loss of territory that would weaken the economic prospects of the state or strengthen the rivals of the state.

Suicide terrorism makes punishment more effective than in international military coercion. Targets remain willing to countenance high costs for important goals, but administrative, economic, or military adjustments to prevent suicide attack are harder, while suicide attackers themselves are unlikely to be deterred by the threat of retaliation. Accordingly, suicide attack is likely to present a threat of continuing limited civilian punishment that the target government cannot completely eliminate, and the upper bound on what punishment can gain for coercers is recognizably higher in suicidal terrorism than in international military coercion.

The data on suicide terrorism from 1980 to 2001 support this conclusion. While suicide terrorism has achieved modest or very limited goals, it has so far failed to compel target democracies to abandon goals central to national wealth or security. When the United States withdrew from Lebanon in 1984, it had no important security, economic, or even ideological interests at stake. Lebanon was largely a humanitarian mission and not viewed as central to the national welfare of the United States. Israel withdrew from most of Lebanon in June 1985 but remained in a security buffer on the edge of southern Lebanon for more than a decade afterward, despite the fact that 17 of 22 suicide attacks occurred in 1985 and 1986. Israel's withdrawals from Gaza and the West Bank in 1994 and 1995 occurred at the same time that settlements increased and did little to hinder the IDF's return, and so these concessions were more modest than they may appear.

Sri Lanka has suffered more casualties from suicide attack than Israel but has not acceded to demands that it surrender part of its national territory. Thus, the logic of punishment and the record of suicide terrorism suggests that, unless suicide terrorists acquire far more destructive technologies, suicide attacks for more ambitious goals are likely to fail and will continue to provoke more aggressive military responses.

POLICY IMPLICATIONS FOR CONTAINING SUICIDE TERRORISM

While the rise in suicide terrorism and the reasons behind it seem daunting, there are important policy lessons to learn. The current policy debate is misguided. Offensive military action or concessions alone rarely work for long. For over 20 years, the governments of Israel and other states targeted by suicide terrorism have engaged in extensive military efforts to kill, isolate, and jail suicide terrorist leaders and operatives, sometimes with the help of quite good surveillance of the terrorists' communities. Thus far, they have met with meager success. Although decapitation of suicide terrorist organizations can disrupt their operations temporarily, it rarely yields long-term gains. Of the 11 major suicide terrorist campaigns that had ended as of 2001, only one—the PKK versus Turkey—did so as a result of leadership decapitation, when the leader, in Turkish custody, asked his followers to stop. So far, leadership decapitation has also not ended Al Qaeda's campaign. Although the United States successfully toppled the Taliban in Afghanistan in December 2001, Al Qaeda launched seven successful suicide terrorist attacks from April to December 2002, killing some 250 Western civilians, more than in the three years before September 11, 2001, combined.

Concessions are also not a simple answer. Concessions to nationalist grievances that are widely held in the terrorists' community can reduce popular support for further terrorism, making it more difficult to recruit new suicide attackers and improving the standing of more moderate nationalist elites who are in competition with the terrorists. Such benefits can be realized, however, only if the concessions really do substantially satisfy the nationalist or self-determination aspirations of a large fraction of the community.

Partial, incremental, or deliberately staggered concessions that are dragged out over a substantial period of time are likely to become the worst of both worlds. Incremental compromise may appear—or easily be portrayed—to the terrorists' community as simply delaying tactics and, thus, may fail to reduce, or actually increase, their distrust that their main concerns will ever be met. Further, incrementalism provides time and opportunity for the terrorists to intentionally provoke the target state in hopes of derailing the smooth progress of negotiated compromise in the short term, so that they can reradicalize their own community and actually escalate their efforts toward even greater gains in the long term. Thus, states that are willing to make concessions should do so in a single step if at all possible.

Advocates of concessions should also recognize that, even if they are successful in undermining the terrorist leaders' base of support, almost any concession at all will tend to encourage the terrorist leaders further about their own coercive effectiveness. Thus, even in the aftermath of a real settlement with the opposing community, some terrorists will remain motivated to continue attacks and, for the medium term, may be able to do so, which in term would put a premium on combining concessions with other solutions.

Given the limits of offense and of concessions, homeland security and defensive efforts generally must be a core part of any solution. Undermining the feasibility of suicide terrorism is a difficult task. After all, a major advantage of suicide attack is that it is more difficult to prevent than other types of attack. However, the difficulty of achieving perfect security should not keep us from taking serious measures to prevent would-be terrorists from easily entering their target society. As Chaim Kaufmann has shown, even intense ethnic civil wars can often be stopped by demographic separation because it greatly reduces both means and incentives for the sides to attack each other. This logic may apply with even more force to the related problem of suicide terrorism, since, for suicide attackers, gaining physical access to the general area of the target is the only genuinely demanding part of an operation, and as we have seen, resentment of foreign occupation of their national homeland is a key part of the motive for suicide terrorism.

The requirements for demographic separation depend on geographic and other circumstances that may not be attainable in all cases. For example, much of Israel's difficulty in containing suicide terrorism derives from the deeply intermixed settlement patterns of the West Bank and Gaza, which make the effective length of the border between Palestinian and Jewish settled areas practically infinite and have rendered even very intensive Israeli border control efforts ineffective. As a result, territorial concessions could well encourage terrorists leaders to strive for still greater gains while greater repression may only exacerbate the conditions of occupation that cultivate more recruits for terrorist organizations. Instead, the best course to improve Israel's security may well be a combined strategy: abandoning territory on the West Bank along with an actual wall that physically separates the populations.

Similarly, if Al Qaeda proves able to continue suicide attacks against the American homeland, the United States should emphasize improving its domestic security. In the short term, the United States should adopt stronger border controls to make it more difficult for suicide attackers to enter the United States. In the long term, the United States should work toward energy independence and, thus, reduce the need for American troops in the Persian Gulf countries where their presence has helped recruit suicide terrorists to attack America. These measures will not provide a perfect solution, but they may make it far more difficult for Al Qaeda to continue attacks in the United States, especially spectacular attacks that require elaborate coordination.

Perhaps most important, the close association between foreign military occupations and the growth of suicide terrorist movements in the occupied regions should give pause to those who favor solutions that involve conquering countries in order to transform their political systems. Conquering countries may disrupt terrorist operations in the short term, but it is important to recognize that occupation of more countries may well increase the number of terrorists coming at us.

THE SPREAD OF
▮ NUCLEAR WEAPONS

Nuclear Instability in South Asia
▮ SCOTT D. SAGAN

The emerging nuclear history of India and Pakistan strongly supports the pessimistic predictions of organizational theorists. Military organizational behavior has led to serious problems in meeting all three requirements for stable nuclear deterrence—prevention of preventive war during periods of transition when one side has a temporary advantage, the development of survivable second-strike forces, and avoidance of accidental nuclear war. . . . These problems have now appeared in India and Pakistan.

It should be acknowledged from the start that there are important differences between the nuclear relationship emerging between India and Pakistan and the cold war system that developed over time between the United States and the Soviet Union. While the differences are clear, however, the significance of these differences is not. For example, the nuclear arsenals in South Asia are, and are likely to remain, much smaller and less sophisticated than were the U.S. and Soviet arsenals. This should make each arsenal both more vulnerable to a counterforce attack (an attack on the adversary's own nuclear forces) and less capable of mounting counterforce attacks, and thus the net effect is uncertain. There are also important differences in civil-military relations in the two cases, but these differences, too, are both stabilizing and potentially destabilizing. The Soviets and the Americans both eventually developed an "assertive" command system with tight high-level civilian control over their nuclear weapons. Also India has an extreme system of assertive civilian control of the military, with (at least until recently) very little direct military influence on any aspect of nuclear weapons policy. Pakistan, however, is at the other end of the spectrum, with the military in complete control of the nuclear arsenal, and with only marginal influence from civilian political leaders, even during the periods when there was a civilian-led government in Islamabad. There are, finally, important differences in mutual understanding, proximity, and hostility. India and Pakistan share a common colonial and pre-colonial history, have some common cultural roots, and share a common border; they also have engaged in four wars against each other, and are involved in a violent fifty-year dispute about the status of Kashmir. In contrast, the Americans and Soviets were on opposite sides of the globe and viewed each other as mysterious, often unpredictable adversaries. The cold war superpowers were involved in a deep-seated ideological rivalry, but held no disputed territory between them and had no enduring history of armed violence against each other.

There is also, however, a crucially important similarity between the nuclear conditions that existed in cold war and those that exist in South Asia today. In both cases, the parochial interests and routine behaviors of the organizations that manage nuclear weapons limit the stability of nuclear deterrence. The newest nuclear weapons will not make exactly the same mistakes with nuclear weapons as did their superpower predecessors. They are, however, also unlikely to meet with complete success in the difficult effort to control these weapons and maintain nuclear peace.

THE PROBLEM OF PREVENTIVE WAR

Pakistan has been under direct military rule for almost half of its existence, and some analysts have argued that the organizational biases of its military leaders had strong effects on strategic decisions concerning the initiation and conduct of the 1965 and 1971 wars with India. In contrast, India has a sustained tradition of strict civilian control over the military since its independence. These patterns of civil-military relations influence nuclear weapons doctrine and operations. In India, the military has traditionally not been involved in decisions concerning nuclear testing, design, or even command and control. In Pakistan, the military largely runs the nuclear weapons program; even during the periods in which civilian prime ministers have held the reins of government, they have neither been told the full details of the nuclear weapons program nor been given direct control over the operational arsenal.

An organizational theory lens suggests that it is very fortunate that it was India, not Pakistan, that was the first to develop nuclear weapons in South Asia. Military rule in Islamabad (and military influence during periods of civilian rule) certainly has played an important role in Pakistani decision making concerning the use of force (see the discussion of the Kargil conflict below). But the Pakistani military did not possess nuclear weapons before India tested in 1974, and thus was not in a position to argue that preventive war now was better than war later after India developed a rudimentary arsenal.

The preventive war problem in South Asia is a complex one, however, and new evidence suggests that military influence in India produced serious risks of preventive war in the 1980s, despite strong institutionalized civilian control. The government of Prime Minister Indira Gandhi considered, but then rejected, plans to attack Pakistan's Kahuta nuclear facility in the early 1980s, a preventive attack plan that was recommended by senior Indian military leaders. Yet, as occurred in the United States, the preferences of senior officers did not suddenly change when civilian leaders ruled against preventive war. Instead, the beliefs went underground, only to resurface later in a potentially more dangerous form.

These beliefs emerged from the shadows during the 1986–87 "Brasstacks" crisis. This serious crisis began in late 1986 when the Indian military initiated a massive military exercise in Rajasthan, involving an estimated 250,000 troops and 1,500 tanks, including the issuance of live ammunition to troops and concluding with a simulated "counter-offensive" attack, including Indian Air Force strikes, into Pakistan. The Pakistani military, fearing that the exercise might turn into a large-scale attack, alerted military forces and conducted exercises along the border, which led to Indian military counter-movements closer to the border and an operational Indian Air Force alert. The resulting crisis produced a flurry of diplomatic activity and was resolved only after direct intervention by the highest political authorities.

The traditional explanation for the Brasstacks crisis has been that it was an accidental crisis, caused by Pakistan's misinterpretation of an inadvertently provocative Indian Army exercise. For example, Devin Hagerty's detailed examination of "NewDelhi's intentions in conducting Brasstacks" concludes that "India's conduct of 'normal' exercises rang alarm bells in Pakistan; subsequently, the logic of the security dilemma structured both sides' behavior, with each interpreting the other's defensive moves as preparations for offensive action.[1] A stronger explanation, however, unpacks "New Delhi's intentions" to look at what different Indian decision makers in the capital wanted to do before and during the crisis.

The key is to understand the preventive-war thinking of the then-Indian chief of the Army Staff, General Krishnaswami Sundarji. Sundarji apparently believed that India's security would be greatly eroded by Pakistani development of a usable nuclear arsenal and thus deliberately designed the Brasstacks exercise in hopes of provoking a Pakistani military response. He hoped that this would then provide India with an excuse to implement existing contingency plans to go on the offensive against Pakistan and to take out its nuclear program in a preventive strike. According to the memoirs of Lieutenant General P. N. Hoon, the commander in chief of the Western Army during Brasstacks:

> Brasstacks was no military exercise. It was a plan to build up a situation for a fourth war with Pakistan. And what is even more shocking is that the Prime Minister, Mr. Rajiv Gandhi, was not aware of these plans for war.

The preventive war motivation behind Sundarji's plans helps to explain why the Indian military did not provide full notification of the exercise to the Pakistanis and then failed to use the special hotline to explain their operations when information was requested by Pakistan during the crisis. A final piece of evidence confirms that Sundarji advocated a preventive strike against Pakistan during the crisis. Considerations of an attack on Pakistani nuclear facilities went all the way up to the most senior decision makers in New Delhi in January 1987:

> [Prime Minister] Rajiv [Gandhi] now considered the possibility that Pakistan might initiate war with India. In a meeting with a handful of senior bureaucrats and General Sundarji, he contemplated beating Pakistan to the draw by launching a preemptive attack on the Army Reserve South. This would have included automatically an attack on Pakistan's nuclear facilities to remove the potential for a Pakistani nuclear riposte to India's attack. Relevant government agencies were not asked to contribute analysis or views to the discussion. Sundarji argued that India's cities could be protected from a Pakistani counterattack (perhaps a nuclear one), but, upon being probed, could not say how. One important advisor from the Ministry of Defense argued eloquently that 'India and Pakistan have already fought their last war, and there is too much to lose in contemplating another one.' This view ultimately prevailed.

THE KARGIL CONFLICT AND FUTURE PROBLEMS

Optimists cannot accept that the Brasstacks crisis may have been a deliberate attempt to spark a preventive attack, but they might be reassured by the final outcome, as senior political leaders stepped in to stop further escalation. The power of nuclear deterrence to prevent war in South Asia, optimists insist, has been demonstrated in repeated crises: the Indian preventive attack discussions in 1984; the Brasstacks crisis; and the 1990 Kashmir crisis. "There is no more ironclad law in international relations theory than this," Devin Hagerty's detailed study concludes, "nuclear states do not fight wars with each other."[2]

In the spring and summer of 1999, however, one year after the exchange of nuclear tests, India and Pakistan did fight a war in the mountains along the line of control separating the portions of Kashmir controlled by each country, near the Indian town of Kargil. The conflict began in May, when the Indian intelligence services discovered what appeared to be Pakistani regular forces lodged in mountain redoubts on the Indian side of the line of control. For almost two months, Indian Army units attacked the Pakistani forces and Indian Air Force jets bombed their bases high in the Himalayan peaks. Although the Indian forces carefully stayed on their side of the line of control in Kashmir, Indian prime minister Atal Bihari Vajpayee informed the U.S. government that he might have to order attacks into Pakistan. U.S. spy satellites revealed that Indian tanks and heavy artillery were being prepared for a counter-offensive in Rajasthan. The fighting ended in July, when Pakistani prime minister Nawaz Sharif flew to Washington and, after receiving "political cover" in the form of statement that President Bill Clinton would "take a personal interest" in resolving the Kashmir problem, pledged to withdraw forces to the Pakistani side of the line of control. Over one thousand Indian and Pakistani soldiers died in the conflict, and Sharif's decision to pull out was one of the major causes of the coup that overthrew his regime in October 1999.

The 1999 Kargil conflict is disturbing not only because it demonstrates that nuclear-armed states can fight wars, but also because the organizational biases of the Pakistani military were a major cause of the conflict. Moreover, such biases continue to exist and could play a role in starting crises in the future. This increases the dangers of both a preventive and preemptive strike if war is considered inevitable, as well as the risk of a deliberate, but limited, use of nuclear weapons on the battlefield.

Three puzzling aspects of the Kargil conflict are understandable from an organizational perspective. First, in late 1998, the Pakistani military planned the Kargil operation, paying much more attention, as organization theory would predict, to the tactical effects of the surprise military maneuver than to the broader strategic consequences. Ignoring the likely international reaction and the predictable domestic consequences of the military incursion in India, however, proved to be a significant factor in the ultimate failure of the Kargil operation.

Second, the Pakistani Army also started the operation with the apparent belief—following the logic of what has been called the "stability/instability paradox"—that a "stable nuclear balance" between India and Pakistan permitted more offensive actions to take place with impunity in Kashmir. It is important to note that this belief was more strongly held by senior military officers than by civilian leaders. For example, at the height of the fighting near Kargil, Pakistani Army leaders stated that "there is almost a red alert situation," but they nevertheless insisted "there is no chance of the Kargil conflict leading to a full-fledged war between the two sides."[3] Although Prime Minister Nawaz Sharif apparently approved the plan to move forces across the line of control, it is not clear that he was fully briefed on the nature, scope, or potential consequences of the operation. The prime minister's statement that he was "trying to avoid nuclear war" and his suggestion that he feared "that India was getting ready to launch a full-scale military operation against Pakistan" provide a clear contrast to the confident military assessment that there was virtually no risk of an Indian counterattack or escalation to nuclear war.

Third, the current Pakistani military government's interpretation of the Kargil crisis, at least in public, is that Nawaz Sharif lost courage and backed down unnecessarily. This view is not widely shared by Pakistani scholars and journalists, but such a "stab in the back" thesis does serve the parochial self-interests of the Pakistani army, which does not want to acknowledge its errors or those of the current Musharraf regime. The New Delhi government's interpretation, however, is that the Indian threats that military escalation—a counterattack across the international border—would be ordered, if necessary, forced Pakistan to retreat. These different "lessons learned" could produce ominous outcomes in future crises: each side believes that the Kargil conflict proved that if its government displays resolve and threatens to escalate to new levels of violence, the other side will exhibit restraint and back away from the brink.

Future military crises between India and Pakistan are likely to be nuclear crises. Proliferation optimists are not concerned about this likelihood, however, since they argue that the danger of preventive war, if it ever existed at all, has been eliminated by the development of deliverable nuclear weapons in both countries after May 1998. The problem of preventive war during periods of transition in South Asia is only of historical interest now, optimists would insist.

I am not convinced by this argument for two basic reasons. First, there is an arms race looming on the horizon in South Asia. The Indian government has given strong support to the Bush administration's plans to develop missile defense technology and has expressed interest in eventually procuring or developing its own missile defense capability. I believe that the Indian nuclear program is strongly influenced by the fact that hawkish nuclear policies are popular among Indian voters and thus serve the domestic political interests of Indian politicians. China is likely to respond to the U.S. decision to build national missile defenses by increasing the size and readiness of its own missile force. This will in turn encourage the Indian government to increase its own missile deployments and develop defense technology.

These deployments in India, however, will threaten the smaller nuclear deterrent forces in Pakistan, and this would inevitably reopen the window of opportunity for preventive war considerations. Military biases, under the preventive war logic of "better now than later," could encourage precipitous action in either country if the government had even a fleeting moment of superiority in this new kind of arms race.

The second reason to be pessimistic is that, in serious crises, attacks might be initiated based on the belief that an enemy's use of nuclear weapons is imminent and unavoidable. While it is clear that the existence of nuclear weapons in South Asia made both governments cautious in their use of conventional military force in 1999, it is also clear that Indian leaders were prepared to escalate the conflict if necessary. Pakistani political authorities, however, made nuclear threats during the crisis, suggesting that nuclear weapons would be used precisely under such conditions. Moreover, according to U.S. officials the Pakistani military, apparently without the Prime Minister's knowledge took initial steps to alert its nuclear forces during the Kargil conflict.

This dangerous alerting pattern was repeated in the South Asian crises that occurred after the September 11, 2001, terrorist attacks in the United States and the December 13, 2001, terrorist attack on the Parliament in New Delhi. In both cases, the Pakistani government feared that its nuclear forces would be attacked and therefore took alert measures to disperse the nuclear weapons and missiles to new locations away from their storage sites. Pakistani fears that attacks on their nuclear arsenal were being planned may not have been entirely fanciful.

After the September 11 Pentagon and World Trade Center attacks, President Bush warned Islamabad that Pakistan would either side with the United States in the new war against terrorism or else be treated as a terrorist state. The development of military plans for U.S. commando raids against the Pakistani nuclear weapons sites was soon widely reported. President Musharraf defused the crisis by deciding to abandon support for the Taliban regime in Afghanistan and to provide logistical and intelligence support for the U.S. war there.

After the December 13 terrorist attack against the Indian Parliament, the Indian government sent massive military forces to the Pakistani border and threatened to attack unless Musharraf cracked down on the radical Islamic groups that supported terrorist operations in Kashmir and New Delhi. Before Musharraf could respond, General S. Padmanabhan, the Indian Army chief, issued a bellicose statement announcing that the military buildup "was not an exercise": "A lot of viable options (beginning from a strike on the camps to a full conventional war) are available. We can do it. . . . If we go to war, jolly good."[4] Senior Indian political authorities criticized the Army chief for making the statement, and diplomats in New Delhi speculated that General Padmanabhan had deliberately made it more difficult for the Pakistanis to back down in this crisis, thus increasing the likelihood of war. Again, President Musharraf defused the crisis, at least temporarily, by initiating a crackdown on Islamic Jihadi groups promoting terrorism in Kashmir and the rest of India.

What lessons should be drawn from these dangerous crises? Optimists will look at only the final result and assume that it was inevitable: Deterrence and coercion worked, as serious threats were issued, the Pakistani president compromised and no war occurred. At a deeper level, however, two more ominous lessons should be learned. First, President Musharraf's decision to back down was by no means inevitable, and he was subject to significant criticism from Islamic parties and some military circles for his conciliatory stance. Other Pakistani leaders could have gone the other way, and, indeed, Musharraf may be less prone to compromise in the future precisely because he was forced to change policies under the threat of attack in these crises. Second, the Pakistani fear that a preventive or preemptive strike against its nuclear arsenal was imminent forced it to take very dangerous military alerting steps in both crises. Taking nuclear weapons and missiles out of their more secure storage locations and deploying them into the field may make the forces less vulnerable to an enemy attack, but it makes the weapons more vulnerable to theft or internal attacks by terrorist organizations. Given the number of al Qaeda members and supporters in Pakistan, this hidden terrorist problem may well have been the most serious nuclear danger of the crises. In short, the crises of 2001 and 2002 demonstrate that nuclear weapons in South Asia may well produce a modicum of restraint, but also momentous dangers.

In future crises in South Asia, the likelihood of either a preventive or preemptive attack will be strongly influenced by a complex mixture of perceptions of the adversary's intent, estimates about its future offensive and defensive capabilities, and estimates of the vulnerability of its current nuclear arsenal. Organizational biases could encourage worst-case assumptions about the adversary's intent and pessimistic beliefs about the prospects for successful strategic deterrence over the long term. Unfortunately, as will be seen below, inherent organizational characteristics can also produce vulnerabilities to an enemy strike.

SURVIVABILITY OF NUCLEAR FORCES IN SOUTH ASIA

The fear of retaliation is central to successful deterrence, and the second requirement for stability with nuclear weapons is therefore the development of secure, second-strike forces. Unfortunately, there are strong reasons to be concerned about the ability of the Indian and Pakistani military to maintain survivable forces. Two problems can already be seen to have reduced (at least temporarily) the survivability of nuclear forces in Pakistan. First, there is evidence that the Pakistani military, as was the case in the cold war examples cited earlier, deployed its missile forces, following standard operating procedures, in ways that produce signatures giving away their deployment locations. Indian intelligence officers, for example, identified the locations of planned Pakistani deployments of M-11 missiles by spotting the placement of "secret" defense communication terminals nearby. A second, and even more dramatic, example follows a cold war precedent quite closely. Just as the road engineers in the Soviet Union inadvertently gave away the location of their ICBMs because construction crews built roads with wide-radius turns next to the missile silos, Pakistani road construction crews have inadvertently signaled the location of the "secret" M-11 missiles by placing wide-radius roads and roundabouts outside newly constructed garages at the Sargodha military base.

Finally, analysts should also not ignore the possibility that Indian or Pakistani intelligence agencies could intercept messages revealing the "secret" locations of otherwise survivable military forces, an absolutely critical issue with small or opaque nuclear arsenals. The history of the 1971 war, for example, demonstrates that both states' intelligence agencies were able to intercept critical classified messages sent by and to the other side. . . .

Perhaps most dramatically, on December 12, 1971, the Indians intercepted a radio message scheduling a meeting of high-level Pakistani officials at Government House in Dacca, which led to an air attack on the building in the middle of the meeting. . . .

NORMAL ACCIDENTS AND UNAUTHORIZED USE IN NUCLEAR SOUTH ASIA

Will the Indian and Pakistani nuclear arsenals be more safe and secure than were the U.S. and Soviet arsenals during the cold war? It is clear that the emerging South Asian nuclear deterrence system is both smaller and less complex today than was the case in the United States or Soviet Union at the height of the cold war. It is also clear, however, that the South Asian nuclear relationship is inherently more tightly coupled because of geographical proximity. With inadequate warning systems in place and with weapons with short flight times emerging in the region, the time-lines for decision making are highly compressed and the danger that one accident could lead to another and then lead to a catastrophic accidental war is high and growing. The proximity of New Delhi and Islamabad to their potential adversary's border poses particular concerns about rapid "decapitation" attacks on national capitals. Moreover, there are legitimate concerns about social stability and support for terrorists inside Pakistan, problems that could compromise nuclear weapons safety and security.

Proliferation optimists will cite the small sizes of India and Pakistan's nuclear arsenals as a reason to be less worried about these problems. Yet the key from a normal accidents perspective is not the numbers, but rather the structure of the arsenal. Here there is both good and bad news. The good news is that under normal peacetime conditions, neither the Indians, nor the Pakistanis regularly deploy nuclear forces mated with delivery systems in the field. The bad news, however, is two-fold. First, Pakistani nuclear weapons do not have PALs (Permissive Action Links, the advanced electronic locks on U.S. nuclear weapons that require a special code for the weapons' activation) on them. Second, Pakistan has started to alert its nuclear weapons in crises; it did so in 1999 during the Kargil crisis and then again in September and December of 2001, in response to fears of Indian (and maybe U.S.) military action after the terrorist attacks in New York, Washington, and New Delhi.

From an organizational perspective, it is not surprising to find evidence of serious accidents emerging in the Indian nuclear and missile programs. . . . The false warning incident that occurred just prior to the Pakistani nuclear tests in May 1998 . . . demonstrat[es] the dangers of accidental war in South Asia. During the crucial days just prior to Prime Minister Sharif's decision to order the tests of Pakistani nuclear weapons, senior military intelligence officers informed him that the Indian and Israeli air forces were about to launch a preventive strike on the test site. The incident is shrouded in mystery, and the cause of this warning message is not clear. Although it is certainly possible that Pakistani intelligence officers simply misidentified aircraft in the region, a more likely explanation is that Inter-Service Intelligence (ISI) officials did not believe there was any threat of an imminent Indian-Israeli attack in 1998, but deliberately concocted (or exaggerated) the warning of a preventive strike to force the prime minister, who was wavering under U.S. pressure, to test the weapons immediately. It is not clear which of these is the more worrisome interpretation of the incident: false warnings could be catastrophic in a crisis whether they are deliberate provocations by rogue intelligence officers, or genuinely believed, but inaccurate, reports of imminent or actual attack.

It is important to note that the possibility of a false warning producing an accidental nuclear war in South Asia is reduced, but is by no means eliminated, by India's adoption of a nuclear no-first-use policy. Not only might the Pakistani government, following its stated first-use doctrine, respond to intelligence (in this case false) that India was about to attack successfully a large portion of Pakistani nuclear forces, but either government could misidentify an accidental nuclear detonation occurring during transport and alert activities at one of their own military bases as the start of a counterforce attack by the other state. Pakistani officials should be particularly sensitive to this possibility because of the 1988 Ojheri incident, in which a massive conventional munitions explosion at a secret ammunition dump near Rawalpindi caused fears among some decision makers that an Indian attack had begun. The possibility of this kind of accident producing a false warning of an attack cannot, however, be ruled out in India, either, as long as the government plans to alert forces or mate nuclear weapons to delivery vehicles during crises.

In addition, there should be serious concern about whether both countries can maintain centralized control over their nuclear weapons. Although government policy in this regard is, for obvious reasons, kept classified, it is known that Pakistan has no personnel reliability program (PRP) for the officers who control the arsenal or the guards who protect the weapons storage sites. In the United States, the program is a set of psychological tests and organizational checks; each year, between 2.5 percent and 5.0 percent of previously PRP certified individuals have been decertified, that is, deemed unsuitable for nuclear weapons related duties. Presumably, similarly low, but still significant, percentages of officers, soldiers, and civilians in other countries would be of questionable reliability as guardians of the arsenal. This personnel reliability problem is serious in India, where civilian custodians maintain custody of the nuclear weapons; it is particularly worrisome in Pakistan, where the weapons are controlled by a professional military organization facing the difficult challenge of maintaining discipline while dealing with a failing economy, serious social problems, and growing religious fundamentalism. This situation increases the risk of accidents and of unauthorized use, such as theft or use by terrorists groups.

Finally, there is evidence that neither the Indian nor the Pakistani military has focused sufficiently on the danger that a missile test launch during a crisis could be misperceived as the start of a nuclear attack. There was an agreement, as part of the Lahore accords in January 1999, to provide advance notification of missile tests, but even such an agreement is not a fool-proof solution, as the Russians discovered in January 1995 when a bureaucratic snafu in Moscow led to a failure to pass on advance notification of a Norwegian weather rocket launch, that resulted in serious false warning of a missile attack. Moreover, both the Pakistanis and the Indians appear to be planing to use their missile test facilities for actual nuclear weapons launches in war. In India, Wheeler Island is reportedly being used like Vandenberg air force base, a test site in peacetime and crises, and a launch site in war. During Kargil, according to the Indian Army chief of staff, nuclear alert activities were also detected at "some of Pakistan's launch areas—some of the areas where they carried out tests earlier of one of their missiles."[5]

Nuclear South Asia will be a dangerous place, not because of ill will or irrationality among government leaders, nor because of any unique cultural inhibitions against strategic thinking in both countries. India and Pakistan face a dangerous nuclear future because they have become like other nuclear powers. Their leaders seek security through nuclear deterrence, but imperfect humans inside imperfect organizations control their nuclear weapons. If my theories are right, these organizations will someday fail to produce secure nuclear deterrence. Unfortunately the evidence from these first years of South Asia's nuclear history suggests that the pessimistic predictions of organization theory are likely to come true, even though I cannot predict the precise pathway by which deterrence will break down.

The organizational perspective suggests that there are more similarities than differences between nuclear powers in the way they manage, or at least try to manage, nuclear weapons operations. There is, however, one important structural difference between the new nuclear powers and their cold war predecessors Just as each new child is born into a different family, each new nuclear power is born into a different nuclear system in which nuclear states influence each other's behavior. Some observers believe that the possibility that other nuclear powers—such as the United States or China—can intervene in future crises in South Asia may be a major constraint on undesired escalation. I fear the opposite: the possibility of intervention may encourage the governments of India and Pakistan to engage in risky behavior, initiating crises or making limited uses of force, precisely because they anticipate (correctly or incorrectly) that other nuclear powers may bail them out diplomatically if the going gets rough.

The possibility that other nuclear states might be able to influence nuclear behavior in South Asia does, however, lead to one final optimistic note. There are many potential unilateral steps and bilateral agreements that could be instituted to reduce the risk of nuclear war between India and Pakistan, and the U.S. government can play a useful role in helping to facilitate such agreements. Many, though not all, of the problems identified in this article can be reduced if nuclear weapons in both countries are maintained in a de-alerted state, with warheads removed from delivery vehicles. U.S. assistance could be helpful in providing the arms verification technology that could permit such de-alerting (or non-alerting in this case) to take place within a cooperative framework. The United States could also be helpful in providing intelligence and warning information, on a case-by-case basis, in peacetime or in crises to reduce the danger of false alarms. Finally, increased security of storage sites and safer management of nuclear weapons operations can be encouraged by sharing better security devices for storage sites and discussing organizational "best practices."

There will be no progress on any of these issues, however, unless Indians, Pakistanis, and Americans stop denying that serious problems exist A basic awareness of nuclear command and control problems exists in New Delhi and Islamabad, but unfortunately Indian and Pakistani leaders too often trivialize them. The United States, in turn, refused to assist the Indians and Pakistanis in developing improved safety and security for their nuclear weapons until after the terrorist attacks on September 11, 2001. Washington officials argued before the September 11 attacks that any assistance in this area would "reward' Islamabad and New Delhi for testing, and signal to other potential nuclear weapons states that the United States was not serious about its nonproliferation goals. The September 11 attacks led the U.S. government to switch its position, and Pakistani officials accepted, at least in principle, that some assistance with their nuclear weapons security could be useful. It is crucial that such efforts to improve Pakistani nuclear security measures be fully implemented and eventually be extended to India.

Nuclear weapons will remain in Pakistan and India for the foreseeable future, and the conflict over Kashmir will continue to smolder, threatening to erupt into a wider and more dangerous war. The deep political problems between the two South Asian nuclear states may someday be resolved, and the U.S. government should encourage progress toward that end. In the meantime, the U.S. government should do whatever it can to reduce the risk that India and Pakistan will use nuclear weapons against each other.

NOTES

1. Devin T. Hagerty, *The Consequences of Nuclear Proliferation* (Cambridge, Mass., MIT Press, 1998), p. 92, 106.
2. Hagerty, *The Consequences of Nuclear Proliferation,* p. 184.
3. Ihtashamul Haque, "Peace Linked to Kashmir Solution," *Dawn Wire Service,* June 26, 1999.
4. "Army Ready for War, Says Chief," *The Statesman* (India), January 12, 2002.
5. Raj Chenagappa, "Pakistan Tried Nuclear Blackmail," *The Newspaper Today,* January 12, 2000. www.thenewspapertoday.com/interview/index.phtml?INTERVIEWINT_PADCOUNT.

Nuclear Stability in South Asia

■ KENNETH N. WALTZ

The American government and most American journalists look on the blossoming of nuclear forces in South Asia as an ominous event, different in implication and effect from all the similar events that we worried about throughout the cold war. A 1998 *New York Times* headline, for example, proclaimed that "India's Arms Race Isn't Safe Like the Cold War." Few thought the American-Soviet arms race safe at the time, and for good reasons few Indians and Pakistanis expect an arms race now. Most of the alarmist predictions about the fate of the subcontinent display forgetfulness about the past and confusion over the effects of nuclear weapons. In the same *New York Times* article, Joseph Cirincione, director of the Non-Proliferation Project at the Carnegie Endowment, reports that Pentagon war games between Pakistan and India always end with a nuclear exchange. Has everyone in that building forgotten that deterrence works precisely because nuclear states fear that conventional military engagements may escalate to the nuclear level, and therefore they draw back from the brink? Admiral David E. Jeremiah, once vice-chairman of the Joint Chiefs of Staff, laments the cultural mindset that leads Americans to believe that "everybody thinks like us," and a longtime president of the Henry L. Stimson Center, Michael Krepon, worries that because of the Pressler Amendment, which cut off aid to nations developing nuclear weapons, Pakistani officers have not had the benefit of attending our military schools. One's reaction to both statements may well be "thank goodness."

The Brookings Institution totaled up the cost of American nuclear weapons over the decades and arrived at the figure of 5.5 trillion dollars. Strobe Talbott, when he was deputy secretary of state, implied that military competition between Pakistan and India will cause them to spend on a proportionate scale. When asked why we should not provide India and Pakistan with advice about, and equipment for safe deterrence, he retorted that "if they locked themselves into the mentality of MAD (Mutual Assured Destruction), they will then be tempted into—like us— a considerable escalation of the arms race."[1] Yet nuclear states need race only to the second-strike level, which is easy to achieve and maintain. Indian and

Pakistani leaders have learned from our folly. A minimal deterrent deters as well as a maximal one. Homi Jehangar Bhabha, father of the Indian bomb, called this "absolute deterrence." K. Subrahmanyam, a foremost strategist, emphasizes that Indians have learned that to build large forces is wasteful and foolish. An arsenal of about sixty weapons, he believes, will deter either Pakistan or China; and Pakistan might need, say, twenty to deter India. Some have claimed that no nuclear country has been satisfied with having only a minimum deterrent. Yet China, with even today only about twenty ICBMs, has been content with small numbers; and India and Pakistan would follow its example were it not for the disruptive effects of American missile defenses on the strategic arms balance in Asia. Political as well as economic constraints on both countries ensure this. Talbott has discerned a global trend away from reliance on nuclear weapons."[2] The United States does rely less on nuclear weapons now because it is the world's dominant conventional power, spending as much on its armed forces in the year 2000 as the next eight big spenders combined. Partly for that reason, some other countries rely more on their nuclear weapons—Russia, for example, with its conventional forces in shambles. Countries that once counted on one of the two great powers for military assistance are now concerned to provide security for themselves: Pakistan, India, Iraq, Japan, and North Korea are all examples.

India tested its "peaceful bomb" in 1974. Its next tests came twenty-four years later. The United States complained loudly both times. Yet the United States tested nuclear weapons many times yearly for many years on end—more than a thousand above and below ground, which is more than the tests of all other countries combined. America's excuse was, at first, that it anticipated a mortal threat from the Soviet Union and, later, that it actually faced such a threat. America's nonproliferation policy denies that such reasoning can legitimate other countries' entering the tight circle of nuclear powers. Nevertheless, the reasoning the United States applied to itself applies to India and to Pakistan as well. Does anyone believe that testing nuclear warheads is something that, in their place, we would not have done?

The question raised by India's and Pakistan's nuclear tests is not whether they should have been conducted, but whether their security requires their becoming nuclear powers. Some countries need nuclear weapons; some do not. Brazil and Argentina set themselves on course to become nuclear states. Both decided to abandon the effort. Neither posed a threat to the other. South Africa became a nuclear state and then, finding no commensurate threat, reversed its policy.

Pakistan obviously needs nuclear weapons. When asked why nuclear weapons are so popular in Pakistan, former prime minister Benazir Bhutto answered, "It's our history. A history of three wars with a larger neighbor. India is five times larger than we are. Their military strength is five times larger. In 1971, our country was disintegrated. So the security issue for Pakistan is an issue of survival." From the other side, Shankar Bajpai, former Indian ambassador to Pakistan, China, and the United States, has said that "Pakistan's quest for a nuclear capability steams from its fear of its larger neighbor, removing that fear should open up immense possibilities"— possibilities for a less worried and more relaxed life. Shamshad Ahmad, Pakistan's foreign secretary, has echoed their thoughts: "In South Asia nuclear deterrence may . . . usher in an era of durable peace between Pakistan and India providing the requisite incentives for resolving all outstanding issues, especially Jammu and Kashmir."[3] In recent years, some Indians and Pakistanis have begun to talk about a peaceful accommodation, and according to a *New York Times* reporter, "just about everybody" in Kashmir "cites the two countries' possession of nuclear weapons as a factor pushing towards peace."[4]

In the 1980s, after the Soviet occupation of Afghanistan, the United States, knowing of Pakistan's nuclear progress, nevertheless continued to supply Pakistan with sophisticated conventional weapons. The United States did not care much about Pakistan's nuclear progress as long as Soviet worries dominated American policy. Once the Soviet Union went into steep decline and then disappeared, America dropped Pakistan, with a speed that surprised not only Pakistan but India as well. For Pakistan to compete conventionally with India was economically impossible. Nuclear weapons linked to a sensible strategy are a low cost way of leveling the playing field. Understandably Pakistan felt itself pressed to follow the nuclear course.

Can India be seen in a similar light? With its superior conventional forces, it needed no nuclear weapons to protect itself against a Pakistan that lacked them, but what about China? Americans think of India as the dominant power in South Asia. India feels differently. India is part of a hostile world. With a Muslim minority of about 150 million, it adjoins Muslim Pakistan, and beyond lies a Muslim world becoming more fundamentalist and more hostile. To the north is an increasingly nationalist, steadily more powerful, and potentially unstable China. The United States has reinforced India's worries about a Chinese-Pakistani-American axis, notably when America "tilted" toward Pakistan in the 1971 war with India. In the middle of the war, Henry Kissinger told Mao Zedong, "We want to keep the pressure on India both militarily and politically," adding that if China "took measures to protect its security, the US would oppose efforts of others to interfere."[5] In a show of support for Pakistan, the American navy moved the aircraft carrier *Enterprise* into the Indian Ocean. To this day, Indians consider this an attempt to hold them in nuclear awe. They call it blackmail. India continues to believe that America favors China over India. A professor at Jawaharlal Nehru University found nuclear cooperation between Beijing and Islamabad "unprecedented in the history of international relations."[6] And an Indian minister of defense wondered, as many Indians do, "why India and Pakistan should be seen as blowing each other up when nuclear weapons in the hands of the United States and China are seen as stabilizing factors."[7] That the United States seems to trust China as an old nuclear power, and not India as a new one, is a cause of bitter resentment.

The decision to make nuclear weapons was a momentous one for India. The tests of May 1998 were overwhelmingly popular with the public at large, but the decision emerged over decades, with much opposition along the way. Even today, Indians who view nuclear deterrence as a difficult and demanding task believe that India will be unable to develop and deploy a nuclear force sufficient for the deterrence of China. In their view, the main effect of India's developing nuclear capabilities was to cause Pakistan to develop its own. India is therefore worse off with nuclear weapons than it would have been without them. The Indian view that carried the day rests on the contrary argument: namely, that it does not take much to deter.

Is it farfetched for India to worry about a Chinese threat to its security? Any country has trouble seeing the world as others do. Let's try. If the United States shared a two-thousand-mile border with a country that was more populous, more prosperous, more heavily armed, and in possession of nuclear weapons, we would react militarily and, judging from our response to the Soviet Union, more vigorously than India has done. What *is* farfetched is for the United States to worry about a Chinese threat to its security and then wonder why India does too.

Kanti Bajpai, a professor at Nehru University, strongly opposes India's nuclear armament. He doubts that India's nuclear deterrent would dissuade China from seizing Arunachal Pradesh in the northeast or Pakistan from seizing Kashmir in the northwest. This is comparable to the worry, dreamt up in the 1960s, about a "Hamburg grab." Some American military commentators worried that the Soviet Union might suddenly seize Hamburg, which jutted into East Germany, and then in effect: ask, "Is NATO's fighting to regain Hamburg worth risking a nuclear conflagration?" Similarly, Kanti Bajpai imagines "a quick grabbing thrust into the two states, backed by nuclear weapons, in the hope of presenting India with a fait accompli."[8] Such worries are as fanciful as American worries were in the cold war. The invader would have to assemble troops near the border. India would then alert its forces, including nuclear ones. With the potential crisis easily foreseeable, why would China or Pakistan run such risks?

One answer to the question is that Pakistan did move troops across the line of control into Kashmir and fight for a time at a fairly high level in the engagement known as Kargil. Joseph Cirincione voices widespread fears when, with the Kashmir conflict in mind, he says, "Just assemble all the risk factors and multiply it out. . . . This is the most dangerous and unstable military situation in the world."[9] His pronouncement repeats the tired old error of inferring from the conventional past what the nuclear future holds, a mistake made almost every time another country gets nuclear weapons. With nuclear weapons added, conventionally dangerous and unstable situations become safer and stabler ones. Nuclear weapons produce what Joseph Nye calls the "crystal ball" effect. Everyone knows that if force gets out of hand all the parties to a conflict face catastrophe. With conventional weapons, the crystal ball is clouded. With nuclear weapons, it is perfectly clear.

What reasons do we have to believe that India's and Pakistan's crystal balls are clouded? Well, again, Kargil. Some observers worry that Pakistan may believe that it can safely raise the level of conventional violence since nuclear weapons limit the extent of India's response. But, of course, they also limit the size and scope of Pakistan's attack, since Pakistan knows it could face nuclear retaliation. And the same reasoning applies to India. It's the same old story: In the presence of nuclear weapons, a country can achieve a significant victory only by risking devastating retaliation.

Sagan calls Kargil the fourth Indian-Pakistani war because it fits the social science definition holding that a military encounter is a war if it produces more than one thousand battle-related deaths. If Kargil is called a war, then the definition of war requires revision; and now that both countries have nuclear weapons the fifth "war" will be no worse than the so-called fourth one. The late Pakistani chief of the army staff, General Mirza Aslam Beg, remarked that India and Pakistan can no longer fight even a conventional war over Kashmir, and his counterpart, the chief of the Indian army staff, General Krishnaswami Sundarji concurred. Kargil showed once again that deterrence does not firmly protect disputed areas but does limit the extent of the violence. Indian rear admiral Raja Menon put the larger point simply: "The Kargil crisis demonstrated that the subcontinental nuclear threshold probably lies territorially in the heartland of both countries, and not on the Kashmir cease-fire line."[10]

The obvious conclusion to draw from Kargil is that the presence of nuclear weapons prevented escalation from major skirmish to full-scale war. This contrasts starkly with the bloody 1965 war, in which both parties were armed only with conventional weapons.

Another question is whether India and Pakistan can firmly control and safely deploy nuclear forces sufficient to deter. Because I said enough about the ease of deterrence in chapter 8, I shall concentrate on questions of safety and control. Sagan claims that "the emerging history of nuclear India and nuclear Pakistan strongly supports the pessimistic predictions of organizational theorists." Yet the evidence, accumulated over five decades, shows that nuclear states fight with nuclear states only at low levels, that accidents seldom occur, and that when they do they never have bad effects. If nuclear pessimists were right, nuclear deterrence would have failed again and again. Nuclear pessimists deal with the potential causes of catastrophe; optimists, with the effects the causes do *not* produce. Since the evidence fails to support the predictions of pessimists, one wonders why the spread of nuclear weapons to South Asia should have bad rather that good effects. What differences in the situation of India and Pakistan may cause their fates to depart from the nuclear norm? If they and their situations are different, then the happy history of the nuclear past does not forecast their futures. American commentators dwell on the differences between the United States and the Soviet Union earlier and India and Pakistan today. Among the seeming differences, these are given prominence: differences in the states involved, differences in their histories of conflict, and differences in the distance between the competing parties. I consider them in turn.

DOES DETERRENCE DEPEND ON WHO IS DETERRING WHOM?

For decades we believed that we were trying to deter two monstrous countries—one an "evil empire" and the other a totalitarian country ruled by a megalomaniac. Now we learn that deterrence worked in the past because the United States, the Soviet Union, and China were settled and sensible societies. Karl Kaiser, of the Research Institute of the German Society for Foreign Affairs, and Arthur G. Rubinoff of the University of Toronto, for example, argue that the success of deterrence depends on its context, that is, on who the countries are and on how they relate to each other. In Kaiser's view, "the stability of nuclear deterrence between East and West rest[ed] on a multitude of military and political factors which in other regions are either totally missing or are only partially present." In Rubinoff's view, it is foolish to compare the American-Soviet conflict with South Asia, where the dynamics are "reminiscent of the outbreak of the First World War." Reminiscence flickers, however, since no one then had nuclear weapons. With a Hindu chauvinist in power in New Delhi and an Islamic party governing India, Rubinoff finds "no resemblance to the deterrent situation that characterized the U.S.-Soviet conflict."[11] That statement may once have applied to India and Pakistan, but only until they armed themselves with nuclear weapons. The history of the cold war shows that what matters is not the character of the countries that have nuclear weapons but the fact that they have them. Differences among nuclear countries abound, but for keeping the peace what difference have they made?

Whatever the identity of rulers, and whatever the characteristics of their states, the national behaviors they produce are strongly conditioned by the world outside. With conventional weapons, a defensive country has to ask itself how much power it must harness to its policy in order to dissuade an aggressive state from striking. Countries willing to run high risks are hard to dissuade. The characteristics of governments and the temperaments of leaders have to be carefully weighed. With nuclear weapons, any state will be deterred by another state's second-strike forces, one need not be preoccupied with the qualities of the state that is to be deterred or scrutinize its leaders. In a nuclear world, any state—whether ruled by a Stalin, a Mao Zedong, a Saddam Hussein, or a Kim Jong Il—will be deterred by the knowledge that aggressive actions may lead to its own destruction.

DOES DETERRENCE DEPEND ON THE DETERRERS' RECENT HISTORY?

India and Pakistan have fought three wars in little more than fifty years and Kashmir is a bone in the throat of Pakistan. In contrast, America and Russia have never fought a war against each other. Yet some other nuclear countries look more like India and Pakistan, and nuclear weapons have kept the peace between them. Russia and China have suffered numerous military invasions by one another over the centuries. In the 1960s, when both had nuclear weapons, skirmishes broke out from time to time along the Siberian frontier, and the fighting was on a fairly large scale. The bitterness of the antagonists rivalled that between India and Pakistan fueled by ethnic resentments and ideological differences.

Clashes between nuclear countries over peripheral areas are hardly the exception. Of today's eight nuclear countries, five have fought their neighbors in the past half century: Russia, China, Israel, Pakistan, and India. Those who believe that the South Asian situation is without parallel often ignore the Middle East. The parallel is not exact, but it is instructive. The Middle East is unrivalled for long-standing conflict, irreconcilable disputes, feelings of distrust and hatred, and recurrent wars. In 1973, two nonnuclear Arab countries, Egypt and Syria, attacked Israel and fought what by anyone's definition was a war. Limited in extent by one side's nuclear weapons, it nonetheless did not spiral out of control.

DOES DETERRENCE DEPEND ON DISTANCE?

Proximity is a constantly emphasized difference between the relations of India and Pakistan and that of the United States and the Soviet Union. America and Russia are separated by vast distances; Pakistan and India live cheek by jowl. They continually rub against each other in irritating and dangerous ways. George Perkovich had this in mind when he expressed his fear that "Somebody blows up something big and India says, 'That's it, and takes out targets. Then you're of your way. Who's going to back down?'"[12] Much the same fears in much the same words were expressed during the cold war. The two antagonists might "go to the brink"; one would slip over the edge, and once the exchange of warheads began neither side would be willing to stop it by giving in to the other. In actuality, however, backing down in times of crisis proved not to be such a big problem. Never do two countries share a common interest more completely than when they are locked in death's embrace. Each may want something else as well, but both want most of all to get out of the dire situation they are in. During the Kargil fighting, India went to "Readiness State 3," which means that warheads were prepared for placement on delivery vehicles, and Pakistan apparently took similar steps. These were seen as rash and dangerous moves, but what does one expect? The United States and the Soviet Union alerted their forces a number of times. Doing so is a way of saying, "This is getting serious, and we both had better calm down." Despite the pessimism engendered by the history of South Asia, Indian-Pakistani wars have been, as wars go, quite restrained. As Admiral Menon has written, "Any analysis of the three wars fought often refers to the rather gentlemanly manner in which they were fought with care taken to avoid civilian casualties."[13] Pakistan's 1999 thrust into Kashmir may have been rash, yet as Menon has rightly said, "Subsequent Pakistani attempts to signal an unwillingness to escalate were mature and sober."[14] And in the Kargil campaign, India never sent its troops across the line of control.

History tells us only what we want to know. A pair of *New York Times* journalists contrasts then with now by claiming that, except in Cuba, "the Americans and Soviets took care not to place their troops in direct military confrontation."[15] What, then, were NATO and Warsaw Treaty Organization troops doing in the middle of Europe, where confrontation was a constant and serious business?

Proximity does make warning time short. Missiles can fly between Islamabad and New Delhi in less than five minutes. Yet nuclear countries in the past have often been close militarily if not geographically. Cuba is only ninety miles from American shores, and that is proximity enough. The United States flew planes at the Soviet Union's borders and across them, believing its radars would not spot them. American bravado continues. In April 2001, an American surveillance plane was struck by a Chinese plane over waters near China. Close surveillance is provocative even if international legalities are nicely observed. As President Dwight D. Eisenhower said when an American plane went down thirty-two miles from the Chinese coast in August 1956, "If planes were flying 20 to 50 miles from our shores, we would be very likely to shoot them down if they came in closer, whether through error or not."[16]

Operation Brasstacks was an all-service Indian operation staged in 1987. As Sagan says, it is widely believed that General Sundarji intended it to be a prelude to a war in which India would destroy Pakistan's nuclear facilities. Sundarji may have thought that even if Pakistan had a few bombs, India would be able to destroy them on the ground. In retrospect, Brasstacks looks more like a typical instance of Indian failure to coordinate policies among the Prime Minister's Office, the External Affairs Ministry, the Defense Ministry, and the military services.

Brasstacks is not something new in the nuclear annals. It pales in comparison to provocative acts by the United States and the Soviet Union. In 1983, for example, Able Archer—a recurrent NATO military exercise—was more extensive than ever before. It was held at a time of extraordinary tension. The Soviets believed that surprise was the key to American war plans. During the exercise, the simulated alert of NATO nuclear forces was thought by the Soviets to be a real one. American Pershing II missiles were to be deployed in Europe soon. The Soviets believed that some of them, with their fifty-kiloton payload, fifty-meter accuracy, and ten-minute delivery time to Moscow, had already arrived. Early in the Reagan administration, Defense Secretary Caspar Weinberger and other officials proclaimed that it was our aim to be able to fight, sustain, and win a nuclear war. With some reason, Soviet leaders believed it was about to begin.

Vast distances lie between the United States and Russia. What difference do these distances make when American troops and missiles are stationed in Europe and Northeast Asia? Those who believe that the Indian-Pakistani confrontation is without precedent have either little knowledge of cold war history or oddly defective memories.

Proximity shortens the time between launch and landing. With little warning time, quick decisions would seem to be required. Acting on early warnings of incoming missiles that may turn out to be false could be fatal to both sides. The notion that deterrence demands the threat of swift retaliation was ingrained in American and Russian thinking, and it remains so today, with both forces still on hair-trigger alert. Yet deterrence of a would-be attacker does not depend on the belief that retaliation will be prompt, but only on the belief that the attacked may in due course retaliate. As K. Subrahmanyam has put it, "The strike back need not be highly time-critical."[17] A small force may be a vulnerable force, but smaller is worse than bigger only if the attacker believes he can destroy *all* of the force before *any* of it can be launched.

Students of organizations rightly worry about complex and tightly-coupled systems because they are susceptible to damaging accidents. They wrongly believe that conflicting nuclear states should be thought of as a tightly-coupled system. Fortunately, nuclear weapons loosen the coupling of states by lessening the effects of proximity and by cutting through the complexities of conventional confrontations. Organizational theorists fail to distinguish between the technical complexities of nuclear-weapons systems and the simplicity of the situations they create.

Sagan points out that the survival of Indian and Pakistani forces cannot be guaranteed. But neither can their complete destruction, and that is what matters. Oddly, many pessimists believe that countries with small and technologically limited nuclear forces may be able to accomplish the difficult feat of making a successful first strike but not the easy one of making their own nuclear force appear to be invulnerable. They overlook a basic nuclear truth: If some part of a force is invulnerable, all of the force is invulnerable. Destroying even a major portion of a nuclear force does no good because of the damage a small number of surviving warheads can do. Conventional weapons put a premium on striking first to gain the initial advantage and set the course of the war. Nuclear weapons eliminate this premium. The initial advantage is insignificant if the cost of gaining it is half a dozen cities.

More important than the size of arsenals, the sophistication of command and control, the proximity of competitors, and the history of the relations, are the sensibilities of leaders. Fortunately, nuclear weapons make leaders behave sensibly even though under other circumstances they might be brash and reckless.

The South Asian situation, said so often to be without precedent, finds precedents galore. Rather than assuming that the present differs significantly from the past, we should emphasize the similarities and learn from them. Fortunately, India and Pakistan have learned from their nuclear predecessors. . . .

Sagan believes that future Indian-Pakistani crises may be nuclear. Once countries have nuclear weapons any confrontation that merits the term "crisis" is a nuclear one. With conventional weapons, crises tend toward instability. Because of the perceived, or misperceived, advantage of striking first, war may be the outcome. Nuclear weapons make crises stable, which is an important reason for believing that India and Pakistan are better off with than without them.

Yet because nuclear weapons limit escalation, they may tempt countries to fight small wars. Glenn Snyder long ago identified the strategic stability/tactical instability paradox. Benefits carry costs in the nuclear business just as they do in other endeavors. The possibility of fighting at low levels is not a bad price to pay for the impossibility of fighting at high levels. This impossibility becomes obvious, since in the presence of nuclear weapons no one can score major gains, and all can lose catastrophically.

Sagan carries Snyder's logic a step farther by arguing that Pakistan and India may nevertheless fight to a higher level of violence, believing that if one side or the other begins to lose control, a third party will step in to prevent the use of nuclear weapons. The idea is a hangover from cold war days when the United States and the Soviet Union thought they had compelling reasons to intervene in other countries' conflicts. The end of the cold war reduced the incentives for such intervention. As K. Subrahmanyam has said, "In a world dominated by the Cold War, there was a certain predictability that any Chinese nuclear threat to India would be countervailed by one or the other super power or both. In the aftermath of the Cold War that predictability has disappeared."[18] Intervention by a third party during low-level fighting would still be possible, but neither side could count on it.

Kanti Bajpai spotted another consequence of nuclear weapons that may be harmful: They may drive the antagonists apart by removing the need to agree. Since deterrence works, Bajpai wonders why countries would try to settle their differences. India and Pakistan, however, did not reach agreement on Kashmir or on other issues when neither had nuclear weapons; now both sides have at least an incentive to discuss their problems.

Crises on the subcontinent recur, and when they do, voices of despair predict a conventional clash ending in nuclear blasts. On December 13, 2001, five gunmen attacked the Indian Parliament. Fourteen people died, including the gunmen.

India, blaming Pakistani terrorists, mounted its largest mobilization in the past thirty years and massed troops and equipment along the India-Pakistan border. As in the crisis of 1990, the United States deployed its diplomats, this time dispatching Secretary of State Colin Powell to calm the contestants. Tempers on both sides flared, bombast filled the air, and an American commentator pointed out once again that all of the American military's war games show that a conventional Indian-Pakistani war will end in a nuclear conflagration. Both India and Pakistan claimed that they could fight conventionally in the face of nuclear weapons. What reason do we have to believe that military and civilian leaders on either side fail to understand the dangers of fighting a conventional war against a nuclear neighbor? The statements of Pakistan's leader, General Musharraf, were mainly conciliatory. Indian military leaders emphasized that any military engagements would have to be limited to such targets as guerrilla training camps and military facilities used by extremists. As an astute analyst put it, "India's way of looking at this is that we're not threatening Pakistan's core interests, so they would have no incentive to launch their weapons."[19] Indian leaders made it clear that they intended to pressure Pakistan to control military intrusions by irregular forces. Pakistan made it clear that its pressure for a Kashmiri settlement would be unremitting. Except to alarmist observers, mainly American, neither side looked as though it would cross or even approach the nuclear threshold. The proposition that nuclear weapons limit the extent of fighting and ultimately preserve peace again found vindication.

Are India and Pakistan worse or better off now that they have nuclear weapons? Are their futures dimmer or brighter? I will surprise no one by saying "brighter." I have looked in vain for important differences between the plight of India and Pakistan and that of other nuclear countries. Nuclear weapons put all countries that possess them in the same boat. South Asia is said to be the "acid test" for deterrence optimists. So far, nuclear deterrence has passed all of the many tests it has faced.

NOTES

1. Quoted in Steven Erlanger, "India's Arms Race Isn't Safe Like the Cold War," *New York Times*, July 12, 1998, section 4, p. 18.
2. Strobe Talbott, "Dealing with the Bomb in South Asia," *Foreign Affairs* 78, no. 2 (March/April 1999), p. 117.
3. Claudia Dreifus, "Benazir Bhutto," *New York Times Magazine*, May 15, 1994, p. 39; K. Shankar Bajpai, "Nuclear Exchange," *Far Eastern Economic Review*, June 24, 1993, p. 24; Shamshad Ahmad, "The Nuclear Subcontinent: Bringing Stability to South Asia," *Foreign Affairs* 78, no. 4 (July/August 1999), p. 125.
4. John F. Burns, "War-Weary Kashmiris Contemplate the Price of Peace," *New York Times*, July 11, 2001, p. A3.
5. Quoted in Jonathan Spence, "Kissinger and the Emperor," *New York Review of Books*, March 4, 1999, p. 21.
6. Amitabh Maltoo, "India's Nuclear Policy in an Anarchic World," in Mattoo, ed., *India's Nuclear Deterrent: Pokhran II and Beyond* (New Delhi: Har-Anand, 1999), p. 22.

7. George Fernandes, quoted in John F. Burns, "Indian Defense Chief Calls U.S. Hypocritical," *New York Times,* June 18, 1998, p. A6.

8. Kanti Bajpai, "The Fallacy of an Indian Deterrent," in Amitabh Mattoo, ed., *India's Nuclear Deterrent,* p. 183. China does not recognize Arunachal Pradesh or Sikkim as parts of India.

9. Quoted in Erlanger, "India's Arms Race Isn't Safe Like the Cold War."

10. Raja Menon, *A Nuclear Strategy for India* (New Delhi: Sage, 2000), p. 116.

11. Karl Kaiser, "Nonproliferation and Nuclear Deterrence, *Survival* 31, no. 2 (March/April, 1989), p. 125; Arthur G. Rubinoff, "The Failure of Nuclear Deterrence in South Asia," *Toronto Globe and Mail,* June 1, 1998, p. A17.

12. Quoted in Celia W. Dugger and Barry Bearak, "You've Got the Bomb. So Do I. Now I Dare You to Fight," *New York Times,* January 16, 2000. sec. 4, p. 1.

13. Menon, *A Nuclear Strategy for India,* p. 293.

14. *Ibid.,* p. 197.

15. Celia W. Dugger and Barry Bearak, "You've Got the Bomb. So Do I. Now I Dare You to Fight," *New York Times,* January 16, 2000, section 4, p. 1.

16. James Bamford, "The Dangers of Spy Planes," *New York Times,* April 5, 2001, p. A21.

17. K. Subrahmanyan, "Nuclear Force Design and Minimum Deterrence Strategy," in Bharat Kamad, ed., *Future Imperiled: India's Security in the 1990s and Beyond* (New Delhi: Viking, 1994).

18. *Ibid.,* p. 186.

19. The analyst is Commodore Uday Bhaskar, deputy directory of the Institute for Defense Studies and Analysis, quoted in Rajiv Chandrasekaran "For India, Deterrence May Not Prevent War," *Washington Post Foreign Service,* January 17, 2002, p. A1.

PART 3 The International Political Economy

In Part One, we examined the meaning of anarchy and saw the consequences for state behavior that flowed from it. In Part Two, we analyzed in more detail one of the primary instruments that states can and must use, namely, military power. In Part Three, we are concerned with the other primary instrument of state action, economic power.

Disparities in power, as we saw earlier, have important effects on state behavior. Such disparities occur not simply because of the differences in the military power that states wield but also because of the differences in economic resources that they generate. In the first instance, the force that a nation can wield is dependent in part on the economic wealth that it can muster to support and sustain its military forces. Wealth is therefore a component of state power. But the generation of wealth, unlike the generation of military power, is also an end of state action. Except in the rarest of circumstances, military power is never sought as an end in itself, but rather is acquired as a means to attain security or the other ends that a state pursues. By contrast, wealth is both a component of state power and a good that can be consumed by its citizenry. Force is mustered primarily for the external arena. Wealth is sought for both the external and the domestic arena. Moreover, wealth and power differ in the degree to which states can pursue each without detriment to the positions and interests of other nations. No situation in international politics is ever totally cooperative or conflictual, but the potential for cooperative behavior is greater in the realm of wealth than in the realm of power.

It is the duality of economic power (as a component and end of state action) and its greater potential for common gains that makes the analysis of the role it plays in state behavior and international interactions complex and elusive. The study of international political economy, as it has been traditionally understood, encompasses both these aspects of economic power.

PERSPECTIVES ON POLITICAL ECONOMY

"The science of economics presupposes a given political order, and cannot be profitably studied in isolation from politics." So wrote E. H. Carr in his seminal work, *The Twenty Years' Crisis*, in 1939. Fifty years earlier, in an essay entitled "Socialism:

Utopian or Scientific" Karl Marx's coauthor, Friedrich Engels asserted: "The materialist conception of history starts from the proposition that the production of the means to support human life . . . is the basis of all social structure. . . . " These two views—that economic processes are not autonomous but require political structures to support them and that economic factors determine the social and political structures of states—represent the polar extremes on the relationship of politics and economics.

Which view is correct? To this question there is no simple or single answer. Any reply is as much philosophical as it is empirical. The economic interests of individuals in a state and of states within the international arena do powerfully affect the goals that are sought and the degree of success with which they are attained. But the political structure of international action is also a constraint. Anarchy makes cooperative actions more difficult to attain than would otherwise be the case and requires that statesmen consider both relative and absolute positions when framing actions in the international economic realm. And often in international politics the imperatives of security and survival override the dictates of economic interests. War, after all, almost never pays in a strict balance-sheet sense, particularly when waged between states of roughly equal power. The economic wealth lost in fighting is usually not recouped in the peace that follows.

The best answers to the question, what is the relation between politics and economics in international affairs, have been given by the classical theorists of international politics. Robert Gilpin examines three schools of thought—the liberals, the Marxists, and the mercantilists. Unlike the other two, liberal political economists have stressed the cooperative, not the conflictual, nature of international economic relations. They have extended Adam Smith's arguments about the domestic economy to the international economy. Smith argued that the specialization of function by individuals within a state, together with their unfettered pursuit of their own self-interests, would increase the wealth of a nation and thereby benefit all. Collective harmony and national wealth could thus be the product of self-interested behavior, if only the government would provide as little restraint on individual action as was necessary. The eighteenth-century philosophers and the nineteenth- and twentieth-century free traders argued that what was good for individuals within a state would also be good for states in the international arena. By trading freely with one another, states could specialize according to their respective comparative advantages and the wealth of all nations would, as a consequence, increase. "Make trade not war" has been the slogan of the liberal free traders.

By contrast, both mercantilists and Marxists have seen state relations as inherently conflictual. For Marxists, this is so because capitalists within and among states compete fiercely with one another to maximize their profits. Driven by their greed, they are incapable of cooperating with one another. Because a state's policy is determined by the capitalist ruling class, states will wage wars for profit and, under Lenin's dictum, will wage wars to redivide the world's wealth. Imperialism as the highest stage of capitalism is a classic zero-sum situation. Mercantilists also argue that economic factors make relations among states conflictual. Their analysis, however, rests not on the externalization of class conflict, but on the nature of political and economic power. For eighteenth-century mercantilists, the world's wealth was

fixed and could only be redivided. For nineteenth- and twentieth-century mercantilists, wealth could be increased for all, but because wealth contributes to national
power and power is relative, not absolute, conflict would continue.

All three schools of thought are motivated by their views on the relation of politics to economics. Mercantilists stress the primacy of politics and the consequent
pursuit of national power and relative position in the international arena. Both liberals and Marxists stress the primacy of economics. For the former, the potential
for economic harmony can override the forces of nationalism if only free trade is
pursued. For the latter, economic interests determine political behavior and, since
the first is conflictual, the second must be also. Both liberals and Marxists want to
banish politics from international relations, the former through free trade, the latter through the universal spread of communism. Mercantilists, like realists, view
these prescriptions as naive and believe that the national interests of every state are
only partly determined by their economic interests.

Contemporary writers continue to wrestle with the relation between politics
and economics in international affairs. Robert O. Keohane analyzes what types of
international political structures are conducive to economic cooperation among
nations. He finds the theory of hegemonic stability—that a dominant power is necessary to create and sustain a stable international economic order—a suggestive
but not definitive way to understand the last one hundred years. A hegemonic
power can foster economic cooperation among states, as the United States did
after World War II, but cooperation can occur in the absence of such a power. A
hegemonic power is neither a necessary nor a sufficient condition for interstate
cooperation.

Bruce R. Scott looks at the political-economic relations between rich and poor
states, and asks why the gap between these two has increased during the globalization era of the last twenty years, when, in fact, neoclassical economic theory predicts that the gap should have decreased. According to this theory, in a free global
market poor states lessen the gap because they are supposed to grow faster than
rich states. That this has not happened is due, according to Scott, to the barriers
imposed by the rich states on immigration and agriculture from the poorer states,
and to the inadequate government structures in the poor states that make them
less than ideal outlets for capital investments from the rich states. Thus, the reasons are political-economic in nature, and the fault lies with both the rich and the
poor states.

INTERDEPENDENCE AND GLOBALIZATION

At the beginning of the twenty-first century, which way will the international political economy go? Can the nations of the world muster the political will necessary
to preserve a relatively open international system that has benefited them all, even
if they have benefited unequally? Or, have the political costs of severe economic
dislocations, which the open system of the last two decades has produced, been too
great? Will states lapse into protectionism? Does free trade still make sense when
factor endowments (land, labor, capital, and technology) are no longer fixed and

when, therefore, comparative advantages are no longer static but perhaps can be created behind protectionist barriers?

These are difficult questions to answer. How they are answered depends heavily on how economically interdependent one sees the nations of the world today. "Interdependence" is one of those terms that has developed a myriad of meanings. The most fruitful way to use the term, when considering the relationship between this concept and peaceful cooperation among states, is as follows: Interdependence is the size of the stake that a state believes it has in seeing other states' economies prosper so as to help its own economy prosper too. Interdependence can be high or low. The more highly perceived interdependence is, the larger a state's stake in the economic well-being of the countries with which it heavily interacts; the less interdependence, the smaller is its stake. High levels of interdependence should facilitate cooperation among states for their mutual gain.

After World War II, the United States used its considerable economic and military power to create an open international economic order by working to lower the barriers among nations to the flow of manufactured goods, raw materials other than agriculture, and capital. The result of this international economic openness was a rise in the level of interdependence, particularly among the industrialized nations of the world, but also, to a considerable degree, among the industrializing nations in East Asia and Latin America. But interdependence has its costs as well as its benefits. High levels of participation in the international economy can bring the benefits of efficiency that flow from specialization, but also the destruction of national industries that can no longer compete internationally. States today must reconcile the imperatives of what Robert Gilpin has called "Keynes at home" with "Smith abroad": maintenance of full employment domestically and competitive participation in the international economy. Through exports and capital inflows, interdependence can help a state increase its wealth, but it also brings vulnerabilities that derive from the need to rely partially on others for one's own prosperity. Balancing the two imperatives is a difficult political act.

Interdependence can exist between pairs of countries and can be generated by important but narrow flows of goods. Globalization, as the term indicates, involves most if not all countries and a wide range of economic transactions. The potential loss of autonomy is broader because the nature of national economies, the abilities of states to direct their individual economic and even social policies, and the stability of governments are affected by the movement toward a truly worldwide economy.

The readings in this section explore various aspects of interdependence and globalization. Jeffrey Frankel provides several benchmarks by which to measure the globalization and integration of the world economy today and then provides a tentative balance sheet on the economic and social effects of globalization. Peter F. Drucker locates important changes in the world economy over the past quarter-century. The prices for raw materials have plunged, greatly decreasing the wealth and power of their producers, who are mainly but not exclusively states in the Third World. (Indeed, since Drucker wrote, oil prices have also fallen and so no longer are an exception to his generalization.) Simultaneously, manufacturing has spread to these countries, knowledge-based employment has grown in the developed countries, and movements of capital have greatly increased. Finally, Kenneth N. Waltz argues that the worldwide nature of globalization has been exaggerated and that states—especially powerful ones like the United States—continue to play leading roles and to be guided by political calculations.

THE PROS AND CONS OF GLOBALIZATION

Today's globalization should not only be measured and compared, however; it must also be assessed. Does it benefit all states that become entangled in it, or do a few benefit at the expense of the many? Is heavy participation in the global economy a prerequisite to economic development, or can such participation actually harm development? Does globalization hasten the degradation of the environment, weaken protection of worker rights in both the rich and poor countries, and give too much power to multinational corporations? Globalization may be a fact of today's world, but it is no longer seen as an unalloyed good, as the protests in Seattle in 1999 and in Genoa in 2001 demonstrate.

The three readings in this section take differing stands on these questions. Dani Rodrik asserts that globalization can be a false promise to developing states. He challenges free-trade orthodoxy by showing that high tariff and nontarrif barriers do not necessarily bring with them low growth, and argues that the preparations that poorer states must take to open themselves up to international trade and investment divert precious and scarce resources from the task of economic development. John Micklethwait and Adrian Wooldridge take the opposite view. Global economic growth, they argue, has been aided significantly by the growth in world trade. Globalization can also be a force for protecting the environment because the wealthier states become, the more they tend to clean up their environment. Finally, globalization aids workers because multinational companies generally pay better wages and provide better working conditions than their local competitors. William Finnegan argues for a middle road between these two positions. Increased international trade can benefit the developing states, but, he argues, it does not automatically do so. Markets "can do great things," he says, but they must also be carefully regulated because the powerful hold an advantage over the weaker and are never shy about exploiting it. Those developing economies that have been the most successful in the world economy—South Korea, Taiwan, and Malaysia—are the ones that have protected their fledgling industries until they have grown strong enough to compete with the giants of the developed world.

PERSPECTIVES ON
■ POLITICAL ECONOMY

The Nature of Political Economy

■ ROBERT GILPIN

> *The international corporations have evidently declared ideological war on the "antiquated" nation state. . . . The charge that materialism, moderniza-tion and internationalism is the new liberal creed of corporate capitalism is a valid one. The implication is clear: The nation state as a political unit of democratic decision-making must, in the interest of "progress," yield control to the new mercantile mini-powers.*[1]

> *While the structure of the multinational corporation is a modern concept, designed to meet the requirements of a modern age, the nation state is a very old-fashioned idea and badly adapted to serve the needs of our present com-plex world.*[2]

These two statements—the first by Kari Levitt, a Canadian nationalist, the second by George Ball, a former United States undersecretary of state—express a domi-nant theme of contemporary writings on international relations. International soci-ety, we are told, is increasingly rent between its economic and its political organization. On the one hand, powerful economic and technological forces are creating a highly interdependent world economy, thus diminishing the traditional significance of national boundaries. On the other hand, the nation-state continues to command men's loyalties and to be the basic unit of political decision making. As one writer has put the issue, "The conflict of our era is between ethnocentric nationalism and geocentric technology."[3]

Ball and Levitt represent two contending positions with respect to this conflict. Whereas Ball advocates the diminution of the power of the nation-state in order to give full rein to the productive potentialities of the multinational corporation, Levitt argues for a powerful nationalism which could counterbalance American corporate domination. What appears to one as the logical and desirable consequence of economic rationality seems to the other to be an effort on the part of American imperialism to eliminate all contending centers of power.

Although the advent of the multinational corporation has put the question of the relationship between economics and politics in a new guise, it is an old issue. In the nineteenth century, for example, it was this issue that divided classical liberals like John Stuart Mill from economic nationalists, represented by Georg Friedrich List. Whereas the former gave primacy in the organization of society to economics and the production of wealth, the latter emphasized the political determination of economic relations. As this issue is central both to the contemporary debate on the multinational corporation and to the argument of this study, this chapter analyzes the three major treatments of the relationship between economics and politics—that is, the three major ideologies of political economy.

THE MEANING OF POLITICAL ECONOMY

The argument of this study is that the relationship between economics and politics, at least in the modern world, is a reciprocal one. On the one hand, politics largely determines the framework of economic activity and channels it in directions intended to serve the interests of dominant groups; the exercise of power in all its forms is a major determinant of the nature of an economic system. On the other hand, the economic process itself tends to redistribute power and wealth; it transforms the power relationships among groups. This in turn leads to a transformation of the political system, thereby giving rise to a new structure of economic relationships. Thus, the dynamics of international relations in the modern world is largely a function of the reciprocal interaction between economics and politics.

First of all, what do I mean by "politics" or "economics"? Charles Kindleberger speaks of economics and politics as two different methods of allocating scarce resources: the first through a market mechanism, the latter through a budget.[4] Robert O. Keohane and Joseph Nye, in an excellent analysis of international political economy, define economics and politics in terms of two levels of analysis: those of structure and of process.[5] Politics is the domain "having to do with the establishment of an order of relations, a structure. . . . "[6] Economics deals with "short-term allocative behavior (i.e., holding institutions, fundamental assumptions, and expectations constant). . . . "[7] Like Kindleberger's definition, however, this definition tends to isolate economic and political phenomena except under certain conditions, which Keohane and Nye define as the "politicization" of the economic system. Neither formulation comes to terms adequately with the dynamic and intimate nature of the relationship between the two.

In this study, the issue of the relationship between economics and politics translates into that between wealth and power. According to this statement of the problem, economics takes as its province the creation and distribution of wealth; politics is the realm of power. I shall examine their relationship from several ideological perspectives, including my own. But what is wealth? What is power?

In response to the question, What is wealth?, an economist-colleague responded, "What do you want, my thirty-second or thirty-volume answer?" Basic concepts are elusive in economics, as in any field of inquiry. No unchallengeable definitions are possible. Ask a physicist for his definition of the nature of space, time, and matter, and you will not get a very satisfying response. What you will get is an *operational* definition, one which is usable: It permits the physicist to build an intellectual edifice whose foundations would crumble under the scrutiny of the philosopher.

Similarly, the concept of wealth, upon which the science of economics ultimately rests, cannot be clarified in a definitive way. Paul Samuelson, in his textbook, doesn't even try, though he provides a clue in his definition of economics as "the study of how men and society *choose* . . . to employ *scarce* productive resources . . . to produce various commodities . . . and distribute them for consumption."[8] Following this lead, we can say that wealth is anything (capital, land, or labor) that can generate future income; it is composed of physical assets and human capital (including embodied knowledge).

The basic concept of political science is power. Most political scientists would not stop here; they would include in the definition of political science the purpose for which power is used, whether this be the advancement of the public welfare or the domination of one group over another. In any case, few would dissent from the following statement of Harold Lasswell and Abraham Kaplan:

> The concept of power is perhaps the most fundamental in the whole of political science: The political process is the shaping, distribution, and exercise of power (in a wider sense, of all the deference values, or of influence in general).[9]

Power as such is not the sole or even the principal goal of state behavior. Other goals or values constitute the objectives pursued by nation-states: welfare, security, prestige. But power in its several forms (military, economic, psychological) is ultimately the necessary means to achieve these goals. For this reason, nation-states are intensely jealous of and sensitive to their relative power position. The distribution of power is important because it profoundly affects the ability of states to achieve what they perceive to be their interests.

The nature of power, however, is even more elusive than that of wealth. The number and variety of definitions should be an embarrassment to political scientists. Unfortunately, this study cannot bring the intradisciplinary squabble to an end. Rather, it adopts the definition used by Hans J. Morgenthau in his influential *Politics Among Nations:* "man's control over the minds and actions of other men."[10] Thus, power, like wealth, is the capacity to produce certain results.

Unlike wealth, however, power cannot be quantified; indeed, it cannot be overemphasized that power has an important psychological dimension. Perceptions of power relations are of critical importance; as a consequence, a fundamental task of statesmen is to manipulate the perceptions of other statesmen regarding the distribution of power. Moreover, power is relative to a specific situation or set of circumstances; there is no single hierarchy of power in international relations. Power may take many forms—military, economic, or psychological—though, in the final analysis, force is the ultimate form of power. Finally, the inability to predict the behavior of others or the outcome of events is of great significance. Uncertainty regarding the distribution of power and the ability of the statesmen to control events plays an important role in international relations. Ultimately, the determination of the distribution of power can be made only in retrospect as a consequence of war. It is precisely for this reason that war has had, unfortunately, such a central place in the history of international relations. In short, power is an elusive concept indeed upon which to erect a science of politics.

Such mutually exclusive definitions of economics and politics as these run counter to much contemporary scholarship by both economists and political scientists, for both disciplines are invading the formerly exclusive jurisdictions of the other. Economists, in particular, have become intellectual imperialists; they are applying their analytical techniques to traditional issues of political science with great success. These developments, however, really reinforce the basic premise of this study, namely, the inseparability of economics and politics.

The distinction drawn above between economics as the science of wealth and politics as the science of power is essentially an analytical one. In the real world, wealth and power are ultimately joined. This, in fact, is the basic rationale for a political economy of international relations. But in order to develop the argument of this study, wealth and power will be treated, at least for the moment, as analytically distinct.

To provide a perspective on the nature of political economy, the next section will discuss the three prevailing conceptions of political economy: liberalism, Marxism, and mercantilism. Liberalism regards politics and economics as relatively separable and autonomous spheres of activities; I associate most professional economists as well as many other academics, businessmen, and American officials with this outlook. Marxism refers to the radical critique of capitalism identified with Karl Marx and his contemporary disciples; according to this conception, economics determines politics and political structure. Mercantilism is a more questionable term because of its historical association with the desire of nation-states for a trade surplus and for treasure (money). One must distinguish, however, between the specific form mercantilism took in the seventeenth and eighteenth centuries and the general outlook of mercantilistic thought. The essence of the mercantilistic perspective, whether it is labeled economic nationalism, protectionism, or the doctrine of the German Historical School, is the subservience of economy to the state and its interests—interests that range from matters of domestic welfare to those of international security. It is this more general meaning of mercantilism that is implied by the use of the term in this study.

Following the discussion of these three schools of thought, I shall elaborate my own, more eclectic, view of political economy and demonstrate its relevance for understanding the phenomenon of the multinational corporation.

THREE CONCEPTIONS OF POLITICAL ECONOMY

The three prevailing conceptions of political economy differ on many points. Several critical differences will be examined in this brief comparison. (See Table 1.)

TABLE 1 ■ COMPARISON OF THE THREE CONCEPTIONS OF POLITICAL ECONOMY

	Liberalism	Marxism	Mercantilism
Nature of economic relations	Harmonious	Conflictual	Conflictual
Nature of the actors	Households and firms	Economic classes	Nation-states
Goal of economic activity	Maximization of global welfare	Maximization of class interests	Maximization of national interest
Relationship between economics and politics	Economics *should* determine politics	Economics *does* determine politics	Politics determines economics
Theory of change	Dynamic equilibrium	Tendency toward disequilibrium	Shifts in the distribution of power

The Nature of Economic Relations

The basic assumption of liberalism is that the nature of international economic relations is essentially harmonious. Herein lay the great intellectual innovation of Adam Smith. Disputing his mercantilist predecessors, Smith argued that international economic relations could be made a positive-sum game; that is to say, everyone could gain, and no one need lose, from a proper ordering of economic relations, albeit the distribution of these gains may not be equal. Following Smith, liberalism assumes that there is a basic harmony between true national interest and cosmopolitan economic interest. Thus, a prominent member of this school of thought has written, in response to a radical critique, that the economic efficiency of the sterling standard in the nineteenth century and that of the dollar standard in the twentieth century serve "the cosmopolitan interest in a national form."[11] Although Great Britain and the United States gained the most from the international role of their respective currencies, everyone else gained as well.

Liberals argue that, given this underlying identity of national and cosmopolitan interests in a free market, the state should not interfere with economic transactions across national boundaries. Through free exchange of commodities, removal of restrictions on the flow of investment, and an international division of labor, everyone will benefit in the long run as a result of a more efficient utilization of the world's scarce resources. The national interest is therefore best served, liberals maintain, by a generous and cooperative attitude regarding economic relations with other countries. In essence, the pursuit of self-interest in a free, competitive economy achieves the greatest good for the greatest number in international no less than in the national society.

Both mercantilists and Marxists, on the other hand, begin with the premise that the essence of economic relations is conflictual. There is no underlying harmony; indeed, one group's gain is another's loss. Thus, in the language of game theory, whereas liberals regard economic relations as a non-zero-sum game, Marxists and mercantilists view economic relations as essentially a zero-sum game.

The Goal of Economic Activity

For the liberal, the goal of economic activity is the optimum or efficient use of the world's scarce resources and the maximization of world welfare. While most liberals refuse to make value judgments regarding income distribution, Marxists and mercantilists stress the distributive effects of economic relations. For the Marxist the distribution of wealth among social classes is central; for the mercantilist it is the distribution of employment, industry, and military power among nation-states that is most significant. Thus, the goal of economic (and political) activity for both Marxists and mercantilists is the redistribution of wealth and power.

The State and Public Policy

These three perspectives differ decisively in their view regarding the nature of the economic actors. In Marxist analysis, the basic actors in both domestic and international relations are economic classes; the interests of the dominant class determine the foreign policy of the state. For mercantilists, the real actors in international economic relations are nation-states; national interest determines foreign policy. National interest may at times be influenced by the peculiar economic interests of classes, elites, or other subgroups of the society; but factors of geography, external configurations of power, and the exigencies of national survival are primary in determining foreign policy. Thus, whereas liberals speak of world welfare and Marxists of class interests, mercantilists recognize only the interests of particular nation-states.

Although liberal economists such as David Ricardo and Joseph Schumpeter recognized the importance of class conflict and neoclassical liberals analyze economic growth and policy in terms of national economies, the liberal emphasis is on the individual consumer, firm, or entrepreneur. The liberal ideal is summarized in the view of Harry Johnson that the nation-state has no meaning as an economic entity.[12]

Underlying these contrasting views are differing conceptions of the nature of the state and public policy. For liberals, the state represents an aggregation of private interests: public policy is but the outcome of a pluralistic struggle among interest groups. Marxists, on the other hand, regard the state as simply the "executive committee of the ruling class," and public policy reflects its interests. Mercantilists, however, regard the state as an organic unit in its own right: the whole is greater than the sum of its parts. Public policy, therefore, embodies the national interest or Rousseau's "general will" as conceived by the political elite.

The Relationship between Economics and Politics: Theories of Change

Liberalism, Marxism, and mercantilism also have differing views on the relationship between economics and politics. And their differences on this issue are directly relevant to their contrasting theories of international political change.

Although the liberal ideal is the separation of economics from politics in the interest of maximizing world welfare, the fulfillment of this ideal would have important political implications. The classical statement of these implications was that of Adam Smith in *The Wealth of Nations*.[13] Economic growth, Smith argued, is primarily a function of the extent of the division of labor, which in turn is dependent upon the scale of the market. Thus he attacked the barriers erected by feudal principalities and mercantilistic states against the exchange of goods and the enlargement of markets. If men were to multiply their wealth, Smith argued, the contradiction between political organization and economic rationality had to be resolved in favor of the latter. That is, the pursuit of wealth should determine the nature of the political order.

Subsequently, from nineteenth-century economic liberals to twentieth-century writers on economic integration, there has existed "the dream . . . of a great republic of world commerce, in which national boundaries would cease to have any great economic importance and the web of trade would bind all the people of the world in the prosperity of peace."[14] For liberals the long-term trend is toward world integration, wherein functions, authority, and loyalties will be transferred from "smaller units to larger ones; from states to federalism; from federalism to supranational unions and from these to superstates."[15] The logic of economic and technological development, it is argued, has set mankind on an inexorable course toward global political unification and world peace.

In Marxism, the concept of the contradiction between economic and political relations was enacted into historical law. Whereas classical liberals—although Smith less than others—held that the requirements of economic rationality *ought* to determine political relations, the Marxist position was that the mode of production does in fact determine the superstructure of political relations. Therefore, it is argued, history can be understood as the product of the dialectical process—the contradiction between the evolving techniques of production and the resistant sociopolitical system.

Although Marx and Engels wrote remarkably little on international economics, Engels, in his famous polemic, *Anti-Duhring*, explicitly considers whether economics or politics is primary in determining the structure of international relations.[16] E. K. Duhring, a minor figure in the German Historical School, had argued, in contradiction to Marxism, that property and market relations resulted less from the economic logic of capitalism than from extraeconomic political factors: "The basis of the exploitation of many by man was an historical act of force which created an exploitative economic system for the benefit of the stronger man or class."[17] Since Engels, in his attack on Duhring, used the example of the unification of Germany through the Zollverein or customs union of 1833, his analysis is directly relevant to this discussion of the relationship between economics and political organization.

Engels argued that when contradictions arise between economic and political structures, political power adapts itself to the changes in the balance of economic forces; politics yields to the dictates of economic development. Thus, in the case of nineteenth-century Germany, the requirements of industrial production had become incompatible with its feudal, politically fragmented structure. "Though political reaction was victorious in 1815 and again in 1848," he argued, "it was unable to prevent the growth of large-scale industry in Germany and the growing participation of German commerce in the world market."[18] In summary, Engels wrote, "German unity had become an economic necessity."[19]

In the view of both Smith and Engels, the nation-state represented a progressive stage in human development, because it enlarged the political realm of economic activity. In each successive economic epoch, advances in technology and an increasing scale of production necessitate an enlargement of political organization. Because the city-state and feudalism restricted the scale of production and the division of labor made possible by the Industrial Revolution, they prevented the efficient utilization of resources and were, therefore, superseded by larger political units. Smith considered this to be a desirable objective; for Engels it was an historical necessity. Thus, in the opinion of liberals, the establishment of the Zollverein was a movement toward maximizing world economic welfare;[20] for Marxists it was the unavoidable triumph of the German industrialists over the feudal aristocracy.

Mercantilist writers from Alexander Hamilton to Frederich List to Charles de Gaulle, on the other hand, have emphasized the primacy of politics; politics, in this view, determines economic organization. Whereas Marxists and liberals have pointed to the production of wealth as the basic determinant of social and political organization, the mercantilists of the German Historical School, for example, stressed the primacy of national security, industrial development, and national sentiment in international political and economic dynamics.

In response to Engels's interpretation of the unification of Germany, mercantilists would no doubt agree with Jacob Viner that "Prussia engineered the customs union primarily for political reasons, in order to gain hegemony or at least influence over the lesser German states. It was largely in order to make certain that the hegemony should be Prussian and not Austrian that Prussia continually opposed Austrian entry into the Union, either openly or by pressing for a customs union tariff lower than highly protectionist Austria could stomach."[21] In pursuit of this strategic interest, it was "Prussian might, rather than a common zeal for political unification arising out of economic partnership, [that] . . . played the major role."[22]

In contrast to Marxism, neither liberalism nor mercantilism has a developed theory of dynamics. The basic assumption of orthodox economic analysis (liberalism) is the tendency toward equilibrium; liberalism takes for granted the existing social order and given institutions. Change is assumed to be gradual and adaptive— a continuous process of dynamic equilibrium. There is no necessary connection between such political phenomena as war and revolution and the evolution of the economic system, although they would not deny that misguided statesmen can blunder into war over economic issues or that revolutions are conflicts over the distribution of wealth; but neither is inevitably linked to the evolution of the productive system. As for mercantilism, it sees change as taking place owing to shifts in the balance of power; yet, mercantilist writers such as members of the German Historical School and contemporary political realists have not developed a systematic theory of how this shift occurs.

On the other hand, dynamics is central to Marxism; indeed Marxism is essentially a theory of social *change*. It emphasizes the tendency toward *dis*equilibrium owing to changes in the means of production and the consequent effects on the ever-present class conflict. When these tendencies can no longer be contained, the sociopolitical system breaks down through violent upheaval. Thus war and revolution are seen as an integral part of the economic process. Politics and economics are intimately joined.

Why an International Economy?

From these differences among the three ideologies, one can get a sense of their respective explanations for the existence and functioning of the international economy.

An interdependent world economy constitutes the normal state of affairs for most liberal economists. Responding to technological advances in transportation and communications, the scope of the market mechanism, according to this analysis, continuously expands. Thus, despite temporary setbacks, the long-term trend is toward global economic integration. The functioning of the international economy is determined primarily by considerations of efficiency. The role of the dollar as the basis of the international monetary system, for example, is explained by the preference for it among traders and nations as the vehicle of international commerce.[23] The system is maintained by the mutuality of the benefits provided by trade, monetary arrangements, and investment.

A second view—one shared by Marxists and mercantilists alike—is that every interdependent international economy is essentially an imperial or hierarchical system. The imperial or hegemonic power organizes trade, monetary, and investment relations in order to advance its own economic and political interests. In the absence of the economic and especially the political influence of the hegemonic power, the system would fragment into autarkic economies or regional blocs. Whereas for liberalism maintenance of harmonious international market relations is the norm, for Marxism and mercantilism conflicts of class or national interests are the norm.

PERSPECTIVE OF THE AUTHOR

My own perspective on political economy rests on what I regard as a fundamental difference in emphasis between economics and politics; namely, the distinction between absolute and relative gains. The emphasis of economic science—or, at least, of liberal economics—is on *absolute* gains; the ultimate defense of liberalism is that over the long run everyone gains, albeit in varying degrees, from a liberal economic regime. Economics, according to this formulation, need not be a zero-sum game. Everyone can gain in wealth through a more efficient division of labor; moreover, everyone can lose, in absolute terms, from economic inefficiency. Herein lies the strength of liberalism.

This economic emphasis on absolute gains is in fact embodied in what one can characterize as the ultimate ideal of liberal economics: the achievement of a "Pareto optimum" world. Such a properly ordered world would be one wherein "by improving the position of one individual (by adding to his possessions) no one else's position is deteriorated." As Oskar Morgenstern has observed, "[e]conomic literature is replete with the use of the Pareto optimum thus formulated or in equivalent language."[24] It is a world freed from "interpersonal comparisons of utility," and thus a world freed from what is central to politics, i.e., ethical judgment and conflict regarding the just and relative distribution of utility. That the notion of a Pareto optimum is rife with conceptual problems and is utopian does not detract from its centrality as the implicit objective of liberal economics. And this emphasis of economics on absolute gains for all differs fundamentally from the nature of political phenomena as studied by political scientists: viz., struggles for power as a goal itself or as a means to the achievement of other goals.

The essential fact of politics is that power is always relative; one state's gain in power is by necessity another's loss. Thus, even though two states may be gaining absolutely in wealth, in political terms it is the effect of these gains on relative power positions which is of primary importance. From this *political* perspective, therefore, the mercantilists are correct in emphasizing that in power terms, international relations is a zero-sum game.

In a brilliant analysis of international politics, the relativity of power and its profound implications were set forth by Jean-Jacques Rousseau:

> The state, being an artificial body is not limited in any way. . . . It can always increase; it always feels itself weak if there is another that is stronger. Its security and preservation demand that it make itself more powerful than its neighbors. It can increase, nourish and exercise its power only at their expense . . . while the inequality of man has natural limits that between societies can grow without cease, until one absorbs all the others. . . . Because the grandeur of the state is purely relative it is forced to compare itself with that of the others. . . . It is in vain that it wishes to keep itself to itself; it becomes small or great, weak or strong, according to whether its neighbor expands or contracts, becomes stronger or declines. . . .
>
> The chief thing I notice is a patent contradiction in the condition of the human race. . . . Between man and man we live in the condition of the civil state, subjected to laws; between people and people we enjoy natural liberty, which makes the situation worse. Living at the same time in the social order and in the state of nature, we suffer from the inconveniences of both without finding . . . security in either. . . . We see men united by artificial bonds, but united to destroy each other; and all the horrors of war take birth from the precautions they have taken in order to prevent them. . . . War is born of peace, or at least of the precautions which men have taken for the purpose of achieving durable peace.[25]

Because of the relativity of power, therefore, nation-states are engaged in a neverending struggle to improve or preserve their relative power positions.

This rather stark formulation obviously draws too sharp a distinction between economics and politics. Certainly, for example, liberal economists may be interested in questions of distribution; the distributive issue was, in fact, of central concern to Ricardo and other classical writers. However, when economists stop taking the system for granted and start asking questions about distribution, they have really ventured into what I regard as the essence of politics, for distribution is really a political issue. In a world in which power rests on wealth, changes in the relative distribution of wealth imply changes in the distribution of power and in the political system itself. This, in fact, is what is meant by saying that politics is about relative gains. Politics concerns the efforts of groups to redistribute gains to their own advantage.

Similarly, to argue that politics is about relative gains is not to argue that it is a constant-sum game. On the contrary, man's power over nature and his fellow man has grown immensely in absolute terms over the past several centuries. It is certainly the case that everyone's absolute capabilities can increase due to the development of new weaponry, the expansion of productive capabilities, or changes in the political system itself. Obviously such absolute increases in power are important politically. Who can deny, for example, that the advent of nuclear weapons has profoundly altered international politics? Obviously, too, states can negotiate disarmament and other levels of military capability.

Yet recognition of these facts does not alter the prime consideration that changes in the relative distribution of power are of fundamental significance politically. Though all may be gaining or declining in absolute capability, what will concern states principally are the effects of these absolute gains or losses on relative positions. How, for example, do changes in productive capacity or military weaponry affect the ability of one state to impose its will on another? It may very well be that in a particular situation absolute gains will not affect relative positions. But the efforts of groups to cause or prevent such shifts in the relative distribution of power constitute the critical issue of politics.

This formulation of the nature of politics obviously does not deny that nations may cooperate in order to advance their mutual interest. But even cooperative actions may have important consequences for the distribution of power in the system. For example, the Strategic Arms Limitation Talks (SALT) between the United States and the Soviet Union are obviously motivated by a common interest in preventing thermonuclear war. Other states will also benefit if the risk of war between the superpowers is reduced. Yet, SALT may also be seen as an attempt to stabilize the international distribution of power to the disadvantage of China and other third powers. In short, in terms of the system as a whole, political cooperation can have a profound effect on the relative distribution of power among nation-states.

The point may perhaps be clarified by distinguishing between two aspects of power. When one speaks of absolute gains in power, such as advances in economic capabilities or weapons development, one is referring principally to increases in physical or material capabilities. But while such capabilities are an important component of power, power, as we have seen, is more than physical capability. Power is also a psychological relationship: Who can influence whom to do what? From this perspective, what may be of most importance is how changes in capability affect this psychological relationship. Insofar as they do, they alter the relative distribution of power in the system.

In a world in which power rests increasingly on economic and industrial capabilities, one cannot really distinguish between wealth (resources, treasure, and industry) and power as national goals. In the short run there may be conflicts between the pursuit of power and the pursuit of wealth; in the long run the two pursuits are identical. Therefore, the position taken in this study is similar to Viner's interpretation of classical mercantilism:

What then is the correct interpretation of mercantilist doctrine and practice with respect to the roles of power and plenty as ends of national policy? I believe that practically all mercantilists, whatever the period, country, or status of the particular individual, would have subscribed to all of the following propositions: (1) wealth is an absolutely essential means to power, whether for security or for aggression; (2) power is essential or valuable as a means to the acquisition or retention of wealth; (3) wealth and power are each proper ultimate ends of national policy; (4) there is long-run harmony between these ends, although in particular circumstances it may be necessary for a time to make economic sacrifices in the interest of military security and therefore also of long-run prosperity.[26]

This interpretation of the role of the economic motive in international relations is substantially different from that of Marxism. In the Marxist framework of analysis, the economic factor is reduced to the profit motive, as it affects the behavior of individuals or firms. Accordingly, the foreign policies of capitalist states are determined by the desire of capitalists for profits. This is, in our view, far too narrow a conception of the economic aspect of international relations. Instead, in this study we label "economic" those sources of wealth upon which national power and domestic welfare are dependent.

Understood in these broader terms, the economic motive and economic activities are fundamental to the struggle for power among nation-states. The objects of contention in the struggles of the balance of power include the centers of economic power. As R. G. Hawtrey has expressed it, "the political motives at work can only be expressed in terms of the economic. Every conflict is one of power and power depends on resources."[27] In pursuit of wealth *and* power, therefore, nations (capitalist, socialist, or fascist) contend over the territorial division and exploitation of the globe.

Even at the level of peaceful economic intercourse, one cannot separate out the political element. Contrary to the attitude of liberalism, international economic relations are in reality political relations. The interdependence of national economies creates economic power, defined as the capacity of one state to damage another through the interruption of commercial and financial relations.[28] The attempts to create and to escape from such dependency relationships constitute an important aspect of international relations in the modern era.

The primary actors in the international system are nation-states in pursuit of what they define as their national interest. This is not to argue, however, that nation-states are the only actors, nor do I believe that the "national interest" is something akin to Rousseau's "general will"—the expression of an organic entity separable from its component parts. Except in the abstract models of political scientists, it has never been the case that the international system was composed solely of nation-states. In an exaggerated acknowledgment of the importance of nonstate or transnational actors at an earlier time, John A. Hobson asked rhetorically whether "a great war could be undertaken by any European state, or a great state loan subscribed, if the House of Rothschild and its connexions set their face against it."[29] What has to be explained, however, are the economic and political circumstances that enable such transnational actors to play their semi-independent role in international affairs. The argument of this study is that the primary determinants of the role played by these non-state actors are the larger configurations of power among nation-states. What is determinant is the interplay of national interests.

As for the concept of "national interest," the national interest of a given nation-state is, of course, what its political and economic elite determines it to be. In part, as Marxists argue, this elite will define it in terms of its own group or class interests. But the national interest comprehends more than this. More general influences, such as cultural values and considerations relevant to the security of the state itself—geographical position, the evolution of military technology, and the international distribution of power—are of greater importance. There is a sense, then, in which the factors that determine the national interest are objective. A ruling elite that fails to take these factors into account does so at its peril. In short, then, there is a basis for considering the nation-state itself as an actor pursuing its own set of security, welfare, and status concerns in competition or cooperation with other nation-states.

Lastly, in a world of conflicting nation-states, how does one explain the existence of an interdependent international economy? Why does a liberal international economy—that is, an economy characterized by relatively free trade, currency convertibility, and freedom of capital movement—remain intact rather than fragment into autarkic national economies and regional or imperial groupings? In part, the answer is provided by liberalism: economic cooperation, interdependence, and an international division of labor enhance efficiency and the maximization of aggregate wealth. Nation-states are induced to enter the international system because of the promise of more rapid growth; greater benefits can be had than could be obtained by autarky or a fragmentation of the world economy. The historical record suggests, however, that the existence of mutual economic benefits is not always enough to induce nations to pay the costs of a market system or to forgo opportunities of advancing their own interests at the expense of others. There is always the danger that a nation may pursue certain short-range policies, such as the imposition of an optimum tariff, in order to maximize its own gains at the expense of the system as a whole.

For this reason, a liberal international economy requires a power to manage and stabilize the system. As Charles Kindleberger has convincingly shown, this governance role was performed by Great Britain throughout the nineteenth century and up to 1931, and by the United States after 1945.[30] The inability of Great Britain in 1929 to continue running the system and the unwillingness of the United States to assume this responsibility led to the collapse of the system in the "Great Depression." The result was the fragmentation of the world economy into rival economic blocs. Both dominant economic powers had failed to overcome the divisive forces of nationalism and regionalism.

The argument of this study is that the modern world economy has evolved through the emergence of great national economies that have successively become dominant. In the words of the distinguished French economist François Perroux, "the economic evolution of the world has resulted from a succession of dominant economies, each in turn taking the lead in international activity and influence. . . . Throughout the nineteenth century the British economy was the dominant economy in the world. From the [eighteen] seventies on, Germany was dominant in respect to certain other Continental countries and in certain specified fields. In the twentieth century, the United States economy has clearly been and still is the internationally dominant economy."[31]

An economic system, then, does not arise spontaneously owing to the operation of an invisible hand and in the absence of the exercise of power. Rather, every economic system rests on a particular political order; its nature cannot be understood aside from politics. This basic point was made some years ago by E. H. Carr when he wrote that "the science of economics presupposes a given political order, and cannot be profitably studied in isolation from politics."[32] Carr sought to convince his fellow Englishmen that an international economy based on free trade was not a natural and inevitable state of affairs but rather one that reflected the economic and political interests of Great Britain. The system based on free trade had come into existence through, and was maintained by, the exercise of British economic and military power. With the rise after 1880 of new industrial and military powers with contrasting economic interests—namely, Germany, Japan, and the United States—an international economy based on free trade and British power became less and less viable. Eventually this shift in the locus of industrial and military power led to the collapse of the system in World War I. Following the interwar period, a liberal international economy was revived through the exercise of power by the world's newly emergent dominant economy—the United States.

Accordingly, the regime of free investment and the preeminence of the multinational corporation in the contemporary world have reflected the economic and political interests of the United States. The multinational corporation has prospered because it has been dependent on the power of, and consistent with the political interests of, the United States. This is not to deny the analyses of economists who argue that the multinational corporation is a response to contemporary technological and economic developments. The argument is rather that these economic and technological factors have been able to exercise their profound effects because the United States—sometimes with the cooperation of other states and sometimes over their opposition—has created the necessary political framework. As former Secretary of the Treasury Henry Fowler stated several years ago, "it is . . . impossible to overestimate the extent to which the efforts and opportunities for American firms abroad depend upon the vast presence and influence and prestige that America holds in the world."[33]

By the mid-1970s, however, the international distribution of power and the world economy resting on it were far different from what they had been when Fowler's words were spoken. The rise of foreign economic competitors, America's growing dependence upon foreign sources of energy and other resources, and the expansion of Soviet military capabilities have greatly diminished America's presence and influence in the world. One must ask if, as a consequence, the reign of the American multinationals over international economic affairs will continue into the future.

In summary, although nation-states, as mercantilists suggest, do seek to control economic and technological forces and channel them to their own advantage, this is impossible over the long run. The spread of economic growth and industrialization cannot be prevented. In time the diffusion of industry and technology undermines the position of the dominant power. As both liberals and Marxists have emphasized, the evolution of economic relations profoundly influences the nature of the international political system. The relationship between economics and politics is a reciprocal one.

Although economic and accompanying political change may well be inevitable, it is not inevitable that the process of economic development and technological advance will produce an increasingly integrated world society. In the 1930s, Eugene Staley posed the issue:

> A conflict rages between technology and politics. Economics, so closely linked to both, has become the major battlefield. Stability and peace will reign in the world economy only when, somehow, the forces on the side of technology and the forces on the side of politics have once more become accommodated to each other.[34]

Staley believed, as do many present-day writers, that politics and technology must ultimately adjust to one another. But he differed with contemporary writers with regard to the inevitability with which politics would adjust to technology. Reflecting the intense economic nationalism of the period in which he wrote, Staley pointed out that the adjustment may very well be the other way around. As he reminds us, in his own time and in earlier periods economics has had to adjust to political realities: "In the 'Dark Ages' following the collapse of the Roman Empire, technology adjusted itself to politics. The magnificent Roman roads fell into disrepair, the baths and aqueducts and amphitheatres and villas into ruins. Society lapsed back to localism in production and distribution, forgot much of the learning and the technology and the governmental systems of earlier days."[35]

CONCLUSION

The purpose of this chapter has been to set forth the analytical framework that will be employed in this study. This framework is a statement of what I mean by "political economy." In its eclecticism it has drawn upon, while differing from, the three prevailing perspectives of political economy. It has incorporated their respective strengths and has attempted to overcome their weaknesses. In brief, political economy in this study means the reciprocal and dynamic interaction in international relations of the pursuit of wealth and the pursuit of power. In the short run, the distribution of power and the nature of the political system are major determinants of the framework within which wealth is produced and distributed. In the long run, however, shifts in economic efficiency and in the location of economic activity tend to undermine and transform the existing political system. This political transformation in turn gives rise to changes in economic relations that reflect the interests of the politically ascendant state in the system.

NOTES

1. Kari Levitt, "The Hinterland Economy," *Canadian Forum* 50 (July–August 1970): p. 163.
2. George W. Ball, "The Promise of the Multinational Corporation," *Fortune,* June 1, 1967, p. 80.

3. Sidney Rolfe, "Updating Adam Smith," *Interplay* (November 1968): p. 15.

4. Charles Kindleberger, *Power and Money: The Economics of International Politics and the Politics of International Economics* (New York: Basic Books, 1970), p. 5.

5. Robert Keohane and Joseph Nye, "World Politics and the International Economic System," in C. Fred Bergsten, ed., *The Future of the International Economic Order: An Agenda for Research* (Lexington, Mass.: D.C. Heath, 1973), p. 116.

6. Ibid.

7. Ibid., p. 117.

8. Paul Samuelson, *Economics: An Introductory Analysis* (New York: McGraw-Hill, 1967), p. 5.

9. Harold Lasswell and Abraham Kaplan, *Power and Society: A Framework for Political Inquiry* (New Haven, Conn.: Yale University Press, 1950), p. 75.

10. Hans Morgenthau, *Politics Among Nations* (New York: Alfred A. Knopf), p. 26. For a more complex but essentially identical view, see Robert Dahl, *Modern Political Analysis* (Englewood Cliffs, N.J.: Prentice-Hall, 1963).

11. Kindleberger, *Power and Money*, p. 227.

12. For Johnson's critique of economic nationalism, see Harry Johnson, ed., *Economic Nationalism in Old and New States* (Chicago: University of Chicago Press, 1967).

13. Adam Smith, *The Wealth of Nations* (New York: Modern Library, 1937).

14. J. B. Condliffe, *The Commerce of Nations* (New York: W. W. Norton, 1950), p. 136.

15. Amitai Etzioni, "The Dialectics of Supranational Unification" in *International Political Communities* (New York: Doubleday, 1966), p. 147.

16. The relevant sections appear in Ernst Wangerman, ed., *The Role of Force in History: A Study of Bismarck's Policy of Blood and Iron,* trans. Jack Cohen (New York: International Publishers, 1968).

17. Ibid., p. 12.

18. Ibid., p. 13.

19. Ibid., p. 14.

20. Gustav Stopler, *The German Economy* (New York: Harcourt, Brace and World, 1967), p. 11.

21. Jacob Viner, *The Customs Union Issue,* Studies in the Administration of International Law and Organization, no. 10 (New York: Carnegie Endowment for International Peace, 1950), pp. 98–99.

22. Ibid., p. 101.

23. Richard Cooper, "Eurodollars, Reserve Dollars, and Asymmetries in the International Monetary System," *Journal of International Economics* 2 (September 1972): pp. 325–44.

24. Oskar Morgenstern, "Thirteen Critical Points in Contemporary Economic Theory: An Interpretation," *Journal of Economic Literature* 10 (December 1972): p. 1169.

25. Quoted in F. H. Hinsley, *Power and the Pursuit of Peace* (Cambridge: Cambridge University Press, 1963), pp. 50–51.

26. Jacob Viner, "Power versus Plenty as Objectives of Foreign Policy in the Seventeenth and Eighteenth Centuries," in *The Long View and the Short: Studies in Economic Theory and Practice* (Glencoe, Ill.: The Free Press, 1958), p. 286.

27. R. G. Hawtrey, *Economic Aspects of Sovereignty* (London: Longmans, Green, 1952), p. 120.

28. Albert Hirshman, *National Power and the Structure of Foreign Trade* (Berkeley: University of California Press, 1969), p. 16.

29. John A. Hobson, *Imperialism: A Study* (1902; 3rd ed., rev., London: G. Allen and Unwin, 1938), p. 57.

30. Charles Kindleberger, *The World in Depression 1929–1939* (Berkeley: University of California Press, 1973), p. 293.
31. François Perroux, "The Domination Effect and Modern Economic Theory," in *Power in Economics*, ed. K. W. Rothschild (London: Penguin, 1971), p. 67.
32. E. H. Carr, *The Twenty Years' Crisis, 1919–1939* (New York: Macmillan, 1951), p. 117.
33. Quoted in Kari Levitt, *Silent Surrender: The American Economic Empire in Canada* (New York: Liveright Press, 1970), p. 100.
34. Eugene Staley, *World Economy in Transition: Technology vs. Politics, Laissez Faire vs. Planning, Power vs. Welfare* (New York: Council on Foreign Relations [under the auspices of the American Coordinating Committee for International Studies], 1939), pp. 51–52.
35. Ibid., p. 52.

Hegemony in the World Political Economy

▬▬▬ ROBERT O. KEOHANE

It is common today for troubled supporters of liberal capitalism to look back with nostalgia on British preponderance in the nineteenth century and American dominance after World War II. Those eras are imagined to be simpler ones in which a single power, possessing superiority of economic and military resources, implemented a plan for international order based on its interests and its vision of the world. As Robert Gilpin has expressed it, "the *Pax Britannica* and *Pax Americana*, like the *Pax Romana,* ensured an international system of relative peace and security. Great Britain and the United States created and enforced the rules of a liberal international economic order."

Underlying this statement is one of the two central propositions of the theory of hegemonic stability:[1] that order in world politics is typically created by a single dominant power. Since regimes constitute elements of an international order, this implies that the formation of international regimes normally depends on hegemony. The other major tenet of the theory of hegemonic stability is that the maintenance of order requires continued hegemony. As Charles P. Kindleberger has said, "For the world economy to be stabilized, there has to be a stabilizer, one stabilizer."[2] This implies that cooperation, . . . [the] mutual adjustment of state policies to one another, also depends on the perpetuation of hegemony.

I discuss hegemony before elaborating my definitions of cooperation and regimes because my emphasis on how international institutions such as regimes facilitate cooperation only makes sense if cooperation and discord are not determined simply by interests and power. In this chapter I argue that a deterministic version of the theory of hegemonic stability, relying only on the realist concepts of interests and power, is indeed incorrect. There is some validity in a modest version of the first proposition of the theory of hegemonic stability—that hegemony can facilitate a certain type of cooperation—but there is little reason to believe that hegemony is either a necessary or a sufficient condition for the emergence of cooperative relationships. Furthermore, and even more important for the argument presented here, the second major proposition of the theory is erroneous: Cooperation does not necessarily require the existence of a hegemonic leader after international regimes have been established. Post-hegemonic cooperation is also possible. . . .

The task of the present chapter is to explore in a preliminary way the value and limitations of the concept of hegemony for the study of cooperation. The first section analyzes the claims of the theory of hegemonic stability; the second section briefly addresses the relationship between military power and hegemony in the world political economy; and the final section seeks to enrich our understanding of the concept by considering Marxian insights. Many Marxian interpretations of hegemony turn out to bear an uncanny resemblance to Realist ideas, using different language to make similar points. Antonio Gramsci's conception of ideological hegemony, however, does provide an insightful supplement to purely materialist arguments, whether Realist or Marxist.

EVALUATING THE THEORY OF HEGEMONIC STABILITY

The theory of hegemonic stability, as applied to the world political economy, defines hegemony as preponderance of material resources. Four sets of resources are especially important. Hegemonic powers must have control over raw materials, control over sources of capital, control over markets, and competitive advantages in the production of highly valued goods.

The importance of controlling sources of raw materials has provided a traditional justification for territorial expansion and imperialism, as well as for the extension of informal influence. . . . [S]hifts in the locus of control over oil affected the power of states and the evolution of international regimes. Guaranteed access to capital, though less obvious as a source of power, may be equally important. Countries with well-functioning capital markets can borrow cheaply and may be able to provide credit to friends or even deny it to adversaries. Holland derived political and economic power from the quality of its capital markets in the seventeenth century; Britain did so in the eighteenth and nineteenth centuries; and the United States has similarly benefited during the last fifty years.

Potential power may also be derived from the size of one's market for imports. The threat to cut off a particular state's access to one's own market, while allowing other countries continued access, is a "potent and historically relevant weapon of economic 'power'."[3] Conversely, the offer to open up one's own huge market to other exporters, in return for concessions or deference, can be an effective means of influence. The bigger one's own market, and the greater the government's discretion in opening it up or closing it off, the greater one's potential economic power.

The final dimension of economic preponderance is competitive superiority in the production of goods. Immanuel Wallerstein has defined hegemony in economic terms as "a situation wherein the products of a given core state are produced so efficiently that they are by and large competitive even in other core states, and therefore the given core state will be the primary beneficiary of a maximally free world market."[4] As a definition of economic preponderance this is interesting but poorly worked out, since under conditions of overall balance of payments equilibrium each unit—even the poorest and least developed—will have some comparative advantage. The fact that in 1960 the United States had a trade deficit in textiles and apparel and in basic manufactured goods (established products not, on the whole, involving the use of complex or new technology) did not indicate that it had lost predominant economic status.[5] Indeed, one should expect the economically preponderant state to import products that are labor-intensive or that are produced with well-known production techniques. Competitive advantage does not mean that the leading economy exports *everything*, but that it produces and exports the most profitable products and those that will provide the basis for producing even more advanced goods and services in the future. In general, this ability will be based on the technological superiority of the leading country, although it may also rest on its political control over valuable resources yielding significant rents.

To be considered hegemonic in the world political economy, therefore, a country must have access to crucial raw materials, control major sources of capital, maintain a large market for imports, and hold comparative advantages in goods with high value added, yielding relatively high wages and profits. It must also be stronger, on these dimensions taken as a whole, than any other country. The theory of hegemonic stability predicts that the more one such power dominates the world political economy, the more cooperative will interstate relations be. This is a parsimonious theory that relies on . . . a "basic force model," in which outcomes reflect the tangible capabilities of actors.

Yet, like many such basic force models, this crude theory of hegemonic stability makes imperfect predictions. In the twentieth century it correctly anticipates the relative cooperativeness of the twenty years after World War II. It is at least partially mistaken, however, about trends of cooperation when hegemony erodes. Between 1900 and 1913 a decline in British power coincided with a decrease rather than an increase in conflict over commercial issues. . . . [R]ecent changes in international regimes can only partially be attributed to a decline in American power. How to interpret the prevalence of discord in the interwar years is difficult, since it is not clear whether any country was hegemonic in material terms during those two decades. The United States, though considerably ahead in productivity, did not replace Britain as the most important financial center and lagged behind in volume of trade. Although American domestic oil production was more than sufficient for domestic needs during these years, Britain still controlled the bulk of major Middle Eastern oil fields. Nevertheless, what prevented American leadership of a cooperative world political economy in these years was less lack of economic resources than an absence of political willingness to make and enforce rules for the system. Britain, despite its efforts, was too weak to do so effectively. The crucial factor in producing discord lay in American politics, not in the material factors to which the theory points.

Unlike the crude basic force model, a refined version of hegemonic stability theory does not assert an automatic link between power and leadership. Hegemony is defined as a situation in which "one state is powerful enough to maintain the essential rules governing interstate relations, and willing to do so."[6] This interpretive framework retains an emphasis on power but looks more seriously than the crude power theory at the internal characteristics of the strong state. It does not assume that strength automatically creates incentives to project one's power abroad. Domestic attitudes, political structures, and decision making processes are also important.

This argument's reliance on state decisions as well as power capabilities puts it into the category of what March calls "force activation models." Decisions to exercise leadership are necessary to "activate" the posited relationship between power capabilities and outcomes. Force activation models are essentially *post hoc* rather than *a priori*, since one can always "save" such a theory after the fact by thinking of reasons why an actor would not have wanted to use all of its available potential power. In effect, this modification of the theory declares that states with preponderant resources will be hegemonic except when they decide not to commit the necessary effort to the tasks of leadership, yet it does not tell us what will determine the latter decision. As a causal theory this is not very helpful, since whether a given configuration of power will lead the potential hegemon to maintain a set of rules remains indeterminate unless we know a great deal about its domestic politics.

Only the cruder theory generates predictions. When I refer without qualification to the theory of hegemonic stability, therefore, I will be referring to this basic force model. We have seen that the most striking contention of this theory—that hegemony is both a necessary and a sufficient condition for cooperation—is not strongly supported by the experience of this century. Taking a longer period of about 150 years, the record remains ambiguous. International economic relations were relatively cooperative both in the era of British hegemony during the mid-to-late nineteenth century and in the two decades of American dominance after World War II. But only in the second of these periods was there a trend toward the predicted disruption of established rules and increased discord. And a closer examination of the British experience casts doubt on the causal role of British hegemony in producing cooperation in the nineteenth century.

Both Britain in the nineteenth century and the United States in the twentieth met the material prerequisites for hegemony better than any other states since the Industrial Revolution. In 1880 Britain was the financial center of the world, and it controlled extensive raw materials, both in its formal empire and through investments in areas not part of the Imperial domain. It had the highest per capita income in the world and approximately double the share of world trade and investment of its nearest competitor, France. Only in the aggregate size of its economy had it already fallen behind the United States.[7] Britain's share of world trade gradually declined during the next sixty years, but in 1938 it was still the world's largest trader, with 14 percent of the world total. In the nineteenth century Britain's relative labor productivity was the highest in the world, although it declined rather precipitously thereafter. As Table 1 shows, Britain in the late nineteenth century and the United States after World War II were roughly comparable in their proportions of world trade, although until 1970 or so the United States had maintained much higher levels of relative productivity than Britain had done three-quarters of a century earlier.

TABLE 1 ■ MATERIAL RESOURCES OF BRITAIN AND THE UNITED STATES AS HEGEMONS: PROPORTIONS OF WORLD TRADE AND RELATIVE LABOR PRODUCTIVITY

	Proportion of world trade	Relative labor productivity*
Britain, 1870	24.0	1.63
Britain, 1890	18.5	1.45
Britain, 1913	14.1	1.15
Britain, 1938	14.0	.92
United States, 1950	18.4	2.77
United States, 1960	15.3	2.28
United States, 1970	14.4	1.72
United States, 1977	13.4	1.45

*As compared with the average rate of productivity in the other members of the world economy. *Source:* David A. Lake, "International Economic Structures and American Foreign Economic Policy, 1887–1934," *World Politics,* vol. 35, no. 4 (July 1983), table 1 (p. 525) and table 3 (p. 541).

Yet, despite Britain's material strength, it did not always enforce its preferred rules. Britain certainly did maintain freedom of the seas. But it did not induce major continental powers, after the 1870s, to retain liberal trade policies. A recent investigation of the subject has concluded that British efforts to make and enforce rules were less extensive and less successful than hegemonic stability theory would lead us to believe they were.[8]

Attempts by the United States after World War II to make and enforce rules for the world political economy were much more effective than Britain's had ever been. America after 1945 did not merely replicate earlier British experience; on the contrary, the differences between Britain's "hegemony" in the nineteenth century and America's after World War II were profound. As we have seen, Britain had never been as superior in productivity to the rest of the world as the United States was after 1945. Nor was the United States ever as dependent on foreign trade and investment as Britain. Equally important, America's economic partners—over whom its hegemony was exercised, since America's ability to make the rules hardly extended to the socialist camp—were also its military allies; but Britain's chief trading partners had been its major military and political rivals. In addition, one reason for Britain's relative ineffectiveness in maintaining a free trade regime is that it had never made extensive use of the principle of reciprocity in trade.[9] It thus had sacrificed potential leverage over other countries that preferred to retain their own restrictions while Britain practiced free trade. The policies of these states might well have been altered had they been confronted with a choice between a closed British market for their exports on the one hand and mutual lowering of barriers on the other. Finally, Britain had an empire to which it could retreat, by selling less advanced goods to its colonies rather than competing in more open markets. American hegemony, rather than being one more instance of a general phenomenon, was essentially unique in the scope and efficacy of the instruments at the disposal of a hegemonic state and in the degree of success attained.

That the theory of hegemonic stability is supported by only one or at most two cases casts doubt on its general validity. Even major proponents of the theory refrain from making such claims. In an article published in 1981, Kindleberger seemed to entertain the possibility that two or more countries might "take on the task of providing leadership together, thus adding to legitimacy, sharing the burdens, and reducing the danger that leadership is regarded cynically as a cloak for domination and exploitation."[10] In *War and Change in World Politics,* Gilpin promulgated what appeared to be a highly deterministic conception of hegemonic cycles: "the conclusion of one hegemonic war is the beginning of another cycle of growth, expansion, and eventual decline."[11] Yet he denied that his view was deterministic, and he asserted that "states can learn to be more enlightened in their definitions of their interests and can learn to be more cooperative in their behavior."[12] Despite the erosion of hegemony, "there are reasons for believing that the present disequilibrium in the international system can be resolved without resort to hegemonic war."[13]

The empirical evidence for the general validity of hegemonic stability theory is weak, and even its chief adherents have doubts about it. In addition, the logical underpinnings of the theory are suspect. Kindleberger's strong claim for the necessity of a single leader rested on the theory of collective goods. He argued that "the danger we face is not too much power in the international economy, but too little, not an excess of domination, but a superfluity of would-be free riders, unwilling to mind the store, and waiting for a storekeeper to appear."[14] . . . [S]ome of the "goods" produced by hegemonic leadership are not genuinely collective in character, although the implications of this fact are not necessarily as damaging to the theory as might be imagined at first. More critical is the fact that in international economic systems a few actors typically control a preponderance of resources. This point is especially telling, since the theory of collective goods does not properly imply that cooperation among a few countries should be impossible. Indeed, one of the original purposes of Olson's use of the theory was to show that in systems with only a few participants these actors "can provide themselves with collective goods without relying on any positive inducements apart from the good itself."[15] Logically, hegemony should not be a necessary condition for the emergence of cooperation in an oligopolistic system.

The theory of hegemonic stability is thus suggestive but by no means definitive. Concentrated power alone is not sufficient to create a stable international economic order in which cooperation flourishes, and the argument that hegemony is necessary for cooperation is both theoretically and empirically weak. If hegemony is redefined as the ability and willingness of a single state to make and enforce rules, furthermore, the claim that hegemony is sufficient for cooperation becomes virtually tautological.

The crude theory of hegemonic stability establishes a useful, if somewhat simplistic, starting-point for an analysis of changes in international cooperation and discord. Its refined version raises a looser but suggestive set of interpretive questions for the analysis of some eras in the history of the international political economy. Such an interpretive framework does not constitute an explanatory systemic theory, but it can help us think of hegemony in another way—less as a concept that helps to explain outcomes in terms of power than as a way of describing an international system in which leadership is exercised by a single state. Rather than being a component of a scientific generalization—that power is a necessary or sufficient condition for cooperation—the concept of hegemony, defined in terms of willingness as well as ability to lead, helps us think about the incentives facing the potential hegemon. Under what conditions, domestic and international, will such a country decide to invest in the construction of rules and institutions?

Concern for the incentives facing the hegemon should also alert us to the frequently neglected incentives facing other countries in the system. What calculus do they confront in considering whether to challenge or defer to a would-be leader? Thinking about the calculations of secondary powers raises the question of deference. Theories of hegemony should seek not only to analyze dominant powers' decisions to engage in rule-making and rule-enforcement, but also to explore why secondary states defer to the leadership of the hegemon. That is, they need to account for the legitimacy of hegemonic regimes and for the coexistence of cooperation, . . . with hegemony. We will see later that Gramsci's notion of "ideological hegemony" provides some valuable clues helping us understand how cooperation and hegemony fit together.

MILITARY POWER AND HEGEMONY IN THE WORLD POLITICAL ECONOMY

Before taking up these themes, we need to clarify the relationship between this analysis of hegemony in the world political economy and the question of military power. A hegemonic state must possess enough military power to be able to protect the international political economy that it dominates from incursions by hostile adversaries. This is essential because economic issues, if they are crucial enough to basic national values, may become military-security issues as well. For instance, Japan attacked the United States in 1941 partly in response to the freezing of Japanese assets in the United States, which denied Japan "access to all the vitally needed supplies outside her own control, in particular her most crucial need, oil."[16] During and after World War II the United States used its military power to assure itself access to the petroleum of the Middle East; and at the end of 1974 Secretary of State Henry A. Kissinger warned that the United States might resort to military action if oil-exporting countries threatened "some actual strangulation of the industrialized world."[17]

Yet the hegemonic power need not be militarily dominant worldwide. Neither British nor American power ever extended so far. Britain was challenged militarily during the nineteenth century by France, Germany, and especially Russia; even at the height of its power after World War II the United States confronted a recalcitrant Soviet adversary and fought a war against China. The military conditions for economic hegemony are met if the economically preponderant country has sufficient military capabilities to prevent incursions by others that would deny it access to major areas of its economic activity.

The sources of hegemony therefore include sufficient military power to deter or rebuff attempts to capture and close off important areas of the world political economy. But in the contemporary world, at any rate, it is difficult for a hegemon to use military power directly to attain its economic policy objectives with its military partners and allies. Allies cannot be threatened with force without beginning

to question the alliance; nor are threats to cease defending them unless they conform to the hegemon's economic rules very credible except in extraordinary circumstances. Many of the relationships within the hegemonic international political
economy dominated by the United States after World War II approximated more
closely the ideal type of "complex interdependence"—with multiple issues, multiple channels of contact among societies, and inefficacy of military force for most
policy objectives—than the converse ideal type of realist theory.[18]

This does not mean that military force has become useless. It has certainly
played an indirect role even in U.S. relations with its closest allies, since Germany
and Japan could hardly ignore the fact that American military power shielded them
from Soviet pressure. It has played a more overt role in the Middle East, where
American military power has occasionally been directly employed and has always
cast a shadow and where U.S. military aid has been conspicuous. Yet changes in
relations of military power have not been the major factors affecting patterns of
cooperation and discord among the advanced industrialized countries since the
end of World War II. Only in the case of Middle Eastern oil have they been highly
significant as forces contributing to changes in international economic regimes,
and even in that case . . . shifts in economic interdependence, and therefore in
economic power, were more important. Throughout the period between 1945 and
1983 the United States remained a far stronger military power than any of its allies
and the only country capable of defending them from the Soviet Union or of intervening effectively against serious opposition in areas such as the Middle East. . . .

Some readers may wish to criticize this account by arguing that military power
has been more important than claimed here. By considering military power only as
a background condition for postwar American hegemony rather than as a variable,
I invite such a debate. Any such critique, however, should keep in mind what I am
trying to explain [here] . . . not the sources of hegemony (in domestic institutions,
basic resources, and technological advances any more than in military power), but
rather the effects of changes in hegemony on cooperation among the advanced
industrialized countries. I seek to account for the impact of American dominance
on the creation of international economic regimes and the effects of an erosion of
that preponderant position on those regimes. Only if *these* problems—not other
questions that might be interesting—could be understood better by exploring
more deeply the impact of changes in relations of military power would this hypothetical critique be damaging to my argument.

MARXIAN NOTIONS OF HEGEMONY

For Marxists, the fundamental forces affecting the world political economy are
those of class struggle and uneven development. International history is dynamic
and dialectical rather than cyclical. The maneuvers of states reflect the stages of
capitalist development and the contradictions of that development. For a Marxist, it is futile to discuss hegemony, or the operation of international institutions,
without understanding that they operate, in the contemporary world system,
within a capitalist context shaped by the evolutionary patterns and functional
requirements of capitalism. Determinists may call these requirements laws.

Historicists may see the patterns as providing some clues into a rather open-ended process that is nevertheless affected profoundly by what has gone before: people making their own history, but not just as they please.

Any genuinely Marxian theory of world politics begins with an analysis of capitalism. According to Marxist doctrine, no smooth and progressive development of productive forces within the confines of capitalist relations of production can persist for long. Contradictions are bound to appear. It is likely that they will take the form of tendencies toward stagnation and decline in the rate of profit, but they may also be reflected in crises of legitimacy for the capitalist state, even in the absence of economic crises.[19] Any "crisis of hegemony" will necessarily be at the same time—and more fundamentally—a crisis of capitalism.

For Marxists, theories of hegemony are necessarily partial, since they do not explain changes in the contradictions facing capitalism. Nevertheless, Marxists have often used the concept of hegemony, implicitly defined simply as dominance, as a way of analyzing the surface manifestations of world politics under capitalism. For Marxists as well as mercantilists, wealth and power are complementary; each depends on the other. . . . [T]he analyses of the Marxist Fred Block and the Realist Robert Gilpin are quite similar: both emphasize the role of U.S. hegemony in creating order after the Second World War and the disturbing effects of the erosion of American power.

Immanuel Wallerstein's work also illustrates this point. He is at pains to stress that modern world history should be seen as the history of capitalism as a world system. Apart from "relatively minor accidents" resulting from geography, peculiarities of history, or luck, "it is the operations of the world-market forces which accentuate the differences, institutionalize them, and make them impossible to surmount over the long run."[20] Nevertheless, when considering particular epochs, Wallerstein emphasizes hegemony and the role of military force. Dutch economic hegemony in the seventeenth century was destroyed not by the operation of the world-market system or contradictions of capitalism, but by the force of British and French arms.[21]

The Marxian adoption of mercantilist categories raises analytical ambiguities having to do with the relationship between capitalism and the state. Marxists who adopt this approach have difficulty maintaining a class focus, since their unit of analysis shifts to the country, rather than the class, for purposes of explaining international events. This is a problem for both Block and Wallerstein, as it often appears that their embrace of state-centered analysis has relegated the concept of class to the shadowy background of political economy. The puzzle of the relationship between the state and capitalism is also reflected in the old debate between Lenin and Kautsky about "ultra-imperialism."[22] Lenin claimed that contradictions among the capitalist powers were fundamental and could not be resolved, against Kautsky's view that capitalism could go through a phase in which capitalist states could maintain unity for a considerable period of time.

The successful operation of American hegemony for over a quarter-century after the end of World War II supports Kautsky's forecast that ultra-imperialism could be stable and contradicts Lenin's thesis that capitalism made inter-imperialist war inevitable. It does not, however, resolve the issue of whether ultra-imperialism could be maintained in the absence of hegemony. An analysis of the contemporary situation in Marxian terminology would hold that one form of ultra-imperialism—American hegemony—is now breaking down, leading to increased disorder, and that the issue at present is "whether all this will ultimately result in a new capitalist world order, in a revolutionary reconstitution of world society, or in the common ruin of the contending classes and nations."[23] The issue from a Marxian standpoint is whether ultra-imperialism could be revived by new efforts at inter-capitalist collaboration or, on the contrary, whether fundamental contradictions in capitalism or in the coexistence of capitalism with the state system prevent any such recovery.

The key question of this book—how international cooperation can be maintained among the advanced capitalist states in the absence of American hegemony—poses essentially the same problem. The view taken here is similar to that of Kautsky and his followers, although the terminology is different. My contention is that the common interests of the leading capitalist states, bolstered by the effects of existing international regimes (mostly created during a period of American hegemony), are strong enough to make sustained cooperation possible, though not inevitable. One need not go so far as . . . the "internationalization of capital" to understand the strong interests that capitalists have in maintaining some cooperation in the midst of rivalry. Uneven development in the context of a state system maintains rivalry and ensures that cooperation will be incomplete and fragile . . . but it does not imply that the struggle must become violent or that compromises that benefit all sides are impossible.

Despite the similarities between my concerns and those of many Marxists, I do not adopt their categories in this study. Marxian explications of the "laws of capitalism" are not sufficiently well established that they can be relied upon for inferences about relations among states in the world political economy or for the analysis of future international cooperation. Insofar as there are fundamental contradictions in capitalism, they will surely have great impact on future international cooperation; but the existence and nature of these contradictions seem too murky to justify incorporating them into my analytical framework.

As this discussion indicates, Marxian insights into international hegemony derive in part from combining Realist conceptions of hegemony as dominance with arguments about the contradictions of capitalism. But this is not the only Marxian contribution to the debate. In the thought of Antonio Gramsci and his followers, hegemony is distinguished from sheer dominance. As Robert W. Cox has expressed it:

> Antonio Gramsci used the concept of hegemony to express a unity between objective material forces and ethico-political ideas—in Marxian terms, a unity of structure and superstructure—in which power based on dominance over production is rationalized through an ideology incorporating compromise or consensus between dominant and subordinate groups. A hegemonial structure of world order is one in which power takes a primarily consensual form, as distinguished from a non-hegemonic order in which there are manifestly rival powers and no power has been able to establish the legitimacy of its dominance.[24]

The value of this conception of hegemony is that it helps us understand the willingness of the partners of a hegemon to defer to hegemonial leadership. Hegemons require deference to enable them to construct a structure of world capitalist order. It is too expensive, and perhaps self-defeating, to achieve this by force; after all, the key distinction between hegemony and imperialism is that a hegemon, unlike an empire, does not dominate societies through a cumbersome political superstructure, but rather supervises the relationships between politically independent societies through a combination of hierarchies of control and the operation of markets.[25] Hegemony rests on the subjective awareness by elites in secondary states that they are benefiting, as well as on the willingness of the hegemon itself to sacrifice tangible short-term benefits for intangible long-term gains.

Valuable as the conception of ideological hegemony is in helping us understand deference, it should be used with some caution. First, we should not assume that leaders of secondary states are necessarily the victims of "false consciousness" when they accept the hegemonic ideology, or that they constitute a small, parasitical elite that betrays the interests of the nation to its own selfish ends. It is useful to remind ourselves, as Robert Gilpin has, that during both the *Pax Britannica* and the *Pax Americana* countries other than the hegemon prospered, and that indeed many of them grew faster than the hegemon itself.[26] Under some conditions—not necessarily all—it may be not only in the self-interest of peripheral elites, but conducive to the economic growth of their countries, for them to defer to the hegemon.[27]

We may also be permitted to doubt that ideological hegemony is as enduring internationally as it is domestically. The powerful ideology of nationalism is not available for the hegemon, outside of its own country, but rather for its enemies. Opponents of hegemony can often make nationalism the weapon of the weak and may also seek to invent cosmopolitan ideologies that delegitimize hegemony, such as the current ideology of a New International Economic Order, instead of going along with legitimating ones. Thus the potential for challenges to hegemonic ideology always exists.

CONCLUSIONS

Claims for the general validity of the theory of hegemonic stability are often exaggerated. The dominance of a single great power may contribute to order in world politics, in particular circumstances, but it is not a sufficient condition and there is little reason to believe that it is necessary. But Realist and Marxian arguments about hegemony both generate some important insights.

Hegemony is related in complex ways to cooperation and to institutions such as international regimes. Successful hegemonic leadership itself depends on a certain form of asymmetrical cooperation. The hegemon plays a distinctive role, providing its partners with leadership in return for deference; but, unlike an imperial power, it cannot make and enforce rules without a certain degree of consent from other sovereign states. As the interwar experience illustrates, material predominance alone does not guarantee either stability or effective leadership. Indeed, the hegemon may have to invest resources in institutions in order to ensure that its preferred rules will guide the behavior of other countries.

Cooperation may be fostered by hegemony, and hegemons require cooperation to make and enforce rules. Hegemony and cooperation are not alternatives; on the contrary, they are often found in symbiotic relationships with one another. To analyze the relationships between hegemony and cooperation, we need a conception of cooperation that is somewhat tart rather than syrupy-sweet. It must take into account the facts that coercion is always possible in world politics and that conflicts of interest never vanish even when there are important shared interests. . . . [C]ooperation should be defined not as the absence of conflict— which is always at least a potentially important element of international relations— but as a process that involves the use of discord to stimulate mutual adjustment.

NOTES

1. Robert O. Keohane, "The Theory of Hegemonic Stability and Changes in International Economic Regimes, 1967–1977," in Ole Holsti et al., *Change in the International System* (Boulder, Colo.: Westview Press, 1980), pp. 131–162.
2. Charles P. Kindleberger, *The World in Depression, 1929–1939* (Berkeley: University of California Press, 1973), p. 305.
3. Timothy J. McKeown, "Hegemonic Stability Theory and Nineteenth Century Tariff Levels in Europe," *International Organization*, vol. 37, no. 1 (Winter 1980), p. 78.
4. Immanuel Wallerstein, *The Modern World-System II: Mercantilism and the Consolidation of the European World-Economy. 1600–1750* (New York: Academic Press, 1980), p. 38.
5. Stephen D. Krasner, "United States Commercial and Monetary Policy: Unravelling the Paradox of External Strength and Internal Weakness," in Peter J. Katzenstein, ed., *Between Power and Plenty: Foreign Economic Policies of Advanced Industrial States* (Madison: University of Wisconsin Press, 1978), pp. 68–69.
6. Robert O. Keohane and Joseph S. Nye, *Power and Interdependence: World Politics in Transition* (Boston: Little, Brown), p. 44.
7. Stephen D. Krasner, "State Power and the Structure of International Trade," *World Politics*, vol. 28, no. 3 (April 1976), p. 333.
8. McKeown, p. 88.
9. Ibid.
10. Charles P. Kindleberger, "Dominance and Leadership in the International Economy," *International Studies Quarterly*, vol. 25, no. 3 (June 1981), p. 252.
11. Robert Gilpin, *War and Change in World Politics* (Cambridge: Cambridge University Press, 1981), p. 210.
12. Ibid., p. 227.
13. Ibid., p. 234.
14. Ibid., p. 253.
15. Mancur Olson, quoted in McKeown, p. 79.
16. Paul Schroeder, *The Axis Alliance and Japanese-American Relations* (Ithaca, N.Y.: Cornell University Press, 1958), p. 53.
17. Seyom Brown, *The Faces of Power: Constancy and Change in United States Foreign Policy from Truman to Reagan* (New York: Columbia University Press, 1983), p. 428.
18. Keohane and Nye, chap. 2.
19. Jurgen Haberman, *Legitimation Crisis* (London: Heinemann, 1976).

20. Immanuel Wallerstein, *The Capitalist World Economy* (Cambridge: Cambridge University Press, 1979), p. 21.

21. Wallerstein, *The Modern World-System II*, pp. 38–39.

22. V. I. Lenin, *Imperialism: The Highest Stage of Capitalism* (New York: International Publishers, 1939), pp. 93–94.

23. Giovanni Arrighi, "A Crisis of Hegemony," in Samir Amin, Giovanni Arrighi, Andre Gunder Frank, and Immanuel Wallerstein, *Dynamics of Global Crisis* (New York: Monthly Review Press, 1982), p. 108.

24. Robert W. Cox, "Social Forces, States, and World Orders: Beyond International Relations Theory," *Journal of International Studies, Millennium*, vol. 10, no. 2 (Summer 1981), p. 153, note 27.

25. Immanuel Wallerstein, *The Modern World System: Capitalist Agriculture and the Origins of the European World-Economy in the Sixteenth Century* (New York: Academic Press, 1974), pp. 15–17.

26. Robert Gilpin, pp. 175–185.

27. This is not to say that hegemony in general benefits small or weak countries. There certainly is no assurance that this will be the case. Hegemons may prevent middle-sized states from exploiting small ones and may construct a structure of order conducive to world economic growth; but they may also exploit smaller states economically or distort their patterns of autonomous development through economic, political, or military intervention. The issue of whether hegemony helps poor countries cannot be answered unconditionally, because too many other factors intervene. Until a more complex and sophisticated theory of the relationships among hegemony, other factors, and welfare is developed, it remains an empirically open question.

The Great Divide in the Global Village

BRUCE R. SCOTT

INCOMES ARE DIVERGING

Mainstream economic thought promises that globalization will lead to a widespread improvement in average incomes. Firms will reap increased economies of scale in a larger market, and incomes will converge as poor countries grow more rapidly than rich ones. In this "win-win" perspective, the importance of nation-states fades as the "global village" grows and market integration and prosperity take hold.

But the evidence paints a different picture. Average incomes have indeed been growing, but so has the income gap between rich and poor countries. Both trends have been evident for more than 200 years, but improved global communications have led to an increased awareness among the poor of income inequalities and heightened the pressure to emigrate to richer countries. In response, the industrialized nations have erected higher barriers against immigration, making the world economy seem more like a gated community than a global village. And although international markets for goods and capital have opened up since World War II and multilateral organizations now articulate rules and monitor the world economy, economic inequality among countries continues to increase. Some two billion people earn less than $2 per day.

At first glance, there are two causes of this divergence between economic theory and reality. First, the rich countries insist on barriers to immigration and agricultural imports. Second, most poor nations have been unable to attract much foreign capital due to their own government failings. These two issues are fundamentally linked: by forcing poor people to remain in badly governed states, immigration barriers deny those most in need the opportunity to "move up" by "moving out." In turn, that immobility eliminates a potential source of pressure on ineffective governments, thus facilitating their survival.

Since the rich countries are unlikely to lower their agricultural and immigration barriers significantly, they must recognize that politics is a key cause of economic inequality. And since most developing countries receive little foreign investment, the wealthy nations must also acknowledge that the "Washington consensus," which assumes that free markets will bring about economic convergence, is mistaken. If they at least admit these realities, they will abandon the notion that

Reprinted by permission of *Foreign Affairs* (Vol. 80, No. 1, January/February 2001). Copyright © 2001 by the Council on Foreign Relations, Inc.

their own particular strategies are the best for all countries. In turn, they should allow poorer countries considerable freedom to tailor development strategies to their own circumstances. In this more pragmatic view, the role of the state becomes pivotal.

Why have economists and policymakers not come to these conclusions sooner? Since the barriers erected by rich countries are seen as vital to political stability, leaders of those countries find it convenient to overlook them and focus instead on the part of the global economy that has been liberalized. The rich countries' political power in multilateral organizations makes it difficult for developing nations to challenge this self-serving world-view. And standard academic solutions may do as much harm as good, given their focus on economic stability and growth rather than on the institutions that underpin markets. Economic theory has ignored the political issues at stake in modernizing institutions, incorrectly assuming that market-based prices can allocate resources appropriately.

The fiasco of reform in Russia has forced a belated reappraisal of this blind trust in markets. Many observers now admit that the transition economies needed appropriate property rights and an effective state to enforce those rights as much as they needed the liberalization of prices. Indeed, liberalization without property rights turned out to be the path to gangsterism, not capitalism. China, with a more effective state, achieved much greater success in its transition than did Russia, even though Beijing proceeded much more slowly with liberalization and privatization.

Economic development requires the transformation of institutions as well as the freeing of prices, which in turn requires political and social modernization as well as economic reform. The state plays a key role in this process; without it, developmental strategies have little hope of succeeding. The creation of effective states in the developing world will not be driven by familiar market forces, even if pressures from capital markets can force fiscal and monetary discipline. And in a world still governed by "states rights," real progress in achieving accountable governments will require reforms beyond the mandates of multilateral institutions.

GO WITH THE FLOW

In theory, globalization provides an opportunity to raise incomes through increased specialization and trade. This opportunity is conditioned by the size of the markets in question, which in turn depends on geography, transportation costs, communication networks, and the institutions that underpin markets. Free trade increases both the size of the market and the pressure to improve economic performance. Those who are most competitive take advantage of the enhanced market opportunities to survive and prosper.

Neoclassical economic theory predicts that poor countries should grow faster than rich ones in a free global market. Capital from rich nations in search of cheaper labor should flow to poorer economies, and labor should migrate from low-income areas toward those with higher wages. As a result, labor and capital costs—and eventually income—in rich and poor areas should eventually converge.

The U.S. economy demonstrates how this theory can work in a free market with the appropriate institutions. Since the 1880s, a remarkable convergence of incomes among the country's regions has occurred. The European Union has witnessed a similar phenomenon, with the exceptions of Greece and Italy's southern half, the *Mezzogiorno*. What is important, however, is that both America and the EU enjoy labor and capital mobility as well as free internal trade.

But the rest of the world does not fit this pattern. The most recent *World Development Report* shows that real per capita incomes for the richest one-third of countries rose by an annual 1.9 percent between 1970 and 1995, whereas the middle third went up by only 0.7 percent and the bottom third showed no increase at all. In the Western industrial nations and Japan alone, average real incomes have been rising about 2.5 percent annually since 1950—a fact that further accentuates the divergence of global income. These rich countries account for about 60 percent of world GDP but only 15 percent of world population.

Why is it that the poor countries continue to fall further behind? One key reason is that most rich countries have largely excluded the international flow of labor into their markets since the interwar period. As a result, low-skilled labor is not free to flow across international boundaries in search of more lucrative jobs. From an American or European perspective, immigration appears to have risen in recent years, even approaching its previous peak of a century ago in the United States. Although true, this comparison misses the central point. Billions of poor people could improve their standard of living by migrating to rich countries. But in 1997, the United States allowed in only 737,000 immigrants from developing nations, while Europe admitted about 665,000. Taken together, these flows are only 0.04 percent of all potential immigrants.

The point is not that the rich countries should permit unfettered immigration. A huge influx of cheap labor would no doubt be politically explosive; many European countries have already curtailed immigration from poor countries for fear of a severe backlash. But the more salient issue is that rich nations who laud liberalism and free markets are rejecting those very principles when they restrict freedom of movement. The same goes for agricultural imports. Both Europe and Japan have high trade barriers in agriculture, while the United States remains modestly protectionist.

Mainstream economic theory does provide a partial rationalization for rich-country protectionism: Immigration barriers need not be a major handicap to poor nations because they can be offset by capital flows from industrialized economies to developing ones. In other words, poor people need not demand space in rich countries because the rich will send their capital to help develop the poor countries. This was indeed the case before World War I, but it has not been so since World War II.

But the question of direct investment, which typically brings technologies and know-how as well as financial capital, is more complicated than theories would predict. The total stock of foreign direct investment did rise almost sevenfold from 1980 to 1997, increasing from 4 percent to 12 percent of world GDP during that period. But very little has gone to the poorest countries. In 1997, about 70 percent went from one rich country to another, 8 developing countries received about

20 percent, and the remainder was divided among more than 100 poor nations. According to the World Bank, the truly poor countries received less than 7 percent of the foreign direct investment to all developing countries in 1992–98. At the same time, the unrestricted opening of capital markets in developing countries gives larger firms from rich countries the opportunity for takeovers that are reminiscent of colonialism. It is not accidental that rich countries insist on open markets where they have an advantage and barriers in agriculture and immigration, where they would be at a disadvantage.

As for the Asian "tigers," their strong growth is due largely to their high savings rate, not foreign capital. Singapore stands out because it has enjoyed a great deal of foreign investment, but it has also achieved one of the highest domestic-savings rates in the world, and its government has been a leading influence on the use of these funds. China is now repeating this pattern, with a savings rate of almost 40 percent of GDP. This factor, along with domestic credit creation, has been its key motor of economic growth. China now holds more than $100 billion in low-yielding foreign-exchange reserves, the second largest reserves in the world.

In short, global markets offer opportunities for all, but opportunities do not guarantee results. Most poor countries have been unable to avail themselves of much foreign capital or to take advantage of increased market access. True, these countries have raised their trade ratios (exports plus imports) from about 35 percent of their GDP in 1981 to almost 50 percent in 1997. But without the Asian tigers, developing-country exports remain less than 25 percent of world exports.

Part of the problem is that the traditional advantages of poor countries have been in primary commodities (agriculture and minerals), and these categories have shrunk from about 70 percent of world trade in 1900 to about 20 percent at the end of the century. Opportunities for growth in the world market have shifted from raw or semiprocessed commodities toward manufactured goods and services—and, within these categories, toward more knowledge-intensive segments. This trend obviously favors rich countries over poor ones, since most of the latter are still peripheral players in the knowledge economy. (Again, the Asian tigers are the exception. In 1995, they exported as much in high-technology goods as did France, Germany, Italy, and Britain combined—which together have three times the population of the tigers.)

ONE COUNTRY, TWO SYSTEMS

Why is the performance of poor countries so uneven and out of sync with theoretical forecasts? Systemic barriers at home and abroad inhibit the economic potential of poorer nations, the most formidable of these obstacles being their own domestic political and administrative problems. These factors, of course, lie outside the framework of mainstream economic analysis. A useful analogy is the antebellum economy of the United States, which experienced a similar set of impediments.

Like today's "global village," the U.S. economy before the Civil War saw incomes diverge as the South fell behind the North. One reason for the Confederacy's secession and the resulting civil war was Southern recognition that it was falling behind in both economic and political power, while the richer and more populous North was attracting more immigrants. Half of the U.S. population lived in the North in 1780; by 1860, this share had climbed to two-thirds. In 1775, incomes in the five original Southern states equaled those in New England, even though wealth (including slaves) was disproportionately concentrated in the South. By 1840, incomes in the northeast were about 50 percent higher than those in the original Southern states; the North's railroad mileage was about 40 percent greater (and manufacturing investment four times higher) than the South's. As the economist Robert Fogel has pointed out, the South was not poor—in 1860 it was richer than all European states except England—but Northern incomes were still much higher and increasing.

Why had Southern incomes diverged from those in the North under the same government, laws, and economy? Almost from their inception, the Southern colonies followed a different path from the North—specializing in plantation agriculture rather than small farms with diversified crops—due to geography and slavery. Thanks to slave labor, Southerners were gaining economies of scale and building comparative advantage in agriculture, exporting their goods to world markets and the North. Gang labor outproduced "free" (paid) labor. But the North was building even greater advantages by developing a middle class, a manufacturing sector, and a more modern social and political culture. With plans to complete transcontinental railroads pending, the North was on the verge of achieving economic and political dominance and the capacity to shut off further expansion of slavery in the West. The South chose war over Northern domination—and modernization.

Although the Constitution guaranteed free trade and free movement of capital and labor, the institution of slavery meant that the South had much less factor mobility than the North. It also ensured less development of its human resources, a less equal distribution of income, a smaller market for manufactures, and a less dynamic economy. It was less attractive to both European immigrants and external capital. With stagnant incomes in the older states, it was falling behind. In these respects, it was a forerunner of many of today's poor countries, especially those in Latin America.

What finally put the South on the path to economic convergence? Four years of civil war with a total of 600,000 deaths and vast destruction of property were only a start. Three constitutional amendments and twelve years of military "reconstruction" were designed to bring equal rights and due process to the South. But the reestablishment of racial segregation following Reconstruction led to sharecropping as former slaves refused to return to the work gangs. Labor productivity dropped so much that Southern incomes fell to about half of the North's in 1880. In fact, income convergence did not take off until the 1940s, when a wartime boom in the North's industrial cities attracted Southern migrants in search of better jobs. At the same time, the South began drawing capital as firms sought lower wages, an anti-union environment, and military contracts in important congressional districts. But this process did not fully succeed until the 1960s, as new federal laws and federal troops brought full civil rights to the South and ensured that the region could finally modernize.

THE GREAT DIVIDE

Although slavery is a rarity today, the traditional U.S. divide between North and South provides a good model for understanding contemporary circumstances in many developing countries. In the American South, voter intimidation, segregated housing, and very unequal schooling were the rule, not the exception—and such tactics are repeated today by the elites in today's poor countries. Brazil, Mexico, and Peru had abundant land relative to population when the Europeans arrived, and their incomes roughly approximated those in North America, at least until 1700. The economists Stanley Engerman and Kenneth Sokoloff have pointed out that these states, like the Confederacy, developed agricultural systems based on vast landholdings for the production of export crops such as sugar and coffee. Brazil and many Caribbean islands also adopted slavery, while Peru and Mexico relied on forced indigenous labor rather than African slaves.

History shows that the political development of North America and developing nations—most of which were colonized by Europeans at some point—was heavily influenced by mortality. In colonies with tolerable death rates (Australia, Canada, New Zealand, and the United States), the colonists soon exerted pressure for British-style protections of persons and property. But elsewhere (most of Africa, Latin America, Indonesia, and to a lesser degree, India), disease caused such high mortality rates that the few resident Europeans were permitted to exploit a disenfranchised laboring class, whether slave or free. When the colonial era ended in these regions, it was followed by "liberationist" regimes (often authoritarian and incompetent) that maintained the previous system of exploitation for the advantage of a small domestic elite. Existing inequalities within poor countries continued; policies and institutions rarely protected individual rights or private initiative for the bulk of the population and allowed elites to skim off rents from any sectors that could bear it. The economist Hernando de Soto has shown how governments in the developing world fail to recognize poor citizens' legal titles to their homes and businesses, thereby depriving them of the use of their assets for collateral. The losses in potential capital to these countries have dwarfed the cumulative capital inflows going to these economies in the last century.

The legacy of these colonial systems also tends to perpetuate the unequal distribution of income, wealth, and political power while limiting capital mobility. Thus major developing nations such as Brazil, China, India, Indonesia, and Mexico are experiencing a divergence of incomes by province within their economies, as labor and capital fail to find better opportunities. Even in recent times, local elites have fought to maintain oppressive conditions in Brazil, El Salvador, Guatemala, Mexico, Nicaragua, and Peru. Faced with violent intimidation, poor people in these countries have suffered from unjust law enforcement similar to what was once experienced by black sharecroppers in the American South.

Modernization and economic development inevitably threaten the existing distribution of power and income, and powerful elites continue to protect the status quo—even if it means that their society as a whole falls further behind. It takes more than a constitution, universal suffrage, and regular elections to achieve governmental accountability and the rule of law. It may well be that only the right of exit—emigration—can peacefully bring accountability to corrupt and repressive regimes. Unlike the U.S. federal government, multilateral institutions lack the legitimacy to intervene in the internal affairs of most countries. Europe's economic takeoff in the second half of the nineteenth century was aided by the emigration of 60 million people to North America, Argentina, Brazil, and Australia. This emigration—about 10 percent of the labor force—helped raise European wages while depressing inflated wages in labor-scarce areas such as Australia and the United States. A comparable out-migration of labor from today's poor countries would involve hundreds of millions of people.

Of course, Latin America has seen some success. Chile has received the most attention for its free market initiatives, but its reforms were implemented by a brutally repressive military regime—hardly a model for achieving economic reform through democratic processes. Costa Rica would seem to be a much better model for establishing accountability, but its economic performance has not been as striking as Chile's.

Italy, like the United States in an earlier era, is another good example of "one country, two systems." Italy's per capita income has largely caught up with that of its European neighbors over the past 20 years, even exceeding Britain's and equaling France's in 1990, but its *Mezzogiorno* has failed to keep up. Whereas overall Italian incomes have been converging toward those of the EU, *Mezzogiorno* incomes have been diverging from those in the north. Southern incomes fell from 65 percent of the northern average in 1975 to 56 percent 20 years later; in Calabria, they fell to 47 percent of the northern average. Southern unemployment rose from 8 percent in 1975 to 19 percent in 1995—almost three times the northern average. In short, 50 years of subsidies from Rome and the EU have failed to stop the *Mezzogiorno* from falling further behind. Instead, they have yielded local regimes characterized by greatly increased public-sector employment, patronage, dependency, and corruption—not unlike the results of foreign aid for developing countries. And the continuing existence of the Mafia further challenges modernization.

Democracy, then, is not enough to ensure that the governed are allowed to reap the gains of their own efforts. An effective state requires good laws as well as law enforcement that is timely, even-handed, and accessible to the poor. In many countries, achieving objective law enforcement means reducing the extralegal powers of vested interests. When this is not possible, the only recourse usually available is emigration. But if the educated elite manages to emigrate while the masses remain trapped in a society that is short of leaders, the latter will face even more formidable odds as they try to create effective institutions and policies. Although Italians still emigrate from south to north, the size of this flow is declining, thanks in part to generous transfer payments that allow them to consume almost as much as northerners. In addition, policymaking for the *Mezzogiorno* is still concentrated in Rome.

The immigration barriers in rich countries not only foreclose opportunities in the global village to billions of poor people, they help support repressive, pseudo-democratic governments by denying the citizens of these countries the right to vote against the regime with their feet. In effect, the strict dictates of sovereignty allow wealthy nations to continue to set the rules in their own favor while allowing badly governed poor nations to continue to abuse their own citizens and retard economic development. Hence the remedy for income divergence must be political as well as economic.

GETTING INSTITUTIONS RIGHT

According to economic theory, developing nations will create and modernize the institutions needed to underpin their markets so that their markets and firms can gradually match the performance of rich countries. But reality is much more complex than theory. For example, de Soto's analysis makes clear that effectively mobilizing domestic resources offers a much more potent source of capital for most developing nations than foreign inflows do. Yet mainstream economists and their formal models largely ignore these resources. Western economic advisers in Russia were similarly blindsided by their reliance on an economic model that had no institutional context and no historical perspective. Economists have scrambled in recent years to correct some of these shortcomings, and the Washington consensus now requires the "right" institutions as well as the "right" prices. But little useful theory exists to guide policy when it comes to institutional analysis, and gaps in the institutional foundations in most developing countries leave economic models pursuing unrealistic solutions or worse.

The adjustment of institutions inevitably favors certain actors and disadvantages others. As a result, modernization causes conflict that must be resolved through politics as well as economics. At a minimum, successful development signifies that the forces for institutional change have won out over the status quo. Achieving a "level playing field" signifies that regulatory and political competition is well governed.

Economists who suggest that all countries must adopt Western institutions to achieve Western levels of income often fail to consider the changes and political risks involved. The experts who recommended that formerly communist countries apply "shock therapy" to markets and democracy disregarded the political and regulatory issues involved. Each change requires a victory in the "legislative market" and successful persuasion within the state bureaucracy for political approval. Countries with lower incomes and fewer educated people than Russia face even more significant developmental challenges just to achieve economic stability, let alone attract foreign investment or make effective use of it. Institutional deficiencies, not capital shortages, are the major impediment to development, and as such they must be addressed before foreign investors will be willing to send in capital.

Although price liberalization can be undertaken rapidly, no rapid process (aside from revolution) exists for an economy modernizing its institutions. Boris Yeltsin may be credited with a remarkable turnover, if not a coup d'état, but his erratic management style and the lack of parliamentary support ensured that his government would never be strong. In these circumstances, helping the new Russian regime improve law enforcement should have come ahead of mass privatization. Launching capitalism in a country where no one other than apparatchiks had access to significant amounts of capital was an open invitation to gangsterism and a discredited system. Naive economic models made for naive policy recommendations.

HOW THE WEST WON

The state's crucial role is evident in the West's economic development. European economic supremacy was forged not by actors who followed a "Washington consensus" model but by strong states. In the fifteenth century, European incomes were not much higher than those in China, India, or Japan. The nation-state was a European innovation that replaced feudalism and established the rule of law; in turn, a legal framework was formed for effective markets. Once these countries were in the lead, they were able to continuously increase their edge through technological advances. In addition, European settlers took their civilization with them to North America and the South Pacific, rapidly raising these areas to rich-country status as well. Thus Europe's early lead became the basis for accumulating further advantages with far-reaching implications.

Europe's rise to economic leadership was not rapid at first. According to the economist Angus Maddison, Europe's economy grew around 0.07 percent a year until 1700; only after 1820 did it reach one percent. But the pace of technological and institutional innovation accelerated thereafter. Meanwhile, discovery of new markets in Africa, Asia, and the Americas created new economic opportunities. Secular political forces overthrew the hegemony of the Catholic Church. Feudalism was eroded by rising incomes and replaced by a system that financed government through taxes, freeing up land and labor to be traded in markets. Markets permitted a more efficient reallocation of land and labor, allowing further rises in incomes. Effective property rights allowed individuals to keep the fruits of their own labor, thereby encouraging additional work. And privatization of common land facilitated the clearing of additional acreage.

The nation-state helped forge all these improvements. It opened up markets by expanding territory; reduced transaction costs; standardized weights, measures, and monetary units; and cut transport costs by improving roads, harbors, and canals. In addition, it was the state that established effective property rights. The European state system thrived on flexible alliances, which constantly changed to maintain a balance of power. Military and economic rivalries prompted states to promote development in agriculture and commerce as well as technological innovation in areas such as shipping and weaponry. Absent the hegemony of a single church or state, technology was diffused and secularized. Clocks, for instance, transferred timekeeping from the monastery to the village clock tower; the printing press did much the same for the production and distribution of books.

Europe's development contrasts sharply with Asia's. In the early modern era, China saw itself as the center of the world, without real rivals. It had a much larger population than Europe and a far bigger market as well. But though the Chinese pioneered the development of clocks, the printing press, gunpowder, and iron, they did not have the external competitive stimulus to promote economic development. Meanwhile, Japan sealed itself off from external influences for more than

200 years, while India, which had continuous competition within the subcontinent, never developed an effective national state prior to the colonial era.

The Europeans also led in establishing accountable government, even though it was achieved neither easily nor peacefully. Most European states developed the notion that the sovereign (whether a monarch or a parliament) had a duty to protect subjects and property in return for taxes and service in the army. Rulers in the Qing, Mughal, and Ottoman Empires, in contrast, never recognized a comparable responsibility to their subjects. During the Middle Ages, Italy produced a number of quasi-democratic city-states, and in the seventeenth century Holland created the first modern republic after a century of rebellion and warfare with Spain. Britain achieved constitutional monarchy in 1689, following two revolutions. After a bloody revolution and then dictatorship, France achieved accountable government in the nineteenth century.

Europe led the way in separating church and state—an essential precursor to free inquiry and adoption of the scientific method—after the Thirty Years' War. The secular state in turn paved the way for capitalism and its "creative destruction." Creative destruction could hardly become the norm until organized religion lost its power to execute as heretics those entrepreneurs who would upset the status quo. After the Reformation, Europeans soon recognized another fundamental tenet of capitalism: the role of interest as a return for the use of capital. Capitalism required that political leaders allow private hands to hold power as well as wealth; in turn, power flowed from the rural nobility to merchants in cities. European states also permitted banks, insurance firms, and stock markets to develop. The "yeast" in this recipe lay in the notion that private as well as state organizations could mobilize and reallocate society's resources—an idea with profound social, political, and economic implications today.

Most of Europe's leading powers did not rely on private initiative alone but adopted mercantilism to promote their development. This strategy used state power to create a trading system that would raise national income, permitting the government to enhance its own power through additional taxes. Even though corruption was sometimes a side effect, the system generally worked well. Venice was the early leader, from about 1000 to 1500; the Dutch followed in the sixteenth and seventeenth centuries; Britain became dominant in the eighteenth century. In Britain, as in the other cases, mercantilist export promotion was associated with a dramatic rise in state spending and employment (especially in the navy), as well as "crony capitalism." After World War II, export-promotion regimes were adopted by Japan, South Korea, Singapore, and Taiwan with similar success. Today, of course, such strategies are condemned as violations of global trade rules, even for poor countries.

Finally, geography played a pivotal role in Europe's rise, providing a temperate climate, navigable rivers, accessible coastline, and defensible boundaries for future states. In addition, Europe lacked the conditions for the production of labor-intensive commodities such as coffee, cotton, sugar, or tobacco—production that might have induced the establishment of slavery. Like in the American North, European agriculture was largely rain-fed, diversified, and small-scale.

Europe's rise, then, was partly due to the creation and diffusion of technological innovations and the gradual accumulation of capital. But the underlying causes were political and social. The creation of the nation-state and institutionalized state rivalry fostered government accountability. Scientific enlightenment and upward social mobility, spurred by healthy competition, also helped Europe achieve such transformations. But many of today's developing countries still lack these factors crucial for economic transformation.

PLAYING CATCH-UP

Globalization offers opportunities for all nations, but most developing countries are very poorly positioned to capitalize on them. Malarial climates, limited access to navigable water, long distances to major markets, and unchecked population growth are only part of the problem. Such countries also have very unequal income structures inherited from colonial regimes, and these patterns of income distribution are hard to change unless prompted by a major upheaval such as a war or a revolution. But as serious as these disadvantages are, the greatest disadvantage has been the poor quality of government.

If today's global opportunities are far greater and potentially more accessible than at any other time in world history, developing countries are also further behind than ever before. Realistic political logic suggests that weak governments need to show that they can manage their affairs much better before they pretend to have strategic ambitions. So what kind of catch-up models could they adopt?

Substituting domestic goods for imports was the most popular route to economic development prior to the 1980s. But its inward orientation made those who adopted it unable to take advantage of the new global opportunities and ultimately it led to a dead end. Although the United States enjoyed success with such a strategy from 1790 until 1940, no developing country has a home market large enough to support a modern economy today. The other successful early growth model was European mercantilism, namely export promotion, as pioneered by Venice, the Dutch republic, Britain, and Germany. Almost all of the East Asian success stories, China included, are modern versions of the export-oriented form of mercantilism.

For its part, free trade remains the right model for rich countries because it provides decentralized initiatives to search for tomorrow's market opportunities. But it does not necessarily promote development. Britain did not adopt free trade until the 1840s, long after it had become the world's leading industrial power. The prescription of lower trade barriers may help avoid even worse strategies at the hands of bad governments, but the Washington-consensus model remains best suited for those who are ahead rather than behind.

Today's shareholder capitalism brings additional threats to poor countries, first by elevating compensation for successful executives, and second by subordinating all activities to those that maximize shareholder value. Since 1970, the estimated earnings of an American chief executive have gone from 30 times to 450 times that of the average worker. In the leading developing countries, this ratio is still less than 50. Applying a similar "market-friendly" rise in executive compensation within the developing world would therefore only aggravate the income gap, providing new ammunition for populist politicians. In addition, shareholder capitalism calls for narrowing the managerial focus to the interests of shareholders, even if this means dropping activities that offset local market imperfections. A leading South African bank has shed almost a million small accounts—mostly held by blacks—to raise its earnings per share. Should this bank, like its American counterparts, have an obligation to serve its community, including its black members, in return for its banking license?

Poor nations must improve the effectiveness of their institutions and bureaucracies in spite of entrenched opposition and poorly paid civil servants. As the journalist Thomas Friedman has pointed out, it is true that foreign-exchange traders can dump the currencies of poorly managed countries, thereby helping discipline governments to restrain their fiscal deficits and lax monetary policies. But currency pressures will not influence the feudal systems in Pakistan and Saudi Arabia, the theocracies in Afghanistan and Iran, or the kleptocracies in Kenya or southern Mexico. The forces of capital markets will not restrain Brazilian squatters as they take possession of "public lands" or the slums of Rio de Janeiro or São Paulo, nor will they help discipline landlords and vigilantes in India's Bihar as they fight for control of their state. Only strong, accountable government can do that.

LOOKING AHEAD

Increased trade and investment have indeed brought great improvements in some countries, but the global economy is hardly a win-win situation. Roughly one billion people earn less than $1 per day, and their numbers are growing. Economic resources to ameliorate such problems exist, but the political and administrative will to realize the potential of these resources in poor areas is lacking. Developing-nation governments need both the pressure to reform their administrations and institutions, and the access to help in doing so. But sovereignty removes much of the external pressure, while immigration barriers reduce key internal motivation. And the Washington consensus on the universality of the rich-country model is both simplistic and self-serving.

The world needs a more pragmatic, country-by-country approach, with room for neomercantilist regimes until such countries are firmly on the convergence track. Poor nations should be allowed to do what today's rich countries did to get ahead, not be forced to adopt the laissez-faire approach. Insisting on the merits of comparative advantage in low-wage, low-growth industries is a sure way to stay poor. And continued poverty will lead to rising levels of illegal immigration and low-level violence, such as kidnappings and vigilante justice, as the poor take the only options that remain. Over time, the rich countries will be forced to pay more attention to the fortunes of the poor—if only to enjoy their own prosperity and safety.

Still, the key initiatives must come from the poor countries, not the rich. In the last 50 years, China, India, and Indonesia have led the world in reducing poverty.

In China, it took civil war and revolution, with tens of millions of deaths, to create a strong state and economic stability; a de facto coup d'état in 1978 brought about a very fortunate change of management. The basic forces behind Chinese reform were political and domestic, and their success depended as much on better using resources as opening up markets. Meanwhile, the former Soviet Union and Africa lie at the other extreme. Their economic decline stems from their failure to maintain effective states and ensure the rule of law.

It will not be surprising if some of today's states experience failure and economic decline in the new century. Argentina, Colombia, Indonesia, and Pakistan will be obvious cases to watch, but other nations could also suffer from internal regional failures—for example, the Indian state of Bihar. Income growth depends heavily on the legal, administrative, and political capabilities of public actors in sovereign states. That is why, in the end, external economic advice and aid must go beyond formal models and conform to each country's unique political and social context.

INTERDEPENDENCE AND
■ GLOBALIZATION

Globalization of the International Economy

■ JEFFREY FRANKEL

Economic globalization is one of the most powerful forces to have shaped the postwar world. In particular, international trade in goods and services has become increasingly important over the past fifty years, and international financial flows over the past thirty years. This chapter documents quantitatively the process of globalization for trade and finance. It then briefly goes beyond the causes of international economic integration to consider its effects, concluding that globalization is overall a good thing, not just for economic growth but also when noneconomic goals are taken into account.

The two major drivers of economic globalization are reduced costs to transportation and communication in the private sector and reduced policy barriers to trade and investment on the part of the public sector. Technological progress and innovation have long been driving the costs of transportation and communication steadily lower. In the postwar period we have seen major further cost-saving advances, even within ocean shipping: supertankers, roll-on-roll-off ships, and containerized cargo. Between 1920 and 1990 the average ocean freight and port charges per short ton of U.S. import and export cargo fell from $95.00 to $29.00 (in 1990 dollars). An increasing share of cargo goes by air. Between 1930 and 1990, average air transport revenue per passenger mile fell from $0.68 to $0.11. Jet air shipping and refrigeration have changed the status of goods that had previously been classified altogether as not tradable internationally. Now fresh-cut flowers, perishable broccoli and strawberries, live lobsters, and even ice cream are sent between continents. Communications costs have fallen even more rapidly. Over this period the cost of a three-minute telephone call from New York to London fell from $244.65 to $3.32. Recent inventions such as faxes and the Internet require no touting.

It is easy to exaggerate the extent of globalization. Much excited discussion of the topic makes it sound as though the rapid increase in economic integration across national borders is unprecedented. Some commentators imply that it has now gone so far that it is complete; one hears that distance and national borders no longer matter, that the nation-state and geography are themselves no longer relevant for economic purposes, and that it is now as easy to do business with a customer across the globe as across town. After all, has not the World Wide Web reduced cross-border barriers to zero?

It would be a mistake for policymakers or private citizens to base decisions on the notion that globalization is so new that the experience of the past is not relevant, or that the phenomenon is now irreversible, or that national monetary authorities are now powerless in the face of the global marketplace, or that the quality of life of Americans—either economic or noneconomic aspects—is determined more by developments abroad than by American actions at home.

It is best to recognize that at any point in history many powerful forces are working to drive countries apart, at the same time as other powerful forces are working to shrink the world. In the 1990s, for example, at the same time that forces such as the Internet and dollarization have led some to proclaim the decline of the nation-state, more new nations have been created (out of the ruins of the former Soviet bloc) than in any decade other than the decolonizing 1960s, each with its own currencies and trade policies. The forces of shrinkage have dominated in recent decades, but the centrifugal forces are important as well.

TWO BENCHMARKS FOR MEASURING ECONOMIC INTEGRATION

The overall post–World War II record of economic integration across national borders, powerful as it has been, is, in two respects, not as striking as widely believed. The first perspective is to judge by the standard of 100 years ago. The second is to judge by the standard of what it would mean to have truly perfect global integration.

Judging Globalization 2000 by the Standard of 1900

The globalization that took place in the nineteenth century was at least as impressive as the current episode. The most revolutionary breakthroughs in transportation and communication had already happened by 1900—for example, the railroad, steamship, telegraph, and refrigeration. Freight rates had fallen sharply throughout the century. An environment of political stability was provided by the Pax Britannica, and an environment of monetary stability was provided by the gold standard. Kevin O'Rourke and Jeffrey Williamson show that, as a result of rapidly growing trade, international differences in commodity prices narrowed dramatically.

It is inescapable to invoke a particularly famous quote from John Maynard Keynes: "What an extraordinary episode in the progress of man that age was which came to an end in August 1914! . . . The inhabitant of London could order by telephone, sipping his morning tea in bed, the various products of the whole earth . . . he could at the same time and by the same means adventure his wealth in the natural resources and new enterprise of any quarter of the world."[1]

The world took a giant step back from economic globalization during the period 1914–1944. Some of the causes of this retrogression were isolationist sentiments in the West that followed World War I, the monetary instability and economic depression that plagued the interwar period, increases in tariffs and other trade barriers including most saliently the adoption by the U.S. Congress of the Smoot-Hawley tariff of 1930, the rise of the fascist bloc in the 1930s, and the rise of the communist bloc in the 1940s. All of these factors pertain to barriers that were created by governments, in contrast to the forces of technology and the private marketplace, which tend to reduce barriers. As a result, the world that emerged in 1945 was far more fragmented economically than the world that had turned to war in 1914.

The victors, however, were determined not to repeat the mistakes they had made at the time of the first world war. This time, they would work to promote economic integration in large part to advance long-term political goals. To govern international money, investment, and trade, they established multilateral institutions— the International Monetary Fund, World Bank, and General Agreement on Tariffs and Trade. The United States initially led the way by reducing trade barriers and making available gold-convertible dollars.

By one basic measure of trade, exports or imports of merchandise as a fraction of total output, it took more than twenty-five years after the end of World War II before the United States around 1970 reached the same level of globalization that it had experienced on the eve of World War I. This fraction continued to increase rapidly between 1971 and 1997—reaching about 9 percent today, still far lower than that in Britain throughout the late and early twentieth centuries. By other measures, some pertaining to the freedom of factor movements, the world even by the turn of the millennium was no more integrated than that of the preceding turn of the century.

Most people find it surprising that trade did not reattain its pre–World War I importance until the early 1970s. The significance of the comparison with 100 years ago goes well beyond factoids that economic historians enjoy springing on the uninitiated. Because technological know-how is irreversible—or was irreversible over the second millennium, if not entirely over the first—there is a tendency to see globalization as irreversible. But the political forces that fragmented the world for thirty years (1914–44) were evidently far more powerful than the accretion of technological progress in transport that went on during that period. The lesson is that nothing is inevitable about the process of globalization. For it to continue, world leaders must make choices of the sort made in the aftermath of World War II, instead of those made in the aftermath of World War I.

Share of output sold at home

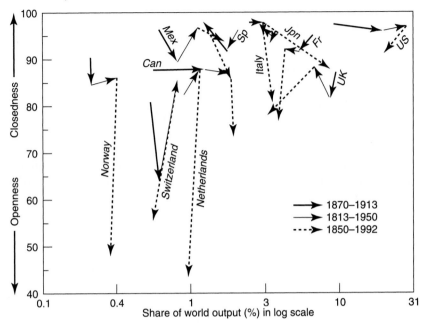

FIGURE 1 ■ Country Size (Share of World Output) versus Closedness (Sales at Home/Total Output)
Source: Author's calculations and data from Angus Maddison, Monitoring the World Economy *(Paris: Development Center of the Organization for Economic Cooperation and Development, 1995).*
*Note: Closedness = (1 − (x/GDP))*100.*

Judging by the Globalization 2000 Standard of Perfect International Integration

Perhaps perfect economic integration across national borders is a straw man. . . . But straw men have their purposes, and in this case ample rhetoric exists to justify the interest. A good straw man needs to be substantial enough to impress the crows and yet not so substantial that he can't be knocked flat. On both scores the proposition of complete international integration qualifies admirably.

Consider again the basic statistics of trade integration—a country's total exports of goods and services, or total imports, as a fraction of GDP. With the rapid increase in services included, these ratios now average 12 percent for the United States. The current level of trade likely represents a doubling from 100 years ago. As remarkable as is this evidence of declining transportation costs, tariffs, and other barriers to trade, it is still very far from the condition that would prevail if these costs and barriers were zero. More sophisticated statistics below will document this claim. But a very simple calculation is sufficient to make the point. U.S. output is about one-fourth of gross world product. The output of producers in other countries is thus about three-fourths of gross world product. If Americans were prone to buy goods and services from foreign producers as easily as from domestic producers, then foreign products would constitute a share of U.S. spending equal to that of the spending of the average resident of the planet. The U.S. import-GDP ratio would equal .75. The same would be true of the U.S. export-GDP ratio. And yet these ratios are only about one-sixth of this hypothetical level (12 percent /75 percent=one-sixth). In other words, globalization would have to increase another sixfold, as measured by the trade ratio, before it would literally be true that Americans did business as easily across the globe as across the country.

Other countries are also a long way from perfect openness in this sense. The overall ratio of merchandise trade to output worldwide is about twice the U.S. ratio. This is to be expected, as other countries are smaller. For the other two large economies—Japan and the European Union considered as a whole—the ratio is closer to the U.S. level. In almost all cases, the ratio falls far short of the level that would prevail in a perfectly integrated world. In Figure 1, the vertical dimension represents the share of a country's output that is sold to its fellow citizens, rather than exported. The downward movement for most countries illustrates that they have become more open over the past 130 years. (One can also see that the integration trend was interrupted during the interwar period.) The United States is still far from perfect openness: the share of output sold at home is disproportionate to the share of world output. Other countries have a higher ratio of trade to GDP than the United States as a result of being smaller and less self-sufficient. Nonetheless, they are similarly far from perfect openness.

Why is globalization still so far from complete? To get an idea of the combination of transportation costs, trade barriers, and other frictions that remains yet to be dismantled, we must delve more deeply into the statistics.

STATISTICAL MEASURES OF ECONOMIC INTEGRATION

It can be instructive to look at direct measures of how some of the barriers to transborder integration have changed during the twentieth century—the level of tariffs on manufactures as an illustration of trade policy, or the price of a trans-Atlantic telephone call as an illustration of technological change in communications and transportation. Nevertheless, the political and physical determinants are too numerous and varied to be aggregated into a few key statistics that are capable of measuring the overall extent of integration in trade or finance. Tariff rates, for example, differ tremendously across commodities, and there is no single sensible way to aggregate them. The situation is even worse for nontariff barriers. Alternative possible measures of the importance of tariffs and other trade barriers have very low correlation with each other. . . .

It is more rewarding to look at summary measures of the *effects* of cross-border barriers on the patterns of trade and investment than to look at measures of the barriers themselves. Two sorts of measures are in use: those pertaining to quantities and those pertaining to prices.

Measures of quantities might appear more direct: "just how big are international flows?" But economists often prefer to look at price measures. In the first place, the quality of the data is often higher for prices than quantities. (This is particularly true of data on international financial markets—the data on the prices of foreign securities are extremely good, the data on aggregate international trade in securities are extremely bad.) In the second place, even at a conceptual level, international differentials in the prices of specific goods or specific assets, which measure the ability of international arbitrage to hold these prices in line, are more useful indicators of the extent of integration in a causal sense. Consider the example of U.S. trade in petroleum products. It is not especially large as a percentage of total U.S. output or consumption of petroleum products. And yet arbitrage ties the price of oil within the United States closely to the price in the world market. Even a pair of countries that records no bilateral oil trade whatsoever will find that their prices move closely together. It is the absence of barriers and the *potential* for large-scale trade that keeps prices in line and makes the markets integrated in the most meaningful sense, not the magnitude of trade that takes place.

The Ability of Arbitrage to Eliminate International Differentials in Goods Prices

According to basic economic theory, arbitrage, defined as the activity of buying an item in a place where it is cheap and simultaneously selling the same item where it is expensive, should drive prices into equality. Its failure to do so perfectly is a source of repeated surprise to economists (though perhaps to nobody else). Often the explanation is that the commodities in question are not in fact identical. Brand names matter, if for no other reason than matters of retailing, warranty, and customer service. A BMW is certainly not the same automobile as a Lexus, and even a BMW sold in Germany is not the same as a BMW sold in the United States (different air pollution control equipment, for example). When the comparison across countries uses aggregate price indexes, as in standard tests of "purchasing power parity," it is no surprise to find only weak evidence of arbitrage. The finding of international price differentials is more surprising in the case of nondifferentiated non-brand-name commodities such as standardized ball bearings. Tests find that price differentials for specific goods are far larger across national borders than they are within countries. Exchange rate variability is a likely culprit.

Even more surprising is the paucity of evidence of a tendency for price differentials to diminish over the long sweep of history. Kenneth Froot, Michael Kim, and Kenneth Rogoff have obtained data on prices in England and Holland since the year 1273 for eight commodities (barley, butter, cheese, eggs, oats, peas, silver, and wheat).[2] Deviations from the so-called Law of One Price across the English Channel are no smaller or less persistent now than they were in the past, even though technological progress has certainly reduced the cost of shipping these products dramatically. Evidently other forces have counteracted the fall in transport costs; candidates are trade barriers under Europe's Common Agricultural Policy and volatility in the exchange rate between the guilder and the pound.

Factors Contributing to Home-Country Bias in Trade

Geography in general—and distance in particular—remain far more important inhibitions to trade than widely believed.

Distance

Distance is still an important barrier to trade and not solely because of physical shipping costs. The effects of informational barriers are observed to decrease with proximity and with linguistic, cultural, historical, and political links. We might call it social distance. Hans Linnemann called it "psychic distance," and Peter Drysdale and Ross Garnaut named it "subjective resistance."[3]

Among many possible proofs that distance is still important, one of the simplest is the observed tendency toward geographical agglomeration of industries. The tendency for industry to concentrate regionally is evidence both of costs to transportation and communication and of increasing returns to scale in production.

The agglomeration occurs even in sectors where physical transport costs are negligible, as in financial services or computer software. Financial firms concentrate in Manhattan and information technology firms concentrate in Silicon Valley. The reason they choose to locate near each other is not because they are trading physical commodities with each other and wish to save on shipping costs. Rather, face-to-face contact is important for exchanging information and negotiating deals.

The importance of distance is also revealed by analysis of data on prices of goods in different locations. If transport costs and other costs of doing business at a distance are important, then arbitrage should do a better job of keeping prices of similar goods in line when they are sold at locations close together rather than far apart. Charles Engel and John Rogers study prices in fourteen consumption categories for twenty-three Canadian and U.S. cities. They find that the distance between two North American cities significantly affects the variability of their relative prices. . . .

Statistical estimates find highly significant effects of distance on bilateral trade. When the distance between two countries is increased by 1 percent, trade between them falls by 0.7 to 1.0 percent. This statistic, like the others that follow, pertains to the effect in isolation, holding constant other effects on trade, such as the size of the trading partners. . . .

Other Geographical Variables

Other physical attributes of location also have statistically significant effects. Landlocked countries engage in less trade by a factor of about one-third, holding other factors equal. Two countries that are adjacent to each other trade about 80 percent more than two otherwise similar countries.

Linguistic and Colonial Factors

Linguistic barriers remain an impediment to trade. Two countries that speak the same language trade about 50 percent more than two otherwise similar countries. The multitude of languages is one of the reasons why economic integration remains far from complete in the European Union.

Colonial links have also been important historically. In 1960, the year when the break-up of the largest colonial empires began in earnest, trade between colonies and the colonial power was on average two to four times greater than for otherwise similar pairs of countries. This effect, already reduced from an earlier peak in the colonial era, has continued to decline in the 1970s and 1980s. But it has not disappeared. Indeed, if small dependencies are included in the sample, then two units that share the same colonizer still trade on average an estimated 80 percent more with each other than two otherwise similar countries (as recently as 1990). In addition, if one of the pair is the colonial mother country, trade is five to nine times greater than it would otherwise be.

Military Factors

The effects on bilateral trade of politico-military alliances, wars, have also been examined. Theoretically and empirically (in the gravity framework) trade is generally higher among countries that are allies and lower among countries that are actual or potential adversaries. Understandably, if two countries are currently at war, there is usually a negative effect on trade. It runs as high as a 99 percent reduction in 1965. More typical is an 82 percent reduction in 1990.[4]

Free Trade Areas

Regional trading arrangements reduce tariffs and other trade barriers within a group of countries, though there is a range from mild preferential trading arrangements to full-fledged economic unions. Often the members of such groups are already tightly linked through proximity, common language, or other ties. But even holding constant for such factors, in the gravity model, the formation of a free trade area is estimated on average to raise trade by 70 to 170 percent. A serious common market, such as the European Union, can have a bigger effect. Nevertheless, in each of the EU member countries, a large bias toward trade within that country remains.

Political Links

A naive economist's view would be that once tariffs and other explicit trade barriers between countries are removed, and geographic determinants of transportation costs are held constant, trade should move as easily across national boundaries as within them. But this is far from the case in reality. If two geographic units belong to the same sovereign nation, such as France and its overseas departments, trade is roughly tripled. Thus political relationships among geographic units have larger effects on trade than such factors as explicit trade policies or linguistic barriers.

Common Country

Even after adjusting for distance (including noncontiguity) and linguistic barriers, all countries still exhibit a substantial bias toward buying domestic goods rather than foreign. . . .

There would be some great advantages of having data at the level of states or provinces within countries. We would be able to ascertain how trade between two geographical entities is affected by their common membership in a political union. We have learned that when two geographical units share such links as speaking a common language, their bilateral trade is clearly boosted. It stands to reason that when two units share a common cultural heritage or legal system, their trade will be enhanced by even more. Data are not generally available on trade among U.S. states, Japanese prefectures, German länder, British counties, or French departments. But there do exist data on trade undertaken by Canadian provinces, among one another and with major American states. They show a strong intranational bias to trade. Ontario exports three times as much to British Columbia as to California, even though the latter has ten times as many people. (The figures are for 1988.) . . .

Currencies

There has long been reason to suspect that the existence of different currencies, and especially the large fluctuation in the exchange rates between currencies since the break-up of the Bretton Woods monetary system in 1971, has been a barrier to international trade and investment. Exchange rate fluctuations are clearly related to the failures of the law of one price observed in goods markets. When it is observed that, for example, Canadians and Americans trade far more with their countrymen than with each other, in a context where trade barriers, geography, and linguistic barriers have been eliminated, the currency difference is one of the prime suspects. . . .

Promoting trade and finance is one of several motivations for the recent adoption of common currencies or currency boards by roughly twenty countries over the past decade (including the eleven members of the European Economic and Monetary Union in 1999). At the same time, however, approximately the same number of new currencies have come into existence, as a result of the breakup of the former Soviet bloc.

Measures of Financial Market Integration

The delegates who met at Bretton Woods in 1944 had a design for the world monetary system that explicitly did not accord financial markets the presumption that was accorded trade in goods, the presumption that international integration was unambiguously good and that barriers should be liberalized as rapidly as possible. Although economic theory can make as elegant a case in favor of free trade in assets as for free trade in goods and services, the delegates had been persuaded by the experience of the 1930s that some degree of controls on international capital movements was desirable. It was not until the final 1973 breakdown of the system of fixed exchange rates that Germany and the United States removed their capital controls. Japan and the United Kingdom kept theirs until the end of the 1970s, and most other European countries did not liberalize until the end of the 1980s. Many emerging-market countries also opened up to large-scale international capital movements in the 1990s (though the subsequent crises have convinced some observers that those delegates at Bretton Woods might have had it right in the first place).

Tests regarding financial markets show international integration that has increased tremendously over the past thirty years but that is less complete than often supposed. This generalization applies to quantity-based tests as well as to price-based tests.

It is true that the gross volume of cross-border capital flows has grown very large. Perhaps the most impressive and widely cited statistic is the gross volume of turnover in foreign exchange markets: $1.5 trillion per day worldwide, by April

1998, which is on the order of a hundred times greater than the volume of trade in goods and services. *Net* capital flows are for most purposes more interesting than gross flows, however. Net capital flows today are far smaller as a share of GDP than were pre-World War I net flows out of Great Britain and into such land-abundant countries as Argentina, Australia, and Canada. Furthermore, Martin Feldstein and Charles Horioka argued in a very influential paper that net capital flows are far smaller than one would expect them to be in a world of perfect international capital mobility: a country that suffers a shortfall in national saving tends to experience an almost commensurate fall in investment, rather than making up the difference by borrowing from abroad. Similarly, investors in every country hold far lower proportions of their portfolios in the form of other countries' securities than they would in a well-diversified portfolio, a puzzle known as home country bias. Evidently, imperfect information and transactions costs are still important barriers to cross-country investment.

The ability of arbitrage to equate asset prices or rates of return across countries has been widely tested. One would expect that in the absence of barriers to cross-border financial flows, arbitrage would bring interest rates into equality. But the answer depends on the precise condition tested. Interest rates that have had the element of exchange risk removed by forward market cover are indeed virtually equated across national borders among industrialized countries, showing that they have few controls on international capital movements. But interest rates seem not to be equalized across countries when they are adjusted for expectations of exchange rate changes rather than for forward exchange rates, and interest rates are definitely not equalized when adjusted for expected inflation rates. Evidently, currency differences are important enough to drive a wedge between expected rates of return. Furthermore, residual transactions costs or imperfect information apparently affects cross-border investment in equities. They discourage investors altogether from investing in some information-intensive assets, such as mortgages, across national borders. Furthermore, country risk still adds a substantial penalty wedge to all investments in developing countries.

In short, though international financial markets, much like goods markets, have become far more integrated in recent decades, they have traversed less of the distance to perfect integration than is widely believed. Globalization is neither new, nor complete, nor irreversible.

The Impact of Economic Globalization

What are the effects of globalization and its merits? We must acknowledge a lower degree of certainty in our answers. It becomes harder to isolate cause and effect. Moreover, once we extend the list of objectives beyond maximizing national incomes, value judgments come into play. Nevertheless, economic theory and empirical research still have much to contribute.

The Effect of Trade on the Level and Growth of Real Income

Why do economists consider economic integration so important? What are the benefits of free trade for the economy?

The Theoretical Case for Trade

Classical economic theory tells us that there are national gains from trade, associated with the phrase "comparative advantage." Over the past two decades, scholars have developed a "new trade theory." It suggests the existence of additional benefits from trade, which are termed dynamic. We consider each theory in turn.

The classical theory goes back to Adam Smith and David Ricardo. Adam Smith argued that specialization—the division of labor—enhances productivity. David Ricardo extended this concept to trade between countries. The notion is that trade allows each country to specialize in what it does best, thus maximizing the value of its output. If a government restricts trade, resources are wasted in the production of goods that could be imported more cheaply than they can be produced domestically.

What if one country is better than anyone else at producing *every* good? The argument in favor of free trade still carries the day. All that is required is for a country to be *relatively* less skilled than another in the production of some good in order for it to benefit from trade. This is the doctrine of comparative advantage—the fundamental (if perhaps counterintuitive) principle that underlies the theory of international trade. It makes sense for Michael Jordan to pay someone else to mow his lawn, even if Jordan could do it better himself, because he has a comparative advantage at basketball over lawn mowing. Similarly, it makes sense for the United States to pay to import certain goods that can be produced more efficiently abroad (apparel, shoes, tropical agriculture, consumer electronics), because the United States has a comparative advantage in other goods (aircraft, financial services, wheat, and computer software).

This is the classical view of the benefits of free trade in a nutshell. Two key attributes of the classical theory are worth flagging. First, it assumes perfect competition, constant returns to scale, and fixed technology, assumptions that are not very realistic. Second, the gains from trade are primarily static in nature—that is, they affect the *level* of real income. The elimination of trade barriers raises income, but this is more along the lines of a one-time increase.

What of the "new trade theory"? It is more realistic than the classical theory, in that it takes into account imperfect competition, increasing returns to scale, and changing technology. It can be viewed as providing equally strong, or stronger, support for the sort of free trade policies that the United States has followed throughout the postwar period, that is, multilateral and bilateral negotiations to reduce trade barriers, than did the classical theory.

To be sure, these theories say that, under certain very special conditions, one country can get ahead by interventions (for example, subsidies to strategic sectors), provided the government gets it exactly right and provided the actions of other countries are taken as given. But these theories also tend to have the property that a world in which everyone is subsidizing at once is a world in which everyone is worse off, and that we are all better off if we can agree to limit subsidies or other interventions.

Bilateral or multilateral agreements where other sides make concessions to U.S. products, in return for whatever concessions the United States makes, are virtually the only sorts of trade agreements the United States has made. Indeed, most recent trade agreements (like the North American Free Trade Agreement and

China's accession to the WTO) have required much larger reductions in import barriers by U.S. trading partners than by the United States. The reason is that their barriers were higher than those of the United States to start with. But the natural implication is that such agreements raise foreign demand for U.S. products by more than they raise U.S. demand for imports. Hence the United States is likely to benefit from a positive "terms of trade effect." This just adds to the usual benefits of increased efficiency of production and gains to consumers from international trade.

Furthermore, even when a government does not fear retaliation from abroad for trade barriers, intervention in practice is usually based on inadequate knowledge and is corrupted by interest groups. Seeking to rule out all sector-specific intervention is the most effective way of discouraging rent-seeking behavior. Globalization increases the number of competitors operating in the economy. Not only does this work to reduce distortionary monopoly power in the marketplace (which is otherwise exercised by raising prices), it can also reduce distortionary corporate power in the political arena (which is exercised by lobbying).

Most important, new trade theory offers reason to believe that openness can have a permanent effect on a country's rate of growth, not just the level of real GDP. A high rate of economic interaction with the rest of the world speeds the absorption of frontier technologies and global management best practices, spurs innovation and cost-cutting, and competes away monopoly.

These dynamic gains come from a number of sources. They include the benefits of greater market size and enhanced competition. Other sources include technological improvements through increased contact with foreigners and their alternative production styles. Such contact can come, for example, from direct investment by foreign firms with proprietary knowledge or by the exposure to imported goods that embody technologies developed abroad. Each of these elements of international trade and interactions has the effect of promoting growth in the domestic economy. When combined with the static effects, there is no question that the efforts to open markets, when successful, can yield significant dividends.

The Empirical Case for Trade

Citing theory is not a complete answer to the question, "how do we know that trade is good?" We need empirical evidence. Economists have undertaken statistical tests of the determinants of countries' growth rates. Investment in physical capital and investment in human capital are the two factors that emerge the most strongly. But other factors matter. Estimates of growth equations have found a role for openness, measured, for example, as the sum of exports and imports as a share of GDP. David Romer and I look at a cross-section of 100 countries during the period since 1960. The study sought to address a major concern about simultaneous causality between growth and trade: does openness lead to growth, or does growth lead to openness? We found that the effect of openness on growth is even stronger when we correct for the simultaneity compared with standard estimates.

The estimate of the effect of openness on income per capita ranges from 0.3 to 3.0. Consider a round middle number such as 1.0. The increase in U.S. openness since the 1950s is 0.12. Multiplying the two numbers together implies that the increased integration has had an effect of 12 percent on U.S. income. More dramatically, compare a stylized Burma, with a ratio close to zero, versus a stylized

Singapore, with a ratio close to 100 percent. Our ballpark estimate, the coefficient of 1.0, implies that Singapore's income is 100 percent higher than Burma's as a result of its openness. The fact that trade can affect a country's growth rate—as opposed to affecting the level of its GDP in a "one-shot" fashion—makes the case for trade liberalization even more compelling. . . .

Macroeconomic Interdependence

Trade and financial integration generally increase the transmission of business cycle fluctuations among countries. Floating exchange rates give countries some insulation against one another's fluctuations. When capital markets are highly integrated, floating rates do not give complete insulation, as the post-1973 correlation among major industrialized economies shows. But international transmission can be good for a country as easily as bad, as happens when adverse domestic developments are in part passed off to the rest of the world. The trade balance can act as an important automatic stabilizer for output and employment, improving in recessions and worsening in booms.

Contagion of financial crises is more worrying. The decade of the 1990s alone abounds with examples: the 1992–93 crises in the European exchange rate mechanism, the "tequila crisis" that began with the December 1994 devaluation of the Mexican peso, and the crises in East Asia and emerging markets worldwide from July 1997 to January 1999. Evidently when one country has a crisis it affects others. There is now a greater consensus among economists than before that not all of the observed volatility, or its cross-country correlation, can be attributed to efficient capital markets punishing or rewarding countries based on a rational evaluation of the economic fundamentals. It is difficult to do justice in one paragraph to a discussion that is as voluminous and vigorous as the debate over the welfare implications of the swelling international capital flows. Still, the majority view remains that countries are overall better off with modern globalized financial markets than without them.

The Effect of Trade on Other Social Goals

Many who fear globalization concede that trade has a positive effect on aggregate national income but suspect that it has adverse effects on other highly valued goals such as labor rights, food safety, culture, and so forth. Here we consider only two major values—equality and the environment—and briefly at that.

Income Distribution

International trade and investment can be a powerful source of growth in poor countries, helping them catch up with those who are ahead in endowments of capital and technology. This was an important component of the spectacular growth of East Asian countries between the 1960s and the 1990s, which remains a miracle even in the aftermath of the 1997–98 currency crises. By promoting convergence, trade can help reduce the enormous worldwide inequality in income. Most of those who are concerned about income distribution, however, seem more motivated by within-country equality than global equality.

A standard textbook theory of international trade, the Heckscher-Ohlin-Samuelson model, has a striking prediction to make regarding within-country income distribution. It is that the scarce factors of production will lose from trade, and the abundant factors will benefit. This means that in rich countries, those who have capital and skills will benefit at the expense of unskilled labor, whereas in poor countries it will be the other way around. The same prediction holds for international capital mobility (or, for that matter, for international labor mobility). It has been very difficult, however, to find substantial direct evidence of the predictions of the model during the postwar period, including distribution effects within either rich or poor countries. Most likely the phenomena of changing technology, intra-industry trade, and worker ties to specific industries are more important today than the factor endowments at the heart of the Heckscher-Ohlin-Samuelson model.

In the United States, the gap between wages paid to skilled workers and wages paid to unskilled workers rose by 18 percentage points between 1973 and 1995 and then leveled off. The fear is that trade is responsible for some of the gap, by benefiting skilled workers more than unskilled workers. Common statistical estimates—which typically impose the theoretical framework rather than testing it—are that between 5 and 30 percent of the increase is attributable to trade. Technology, raising the demand for skilled workers faster than the supply, is the major factor responsible for the rest. One of the higher estimates is that trade contributes one-third of the net increase in the wage gap.

On a sample of seventy-three countries, Chakrabarti finds that trade actually reduces inequality, as measured by the Gini coefficient. This relationship also holds for each income class.

Clearly, income distribution is determined by many factors beyond trade. One is redistribution policies undertaken by the government. In some cases such policies are initiated in an effort to compensate or "buy off" groups thought to be adversely affected by trade. But a far more important phenomenon is the tendency for countries to implement greater redistribution as they grow richer.

A long-established empirical regularity is the tendency for income inequality to worsen at early stages of growth and then to improve at later stages. The original explanation for this phenomenon, known as the Kuznets curve, had to do with rural-urban migration. But a common modern interpretation is that income redistribution is a "superior good"—something that societies choose to purchase more of, even though at some cost to aggregate income, as they grow rich enough to be able to afford to do so. If this is right, then trade can be expected eventually to raise equality, by raising aggregate income.

Environment

Similar logic holds that trade and growth can also be good for the environment, once the country gets past a certain level of per capita income. Gene Grossman and Alan Krueger found what is called the environmental Kuznets curve: growth is bad for air and water pollution at the initial stages of industrialization but later on reduces pollution as countries become rich enough to pay to clean up their environments. . . . A key point is that popular desires need not translate automatically into environmental quality; rather government intervention is usually required to address externalities.

The idea that trade can be good for environment is surprising to many. The pollution-haven hypothesis instead holds that trade encourages firms to locate production of highly polluting sectors in low-regulation countries in order to stay competitive. But economists' research suggests that environmental regulation is not a major determinant of firms' ability to compete internationally. Furthermore, running counter to fears of a "race to the bottom," is the Pareto-improvement point: trade allows countries to attain more of whatever their goals are, including higher market-measured income for a given level of environmental quality or a better environment for a given level of income. . . .

The econometric studies of the effects of trade and growth on the environment get different results depending on what specific measures of pollution they use. There is a need to look at other environmental criteria as well. It is difficult to imagine, for example, that trade is anything but bad for the survival of tropical hardwood forests or endangered species, without substantial efforts by governments to protect them.

The argument that richer countries will take steps to clean up their environments holds only for issues when the effects are felt domestically—where the primary "bads," such as smog or water pollution, are external to the firm or household but internal to the country. Some environmental externalities that have received increased attention in recent decade, however, are global. Biodiversity, overfishing, ozone depletion, and greenhouse gas emissions are four good examples. A ton of carbon dioxide has the same global warming effect regardless of where in the world it is emitted. In these cases, individual nations can do little to improve the environment on their own, no matter how concerned their populations or how effective their governments. For each of the four examples, governments have negotiated international treaties in an attempt to deal with the problem. But only the attempt to address ozone depletion, the Montreal Protocol, can be said as yet to have met with much success.

Is the popular impression then correct, that international trade and finance exacerbates these global environmental externalities? Yes, but only in the sense that trade and finance promote economic growth. Clearly if mankind were still a population of a few million people living in preindustrial poverty, greenhouse gas emissions would not be a big issue. Industrialization leads to environmental degradation, and trade is part of industrialization. But virtually everyone wants industrialization, at least for themselves. Deliberate self-impoverishment is not a promising option. Once this point is recognized, there is nothing special about trade compared with the other sources of economic growth: capital accumulation, rural-urban migration, and technological progress. . . .

SUMMARY OF CONCLUSIONS

This chapter gives confident answers to questions about the extent and sources of economic globalization and moderately confident answers to some questions about its effects.

The world has become increasingly integrated with respect to trade and finance since the end of World War II, owing to declining costs to transportation and communication and declining government barriers. The phenomenon is neither new nor complete, however. Globalization was more dramatic in the half-century preceding World War I, and much of the progress during the last half-century has merely reversed the closing off that came in between. In the second regard, globalization is far from complete. Contrary to popular impressions, national borders and geography still impede trade and investment substantially. A simple calculation suggests that the ratio of trade to output would have to increase at least another sixfold before it would be true that Americans trade across the globe as readily as across the country. Such barriers as differences in currencies, languages, and political systems each have their own statistically estimated trade-impeding influences, besides the remaining significant effects of distance, borders, and other geographical and trade policy variables.

The chapter's discussion of the impacts of economic globalization has necessarily been exceedingly brief. Both theory and evidence are read as clearly supportive of the proposition that trade has a positive effect on real incomes. This is why economists believe it is important that the process of international integration be allowed to continue, especially for the sake of those countries that are still poor.

Effects on social values other than aggregate incomes can be positive or negative, depending on the details, and the statistical evidence does not always give clear-cut answers about the bottom line. In the two most studied cases, income distribution and environmental pollution, there seems to be a pattern whereby things get worse in the early stages of industrialization but then start to get better at higher levels of income. Societies that become rich in terms of market-measured output choose to improve their quality of life in other ways as well. It is possible that the same principle extends to noneconomic values such as safety, human rights, and democracy. In short, there is reason to hope that, aside from the various more direct effects of trade on noneconomic values, there is a general indirect beneficial effect that comes through the positive effect of trade on income. . . .

NOTES

1. John Maynard Keynes, *The Economic Consequences of The Peace* (Harcourt Brace, and Howe (1920).
2. Kenneth Froot, Michael Kim, and Kenneth Rogoff, "The Law of One Price over 700 Years," Working Paper 5132 (Cambridge, Mass.: National Bureau of Economic Research, May 1995).
3. Hans Linnemann, *An Econometric Study of International Trade Flows* (Amsterdam: North-Holland, 1960); and Peter Drysdale and Ross Garnaut, "Trade Intensities and the Analysis of Bilateral Trade Flows in a Many-Country World," *Hitotsubashi Journal of Economics*, vol. 22 (1982), pp. 62–84.
4. Edward Mansfield, "Effects of International Politics on Regionalism in International Trade," in Kym Anderson and Richard Blackhurst, eds., *Regional Integration and the Global Trading System* (Harvester Wheatsheaf, 1993); Edward Mansfield and Rachel Bronson, "The Political Economy of Major-Power Trade Flows," in Edward Mansfield and Helen Milner, eds., *The Political Economy of Regionalism* (Columbia University Press 1997); and Joanne Gowa and Edward Mansfield, "Power Politics and International Trade," *American Political Science Review*, vol. 87 (June 1993), pp. 408–20.

The Changed World Economy

PETER F. DRUCKER

The talk today is of the "changing world economy." I wish to argue that the world economy is not "changing"; it has *already changed*—in its foundations and in its structure—and in all probability the change is irreversible.

Within the last decade or so, three fundamental changes have occurred in the very fabric of the world economy:

- The primary-products economy has come "uncoupled" from the industrial economy.
- In the industrial economy itself, production has come "uncoupled" from employment.
- Capital movements rather than trade (in both goods and services) have become the driving force of the world economy. The two have not quite come uncoupled, but the link has become loose, and worse, unpredictable.

These changes are permanent rather than cyclical. We may never understand what caused them—the causes of economic change are rarely simple. It may be a long time before economic theorists accept that there have been fundamental changes, and longer still before they adapt their theories to account for them. Above all, they will surely be most reluctant to accept that it is the world economy in control, rather than the macroeconomics of the nation-state on which most economic theory still exclusively focuses. Yet this is the clear lesson of the success stories of the last 20 years—of Japan and South Korea; of West Germany (actually a more impressive though far less flamboyant example than Japan); and of the one great success within the United States, the turnaround and rapid rise of an industrial New England, which only 20 years ago was widely considered moribund.

Practitioners, whether in government or in business, cannot wait until there is a new theory. They have to act. And their actions will be more likely to succeed the more they are based on the new realities of a changed world economy.

First, consider the primary-products economy. The collapse of non-oil commodity prices began in 1977 and has continued, interrupted only once (right after the 1979 petroleum panic), by a speculative burst that lasted less than six months; it was followed by the fastest drop in commodity prices ever registered. By early

1986 raw material prices were at their lowest levels in recorded history in relation to the prices of manufactured goods and services—in general as low as at the depths of the Great Depression, and in some cases (e.g., lead and copper) lower than their 1932 levels.[1]

This collapse of prices and the slowdown of demand stand in startling contrast to what had been confidently predicted. Ten years ago the Club of Rome declared that desperate shortages for *all* raw materials were an absolute certainty by the year 1985. In 1980 the Carter Administration's *Global 2000 Report to the President: Entering the Twenty-First Century* concluded that world demand for food would increase steadily for at least 20 years; that worldwide food production would fall except in developed countries; and that real food prices would double. This forecast helps to explain why American farmers bought up all available farmland, thus loading on themselves the debt burden that now so threatens them.

Contrary to all these expectations, global agricultural output actually rose almost one-third between 1972 and 1985 to reach an all-time high. It rose the fastest in less-developed countries. Similarly, production of practically all forest products, metals and minerals has gone up between 20 and 35 percent in the last ten years—again with the greatest increases in less-developed countries. There is not the slightest reason to believe that the growth rates will slacken, despite the collapse of commodity prices. Indeed, as far as farm products are concerned, the biggest increase—at an almost exponential rate of growth—may still be ahead.[2]

Perhaps even more amazing than the contrast between such predictions and what has happened is that the collapse in the raw materials economy seems to have had almost no impact on the world industrial economy. If there was one thing considered "proven" beyond doubt in business cycle theory, it is that a sharp and prolonged drop in raw material prices inevitably, and within 18 to 30 months, brings on a worldwide depression in the industrial economy.[3] While the industrial economy of the world today is not "normal" by any definition of the term, it is surely not in a depression. Indeed, industrial production in the developed non-communist countries has continued to grow steadily, albeit at a somewhat slower rate in Western Europe.

Of course, a depression in the industrial economy may only have been postponed and may still be triggered by a banking crisis caused by massive defaults on the part of commodity-producing debtors, whether in the Third World or in Iowa. But for almost ten years the industrial world has run along as though there were no raw material crisis at all. The only explanation is that for the developed countries—excepting only the Soviet Union—the primary-products sector has become marginal where before it had always been central.

In the late 1920s, before the Great Depression, farmers still constituted nearly one-third of the U.S. population and farm income accounted for almost a quarter of the gross national product. Today they account for less than 5 percent of population and even less of GNP. Even adding the contribution that foreign raw material and farm producers make to the American economy through their purchases of American industrial goods, the total contribution of the raw material and food producing economies of the world to the American GNP is, at most, one-eighth. In most other developed countries, the share of the raw materials sector is even lower. Only in the Soviet Union is the farm still a major employer, with almost a quarter of the labor force working on the land.

The raw material economy has thus come uncoupled from the industrial economy. This is a major structural change in the world economy, with tremendous implications for economic and social policy as well as economic theory, in developed and developing countries alike.

For example, if the ratio between the prices of manufactured goods and the prices of non-oil primary products (that is, foods, forest products, metals and minerals) had been the same in 1985 as it had been in 1973, the 1985 U.S. trade deficit might have been a full one-third less—$100 billion as against an actual $150 billion. Even the U.S. trade deficit with Japan might have been almost one-third lower, some $35 billion as against $50 billion. American farm exports would have bought almost twice as much. And industrial exports to a major U.S. customer, Latin America, would have held; their near-collapse alone accounts for a full one-sixth of the deterioration in the U.S. foreign trade over the past five years. If primary-product prices had not collapsed, America's balance of payments might even have shown a substantial surplus.

Conversely, Japan's trade surplus with the world might have been a full 20 percent lower. And Brazil in the last few years would have had an export surplus almost 50 percent higher than its current level. Brazil would then have had little difficulty meeting the interest on its foreign debt and would not have had to endanger its economic growth by drastically curtailing imports as it did. Altogether, if raw material prices in relationship to manufactured goods prices had remained at the 1973 or even the 1979 level, there would be no crisis for most debtor countries, especially in Latin America.[4]

What accounts for this change?

Demand for food has actually grown almost as fast as the Club of Rome and the *Global 2000 Report* anticipated. But the supply has grown much faster; it not only has kept pace with population growth, it has steadily outrun it. One cause of this, paradoxically, is surely the fear of worldwide food shortages, if not world famine, which resulted in tremendous efforts to increase food output. The United States led the parade with a farm policy of subsidizing increased food production. The European Economic Community followed suit, and even more successfully. The greatest increases, both in absolute and in relative terms, however, have been in developing countries: in India, in post-Mao China and in the rice-growing countries of Southeast Asia.

And there is also the tremendous cut in waste. In the 1950s, up to 80 percent of the grain harvest of India fed rats and insects rather than human beings. Today in most parts of India the wastage is down to 20 percent. This is largely the result of unspectacular but effective "infrastructure innovations" such as small concrete storage bins, insecticides and three-wheeled motorized carts that take the harvest straight to a processing plant instead of letting it sit in the open for weeks.

It is not fanciful to expect that the true "revolution" on the farm is still ahead. Vast tracts of land that hitherto were practically barren are being made fertile, either through new methods of cultivation or through adding trace minerals to the soil. The sour clays of the Brazilian highlands or the aluminum-contaminated soils of neighboring Peru, for example, which never produced anything before, now produce substantial quantities of high-quality rice. Even greater advances have been registered in biotechnology, both in preventing diseases of plants and animals and in increasing yields.

In other words, just as the population growth of the world is slowing down quite dramatically in many regions, food production is likely to increase sharply.

Import markets for food have all but disappeared. As a result of its agricultural drive, Western Europe has become a substantial food exporter plagued increasingly by unsalable surpluses of all kinds of foods, from dairy products to wine, from wheat to beef. China, some observers predict, will have become a food exporter by the year 2000. India is about at that stage, especially with wheat and coarse grains. Of all major non-communist countries only Japan is still a substantial food importer, buying abroad about one-third of its food needs. Today most of this comes from the United States. Within five or ten years, however, South Korea, Thailand and Indonesia—low-cost producers that are fast increasing food output— are likely to try to become Japan's major suppliers.

The only remaining major food buyer on the world market may then be the Soviet Union—and its food needs are likely to grow.[5] However, the food surpluses in the world are so large—maybe five to eight times what the Soviet Union would ever need to buy—that its food needs are not by themselves enough to put upward pressure on world prices. On the contrary, the competition for access to the Soviet market among the surplus producers—the United States, Europe, Argentina, Australia, New Zealand (and probably India within a few years)—is already so intense as to depress world food prices.

For practically all non-farm commodities, whether forest products, minerals or metals, world demand is shrinking—in sharp contrast to what the Club of Rome so confidently predicted. Indeed, the amount of raw material needed for a given unit of economic output has been dropping for the entire century, except in wartime. A recent study by the International Monetary Fund calculates the decline as one and one-quarter percent a year (compounded) since 1900.[6] This would mean that the amount of industrial raw materials needed for one unit of industrial production is now no more than two-fifths of what it was in 1900. And the decline is accelerating. The Japanese experience is particularly striking. In 1984, for every unit of industrial production, Japan consumed only 60 percent of the raw materials consumed for the same volume of industrial production in 1973, 11 years earlier.

Why this decline in demand? It is not that industrial production is fading in importance as the service sector grows—a common myth for which there is not the slightest evidence. What is happening is much more significant. Industrial production is steadily switching away from heavily material-intensive products and processes. One of the reasons for this is the new high-technology industries. The raw materials in a semiconductor microchip account for 1 to 3 percent of total production cost; in an automobile their share is 40 percent, and in pots and pans 60 percent. But also in older industries the same scaling down of raw material needs goes on, and with respect to old products as well as new ones. Fifty to 100 pounds of fiberglass cable transmit as many telephone messages as does one ton of copper wire.

This steady drop in the raw material intensity of manufacturing processes and manufacturing products extends to energy as well, and especially to petroleum. To produce 100 pounds of fiberglass cable requires no more than 5 percent of the energy needed to produce one ton of copper wire. Similarly, plastics, which are increasingly replacing steel in automobile bodies, represent a raw material cost, including energy, of less than half that of steel.

Thus it is quite unlikely that raw material prices will ever rise substantially as compared to the prices of manufactured goods (or high-knowledge services such as information, education or health care) except in the event of a major prolonged war.

One implication of this sharp shift in the terms of trade of primary products concerns the developed countries, both major raw material exporters like the United States and major raw material importing countries such as Japan. For two centuries the United States has made maintenance of open markets for its farm products and raw materials central to its international trade policy. This is what it has always meant by an "open world economy" and by "free trade."

Does this still make sense, or does the United States instead have to accept that foreign markets for its foodstuffs and raw materials are in a long-term and irreversible decline? Conversely, does it still make sense for Japan to base its international economic policy on the need to earn enough foreign exchange to pay for imports of raw materials and foodstuffs? Since Japan opened to the outside world 120 years ago, preoccupation—amounting almost to a national obsession—with its dependence on raw material and food imports has been the driving force of Japan's policy, and not in economics alone. Now Japan might well start out with the assumption—a far more realistic one in today's world—that foodstuffs and raw materials are in permanent oversupply.

Taken to their logical conclusion, these developments might mean that some variant of the traditional Japanese policy—highly mercantilist with a strong de-emphasis of domestic consumption in favor of an equally strong emphasis on capital formation, and protection of infant industries—might suit the United States better than its own tradition. The Japanese might be better served by some variant of America's traditional policies, especially a shifting from favoring savings and capital formation to favoring consumption. Is such a radical break with more than a century of political convictions and commitments likely? From now on the fundamentals of economic policy are certain to come under increasing criticism in these two countries—and in all other developed countries as well.

These fundamentals will, moreover, come under the increasingly intense scrutiny of major Third World nations. For if primary products are becoming of marginal importance to the economies of the developed world, traditional development theories and policies are losing their foundations.[7] They are based on the assumption—historically a perfectly valid one—that developing countries pay for imports of capital goods by exporting primary materials—farm and forest products, minerals, metals. All development theories, however much they differ otherwise, further assume that raw material purchases by the industrially developed countries must rise at least as fast as industrial production in these countries. This in turn implies that, over any extended period of time, any raw material producer becomes a better credit risk and shows a more favorable balance of trade. These premises have become highly doubtful. On what foundation, then, can economic development be based, especially in countries that do not have a large enough population to develop an industrial economy based on the home market? As we shall presently see, these countries can no longer base their economic development on low labor costs.

The second major change in the world economy is the uncoupling of manufacturing production from manufacturing employment. Increased manufacturing production in developed countries has actually come to mean *decreasing* blue-collar employment. As a consequence, labor costs are becoming less and less important as a "comparative cost" and as a factor in competition.

There is a great deal of talk these days about the "de-industrialization" of America. In fact, manufacturing production has risen steadily in absolute volume and has remained unchanged as a percentage of the total economy. Since the end of the Korean War, that is, for more than 30 years, it has held steady at 23–24 percent of America's total GNP. It has similarly remained at its traditional level in all of the other major industrial countries.

It is not even true that American industry is doing poorly as an exporter. To be sure, the United States is importing from both Japan and Germany many more manufactured goods than ever before. But it is also exporting more, despite the heavy disadvantages of an expensive dollar, increasing labor costs and the near-collapse of a major industrial market, Latin America. In 1984—the year the dollar soared—exports of American manufactured goods rose by 8.3 percent; and they went up again in 1985. The share of U.S.-manufactured exports in world exports was 17 percent in 1978. By 1985 it had risen to 20 percent—while West Germany accounted for 18 percent and Japan 16. The three countries together thus account for more than half of the total.

Thus it is not the American economy that is being "de-industrialized." It is the American labor force.

Between 1973 and 1985, manufacturing production (measured in constant dollars) in the United States rose by almost 40 percent. Yet manufacturing employment during that period went down steadily. There are now five million fewer people employed in blue-collar work in American manufacturing industry than there were in 1975.

Yet in the last 12 years total employment in the United States grew faster than at any time in the peacetime history of any country—from 82 to 110 million between 1973 and 1985—that is, by a full one-third. The entire growth, however, was in non-manufacturing, and especially in non-blue-collar jobs.

The trend itself is not new. In the 1920s one out of every three Americans in the labor force was a blue-collar worker in manufacturing. In the 1950s the figure was one in four. It now is down to one in every six—and dropping. While the trend has been running for a long time, it has lately accelerated to the point where—in peacetime at least—no increase in manufacturing production, no matter how large, is likely to reverse the long-term decline in the number of blue-collar jobs in manufacturing or in their proportion of the labor force.

This trend is the same in all developed countries, and is, indeed, even more pronounced in Japan. It is therefore highly probable that in 25 years developed countries such as the United States and Japan will employ no larger a proportion of the labor force in manufacturing than developed countries now employ in farming—at most, 10 percent. Today the United States employs around 18 million people in blue-collar jobs in manufacturing industries. By 2010, the number is likely to be no more than 12 million. In some major industries the drop will be even sharper. It is quite unrealistic, for instance, to expect that the American automobile industry will employ more than one-third of its present blue-collar force 25 years hence, even though production might be 50 percent higher.

If a company, an industry or a country does not in the next quarter century sharply increase manufacturing production and at the same time sharply reduce the blue-collar work force, it cannot hope to remain competitive—or even to remain "developed." It would decline fairly fast. Britain has been in industrial decline for the last 25 years, largely because the number of blue-collar workers per unit of manufacturing production went down far more slowly than in all other non-communist developed countries. Even so, Britain has the highest unemployment rate among non-communist developed countries—more than 13 percent.

The British example indicates a new and critical economic equation: a country, an industry or a company that puts the preservation of blue-collar manufacturing jobs ahead of international competitiveness (which implies a steady shrinkage of such jobs) will soon have neither production nor jobs. The attempt to preserve such blue-collar jobs is actually a prescription for unemployment.

So far, this concept has achieved broad national acceptance only in Japan.[8] Indeed, Japanese planners, whether in government or private business, start out with the assumption of a doubling of production within 15 to 20 years based on a cut in blue-collar employment of 25 to 40 percent. A good many large American companies such as IBM, General Electric and the big automobile companies have similar forecasts. Implicit in this is the conclusion that a country will have less overall unemployment the faster it shrinks blue-collar employment in manufacturing.

This is not a conclusion that American politicians, labor leaders or indeed the general public can easily understand or accept. What confuses the issue even more is that the United States is experiencing several separate and different shifts in the manufacturing economy. One is the acceleration of the substitution of knowledge and capital for manual labor. Where we spoke of mechanization a few decades ago, we now speak of "robotization" or "automation." This is actually more a change in terminology than a change in reality. When Henry Ford introduced the assembly line in 1909, he cut the number of man-hours required to produce a motor car by some 80 percent in two or three years—far more than anyone expects to result from even the most complete robotization. But there is no doubt that we are facing a new, sharp acceleration in the replacement of manual workers by machines—that is, by the products of knowledge.

A second development—and in the long run this may be even more important—is the shift from industries that were primarily labor-intensive to industries that, from the beginning, are knowledge-intensive. The manufacturing costs of the semiconductor microchip are about 70 percent knowledge—that is, research, development and testing—and no more than 12 percent labor. Similarly with prescription drugs, labor represents no more than 15 percent, with knowledge representing almost 50 percent. By contrast, in the most fully robotized automobile plant labor would still account for 20 to 25 percent of the costs.

Another perplexing development in manufacturing is the reversal of the dynamics of size. Since the early years of this century, the trend in all developed countries has been toward ever larger manufacturing plants. The economies of scale greatly favored them. Perhaps equally important, what one might call the "economies of management" favored them. Until recently, modern management techniques seemed applicable only to fairly large units.

This has been reversed with a vengeance over the last 15 to 20 years. The entire shrinkage in manufacturing jobs in the United States has occurred in large companies, beginning with the giants in steel and automobiles. Small and especially medium-sized manufacturers have either held their own or actually added employees. In respect to market standing, exports and profitability too, smaller and middle-sized businesses have done remarkably better than big ones. The reversal of the dynamics of size is occurring in the other developed countries as well, even in Japan where bigger was always better and biggest meant best. The trend has reversed itself even in old industries. The most profitable automobile company these last years has not been one of the giants, but a medium-sized manufacturer in Germany—BMW. The only profitable steel companies, whether in the United States, Sweden or Japan, have been medium-sized makers of specialty products such as oil drilling pipe.

In part, especially in the United States, this is a result of a resurgence of entrepreneurship.[9] But perhaps equally important, we have learned in the last 30 years how to manage the small and medium-sized enterprise to the point where the advantages of smaller size, e.g., ease of communications and nearness to market and customer, increasingly outweigh what had been forbidding management limitations. Thus in the United States, but increasingly in the other leading manufacturing nations such as Japan and West Germany as well, the dynamism in the economy has shifted from the very big companies that dominated the world's industrial economy for 30 years after World War II to companies that, while much smaller, are professionally managed and largely publicly financed.

Two distinct kinds of "manufacturing industry" are emerging. One is material-based, represented by the industries that provided economic growth in the first three-quarters of this century. The other is information- and knowledge-based: pharmaceuticals, telecommunications, analytical instruments and information processing such as computers. It is largely the information-based manufacturing industries that are growing.

These two groups differ not only in their economic characteristics but especially in their position in the international economy. The products of material-based industries have to be exported or imported as "products." They appear in the balance of trade. The products of information-based industries can be exported or imported both as "products" and as "services," which may not appear accurately in the overall trade balance.

An old example is the printed book. For one major scientific publishing company, "foreign earnings" account for two-thirds of total revenues. Yet the company exports few, if any, actual books—books are heavy. It sells "rights," and the "product" is produced abroad. Similarly, the most profitable computer "export sales" may actually show up in trade statistics as an "import." This is the fee some of the world's leading banks, multinationals and Japanese trading companies get for processing in their home office data arriving electronically from their branches and customers around the world.

In all developed countries, "knowledge" workers have already become the center of gravity of the labor force. Even in manufacturing they will outnumber blue-collar workers within ten years. Exporting knowledge so that it produces license income, service fees and royalties may actually create substantially more jobs than exporting goods.

This in turn requires—as official Washington seems to have realized—far greater emphasis in trade policy on "invisible trade" and on abolishing the barriers to the trade in services. Traditionally, economists have treated invisible trade as a stepchild, if they noted it at all. Increasingly, it will become central. Within 20 years major developed countries may find that their income from invisible trade is larger than their income from exports.

Another implication of the "uncoupling" of manufacturing production from manufacturing employment is, however, that the choice between an industrial policy that favors industrial *production* and one that favors industrial *employment* is going to be a singularly contentious political issue for the rest of this century. Historically these have always been considered two sides of the same coin. From now on the two will increasingly pull in different directions; they are indeed already becoming alternatives, it not incompatible.

Benign neglect—the policy of the Reagan Administration these last few years—may be the best policy one can hope for, and the only one with a chance of success. It is probably not an accident that the United States has, after Japan, by far the lowest unemployment rate of any industrially developed country. Still, there is surely need also for systematic efforts to retrain and to place redundant blue-collar workers—something no one as yet knows how to do successfully.

Finally, low labor costs are likely to become less of an advantage in international trade simply because in the developed countries they are going to account for less of total costs. Moreover, the total costs of automated processes are lower than even those of traditional plants with low labor costs; this is mainly because automation eliminates the hidden but high costs of "not working," such as the expense of poor quality and rejects, and the costs of shutting down the machinery to change from one model of a product to another. Consider two automated American producers of televisions, Motorola and RCA. Both were almost driven out of the market by imports from countries with much lower labor costs. Both subsequently automated, with the result that these American-made products now successfully compete with foreign imports. Similarly, some highly automated textile mills in the Carolinas can underbid imports from countries with very low labor costs such as Thailand. On the other hand, although some American semiconductor companies have lower labor costs because they do the labor-intensive work off-shore, e.g., in West Africa, they are still the high-cost producers and easily underbid by the heavily automated Japanese. . . .

The third major change that has occurred in the world economy is the emergence of the "symbol" economy—capital movements, exchange rates and credit flows—as the flywheel of the world economy, in place of the "real" economy—the flow of goods and services. The two economies seem to be operating increasingly independently. This is both the most visible and the least understood of the changes. . . .

Traditional international economic theory is still neoclassical, holding that trade in goods and services determines international capital flows and foreign exchange rates. Capital flows and foreign exchange rates since the first half of the 1970s have, however, moved quite independently of foreign trade, and indeed (e.g., in the rise of the dollar in 1984–85) have run counter to it. . . .

From now on exchange rates between major currencies will have to be treated in economic theory and business policy alike as a "comparative-advantage" factor, and a major one.

Economic theory teaches that the comparative-advantage factors of the "real" economy—comparative labor costs and labor productivity, raw material costs, energy costs, transportation costs and the like—determine exchange rates. Practically all businesses base their policies on this notion. Increasingly, however, it is exchange rates that decide how labor costs in country A compare to labor costs in country B. Exchange rates are thus a major "comparative cost" and one totally beyond business control. Any firm exposed to the international economy has to realize that it is in two businesses at the same time. It is both a maker of goods (or a supplier of services) and a "financial" business. It cannot disregard either.

Specifically, the business that sells abroad—whether as an exporter or through a subsidiary—will have to protect itself against three foreign exchange exposures: proceeds from sales, working capital devoted to manufacturing for overseas markets, and investments abroad. This will have to be done whether the business expects the value of its own currency to go up or down. Businesses that buy abroad will have to do likewise. Indeed, even purely domestic businesses that face foreign competition in their home market will have to learn to hedge against the currency in which their main competitors produce. If American businesses had been run this way during the years of the overvalued dollar, from 1982 through 1985, most of the losses in market standing abroad and in foreign earnings might have been prevented. They were management failures, not acts of God. Surely stockholders, but also the public in general, have every right to expect management to do better the next time around. . . .

We are left with one conclusion: economic dynamics have decisively shifted from the national economy to the world economy. . . .

NOTES

1. When the price of petroleum dropped to $15 a barrel in February 1986, it was actually below its 1933 price (adjusted for the change in the purchasing power of the dollar). It was still, however, substantially higher than its all-time low in 1972–73, which in 1986 dollars amounted to $7–$8 a barrel.
2. On this see two quite different discussions by Dennis Avery, "U.S. Farm Dilemma: The Global Bad News Is Wrong," *Science,* Oct. 25, 1985; and Barbara Insel, "A World Awash in Grain," *Foreign Affairs,* Spring 1985.

3. The business cycle theory was developed just before World War I by the Russian mathematical economist Nikolai Kondratieff, who made comprehensive studies of raw material price cycles and their impacts all the way back to 1797.

4. These conclusions are based on static analysis, which presumes that which products are bought and sold is not affected by changes in price. This is of course unrealistic, but the flaw should not materially affect the conclusions.

5. Although the African famine looms large in our consciousness, the total population of the affected areas is far too small to make any dent in world food surpluses.

6. David Sapsford, *Real Primary Commodity Prices: An Analysis of Long-Run Movements*, International Monetary Fund Internal Memorandum, May 17, 1985, (unpublished).

7. This was asserted as early as 1950 by the South American economist Raúl Prebisch in *The Economic Development of Latin America and Its Principal Problems* (E/CN.12/89/REV.1), United Nations Economic Commission for Latin America. But then no one, including myself, believed him.

8. The Japanese government, for example, sponsors a finance company that makes long-term, low interest loans to small manufacturers to enable them to automate rapidly.

9. On this see my book, *Innovation and Entrepreneurship: Practice and Principles*, New York: Harper & Row, 1985.

Globalization and Governance

KENNETH N. WALTZ

In 1979 I described the interdependence of states as low but increasing. It has increased, but only to about the 1910 level if measured by trade or capital flows as a percentage of GNP; lower if measured by the mobility of labor, and lower still if measured by the mutual military dependence of states. Yet one feels that the world has become a smaller one. International travel has become faster, easier, and cheaper; music, art, cuisines, and cinema have all become cosmopolitan in the world's major centers and beyond. The *Peony Pavilion* was produced in its entirety for the first time in 400 years, and it was presented not in Shanghai or Beijing, but in New York. Communication is almost instantaneous, and more than words can be transmitted, which makes the reduced mobility of labor of less consequence. High-technology jobs can be brought to the workers instead of the workers to the jobs; foreigners can become part of American design teams without leaving their homelands. Before World War I, the close interdependence of states was thought of as heralding an era of peace among nations and democracy and prosperity within them. Associating interdependence, peace, democracy, and prosperity is nothing new. In his much translated and widely read book, *The Great Illusion* (1933), Norman Angell summed up the texts of generations of classical and neo-classical economists and drew from them the dramatic conclusion that wars would no longer be fought because they would not pay. World War I instead produced the great disillusion, which reduced political optimism to a level that remained low almost until the end of the Cold War. I say "almost" because beginning in the 1970s a new optimism, strikingly similar in content to the old, began to resurface. Interdependence was again associated with peace and peace increasingly with democracy, which began to spread wonderfully to Latin America, to Asia, and with the Soviet Union's collapse, to Eastern Europe. Francis Fukuyama (1992) foresaw a time when all states would be liberal democracies and, more recently, Michael Doyle (1997) projected the year for it to happen as lying between 2050 and 2100. John Mueller (1989), heralding the disappearance of war among the world's advanced countries, argued that Norman Angell's premises were right all along, but that he had published his book prematurely.

Robert Keohane and Joseph Nye in their 1977 book, *Power and Interdependence,* strengthened the notion that interdependence promotes peace and limits

From "Globalization and Governance" by Kenneth N. Waltz from *PS: Political Science and Politics,* Vol. 32, No. 4 (December 1999) pp. 693-700 with minor revisions. Copyright © 1999 by Cambridge University Press. Reprinted with the permission of Cambridge University Press.

the use of force by arguing that simple interdependence had become complex interdependence, binding the economic and hence the political interests of states ever more tightly together. Now, we hear from many sides that interdependence has reached yet another height, transcending states and making *The Borderless World,* which is the title and theme of Kenichi Ohmae's 1990 book. People, firms, markets matter more; states matter less. Each tightening of the economic screw raises the benefits of economic exchange and makes war among the more advanced states increasingly costly. The simple and plausible propositions are that as the benefits of peace rise, so do the costs of war. When states perceive wars to be immensely costly, they will be disinclined to fight them. War becomes rare, but is not abolished because even the strongest economic forces cannot conquer fear or eliminate concern for national honor (Friedman 1999, 196–97).

Economic interests become so strong that markets begin to replace politics at home and abroad. That economics depresses politics and limits its significance is taken to be a happy thought. The first section of this paper examines its application domestically; the second, internationally.

THE STATE OF THE STATE

Globalization is the fad of the 1990s, and globalization is made in America. Thomas Friedman's *The Lexus and the Olive Tree* is a celebration of the American way, of market capitalism and liberal democracy. Free markets, transparency, and flexibility are the watchwords. The "electronic herd" moves vast amounts of capital in and out of countries according to their political and economic merits. Capital moves almost instantaneously into countries with stable governments, progressive economies, open accounting, and honest dealing, and out of countries lacking those qualities. States can defy the "herd," but they will pay a price, usually a steep one, as did Thailand, Malaysia, Indonesia, and South Korea in the 1990s. Some countries may defy the herd inadvertently (the countries just mentioned); others, out of ideological conviction (Cuba and North Korea); some, because they can afford to (oil-rich countries); others, because history has passed them by (many African countries).

Countries wishing to attract capital and to gain the benefits of today's and tomorrow's technology have to don the "golden straitjacket," a package of policies including balanced budgets, economic deregulation, openness to investment and trade, and a stable currency. The herd decides which countries to reward and which to punish, and nothing can be done about its decisions. In September 1997, at a World Bank meeting, Malaysia's prime minister, Dr. Mahathir Mohammad, complained bitterly that great powers and international speculators had forced Asian countries to open their markets and had manipulated their currencies in order to destroy them. Friedman (1999, 93) wonders what Robert Rubin, then-U.S. treasury secretary, might have said in response. He imagines it would have been something like this: "What planet are you living on? . . . Globalization isn't a choice, it's a reality, . . . and the only way you can grow at the speed that your people want to grow is by tapping into the global stock and bond markets, by seeking out multinationals to invest in your country, and by selling into the global trading system what your factories produce. And the most basic truth about globalization is this: *No one is in charge.*"

The herd has no telephone number. When the herd decides to withdraw capital from a country, there is no one to complain to or to petition for relief. Decisions of the herd are collective ones. They are not made; they happen, and they happen because many investors individually make decisions simultaneously and on similar grounds to invest or to withdraw their funds. Do what displeases the herd, and it will trample you into the ground. Globalization is shaped by markets, not by governments.

Globalization means homogenization. Prices, products, wages, wealth, and rates of interest and profit tend to become the same all over the world. Like any powerful movement for change, globalization encounters resistance—in America, from religious fundamentalists; abroad, from anti-Americanists; everywhere from cultural traditionalists. And the resisters become bitter because consciously or not they know they are doomed. Driven by technology, international finance sweeps all before it. Under the protection of American military power, globalization proceeds relentlessly. As Friedman proclaims: "America truly is the ultimate benign hegemony" (375).

The "end of the Cold War and the collapse of communism have discredited all models other than liberal democracy." The statement is by Larry Diamond, and Friedman repeats it with approval. There is one best way, and America has found it. "It's a post-industrial world, and America today is good at everything that is post-industrial" (145, 303). The herd does not care about forms of government as such, but it values and rewards "stability, predictability, transparency, and the ability to transfer and protect its private property." Liberal democracies represent the one best way. The message to all governments is clear: Conform or suffer.

There is much in what Friedman says, and he says it very well. But how much? And, specifically, what is the effect of closer interdependence on the conduct of the internal and external affairs of nations?

First, we should ask how far globalization has proceeded? As everyone knows, much of the world has been left aside: most of Africa and Latin America, Russia, all of the Middle East except Israel, and large parts of Asia. Moreover, for many countries, the degree of participation in the global economy varies by region. Northern Italy, for example, is in; southern Italy is out. In fact, globalization is not global but is mainly limited to northern latitudes. Linda Weiss points out that, as of 1991, 81% of the world stock of foreign direct investment was in high-wage countries of the north: mainly the United States, followed by the United Kingdom, Germany, and Canada. She adds that the extent of concentration has grown by 12 points since 1967 (Weiss 1998; cf., Hirst and Thompson 1996, 72).

Second, we should compare the interdependence of nations now with interdependence earlier. The first paragraph of this paper suggests that in most ways we have not exceeded levels reached in 1910. The rapid growth of international trade and investment from the middle 1850s into the 1910s preceded a prolonged period of war, internal revolution, and national insularity. After World War II, protectionist policies lingered as the United States opened its borders to trade while taking a relaxed attitude toward countries that protected their markets during the years of recovery from war's devastation. One might say that from 1914 into the 1960s an interdependence deficit developed, which helps to explain the steady growth of interdependence thereafter. Among the richest 24 industrial economies (the OECD countries), exports grew at about twice the rate of GDP after 1960. In 1960, exports were 9.5% of their GDPs; in 1900, 20.5% (Wade 1996, 62; cf., Weiss 1998, 171). Finding that 1999 approximately equals 1910 in extent of interdependence is hardly surprising. What is true of trade also holds for capital flows, again as a percentage of GDP (Hirst and Thompson 1996, 36).

Third, money markets may be the only economic sector one can say has become truly global. Finance capital moves freely across the frontiers of OECD countries and quite freely elsewhere (Weiss 1998, xii). Robert Wade notes that real interest rates within northern countries and between northern and southern countries vary by no more than 5%. This seems quite large until one notices variations across countries of 10 to 50 times in real wages, years of schooling, and numbers of working scientists. Still, with the movement of financial assets as with commodities, the present remains like the past. Despite today's ease of communication, financial markets at the turn of the previous century were at least as integrated as they are now (Wade 1996, 73–75).

Obviously, the world is not one. Sadly, the disparities of the North and South remain wide. Perhaps surprisingly, among the countries that are thought of as being in the zone of globalization, differences are considerable and persistent. To take just one example, financial patterns differ markedly across countries. The United States depends on capital imports, Western Europe does not, and Japan is a major capital exporter. The more closely one looks, the more one finds variations. That is hardly surprising. What looks smooth, uniform, and simple from a distance, on closer inspection proves to be pockmarked, variegated, and complex. Yet here, the variations are large enough to sustain the conclusion that globalization, even within its zone, is not a statement about the present, but a prediction about the future.

Many globalizers underestimate the extent to which the new looks like the old. In any competitive system the winners are imitated by the losers, or they continue to lose. In political as in economic development, latecomers imitate the practices and adopt the institution of the countries who have shown the way. Occasionally, someone finds a way to outflank, to invent a new way, or to ingeniously modify an old way to gain an advantage; and then the process of imitation begins anew. That competitors begin to look like one another if the competition is close and continuous is a familiar story. Competition among states has always led some of them to imitate others politically, militarily, and economically; but the apostles of globalization argue that the process has now sped up immensely and that the straitjacket allows little room to wiggle. In the old political era, the strong vanquished the weak; in the new economic era, "the fast eat the slow" (Klaus Schwab quoted in Friedman 1999, 171). No longer is it "Do what the strong party says or risk physical punishment"; but instead "Do what the electronic herd requires or remain impoverished." But then, in a competitive system there are always winners and losers. A few do exceptionally well, some get along, and many bring up the rear.

States have to conform to the ways of the more successful among them or pay a stiff price for not doing so. We then have to ask what is the state of the state? What becomes of politics within the coils of encompassing economic processes? The message of globalizers is that economic and technological forces impose near uniformity of political and economic forms and functions on states. They do so because the herd is attracted only to countries with reliable, stable, and open governments—that is, to liberal democratic ones.

Yet a glance at just the past 75 years reveals that a variety of political-economic systems have produced impressive results and were admired in their day for doing so. In the 1930s and again in the 1950s, the Soviet Union's economic growth rates were among the world's highest, so impressive in the '50s that America feared being overtaken and passed by. In the 1960s President Kennedy got "the country moving again," and America's radically different system gained world respect. In the '70s, Western European welfare states with managed and directed economics were highly regarded. In the late '70s and through much of the '80s, the Japanese brand of neomercantilism was thought to be the wave of the future; and Western Europe and the United States worried about being able to keep up. Imitate or perish was the counsel of some; pry the Japanese economy open and make it compete on our grounds was the message of others. America did not succeed in doing much of either. Yet in the 1990s, its economy has flourished. Globalizers offer it as the ultimate political-economic model—and so history again comes to an end. Yet it is odd to conclude from a decade's experience that the one best model has at last appeared. Globalization, if it were realized, would mean a near uniformity of conditions across countries. Even in the 1990s, one finds little evidence of globalization. The advanced countries of the world have enjoyed or suffered quite different fates. Major Western European countries were plagued by high and persistent unemployment; Northeast and Southeast Asian countries experienced economic stagnation or collapse while China continued to do quite well; and we know about the United States.

Variation in the fortunes of nations underlines the point: The country that has done best, at least lately, is the United States. Those who have fared poorly have supposedly done so because they have failed to conform to the American Way. Globalizers do not claim that globalization is complete, but only that it is in process and that the process is irreversible. Some evidence supports the conclusion; some does not. Looking at the big picture, one notices that nations whose economies have faltered or failed have been more fully controlled, directed, and supported governmentally than the American economy. Soviet-style economies failed miserably; in China, only the free-market sector flourishes; the once much-favored Swedish model has proved wanting. One can easily add more examples. From them it is tempting to leap to the conclusion that America has indeed found, or stumbled onto, the one best way.

Obviously, Thomas Friedman thinks so. Tip O'Neill, when he was a congressman from Massachusetts, declared that all politics are local. Wrong, Friedman says, all politics have become global. "The electronic herd," he writes, "turns the whole world into a parliamentary system, in which every government lives under the fear of a no-confidence vote from the herd" (1999, 62, 115).

I find it hard to believe that economic processes direct or determine a nation's policies, that spontaneously arrived at decisions about where to place resources reward or punish a national economy so strongly that a government either does what pleases the "herd" or its economy fails to prosper or even risks collapse. We all recall recent cases, some of them mentioned above, that seem to support Friedman's thesis. Mentioning them both makes a point and raises doubts.

First, within advanced countries at similar levels of development that are closely interrelated, one expects uniformities of form and function to be most fully displayed. Yet Stephen Woolcock, looking at forms of corporate governance within the European community, finds a "spectrum of approaches" and expects it to persist for the foreseeable future (1996, 196). Since the 1950s, the economies of Germany and France have grown more closely together as each became the principal trading partner of the other. Yet a study of the two countries concludes that France has copied German policies but has been unwilling or unable to copy institutions (Boltho 1996). GDP per work hour among seven of the most prosperous countries came close together between the 1950s and the 1980s (Boyer 1996, 37). Countries at a high level of development do tend to converge in productivity, but that is something of a tautology.

Second, even if all politics have become global, economies remain local perhaps to a surprising extent. Countries with large economies continue to do most of their business at home. Americans produce 88% of the goods they buy. Sectors that are scarcely involved in international trade, such as government, construction, nonprofit organizations, utilities, and wholesale and retail trade employ 82% of Americans (Lawrence 1997, 21). As Paul Krugman says, "The United States is still almost 90% an economy that produces goods and services for its own use" (1997, 166). For the world's three largest economies—the United States, Japan, and the European Union—taken as a unit, exports are 12% or less of GDP (Weiss 1998, 176). What I found to be true in 1970 remains true today: The world is less interdependent than is usually supposed (Waltz 1970). Moreover, developed countries, oil imports aside, do the bulk of their external business with one another, and that means that the extent of their dependence on commodities that they could not produce for themselves is further reduced.

Reinforcing the parochial pattern of productivity, the famous footloose corporations in fact turn out to be firmly anchored in their home bases. One study of the world's 100 largest corporations concludes that not one of them could be called truly "global" or "footloose." Another study found one multinational corporation that seemed to be leaving its home base: Britain's chemical company, ICI (Weiss 1998, 18, 22; cf., Hirst and Thompson 1996, 82–93, 90, 95ff.). On all the important counts—location of most assets, site of research and development, ownership, and management—the importance of a corporation's home base is marked. And the technological prowess of corporations corresponds closely to that of the countries in which they are located.

Third, the *"transformative capacity"* of states, as Linda Weiss emphasizes, is the key to their success in the world economy (Weiss 1998, xii). Because technological innovation is rapid, and because economic conditions at home and abroad change often, states that adapt easily have considerable advantages. International politics remains inter-national. As the title of a review by William H. McNeill (1997) puts it, "Territorial States Buried Too Soon." Global or world politics has not taken over from national politics. The twentieth century was the century of the nation-state. The twenty-first will be too. Trade and technology do not determine a single best way to organize a polity and its economy. National systems display a great deal of resilience. States still have a wide range of choice. Most states survive, and the units that survive in competitive systems are those with the ability to adapt. Some do it well, and they grow and prosper. Others just manage to get along. That's the way it is in competitive systems. In this spirit, Ezra Taft Benson, when he was President Eisenhower's secretary of agriculture, gave this kindly advice to America's small farmers: "Get big or get out." Success in competitive systems requires the units of the system to adopt ways they would prefer to avoid.

States adapt to their environment. Some are light afoot, and others are heavy. The United States looked to be heavy afoot in the 1980s when Japan's economy was booming. Sometimes it seemed that MITI (Ministry of International Trade and Industry) was manned by geniuses who guided Japan's economy effortlessly to its impressive accomplishments. Now it is the United States that appears light afoot, lighter than any other country. Its government is open: Accurate financial information flows freely, most economic decisions are made by private firms. These are the characteristics that make for flexibility and for quick adaptation to changing conditions.

Competitive systems select for success. Over time, the qualities that make for success vary. Students of American government point out that one of the advantages of a federal system is that the separate states can act as laboratories for social-economic experimentation. When some states succeed, others may imitate them. The same thought applies to nations. One must wonder who the next winner will be.

States adapt; they also protect themselves. Different nations, with distinct institutions and traditions, protect themselves in different ways. Japan fosters industries, defends them, and manages its trade. The United States uses its political, economic, and military leverage to protect itself and manipulate international events to promote its interests. Thus, as David E. Spiro elaborately shows, international markets and institutions did not recycle petrodollars after 1974. The United States did. Despite many statements to the contrary, the United States worked effectively through different administrations and under different cabinet secretaries to undermine markets and thwart international institutions. Its leverage enabled it to manipulate the oil crisis to serve its own interests (1999, chap. 6).

Many of the interdependers of the 1970s expected the state to wither and fade away. Charles Kindleberger wrote in 1969 that "the nation-state is just about through as an economic unit" (207). Globalizers of the 1990s believe that this time it really is happening. The state has lost its "monopoly over internal sovereignty," Wolfgang H. Reinecke writes, and as "an externally sovereign actor" it "will become a thing of the past" (1997, 137; cf., Thurow 1999). Internally, the state's monopoly has never been complete, but it seems more nearly so now than earlier, at least in well-established states. The range of governmental functions and the extent of state control over society and economy has seldom been fuller than it is now. In many parts of the world the concern has been not with the state's diminished internal powers but with their increase. And although state control has lessened somewhat recently, does anyone believe that the United States and Britain, for example, are back to a 1930s level, let alone to a nineteenth-century level of governmental regulation?

States perform essential political social-economic functions, and no other organization appears as a possible competitor to them. They foster the institutions that make internal peace and prosperity possible. In the state of nature, as Kant put it, there is "no mine and thine." States turn possession into property and thus make saving, production, and prosperity possible. The sovereign state with fixed borders has proved to be the best organization for keeping peace and fostering the conditions for economic well being.[1] We do not have to wonder what happens to society and economy when a state begins to fade away. We have all too many examples. A few obvious ones are China in the 1920s and '30s and again in the 1960s and '70s, post-Soviet Russia, and many African states since their independence. The less competent a state, the likelier it is to dissolve into component parts or to be unable to adapt to transnational developments. Challenges at home and abroad test the mettle of states. Some states fail, and other states pass the tests nicely. In modern times, enough states always make it to keep the international system going as a system of states. The challenges vary; states endure. They have proved to be hardy survivors.

Having asked how international conditions affect states, I now reverse the question and ask how states affect the conduct of international political affairs.

THE STATE IN INTERNATIONAL POLITICS

Economic globalization would mean that the world economy, or at least the globalized portion of it, would be integrated and not merely interdependent. The difference between an interdependent and an integrated world is a qualitative one and not a mere matter of proportionately more trade and a greater and more rapid flow of capital. With integration, the world would look like one big state. Economic markets and economic interests cannot perform the functions of government. Integration requires or presumes a government to protect, direct, and control. Interdependence, in contrast to integration, is "the mere mutualism" of states, as Émile Durkheim put it. It is not only less close than usually thought but also politically less consequential. Interdependence did not produce the world-shaking events of 1989–91. A political event, the failure of one of the world's two great powers, did that. Had the configuration of international politics not fundamentally changed, neither the unification of Germany nor the war against Saddam Hussein would have been possible. The most important events in international politics are explained by differences in the capabilities of states, not by economic forces operating across states or transcending them. Interdependers, and globalizers even more so, argue that the international economic interests of states work against their going to war. True, they do. Yet if one asks whether economic interests or nuclear weapons inhibit war more strongly, the answer obviously is nuclear weapons. European great powers prior to World War I were tightly tied together economically. They nevertheless fought a long and bloody war. The United States and the Soviet Union were not even loosely connected economically. They co-existed peacefully through the four-and-a-half decades of the Cold War. The most important causes of peace, as of war, are found in international-political conditions, including the weaponry available to states. Events following the Cold War dramatically demonstrate the political weakness of economic forces. The integration (not just the interdependence) of the parts of the Soviet Union and of Yugoslavia, with all of their entangling economic interests, did not prevent their disintegration. Governments and people sacrifice welfare and even security to nationalism, ethnicity, and religion.

Political explanations weigh heavily in accounting for international-political events. National *politics*, not international markets, account for many international *economic* developments. A number of students of politics and of economics believe that blocs are becoming more common internationally. Economic interests and market forces do not create blocs; governments do. Without governmental decisions, the Coal and Steel Community, the European Economic Community, and the European Union would not have emerged. The representatives of states negotiate regulations in the European Commission. The Single-Market Act of 1985 provided that some types of directives would require less than a unanimous vote in the Council of Ministers. This political act cleared the way for passage of most of the harmonization standards for Europe (Dumez and Jeunemaître 1996, 229). American governments forged NAFTA; Japan fashioned an East and Southeast Asian producing and trading area. The decisions and acts of a country, or a set of countries arriving at political agreements, shape international political and economic institutions. Governments now intervene much more in international economic matters than they did in the earlier era of interdependence. Before World War I, foreign-ministry officials were famed for their lack of knowledge of, or interest in, economic affairs. Because governments have become much more active in economic affairs at home and abroad, interdependence has become less of an autonomous force in international politics.

The many commentators who exaggerate the closeness of interdependence, and even more so those who write of globalization, think in unit rather than in systemic terms. Many small states import and export large shares of their gross domestic products. States with large GDPs do not. They are little dependent on others, while a number of other states heavily depend on them. The terms of political, economic, and military competition are set by the larger units of the international-political system. Through centuries of multipolarity, with five or so great powers of comparable size competing with one another, the international system was quite closely interdependent. Under bi- and unipolarity the degree of interdependence declined markedly.

States are differentiated from one another not by function but primarily by capability. For two reasons, inequalities across states have greater political impact than inequalities across income groups within states. First, the inequalities of states are larger and have been growing more rapidly. Rich countries have become richer while poor countries have remained poor. Second, in a system without central governance, the influence of the units of greater capability is disproportionately large because there are no effective laws and institutions to direct and constrain them. They are able to work the system to their advantage, as the petrodollar example showed. I argued in 1970 that what counts are states' capacity to adjust to external conditions and their ability to use their economic leverage for political advantage. The United States was then and is still doubly blessed. It remains highly important in the international economy, serving as a principal market for a number of countries and as a major supplier of goods and services, yet its dependence on others is quite low. Precisely because the United States is relatively little dependent on others, it has a wide range of policy choices and the ability both to bring pressure on others and to assist them. The "herd" with its capital may flee from countries when it collectively decides that they are politically and economically unworthy, but some countries abroad, like some firms at home, are so important that they cannot be allowed to fail. National governments and international agencies then come to the rescue. The United States is the country that most often has the ability and the will to step in. The agency that most often acts is the IMF, and most countries think of the IMF as the enforcement arm of the U.S. Treasury (Strange 1996, 192). Thomas Friedman believes that when the "herd" makes its decisions, there is no appeal; but often there is an appeal, and it is for a bail out organized by the United States.

The international economy, like national economies, operates within a set of rules and institutions. Rules and institutions have to be made and sustained. Britain, to a large extent, provided this service prior to World War I; no one did between the wars, and the United States has done so since. More than any other state, the United States makes the rules and maintains the institutions that shape the international political economy.

Economically, the United States is the world's most important country; militarily, it is not only the most important country, it is the decisive one. Thomas Friedman puts the point simply: The world is sustained by "the presence of American power and America's willingness to use that power against those who would threaten the system of globalization. . . . The hidden hand of the market will never work without a hidden fist" (1999, 373). But the hidden fist is in full view. On its military forces, the United States outspends the next six or seven big spenders combined. When force is needed to keep or to restore the peace, either the United States leads the way or the peace is not kept. The Cold War militarized international politics. Relations between the United States and the Soviet Union, and among some other countries as well, came to be defined largely in a single dimension, the military one. As the German sociologist Erich Weede has remarked, "National security decision making in some . . . democracies (most notably in West Germany) is actually penetrated by the United States" (1989, 225). . . .

Many globalizers believe that the world is increasingly ruled by markets. Looking at the state among states leads to a different conclusion. The main difference between international politics now and earlier is not found in the increased interdependence of states but in their growing inequality. With the end of bipolarity, the distribution of capabilities across states has become extremely lopsided.

Rather than elevating economic forces and depressing political ones, the inequalities of international politics enhance the political role of one country. Politics, as usual, prevails over economics.

NOTE

1. The picture of the purpose and the performance of states is especially clear in Thomson and Krasner (1989).

REFERENCES

Angell, Norman. 1933. *The Great Illusion.* New York: G.P. Putnam's Sons.
Boltho, Andrea. 1996. "Has France Converged on Germany?" In *National Diversity and Global Capitalism,* ed. Suzanne Berger and Ronald Dore. Ithaca: Cornell University Press.
Bover, Robert. 1996. "The Convergence Hypothesis Revisited: Globalization But Still the Century of Nations." In *National Diversity and Global Capitalism,* ed. Suzanne Berger and Ronald Dore. Ithaca: Cornell University Press.
Carter, Ashton B., and William J. Perry. 1999. *Preventive Defense: A New Security Strategy for America.* Washington, DC: The Brookings Institution.
———, and John D. Steinbruner. 1992. *A New Concept of Cooperative Security.* Washington, DC: The Brookings Institution.
Doyle, Michael W. 1997. *Ways of War and Peace: Realism, Liberalism, and Socialism.* New York: W.W. Norton.
Dumez, Hervé, and Alain Jeunemaître. 1996. "The Convergence of Competition Policies in Europe: Internal Dynamics and External Imposition." In *National Diversity and Global Capitalism,* ed. Suzanne Berger and Ronald Dore. Ithaca: Cornell University Press.
Fukuyama, Francis. 1992. *The End of History and the Last Man.* New York: Free Press.
Friedman, Thomas L. 1999. *The Lexus and the Olive Tree.* New York: Farrar, Straus, Giroux.
Gardner, Lloyd. 1995. *Pay Any Price: Lyndon Johnson and the Wars for Vietnam.* Chicago: I.R. Dee.
Hist, Paul, and Grahame Thompson. 1996. *Globalization in Question: The International Economy and the Possibilities of Governance.* Cambridge, UK: Polity Press.
Huntington, Samuel P. 1999. "The Lonely Superpower." *Foreign Affairs* 78 (March/April).
Ikenberry, John. 1998/99. "Institutions, Strategic Restraint, and the Persistence of American Postwar Order." *International Security* 23 (Winter): 77–78.
Keohane, Robert O., and Joseph S. Nye. 1977. *Power and Interdependence: World Politics in Transition.* Boston: Little, Brown.
Kindleberger, Charles P. 1969. *American Business Abroad.* New Haven: Yale University Press.
Krugman, Paul. 1997. "Competitiveness: A Dangerous Obsession." In *The New Shape of World Politics.* New York: W.W. Norton and *Foreign Affairs.*
Lawrence, Robert Z. 1997. "Workers and Economists II: Resist the Binge." In *The New Shape of Politics.* New York: W.W. Norton and *Foreign Affairs.*
Mueller, John. 1989. *Retreat from Doomsday: The Obsolescence of Major War.* New York: Basic Books.

McNeill, William H. 1997. "Territorial States Buried Too Soon." *Mershon International Studies Review.*

Nye, Joseph Jr. 1999. "Redefining the National Interest." *Foreign Affairs* 78 (July/August).

Ohmae, Kenichi. 1990. *The Borderless World: Power and Strategy in the Interlinked Economy.* New York: HarperBusiness.

Reinecke, Wolfgang H. 1997. "Global Public Policy." *Foreign Affairs* 76 (November/December).

Spiro, David E. 1999. *The Hidden Hand of American Hegemony: Petrodollar Recycling and International Markets.* Ithaca: Cornell University Press.

Strange, Susan. 1996. *The Retreat of the State: The Diffusion of Power in the World Economy.* Cambridge: Cambridge University Press.

Thomson, Janice E., and Stephen D. Krasner. 1989. "Global Transactions and the Consolidation of Sovereignty." In *Global Changes and Theoretical Challenges: Approaches to World Politics for the 1990s,* ed. Ernst-Otto Czempiel and James N. Rosenau. Lexington, MA: Lexington Books.

Thurow, Lester C. 1999. *Building Wealth: The New Rules for Individuals, Companies, and Nations in a Knowledge-Based Economy.* New York: HarperCollins.

Wade, Robert. 1996. "Globalization and Its Limits: Reports of the Death of the National Economy Are Grossly Exaggerated." In *National Diversity and Global Capitalism,* ed. Suzanne Berger and Ronald Dore. Ithaca: Cornell University Press.

Waltz, Kenneth N. 1970. "The Myth of National Interdependence." In *The International Corporation,* ed. Charles P. Kindleberger. Cambridge, MA: MIT Press.

———. "Structural Realism after the Cold War." Presented at the Annual Meeting of the American Political Science Association, Boston.

Weede, Erich. 1989. "Collective Goods in an Interdependent World: Authority and Order as Determinants of Peace and Prosperity." In *Global Changes and Theoretical Challenges: Approaches to World Politics for the 1990s,* ed. Ernst-Otto Czempiel and James N. Rosenau. Lexington, MA: Lexington Books.

Weiss, Linda. 1998. *The Myth of the Powerless State: Governing the Economy in a Global Era.* Cambridge, UK: Polity Press.

Woolcock, Stephen. 1996. "Competition among Forms of Corporate Governance in the European Community: The Case of Britain." In *National Diversity and Global Capitalism,* ed. Suzanne Berger and Ronald Dore. Ithaca: Cornell University Press.

THE PROS AND CONS OF ■ GLOBALIZATION

Trading in Illusions
■ DANI RODRIK

A senior U.S. Treasury official recently urged Mexico's government to work harder to reduce violent crime because "such high levels of crime and violence may drive away foreign investors." This admonition nicely illustrates how foreign trade and investment have become the ultimate yardstick for evaluating the social and economic policies of governments in developing countries. Forget the slum dwellers or *campesinos* who live amidst crime and poverty throughout the developing world. Just mention "investor sentiment" or "competitiveness in world markets" and policymakers will come to attention in a hurry.

Underlying this perversion of priorities is a remarkable consensus on the imperative of global economic integration. Openness to trade and investment flows is no longer viewed simply as a component of a country's development strategy; it has mutated into the most potent catalyst for economic growth known to humanity. Predictably, senior officials of the World Trade Organization (WTO), International Monetary Fund (IMF), and other international financial agencies incessantly repeat the openness mantra. In recent years, however, faith in integration has spread quickly to political leaders and policymakers around the world.

Joining the world economy is no longer a matter simply of dismantling barriers to trade and investment. Countries now must also comply with a long list of admission requirements, from new patent rules to more rigorous banking standards. The apostles of economic integration prescribe comprehensive institutional reforms that took today's advanced countries generations to accomplish, so that developing countries can, as the cliché goes, maximize the gains and minimize the risks of participation in the world economy. Global integration has become, for all practical purposes, a substitute for a development strategy.

This trend is bad news for the world's poor. The new agenda of global integration rests on shaky empirical ground and seriously distorts policymakers' priorities. By focusing on international integration, governments in poor nations divert human resources, administrative capabilities, and political capital away from more urgent development priorities such as education, public health, industrial capacity, and social cohesion. This emphasis also undermines nascent democratic institutions by removing the choice of development strategy from public debate.

World markets are a source of technology and capital; it would be silly for the developing world not to exploit these opportunities. But globalization is not a shortcut to development. Successful economic growth strategies have always required a judicious blend of imported practices with domestic institutional innovations. Policymakers need to forge a domestic growth strategy by relying on domestic investors and domestic institutions. The costliest downside of the integrationist faith is that it crowds out serious thinking and efforts along such lines.

EXCUSES, EXCUSES

Countries that have bought wholeheartedly into the integration orthodoxy are discovering that openness does not deliver on its promise. Despite sharply lowering their barriers to trade and investment since the 1980s, scores of countries in Latin America and Africa are stagnating or growing less rapidly than in the heyday of import substitution during the 1960s and 1970s. By contrast, the fastest growing countries are China, India, and others in East and Southeast Asia. Policymakers in these countries have also espoused trade and investment liberalization, but they have done so in an unorthodox manner—gradually, sequentially, and only after an initial period of high growth—and as part of a broader policy package with many unconventional features.

The disappointing outcomes with deep liberalization have been absorbed into the faith with remarkable aplomb. Those who view global integration as the prerequisite for economic development now simply add the caveat that opening borders is insufficient. Reaping the gains from openness, they argue, also requires a full complement of institutional reforms.

Consider trade liberalization. Asking any World Bank economist what a successful trade-liberalization program requires will likely elicit a laundry list of measures beyond the simple reduction of tariff and nontariff barriers: tax reform to make up for lost tariff revenues; social safety nets to compensate displaced workers; administrative reform to bring trade practices into compliance with WTO rules; labor market reform to enhance worker mobility across industries; technological assistance to upgrade firms hurt by import competition; and training programs to ensure that export-oriented firms and investors have access to skilled workers. As the promise of trade liberalization fails to materialize, the prerequisites keep expanding. For example, Clare Short, Great Britain's secretary of state for international development, recently added universal provision of health and education to the list.

In the financial arena, integrationists have pushed complementary reforms with even greater fanfare and urgency. The prevailing view in Washington and other Group of Seven (G-7) capitals is that weaknesses in banking systems, prudential regulation, and corporate governance were at the heart of the Asian financial crisis of the late 1990s. Hence the ambitious efforts by the G-7 to establish international codes and standards covering fiscal transparency, monetary and financial policy, banking supervision, data dissemination, corporate governance, and accounting standards. The Financial Stability Forum (FSF)—a G-7 organization with minimal representation from developing nations—has designated 12 of these standards as essential for creating sound financial systems in developing countries. The full FSF compendium includes an additional 59 standards the agency considers "relevant for sound financial systems," bringing the total number of codes to 71. To fend off speculative capital movements, the IMF and G-7 also typically urge developing countries to accumulate foreign reserves and avoid exchange-rate regimes that differ from a "hard peg" (tying the value of one's currency to that of a more stable currency, such as the U.S. dollar) or a "pure float" (letting the market determine the appropriate exchange rate).

A cynic might wonder whether the point of all these prerequisites is merely to provide easy cover for eventual failure. Integrationists can conveniently blame disappointing growth performance or a financial crisis on "slippage" in the implementation of complementary reforms rather than on a poorly designed liberalization. So if Bangladesh's freer trade policy does not produce a large enough spurt in growth, the World Bank concludes that the problem must involve lagging reforms in public administration or continued "political uncertainty" (always a favorite). And if Argentina gets caught up in a confidence crisis despite significant trade and financial liberalization, the IMF reasons that structural reforms have been inadequate and must be deepened.

FREE TRADE-OFFS

Most (but certainly not all) of the institutional reforms on the integrationist agenda are perfectly sensible, and in a world without financial, administrative, or political constraints, there would be little argument about the need to adopt them. But in the real world, governments face difficult choices over how to deploy their fiscal resources, administrative capabilities, and political capital. Setting institutional priorities to maximize integration into the global economy has real opportunity costs.

Consider some illustrative trade-offs. World Bank trade economist Michael Finger has estimated that a typical developing country must spend $150 million to implement requirements under just three WTO agreements (those on customs valuation, sanitary and phytosanitary measures, and trade-related intellectual property rights). As Finger notes, this sum equals a year's development budget for many least-developed countries. And while the budgetary burden of implementing financial codes and standards has never been fully estimated, it undoubtedly entails a substantial diversion of fiscal and human resources as well. Should governments in developing countries train more bank auditors and accountants, even if those investments mean fewer secondary-school teachers or reduced spending on primary education for girls?

In the area of legal reform, should governments focus their energies on "importing" legal codes and standards or on improving existing domestic legal institutions? In Turkey, a weak coalition government spent several months during 1999 gathering political support for a bill providing foreign investors the protection of international arbitration. But wouldn't a better long-run strategy have involved reforming the existing legal regime for the benefit of foreign and domestic investors alike?

In public health, should governments promote the reverse engineering of patented basic medicines and the importation of low-cost generic drugs from "unauthorized" suppliers, even if doing so means violating WTO rules against such practices? When South Africa passed legislation in 1997 allowing imports of patented AIDS drugs from cheaper sources, the country came under severe pressure from Western governments, which argued that the South African policy conflicted with WTO rules on intellectual property.

How much should politicians spend on social protection policies in view of the fiscal constraints imposed by market "discipline"? Peru's central bank holds foreign reserves equal to 15 months of imports as an insurance policy against the sudden capital outflows that financially open economies often experience. The opportunity cost of this policy amounts to almost 1 percent of gross domestic product annually—more than enough to fund a generous antipoverty program.

How should governments choose their exchange-rate regimes? During the last four decades, virtually every growth boom in the developing world has been accompanied by a controlled depreciation of the domestic currency. Yet financial openness makes it all but impossible to manage the exchange rate.

How should policymakers focus their anticorruption strategies? Should they target the high-level corruption that foreign investors often decry or the petty corruption that affects the poor the most? Perhaps, as the proponents of permanent normal trade relations with China argued in the recent U.S. debate, a government that is forced to protect the rights of foreign investors will become more inclined to protect the rights of its own citizens as well. But this is, at best, a trickledown strategy of institutional reform. Shouldn't reforms target the desired ends directly—whether those ends are the rule of law, improved observance of human rights, or reduced corruption?

The rules for admission into the world economy not only reflect little awareness of development priorities, they are often completely unrelated to sensible economic principles. For instance, WTO agreements on anti-dumping, subsidies and countervailing measures, agriculture, textiles, and trade-related intellectual property rights lack any economic rationale beyond the mercantilist interests of a narrow set of powerful groups in advanced industrial countries. Bilateral and regional trade agreements are typically far worse, as they impose even tighter prerequisites on developing countries in return for crumbs of enhanced "market access." For example, the African Growth and Opportunity Act signed by U.S.

President Clinton in May 2000 provides increased access to the U.S. market only if African apparel manufacturers use U.S.-produced fabric and yarns. This restriction severely limits the potential economic spillovers in African countries.

There are similar questions about the appropriateness of financial codes and standards. These codes rely heavily on an Anglo-American style of corporate governance and an arm's-length model of financial development. They close off alternative paths to financial development of the sort that have been followed by many of today's rich countries (for example, Germany, Japan, or South Korea).

In each of these areas, a strategy of "globalization above all" crowds out alternatives that are potentially more development-friendly. Many of the institutional reforms needed for insertion into the world economy can be independently desirable or produce broader economic benefits. But these priorities do not necessarily coincide with the priorities of a comprehensive development agenda.

ASIAN MYTHS

Even if the institutional reforms needed to join the international economic community are expensive and preclude investments in other crucial areas, pro-globalization advocates argue that the vast increases in economic growth that invariably result from insertion into the global marketplace will more than compensate for those costs. Take the East Asian tigers or China, the advocates say. Where would they be without international trade and foreign capital flows?

That these countries reaped enormous benefits from their progressive integration into the world economy is undeniable. But look closely at what policies produced those results, and you will find little that resembles today's rule book.

Countries like South Korea and Taiwan had to abide by few international constraints and pay few of the modern costs of integration during their formative growth experience in the 1960s and 1970s. At that time, global trade rules were sparse and economies faced almost none of today's common pressures to open their borders to capital flows. So these countries combined their outward orientation with unorthodox policies: high levels of tariff and non-tariff barriers, public ownership of large segments of banking and industry, export subsidies, domestic-content requirements, patent and copyright infringements, and restrictions on capital flows (including on foreign direct investment). Such policies are either precluded by today's trade rules or are highly frowned upon by organizations like the IMF and the World Bank.

China also followed a highly unorthodox two-track strategy, violating practically every rule in the guidebook (including, most notably, the requirement of private property rights). India, which significantly raised its economic growth rate in the early 1980s, remains one of the world's most highly protected economies.

All of these countries liberalized trade gradually, over a period of decades, not years. Significant import liberalization did not occur until after a transition to high economic growth had taken place. And far from wiping the institutional slate clean, all of these nations managed to eke growth out of their existing institutions, imperfect as they may have been. Indeed, when some of the more successful Asian economies gave in to Western pressure to liberalize capital flows rapidly, they were rewarded with the Asian financial crisis.

That is why these countries can hardly be considered poster children for today's global rules. South Korea, China, India, and the other Asian success cases had the freedom to do their own thing, and they used that freedom abundantly. Today's globalizers would be unable to replicate these experiences without running afoul of the IMF or the WTO.

The Asian experience highlights a deeper point: A sound overall development strategy that produces high economic growth is far more effective in achieving integration with the world economy than a purely integrationist strategy that relies on openness to work its magic. In other words, the globalizers have it exactly backwards. Integration is the result, not the cause, of economic and social development. A relatively protected economy like Vietnam is integrating with the world economy much more rapidly than an open economy like Haiti because Vietnam, unlike Haiti, has a reasonably functional economy and polity.

Integration into the global economy, unlike tariff rates or capital-account regulations, is not something that policymakers control directly. Telling finance ministers in developing nations that they should increase their "participation in world trade" is as meaningful as telling them that they need to improve technological capabilities—and just as helpful. Policymakers need to know which strategies will produce these results, and whether the specific prescriptions that the current orthodoxy offers are up to the task.

TOO GOOD TO BE TRUE

Do lower trade barriers spur greater economic progress? The available studies reveal no systematic relationship between a country's average level of tariff and nontariff barriers and its subsequent economic growth rate. If anything, the evidence for the 1990s indicates a positive relationship between import tariffs and economic growth [see chart]. The only clear pattern is that countries dismantle their trade restrictions as they grow richer. This finding explains why today's rich countries, with few exceptions, embarked on modern economic growth behind protective barriers but now display low trade barriers.

The absence of a strong negative relationship between trade restrictions and economic growth may seem surprising in view of the ubiquitous claim that trade liberalization promotes higher growth. Indeed, the economics literature is replete with cross-national studies concluding that growth and economic dynamism are strongly linked to more open trade policies. A particularly influential study finds that economies that are "open," by the study's own definition, grew 2.45 percentage points faster annually than closed ones—an enormous difference.

Upon closer look, however, such studies turn out to be unreliable. In a detailed review of the empirical literature, University of Maryland economist Francisco Rodríguez and I found a major gap between the results that economist have actually obtained and the policy conclusions they have typically drawn. For example, in many cases economists blame poor growth on the government's failure to liberalize trade policies, when the true culprits are ineffective institutions, geographic determinants (such as location in a tropical region), or inappropriate macroeconomic policies (such as an overvalued exchange rate). Once these misdiagnoses are corrected, any meaningful relationship across countries between the level of trade barriers and economic growth evaporates.

The evidence on the benefits of liberalizing capital flows is even weaker. In theory, the appeal of capital mobility seems obvious: If capital is free to enter (and leave) markets based on the potential return on investment, the result will be an efficient allocation of global resources. But in reality, financial markets are inherently unstable, subject to bubbles (rational or otherwise), panics, shortsightedness, and self-fulfilling prophecies. There is plenty of evidence that financial liberalization is often followed by financial crash—just ask Mexico, Thailand, or Turkey—while there is little convincing evidence to suggest that higher rates of economic growth follow capital-account liberalization.

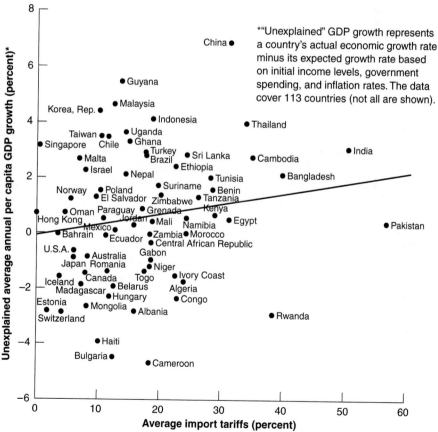

FIGURE 1 ■ HIGH TARIFFS DON'T MEAN LOW GROWTH
Gross Domestic Product (GDP) Growth and Tariff Rates, 1990s
Source: Author's calculations based on World Bank data.

Perhaps the most disingenuous argument in favor of liberalizing international financial flows is that the threat of massive and sudden capital movements serves to discipline policymakers in developing nations who might otherwise manage their economies irresponsibly. In other words, governments might be less inclined to squander their societies' resources if such actions would spook foreign lenders. In practice, however, the discipline argument falls apart. Behavior in international capital markets is dominated by mood swings unrelated to fundamentals. In good times, a government with a chronic fiscal deficit has an easier time financing its spending when it can borrow funds from investors abroad; witness Russia prior to 1998 or Argentina in the 1990s. And in bad times, governments may be forced to adopt inappropriate policies in order to conform to the biases of foreign investors; witness the excessively restrictive monetary and fiscal policies in much of East Asia in the immediate aftermath of the Asian financial crisis. A key reason why Malaysia was able to recover so quickly after the imposition of capital controls in September 1998 was that Prime Minister Mahathir Mohamad resisted the high interest rates and tight fiscal policies that South Korea, Thailand, and Indonesia adopted at the behest of the International Monetary Fund.

GROWTH BEGINS AT HOME

Well-trained economists are justifiably proud of the textbook case in favor of free trade. For all the theory's simplicity, it is one of our profession's most significant achievements. However, in their zeal to promote the virtues of trade, the most ardent proponents are peddling a cartoon version of the argument, vastly overstating the effectiveness of economic openness as a tool for fostering development. Such claims only endanger broad public acceptance of the real article because they unleash unrealistic expectations about the benefits of free trade. Neither economic theory nor empirical evidence guarantees that deep trade liberalization will deliver higher economic growth. Economic openness and all its accouterments do not deserve the priority they typically receive in the development strategies pushed by leading multilateral organizations.

Countries that have achieved long-term economic growth have usually combined the opportunities offered by world markets with a growth strategy that mobilizes the capabilities of domestic institutions and investors. Designing such a growth strategy is both harder and easier than implementing typical integration policies. It is harder because the binding constraints on growth are usually country specific and do not respond well to standardized recipes. But it is easier because once those constraints are targeted, relatively simple policy changes can yield enormous economic payoffs and start a virtuous cycle of growth and additional reform.

Unorthodox innovations that depart from the integration rule book are typically part and parcel of such strategies. Public enterprises during the Meiji restoration in Japan; township and village enterprises in China; an export processing zone in Mauritius; generous tax incentives for priority investments in Taiwan; extensive credit subsidies in South Korea; infant-industry protection in Brazil during the

1960s and 1970s—these are some of the innovations that have been instrumental in kick-starting investment and growth in the past. None came out of a Washington economist's tool kit.

Few of these experiments have worked as well when transplanted to other settings, only underscoring the decisive importance of local conditions. To be effective, development strategies need to be tailored to prevailing domestic institutional strengths. There is simply no alternative to a homegrown business plan. Policymakers who look to Washington and financial markets for the answers are condemning themselves to mimicking the conventional wisdom du jour, and to eventual disillusionment.

Why the Globalization Backlash Is Stupid

JOHN MICKLETHWAIT AND
ADRIAN WOOLDRIDGE

"GLOBALIZATION MEANS THE TRIUMPH OF GIANT COMPANIES"

Nonsense. If you listen to antiglobalists, we live in a world of "Disneyfication" and "Coca-Colonization" in which giant companies simultaneously trample over their smaller commercial rivals and turn national governments into helpless lackeys. They are wrong on both counts.

The proportion of output from big companies has declined, not increased. Globalization radically shifts the balance of advantage from incumbents to challengers. Incumbents could once protect themselves behind lofty barriers such as the high cost of capital, the difficulty of acquiring new technology, or the importance of close relationships with national governments. Globalization reduces the importance of all these things. Lower barriers make capital easier to raise, technology easier to buy, markets easier to reach, and ties with national governments ever less important. You no longer have to be a multinational to have the reach of one.

By all rights, Motorola Inc. ought to be the undisputed ruler of the wireless world. The company was the first to mass-produce car phones. It also sits in the heart of the world's biggest market for them. But it has been humbled by Nokia Corp., a relatively small company from Finland that only a decade ago was more interested in bathroom tissue than mobile phones. Nokia's only weapons were better phones and better management. Against these, mere size proved a puny defense—which helps explain why giants such as AT&T Corp. and General Motors Corp. (GM) now look so vulnerable.

The idea that companies are now more important than governments is equally misleading. Far from getting smaller, governments in most Western countries remain colossal, consuming more than 40 percent of Western Europe's gross domestic product (GDP), for example. They continue to expand their influence over corporate behavior through regulatory policy. Bill Gates rapidly discovered that a rather obscure Justice Department antitrust lawyer, Joel Klein, was a much more fearsome opponent than any mere company. Jack Welch, the face of American Big Business, met his Waterloo in Belgium when the similarly anonymous bureaucrats of the European Commission blocked what would have been the biggest merger in history, that between General Electric and Honeywell.

As for the oft-quoted "statistics" about so many companies being bigger than countries—the idea that GM is as big as Denmark—these compare sales figures with GDP. Since GDP measures value added, the correct corporate comparison is profits. As Martin Wolf of the *Financial Times* has pointed out, GM then slides from being as large as the 23rd biggest country to the 55th, about the same size as a basket case like Ukraine.

"GLOBALIZATION IS DESTROYING THE ENVIRONMENT"

Not really.   This myth provides a prime example of a conceit that underlies a great deal of antiglobal thinking. Take one self-evident truth that all sensible people can agree upon—business of all sorts tends to despoil the environment. Then repeat that observation in highly emotive language, ignoring all other mitigating factors. Then heap all the blame on global companies, global regulators, and indeed globalization itself, when the bulk of the damage is done by local governments, local companies, and even local voters. And, whatever happens, keep running away from the really hard question: How much is greenery worth?

A good starting point is that almost all business that produces a physical product tends to be dirty. Until relatively recently, businesspeople were reluctant to admit this reality. That not only made them look shifty, it also meant that they never made arguments about the choices involved. For instance, during the furor in 1995 over the offshore disposal of its Brent Spar oil rig, Shell failed to argue with any force that Greenpeace's demand that the rig be disposed of on land was by no means the greener solution.

Nowadays, business, particularly multinational business, is better behaved. Businesspeople have not become softer. They have simply wised up to two things. The first is that dirty factories lose them consumers. The second is that environmental regulations are not prohibitively expensive, particularly for multinationals. A 1990 study by the U.S. Environmental Protection Agency, for instance, found that even the most polluting industries don't have to spend more than 2 percent of their revenues on being good environmental citizens. Go to a ghastly eyesore in the Third World, such as Cubatão, the capital of Brazil's chemical business (once dubbed the most polluted city on earth), and you find that multinational companies tend to be cleaner than their Brazilian counterparts—and keener to abide by international standards.

What about the idea that trade, by increasing business activity generally, harms the environment? This is certainly true in the short term. If open borders increase the market for a chemical factory in Lagos, the factory will create more chemicals. But as countries grow richer, they also tend to clean up their act: An elaborate index of environmental sustainability in 122 countries prepared for the World Economic Forum this year showed a strong correlation between a country's greenness and wealth (though, to be fair, an even stronger one with its lack of corruption). More generally, although environmentalism is a good thing, it must be balanced against other virtues, including, from a developing country's point of view, economic growth. It is patronizing for rich-world greens to decide that Africans should not tolerate dirtier air and water in exchange for more wealth.

Alas, the cost of the environment is nearly always tabulated incorrectly. In China, according to the World Bank, air and water pollution cost $54 billion a year—8 percent of the country's GDP. But it is not the polluting companies that bear this price. For that matter, what incentive do Indian polluters have to stop throwing rubbish into the Ganges that then wrecks Bangladesh's rice paddies? One reason why fish stocks are alarmingly low globally is because the seas of the world provide a textbook example of the "tragedy of the commons." Because nobody owns them, nobody feels responsible for them. If a Norwegian fisherman does not pillage them, then his British rival will. This dynamic is also dramatically evident in the current impasse over global warming.

But blaming these things on globalization seems a spurious way to let local politicians off the hook. The right way to protest, say, George W. Bush's decision to junk the Kyoto Protocol is not to blame "the market," but Bush himself. And how exactly would a less interlinked world help? Global warming would not go away if trade barriers went up. Far from being caused by unfettered capitalism, environmental damage is often caused by exactly the opposite. One reason fishing fleets can continue to ravage the oceans is because governments spend $21 billion a year supporting them. Brazil's government initially spurred on the despoliation of the rain forest. The World-watch Institute reckons that there are $650 billion worth of subsidies going to environmentally destructive activities. On the other hand, globalization sometimes directly benefits the environment by promoting things such as trade in pollution-control technology and the privatization of state-owned companies, which become less polluting as they are restructured.

"GLOBALIZATION MAKES GEOGRAPHY IRRELEVANT"

Wrong again.   You might think that the death of distance also means the death of geography. The truth is probably the opposite. If most tangible resources are within anyone's reach, then what matters are the intangible things, which in turn means proximity to people.

The world economy is visibly organizing itself around various clusters of excellence, most obviously Hollywood, Silicon Valley, and Wall Street. The main challenge for companies in a global economy is to situate themselves in various centers of excellence and weave together different centers of excellence into a global production network. The main challenge for communities is to invest in their comparative advantage. Look at the way that Miami has exploited its connections with Latin America. Or the way that the energy cluster in Houston has used its expertise in oil to move into gas, electricity, and energy trading.

The idea that businesses can simply up-sticks and move is also rubbish. Considerable publicity has been given to the few Swedish and German companies that have eventually moved some operations out of their highly taxed homelands; the real story is how long those firms stuck it out. Wander around Los Angeles, America's main manufacturing center, and you will find squadrons of low-tech factories churning out toys, furniture, and clothes, all of which could probably be made cheaper elsewhere. They stay partly for personal reasons (many are family-owned), partly because they can compensate for high labor costs by using more machines, but mostly because Los Angeles is a hub for all three industries—a place where designers, suppliers, and distributors are just around the corner.

Finally, borders remain much more important than many people imagine. Canada and the United States are both English-speaking countries and members of the North American Free Trade Agreement. But the average Canadian province does 12 times as much trade in goods and 40 times as much trade in services with another Canadian province as it does with an American state of the same size and proximity. Similar figures exist for the European Union (EU) countries.

"GLOBALIZATION MEANS AMERICANIZATION"

Not necessarily.   True, globalization certainly tilts the playing field in favor of liberal virtues such as accountability, transparency, and individual rights that are often deemed to be American.

Yet does this mean Americanization? Foreign dictators who want to use xenophobia to prop up their positions would no doubt argue that it does. But the United States has no monopoly on liberal virtues. Classical liberalism was first developed by a group of British thinkers—John Locke, David Hume, and Adam Smith. We still use a French phrase, laissez faire, when we invoke the ideal of a free market economy. The first joint stock company was developed in Britain rather than the United States. Indeed, American democracy was arguably the product of British corporations such as the Virginia Company. For all its bureaucracy, the EU now enshrines liberal values such as democratic representation and individual rights every bit as firmly as the U.S. Constitution.

Certainly, Europe is now moving closer to the Anglo-American shareholder model of capitalism than it had in the immediate postwar years. A popular share-owning culture is slowly putting down roots in Europe. The euro, like the single market before it, is forcing European companies to slim. But these developments do not mean that European companies or European society will become mere facsimiles of America. Europeans will probably continue to put much more emphasis on social solidarity than the United States. France's tight labor laws (including a relatively new 35-hour week) have not stopped its global companies from being competitive, though they have arguably kept its unemployment rate unnecessarily high. The Nordic countries, whose economic performance has matched America's, argue that their well-developed welfare states make their economies more flexible because people are not afraid to change jobs. There are growing signs that Europe (with a potential internal market of 500 million people) is beginning to flex its muscles against the United States, whether it be through vetoing mergers, building its own army, or generally disagreeing with American foreign policy in areas such as the Middle East.

Nor does globalization necessarily mean the Americanization of popular culture. True, American films can be seen almost all over the world, the Big Mac™ is the closest thing we have to a universal food, and Britney Spears is hard to avoid, even if you are in Tibet. But cultural trade is a two-way process. If you look at popular musicals (Andrew Lloyd Webber's) or the bestseller lists (the *Harry Potter* series), Britain continues to exercise a powerful influence on the United States. The most successful programs on American television at the moment are "reality" programs imported from Europe. Foreigners own half of America's top 20 book-publishing houses and half of its film studios. On the whole, consumers have a marked taste for local products, something that is becoming easier to satisfy as technology makes economies of scale less important. The most popular television program in European countries is nearly always a local production. A few years ago hardly any self-respecting European teenager would have been caught listening to local groups. Now France has Air and Sweden has The Cardigans.

But there is a more important reason why globalization does not mean the triumph of a particular nationality. The essence of globalization is that it increases choice. And this includes the choice to live life according to your own lights. A nice example of this is the Bruderhof, a religious group that is rather like the Amish. The Bruderhof reject many features of the modern world. They don't have radios or televisions; they don't approve of feminism and homosexuality. But they have established a highly successful global toy business using a mixture of Japanese management techniques and American technology. The result: They have all the money that they need to keep their community flourishing, but they have not had to abandon their way of life.

"GLOBALIZATION MEANS A RACE TO THE BOTTOM IN LABOR STANDARDS"

No. This argument rests on four misconceptions.

The first is that employers are concerned, above all, with the price of labor. In fact, what really interests them is the value of labor. Some companies will undoubtedly move routine tasks to parts of the world where hourly wages are lower. But in general what employers want is not cheap workers but productive ones. And the most productive workers are usually those with the best education, access to the best machinery, and a support system that includes things like good infrastructure.

If the "race to the bottom" argument were correct, you would expect foreign direct investment (FDI) to be pouring into countries with the lowest wages and the weakest labor standards. Nothing could be further from the truth. The United States is the world's largest recipient of FDI. Year after year the United States has run a net surplus in its capital account (and the inflow of foreign capital has helped to keep interest rates low, build new factories, and bring new production methods to bear on the economy). About 80 percent of U.S. FDI goes to other rich countries. American investment in countries like Mexico and China is a mere fragment of U.S. investment at home.

The second is that globalization is weakening the ties of companies to their home regions. But companies depend on the environment that first created them in all sorts of ways, some obvious, some more subtle. During the Justice Department's investigation of Microsoft, Bill Gates could not have threatened to move his operation to the Bahamas, even though Microsoft has relatively few fixed assets. Microsoft depends not just on a supply of educated workers (who would have refused to move) but also on its close relationship with American universities.

The third idea—that global companies are hostile to "worker protection" such as trade-union rights and labor standards—contains a half-truth. Companies rarely react favorably to unions (or indeed to governments) that want to shackle their freedom of maneuver with inflexible rules about, say, hiring and firing. But, by and large, multinationals are much less hostile to things such as safe working environments, on-the-job training, and opportunities for promotion. Once again, the key factor for companies is boosting productivity rather than lowering the price they pay for labor, so a well-trained and healthy workforce is important. Survey after survey shows multinationals providing higher wages and better working conditions for their employees than their local competitors.

The fourth and largest misconception is that globalization is a zero-sum game: that if the rich are getting richer as a result of globalization, then the poor must be getting poorer. But the argument in favor of globalization is that it can improve the lot of everybody by leading to a more efficient use of resources.

Of course, globalization does not always achieve this goal, and of course it cannot impose efficiency without a certain amount of pain, but in general, globalization improves the living standards of the vast majority of people. In the half century since the foundation of the General Agreement on Tariffs and Trade (GATT), the world economy has grown sixfold, in part because trade has expanded 16-fold. The Organisation for Economic Co-operation and Development calculates that nations that are relatively open to trade grow about twice as fast as those that are relatively closed. Despite the Asian crisis, the World Bank calculates that some 800 million people moved out of absolute poverty in the past decade. And the people left behind still tend to suffer from too little globalization (be it trade barriers to the goods that they produce or restraints on the information they can get at home) rather than too much.

"GLOBALIZATION CONCENTRATES POWER IN UNDEMOCRATIC INSTITUTIONS LIKE THE WTO"

No. Organizations like the World Trade Organization (WTO) and the International Monetary Fund (IMF) are not quite paper tigers. But they are much less powerful than their detractors (and a few of their inmates) imagine. The WTO is essentially an arbitration mechanism: It deals with issues that clashing governments refer to it. The IMF is a crisis management agency. True, it can impose stringent requirements for structural reforms on its clients, and it has often done so with breathtaking arrogance and insensitivity. But governments only resort to the IMF if they are already in serious trouble.

By any conceivable measure, national governments are far more important players in the international order than global institutions. During the Asian crisis, it was the U.S. Treasury Department that decided whether to bail out countries, not the IMF. (And why not? It was writing the checks.) For all the fears in the American heartland about the U.N.'s black helicopters, national governments decide whether to send peacekeeping troops. And now the international institutions face a new constraint. The number of international nongovernmental organizations (NGOs) increased from 6,000 in 1990 to 26,000 by the end of the decade. Visit any old-fashioned multilateral institution and you will find it surrounded by NGOs monitoring it. There are 1,700 clustered around the United Nations' offices in Geneva, for example.

Membership of the WTO suggests that globalization is a bottom-up process. When GATT was founded in 1948, it only had 23 contracting parties, most of them industrialized nations; today the WTO has 142 members, more than three quarters of them developing nations, and 20 more countries are eagerly waiting to join. It may be true that the global civil servants who run most international institutions are not directly elected (just as the heads of civil service departments are not directly elected). But they are accountable to national governments, the majority of which are now democracies.

Indeed, you could argue that the real democratic deficit in global institutions is to be found not in the IMF and the WTO but in the NGOs that protest against them. NGOs claim to represent global civil society (whatever that is). But nobody elects them. They are not accountable to democratic governments. They represent nobody but their members and their activist cadres, which in some of the noisiest cases means a few hundred people.

The Economics of Empire
Notes on the Washington Consensus

████████ WILLIAM FINNEGAN

In early March [2003] President Bush, on the verge of declaring war on Iraq, was asked at a press conference why he thought "so many people around the world take a different view of the threat that Saddam Hussein poses than you and your allies." Mr. Bush replied, "I've seen all kinds of protests since I've been the president. I remember the protests against trade. There was a lot of people who didn't feel like free trade was good for the world. I completely disagree. I think free trade is good for both wealthy and impoverished nations. That didn't change my opinion about trade." . . .

Sometimes known as the Washington Consensus,[1] other times simply as "free trade," this gospel has been the main American ideological export since anti-Communism (to which it is related) lost strategic relevance. It is promulgated directly through U.S. foreign policy and indirectly through multilateral institutions such as the World Bank, the International Monetary Fund, and the World Trade Organization. Its core tenets are deregulation, privatization, "openness" (to foreign investment, to imports), unrestricted movement of capital, and lower taxes. Presented with special force to developing countries as a formula for economic management, it is also, in its fullness, a theory of how the world should be run, under American supervision. Attacking America is, therefore, attacking the theory, and attacking the theory is attacking America.

The possibility that the Marines and high-altitude bombers might need to be involved in spreading the good news about free trade does not, in context, seem far-fetched. Consider "The National Security Strategy of the United States," issued by the White House in September 2002. Presidents are required to submit a security strategy periodically to Congress, but the Bush edition received an unusual amount of attention because of its unprecedented assertion of an American right to strike U.S. enemies preemptively, as well as its vow to maintain American military supremacy over all rivals indefinitely. Just as notable, however, in another way, was the repeated, incongruous insertion of fundamentalist free-trade precepts. The Strategy claims to have discovered "a single sustainable model for national success"—the Washington Consensus. There is, in its authors' view, simply no other way. History has validated this messianic vision, and the American role in leading the world to its realization on this earth. "We will actively work to bring the hope of democracy, development, free markets, and free trade to every corner of the world," the Strategy avows. It even provides a list of policy particulars, such as "lower marginal tax rates" and "pro-growth legal and regulatory policies" (read: weaker environmental and labor laws), that it believes every country should adopt. . . .

But beyond the triumphalist theory—and capitalism obviously has much to be triumphal about—there is the practice. The Washington Consensus has been around long enough now that results are in from many countries, including from some of the most diligent followers of its policy prescriptions. These results are less than encouraging. Argentina, for instance, did everything it was told to do by Washington throughout the 1990s—privatization, deregulation, trade liberalization, tax reform—and found itself a much-touted example of the virtues of *neoliberalismo* until shortly before its collapse in 2001. Today, Argentina is suffering through the worst economic crisis in its history. Yet even major failures seem not to shake the faith of the true believers in the Bush Administration, who include the president. Like other fundamentalisms, market fundamentalism seems impervious to argument or inconvenient facts. Inside the muscular church of laissez-faire, broad-brush ideas—all of them estimable in the abstract—get rolled together into a mesmerizing, internally coherent mantra.

But vulgarity and obtuseness should not be mistaken for sincerity. Not only is the case for President Bush's "opinion" that "free trade is good for both wealthy and impoverished nations" empirically feeble; there is plenty of evidence that rich countries, starting with the United States, have no intention of playing by the trade rules and strictures they foist on poorer, weaker countries as "a single sustainable model." We practice free trade selectively, which is to say not at all, and, when it suits our commercial purposes, we actively prevent poor countries from exploiting their few advantages on the world market. While President Bush extols a simple, sweeping, unexceptionable creed at every opportunity, however inappropriate, his administration, guided by figures such as Trade Representative Zoellick, pursues a far more complex and sophisticated agenda. Theirs is not an ideology of freedom or democracy. It is a system of control. It is an economics of empire. . . .

These pillars of the postwar international financial order were conceived during the latter part of World War II at a conference of American, British, and European economists and civil servants held in Bretton Woods, New Hampshire, and dominated intellectually by John Maynard Keynes. The World Bank was originally intended to help finance the reconstruction of postwar Europe—a project that neither private capital nor shattered states could be expected to undertake. After the Marshall Plan made that purpose redundant, the Bank, looking for a raison d'être, began to concentrate on Asia, Africa, and Latin America, where it loaned money to poor governments, usually for specific projects. Today, the Bank has 9,700 employees, 184 member states, and lends nearly $20 billion a year. The founding purpose of the I.M.F. was to make short-term loans to stabilize currencies and the balance of payments, promote international economic cooperation, and prevent another

Depression. It, too, has changed with the times. Now it makes long-term loans as well, functions almost entirely in the developing world, and, by interpreting its mandate to maintain international financial stability as broadly as possible, seeks to actively manage the economies of many poor countries. Because almost all significant aid and loans to poor countries hinge on the I.M.F.'s assessment of a nation's financial soundness, the Fund has the leverage to dictate public policy in large areas of the globe. Power within the institutions was originally apportioned among governments according to their relative financial strength and contributions, which meant that the United States had the leading role from the start. Although the managing director of the I.M.F. is traditionally a European, the U.S. is the only country with an effective veto over I.M.F. actions. The president of the World Bank has always been an American. The Bank and the I.M.F work together closely. They are the two most powerful financial institutions in the world.

During the Cold War, loans were often nakedly political. Anti-Communist dictators—in Uruguay, Ethiopia, the Philippines—were rewarded. Dictatorships in general were viewed as more reliable than democracies, and useful Communists, such as Ceaușescu, in Romania, also became big clients. Even apartheid South Africa got loans from the World Bank. Robert McNamara, having presided over the Vietnam War, became president of the Bank in 1968. He aggressively expanded its operations, pushing poor countries to accept loans to build factories, highways, huge power projects, vast agro-industrial schemes. This development model had fundamental problems. By 1981, when McNamara retired, abandoned megaprojects littered the Third World, together with uprooted populations, ravaged forests and watersheds, countries no longer able to feed themselves, and an ocean of impossible debt.

Both the Bank and the I.M.F. passed through an ideological looking glass in the 1980s. They had been established and run on Keynesian principles—on assumptions that markets need state guidance, whether to stabilize currencies and prevent panics (I.M.F.) or to build infrastructure necessary for economic development (the Bank). But with the ascendance of Reaganite (and Thatcherite) free-market economics in the West—among their rich-country masters, that is—both institutions changed their operating philosophies. They began pushing policies laissez-faire—what became known as the Washington Consensus.

Unfortunately, they have had even less success with the new philosophy. Financial panics and crises continue to roil the I.M.F.'s clients, from East Asia to Argentina. The idea that open markets and increased trade lead invariably to economic growth may be sound in theory, but it has repeatedly failed the reality test. A recent study found that I.M.F. programs have had, overall, a *negative* effect on economic growth in participating countries. And the World Bank's declared mission of reducing poverty has been a bust so far. More than a billion people are now living on less than one dollar a day—the figure in 1972 was 800 million—while nearly half the world's population is living on less than two dollars a day. When Catherine Caufield began the reporting for her book on the World Bank, *Masters of Illusion,* she asked the Bank to direct her toward some of its most successful projects. The Bank's press officers made repeated promises but produced no list. Finally, as Caufield was leaving for India, which happened to be the Bank's largest client, they came up with the name of one project, the South Bassein Offshore Gas Development Project. Caufield could find no one in India who had heard of it. Later, she discovered that the project was a gas field in the Arabian Sea and was known in India by a different name. The Bank had loaned $772 million to the project and, because no villagers had needed to be resettled from the open sea, had managed to avoid controversy—this was apparently the successful part. The project had taken twice as long as expected to complete, and, according to Bank records, more than a third of the loan had ultimately been written off "due to misprocurement."

Every generation of Bank officials has vowed to improve this record, to start funding projects that benefit not only big business and local elites but also the poor. And the Bank's efforts to promote access to health care and education—projects undertaken with non-governmental organizations (NGOs) and other "civil society" groups—have increased. But many Bank contracts are worth millions, and multinational corporations remain their major beneficiaries. Testifying before Congress in 1995, Lawrence Summers, then of the Treasury Department (now president of Harvard), disclosed that American corporations received $1.35 in procurement contracts for each dollar the American government contributed to the World Bank and other multilateral development banks. This was an unusually candid admission by a leading Bank supporter that one of its main activities is, in fact, corporate welfare. Those donated American dollars come, after all, from ordinary American taxpayers—few of whom know anything about what the World Bank does.

The Bank does many things, of course, and employs many people who are undoubtedly devoted to the idea of reducing poverty. (So does the I.M.F.) It provides technical assistance to poor countries, some of it clearly useful, and even tolerates a degree of internal debate.[2] But both the Bank and the I.M.F. are locked in unhealthy relationships with their client governments. Governments recognize, obviously, that their poverty is a precondition for the flow of aid, and, for the less scrupulous among them, this can turn the poor themselves into a valuable commodity, their pitifulness a resource not to be squandered through amelioration. On the donors' side, lending is essential to the continued health of aid bureaucracies and the advancement of careers—not the best environment in which to make wise decisions. Then there is the merry-go-round of fiscal crises and bailouts, aboard which the Bank and the I.M.F. and rich-country bilateral lenders regularly make new loans to deeply indebted countries in order to avoid the embarrassment of non-performing loans. Because it helps condemn the world's poor to a fate of permanent debt, the Bank's self-description as a "pro-poor" development agency is at best self-deluding. . . . The Bank's core constituencies remain the corporations and the poor-country bureaucrats and politicians whom it enriches. . . .

The handful of countries that have managed to escape mass poverty since the 1950s are concentrated in East Asia—South Korea, Taiwan, Singapore, and, to a lesser extent, Thailand and Malaysia. South Korea and Taiwan followed strongly *dirigiste* industrial policies. High protective tariffs were raised, for instance, around certain fledgling industries. (This is sometimes known as the "infant industry" strategy.) Some of these industries were selected for their export potential, and when they were ready to compete internationally they quickly found markets. The local standard of living began to rise. This development strategy is similar to what all the Western powers once did to encourage their own industries, but it is anathema under the free-trade dogma of the Washington Consensus, and it could not be implemented by any underdeveloped, indebted country today. It relies heavily on tariffs and state planning, and is thus noxious not only to the I.M.F. and the World Bank but, equally as important, to the World Trade Organization, which is the third Bretton Woods institution. The W.T.O. is dedicated, even more unequivocally than the others, to eliminating "barriers to trade."

South Korea, Taiwan, and Singapore also managed, each in its own way, to turn some of the early waves of the current flood of corporate globalization to their advantage. When manufacturing started fleeing the high-wage nations of the West, opening assembly plants in Latin America and Asia, the countries that came to be known as the Asian Tigers successfully imposed local-content laws (requiring that investors buy locally produced components when possible) and consistently cut better deals for the transfer of technical skills to their own workers than, say, Mexico did. Thus, when the multinationals moved on to Indonesia and Vietnam in search of cheaper labor, Taiwan and South Korea were ready to let the sweatshops go and to assume a higher position in the global production chain.

None of this wise planning meant that the Tigers were immune to pressures from the multilateral financial institutions. The I.M.F., in particular, was determined that the newly prosperous East Asian countries liberalize their capital markets, and its success in prying open those markets contributed to the devastating regional economic crisis of 1997–98. In the crisis, only Malaysia seriously defied the stern—and, in retrospect, disastrous—advice of the U.S. Treasury Department not to impose capital controls. (These are laws that impede international investors and speculators—what Thomas L. Friedman, the great sloganeer of globalization, calls "the Electronic Herd"—as they move money in or out of a country.) By no coincidence, Malaysia emerged from the wreckage more quickly and less scathed than any of its neighbors. (Chile, which has made more progress against poverty under neoliberalism than any other Latin American country, also uses capital controls.)

China and India, although poor, have the populational heft to ignore many applications of Western pressure, which has helped each of them ride the globalization wave at least in the right general direction. China offers foreign corporations some of the world's cheapest labor, particularly in what are called export-processing zones, or free-trade zones. EPZs are tax-free manufacturing zones, where local labor and environmental laws (if any) are often relaxed or suspended in order to attract foreign capital. Today, tens of millions of people in more than seventy countries work in EPZs. They are where the American (and Canadian, and Western European) manufacturing jobs go when they go south. Or, rather, parts of the jobs go there, temporarily, because multinational firms have found that it is often most profitable to distribute the different aspects of production and assembly to different contractors and subcontractors, often in different countries, with the lowest-skilled, most tedious, unhealthy, labor-intensive work typically going to the least developed country. Mobility is essential to this arrangement—the ability to quickly transfer operations from country to country in search of the cheapest production costs and least hassle from local authorities. Thus the facilities in EPZs, the vast prefab sheds and plants, are rarely owned by the contractors who use them, let alone by the multinationals who place the orders. They are leased.

EPZs are not a viable development model. Wages are low, and workers are typically drawn not from local communities but from distant villages and rural areas. With the constant threat that companies will pick up and leave if they are taxed or regulated, local governments rarely profit in any significant way. Local-content laws and knowledge transfer are seldom, if ever, part of the package. A few corrupt officials, along with managers drawn from local elites, profit, certainly, but the great influx of foreign technology and capital that EPZs are supposed to bring rarely materializes.

And this seemingly minor, disappointing fact undermines a crucial assumption, widespread in the West, about the new global division of labor. The assumption is that the developed world is turning into one big postindustrial service economy while the rest of the world industrializes, and that, yes, sweatshops, child labor, egregious pollution, health and safety nightmares, and subsistence-level wages come with industrialization, but that any country that wants to develop must go through all that. *We went through it. So did Western Europe.* This assumption, although not usually stated so crudely, underpins every serious argument for corporate-led globalization. The problem is that the industrialization that Indonesia, Honduras, the Philippines, and dozens of other countries are now experiencing is not the same industrialization that we in the West experienced. It's true that people are moving from farms to factories, and that urbanization is occurring at a rapid pace. But exploration and immiseration are not development. And unregulated, untaxed foreign ownership, with profits being remitted to faraway investors, will never build good infrastructure. It is simply not clear how, under the current model, the poor majority in most poor countries will ever benefit from globalization.

China has achieved and maintained impressive growth, even in the present world recession. And yet China, although increasingly integrated into the world economy, and recently admitted to the W.T.O., is following a development path very much its own. It has strict capital controls. It forbids foreigners from owning many forms of stock. It has gone slowly with privatization. (Russia already demonstrated how to do it fast and badly.) The state retains control of the banking system. Still, everybody wants to do business with China, if only because of the size and docility of its labor force and the size of its consumer market, which is expanding swiftly, along with its urban middle class. Politically, China remains, of course, a one-party state—a police state, in fact—nominally Communist, with little interest in human rights, the rule of law, or other democratic niceties that theoretically come with a market economy.

India, the world's largest democracy, has achieved less growth, and it has been racked by battles over some of the main insults of corporate globalization, such as seed patenting and the construction of giant, World Bank-backed dams that have displaced millions of villagers. But the Indian middle class (also growing) has enjoyed the fruits of a technology-led boom, thanks to a thick slice of the world's software programming and back-office work being outsourced to a few Indian firms. The government, meanwhile, has continued to protect many domestic industries—and to use capital controls—basically thumbing its nose at the imprecations of the Bretton Woods institutions to stop.

Most national governments today, though, must struggle in a world economy in which they are dwarfed by global corporations. And those corporations, while gaining power steadily in relation to states (which must compete to lure investment), have also been quietly undergoing a profound self-transformation. This transformation can be seen most easily in two figures: first, the total assets of the 100 largest multinational corporations increased, between 1980 and 1995, by 697 percent; second, the total direct employment of those same corporations during that same period *decreased* by 8 percent. This was more than mere downsizing. These figures demonstrate, again, that a great many of the jobs that left the rich world over the past twenty-five years did not, in fact, rematerialize intact elsewhere, in the Global South, where labor is cheaper. Because the question turned out to be, in many cases, again, not where to produce goods but how to produce them, and the answer turned out to be not by owning factories and having employees but by ordering products from contractors and subcontractors and sub-subcontractors in poor countries. EPZs have been instrumental to the success of this strategy. . . .

The market fundamentalist's version of history and economics is both more scriptural and more expedient than it is factual. The idea, for instance, that greater trade leads to greater general prosperity, which is an unshakable conviction not only among true believers but also among liberal globalizers, including most of the American journalistic establishment and the Democratic Party, is in many cases simply untrue. In Latin America, during the 1960s and 1970s—the decades preceding the great trade boom of globalization—per capita income rose 73 percent. During the last two decades, with trade expanding rapidly under neoliberalism, per capita income rose less than 6 percent. The same dismal pattern appears in the United States. Between 1947 and 1973, economic growth averaged 4 percent and non-managerial wages—that's the pay of more than 80 percent of American workers—rose 63 percent, in real dollars. Since 1973, with international trade soaring, real wages have fallen 4 percent, while economic growth has averaged 3 percent. Nobody knows precisely what effect trade has had on American wages and growth, but even conservative economists ascribe a significant amount of the long-term American wage stagnation to the effects of globalization. These effects, when they are acknowledged at all by free traders, are, we are assured, only temporary. But they have lasted more than a generation now and, as the Springsteen song says about good jobs, "They ain't comin' back." . . .

But even economic growth, which is regarded nearly universally as an overall social good, is not necessarily so. There is growth so unequal that is heightens social conflict and increases repression. There is growth so environmentally destructive that it detracts, in sum, from a community's quality of life. (Trade itself carries vast, and rarely calculated, environmental consequences, with pollution-spreading ships, trucks, and planes rushing goods around the globe.) Then there is the destruction of communities themselves, as nations frantically reshape their economies around exports and specialization—the mass production of those goods that may afford them comparative advantage in the global marketplace. Finally, there is the peculiar way that growth, or gross domestic product, is calculated, which is as a value-free measure of total economic output, one that does not distinguish between costs and benefits. Thus resource extraction is a plus, while resource depletion does not register. Strip-mining, clear-cutting, overfishing, pumping an aquifer (or an oil reserve) dry—these ravages and permanent losses do not figure in the growth equation. Neither is income distribution a factor, meaning that most people may be getting poorer in a context of economic "growth." Medical bills and legal bills all count as growth, leading to an absurdist universe in which, as policy analysts Ted Halstead and Clifford Cobb put it, "the nation's economic hero is a terminal cancer patient who has just gone through a bitterly contested divorce."

This is not to say that the world's poor are not in need of economic growth, in the sense of greater economic opportunity. They are. But the question remains: What policies and incentives will actually provide that opportunity? Increased international trade *can* be beneficial to the poor. *But it is not automatically so.* Markets *can* do great things, and yet they remain flawed, fickle mechanisms that favor those with money, and they must be carefully regulated. . . .

The truth is, no government practices free trade. It is a credo, a chimera, a utopian conceit—a nice idea—as well as a fine club with which to belabor one's political opponents and economic competitors. The E.U. subsidizes its farmers as lavishly as the U.S., and Japan does almost as well by its farmers. The W.T.O. is a tariff-trading bourse, where countries dicker and bicker and hash out compromises under arbitration. Its founding document is more than 27,000 pages long. This is not the yellow brick road to a purified, simplified ("free") global trading system.

But the main problem, from the perspective of poor countries, with the existing system of world finance and trade is simply that the rules drawn up, and the decisions handed down, at the W.T.O., the I.M.F., and other international tribunals, are drawn up and handed down almost entirely by the rich countries. They have the negotiators, the expertise, the financial leverage, and in some cases (such as the I.M.F. and the World Bank) the weighted vote to win virtually every dispute. Even when rich countries clearly violate an agreement, their poor-country counterparts may lack the resources (meaning, often, simply the lawyers) to lodge a successful protest.

Lopsided legal contests in trade courts are not tragedies, of course. Those occur, rather, in what international bureaucrats like to call "the field"—when the European Union decides to dump heavily subsidized powdered milk in Jamaica, say, and Jamaican dairy farmers are forced to throw away hundreds of thousands of gallons of fresh milk; or when the United States decides to off-load vast quantities of subsidized rice in Haiti, putting thousands of small rice farmers out of business and causing a regional rise in child malnutrition. Haiti, although the poorest country in the Western Hemisphere, does well, incidentally, on the I.M.F.'s trade openness rankings.

Beyond the egregious incidents, though, there are the structural obstructions. Rich-country tariffs, for instance. They are, in the aggregate, four times higher against the products of poor countries than against the products of other rich countries. Why? Well, what you got to negotiate *with*, mon? Or consider the twist known as "tariff peaks." These charges, levied at rich-country ports, get higher with the amount of processing that an imported product has undergone. Peanuts? We charge you, assuming that this is an American port, *x*. Peanut butter? We charge you *x* plus *132 percent*. Our peanut-butter companies do not appreciate competition, you see. Canada, Japan, and the E.U. all use tariff peaks to keep out processed foods and other manufactured products. The result is to prevent poor countries from adding any value to their raw commodities—to prevent them, that is, from achieving even the primary stages of industrial development.

It's the perennial mismatch of the powerful center and the weak periphery. In economic policy today, though, it plays out in a particularly perverse way. When a poor country is in recession, for instance, it is usually ordered by its paymasters at the I.M.F. to balance its books. This approach to fiscal management went out in the West with Herbert Hoover. In the rich countries, we run deficits during a recession and apply good countercyclical remedies like lowered interest rates. We don't listen to the I.M.F.'s ultraorthodox prescriptions because we don't owe the I.M.F. money. Austerity, like free trade, is for us to prescribe and for poor countries to practice. Private enterprises in poor countries are expected to compete with rich multinationals when the interest rates that they must pay to raise capital—pushed dizzyingly high under austerity plans—make fair competition impossible. And all this bitter medicine comes in a bottle labeled Economic Freedom. . . .

It's easy to be cynical about the double binds—the rigged world trade system, to be blunt—faced by poor countries. And the bald contradictions of U.S. policy and preachments suggest, certainly, a degree of official cynicism. But nobody really wants to see economies stultify or implode (nobody except, perhaps, a few financial specialists known as vulture capitalists), and the I.M.F.'s great efforts to prevent emerging-economy disasters with emergency bailouts, although frequently unsuccessful, seem basically sincere. The problem lies, rather, with the model.

Even market fundamentalists concede that corporate-led globalization produces both winners and losers. Why should the U.S. government look beyond a strict pro-business definition of the national interest? Because it is *in* our national interest, especially in the longer term, to expand globalization's circle of winners and to throw lifelines to the billions of people struggling to stay afloat in the world economic maelstrom. The U.S. currently enjoys a truly rare global preeminence—military, economic, pop-cultural. But power is not, obviously, the same as legitimacy. And every over-weening, remorseless projection of American power, every unfair trade rule and economic double standard jammed into the global financial architecture, helps erode the legitimacy of American ascendancy in the eyes of the world's poor. This erosion is occurring throughout Latin America, Africa, Asia. At the W.T.O., in response to worldwide protests against the high prices of AIDS drugs, the United States finally acceded, in November 2001, to a historic decision that public health should, after all, be a consideration in some areas of patent protection. Then, in late 2002, under pressure from the big pharmaceuticals, the Bush Administration quietly changed its position and sent Trade Representative Zoellick to kill an agreement allowing poor countries access to generic medicines. Few

Americans noticed. But in Africa, and Asia, and all the countries directly injured by this decision, millions noticed. . . .

American always overestimate the amount of foreign aid we give. In recent national polls, people have guessed, on average, that between 15 and 24 percent of the federal budget goes for foreign aid. In reality, it is less than 1 percent. The U.N. has set a foreign-aid goal for the rich countries of .7 percent of gross national product. A few countries have attained that modest goal, all of them Scandinavian. The U.S. has never come close. Indeed, it comes in dead last, consistently, in the yearly totals of rich-country foreign aid as a percentage of GNP. In 2000, we gave .1 percent. President Bush's dramatic proposal, post-September 11, to increase foreign aid to $15 billion looks rather puny next to the $48 billion increase in this year's $379 billion military budget.

Along with our delusions about foreign aid, there persists a more general belief about the rich world trying to help the poor, at least financially. In fact, the net transfer of moneys each year runs the other way—from the poor countries to the rich, mainly in the form of corporate profits and government debt servicing.

But it is simplistic, even misleading, to talk about whole nations as winners or losers under the current globalization regime, since there are, in every country, significant groups of both winners and losers. In China, with its remarkable growth rate and burgeoning middle class, tens of millions of people have been left unemployed and destitute in the upheavals caused by the arrival of capitalism, while millions more find themselves working seven days a week in dangerous, abysmally paid factory jobs. In dozens of countries, a dominant ethnic minority is reaping most, if not all, of the gains of economic integration while working-class and peasant majorities absorb the shocks and bitter downsides of trade liberalization. Even in the U.S., the foremost proponent of free trade and presumably its great beneficiary, there are those millions of good jobs that disappeared with globalization, leaving their former holders working non-union at Wal-Mart. There is a strong argument that the U.S. may be trading itself into oblivion, for it seems that we began, in 1976, running a trade deficit, leading to an international debt that has since ballooned to $2.4 trillion, or roughly 24 percent of GDP. Our major trading partners have yet to call in these debts, but the national balance sheet looks worse every year. With the economy threatening to slip into Japan-style deflation, life as a debtor nation could become quite unpleasant. In that event, globalization, certainly in this corporate-driven form, may start looking like a bad idea to more and more Americans. . . .

But the daily work of increasing American commercial supremacy, while binding the global economy into stronger, more tightly woven webs of integration, is not for the otherworldly. It's being done quietly, in our name, by trade bureaucrats and proconsuls and "area specialists" even while our leaders speak soothingly of a rising tide of freedom. Restive countries, awakening to some notion of self-interest, may wander off the reservation, of course. More poignantly, transnational capital always has its own logic and pursues its own ends. While we make the world safe for multinational corporations, it is by no means clear that they intend to return the favor.

NOTES

1. The term was coined in 1989 by John Williamson, of the Institute for International Economics, to describe the conventional wisdom at the U.S. Treasury Department, the World Bank, and the International Monetary Fund on policy reforms that would aid development in Latin America. Williamson later expressed dismay at the "populist definition," as he called it, of the term that had taken hold in public debate, where the Washington Consensus became synonymous with market fundamentalism, globally applied.
2. William Easterly, a senior Bank economist, tested the limits of that tolerance in 2001 when he published *The Elusive Quest for Growth,* a book that chronicled the failed development panaceas the Bank has promoted over the years. In a prologue, Easterly applauded the fact that his employer "encourages gadflies like me to exercise intellectual freedom." In the preface to a paperback edition, published in 2002, however, Easterly was obliged to revise this assessment. In truth, the Bank, he had learned, "encourages gadflies like me to find another job."

PART 4

Contemporary World Politics

With the end of the Cold War and start of the "War on Terrorism," we are in a new era of international politics. In Part Four we have picked, for more systematic analysis, five features of this era that we believe are the most important for understanding its major contours and challenges. They are: the future of war, both conventional and unconventional; the uses to which American power should be put; the causes and ways of dealing with domestic collapse and civil wars; the protection of the global environment, especially the gargantuan task of coping with likely climate change; and the effects on world politics being wrought by the rise of new actors and new forces, such as the European Union, nongovernmental organizations (NGOs), transnational corporations, and a more activist commitment to the rule of international law.

CONFLICT, WAR, AND TERRORISM

War is as old as the time when human beings first organized themselves into groups. In the modern era, it has been the great powers that have fought most, and that have always conducted their policies with the possibility of war in mind. Will the world be as ravaged by war in the decades to come as it has been since the dawn of civilization? Or are we now entering a new era when war will disappear or be transformed? If war continues, will it still be waged between the kind of actors who were most prominent in the past?

Robert Jervis, Samuel P. Huntington, and Jessica Stern address the future nature of war and the likely sources of conflict. Jervis argues that war among the rich democracies of North America, Western Europe, and Japan is not only a thing of the past but is no longer even contemplated. Since war among the leading powers has been the motor of traditional international politics, the coming era will be radically different. The rest of the world is not likely to remain at peace, however. Indeed, in much of the Third World, conflicts between, but especially within states rage, and disputes over borders and access to borders and natural resources provide proximate reasons for conflict. Huntington argues that the fault lines of future conflicts will be more civilizational than state-centered in nature. He identifies seven major world civilizations and explains the reasons why political conflicts, and sometimes wars, are more likely to occur among states belonging to different civilizations rather than among states of the same civilization.

The obvious new element of conflict is the War on Terrorism triggered by al Qaeda's attack on the World Trade Center and the Pentagon. Many of the consequences of the American response are discussed in the next section. Here Jessica Stern looks at al Qaeda itself, still a mysterious organization. She tracks how it has changed in response to its ouster from Afghanistan and the related policies of its adversaries. It might be easier for scholars to understand the organization and for the United States and others to deal with it if it remained unchanged. But such stability is precluded by the dynamic nature of politics, in which adversaries constantly anticipate and respond to each other's behavior. While most of al Qaeda's objectives remain the same, not only have the threats to it changed, but so have its opportunities and possible allies.

THE USES OF AMERICAN POWER

Since the collapse of the Soviet Union in 1991, the United States has been the world's strongest economic and military power, and, as a consequence, analysts have argued that we live in a "unipolar" world—one dominated by a single state. Immediately following the end of the Cold War, America's economic and military strength was an important feature of international political life: American military power deployed abroad was a stabilizing influence in key regions, and America's remarkable economic growth in the 1990s helped other states to prosper as well. For many of the conflicts that have erupted since 1991, the United States has been the "911" of the world.

But 9/11 now obviously has an additional meaning, and the use of American power since the terrorist attacks raises a host of new issues. How will the United States pursue its war on terror? To what extent is this largely an American struggle? What is the role of other states, how will they react to the highly assertive American policy, and how heavily should the United States weigh their preferences and interests? These issues are sharply raised by what can be called the "Bush Doctrine" outlined in numerous official documents and presidential speeches and embodied in many American actions, especially the ouster of Saddam Hussein. Many people have attributed the new American policy and the sharp shift in President Bush's policy to a combination of factors, most obviously the terrorist attacks, but also Bush's unilateralist predispositions, his religious beliefs, and the role of neo-conservatives in his administration. While not denying the relevance of these factors, Robert Jervis looks to the structure of the international system for much of the explanation. Realists like Morgenthau and Waltz have stressed that power is checked only by counter-balancing power. A unipolar system will be highly conducive to unilateralism on the part of the leading state as it sees both that no other states can block it and that countries which share its interests are not sufficiently powerful to act on their own, but rather will wait for the leading power to shoulder the burden of action.

Such a policy is natural, but this does not mean it will be in the interests of the world—or even that it well serves the dominant state. G. John Ikenberry focuses on the costs entailed by the United States moving away from its previous pattern of closely working with a wide range of allies and instead reducing the extent to which it allows them to influence its policies. Acting alone has obvious attractions, especially in the face of pressing threats, but for many tasks, such as maintaining the global economy, building norms and institutions that in the long run are in the American interest, and rebuilding failed states, extensive cooperation from others may be more than helpful, it may be essential. Charles Krauthammer largely disagrees. He stresses the extent to which September 11 increased American power and made multilateralism more difficult. Under these circumstances, the United States has little choice but to be highly assertive. If it is not, the result will be a power vacuum and disorder that will end up harming not only the United States, but its allies as well. For Joseph Nye, whether the United States should behave unilaterally or multilaterally depends largely on the circumstances. Working with others usually is in America's interest, and should be what the United States thinks of and tries first. But when vital interests are at stake, when multilateral arrangements can interfere with stability, and when compromising with others compromises essential values or prevents necessary action, the United States should be prepared to act largely on its own if need be.

FAILED STATES, CIVIL WARS, AND NATION-BUILDING

Although civil strife and domestic collapse are as old as history, they have become more prominent after the Cold War and have become even more important recently through the perceived links to terrorism. State failure and civil war are fed by both internal and external causes, which makes them particularly hard to understand and deal with. Because of the growth in the number of states and because of the heightened consequences for regions, if not the entire world, for disturbance in one area these subjects are now high on the agenda of both scholars and policymakers. Because we live in well-established countries with a high degree of public order, most of us too easily forget that this situation is not a natural one, but rather the hard-won result of a broad concatenation of political, economic, and social forces. Under some circumstances, central authority can not only be subject to violent dispute, but can also be so torn apart that it simply disappears, resulting in the national government being replaced by local warlords, roving bands of thugs, and chaos.

Robert Rotberg looks at strong, weak, and collapsing states. He details many of the paths that lead to state collapse, as well as examining states that seemed headed in this direction but saved themselves. State failure and civil war are often reciprocally related, of course. One prominent explanation for these phenomena is the power of deep grievances and divisions within a state, often along ethnic lines. But Paul Collier argues that at least as important are economic factors, both the lack of resources at the disposal of the central government that could allow it to maintain order and the incentives for civil war that are provided by resources that rebels can exploit. Furthermore, he shows that civil wars are like many diseases in that they are both contagious (i.e., being likely to spread to neighbors) and subject to recurrences (i.e., one round of civil strife is likely to lead to others).

Even if the role of ethnicity has sometimes been exaggerated, it often plays a role. Chaim Kaufmann analyzes the nature of ethnic civil wars, shows why they are so intractable, and surveys the various methods of intervening in them. He concludes that physical separation of the warring ethnic groups, either by creating safe areas within a state or by partitioning the state, offers the best long-term hope to stop the killing. Most current discussion focuses not on dividing countries but on rebuilding them. James Dobbins extracts the lessons we can learn from outsiders' attempts at nation-building and democratization since World War II. Germany and Japan are of course marvelous successes, but he shows that the conditions and policies at work may be very hard to replicate.

THE ENVIRONMENT AND CLIMATE CHANGE

Protection of the global environment is not a new issue, but its importance has increased within the last decade, with the greater damage in the form of depletion of the world's fisheries, degradation of the ozone layer, and the threat of global warming and attendant climate change. The United Nations Conference on the Environment held in Rio in 1992 marked a watershed in international awareness of the increasing threat to the global environment.

Truly global environmental threats, as opposed to strictly national ones, are especially difficult to deal with because they are a "commons" problem. In such cases, concertation of state action does not come easy because the situation looks as follows. No single state owns the resource being consumed (or abused), but all use it (or abuse it), and none can be prevented from using and abusing it at will. A commons (or public) good is therefore one that no single individual or entity owns, but that all need and can use. For such goods, no individual or state has an incentive to minimize its exploitation unless it is persuaded that all others will act in similar fashion. This represents a collective action problem: uncoordinated individual action produces collective disaster. This is the "tragedy of the commons" and the message of Garrett Hardin's article.

Not all analysts agree with Hardin's logic, however. Julian L. Simon challenges the view that humankind must husband its natural resources because he argues that their supply is infinite, or at least not finite in an economic sense. He challenges us to think like an economist—to consider not just the absolute supply of a good but rather how much is available at a given price. In this sense, no resource is finite because substitutes are always available if the price of a good rises too high compared to other goods that can be substituted for it. In short, the market will solve the problem of the availability of resources, and by extension, the market can deal with the degradation of the environment when the costs of cleaning it up are built into the price of the goods that contribute to its degradation. Thomas Homer-Dixon takes exception to Simon's view. He gives seven reasons why Simon-type arguments no longer apply in today's world. The taproot of all seven is the continuing growth in the world's population. If it becomes too large, the sheer mass of humanity will overwhelm the ability of humanity to invent its way out of its problems. In Homer-Dixon's eyes, we are at that point now.

Finally, climate change induced by man-made global warming, or what is properly termed "the enhanced greenhouse effect," may be humankind's greatest challenge. Widespread, sustained, and growing use of fossil fuels to develop and sustain modern economies has added enough carbon dioxide to the world's atmosphere to cause the average global temperature to increase by nearly one degree since the onset of the Industrial Revolution. This may sound insignificant, but it is not. The overall change in global temperature from the depths of the last Ice Age until now can be measured within the range of four to nine degrees centigrade. The best estimates of climatologists are that at present and projected rates of fossil fuel burning, the average global temperature will increase from two to six degrees centigrade by the end of the twenty-first century. At the high end of this estimate, we will be in the range within which severe climate change occurred in the past. Climate change raises dangers not only of widespread dislocations but also of catastrophic climate change if warming feeds on itself (warming produces more warming and so on).

Climate change is the biggest commons problem of them all. Every nation contributes to it, although some much more than others. The United States, for example, contributes about one-fifth of the greenhouse gases produced each year. China is also a big contributor, but so, too, are nations that cut down their forests because trees absorb carbon dioxide. Slowing greenhouse gas emissions, and preferably stabilizing them at a safe level, will require a degree of international cooperation not yet achieved in humankind's history. It also will likely involve massive transfers of resources from the rich nations to the poor, adoption of clean and environmentally friendly energy technologies, novel political-economic schemes like emissions trading rights, and sacrifice by both rich and poor.

The nations of the world have been wrestling with this extremely complex problem for a little over a decade. At the Rio Conference in 1992, they committed themselves to a framework convention on dealing with global warming, but they made no specific commitments. Rio was more an exhortation to act than a specific plan for action. At the Kyoto Conference in 1997, the rich developed states did lay out a plan of action that committed them to reduce by 2010 their greenhouse gas emissions from six to eight percent below their 1990 levels. The world's poorer developing states, however, refused to make similar binding commitments, arguing that the developed states had created the problem and therefore should solve it—first by reducing their own emissions and then by giving the developing states the financial resources and technology to build environmentally safe energy industries. The parties to the Kyoto Treaty (called the Annex I countries) have subsequently been engaged in negotiating the specific measures and mechanisms necessary to put the Kyoto commitments into effect, and most of them have ratified the Kyoto Protocol, but the United States, under the Bush administration, decided not to be part of this process, stated that the United States will not ratify the treaty, and withdrew the treaty from Senate consideration. If the world is to deal effectively with global warming, then Third World nations and the United States, both of which refuse to be a party to Kyoto's limits, must somehow be convinced to do their share. Indeed, Third World nations are not likely to agree to help until the United States takes serious action to reduce its greenhouse gas emissions. Thomas Schelling notes the flaws in the Kyoto arrangements, especially its short-run focus, its neglect of technology, and its faulty incentives, and points to more flexible and carefully crafted arrangements as an alternative. The Marshall Plan after World War II, the World Trade Organization, and NATO are perhaps the most successful instances of deep and widespread cooperation and their procedures and approaches, he argues, could be emulated to deal with global warming.

NEW ACTORS AND NEW FORCES IN WORLD POLITICS

The state system we live in today dates roughly from the Peace of Westphalia, which ended the Thirty Years War, one of the bloodiest in human history. Consequently, the modern international system of states has recently celebrated its 350th anniversary. Will it continue? That is, will the state remain the most important, although not the only important, actor in world politics?

The six final selections of this book provide informed speculation on this question. Margaret E. Keck and Kathryn Sikkink provide a more systematic analysis of NGOs and show how transnational networks operate and increasingly affect state action. Many of these actors are deeply concerned about human rights. At bottom, the most fundamental units in the world are not states but individuals, and Rhoda E. Howard and Jack Donnelly argue that, although cultures and systems differ, each individual still has a set of rights by virtue of being human. In the absence of effective international government, there is no choice but to rely on states for the enforcement of human rights. So states are both strengthened because they have assumed new responsibilities and weakened because their sovereignty is challenged by universal norms and outside actors. States are also challenged by the flow of commodities and people that illegally flow across their borders, especially drugs, arms, terrorists, money derived from crime, migrants, and refugees. Moisés Naím examines these and the limited responses available to state authorities. Jack Rakove examines another type of new international actor—the European Union. He assesses the attempt to write its constitution and the tensions between seeking legitimacy by basing it on the consent of the populations, on the one hand, and working through the established states, on the other. In either case, law plays a great role in the EU. More broadly, Steven R. Ratner argues that international law is having greater effect on state action, and by implication, that international politics are becoming more regulated and domestic-like. More international law is being written, and enforcement is being improved.

Whether the forces and actors described above will eventually subvert the state system or instead remain subservient to it, or whether some new patterns now difficult to imagine will emerge, is something we will be able to answer only several decades from now.

CONFLICT, WAR, AND TERRORISM

The Era of Leading Power Peace

ROBERT JERVIS

War and the possibility of war among the great powers has been the motor of international politics, not only strongly influencing the boundaries and distribution of values among them, but deeply affecting their internal arrangements and shaping the fates of the smaller ones. Being seen as an ever-present possibility produced by deeply-rooted factors such as human nature and the lack of world government, this force was expected to continue indefinitely. But I would argue that war among the leading great powers—the most developed states of the United States, West Europe, and Japan—will not occur in the future, and indeed is no longer a source of concern for them (Mueller 1989).

Now, however, the leading states form what Karl Deutsch called a pluralistic security community, a group among whom war is literally unthinkable—i.e., neither the publics nor the political elites nor even the military establishments expect war with each other (Deutsch et al. 1957). No official in the Community would advocate a policy on the grounds that it would improve the state's position in the event of war with other members or allow the state to more effectively threaten them.

Although no one state can move away from the reliance on war by itself lest it become a victim, they can collectively do so if each forsakes the resort to force. This development challenges many of our theories and raises the question of what international politics will be like in the future.

Security communities are not unprecedented. But what is unprecedented is that the states that constitute this one are the leading members of the international system and so are natural rivals who in the past were central to the violent struggle for security, power, and contested values. Winston Churchill exaggerated only

Excerpted/abridged from "Theories of War in an Era of Leading-Power Peace Presidential Address, APSA, 2001" by Robert Jervis from *American Political Science Review*, Vol. 96, No. 1 (March 2002) pp. 1–14. Reprinted with the permission of Cambridge University Press. Portions of the text and some footnotes have been omitted.

slightly when he declared that "people talked a lot of nonsense when they said nothing was ever settled by war. Nothing in history was ever settled *except* by wars" (quoted in Gilbert 1983, 860–61). Even cases of major change without war, such as Britain yielding hegemony in the Western hemisphere to the United States at the turn of the twentieth century, were strongly influenced by security calculations. Threatening war, preparing for it, and trying to avoid it have permeated all aspects of politics, and so a world in which war among the most developed states is unthinkable will be very different from the history with which we are familiar. To paraphrase and extend a claim made by Evan Luard (1986, 77), given the scale and frequency of war among the great powers in the preceding millennia, this is a change of spectacular proportions, perhaps the single most striking discontinuity that the history of international politics has anywhere provided.

Two major states, Russia and China, might fight each other or a member of the Community. But, as I will discuss below, such a conflict would be different from traditional wars between great powers. Furthermore, these countries lack many of the attributes of great powers: their internal regimes are shaky, they are not at the forefront of any advanced forms of technology or economic organization, they can pose challenges only regionally, and they have no attraction as models for others. They are not among the most developed states and I think it would be fair to put them outside the ranks of the great powers as well. But their military potential, their status as nuclear powers, and the size of their economies renders that judgment easily debatable and so I will not press it but rather will argue that the set of states that form the Community are not all the great powers, but all the most developed ones.

CENTRAL QUESTIONS

Five questions arise. First, does the existence of the Community mean the end of security threats to its members, and more specifically to the United States? Second, will the Community endure? Third, what are the causes of its construction and maintenance? Fourth, what are the implications for this transformation for the conduct of international affairs? Finally, what does this say about theories of the causes of war?

CONTINUED THREATS

The fact that the United States is not menaced by the most developed countries does not mean that it does not face any military threats at all. Indeed, some see the United States as no more secure than it was during the Cold War, being imperiled by terrorists and "rogue" states, in addition to Russia and China. But even if I am wrong to believe that these claims are greatly exaggerated, these conflicts do not have the potential to drive world politics the way that clashes among the leading powers did in the past. They do not permeate all facets of international politics and structure state–society relations; they do not represent a struggle for dominance in the international system or a direct challenge to American vital interests.

Recent terrorist attacks are of unprecedented magnitude and will have a significant impact on domestic and international politics, but I do not think they have the potential to be a functional substitute for great power war—i.e., to be the driving force of politics. Despite rhetoric to the contrary, there is little chance that all the countries will unite to combat terrorism; the forms of this scourge are too varied and indeed often are a useful tool for states, and states have many other interests that are at least as important as combating terrorism. Similarly, although the events of September 11 have triggered significant changes in American foreign policy and international alignments, I believe that in a fairly short period of time previous outlooks and conflicts of interest will reassert themselves. Even if this is not the case and if combating terrorism becomes the most important goal for most or all states, the move away from leading power war is still both important and puzzling.

WILL THE SECURITY COMMUNITY LAST?

Predictions about the maintenance of the Community are obviously disputable (indeed, limitations on people's ability to predict could undermine it), but nothing in the short period since the end of the Cold War points to an unraveling. We could make a long list of disputes, but there were at least as many in the earlier period. The Europeans' effort to establish an independent security force is aimed at permitting them to intervene when the United States chooses not to (or perhaps by threatening such action, to trigger American intervention), not at fighting the United States. Even if Europe were to unite either to balance against the United States or because of its own internal dynamics and the world were to become bipolar again, it is very unlikely that suspicions, fears for the future, and conflicts of interest would be severe enough to break the Community.

A greater threat would be the failure of Europe to unite coupled with an American withdrawal of forces, which could lead to "security competition" within Europe (Art 1996a; Mearsheimer 2001, 385–96). Partly general, the fears would focus on Germany. Their magnitude is hard to gauge and it is difficult to estimate what external shocks or kinds of German behavior would activate them. The fact that Thatcher and Mitterrand opposed German unification is surely not forgotten in Germany and is an indication that concerns remain. But this danger is likely to constitute a self-denying prophecy in two ways. First, many Germans are aware of the need not only to reassure others by tying themselves closely to Europe, but also to seek to make it unlikely that future generations of Germans would want to break these bonds even if they could. Second, Americans who worry about the residual danger will favor keeping some troops in Europe as the ultimate intra-European security guarantee.

Expectations of peace close off important routes to war. The main reason for Japanese aggression in the 1930s was the desire for a self-sufficient sphere that would permit Japan to fight the war with the Western powers that was seen as inevitable, not because of particular conflicts, but because it was believed that great powers always fight each other. By contrast, if states believe that a security community will last they will not be hypersensitive to threats from within it and will not feel the need to undertake precautionary measures that could undermine the security of other members. Thus the United States is not disturbed that British and French nuclear missiles could destroy American cities and while those two countries object to American plans for missile defense, they do not feel the need to increase their forces in response. As long as peace is believed to be very likely, the chance of inadvertent spirals of tension and threat is low.

Nevertheless, the point with which I began this section is unavoidable. World politics can change rapidly and saying that nothing foreseeable will dissolve the Community is not the same as saying that it will not dissolve (Betts 1992). To the extent that it rests on democracy and prosperity (see below), anything that would undermine these would also undermine the Community. Drastic climate change could also shake the foundations of much that we have come to take for granted. But it is hard to see how dynamics at the international level (i.e., the normal trajectory of fears, disputes, and rivalries) could produce war among the leading states. In other words, the Community does not have within it the seeds of its own destruction.

Our faith in the continuation of this peace is increased to the extent that we think we understand its causes and have reason to believe that they will continue. This is our next topic.

EXPLANATIONS FOR THE SECURITY COMMUNITY

There are social constructivist, liberal, and realist explanations for the Community which, although proceeding from different assumptions and often using different terms, invoke overlapping factors.

Social Constructivism

Social constructivist accounts stress the role of norms of non-violence and shared identities that, through an interactive process of reciprocal behaviors and expectations, have led the advanced democracies to assume the role of each other's friend. In contradistinction to the liberal and realist explanations, this downplays the importance of material factors and elevates ideas, images of oneself and others, and conceptions of appropriate conduct. The roots of the changes that have produced this enormous shift in international politics among some countries but not others is not specified in detail, but the process is a self-reinforcing one—a benign cycle of behavior, beliefs, and expectations.

People become socialized into attitudes, beliefs, and values that are conducive to peace. Individuals in the Community may see their own country as strong and good—and even better than others—but they rarely espouse the virulent nationalism that was common in the past. Before World War I, one German figure could proclaim that the Germans were "the greatest civilized people known to history" while another declared that the Germans were "the chosen people of this century," which explains "why other people hate us. They do not understand us but they fear our tremendous spiritual superiority." Thomas Macaulay similarly wrote that the British were "the greatest and most highly civilized people that ever the world saw" and were "the acknowledged leaders of the human race in the causes of political improvement," while Senator Albert Beveridge proclaimed that "God has made us the master organizers of the world" (quoted in Van Evera 1984, 27). These sentiments are shocking today because they are so at variance from what we have been taught to think about others and ourselves. We could not adopt these views without rejecting a broad set of beliefs and values. An understanding of the effects of such conceptions led the Europeans, and to an unfortunately lesser extent the Japanese, to de-nationalize and harmonize their textbooks after World War II and has similarly led countries with remaining enemies to follow a different path: The goals for the education of a 12-year-old child in Pakistan include the "ability to know all about India's evil designs about Pakistan; acknowledge and identify forces that may be working against Pakistan; understand the Kashmir problem" (quoted in Kumar 2001, 29).

The central objection to constructionism is that it mistakes effect for cause: its description is correct, but the identities, images, and self-images are superstructure, being the product of peace and of the material incentives discussed below. What is crucial is not people's thinking, but the factors that drive it. The validity of this claim is beyond the reach of current evidence, but it points to a critique of the constructivist argument that the Community will last, which places great faith in the power of socialization and the ability of ideas to replicate and sustain themselves. This conception may betray an excessive faith in the validity of ideas that seem self-evident today, but that our successors might reject. Constructivism may present us with actors who are "over-socialized" (Wrong 1976, ch. 2) and leave too little role for agency in the form of people who think differently, perhaps because their material conditions are different.

Liberalism

The liberal explanation has received most attention. Although it comes in several variants, the central strands are the pacifying effects of democracy and economic interdependence.

Democracy

The members of the Community are democracies, and many scholars argue that democracies rarely if ever fight each other. Although the statistical evidence is, as usual, subject to debate, Jack Levy is correct to claim that it is "as close as anything we have to an empirical law in international politics" (Levy 1989, 88).

Less secure, however, is our understanding of why this is the case. We have numerous explanations, which can be seen as competing or complementary. Democracies are systems of dispersed power, and dispersed power means multiple veto points and groups that could block war. (This seems true almost by definition, but if the accounts of former Soviet leaders are to be trusted, Brezhnev was more constrained by his colleagues than was Nixon, at least where arms control was concerned.) Related are the norms of these regimes: democracies function through compromise, non-violence, and respect for law. To the extent that these values and habits govern foreign policy, they are conducive to peace, especially in relations with other democracies who reciprocate.

Other scholars have argued that the key element lies in the realm of information. By having a relatively free flow of intelligence and encouraging debate, democracies are less likely to make egregious errors in estimating what courses of action will maintain the peace. The other side of the informational coin is that democracies can more effectively telegraph their own intentions, and so avoid both unnecessary spirals of conflict and wars that stem from others' incorrect beliefs that the democracy is bluffing (although an obvious cost is an inability to bluff).

Finally, in a recasting of the traditional argument that democracies are less likely to go to war because those who hold ultimate authority (i.e., the general public) will pay the price for conflict, some argue that the institutional and coalitional nature of democratic regimes requires their leaders to pursue successful policies if they are to stay in office. Thus democracies will put greater efforts into winning wars and be careful to choose to fight only wars they can win. Autocracies have a much narrower base and so can stay in power by buying off their supporters even if their foreign policies are unnecessarily costly. These arguments, while highly suggestive, share with earlier liberal thinking quite stylized assumptions about the preferences of societal actors and pay little attention to how each country anticipates the behavior of others and assesses how others expect it to behave.

These explanations for the democratic peace are thoughtful and often ingenious, but not conclusive. Many of them lead us to expect not only dyadic effects, but monadic ones as well—i.e., democracies should be generally peaceful, not only peaceful toward each other, a finding that most scholars deny. They would also lead us to expect that one democracy would not seek to overthrow another, a proposition that is contradicted by American behavior during the Cold War. Furthermore, most of the arguments are built around dyads but it is not entirely clear that the posited causes would apply as well to multilateral groupings like the Community.

The causal role of democracy is hard to establish because these regimes have been relatively rare until recently, much of the democratic peace can be explained by the Soviet threat, and the same factors that lead countries to become democratic (e.g., being relatively rich and secure) are conducive to peace between them. It is particularly important and difficult to control for the role of common interest, which loomed so large during the Cold War. But interests are not objective and may be strongly influenced by the country's internal regime. Thus the democracies may have made common cause during the Cold War in part because they were democracies; common interest may be a mechanism by which the democratic peace is sustained as much as it is a competing explanation for it (for this and related issues, see Farber and Gowa 1995, 1997; Gartzke 1998, 2000; Maoz 1997; Oneal and Russett 1999; Schweller 2000). Moreover, if democracies are more likely to become economically interdependent with one another, additional common interest will be created. But to bring up the importance of interest is to highlight an ambiguity and raise a question. The ambiguity is whether the theory leads us to expect democracies *never* to fight each other or "merely" to fight *less* than do other dyads. (Most scholars take the latter view, but this does not mean that this is what most versions of the theory actually imply.) The related hypothetical question is: Is it impossible for two democracies to have a conflict of interest so severe that it leads to war? This troubles the stronger version of the argument because it is hard to answer in the affirmative.

But would democracies let such a potent conflict of interest develop? At least as striking as the statistical data is the fact—or rather, the judgment—that the regimes that most disturbed the international order in the twentieth century also devastated their own peoples—the USSR, Germany under the Nazis and, perhaps, under Kaiser Wilhelm. One reason for this connection may be the desire to remake the world (but because the international order was established by countries that were advanced democracies, it may not be surprising that those who opposed it were not). Not all murderous regimes are as ambitious (e.g., Idi Amin's Uganda), and others with both power and grand designs may remain restrained (e.g., Mao's China), but it is hard to understand the disruptive German and Soviet foreign policy without reference to their domestic regimes.

Interdependence

The second leg of the liberal explanation for the Community is the high level of economic interdependence. The basic argument was developed by Cobden, Bright, and the other nineteenth-century British liberals. As the former put it: "Free Trade is God's diplomacy and there is no other certain way of uniting people in bonds of peace." (Quoted in Bourne 1970, 85. For a general treatment of Cobden's views, see Cain 1979. For the most recent evidence, see McMillan 1997; Russett and Oneal 2001, ch. 4; for arguments that interdependence has been exaggerated and misunderstood, see Waltz 1970, 1979 ch. 7, 1999. Most traditional liberal thinking and the rest of my brief discussion assumes symmetry; as Hirschman 1945 showed, asymmetric dependence can provide the basis for exploitative bargaining.) Although the evidence for this proposition remains in dispute, the causal argument is relatively straightforward. "If goods cannot cross borders, armies will" is the central claim, in the words of the nineteenth-century French economist Frederick Bastiat which were often repeated by Secretary of State Cordell Hull (perhaps excessively influenced by the experience of the 1930s). Extensive economic intercourse allows states to gain by trade the wealth that they would otherwise seek through fighting. Relatedly, individuals and groups who conduct these economic relations develop a powerful stake in keeping the peace and maintaining good relations. Thus it is particularly significant that in the contemporary world many firms have important ties abroad and that direct foreign investment holds the fates of important actors hostage to continued good relations. There can be a benign cycle here as increasing levels of trade strengthen the political power of actors who have a stake in deepening these ties.

The liberal view assumes that actors place a high priority on wealth, that trade is a better route to it than conquest, and that actors who gain economically from the exchange are politically powerful. These assumptions are often true, especially in the modern world, but are not without their vulnerabilities. At times honor and glory, in addition to more traditional forms of individual and national interest, can be more salient than economic gain. Thus as the Moroccan crisis of 1911 came to its climax, General von Moltke wrote to his wife: "If we again slip away from this affair with our tail between our legs . . . I shall despair of the future of the German Empire. I shall then retire. But before handing in my resignation I shall move to abolish the Army and to place ourselves under Japanese protectorate; we shall then be in a position to make money without interference and to develop into ninnies" (quoted in Berghahn 1973, 97). Traditional liberal thought understood this well and stressed that economic activity was so potent not only because it gave people an interest in maintaining peace, but because it reconstructed social values to downgrade status and glory and elevate material well-being. It follows that the stability of the Community rests in part upon people giving priority to consumption. Critics decry modern society's embodiment of individualistic, material values, but one can easily imagine that others could generate greater international conflict.

There are four general arguments against the pacific influence of interdependence. First, if it is hard to go from the magnitude of economic flows to the costs that would be incurred if they were disrupted, it is even more difficult to estimate how much political impact these costs will have, which depends on the other considerations in play and the political context. This means that we do not have a theory that tells us the expected magnitude of the effect. Second, even the sign of the effect can be disputed: interdependence can increase conflict as states gain bargaining leverage over each other, fear that others will exploit them, and face additional sources of disputes. These effects might not arise if states expect to remain at peace with each other, however. Third, it is clear that interdependence does not guarantee peace. High levels of economic integration did not prevent World War I, and nations that were much more unified than any security community have peacefully dissolved or fought civil wars. But this does not mean that interdependence is not conducive to peace. Fourth, interdependence may be more an effect than a cause, more the product than a generator of expectations of peace and cooperation.

Realist Explanations

The crudest realist explanation for the Community would focus on the rise of the common threat from Russia and China. While not entirely implausible, this argument does not fit the views espoused by most elites in Japan and Europe, who are relatively unconcerned about these countries and believe that whatever dangers emanate from them would be magnified rather than decreased by a confrontational policy.

American Hegemony

Two other realist accounts are stronger. The first argues that the Community is largely caused by the other enormous change in world politics—the American dominance of world politics. U.S. defense spending, to take the most easily quantifiable indicator, is now greater than that of the next 8 countries combined (O'Hanlon 2001, 4–5). Furthermore, thanks to the Japanese constitution and the integration of armed forces within NATO, America's allies do not have to fear attacks from each other: their militaries (especially Germany's) are so truncated that they could not fight a major war without American assistance or attack each other without undertaking a military buildup that would give others a great deal of warning. American dominance also leads us to expect that key outcomes, from the expansion of NATO, to the American-led wars in Kosovo and the Persian Gulf, to the IMF bailouts of Turkey and Argentina in the spring of 2001, will conform to American preferences.

But closer examination reveals differences between current and past hegemonies. The United States usually gives considerable weight to its partners' views and indeed its own preferences are often influenced by theirs, as was true in Kosovo. For their parts, the other members of the Community seek to harness and constrain American power, not displace it. The American hegemony will surely eventually decay but increased European and Japanese strength need not lead to war, contrary to the expectations of standard theories of hegemony and great power rivalry. Unlike previous eras of hegemony, the current peace seems uncoerced and accepted by most states, which does not fit entirely well with realism.

Nuclear Weapons

The second realist argument was familiar during the Cold War but receives less attention now. This is the pacifying effect of nuclear weapons, which, if possessed in sufficient numbers and invulnerable configurations, make victory impossible and war a feckless option. An immediate objection is that not all the major states in the Community have nuclear weapons. But this is only technically correct: Germany and Japan could produce nuclear weapons if a threat loomed, as their partners fully understand. The other factors discussed in the previous pages may or may not be important; nuclear weapons by themselves would be sufficient to keep the great powers at peace.

While there is a great deal to this argument, it is not without its problems. First, because this kind of deterrence rests on the perceived possibility of war, it may explain peace, but not a security community. Second, mutual deterrence can be used as a platform for hostility, coercion, and even limited wars. In what Glenn Snyder (1965; also see Jervis 1989, 19–23, 74–106) calls the stability-instability paradox, the common realization that all-out war would be irrational provides a license for threats and the use of lower levels of violence. Under some circumstances a state could use the shared fear of nuclear war to exploit others. If the state thinks that the other is preoccupied with the possibility of war and does not anticipate that the state will make the concessions needed to reduce this danger, it will expect the other to retreat and so can stand firm. In other words, the fact that war would be the worst possible outcome for both sides does not automatically lead to uncoerced peace, let alone to a security community.

A Synthetic Interactive Explanation

I think the development and maintenance of the Community is best explained by a combination and reformulation of several factors discussed previously. Even with the qualifications just discussed, a necessary condition is the belief that conquest is difficult and war is terribly costly. When conquest is easy, aggression is encouraged and the security dilemma operates with particular viciousness as even defensive states need to prepare to attack (Van Evera 1999). But when states have modern armies with extensive firepower and, even more, nuclear weapons, it is hard for anyone to believe that war could make sense.

Statesmen must consider the gains that war might bring as well as the costs. Were they to be very high, they might outweigh great expected costs. But, if anything, the expected benefits of war within the Community have declined, in part because the developed countries, including those that lost World War II, are generally satisfied with the status quo. Even in the case that shows the greatest strain—U.S.–Japanese relations—no one has explained how a war could provide either side much gross, let alone net, benefit. It is then hard to locate a problem for which war among the Community members would provide a solution. Furthermore, as liberals have stressed, peace within the Community brings many gains, especially economic.

Of course costs and benefits are subjective, depending as they do on what the actors value, and changes in values are the third leg of my explanation. Most political analysis takes the actors' values for granted because they tend to be widely shared and to change slowly. Their importance and variability becomes clear only when we confront a case like Nazi Germany which, contrary to standard realist conceptions of national interest and security, put everything at risk in order to seek the domination of the Aryan race.

The changes over the last 50–75 years in what the leaders and publics in the developed states value drive some of the calculations of costs and benefits. To start with, war is no longer seen as good in itself; no great power leader today would agree with Theodore Roosevelt that "no triumph of peace is quite so great as the supreme triumph of war" (quoted in Harbaugh 1961, 99). In earlier eras it was commonly believed that war brought out the best in individuals and nations and that the virtues of discipline, risk-taking, and self-sacrifice that war required were central to civilization. Relatedly, honor and glory used to be central values. In a world so constituted, the material benefits of peace would be much less important; high levels of trade, the difficulty of making conquest pay, and even nuclear weapons might not produce peace.

Democracy and identity also operate through what actors value, and may in part be responsible for the decline in militarism just noted. Compromise, consideration for the interests of others, respect for law, and a shunning of violence outside this context all are values that underpin democracy and are reciprocally cultivated by it. The Community also is relatively homogeneous in that its members are all democracies and have values that are compatibly similar. One impulse to war is the desire to change the other country, and this disappears if values are shared. The United States could conquer Canada, for example, but what would be the point when so much of what it wants to see there is already in place?

Central to the rise of the Community is the decline in territorial disputes among its members. Territory has been the most common cause and object of conflicts in the past, and we have become so accustomed to their absence that it is easy to lose sight of how drastic and consequential this change is. Germans no longer care that Alsace and Lorraine are French; the French are not disturbed by the high level of German presence in these provinces. The French furthermore permitted the Saar to return to Germany and are not bothered by this loss, and indeed do not feel it as a loss at all. Although for years the Germans refused to renounce their claims to the "lost territories" to the east, they did so upon unification and few voices were raised in protest.

The causes of these changes in values in general and nationalism and concern with territory in particular are subject to dispute, as are the developments that could reverse them. In particular, it is unclear how much they are rooted in material changes, most obviously the increased destructiveness of war and the unprecedented prosperity that is seen as linked to good political relations, and to what extent they are more autonomous, following out perhaps a natural progression and building on each other. They may be linked (inextricably?) to high levels of consumption, faith in rationality, and the expectation of progress, although it is not unreasonable to argue that this describes Europe in 1914 as well. The decreased salience of territory and decline of territorial disputes is almost surely produced in part by the decoupling of territorial control and national prosperity, and most of the other relationships between material structures and ideational patterns are complex and reciprocal. Just as capitalism is built and sustained by pre-capitalist values and post-materialism may grow from prosperity so the values that sustain the Community can neither be separated nor simply deduced from changes in the means and levels of production and potential destruction.

The increased destructiveness of war, the benefits of peace, and the changes in values interact and reinforce each other. If war were not so dreadful, it could be considered as an instrument for national enrichment; if peace did not seem to bring prosperity and national well-being, violence would at least be contemplated; that military victory is no longer seen as a positive value both contributes to and is in part explained by the high perceived costs of war. Similarly, expectations of peace allow states to value each other's economic and political successes. Although these may incite envy, they no longer produce strong security fears, as they did in the past. The Community may then contain within it the seeds of its own growth through the feedbacks among its elements.

Another dynamic element is crucial as well: the progress of the Community is path-dependent in that without the Cold War it is unlikely that the factors we have discussed could have overcome prevalent fears and rivalries. The conflict with the Soviet Union produced American security guarantees and an unprecedented sense of common purpose among the states that now form the Community. Since the coalition could be undermined by social unrest or political instability, each country sought to see that the others were well off and resisted the temptation to solve its own problems by exporting them to its neighbors. Since the coalition would have been disrupted had any country developed strong grievances against other members, each had reason to moderate its demands and mediate when conflicts developed between others. To cultivate better relations in the future, leaders consciously portrayed the others as partners and sponsored the socialization practices discussed above. The American willingness to engage in extensive cooperation abroad, the European willingness to go far down the road of integration, the

Japanese willingness to tie itself closely to the United States were improbable without the Cold War. But having been established, these forms of cooperation set off positive feedback and are now self-sustaining.

IMPLICATIONS

What are the implications of the existence of the security community for how these states will carry out relations among themselves and for general theories of war and peace?

International Politics Within the Community

In previous eras, no aspect of international politics and few aspects of domestic politics were untouched by the anticipation of future wars among the leading powers. Much will then change in the Community. In the absence of these states amalgamating—a development that is out of the question outside of Europe and unlikely within it—they will neither consider using force against one another nor lose their sovereignty. There will then be significant conflicts of interest without clear means of resolving them. They will continue to be rivals in some respects, and to bargain with each other. Indeed, the stability-instability paradox implies that the shared expectation that disputes will remain peaceful will remove some restraints on vituperation and competitive tactics. The dense network of institutions within the Community should serve to provide multiple means for resolving conflicts, but will also provide multiple ways for a dissatisfied country to show its displeasure and threaten disruption.

The fact that the situation is a new one poses challenges and opportunities for states. What goals will have highest priority? How important will considerations of status be? Will non-military alliances form? Bargaining will continue, and this means that varieties of power, including the ability to help and hurt others, will remain relevant. Threats, bluffs, warnings, the mobilization of resources for future conflicts, intense diplomatic negotiations, and shifting patterns of working with and against others all will remain. But the content of these forms will differ from those of traditional international politics.

Politics within the Community may come to resemble the relations between the United States and Canada and Australia that Keohane and Nye (1977) described as complex interdependence: extensive transnational and transgovernmental relations, bargains carried out across different issue areas, and bargaining power gained through asymmetric dependence but limited by overall common interests. Despite this pathbreaking study, however, we know little about how this kind of politics will be conducted. As numerous commentators have noted, economic issues and economic resources will play large roles, but the changed context will matter. Relative economic advantage was sought in the past in part because it contributed to military security. This no longer being the case, the possibilities for cooperation are increased.

Even though force will not be threatened within the Community, it will remain important in relations among its members. During the Cold War the protection the

United States afforded to its allies gave it an important moral claim and significant bargaining leverage. Despite the decreased level of threat, this will be true for the indefinite future because militarily Japan and Europe need the United States much more than the United States needs them. While the unique American ability to lead military operations like those in the Persian Gulf and Kosovo causes resentments and frictions with its allies, it also gives it a resource that is potent even—or especially—if it is never explicitly brought to the table.

Four Possible Futures

Even within the contours of a Community, there is a significant range of patterns of relations that are possible, four of which can be briefly sketched.

The greatest change would be a world in which national autonomy would be further diminished and the distinctions between domestic and foreign policy would continue to erode. Medieval Europe, with its overlapping forms of sovereignty rather than compartmentalized nation-states, which might dissolve because they are no longer needed to provide security and can no longer control their economies, is one model here. Although most scholars see the reduction of sovereignty and the growth of the power of non-governmental organizations as conducive to peace and harmony, one can readily imagine sharp conflicts, for example among business interests, labor, and environmentalists (many Marxists see class conflicts as increasingly important); between those with different views of the good life; between those calling for greater centralization to solve common problems and those advocating increased local control. But state power and interest would in any case be greatly decreased. The notion of "national interest," always contested, would become even more problematic.

A second world, not completely incompatible with the first, would be one in which states in the Community play a large role, but with more extensive and intensive cooperation. Relations would be increasingly governed by principles and laws, a change that could benignly spill over into relations outside the Community. Although bargaining would not disappear, there would be more joint efforts to solve common problems and the line between "high" and "low" politics would become even more blurred.

In this world, the United States would share more power and responsibility with the rest of the Community than is true today. While popular with scholars at least as likely is a continuation of the present trajectory in which the United States maintains hegemony and rejects significant limitations on its freedom of action. National interests would remain distinct and the United States would follow the familiar pattern in which ambitions and perceived interests expand as power does. Both conflicts of interest and the belief that hegemony best produces collective goods would lead the United States to oppose the efforts of others to become a counterweight if not a rival to it. In effect, the United States would lead an empire, but probably a relatively benign one. Doing so would be rendered more difficult by the fact that the American self-image precludes seeing its role for what it is, in part because of the popularity of values of equality and supranationalism. Other members of the Community would resent seeing their interests overridden by the United States on some occasions, but the exploitation would be limited by their bargaining power and the American realization that excessive discontent would have serious long-term consequences. Others might accept these costs in return for the U.S. security guarantee and the ability to keep their own defense spending very low, especially because the alternative to American-dominated stability might be worse.

The fourth model also starts with the American attempt to maintain hegemony, but this time the costs and dangers of American unilateralism become sufficient to lead others to form a counter-balancing coalition, one that might include Russia and China as well. Europe and Japan might also become more assertive because they fear that the United States will eventually withdraw its security guarantee, thereby accelerating if not creating a rift within the Community. Much that realism stresses—the clash of national interests, the weakness of international institutions, maneuvering for advantage, and the use of power and threats—would come to the fore, but with the vital difference that force would not be contemplated and the military balance would enter in only indirectly, as discussed above. This would be a strange mixture of the new and the familiar, and the central question is what *ultima ratio* will replace cannons. What will be the final arbiter of disputes? What kinds of threats will be most potent? How fungible will the relevant forms of power be?

Outlining these possibilities raises two broad questions that I cannot answer. First, is the future essentially determined, as many structural theories would imply, or does it depend on national choices strongly influenced by variable domestic politics, leaders, and accidents? Second, if the future is not determined, how much depends on choices the United States has yet to make, and what will most influence these choices?

IMPLICATIONS FOR THEORIES OF THE CAUSES OF WAR

Whatever its explanation, the very existence of a security community among the leading powers refutes many theories of the causes of war, or at least indicates they are not universally valid. Thus human nature and the drive for dominance, honor, and glory may exist and contribute to a wide variety of human behaviors but they are not fated to lead to war.

The obvious rebuttal is that war still exists outside the Community and that civil wars continue unabated. But only wars fought by members of the Community have the potential to undermine the argument that, under some conditions, attributes of humans and societies that were seen as inevitably producing wars in fact do not do so. The cases that could be marshalled are the Gulf War and the operation in Kosovo, but they do not help these theories. These wars were provoked by others, gained little honor and glory for the Community, and were fought in a manner that minimized the loss of life on the other side. It would be hard to portray them as manifestations of brutal or evil human nature. Indeed, it is more plausible to see the Community's behavior as consistent with a general trend toward its becoming less violent generally: the abolition of official torture and the decreased appeal of capital punishment, to take the most salient examples (Mueller 1989).

The existence of the Community also casts doubt on theories that argue that the leading powers always struggle for dominance for gain, status, or security, and are willing to use force to this end. Traditional Marxist theories claim that capitalists could never cooperate; proponents of the law of uneven growth see changes in the relative power of major states as producing cycles of domination, stability, challenge, and war. Similarly, "power transitions" in which rising powers catch up with dominant ones are seen to be very difficult to manage peacefully. These theories, like the version of hegemonic stability discussed above, have yet to be tested because the United States has not yet declined. But if the arguments made here are correct, transitions will not have the same violent outcome that they had in the past, leading us to pay greater attention to the conditions under which these theories do and do not hold.

For most scholars, the fundamental cause of war is international anarchy, compounded by the security dilemma. These forces press hardest on the leading powers because while they may be able to guarantee the security of others, no one can provide this escape from the state of nature for them. As we have seen, different schools of thought propose different explanations for the rise of the Community and so lead to somewhat different propositions about the conditions under which anarchy can be compatible with peace. Constructivism stresses the importance of identities and ideas; liberalism argues for the power of material incentives for peace; realism looks at the costs of war and the details of the payoff structure; my composite explanation stresses the interaction among several factors of costs, benefits, values, and path-dependence. But what is most important is that the Community constitutes a proof by existence of uncoerced peace without central authority. Because these countries are the most powerful ones and particularly war-prone, the Community poses a fundamental challenge to our understanding of world politics and our expectations of future possibilities.

REFERENCES

Art, Robert J. 1996. "Why Western Europe Needs the United States and NATO." *Political Science Quarterly* 111 (Spring): 1–39.

Berghahn, V. R. 1973. *Germany and the Approach of War in 1914.* New York: St. Martin's Press.

Betts, Richard. 1992. "Systems of Peace or Causes of War? Collective Security, Arms Control, and the New Europe." *International Security* 17 (Summer): 5–43.

Bourne, Kenneth. 1970. *The Foreign Policy of Victorian England: 1830–1902.* Oxford: Clarendon Press.

Cain, Peter. 1979. "Capitalism, War and Internationalism in the Thought of Richard Cobden." *British Journal of International Studies* 5 (October): 229–47.

Deutsch, Karl W., et al. 1957. *Political Community and the North Atlantic Area: International Organizations in the Light of Historical Experience.* Princeton, NJ: Princeton University Press.

Farber, Henry, and Joanne Gowa. 1995. "Polities and Peace." *International Security* 20 (Fall): 123–46.

Farber, Henry and Joanne Gowa. 1997. "Common Interests or Common Polities?" *Journal of Politics* 59 (May): 123–46.

Gartzke, Erik. 1998. "Kant We All Get Along? Motive, Opportunity, and the Origins of the Democratic Peace." *American Journal of Political Science* 42 (1): 1–27.

Gartzke, Erik. 2000. "Preferences and Democratic Peace." *International Studies Quarterly* 44 (June): 191–212.

Gilbert, Martin. 1983. *Winston S. Churchill,* Volume VI, *Finest Hour 1939–1941.* London: Heinemann.

Harbaugh, William Henry. 1961. *The Life and Times of Theodore Roosevelt.* New York: Collier Books.

Hirschman, Albert O. 1945. *National Power and the Structure of Foreign Trade.* Berkeley and Los Angeles: University of California Press.

Jervis, Robert. 1989. *The Meaning of Nuclear Revolution: Statecraft and the Prospect of Armageddon.* Ithaca, NY: Cornell University Press.

Keohane, Robert O., and Joseph Nye, eds. 1977. *Power and Interdependence: World Politics in Transition.* Boston, MA: Little Brown.

Kumar, Amitava. 2001. "Bristling on the Subcontinent." *The Nation.* April 23, 2001, 29–30.

Levy, Jack S. 1989. "Domestic Politics and War." In *The Origins and Prevention of Major Wars,* eds. Robert I. Rotberg and Theodore K. Rabb. Cambridge: Cambridge University Press. Pp. 79–100.

Luard, Evan. 1986. *War in International Society: A Study in International Sociology.* London: I.B. Tauris.

Maoz, Zeev. 1997. "The Controversy Over the Democratic Peace: Rearguard Action or Cracks in the Wall?" *International Security* 22 (Summer): 162–98.

McMillan, Susan M. 1997. "Interdependence and Conflict." *Mershon International Studies Review* 41, supplement 1 (May): 33–58.

Mearsheimer, John J. 2001. *The Tragedy of Great Power Politics.* New York: Norton.

Mueller, John. 1989. *Retreat from Doomsday: The Obsolescence of Major War.* New York: Basic Books.

O'Hanlon, Michael E. 2001. *Defense Policy Choices for the Bush Administration.* Washington, DC: Brookings Institution Press.

Oneal, John R., and Bruce Russett. 1999. "Is the Liberal Peace Just an Artifact of Cold War Interests? Assessing Recent Critiques." *International Interactions* 25 (3): 213–41.

Russett, Bruce, and John R. Oneal. 2001. *Triangulating Peace: Democracy, Interdependence, and International Organizations.* New York: Norton.

Schweller, Randall L. 2000. "Democracy and the Post–Cold War Era." In *The New World Order,* eds. Birthe Hansen and Bertel Heurlin. New York: St. Martin's Press. Pp. 46–80.

Snyder, Glenn. 1965. "The Balance of Power and the Balance of Terror." In *The Balance of Power,* ed. Paul Seabury. San Francisco: Chandler. Pp. 184–201.

Van Evera, Stephen. 1984. "The Cult of the Offensive and the Origins of the First World War." *International Security* 9 (Summer): 58–107.

Van Evera, Stephen. 1999. *Causes of War: Power and the Roots of Conflict.* Ithaca, NY: Cornell University Press.

Waltz, Kenneth N. 1970. "The Myth of National Interdependence." In *The International Corporation,* ed. Charles P. Kindleberger. Cambridge, MA: MIT Press. Pp. 205–23.

Waltz, Kenneth N. 1979. *Theory of International Politics.* Reading, MA: Addison-Wesley Publishing.

Waltz, Kenneth N. 1999. "Globalization and Governance." *PS: Political Science & Politics* 32 (December): 693–700.

Wrong, Dennis H. 1976. *Skeptical Sociology.* New York: Columbia University Press.

The Clash of Civilizations?

SAMUEL P. HUNTINGTON

THE NEXT PATTERN OF CONFLICT

World politics is entering a new phase, and intellectuals have not hesitated to pro-liferate visions of what it will be—the end of history, the return of traditional rival-ries between nation-states, and the decline of the nation-state from the conflicting pulls of tribalism and globalism, among others. Each of these visions catches aspects of the emerging reality. Yet they all miss a crucial, indeed a central, aspect of what global politics is likely to be in the coming years.

It is my hypothesis that the fundamental source of conflict in this new world will not be primarily ideological or primarily economic. The great divisions among humankind and the dominating source of conflict will be cultural. Nation states will remain the most powerful actors in world affairs, but the principal conflicts of global politics will occur between nations and groups of different civilizations. The clash of civilizations will dominate global politics. The fault lines between civiliza-tions will be the battle lines of the future.

Conflict between civilizations will be the latest phase in the evolution of con-flict in the modern world. For a century and a half after the emergence of the mod-ern international system with the Peace of Westphalia, the conflicts of the Western world were largely among princes—emperors, absolute monarchs, and constitu-tional monarchs attempting to expand their bureaucracies, their armies, their mer-cantilist economic strength, and, most important, the territory they ruled. In the process they created nation-states, and beginning with the French Revolution the principal lines of conflict were between nations rather than princes. In 1793, as R. R. Palmer put it, "The wars of kings were over; the wars of peoples had begun." This nineteenth-century pattern lasted until the end of World War I. Then, as a result of the Russian Revolution and the reaction against it, the conflict of nations yielded to the conflict of ideologies, first among communism, fascism-Nazism, and liberal democracy, and then between communism and liberal democracy. During the Cold War, this latter conflict became embodied in the struggle between the two superpowers, neither of which was a nation-state in the classical European sense and each of which defined its identity in terms of its ideology.

These conflicts between princes, nation-states, and ideologies were primarily conflicts within Western civilization, "Western civil wars," as William Lind has labeled them. This was as true of the Cold War as it was of the world wars and the

Reprinted by permission of *Foreign Affairs*, (Vol. 72, No. 3, Summer 1993). Copyright © 1993 by the Council on Foreign Relations, Inc.

earlier wars of the seventeenth, eighteenth, and nineteenth centuries. With the end of the Cold War, international politics moves out of its Western phase, and its centerpiece becomes the interaction between the West and non-Western civilizations and among non-Western civilizations. In the politics of civilizations, the peoples and governments of non-Western civilizations no longer remain the objects of history as targets of Western colonialism but join the West as movers and shapers of history.

THE NATURE OF CIVILIZATIONS

During the Cold War the world was divided into the First, Second, and Third worlds. Those divisions are no longer relevant. It is far more meaningful now to group countries not in terms of their political or economic systems or in terms of their level of economic development but rather in terms of their culture and civilization.

What do we mean when we talk of a civilization? A civilization is a cultural entity. Villages, regions, ethnic groups, nationalities, religious groups, all have distinct cultures at different levels of cultural heterogeneity. The culture of a village in southern Italy may be different from that of a village in northern Italy, but both will share in a common Italian culture that distinguishes them from German villages. European communities, in turn, will share cultural features that distinguish them from Arab or Chinese communities. Arabs, Chinese, and Westerners, however, are not part of any broader cultural entity. They constitute civilizations. A civilization is thus the highest cultural grouping of people and the broadest level of cultural identity people have short of that which distinguishes humans from other species. It is defined both by common objective elements, such as language, history, religion, customs, institutions, and by the subjective self-identification of people. People have levels of identity: A resident of Rome may define himself with varying degrees of intensity as a Roman, an Italian, a Catholic, a Christian, a European, a Westerner. The civilization to which he belongs is the broadest level of identification with which he intensely identifies. People can and do redefine their identities and, as a result, the composition and boundaries of civilizations change.

Civilizations may involve a large number of people, as with China ("a civilization pretending to be a state," as Lucian Pye put it), or a very small number of people, such as the Anglophone Caribbean. A civilization may include several nation-states, as is the case with Western, Latin American, and Arab civilizations, or only one, as is the case with Japanese civilization. Civilizations obviously blend and overlap, and may include subcivilizations. Western civilization has two major variants, European and North American, and Islam has its Arab, Turkic, and Malay subdivisions. Civilizations are nonetheless meaningful entities, and while the lines between them are seldom sharp, they are real. Civilizations are dynamic; they rise and fall; they divide and merge. And, as any student of history knows, civilizations disappear and are buried in the sands of time.

Westerners tend to think of nation-states as the principal actors in global affairs. They have been that, however, for only a few centuries. The broader reaches of human history have been the history of civilizations. In *A Study of History,* Arnold Toynbee identified 21 major civilizations; only six of them exist in the contemporary world.

WHY CIVILIZATIONS WILL CLASH

Civilization identity will be increasingly important in the future, and the world will be shaped in large measure by the interactions among seven or eight major civilizations. These include Western, Confucian, Japanese, Islamic, Hindu, Slavic-Orthodox, Latin American, and possibly African civilization. The most important conflicts of the future will occur along the cultural fault lines separating these civilizations from one another.

Why will this be the case?

First, differences among civilizations are not only real; they are basic. Civilizations are differentiated from each other by history, language, culture, tradition, and, most important, religion. The people of different civilizations have different views on the relations between God and man, the individual and the group, the citizen and the state, parents and children, husband and wife, as well as differing views of the relative importance of rights and responsibilities, liberty and authority, equality and hierarchy. These differences are the product of centuries. They will not soon disappear. They are far more fundamental than differences among political ideologies and political regimes. Differences do not necessarily mean conflict, and conflict does not necessarily mean violence. Over the centuries, however, differences among civilizations have generated the most prolonged and the most violent conflicts.

Second, the world is becoming a smaller place. The interactions between peoples of different civilizations are increasing; these increasing interactions intensify civilization-consciousness and awareness of differences between civilizations and commonalities within civilizations. North African immigration to France generates hostility among Frenchmen and at the same time increased receptivity to immigration by "good" European Catholic Poles. Americans react far more negatively to Japanese investment than to larger investments from Canada and European countries. . . . The interactions among peoples of different civilizations enhance the civilization-consciousness of people that, in turn, invigorates differences and animosities stretching or thought to stretch back deep into history.

Third, the processes of economic modernization and social change throughout the world are separating people from longstanding local identities. They also weaken the nation-state as a source of identity. In much of the world religion has moved in to fill this gap, often in the form of movements that are labeled "fundamentalist." Such movements are found in Western Christianity, Judaism, Buddhism, and Hinduism, as well as in Islam. In most countries and most religions the people active in fundamentalist movements are young, college-educated, middle-class technicians, professionals, and business persons. . . . The revival of religion . . . provides a basis for identity and commitment that transcends national boundaries and unites civilizations.

Fourth, the growth of civilization-consciousness is enhanced by the dual role of the West. On the one hand, the West is at a peak of power. At the same time, however, and perhaps as a result, a return to the roots phenomenon is occurring among non-Western civilizations. Increasingly one hears references to trends toward a turning inward and "Asianization" in Japan, the end of the Nehru legacy and the "Hinduization" of India, the failure of Western ideas of socialism and nationalism and hence "re-Islamization" of the Middle East. . . . A West at the peak of its power confronts non-Wests that increasingly have the desire, the will, and the resources to shape the world in non-Western ways.

In the past, the elites of non-Western societies were usually the people who were most involved with the West, had been educated at Oxford, the Sorbonne, or Sandhurst, and had absorbed Western attitudes and values. At the same time, the populace in non-Western countries often remained deeply imbued with the indigenous culture. Now, however, these relationships are being reversed. A de-Westernization and indigenization of elites is occurring in many non-Western countries at the same time that Western, usually American, cultures, styles, and habits become more popular among the mass of the people.

Fifth, cultural characteristics and differences are less mutable and hence less easily compromised and resolved than political and economic ones. In the former Soviet Union, communists can become democrats, the rich can become poor and the poor rich, but Russians cannot become Estonians and Azeris cannot become Armenians. In class and ideological conflicts, the key question was "Which side are you on?" and people could and did choose sides and change sides. In conflicts between civilizations, the question is "What are you?" That is a given that cannot be changed. . . . Even more than ethnicity, religion discriminates sharply and exclusively among people. A person can be half-French and half-Arab and simultaneously even a citizen of two countries. It is more difficult to be half-Catholic and half-Muslim.

Finally, economic regionalism is increasing. The proportions of total trade that were intraregional rose between 1980 and 1989 from 51 percent to 59 percent in Europe, 33 percent to 37 percent in East Asia, and 32 percent to 36 percent in North America. The importance of regional economic blocs is likely to continue to increase in the future. On the one hand, successful economic regionalism will reinforce civilization-consciousness. On the other hand, economic regionalism may succeed only when it is rooted in a common civilization. The European Community rests on the shared foundation of European culture and Western Christianity. The success of the North American Free Trade Area depends on the convergence now underway of Mexican, Canadian, and American cultures. Japan, in contrast, faces difficulties in creating a comparable economic entity in East Asia because Japan is a society and civilization unique to itself. However strong the trade and investment links Japan may develop with other East Asian countries, its cultural differences with those countries inhibit and perhaps preclude its promoting regional economic integration like that in Europe and North America.

Common culture, in contrast, is clearly facilitating the rapid expansion of the economic relations between the People's Republic of China and Hong Kong, Taiwan, Singapore, and the overseas Chinese communities in other Asian countries. With the Cold War over, cultural commonalities increasingly overcome ideological differences, and mainland China and Taiwan move closer together. If cultural commonality is a prerequisite for economic integration, the principal East Asian economic bloc of the future is likely to be centered on China. This bloc is, in fact, already coming into existence. . . .

Culture and religion also form the basis of the Economic Cooperation Organization, which brings together ten non-Arab Muslim countries: Iran, Pakistan, Turkey, Azerbaijan, Kazakhstan, Kyrgyzstan, Turkmenistan, Tadjikistan, Uzbekistan, and Afghanistan. One impetus to the revival and expansion of this organization, founded originally in the 1960s by Turkey, Pakistan, and Iran, is the realization by the leaders of several of these countries that they had no chance of admission to the European Community. Similarly, Caricom, the Central American Common Market, and Mercosur rest on common cultural foundations. Efforts to build a broader Caribbean–Central American economic entity bridging the Anglo-Latin divide, however, have to date failed.

As people define their identity in ethnic and religious terms, they are likely to see an "us" versus "them" relation existing between themselves and people of different ethnicity or religion. . . . Most important, the efforts of the West to promote its values of democracy and liberalism as universal values, to maintain its military predominance, and to advance its economic interests engender countering responses from other civilizations. Decreasingly able to mobilize support and form coalitions on the basis of ideology, governments and groups will increasingly attempt to mobilize support by appealing to common religion and civilization identity.

The clash of civilizations thus occurs at two levels. At the micro-level, adjacent groups along the fault lines between civilizations struggle, often violently, over the control of territory and each other. At the macro-level, states from different civilizations compete for relative military and economic power, struggle over the control of international institutions and third parties, and competitively promote their particular political and religious values.

THE FAULT LINES BETWEEN CIVILIZATIONS

The fault lines between civilizations are replacing the political and ideological boundaries of the Cold War as the flash points for crisis and bloodshed. The Cold War began when the Iron Curtain divided Europe politically and ideologically. The Cold War ended with the end of the Iron Curtain. As the ideological division of Europe has disappeared, the cultural division of Europe between Western Christianity, on the one hand, and Orthodox Christianity and Islam, on the other, has reemerged. The most significant dividing line in Europe, as William Wallace has suggested, may well be the eastern boundary of Western Christianity in the year 1500. This line runs along what are now the boundaries between Finland and Russia and between the Baltic states and Russia, cuts through Belarus and Ukraine separating the more Catholic western Ukraine from Orthodox eastern Ukraine, swings westward separating Transylvania from the rest of Romania, and then goes through Yugoslavia almost exactly along the line now separating Croatia and Slovenia from the rest of Yugoslavia. In the Balkans this line, of course, coincides with the historic boundary between the Hapsburg and Ottoman empires. The peoples to the north and west of this line are Protestant or Catholic; they shared the common experiences of European history—feudalism, the Renaissance, the Reformation, the Enlightenment, the French Revolution, the Industrial Revolution; they are generally economically better off than the peoples to the east; and they may now look forward to increasing involvement in a common European economy and to the consolidation of democratic political systems. The peoples to the east and south of this line are Orthodox or Muslim; they historically belonged to the Ottoman or Tsarist empires and were only lightly touched by the shaping events in the rest of Europe; they are generally less advanced economically; they seem much less likely to develop stable democratic political systems. The Velvet Curtain of culture has replaced the Iron Curtain of ideology as the most significant dividing line in Europe. As the events in Yugoslavia show, it is not only a line of difference; it is also at times a line of bloody conflict. . . .

After World War II, the West . . . began to retreat; the colonial empires disappeared; first Arab nationalism and then Islamic fundamentalism manifested themselves; the West became heavily dependent on the Persian Gulf countries for its energy; the oil-rich Muslim countries became money-rich and, when they wished to, weapons-rich. Several wars occurred between Arabs and Israel (created by the West). France fought a bloody and ruthless war in Algeria for most of the 1950s; British and French forces invaded Egypt in 1956; American forces went into Lebanon in 1958; subsequently American forces returned to Lebanon, attacked Libya, and engaged in various military encounters with Iran; Arab and Islamic terrorists, supported by at least three Middle Eastern governments, employed the weapon of the weak and bombed Western planes and installations and seized Western hostages. This warfare between Arabs and the West culminated in 1990, when the United States sent a massive army to the Persian Gulf to defend some Arab countries against aggression by another. In its aftermath NATO planning is increasingly directed to potential threats and instability along its "southern tier."

This centuries-old military interaction between the West and Islam is unlikely to decline. It could become more virulent. The Gulf War left some Arabs feeling proud that Saddam Hussein had attacked Israel and stood up to the West. It also left many feeling humiliated and resentful of the West's military presence in the Persian Gulf, the West's overwhelming military dominance, and their apparent inability to shape their own destiny. Many Arab countries, in addition to the oil exporters, are reaching levels of economic and social development where autocratic forms of government become inappropriate and efforts to introduce democracy become stronger. Some openings in Arab political systems have already occurred. The principal beneficiaries of these openings have been Islamist movements. In the Arab world, in short, Western democracy strengthens anti-Western political forces. This may be a passing phenomenon, but it surely complicated relations between Islamic countries and the West. . . .

On both sides the interaction between Islam and the West is seen as a clash of civilizations. The West's "next confrontation," observes M. J. Akbar, an Indian Muslim author, "is definitely going to come from the Muslim world. It is in the sweep of the Islamic nations from the Maghreb to Pakistan that the struggle for a new world order will begin.". . .

Historically, the other great antagonistic interaction of Arab Islamic civilization has been with the pagan, animist, and now increasingly Christian black peoples to the south. In the past, this antagonism was epitomized in the image of Arab slave dealers and black slaves. It has been reflected in the ongoing civil war in the Sudan between Arabs and blacks, the fighting in Chad between Libyan-supported insurgents and the government, the tensions between Orthodox Christians and Muslims in the Horn of Africa, and the political conflicts, recurring riots, and communal violence between Muslims and Christians in Nigeria. The modernization of Africa and the spread of Christianity are likely to enhance the probability of violence along this fault line. Symptomatic of the intensification of this conflict was Pope John Paul II's speech in Khartoum in February 1993 attacking the actions of the Sudan's Islamist government against the Christian minority there.

On the northern border of Islam, conflict has increasingly erupted between Orthodox and Muslim peoples, including the carnage of Bosnia and Sarajevo, the simmering violence between Serb and Albanian, the tenuous relations between Bulgarians and their Turkish minority, the violence between Ossetians and Ingush, the unremitting slaughter of each other by Armenians and Azeris, the tense relations between Russians and Muslims in Central Asia, and the deployment of Russian troops to protect Russian interests in the Caucasus and Central Asia. Religion reinforces the revival of ethnic identities and restimulates Russian fears about the security of their southern borders. . . .

The conflict of civilizations is deeply rooted elsewhere in Asia. The historic clash between Muslim and Hindu in the subcontinent manifests itself now not only in the rivalry between Pakistan and India but also in intensifying religious strife within India between increasingly militant Hindu groups and India's substantial Muslim minority. The destruction of the Ayodhya mosque in December 1992 brought to the fore the issue of whether India will remain a secular democratic state or become a Hindu one. In East Asia, China has outstanding territorial disputes with most of its neighbors. It has pursued a ruthless policy toward the Buddhist people of Tibet, and it is pursuing an increasingly ruthless policy toward its Turkic-Muslim minority. With the Cold War over, the underlying differences between China and the United States have reasserted themselves in areas such as human rights, trade, and weapons proliferation. These differences are unlikely to moderate. . . .

The same phrase has been applied to the increasingly difficult relations between Japan and the United States. Here cultural difference exacerbates economic conflict. People on each side allege racism on the other, but at least on the American side the antipathies are not racial but cultural. The basic values, attitudes, behavioral patterns of the two societies could hardly be more different. The economic issues between the United States and Europe are no less serious than those between the United States and Japan, but they do not have the same political salience and emotional intensity because the differences between American culture and European culture are so much less than those between American civilization and Japanese civilization.

The interactions between civilizations vary greatly in the extent to which they are likely to be characterized by violence. Economic competition clearly predominates between the American and European subcivilizations of the West and between both of them and Japan. On the Eurasian continent, however, the prolif-eration of ethnic conflict, epitomized at the extreme in "ethnic cleansing," has not been totally random. It has been most frequent and most violent between groups belonging to different civilizations. In Eurasia the great historic fault lines between civilizations are once more aflame. This is particularly true along the boundaries of the crescent-shaped Islamic bloc of nations from the bulge of Africa to central Asia. Violence also occurs between Muslims, on the one hand, and Orthodox Serbs in the Balkans, Jews in Israel, Hindus in India, Buddhists in Burma, and Catholics in the Philippines. Islam has bloody borders.

CIVILIZATION RALLYING: THE KIN-COUNTRY SYNDROME

Groups or states belonging to one civilization that become involved in war with people from a different civilization naturally try to rally support from other mem-bers of their own civilization. As the post–Cold War world evolves, civilization commonality, what H. D. S. Greenway has termed the "kin-country" syndrome, is replacing political ideology and traditional balance of power considerations as the principal basis for cooperation and coalitions. It can be seen gradually emerging in the post–Cold War conflicts in the Persian Gulf, the Caucasus and Bosnia. None of these was a full-scale war between civilizations, but each involved some elements of civilizational rallying, which seemed to become more important as the conflict continued and which may provide a foretaste of the future.

First, in the Gulf War one Arab state invaded another and then fought a coali-tion of Arab, Western, and other states. While only a few Muslim governments overtly supported Saddam Hussein, many Arab elites privately cheered him on, and he was highly popular among large sections of the Arab publics. Islamic fun-damentalist movements universally supported Iraq rather than the Western-backed governments of Kuwait and Saudi Arabia. Forswearing Arab nationalism, Saddam Hussein explicitly invoked an Islamic appeal. He and his supporters attempted to define the war as a war between civilizations. "It is not the world against Iraq," as Safar Al-Hawali, dean of Islamic Studies at the Umm Al-Qura University in Mecca, put it in a widely circulated tape. "It is the West against Islam." Ignoring the rivalry between Iran and Iraq, the chief Iranian religious leader, Ayatollah Ali Khamenei, called for a holy war against the West: "The strug-gle against American aggression, greed, plans, and policies will be counted as a jihad, and anybody who is killed on that path is a martyr." "This is a war," King Hussein of Jordan argued, "against all Arabs and all Muslims and not against Iraq alone.". . .

Second, the kin-country syndrome also appeared in conflicts in the former Soviet Union. Armenian military successes in 1992 and 1993 stimulated Turkey to become increasingly supportive of its religious, ethnic, and linguistic brethren in Azerbaijan. "We have a Turkish nation feeling the same sentiments as the Azer-baijanis," said one Turkish official in 1992. "We are under pressure. Our newspa-pers are full of the photos of atrocities and are asking us if we are still serious about pursuing our neutral policy. Maybe we should show Armenia that there's a big

Turkey in the region." President Turgut Özal agreed, remarking that Turkey should at least "scare the Armenians a little bit." Turkey, Özal threatened again in 1993, would "show its fangs." Turkish Air Force jets flew reconnaissance flights along the Armenian border; Turkey suspended food shipments and air flights to Armenia; and Turkey and Iran announced they would not accept dismemberment of Azerbaijan. In the last years of its existence, the Soviet government supported Azerbaijan because its government was dominated by former communists. With the end of the Soviet Union, however, political considerations gave way to religious ones. Russian troops fought on the side of the Armenians, and Azerbaijan accused the "Russian government of turning 180 degrees" toward support for Christian Armenia.

Third, with respect to the fighting in the former Yugoslavia, Western publics manifested sympathy and support for the Bosnian Muslims and the horrors they suffered at the hands of the Serbs. Relatively little concern was expressed, however, over Croatian attacks on Muslims and participation in the dismemberment of Bosnia-Herzegovina. In the early stages of the Yugoslav breakup, Germany, in an unusual display of diplomatic initiative and muscle, induced the other 11 members of the European Community to follow its lead in recognizing Slovenia and Croatia. As a result of the pope's determination to provide strong backing to the two Catholic countries, the Vatican extended recognition even before the Community did. The United States followed the European lead. Thus the leading actors in Western civilization rallied behind their coreligionists. Subsequently Croatia was reported to be receiving substantial quantities of arms from Central European and other Western countries. Boris Yeltsin's government, on the other hand, attempted to pursue a middle course that would be sympathetic to the Orthodox Serbs but not alienate Russia from the West. Russian conservative and nationalist groups, however, including many legislators, attacked the government for not being more forthcoming in its support for the Serbs. By early 1993 several hundred Russians apparently were serving with the Serbian forces, and reports circulated of Russian arms being supplied to Serbia.

Islamic governments and groups, on the other hand, castigated the West for not coming to the defense of the Bosnians. Iranian leaders urged Muslims from all countries to provide help to Bosnia; in violation of the U.N. arms embargo, Iran supplied weapons and men for the Bosnians; Iranian-supported Lebanese groups sent guerrillas to train and organize the Bosnian forces. In 1993 up to 4,000 Muslims from over two dozen Islamic countries were reported to be fighting in Bosnia. The governments of Saudi Arabia and other countries felt under increasing pressure from fundamentalist groups in their own societies to provide more vigorous support for the Bosnians. By the end of 1992, Saudi Arabia had reportedly supplied substantial funding for weapons and supplies for the Bosnians, which significantly increased their military capabilities vis-à-vis the Serbs. . . .

Civilization rallying to date has been limited, but it has been growing, and it clearly has the potential to spread much further. As the conflicts in the Persian Gulf, the Caucasus, and Bosnia continued, the positions of nations and the cleavages between them increasingly were along civilizational lines. Populist politicians, religious leaders, and the media have found it a potent means of arousing mass support and of pressuring hesitant governments. In the coming years, the local conflicts most likely to escalate into major wars will be those, as in Bosnia and the Caucasus, along the fault lines between civilizations. The next world war, if there is one, will be a war between civilizations.

THE WEST VERSUS THE REST

The West is now at an extraordinary peak of power in relation to other civilizations. Its superpower opponent has disappeared from the map. Military conflict among Western states is unthinkable, and Western military power is unrivaled. Apart from Japan, the West faces no economic challenge. It dominates international political and security institutions and with Japan international economic institutions. Global political and security issues are effectively settled by a directorate of the United States, Britain, and France, world economic issues by a directorate of the United States, Germany, and Japan, all of which maintain extraordinarily close relations with each other to the exclusion of lesser and largely non-Western countries. Decisions made at the U.N. Security Council or in the International Monetary Fund that reflect the interests of the West are presented to the world as reflecting the desires of the world community. The very phrase "the world community" has become the euphemistic collective noun (replacing "the Free World") to give global legitimacy to actions reflecting the interests of the United States and other western powers. Through the IMF and other international economic institutions, the West promotes its economic interests and imposes on other nations the economic policies it thinks appropriate. In any poll of non-Western peoples, the IMF undoubtedly would win the support of finance ministers and a few others, but get an overwhelmingly unfavorable rating from just about everyone else, who would agree with Georgy Arbatov's characterization of IMF officials as "neo-Bolsheviks who love expropriating other people's money, imposing undemocratic and alien rules of economic and political conduct and stifling economic freedom."

Western domination of the U.N. Security Council and its decisions, tempered only by occasional abstention by China, produced U.N. legitimation of the West's use of force to drive Iraq out of Kuwait and its elimination of Iraq's sophisticated weapons and capacity to produce such weapons. . . . The West in effect is using international institutions, military power and economic resources to run the world in ways that will maintain Western predominance, protect Western interests, and promote Western political and economic values.

That at least is the way in which non-Westerners see the new world, and there is a significant element of truth in their view. Differences in power and struggles for military, economic, and institutional power are thus one source of conflict between the West and other civilizations. Differences in culture, that is basic values and beliefs, are a second source of conflict. . . . Western concepts differ fundamentally from those prevalent in other civilizations. Western ideas of individualism, liberalism, constitutionalism, human rights, equality, liberty, the rule of law, democracy, free markets, the separation of church and state, often have little resonance in Islamic, Confucian, Japanese, Hindu, Buddhist, or Orthodox cultures. Western efforts to propagate such ideas produce instead a reaction against "human rights imperialism" and a reaffirmation of indigenous values, as can be seen in the support for religious fundamentalism by the younger genera- tion in non-Western cultures. The very notion that there could be a "universal civ- ilization" is a Western idea, directly at odds with the particularism of most Asian societies and their emphasis on what distinguishes one people from another. . . . These differences are most manifest in the efforts of the United States and other Western powers to induce other peoples to adopt Western ideas concerning democracy and human rights. Modern democratic government originated in the West. When it has developed in non-Western societies it has usually been the product of Western colonialism or imposition.

The central axis of world politics in the future is likely to be, in Kishore Mah- bubani's phrase, the conflict between "the West and the Rest" and the responses of non-Western civilizations to Western power and values.[1] Those responses gen- erally take one or a combination of three forms. At one extreme, non-Western states can, like Burma and North Korea, attempt to pursue a course of isolation, to insulate their societies from penetration or "corruption" by the West, and, in effect, to opt out of participation in the Western-dominated global community. The costs of this course, however, are high, and few states have pursued it exclu- sively. A second alternative, the equivalent of "bandwagoning" in international relations theory, is to attempt to join the West and accept its values and institu- tions. The third alternative is to attempt to "balance" the West by developing eco- nomic and military power and cooperating with other non-Western societies against the West, while preserving indigenous values and institutions; in short, to modernize but not to Westernize.

THE TORN COUNTRIES

In the future, as people differentiate themselves by civilization, countries with large numbers of peoples of different civilizations . . . are candidates for dismem- berment. Some other countries have a fair degree of cultural homogeneity but are divided over whether their society belongs to one civilization or another. These are torn countries. Their leaders typically wish to pursue a bandwagoning strategy and to make their countries members of the West, but the history, culture, and tradi- tions of their countries are non-Western. The most obvious and prototypical torn country is Turkey. The late twentieth-century leaders of Turkey have followed in the Attatürk tradition and defined Turkey as a modern, secular, Western nation- state. They allied Turkey with the West in NATO and in the Gulf War; they applied for membership in the European Community. At the same time, however, elements in Turkish society have supported an Islamic revival and have argued that Turkey is basically a Middle Eastern Muslim society. In addition, while the elite of Turkey has defined Turkey as a Western society, the elite of the West refuses to accept Turkey as such. Turkey will not become a member of the European Com- munity, and the real reason, as President Özal said, "is that we are Muslim and they are Christian and they don't say that." Having rejected Mecca, and then being rejected by Brussels, where does Turkey look? Tashkent may be the answer. The end of the Soviet Union gives Turkey the opportunity to become the leader of a revived Turkic civilization involving seven countries from the borders of Greece to those of China. Encouraged by the West, Turkey is making strenuous efforts to carve out this new identity for itself.

During the past decade Mexico has assumed a position somewhat similar to that of Turkey. Just as Turkey abandoned its historic opposition to Europe and attempted to join Europe, Mexico has stopped defining itself by its opposition to the United States and is instead attempting to imitate the United States and to join it in the North American Free Trade Area. Mexican leaders are engaged in the great task of redefining Mexican identity and have introduced fundamental economic reforms that eventually will lead to fundamental political change. In 1991 a top adviser to President Carlos Salinas de Gortari described at length to me all the changes the Salinas government was making. When he finished, I remarked: "That's most impressive. It seems to me that basically you want to change Mexico from a Latin American country into a North American country." He looked at me with surprise and exclaimed: "Exactly! That's precisely what we are trying to do, but of course we could never say so publicly." As his remark indicates, in Mexico as in Turkey, significant elements in society resist the redefinition of their country's identity. In Turkey, European-oriented leaders have to make gestures to Islam (Özal's pilgrimage to Mecca); so also Mexico's North American-oriented leaders have to make gestures to those who hold Mexico to be a Latin American country (Salinas' Ibero-American Guadalajara summit).

Historically Turkey has been the most profoundly torn country. For the United States, Mexico is the most immediate torn country. Globally the most important torn country is Russia. The question of whether Russia is part of the West or the leader of a distinct Slavic-Orthodox civilization has been a recurring one in Russian history. That issue was obscured by the communist victory in Russia, which imported a Western ideology, adapted it to Russian conditions and then challenged the West in the name of that ideology. The dominance of communism shut off the historic debate over Westernization versus Russification. With communism discredited Russians once again face that question. . . .

To redefine its civilization identity, a torn country must meet three requirements. First, its political and economic elite has to be generally supportive of and enthusiastic about this move. Second, its public has to be willing to acquiesce in the redefinition. Third, the dominant groups in the recipient civilization have to be willing to embrace the convert. All three requirements in large part exist with respect to Mexico. The first two in large part exist with respect to Turkey. It is not clear that any of them exist with respect to Russia's joining the West. The conflict between liberal democracy and Marxism-Leninism was between ideologies which, despite their major differences, ostensibly shared ultimate goals of freedom, equality and prosperity. A traditional, authoritarian, nationalist Russia could have quite different goals. A Western democrat could carry on an intellectual debate with a Soviet Marxist. It would be virtually impossible for him to do that with a Russian traditionalist. If, as the Russians stop behaving like Marxists, they reject liberal democracy and begin behaving like Russians but not like Westerners, the relations between Russia and the West could again become distant and conflictual.

THE CONFUCIAN-ISLAMIC CONNECTION

The obstacles to non-Western countries joining the West vary considerably. They are least for Latin American and East European countries. They are greater for the Orthodox countries of the former Soviet Union. They are still greater for Muslim, Confucian, Hindu, and Buddhist societies. Japan has established a unique position for itself as an associate member of the West: It is in the West in some respects but clearly not of the West in important dimensions. Those countries that for reasons of culture and power do not wish to, or cannot, join the West compete with the West by developing their own economic, military, and political power. They do this by promoting their internal development and by cooperating with other non-Western countries. The most prominent form of this cooperation is the Confucian-Islamic connection that has emerged to challenge Western interests, values, and power.

Almost without exception, Western countries are reducing their military power. . . . China, North Korea, and several Middle Eastern states, however, are significantly expanding their military capabilities. They are doing this by the import of arms from Western and non-Western sources and by the development of indigenous arms industries. One result is the emergence of what Charles Krauthammer has called "Weapon States," and the Weapon Sates are not Western states. Another result is the redefinition of arms control, which is a Western concept and a Western goal. During the Cold War the primary purpose of arms control was to establish a stable military balance between the United States and its allies and the Soviet Union and its allies. In the post–Cold War world the primary objective of arms control is to prevent the development by non-Western societies of military capabilities that could threaten Western interests. The West attempts to do this through international agreements, economic pressure, and controls on the transfer of arms and weapons technologies.

The conflict between the West and the Confucian-Islamic states focuses largely, although not exclusively, on nuclear, chemical, and biological weapons, ballistic missiles, and other sophisticated means for delivering them, and the guidance, intelligence, and other electronic capabilities for achieving that goal. The West promotes nonproliferation as a universal norm and nonproliferation treaties and inspections as means of realizing that norm. It also threatens a variety of sanctions against those who promote the spread of sophisticated weapons and proposes some benefits for those who do not. The attention of the West focuses, naturally, on nations that are actually or potentially hostile to the West.

The non-Western nations, on the other hand, assert their right to acquire and to deploy whatever weapons they think necessary for their security. They also have absorbed, to the full, the truth of the response of the Indian defense minister when asked what lesson he learned from the Gulf War: "Don't fight the United States unless you have nuclear weapons." Nuclear weapons, chemical weapons, and missiles are viewed, probably erroneously, as the potential equalizer of superior Western conventional power. China, of course, already has nuclear weapons; Pakistan and India have the capability to deploy them. North Korea, Iran, Iraq, Libya, and Algeria appear to be attempting to acquire them. A top Iranian official has declared that all Muslim states should acquire nuclear weapons, and in 1988 the president of Iran reportedly issued a directive calling for development of "offensive and defensive chemical, biological, and radiological weapons."

Centrally important to the development of counter-West military capabilities is the sustained expansion of China's military power and its means to create military power. Buoyed by spectacular economic development, China is rapidly increasing its military spending and vigorously moving forward with the modernization of its armed forces. It is purchasing weapons from the former Soviet states; it is developing long-range missiles; in 1992 it tested a one-megaton nuclear device. It is developing power-projection capabilities, acquiring aerial refueling technology, and trying to purchase an aircraft carrier. Its military buildup and assertion of sovereignty over the South China Sea are provoking a multilateral regional arms race in East Asia. China is also a major exporter of arms and weapons technology. It has exported materials to Libya and Iraq that could be used to manufacture nuclear weapons and nerve gas. It has helped Algeria build a reactor suitable for nuclear weapons research and production. China has sold to Iran nuclear technology that American officials believe could only be used to create weapons and apparently has shipped components of 300-mile-range missiles to Pakistan. North Korea has had a nuclear weapons program under way for some while and has sold advanced missiles and missile technology to Syria and Iran. The flow of weapons and weapons technology is generally from East Asia to the Middle East. There is, however, some movement in the reverse direction; China has received Stinger missiles from Pakistan.

A Confucian-Islamic military connection has thus come into being, designed to promote acquisition by its members of the weapons and weapons technologies needed to counter the military power of the West. It may or may not last. At present, however, it is, as Dave McCurdy has said, "a renegades' mutual support pact, run by the proliferators and their backers." A new form of arms competition is thus occurring between Islamic-Confucian states and the West. In an old-fashioned arms race, each side developed its own arms to balance or to achieve superiority against the other side. In this new form of arms competition, one side is developing its arms and the other side is attempting not to balance but to limit and prevent that arms buildup while at the same time reducing its own military capabilities.

IMPLICATIONS FOR THE WEST

This article does not argue that civilization identities will replace all other identities, that nation-states will disappear, that each civilization will become a single coherent political entity, that groups within a civilization will not conflict with and even fight each other. This paper does set forth the hypotheses that differences between civilizations are real and important; civilization-consciousness is increasing; conflict between civilizations will supplant ideological and other forms of conflict as the dominant global form of conflict; international relations, historically a game played out within Western civilization, will increasingly be de-Westernized and become a game in which non-Western civilizations are actors and not simply objects; successful political, security, and economic international institutions are more likely to develop within civilizations than across civilizations; conflicts between groups in different civilizations will be more frequent, more sustained, and more violent than conflicts between groups in the same civilization; violent conflicts between groups in different civilizations are the most likely and most dangerous source of escalation that could lead to global wars; the paramount axis of world politics will be the relations between "the West and the Rest"; the elites in some torn non-Western countries will try to make their countries part of the west, but in most cases face major obstacles to accomplishing this; a central focus of conflict for the immediate future will be between the West and several Islamic-Confucian states.

This is not to advocate the desirability of conflicts between civilizations. It is to set forth descriptive hypotheses as to what the future may be like. If these are plausible hypotheses, however, it is necessary to consider their implications for Western policy. These implications should be divided between short-term advantage and long-term accommodation. In the short term it is clearly in the interest of the West to promote greater cooperation and unity within its own civilization, particularly between its European and North American components; to incorporate into the West societies in Eastern Europe and Latin America whose cultures are close to those of the West; to promote and maintain cooperative relations with Russia and Japan; to prevent escalation of local inter-civilization conflicts into major inter-civilization wars; to limit the expansion of the military strength of Confucian and Islamic states; to moderate the reduction of Western military capabilities and maintain military superiority in East and Southwest Asia; to exploit differences and conflicts among Confucian and Islamic states; to support in other civilizations groups sympathetic to Western values and interests; to strengthen international institutions that reflect and legitimate Western interests and values; and to promote the involvement of non-Western states in those institutions.

In the longer term other measures would be called for. Western civilization is both Western and modern. Non-Western civilizations have attempted to become modern without becoming Western. To date only Japan has fully succeeded in this quest. Non-Western civilizations will continue to attempt to acquire the wealth, technology, skills, machines, and weapons that are part of being modern. They will also attempt to reconcile this modernity with their traditional culture and values. Their economic and military strength relative to the West will increase. Hence the West will increasingly have to accommodate those non-Western modern civilizations whose power approaches that of the West but whose values and interests differ significantly from those of the West. This will require the West to maintain the economic and military power necessary to protect its interests in relation to these civilizations. It will also, however, require the West to develop a more profound understanding of the basic religious and philosophical assumptions underlying other civilizations and the ways in which people in those civilizations see their interests. It will require an effort to identify elements of commonality between Western and other civilizations. For the relevant future, there will be no universal civilization, but instead a world of different civilizations, each of which will have to learn to coexist with the others.

NOTE

1. Kishore Mahbubani, "The West and the Rest," *The National Interest* (Summer 1992), 3–13.

Al Qaeda: The Protean Enemy

JESSICA STERN

WHAT'S NEXT FROM AL QAEDA?

Having suffered the destruction of its sanctuary in Afghanistan two years ago, al Qaeda's already decentralized organization has become more decentralized still. The group's leaders have largely dispersed to Pakistan, Iran, Iraq, and elsewhere around the world (only a few still remain in Afghanistan's lawless border regions). And with many of the planet's intelligence agencies now focusing on destroying its network, al Qaeda's ability to carry out large-scale attacks has been degraded.

Yet despite these setbacks, al Qaeda and its affiliates remain among the most significant threats to U.S. national security today. In fact, according to George Tenet, the CIA's director, they will continue to be this dangerous for the next two to five years. An alleged al Qaeda spokesperson has warned that the group is planning another strike similar to those of September 11. On May 12 [2003], simultaneous bombings of three housing complexes in Riyadh, Saudi Arabia, killed at least 29 people and injured over 200, many of them Westerners. Intelligence officials in the United States, Europe, and Africa report that al Qaeda has stepped up its recruitment drive in response to the war in Iraq. And the target audience for its recruitment has also changed. They are now younger, with an even more "menacing attitude," as France's top investigative judge on terrorism-related cases, Jean-Louis Bruguière, describes them. More of them are converts to Islam. And more of them are women.

What accounts for al Qaeda's ongoing effectiveness in the face of an unprecedented onslaught? The answer lies in the organization's remarkably protean nature. Over its life span, al Qaeda has constantly evolved and shown a surprising willingness to adapt its mission. This capacity for change has consistently made the group more appealing to recruits, attracted surprising new allies, and—most worrisome from a Western perspective—made it harder to detect and destroy. Unless Washington and its allies show a similar adaptability, the war on terrorism won't be won anytime soon, and the death toll is likely to mount.

MALLEABLE MISSIONS

Why do religious terrorists kill? In interviews over the last five years, many terrorists and their supporters have suggested to me that people first join such groups to make the world a better place—at least for the particular populations they aim to serve. Over time, however, militants have told me, terrorism can become a career as much as a passion. Leaders harness humiliation and anomie and turn them into weapons. Jihad becomes addictive, militants report, and with some individuals or groups—the "professional" terrorists—grievances can evolve into greed: for money, political power, status, or attention.

In such "professional" terrorist groups, simply perpetuating their cadres becomes a central goal, and what started out as a moral crusade becomes a sophisticated organization. Ensuring the survival of the group demands flexibility in many areas, but especially in terms of mission. Objectives thus evolve in a variety of ways. Some groups find a new cause once their first one is achieved—much as the March of Dimes broadened its mission from finding a cure for polio to fighting birth defects after the Salk vaccine was developed. Other groups broaden their goals in order to attract a wider variety of recruits. Still other organizations transform themselves into profit-driven organized criminals, or form alliances with groups that have ideologies different from their own, forcing both to adapt. Some terrorist groups hold fast to their original missions. But only the spry survive.

Consider, for example, Egyptian Islamic Jihad (EIJ). EIJ's original objective was to fight the oppressive, secular rulers of Egypt and turn the country into an Islamic state. But the group fell on hard times after its leader, Sheikh Omar Abdel Rahman, was imprisoned in the United States and other EIJ leaders were killed or forced into exile. Thus in the early 1990s, Ayman al-Zawahiri decided to shift the group's sights from its "near enemy"—the secular rulers of Egypt—to the "far enemy," namely the United States and other Western countries. Switching goals in this way allowed the group to align itself with another terrorist aiming to attack the West and able to provide a significant influx of cash: Osama bin Laden. In return for bin Laden's financial assistance, Zawahiri provided some 200 loyal, disciplined, and well-trained followers, who became the core of al Qaeda's leadership.

A second group that has changed its mission over time to secure a more reliable source of funding is the Islamic Movement of Uzbekistan (IMU), which, like EIJ, eventually joined forces with the Taliban and al Qaeda. The IMU's original mission was to topple Uzbekistan's corrupt and repressive post-Soviet dictator, Islam Karimov. Once the IMU formed an alliance with the Taliban's leader, Mullah Omar, however, it began promoting the Taliban's anti-American and anti-Western agenda, also condemning music, cigarettes, sex, and alcohol. This new puritanism reduced its appeal among its original, less-ideological supporters in Uzbekistan—one downside to switching missions.

Even Osama bin Laden himself has changed his objectives over time. The Saudi terrorist inherited an organization devoted to fighting Soviet forces in Afghanistan. But he turned it into a flexible group of ruthless warriors ready to fight on behalf of multiple causes. His first call to holy war, issued in 1992, urged believers to kill American soldiers in Saudi Arabia and the Horn of Africa but barely mentioned Palestine. The second, issued in 1996, was a 40-page document listing atrocities and injustices committed against Muslims, mainly by Western powers. With the release of his third manifesto in February 1998, however, bin Laden began urging his followers to start deliberately targeting American civilians, rather than soldiers. (Some al Qaeda members were reportedly distressed by this shift to civilian targets and left the group.) Although this third declaration mentioned the Palestinian struggle, it was still only one among a litany of grievances. Only in bin Laden's fourth call to arms—issued to the al Jazeera network on October 7, 2001, to coincide with the U.S. aerial bombardment of Afghanistan—did he emphasize Israel's occupation of Palestinian lands and the suffering of Iraqi children under UN sanctions, concerns broadly shared in the Islamic world. By extending his appeal, bin Laden sought to turn the war on terrorism into a war between all of Islam and the West. The events of September 11, he charged, split the world into two camps—believers and infidels—and the time had come for "every Muslim to defend his religion." . . .

One of al Qaeda's aims in fighting the West . . . has become to restore the dignity of humiliated young Muslims. This idea is similar to the anticolonialist theoretician Frantz Fanon's notion that violence is a "cleansing force" that frees oppressed youth from "inferiority complexes," "despair," and "inaction," making them fearless and restoring their self-respect. The real target audience of violent attacks is therefore not necessarily the victims and their sympathizers, but the perpetrators and their sympathizers. Violence becomes a way to bolster support for the organization and the movement it represents. Hence, among the justifications for "special operations" listed in al Qaeda's terrorist manual are "bringing new members to the organization's ranks" and "boosting Islamic morale and lowering that of the enemy." The United States may have become al Qaeda's principal enemy, but raising the morale of Islamist fighters and their sympathizers is now one of its principal goals.

FRIENDS OF CONVENIENCE

Apart from the flexibility of its mission, another explanation for al Qaeda's remarkable staying power is its willingness to forge broad—and sometimes unlikely—alliances. In an effort to expand his network, bin Laden created the International Islamic Front for Jihad Against the Jews and Crusaders (IIF) in February 1998. In addition to bin Laden and EIJ's Zawahiri, members included the head of Egypt's Gama'a al Islamiya, the secretary-general of the Pakistani religious party known as the Jamiat-ul-Ulema-e-Islam (JUI), and the head of Bangladesh's Jihad Movement. Later, the IIF was expanded to include the Pakistani *jihadi* organizations Lashkar-e-Taiba, Harkat-ul-Mujahideen, and Sipah-e-Sahaba Pakistan, the last an anti-Shi'a sectarian party. . . .

Perhaps most surprising (and alarming) is the increasing evidence that al Qaeda, a Sunni organization, is now cooperating with the Shi'a group Hezbollah, considered to be the most sophisticated terrorist group in the world. Hezbollah, which enjoys backing from Syria and Iran, is based in southern Lebanon and in the lawless "triborder" region of South America, where Paraguay, Brazil, and Argentina meet. . . . [This] region has become the world's new Libya, a place where terrorists with widely disparate ideologies—Marxist Colombian rebels, American white supremacists, Hamas, Hezbollah, and others—meet to swap tradecraft. Authorities now worry that the more sophisticated groups will invite the American radicals to help them. Moneys raised for terrorist organizations in the United States are often funneled through Latin America, which has also become an important stopover point for operatives entering the United States. Reports that Venezuela's President Hugo Chávez is allowing Colombian rebels and militant Islamist groups to operate in his country are meanwhile becoming more credible, as are claims that Venezuela's Margarita Island has become a terrorist haven.

As these developments suggest and Tenet confirms, "mixing and matching of capabilities, swapping of training, and the use of common facilities" have become the hallmark of professional terrorists today. This fact has been borne out by the leader of a Pakistani *jihadi* group affiliated with al Qaeda, who recently told me that informal contacts between his group and Hezbollah, Hamas, and others have become common. Operatives with particular skills loan themselves out to different groups, with expenses being covered by the charities that formed to fund the fight against the Soviet Union in Afghanistan.

Meanwhile, the Bush administration's claims that al Qaeda cooperated with the "infidel" (read: secular) Saddam Hussein while he was still in office are now also gaining support, and from a surprising source. Hamid Mir, bin Laden's "official biographer" and an analyst for al Jazeera, spent two weeks filming in Iraq during the war. Unlike most reporters, Mir wandered the country freely and was not embedded with U.S. troops. He reports that he has "personal knowledge" that one of Saddam's intelligence operatives, Farooq Hijazi, tried to contact bin Laden in Afghanistan as early as 1998. At that time, bin Laden was publicly still quite critical of the Iraqi leader, but he had become far more circumspect by November 2001, when Mir interviewed him for the third time. Mir also reports that he met a number of Hezbollah operatives while in Iraq and was taken to a recruitment center there.

NEW-STYLE NETWORKS

Al Qaeda seems to have learned that in order to evade detection in the West, it must adopt some of the qualities of a "virtual network": a style of organization used by American right-wing extremists for operating in environments (such as the United States) that have effective law enforcement agencies. American antigovernment groups refer to this style as "leaderless resistance." The idea was popularized by Louis Beam, the self-described ambassador-at-large, staff propagandist, and "computer terrorist to the Chosen" for Aryan Nations, an American neo-Nazi group. Beam writes that hierarchical organization is extremely dangerous for insurgents, especially in "technologically advanced societies where electronic surveillance can often penetrate the structure, revealing its chain of command." In leaderless organizations, however, "individuals and groups operate independently of each other, and never report to a central headquarters or single leader for direction or instruction, as would those who belong to a typical pyramid organization." Leaders do not issue orders or pay operatives; instead, they inspire small cells or individuals to take action on their own initiative. . . .

The Internet has also greatly facilitated the spread of "virtual" subcultures and has substantially increased the capacity of loosely networked terrorist organizations. For example, Beam's essay on the virtues of "leaderless resistance" has long been available on the Web and, according to researcher Michael Reynolds, has been highlighted by radical Muslim sites. Islamist Web sites also offer on-line training courses in the production of explosives and urge visitors to take action on their own. The "encyclopedia of jihad," parts of which are available on-line, provides instructions for creating "clandestine activity cells," with units for intelligence, supply, planning and preparation, and implementation.

The obstacles these Web sites pose for Western law enforcement are obvious. In one article on the "culture of jihad" available on-line, a Saudi Islamist urges bin Laden's sympathizers to take action without waiting for instructions. "I do not need to meet the Sheikh and ask his permission to carry out some operation," he writes, "the same as I do not need permission to pray, or to think about killing the Jews and the Crusaders that gather on our lands." Nor does it make any difference whether bin Laden is alive or dead: "There are a thousand bin Ladens in this nation. We should not abandon our way, which the Sheikh has paved for you, regardless of the existence of the Sheikh or his absence." And according to U.S. government officials, al Qaeda now uses chat rooms to recruit Latino Muslims with U.S. passports, in the belief that they will arouse less suspicion as operatives than would Arab-Americans. Finally, as the late neo-Nazi William Pierce once told me, using the Web to recruit "leaderless resisters" offers still another advantage: it attracts better-educated young people than do more traditional methods, such as radio programs. . . .

JOINING THE FAMILY

Virtual links are only part of the problem; terrorists, including members of bin Laden's IIF, have also started to forge ties with traditional organized crime groups, especially in India. One particularly troubling example is the relationship established between Omar Sheikh and an ambitious Indian gangster named Aftab Ansari. Asif Reza Khan, the "chief executive" for Ansari's Indian operations, told interrogators that he received military training at a camp in Khost, Afghanistan, belonging to Lashkar-e-Taiba, and that "leaders of different militant outfits in Pakistan were trying to use his network for the purpose of jihad, whereas [Ansari] was trying to use the militants' networks for underworld operations."

Khan told his interrogators that the don provided money and hideouts to his new partners, in one case transferring $100,000 to Omar Sheikh—money that Omar Sheikh, in turn, wired to Muhammad Atta, the lead hijacker in the September 11 attacks. According to Khan, Ansari viewed the $100,000 gift as an "investment" in a valuable relationship.

Still another set of unlikely links has sprung up in American prisons, where Saudi charities now fund organizations that preach radical Islam. According to Warith Deen Umar, who hired most of the Muslim chaplains currently active in New York State prisons, prisoners who are recent Muslim converts are natural recruits for Islamist organizations. Umar, incidentally, told *The Wall Street Journal* that the September 11 hijackers should be honored as martyrs, and he traveled to Saudi Arabia twice as part of an outreach program designed to spread Salafism (a radical Muslim movement) in U.S. prisons.

Another organization now active in U.S. prisons is Jamaat ul-Fuqra, a terrorist group committed to purifying Islam through violence. (Daniel Pearl was abducted and murdered in Pakistan while attempting to interview the group's leader, Sheikh Gilani, to investigate the claim that Richard Reid—who attempted to blow up an international flight with explosives hidden in his shoes—was acting under Gilani's orders.) The group functions much like a cult in the United States; members live in poverty in compounds, some of which are heavily armed. Its members have been convicted of fraud, murder, and several bombings, but so far, most of their crimes have been relatively small scale. Clement Rodney Hampton-El, however, convicted of participating with Omar Abdel Rahman in a 1993 plot to blow up New York City landmarks, was linked to the group, and U.S. law enforcement authorities worry that the Fuqra has since come under the influence of al Qaeda.

Still another surprising source of al Qaeda recruits is Tablighi Jamaat (TJ), a revivalist organization that aims at creating better Muslims through "spiritual jihad": good deeds, contemplation, and proselytizing. According to the historian Barbara Metcalf, TJ has traditionally functioned as a self-help group, much like Alcoholics Anonymous, and most specialists claim that it is no more prone to violence than are the Seventh-Day Adventists, with whom TJ is frequently compared. But several Americans known to have trained in al Qaeda camps were brought to Southwest Asia by TJ and appear to have been recruited into *jihadi* organizations while traveling under TJ auspices. For example, Jose Padilla (an American now being held as an "enemy combatant" for planning to set off a "dirty" radiological bomb in the United States) was a member of TJ, as were Richard Reid and John Walker Lindh (the so-called American Taliban). . . .

Totalitarian Islamist revivalism has become the ideology of the dystopian new world order. In an earlier era, radicals might have described their grievances through other ideological lenses, perhaps anarchism, Marxism, or Nazism. Today they choose extreme Islamism.

Radical transnational Islam, divorced from its countries of origin, appeals to some jobless youths in depressed parts of Europe and the United States. As the French scholar Olivier Roy points out, leaders of radical Islamic groups often come from the middle classes, many of them having trained in technical fields, but their followers tend be working-class dropouts.

Focusing on economic and social alienation may help explain why such a surprising array of groups has proved willing to join forces with al Qaeda. Some white supremacists and extremist Christians applaud al Qaeda's rejectionist goals and may eventually contribute to al Qaeda missions. Already a Swiss neo-Nazi named Albert Huber has called for his followers to join forces with Islamists. Indeed, Huber sat on the board of directors of the Bank al Taqwa, which the U.S. government accuses of being a major donor to al Qaeda. Meanwhile, Matt Hale, leader of the white-supremacist World Church of the Creator, has published a book indicting Jews and Israelis as the real culprits behind the attacks of September 11.

These groups, along with Horst Mahler (a founder of the radical leftist German group the Red Army Faction), view the September 11 attacks as the first shot in a war against globalization, a phenomenon that they fear will exterminate national cultures. Leaderless resisters drawn from the ranks of white supremacists or other groups are not currently capable of carrying out massive attacks on their own, but they may be if they join forces with al Qaeda.

MODERN METHODOLOGY

Al Qaeda has lately adopted innovative tactics as well as new alliances. Two new approaches are particularly alarming to intelligence officials: efforts to use surface-to-air missiles to shoot down aircraft and attempts to acquire chemical, nuclear, or biological weapons.

In November 2002, terrorists launched two shoulder-fired SA-7 missiles at an Israeli passenger jet taking off from Mombasa, Kenya, with 271 passengers on board. Investigators say that the missiles came from the same batch as those used in an earlier, also unsuccessful attack on a U.S. military jet in Saudi Arabia. And intelligence officials believe that Hezbollah contacts were used to smuggle the missiles into Kenya from Somalia.

Meanwhile, according to Barton Gellman of *The Washington Post*, documents seized in Pakistan in March 2003 reveal that al Qaeda has acquired the necessary materials for producing botulinum and salmonella toxins and the chemical agent cyanide—and is close to developing a workable plan for producing anthrax, a far more lethal agent. Even more worrisome is the possibility that al Qaeda, perhaps working with Hezbollah or other terrorist groups, will recruit scientists with access to sophisticated nuclear or biological weapons programs, possibly, but not necessarily, ones that are state-run.

To fight such dangerous tactics, Western governments will also need to adapt. In addition to military, intelligence, and law enforcement responses, Washington should start thinking about how U.S. policies are perceived by potential recruits to terrorist organizations. The United States too often ignores the unintended consequences of its actions, disregarding, for example, the negative message sent by Washington's ongoing neglect of Afghanistan and of the chaos in postwar Iraq. If the United States allows Iraq to become another failed state, groups both inside and outside the country that support al Qaeda's goals will benefit.

Terrorists, after all, depend on the broader population for support, and the right U.S. policies could do much to diminish the appeal of rejectionist groups. It does not make sense in such an atmosphere to keep U.S. markets closed to Pakistani textiles or to insist on protecting intellectual property with regard to drugs that needy populations in developing countries cannot hope to afford.

In countries where extremist religious schools promote terrorism, Washington should help develop alternative schools rather than attempt to persuade the local government to shut down radical *madrasahs*. In Pakistan, many children end up at extremist schools because their parents cannot afford the alternatives; better funding for secular education could therefore make a positive difference.

The appeal of radical Islam to alienated youth living in the West is perhaps an even more difficult problem to address. Uneasiness with liberal values, discomfort with uncertain identities, and resentment of the privileged are perennial problems in modern societies. What is new today is that radical leaders are using the tools of globalization to construct new, transnational identities based on death cults, turning grievances and alienation into powerful weapons. To fight these tactics will require getting the input not just of moderate Muslims, but of radical Islamist revivalists who oppose violence.

To prevent terrorists from acquiring new weapons, meanwhile, Western governments must make it harder for radicals to get their hands on them. Especially important is the need to continue upgrading security at vulnerable nuclear sites, many of which, in Russia and other former Soviet states, are still vulnerable to theft. The global system of disease monitoring—a system sorely tested during the SARS epidemic—should also be upgraded, since biological attacks may be difficult to distinguish from natural outbreaks. Only by matching the radical innovation shown by professional terrorists such as al Qaeda—and by showing a similar willingness to adapt and adopt new methods and new ways of thinking—can the United States and its allies make themselves safe from the ongoing threat of terrorist attack.

THE USES OF AMERICAN
■ POWER

Explaining the Bush Doctrine
■ ROBERT JERVIS

The invasion of Iraq, although important in itself, is even more noteworthy as a manifestation of the Bush Doctrine. In a sharp break from the president's pre-September 11 views that saw American leadership, and especially its use of force, restricted to defending narrow and traditional vital interests, he has enunciated a far-reaching program that calls for something very much like an empire.

The Doctrine has four elements: a strong belief in the importance of a state's domestic regime in determining its foreign policy and the related judgment that this is a time of great opportunity to transform international politics, the perception of great threats that can be defeated only by new and vigorous policies (most notably preventive war), a willingness to act unilaterally when necessary, and as both a cause and a summary of these beliefs, an overriding sense that peace and stability requires the U.S. assert its primacy in world politics. It is of course possible that I am exaggerating and that what we are seeing is mostly an elaborate rationale for the overthrow of Saddam Hussein that will have little relevance beyond that. I think the Doctrine is real, however. It is quite articulate and American policy since the end of the war has been consistent with it.

DEMOCRACY AND LIBERALISM

This is not to say that the Doctrine is entirely consistent, and one component may not fit well with the rest despite receiving pride of place in the "The National Security Strategy of the U.S.," which starts thusly: "The great struggles of the twentieth century between liberty and totalitarianism ended with a decisive victory for the

Reprinted by permission from *Political Science Quarterly*, 118 (Fall 2003): 365-388.

forces of freedom—and a single sustainable model for national success: freedom, democracy, and free enterprise." The spread of these values opens the path to "make the world not just safer but better," a "path [that] is not America's alone. It is open to all."[1] This taps deep American beliefs and traditions enunciated by Woodrow Wilson and echoed by Bill Clinton, and is linked to the belief, common among powerful states, that its values are universal and their spread will benefit the entire world. Just as Wilson sought to "teach [the countries of Latin America] to elect good men," so Bush will bring free markets and free elections to countries without them. This agenda horrifies Realists (and perhaps realists).[2] Some mid-level officials think this is window dressing; by contrast, John Gaddis sees it as the heart of the doctrine,[3] a view that is endorsed by other officials.

The administration's argument is that strong measures to spread democracy are needed and will be efficacious. Indeed, liberating Iraq will not only produce democracy there, but will encourage it in the rest of the Middle East. There is no incompatibility between Islam or any other culture and democracy; the example of political pluralism in one country will be emulated. The implicit belief is that democracy can take hold when the artificial obstacles to it are removed. Far from being the product of unusually propitious circumstances, a free and pluralist system is the natural order that will prevail unless something special intervenes. Furthermore, more democracies will mean greater stability, peaceful relations with neighbors, and less terrorism, comforting claims that evidence indicates is questionable at best.[4] Would a democratic Iraq be stable? Would an Iraq that reflected the will of its people recognize Israel or renounce all claims to Kuwait? Would a democratic Palestinian state be more willing to live at peace with Israel than an authoritarian one, especially if it did not gain all of the territory lost in 1967? Previous experience also calls into question the links between democracy and free markets, each of which can readily undermine the other. But such doubts do not cloud official pronouncements or even the off-the-record comments of top officials. The U.S. now appears to have a faith-based foreign policy.

This (or any other) administration may not act on it. No American government has been willing to sacrifice stability and support of U.S. policy to honor democracy in countries like Algeria, Egypt, Saudi Arabia, and Pakistan. But the current view does parallel Ronald Reagan's policy of not accepting a detente with the USSR that was limited to arms control and insisting on a larger agenda that included human rights within the Soviet Union, and thus implicitly called for new domestic regime. The Bush administration is heir to this tradition when it declares that any agreement with North Korea would have to address a range of problems in addition to nuclear weapons, including "the abominable way [the North] treats its people."[5] The argument is that, as in Iraq, regime change is necessary because tyrannical governments will always be prone to disregard agreements and coerce their neighbors just as they mistreat their own citizens. Notwithstanding their being Realists in their views about how states influence one another, Bush and his colleagues are Liberals in their beliefs about the sources of foreign policy.

Consistent with Liberalism, this perspective is highly optimistic in seeing the possibility of progress. A week after September 11, Bush is reported to have told one of his closest advisers: "We have an opportunity to restructure the world toward freedom, and we have to get it right." He expounded this theme in a formal speech marking the 6-month anniversary of the attack: "When the terrorists are disrupted and scattered and discredited, . . . we will see then that the old and serious disputes can be settled within the bounds of reason, and goodwill, and mutual security. I see a peaceful world beyond the war on terror, and with courage and unity, we are building that world together."[6] In February 2002 the president responded to a reporter's question about the predictable French criticism of his policy by saying that "history has given us a unique opportunity to defend freedom. And we're going to seize the moment, and do it."[7] One month later he declared, "We understand history has called us into action, and we are not going to miss that opportunity to make the world more peaceful and more free."[8]

THREAT AND PREVENTIVE WAR

The second pillar of the Bush doctrine is that we live in a time not only of opportunity, but of great threat, posed primarily by terrorists and rogue states. Optimism and pessimism are linked in the belief that if the U.S. does not make the world better, it will grow more dangerous. As Bush said in his West Point address of June 1, 2002:

> Today our enemies see weapons of mass destruction as weapons of choice. For rogue states these weapons are tools of intimidation and military aggression against their neighbors. These weapons may also allow these states to attempt to blackmail the U.S. and our allies to prevent us from deterring or repelling the aggressive behavior of rogue states. Such states also see these weapons as their best means of overcoming the conventional superiority of the U.S.

These threats cannot be contained by deterrence. Terrorists are fanatics and there is nothing that they value that we can hold at risk; rogues like Iraq are risk-acceptant and accident prone. The heightened sense of vulnerability increases the dissatisfaction with deterrence, but it is noteworthy that this stance taps into the long-standing Republican critique of many American Cold War policies. One wing of the party always sought defense rather than deterrence (or, to be more precise, deterrence by denial instead of deterrence by punishment), and this was reflected in the search for escalation dominance, multiple nuclear options, and defense against ballistic missiles.[9]

Because even defense may not be possible against terrorists or rogues, the U.S. must be ready to wage preventive wars and to act "against . . . emerging threats before they are fully formed," as Bush puts it.[10] Prevention is not a new element in world politics, although Dale Copeland's important treatment exaggerates its previous centrality.[11] Israel launched a preventive strike against the Iraqi nuclear program in 1981, during the Cold War U.S. officials contemplated attacking the USSR and the PRC before they could develop robust nuclear capabilities,[12] and the Monroe Doctrine and westward expansion in the 19th century stemmed in part from the American desire to prevent any European power from establishing a presence that could menace it.

The U.S. was a weak country at that time; now the preventive war doctrine is based on strength, and on the associated desire to ensure the maintenance of American dominance. Critics argue that preventive wars are rarely necessary because deterrence can be effective and many threats are exaggerated or can be met with strong but less militarized policies. Libya, for example, once the leading rogue, now seems to be outside of the Axis of Evil. Bismarck called preventive wars "suicide for fear of death," and although the disparity of power between the U.S. and its adversaries means this is no longer the case, the argument for such wars implies a high degree of confidence that the future will be bleak unless they are undertaken, or at least a belief that this world will be worse than the likely one produced by the war.

This policy then faces three large obstacles. First, by definition, the relevant information is hard to obtain because it involves predictions about threats that reside sometime in the future. Thus while in retrospect it is easy to say that the Western allies should have stopped Hitler long before 1939, at the time it was far from clear that he would turn out to be such a menace. No one who reads Neville Chamberlain's speeches can believe that he was a fool. In some cases, a well placed spy might be able to provide solid evidence that the other had to be stopped, but in many other cases—perhaps including Nazi Germany—even this would not be sufficient because leaders do not themselves know how they will act in the future. The Bush Doctrine implies that the problem is not so difficult because the state's foreign policy is shaped if not determined by its domestic political system. Thus knowing that North Korea, Iran, and Syria are brutal dictatorships tells us that they will seek to dominate their neighbors, sponsor terrorism, and threaten the United States. But while the generalization that states that oppress their own people will disturb the international system fits many cases, it is far from universal, which means that such short-cuts to the assessment process are fallible. Second and relatedly, even information on capabilities and past behavior may be difficult to come by, as the case of Iraq shows. Saddam's links to terrorists were murky and remain subject to debate, and while much remains unclear, it seems that the U.S. and Britain not only publicly exaggerated but also privately overestimated the extent of his WMD program.

Third, unless all challengers are deterred by the exercise of the Doctrine in Iraq, preventive war will have to be repeated as other threats reach a similar threshold. Doing so will require sustained domestic if not international support, which is made less likely by the first two complications. The very nature of a preventive war means that the evidence is ambiguous and the supporting arguments are subject to rebuttal. If Britain and France had gone to war with Germany before 1939, large segments of the public would have believed that the war was not necessary. If it had gone badly, the public would have wanted to sue for peace; if it had gone well, public opinion would have questioned its wisdom. While it is too early to say how American opinion will view Saddam's overthrow (and opinion is likely to change over time), a degree of skepticism that will inhibit the repetition of this policy seems probable.

National leaders are aware of these difficulties and generally hesitate to take strong actions in the face of such uncertainty. While one common motive for war has been the belief that the situation will deteriorate unless the state acts strongly now, and indeed this kind of fear drives the security dilemma, leaders usually put off decisions if they can. They know that many potential threats will never eventuate or will be made worse by precipitous military action, and they are predisposed to postpone, to await further developments and information, to kick the can down the road. In rejecting this approach (in Iraq, if not in North Korea), Bush and his colleagues are behaving unusually, although this does not mean they are wrong.

Part of the reason for their stance is the feeling of vulnerability and the consequent belief that the risks and costs of inaction are unacceptably high. Note one of the few lines that brought applause in Bush's Cincinnati speech of October 7, 2002 and that shows the powerful psychological link between September 11 and the drive to depose Saddam: "We will not live in fear." Taken literally, this makes no sense. Unfortunately, fear is often well-founded. What it indicates is an understandable desire for a safer world, despite that fact that the U.S. did live in fear throughout the Cold War and survive quite well. But if the sentence has little logical meaning, the emotion it embodies is an understandable fear of fear, a drive to gain certainty, an impulse to assert control by acting.

This reading of Bush's statement is consistent with my impression that many people who opposed invading Iraq before September 11 but altered their positions afterwards had not taken terrorism terribly seriously before 9/11, a category that includes George Bush.[13] Those who had studied the subject were of course surprised by the timing and method of the attacks, but not that they took place, and so changed their beliefs only incrementally. But Bush frequently acknowledges, indeed stresses, that he was shocked by the assault, which greatly increased his feelings of danger and led him to feel that drastically different policies were necessary. As he put it in his Cincinnati speech: "On September 11th, 2001, America felt its vulnerability." It is no accident that this sentence comes between two paragraphs about the need to disarm Iraq. Three months later in response to an accusation that he always wanted to invade Iraq, Bush replied: "prior to September 11, we were discussing smart sanctions. . . . After September 11, the doctrine of containment just doesn't hold any water. . . . My vision shifted dramatically after September 11, because I now realize the stakes, I realize the world has changed."[14] Secretary of Defense Donald Rumsfeld similarly explained that the U.S. "did not act in Iraq because we had discovered dramatic new evidence of Iraq's pursuit of weapons of mass murder. We acted because we saw the existing evidence in a new light, through the prism of our experience on September 11."[15] The claim that some possibilities are unlikely enough to be put aside lost plausibility in face of the obvious retort: "What could be less likely than terrorists flying airplanes into the World Trade Center and the Pentagon?" During the Cold War, Bernard Brodie expressed his exasperation with wild suggestions about military actions the USSR might undertake: "All sorts of notions and propositions are churned out, and often presented for consideration with the prefatory words: 'It is conceivable that . . . ' Such words establish their own truth, for the fact that someone has conceived of whatever proposition follows is enough to establish that it is conceivable. Whether it is worth a second thought, however, is another matter."[16] Worst case analysis is now hard to dismiss.

UNILATERALISM

The perceived need for preventive wars is linked to the fundamental unilateralism of the Bush Doctrine since it is hard to get a consensus for such strong actions and other states have every reason to let the dominant power carry the full burden. Unilateralism also has deep roots in the non-northeastern parts of the Republican Party, was well represented in the Reagan Administration, draws on long-standing American political traditions, and was part of Bush's outlook before September 11. Of course, assistance from others was needed in Afghanistan and solicited in Iraq. But these should not be mistaken for joint ventures as the U.S. did not bend its policy to meet others' preferences. In stressing that the U.S. is building coalitions in the plural rather than an alliance (the mission determines the coalition, in Rumsfeld's phrase), American leaders have made it clear that they will forego the participation of any particular country rather than compromise.

Even before September 11 Bush displayed little willingness to cater to world public opinion or to heed the cries of outrage from European countries as the U.S. interpreted its interests, and the interests of the world, in its own way. Thus the Bush administration walked away from the Kyoto Treaty, the International Criminal Court, and the protocol implementing the ban on biological weapons rather than trying to work within these frameworks and modify them. The U.S. also ignored European criticisms of its Middle Eastern policy. On a smaller scale, it forced out the heads of the Organization for the Prohibition of Chemical Weapons and the Intergovernmental Panel on Climate Change. In response to this kind of behavior, European diplomats can only say: "Big partners should consult with smaller partners."[17] The operative word is "should." When in the wake of the overthrow of Saddam, Chirac declares: "We are no longer in an era where one or two countries control the fate of another country," he describes the world as he would like it to be, not as it is.[18]

The administration has defended each of its actions, but not its general stance. The most principled, persuasive, and perhaps correct defense is built around the difficulty in procuring public goods. As long as leadership is shared, very little will happen because no one actor will be willing to shoulder the costs and the responsibilities. "At this moment in history, if there is a problem, we're expected to deal with it," is how Bush explains it; "We are trying to lead the world," is what one administration official said when the U.S. blocked language in a UN declaration on child health that might be read as condoning abortion.[19] This is not entirely hypocritical: many of the countries that endorsed the Kyoto protocol had grave reservations but were unwilling to stand up to strongly committed domestic groups.

Indeed, real consultation is likely to produce inaction, as was true in 1993 when Clinton called for "lift and strike" in Yugoslavia (i.e., lifting the arms embargo against Bosnia and striking Serbian forces). But because he believed in sharing power and was unwilling to move on his own, he sent Secretary of State Christopher to ascertain European views. This multilateral and democratic procedure did not work because the Europeans did not want to be put on the spot, and in the face of apparent American indecision they refused to endorse such a strong policy. If the U.S. had informed the Europeans rather than consulted them, they probably would have complained, but gone along; what critics call unilateralism often is effective leadership. Could Arafat have been moved from his central position if the U.S. had sought consensus rather than staking out its own position? Bush could also argue that just as Reagan's ignoring the sophisticated European counsels to moderate his rhetoric led to the delegitimation of the Soviet system, so his insistence on confronting tyrants has slowly brought others around to his general perspective, if not to his particular policies.

AMERICAN HEGEMONY

The final element of the Doctrine, which draws together the others, is the establishment of American hegemony, primacy, or empire. In the Bush Doctrine there are no universal norms or rules governing all states. On the contrary, order can be maintained only if the dominant power behaves quite differently from the others. Thus the administration is not worried that its preventive war doctrine or attacking Iraq without Security Council endorsement will set a precedent for others because the dictates that apply to them do not bind the United States. Similarly, the U.S. sees no contradiction between expanding the ambit of nuclear weapons to threaten their employment even if others have not used WMD first on the one hand and a vigorous anti-proliferation policy on the other. American security, world stability, and the spread of liberalism require the U.S. to act in ways others cannot and must not. This is not a double standard, but is what world order requires.

Hegemony is implied when the Bush Nuclear Posture Review talks of dissuading future military competitors. At first glance this seems to refer to Russia and China, but the point applies to the countries of Western Europe as well, either individually or as a unit. This was clear in the draft defense guidance written by Paul Wolfowitz for Dick Cheney at the end of the first Bush administration and also was implied by President Bush when he declared to the graduating cadets at West Point: "America has, and intends to keep, military strengths beyond challenge—thereby making the destabilizing arms races of other eras pointless, and limiting rivalries to trade and other pursuits of peace."[20] This would mean not only sustaining such a high level of military spending that no other country or group of countries would be tempted to challenge it, but also using force on behalf of others so they will not need to develop potent military establishments of their own. In an implicit endorsement of hegemonic stability theory, the driving belief is that the world cannot afford to return to traditional multipolar balance of power politics, which would inevitably turn dangerous and destructive.

HOW DID WE GET HERE?

Although many observers—myself included—were taken by surprise by this turn in American policy, we probably should not have been. It is consistent with standard patterns of international politics and with much previous American behavior in the Cold War. Until recently, however, it did not seem clear that the U.S. would in fact behave in a highly unilateral fashion and assert its primacy. The new American stance was precipitated if not caused by the interaction between the terrorist attacks and the election of George Bush, who brought to the office a more unilateral outlook than his predecessors and his domestic opponents. Bush's response to September 11 may parallel his earlier religious conversion and owe something to his religious beliefs, especially in his propensity to see the struggle as one between good and evil. There is reason to believe that just as his coming to Christ gave meaning to his previously aimless and dissolute personal life, so the war on terrorism has become not only the defining characteristic of his foreign policy, but also his sacred mission. An associate of the president reports: "I believe the president was sincere, after 9/11, thinking 'This is what I was put on this earth for.'"[21] We can only speculate on what President Gore would have done. My estimate is that he would have invaded Afghanistan, but not proceeded against Iraq, nor would he have moved away from treaties and other arrangements over a wide range of issues. To some extent, then, the current assertion of strong American hegemony may be an accident.

But it was an accident waiting to happen. To start with, there are structural reasons to have expected a large terrorist attack. Bin Laden had attacked American interests abroad and from early on sought to strike its homeland. His enmity stemmed primarily from the establishment of U.S. bases in Saudi Arabia, which was a product of America's world-wide responsibilities. (Ironically, the overthrow of Saddam is likely to permit the U.S. to greatly reduce its presence in Saudi Arabia, although I doubt if bin Laden expected this result to follow from his attack or that he will now be satisfied.) Furthermore, al Qaeda was not the only group targeting the U.S.; as Richard Betts has argued, terrorism is the obvious weapon of weak actors against the leading state.[22]

Even without terrorism, both internal and structural factors predisposed the U.S. to assert its dominance. I think the latter are more important, but it is almost a truism of the history of American foreign relations that the U.S. rarely if ever engages in deeply cooperative ventures with equals.[23] Unlike the European states who were surrounded by peers, once the U.S. had established its regional dominance, it had great choice about the terms on which it would work with others. Thus when the U.S. intervened in World War I, it insisted that the coalition be called the "Allied and Associated Powers"—i.e., it was an associate, with freedom of action, not an ally. The structure of the American government, its weak party system, its domestic diversity, and its political traditions, all make sustained cooperation difficult. It would be an exaggeration to say that unilateralism is the American way of foreign policy, but there certainly is a strong pull in this direction.

More importantly, the U.S. may be acting like a normal state that has gained a position of dominance. There are four facets to this argument. First and most general is the core of the Realist outlook that power is checked most effectively and often only by counter-balancing power. It follows that states that are not subject to external restraints tend to feel few restraints at all. As Edmund Burke put it, in a position endorsed by Hans Morgenthau: "I dread our *own* power and our *own* ambition; I dread our being too much dreaded. It is ridiculous to say that we are not men, and that, as men, we shall never wish to aggrandize ourselves."[24] With this as one of his driving ideas, Waltz saw the likelihood of current behavior from the start of the post-Cold War era:

> The powerful state may, and the United States does, think of itself as acting for the sake of peace, justice, and well-being in the world. But these terms will be defined to the liking of the powerful, which may conflict with the preferences and the interests of others. In international politics, overwhelming power repels and leads others to try to balance against it. With benign intent, the United States has behaved, and until its power is brought into a semblance of balance, will continue to behave in ways that annoy and frighten others.[25]

Parts of the Bush Doctrine are unique to the circumstances, but it is the exception rather than the rule for states to stay on the path of moderation when others do not force them to do so.[26]

Second, states' definitions of their interests tend to expand as their power does. It then becomes worth pursuing a whole host of objectives that were out of reach when the state's security was in doubt and all efforts had to be directed to primary objectives. Under the new circumstances, states seek what Wolfers called "milieu goals."[27] The hope of spreading democracy and liberalism throughout the world has always been an American goal, but the lack of a peer competitor now makes it more realistic—although perhaps not very realistic—to actively strive for it. Seen in this light, the administration's perception that this is a time of great opportunity in the Middle East is the product not so much of the special circumstances in the region, but of the enormous resources at America's disposal.

More specifically, the quick American victory in Afghanistan probably contributed to the expansion of American goals, just as the easy military victory in Iraq will encourage the pursuit of a wider agenda, if not threatening force against other tyrants ("moving down the list," in the current phrase). Bush's initial speech after September 11 declared war on terrorists "with a global reach." This was ambitious, but at least the restriction to these kinds of terrorists meant that many others were not of concern. The modifier was dropped in the wake of Afghanistan, however. Not only did rhetoric shift to seeing terrorism in general as a menace to civilization and "the new totalitarian threat,"[28] but the U.S. sent first military trainers and then a combat unit to the Philippines to attack guerrillas who posed only a minimal threat to Americans and who have no significant links to Al Qaeda. Furthermore, at least up until a point, the exercise of power can increase power as well as interests. I do not think that the desire to control a large supply of oil was significant motivation for the Iraqi war, but it will give the U.S. an additional instrument of influence.

A third structural explanation for American behavior is that increased relative power brings with it new fears. The reasons are both objective and subjective. As Wolfers notes in his classic essay on "National Security as Ambiguous Symbol," the latter can diverge from the former.[29] In one manifestation of this, as major threats disappear, people psychologically elevate ones that were previously seen as quite manageable. Indeed people now seem to be as worried as they were during the height of the Cold War despite the fact that a terrorist or rogue attack, even with WMD, could cause only a small fraction of World War III's devastation. But there is more to it than psychology. A dominant state acquires an enormous stake in the world order and interests spread throughout the globe. Most countries are primarily concerned with what happens in their immediate neighborhoods; the world is the hegemon's neighborhood, and it is not only hubris that leads it to be concerned with anything that happens anywhere. The result is a fusion of narrow and broad self-interest. At a point when most analysts were worried about the decline of American power, not its excesses, Waltz noted that for the U.S., "like some earlier great powers. . . . the interest of the country in security came to be identified with the maintenance of a certain world order. For countries at the top, this is predictable behavior. . . . Once a state's interests reach a certain extent, they become self-reinforcing."[30]

The historian John S. Galbraith explored the related dynamic of the "turbulent frontier" that produced the unintended expansion of colonialism. As a European power gained an enclave in Africa or Asia, usually along the coast or river, it also gained an unpacified boundary that had to be policed. This led to further expansion of influence and often of settlement, and this in turn produced a new area that had to be protected and a new zone of threat.[31] There were few natural limits to this process. There are not likely to be many now. The wars in Afghanistan and Iraq have led to the establishment of U.S. bases and security commitments in central Asia, an area previously beyond reach. It is not hard to imagine how the U.S. could be drawn further into politics in the region, and to find itself using force to oppose terrorist or guerrilla movements that arise there, perhaps in part in reaction to the American presence. The same dynamic could play out in Colombia.

The fourth facet can be seen as a broader conception of the previous point. As Realists stress, even states that find the status quo acceptable have to worry about the future. Indeed, the more an actor sees the current situation as satisfactory, the more it will expect the future to be worse. Psychology plays a role here too: prospect theory argues that actors are prone to accept great risks when they believe they will suffer losses unless they act boldly. The adoption of a preventive war doctrine may be a mistake, especially if taken too far, but is not foreign to normal state behavior, as I noted earlier, and appeals to states that have a valued position to maintain. However secure states are, only rarely can they be secure enough, and if they are currently very powerful they will have strong reasons to act now to prevent a deterioration that could allow others to harm them in the future.

All this means that under the Bush Doctrine the U.S. is not a status quo power. Its motives may not be selfish, but the combination of power, fear, and perceived opportunity lead it to seek to reshape world politics and the societies of many of its members. This tracks with and extends traditional ideas in American foreign relations held by both liberals and conservatives that saw the U.S. as a revolutionary country. As the first modern democracy, the U.S. was founded on principles of equality, progress, and a government subordinate to civil society that, while initially being uniquely American, had universal applicability. Indeed, because a state's foreign policy is inseparable from its domestic regime, a safe and peaceful world required the spread of these arrangements. Under current conditions of terrorism and WMD, tyrannical governments pose too much of a potential if not actual danger to be tolerated. The world cannot stand still: without strong

American intervention, the international environment will become more menacing to America and its values, but strong action can increase its security and produce a better world. In a process akin to the deep security dilemma,[32] in order to protect itself the U.S. is impelled to act in a way that will increase or at least bring to the surface conflicts with others. Even if the prevailing situation is satisfactory, it cannot be maintained by purely defensive measures. Making the world safe for American democracy is believed to require that dictatorial regimes be banished, or at least kept from weapons of mass destruction.

Although not mentioned in the pronouncements, the Bush Doctrine is made possible by the existence of a security community among the world's most powerful and developed states (the U.S., West Europe, and Japan).[33] The lack of fears of war among these countries allows the U.S. to focus on other dangers and to pursue other goals. Furthermore, the development of the security community gives the U.S. a position that it now wants to preserve.

CONCLUSION

The war against Saddam marks out the path on which the U.S. is embarked and illuminates the links between preventive war and hegemony, which was much of the reason for the opposition at home and abroad. Bush's goals are extraordinarily ambitious, involving remaking not only international politics but recalcitrant societies as well, which is seen as an end in itself and a means to American security. For better or (and?) for worse, the U.S. has set itself tasks that prudent states would shun. As a result, it will be infringing on what adversaries (if not allies) see as their vital interests. Coercion and especially deterrence may be insufficient for these tasks because these instruments share with traditional diplomacy the desire to minimize conflict by limiting one's own claims to interests that others can afford to respect. States that seek more need to be highly assertive if not aggressive (which provides additional reasons to question the goals themselves). The beliefs of Bush and his colleagues that Saddam's regime would have been an unacceptable menace to American interests if it had been allowed to obtain nuclear weapons not only tell us about their fears for the limits of U.S. influence that might have been imposed, but also speak volumes about the expansive definition of U.S. interests that they hold.[34]

Indeed, the war is hard to understand if the only object was to disarm Saddam or even to remove him from power. Even had the inflated estimates of his WMD capability been accurate, the danger was simply too remote to justify the effort. But if changing the Iraqi regime was expected to bring democracy and stability to the Middle East, discourage tyrants and energize reformers throughout the world, and demonstrate the American willingness to provide a high degree of what it considers world order whether others like it or not, then, as part of a larger project, the war makes sense. Those who find both the hopes and the fears excessive if not delusional agree with the great British statesman Lord Salisbury when he tried to bring some perspective to the Eastern Crisis of 1877–78: "It has generally been acknowledged to be madness to go to war for an idea, but if anything is more unsatisfactory, it is to go to war against a nightmare."[35]

We can only speculate about the crucial question of whether the Bush Doctrine will work. Contrary to the common impression, democracies, and especially the U.S., do not find it easy to sustain a clear line of policy when the external environment is not compelling. Significant casualties will surely be corrosive, and when the going gets tough I think the U.S. will draw back.

Furthermore, while the U.S. is indeed the strongest country in the world, its power is still subject to two familiar limitations: it is harder to build than to destroy, and success depends on others' decisions because their cooperation is necessary for the state to reach its goals. The war in Iraq has increased the risks that others face in pursuing nuclear weapons, but it has also increased their incentives to do so. Amid the debate about what these weapons can accomplish, everyone agrees that they can deter invasion, which makes them very attractive to states who fear they might be in the American gun sights. Both Waltz's argument that proliferation will produce stability and the contrary and more common claim that it would make the world more dangerous imply that the spread of nuclear weapons will reduce American influence because others will have less need of its security guarantees and will be able to fend off its threats to their vital interests. The American attempt to minimize the ability of others to resist U.S. pressures is the mark of a country bent not on maintaining the status quo, but on fashioning a new and better order.

Russia and traditional American allies may see themselves better off with U.S. as an assertive hegemon, allowing them to gain the benefits of world order while being spared the costs, and they may conclude that any challenge would fail or bring with it dangerous rivalry. Indeed without the war in Iraq I doubt that the spring of 2003 would have seen the degree of cooperation that the U.S. obtained from Europe in combatting the Iranian nuclear program and from Japan and the PRC in containing North Korea. But I suspect that much will depend on allies' answers to several questions: Can the American domestic political system sustain the Bush Doctrine over the long run? Will the U.S. be open to allied influence and values? Will it put pressure on Israel as well as on the Arabs to reach a settlement? More generally, will it seek to advance the broad interests of the diverse countries and people in the world or will it exploit its power for its own narrower political, economic, and social interests? Bush's world gives little place for other states—even democracies—except as members of a supporting cast. Conflating broader with narrower interests and believing that one has a monopoly on wisdom are familiar patterns for dominant powers, and ones that rarely sit well with other powerful states.

NOTES

1. White House, "The National Security Strategy of the United States," (Washington, D.C.: September 2002), pp. i, 1. Bush's West Point speech similarly declared: "Moral truth is the same in every culture, in every time, and in every place. . . . We are in a conflict between good and evil." "When it comes to the common rights and needs of men and women, there is no clash of civilizations." "Remarks by the President at 2002 Grad-

uation Exercise of the Unites States Military Academy," White House Press Release, June 1, 2002, p. 3.

2. Thus Samuel Huntington, who agrees that a state's foreign policy is strongly influenced by its domestic regime, argues that conflict can be reduced only by not pushing Western values on other societies: *The Clash of Civilizations and the Remaking of the World Order* (New York: Simon and Schuster, 1996).

3. John Lewis Gaddis, "Bush's Security Strategy," *Foreign Policy,* No. 133, November/December 2002, pp. 50–57.

4. Edward Mansfield and Jack Snyder, *Democratization and War* (Cambridge: MIT Press, forthcoming).

5. Quoted in David Sanger, "U.S. to Withdraw From Arms Accord With North Korea," *New York Times,* October 20, 2002.

6. Quoted in Frank Bruni, "For President, a Mission and a Role in History," ibid, September 22, 2001; "President Thanks World Coalition for Anti-Terrorism Efforts," White House Press Release, March 11, 2002, pp. 3–4; also see "Remarks by the President at 2002 Graduation Exercise," pp. 4–5.

7. "President Bush, Prime Minister Koizumi Hold Press Conference," White House Press Release, February 18, 2002, p. 6.

8. "President, Vice President Discuss the Middle East," White House Press Release, March 21, 2002, p. 2.

9. It is no accident that the leading theorist of this school of thought, Albert Wohlstetter, trained and sponsored many of the driving figures of the Bush administration, such as Paul Wolfowitz and Richard Perle.

10. Letter accompanying "National Security Strategy of the U.S.," p. ii. Calling this aspect of the doctrine and our policy against Iraq "preemptive," as the Bush administration does, is to do violence to the English language. No one thought that Iraq was about to attack anyone; rather the argument was that Iraq and perhaps others are terrible menaces that eventually will do the U.S. great harm and must be dealt with as soon as possible, before the harm has been inflicted and while prophylactic actions can be taken at reasonable cost. For a study of cases, see Robert Litwak, "The New Calculus of Preemption," *Survival,* vol. 44, Winter 2002–03, pp. 53–79.

11. Dale Copeland, *The Origins of Major War* (Ithaca, NY: Cornell University Press, 2000); also see John Mearsheimer, *Tragedy of Great Power Politics* (New York: Norton, 2001). For important conceptual distinctions and propositions, see Jack Levy, "Declining Power and the Preventive Motivation for War," *World Politics,* vol. 40, October 1987, pp. 82–107 and, for a study that is skeptical of the general prevalence of preventive wars but presents one example, Levy and Joseph Gochal, "Democracy and Preventive War: Israel and the 1956 Sinai Campaign," *Security Studies,* vol. 11, Winter 2001/2, pp. 1–49. On the U.S. experience, see Art, *Grand Strategy for America,* pp. 181–97. Randall Schweller argues that democratic states fight preventively only under very restrictive circumstances: "Domestic Structure and Preventive War: Are Democracies More Pacific?" *World Politics,* vol. 44, January 1992, pp. 235–69, and notes the unusual nature of the Israeli cases. For the argument that states are generally well served resisting the temptation to fight preventively, see Richard Betts, "Striking First: A History of Thankfully Lost Opportunities," *Ethics and International Affairs,* vol. 17, No. 1, 2003, pp. 17–24. For a review of power transition theory, which in one interpretation is driven by preventive motivation, see Jacek Kugler and Douglas Lemke, *Parity and War: Evaluations and Extensions of The War Ledger* (Ann Arbor: University of Michigan Press, 1996).

12. Marc Trachtenberg, *History and Strategy* (Princeton: Princeton University Press, 1991), ch. 3; William Burr and Jeffrey Richelson, "Whether to 'Strangle the Baby in the Cradle': The United States and the Chinese Nuclear Program, 1960–64," *International Security,* vol. 25, Winter 2000/01, pp. 54–99. Gregory Mitrovich shows how much of American early Cold War policy was driven by the fear that it could not sustain a prolonged confrontation: *Undermining the Kremlin: America's Strategy to Subvert the Soviet Bloc, 1947–1956* (Ithaca, NY: Cornell University Press, 2000).

13. According to Robert Woodward, George Tenet believed that "Bush had been the least prepared of all of [the administration leaders] for the terrorist attacks": *Bush at War* (New York: Simon and Schuster, 2002), p. 318. Before then his administration had concentrated on Russia and the PRC.

14. *New York Times,* February 1, 2003.

15. Quoted in James Risen, David Sanger, and Thom Shanker, "In Sketchy Data, Trying to Gauge Iraq Threat," ibid., July 20, 2003.

16. Bernard Brodie, "The Development of Nuclear Strategy," *International Security,* vol. 2, Spring 1978, p. 83.

17. Quoted in Steven Erlanger, "Bush's Move On ABM Pact Gives Pause to Europeans," *New York Times,* December 13, 2001; also see Suzanne Daley, "Many in Europe Voice Worry that U.S. Will Not Consult Them," ibid, January 31, 2002; Erlanger, "Protests, and Friends Too, Await Bush in Europe," ibid, May 22, 2002; Elizabeth Becker, "U.S. Unilateralism Worries Trade Officials," ibid, March 17, 2003.

18. Quoted in Karen DeYoung, "Chirac Moves To Repair U.S. Ties," *Washington Post,* April 16, 2003.

19. Quoted in Bob Woodward interview with Bush in ibid, November 19, 2002 (also see Woodward, *Bush at War* p. 281); quoted in Somini Sengupta, "U.N. Forum Stalls on Sex Education and Abortion Rights," *New York Times,* 10 May 2002.

20. "Remarks by the President at 2002 Graduation Exercise," p. 4. The Wolfowitz draft is summarized in stories in the *New York Times,* March 8 and May 24, 1992. Also see Zalmay Khalilzad, *From Containment to Global Leadership? America and the World After the Cold War* (Santa Monica, CA: RAND, 1995), and Robert Kagan and William Kristol, eds., *Present Dangers: Crisis and Opportunity in American Foreign and Defense Policy* (San Francisco: Encounter Books, 2000). This stance gives others incentives to develop asymmetric responses, of which terrorism is only the most obvious example. For possible PRC options, see Thomas Christensen, "Posing Problems Without Catching Up: China's Rise and Challenges for U.S. Security Policy," *International Security,* vol. 25, Spring 2001, pp. 5–40.

21. Quoted in James Harding, "Conflicting Views From Two Bush Camps," *Financial Times,* March 20, 2003; for a perceptive analysis, see Bruni, "For President, a Mission and a Role in History." Also see Woodward, *Bush at War,* pp. 102, 205, 281.

22. Richard Betts, "The Soft Underbelly of American Primacy: Tactical Advantages of Terror," *Political Science Quarterly,* vol. 117, Spring 2002, pp. 19–36.

23. See, for example, Jesse Helms' defense of unilateralism as the only way consistent with American interests and traditions: "American Sovereignty and the UN," *National Interest,* No. 62, Winter 2000/01, pp. 31–34. For a discussion of historical, sociological, and geographical sources of the moralistic outlook in American foreign policy, see Arnold Wolfers, *Discord and Collaboration* (Baltimore: Johns Hopkins University Press, 1962), chapter 15, and Louis Hartz, *The Liberal Tradition in America* (New York: Harcourt, Brace, 1955), chapter 11. For a discussion of current U.S. policy in terms of its self-image as an exceptional state, see Stanley Hoffmann, "The High and the Mighty," *American Prospect,* vol. 1, January 2003, pp. 28–31.

24. Quoted in Hans Morgenthau, *Politics Among Nations*, 5th ed, revised (New York: Knopf, 1978), pp. 169–70, emphasis in the original.
25. Kenneth Waltz, "America as a Model for the World? A Foreign Policy Perspective," *PS: Political Science and Politics*, vol. 24, December 1991, p. 69.
26. Alexander Wendt and, more persuasively, Paul Schroeder would disagree or at least modify this generalization, arguing that prevailing ideas can and have led to more moderate and consensual behavior: Wendt, *Social Theory of International Politics* (New York: Cambridge University Press, 1999); Schroeder, *The Transformation of European Politics, 1763–1848* (New York: Oxford University Press, 1994), and "Does the History of International Politics Go Anywhere?" in David Wetzel and Theodore Hamerow, eds., *International Politics and German History* (Westport: Praeger, 1997), pp 15–36. This is a central question of international politics and history that I cannot fully discuss here, but believe that at least the mild statement that unbalanced power is dangerous can easily be sustained.
27. Wolfers, *Discord and Collaboration*, chapter 5.
28. "President Thanks World Coalition for Anti-Terrorism Efforts"; David Sanger, "In Reichstag, Bush Condemns Terror as New Despotism," *New York Times*, 24 May 2002. Also see "Remarks by President at 2002 Graduation Exercise," p. 3. The question of how broad the target should be was debated within the administration from the start, with Bush initially insisting on a focus on Al Qaeda: Woodward, *Bush at War*, p. 48.
29. *Discord and Collaboration*, chapter 10.
30. Kenneth Waltz, *Theory of International Politics* (Reading, MA.: Addison-Wesley, 1979), p. 200.
31. John S. Galbraith, "The 'Turbulent Frontier' as a Factor in British Expansion," *Comparative Studies in Society and History*, vol. 2, January 1960, pp. 34–48; *Reluctant Empire: British Policy on the South African Frontier, 1834–1854* (Berkeley: University of California Press, 1963). Also see Ronald Robinson and John Gallager with Alice Denny, *Africa and the Victorians: The Official Mind of Imperialism* (London: Macmillan, 1961). A related imperial dynamic that is likely to recur is that turning a previously recalcitrant state into a client usually weakens it internally and requires further intervention.
32. Robert Jervis, "Was the Cold War a Security Dilemma?" *Journal of Cold War History*, vol. 3, Winter 2001, pp. 36–60; also see Paul Roe, "Former Yugoslavia: The Security Dilemma That Never Was?" *European Journal of International Relations*, vol. 6, September 2000, pp. 373–93. The current combination of fear and hope that produces offensive actions for defensive motives resembles the combination that produced the pursuit of preponderance in the aftermath of World War II.
33. Robert Jervis, "Theories of War in an Era of Leading Power Peace," *American Political Science Review*, vol. 96, March 2003, pp. 1–14.
34. I have discussed how Bush's policy toward Iraq does and does not fit with deterrence thinking in "The Confrontation Between Iraq and the U.S.: Implications for the Theory and Practice of Deterrence," *European Journal of International Relations*, vol. 9, No. 2, June 2003, pp. 315–37.
35. Quoted in R. W. Seton-Watson, *Disraeli, Gladstone, and the Eastern Question* (New York: Norton, 1972), p. 222.

America's Imperial Ambition

![] G. JOHN IKENBERRY

THE LURES OF PREEMPTION

In the shadows of the Bush administration's war on terrorism, sweeping new ideas are circulating about U.S. grand strategy and the restructuring of today's unipolar world. They call for American unilateral and preemptive, even preventive, use of force, facilitated if possible by coalitions of the willing—but ultimately unconstrained by the rules and norms of the international community. And the extreme, these notions form a neoimperial vision in which the United States arrogates to itself the global role of setting standards, determining threats, using force, and meting out justice. It is a vision in which sovereignty becomes more absolute for America even as it becomes more conditional for countries that challenge Washington's standards of internal and external behavior. It is a vision made necessary—at least in the eyes of its advocates—by the new and apocalyptic character of contemporary terrorist threats and by America's unprecedented global dominance. These radical strategic ideas and impulses could transform today's world order in a way that the end of the Cold War, strangely enough, did not. . . .

America's nascent neoimperial grand strategy threatens to rend the fabric of the international community and political partnerships precisely at a time when that community and those partnerships are urgently needed. It is an approach fraught with peril and likely to fail. It is not only politically unsustainable but diplomatically harmful. And if history is a guide, it will trigger antagonism and resistance that will leave America in a more hostile and divided world.

PROVEN LEGACIES

The mainstream of American foreign policy has been defined since the 1940s by two grand strategies that have built the modern international order. One is realist in orientation, organized around containment, deterrence, and the maintenance of the global balance of power. Facing a dangerous and expansive Soviet Union after 1945, the United States stepped forward to fill the vacuum left by a waning British Empire and a collapsing European order to provide a counterweight to Stalin and his Red Army.

The touchstone of this strategy was containment, which sought to deny the Soviet Union the ability to expand its sphere of influence. Order was maintained by managing the bipolar balance between the American and Soviet camps. Stability was achieved through nuclear deterrence. For the first time, nuclear weapons and the doctrine of mutual assured destruction made war between the great powers irrational. But containment and global power-balancing ended with the collapse of the Soviet Union in 1991. Nuclear deterrence is no longer the defining logic of the existing order, although it remains a recessed feature that continues to impart stability in relations among China, Russia, and the West.

This strategy has yielded a bounty of institutions and partnerships for America. The most important have been the NATO and U.S.-Japan alliances, American-led security partnerships that have survived the end of the Cold War by providing a bulwark for stability through commitment and reassurance. The United States maintains a forward presence in Europe and East Asia; its alliance partners gain security protection as well as a measure of regularity in their relationship with the world's leading military power. But Cold War balancing has yielded more than a utilitarian alliance structure; it has generated a political order that has value in itself.

This grand strategy presupposes a loose framework of consultations and agreements to resolve differences: the great powers extend to each other the respect of equals, and they accommodate each other until vital interests come into play. The domestic affairs of these states remain precisely that—domestic. The great powers compete with each other, and although war is not unthinkable, sober statecraft and the balance of power offer the best hope for stability and peace. . . .

The other grand strategy, forged during World War II as the United States planned the reconstruction of the world economy, is liberal in orientation. It seeks to build order around institutionalized political relations among integrated market democracies, supported by an opening of economies. This agenda was not simply an inspiration of American businessmen and economists, however. There have always been geopolitical goals as well. Whereas America's realist grand strategy was aimed at countering Soviet power, its liberal grand strategy was aimed at avoiding a return to the 1930s, an era of regional blocs, trade conflict, and strategic rivalry. Open trade, democracy, and multilateral institutional relations went together. Underlying this strategy was the view that a rule-based international order, especially one in which the United States uses its political weight to derive congenial rules, will most fully protect American interests, conserve its power, and extend its influence.

This grand strategy has been pursued through an array of postwar initiatives that look disarmingly like "low politics": the Bretton Woods institutions, the World Trade Organization (WTO), and the Organization for Economic Cooperation and Development are just a few examples. Together, they form a complex layer cake of integrative initiatives that bind the democratic industrialized world together. During the 1990s, the United States continued to pursue this liberal grand strategy. Both the first Bush and the Clinton administrations attempted to articulate a vision of world order that was not dependent on an external threat or an explicit policy of balance of power. Bush the elder talked about the importance of the transatlantic community and articulated ideas about a more fully integrated Asia-Pacific region. In both cases, the strategy offered a positive vision of alliance and partnership built around common values, tradition, mutual self-interest, and the preservation of stability. The Clinton administration likewise attempted to describe the post–Cold War order in terms of the expansion of democracy and open markets. In this vision, democracy provided the foundation for global and regional community, and trade and capital flows were forces for political reform and integration. . . .

AMERICA'S HISTORIC BARGAINS

These two grand strategies are rooted in divergent, even antagonistic, intellectual traditions. But over the last 50 years they have worked remarkably well together. The realist grand strategy created a political rationale for establishing major security commitments around the world. The liberal strategy created a positive agenda for American leadership. The United States could exercise its power and achieve its national interests, but it did so in a way that helped deepen the fabric of international community. American power did not destabilize world order; it helped create it. The development of rule-based agreements and political-security partnerships was good both for the United States and for much of the world. By the end of the 1990s, the result was an international political order of unprecedented size and success: a global coalition of democratic states tied together through markets, institutions, and security partnerships.

This international order was built on two historic bargains. One was the U.S. commitment to provide its European and Asian partners with security protection and access to American markets, technology, and supplies within an open world economy. In return, these countries agreed to be reliable partners providing diplomatic, economic, and logistical support for the United States as it led the wider Western postwar order. The other is the liberal bargain that addressed the uncertainties of American power. East Asian and European states agreed to accept American leadership and operate within an agreed-upon political-economic system. The United States, in response, opened itself up and bound itself to its partners. In effect, the United States built an institutionalized coalition of partners and reinforced the stability of these mutually beneficial relations by making itself more "user-friendly"—that is, by playing by the rules and creating ongoing political processes that facilitated consultation and joint decision-making. The United States made its power safe for the world, and in return the world agreed to live within the U.S. system. These bargains date from the 1940s, but they continue to shore up the post–Cold War order. The result has been the most stable and prosperous international system in world history. But new ideas within the Bush administration—crystallized by September 11 and U.S. dominance—are unsettling this order and the political bargains behind it.

A NEW GRAND STRATEGY

For the first time since the dawn of the Cold War, a new grand strategy is taking shape in Washington. It is advanced most directly as a response to terrorism, but it also constitutes a broader view about how the United States should wield power and organize world order. According to this new paradigm, America is to be less bound to its partners and to global rules and institutions while it steps forward to play a more unilateral and anticipatory role in attacking terrorist threats and confronting rogue states seeking WMD. The United States will use its unrivaled military power to manage the global order. . . .

The new strategy maintains that the Cold War concept of deterrence is outdated. Deterrence, sovereignty, and the balance of power work together. When deterrence is no longer viable, the larger realist edifice starts to crumble. The threat today is not other great powers that must be managed through second-strike nuclear capacity but the transnational terrorist networks that have no home address. They cannot be deterred because they are either willing to die for their cause or able to escape retaliation. The old defensive strategy of building missiles and other weapons that can survive a first strike and be used in a retaliatory strike to punish the attacker will no longer ensure security. The only option, then, is offense.

The use of force, this camp argues, will therefore need to be preemptive and perhaps even preventive—taking on potential threats before they can present a major problem. But this premise plays havoc with the old international rules of self-defense and United Nations norms about the proper use of force. Rumsfeld has articulated the justification for preemptive action by stating that the "absence of evidence is not evidence of absence of weapons of mass destruction." But such an approach renders international norms of self-defense—enshrined by Article 51 of the UN Charter—almost meaningless. The administration should remember that when Israeli jets bombed the Iraqi nuclear reactor at Osirak in 1981 in what Israel described as an act of self-defense, the world condemned it as an act of aggression. Even British Prime Minister Margaret Thatcher and the American ambassador to the UN, Jeane Kirkpatrick, criticized the action, and the United States joined in passing a UN resolution condemning it.

The Bush administration's security doctrine takes this country down the same slippery slope. Even without a clear threat, the United States now claims a right to use preemptive or preventive military force. At West Point, Bush put it succinctly when he stated that "the military must be ready to strike at a moment's notice in any dark corner of the world. All nations that decide for aggression and terror will pay a price." The administration defends this new doctrine as a necessary adjustment to a more uncertain and shifting threat environment. This policy of no regrets errs on the side of action—but it can also easily become national security by hunch or inference, leaving the world without clear-cut norms for justifying force. . . .

No one in the Bush administration argues that NATO or the U.S.-Japan alliance should be dismantled. Rather, these alliances are now seen as less useful to the United States as it confronts today's threats. Some officials argue that it is not that the United States chooses to depreciate alliance partnerships, but that the Europeans are unwilling to keep up. Whether that is true, the upgrading of the American military, along with its sheer size relative to the forces of the rest of the world, leaves the United States in a class by itself. In these circumstances, it is increasingly difficult to maintain the illusion of true alliance partnership. America's allies become merely strategic assets that are useful depending on the circumstance. The United States still finds attractive the logistical reach that its global alliance system provides, but the pacts with countries in Asia and Europe become more contingent and less premised on a vision of a common security community. . . .

In this brave new world, neoimperial thinkers contend that the older realist and liberal grand strategies are not very helpful. American security will not be ensured, as realist grand strategy assumes, by the preservation of deterrence and stable relations among the major powers. In a world of asymmetrical threats, the global balance of power is not the linchpin of war and peace. Likewise, liberal strategies of building order around open trade and democratic institutions might have some long-term impact on terrorism, but they do not address the immediacy of the threats. Apocalyptic violence is at our doorstep, so efforts at strengthening the rules and institutions of the international community are of little practical value. If we accept the worst-case imagining of "we don't know what we don't know," everything else is secondary: international rules, traditions of partnership, and standards of legitimacy. It is a war. And as Clausewitz famously remarked, "War is such a dangerous business that the mistakes which come from kindness are the very worst."

IMPERIAL DANGERS

Pitfalls accompany this neoimperial grand strategy, however. Unchecked U.S. power, shorn of legitimacy and disentangled from the postwar norms and institutions of the international order, will usher in a more hostile international system, making it far harder to achieve American interests. The secret of the United States' long brilliant run as the world's leading state was its ability and willingness to exercise power within alliance and multinational frameworks, which made its power and agenda more acceptable to allies and other key states around the world. This achievement has now been put at risk by the administration's new thinking.

The most immediate problem is that the neoimperialist approach is unsustainable. Going it alone might well succeed in removing Saddam Hussein from power, but it is far less certain that a strategy of counterproliferation, based on American willingness to use unilateral force to confront dangerous dictators, can work over the long term. An American policy that leaves the United States alone to decide which states are threats and how best to deny them weapons of mass destruction will lead to a diminishment of multilateral mechanisms—most important of which is the nonproliferation regime. . . .

Another problem follows. The use of force to eliminate WMD capabilities or overturn dangerous regimes is never simple, whether it is pursued unilaterally or by a concert of major states. After the military intervention is over, the target country has to be put back together. Peacekeeping and state building are inevitably required, as are long-term strategies that bring the UN, the World Bank, and the major powers together to orchestrate aid and other forms of assistance. This is not heroic work, but it is utterly necessary. Peacekeeping troops may be required for many years, even after a new regime is built. Regional conflicts inflamed by outside military intervention must also be calmed. This is the "long tail" of burdens and commitments that comes with every major military action.

When these costs and obligations are added to America's imperial military role, it becomes even more doubtful that the neoimperial strategy can be sustained at home over the long haul—the classic problem of imperial overstretch. The United States could keep its military predominance for decades if it is supported by a growing and increasingly productive economy. But the indirect burdens of cleaning up the political mess in terrorist-prone failed states levy a hidden cost. Peacekeeping and state building will require coalitions of states and multilateral agencies that can be brought into the process only if the initial decisions about military intervention are hammered out in consultation with other major states. America's older realist and liberal grand strategies suddenly become relevant again.

A third problem with an imperial grand strategy is that it cannot generate the cooperation needed to solve practical problems at the heart of the U.S. foreign policy agenda. In the fight on terrorism, the United States needs cooperation from European and Asian countries in intelligence, law enforcement, and logistics. Outside the security sphere, realizing U.S. objectives depends even more on a continuous stream of amicable working relations with major states around the world. It needs partners for trade liberalization, global financial stabilization, environmental protection, deterring transnational organized crime, managing rise of China, and a host of other thorny challenges. But it is impossible to expect would-be partners to acquiesce to America's self-appointed global security protectorate and then pursue business as usual in all other domains.

The key policy tool for states confronting a unipolar and unilateral America is to withhold cooperation in day-to-day relations with the United States. One obvious means is trade policy; the European response to the recent American decision to impose tariffs on imported steel is explicable in these terms. This particular struggle concerns specific trade issues, but it is also a struggle over how Washington exercises power. The United States may be a unipolar military power, but economic and political power is more evenly distributed across the globe. The major states may not have much leverage in directly restraining American military policy, but they can make the United States pay a price in other areas.

Finally, the neoimperial grand strategy poses a wider problem for the maintenance of American unipolar power. It steps into the oldest trap of powerful imperial states: self-encirclement. When the most powerful state in the world throws its weight around, unconstrained by rules or norms of legitimacy, it risks a backlash. Other countries will bridle at an international order in which the United States plays only by its own rules. The proponents of the new grand strategy have assumed that the United States can single-handedly deploy military power abroad and not suffer untoward consequences; relations will be coarser with friends and allies, they believe, but such are the costs of leadership. But history shows that powerful states tend to trigger self-encirclement by their own overestimation of their power. Charles V, Louis XIV, Napoleon, and the leaders of post-Bismarck Germany sought to expand their imperial domains and impose a coercive order on others. Their imperial orders were all brought down when other countries decided they were not prepared to live in a world dominated by an overweening coercive state. America's imperial goals and modus operandi are much more limited and benign than were those of age-old emperors. But a hard-line imperial grand strategy runs the risk that history will repeat itself. . . .

BRING IN THE OLD

Bush has not fully articulated a vision of postwar international order, aside from defining the struggle as one between freedom and evil. The world has seen Washington take determined steps to fight terrorism, but it does not yet have a sense of Bush's larger, positive agenda for a strengthened and more decent international order.

This failure explains why the sympathy and goodwill generated around the world for the United States after September 11 quickly disappeared. Newspapers that once proclaimed, "We are all Americans," now express distrust toward America. The prevailing view is that the United States seems prepared to use its power to go after terrorists and evil regimes, but not to use it to help build a more stable and peaceful world order. The United States appears to be degrading the rules and institutions of international community, not enhancing them. To the rest of the world, neoimperial thinking has more to do with exercising power than with exercising leadership.

In contrast, America's older strategic orientations—balance-of-power realism and liberal multilaterialism—suggest a mature world power that seeks stability and pursues its interests in ways that do not fundamentally threaten the positions of other states. They are strategies of co-option and reassurance. The new imperial grand strategy presents the United States very differently: a revisionist state seeking to parlay its momentary power advantages into a world order in which it runs the show. Unlike the hegemonic states of the past, the United States does not seek territory or outright political domination in Europe or Asia; "America has no empire to extend or utopia to establish," Bush noted in his West Point address. But the sheer power advantages that the United States possesses and the doctrines of preemption and counterterrorism that it is articulating do unsettle governments and people around the world. The costs could be high. The last thing the United States wants is for foreign diplomats and government leaders to ask, How can we work around, undermine, contain, and retaliate against U.S. power?

Rather than invent a new grand strategy, the United States should reinvigorate its older strategies, those based on the view that America's security partnerships are not simply instrumental tools but critical components of an American-led world political order that should be preserved. U.S. power is both leveraged and made more legitimate and user-friendly by these partnerships. The neoimperial thinkers are haunted by the specter of catastrophic terrorism and seek a radical reordering of America's role in the world. America's commanding unipolar power and the advent of frightening new terrorist threats feed this imperial temptation. But it is a grand strategic vision that, taken to the extreme, will leave the world more dangerous and divided—and the United States less secure.

The Unipolar Moment Revisited

▬▬▬ CHARLES KRAUTHAMMER

In late 1990, shortly before the collapse of the Soviet Union, it was clear that the world we had known for half a century was disappearing. The question was what would succeed it. I suggested then that we had already entered the "unipolar moment." The gap in power between the leading nation and all the others was so unprecedented as to yield an international structure unique to modern history: unipolarity.

At the time, this thesis was generally seen as either wild optimism or simple American arrogance. The conventional wisdom was that with the demise of the Soviet empire the bipolarity of the second half of the 20th century would yield to multipolarity. The declinist school, led by Paul Kennedy, held that America, suffering from "imperial overstretch", was already in relative decline. The Asian enthusiasm, popularized by (among others) James Fallows, saw the second coming of the Rising Sun. The conventional wisdom was best captured by Senator Paul Tsongas: "The Cold War is over; Japan won."

They were wrong, and no one has put it more forcefully than Paul Kennedy himself in a classic recantation published earlier this year. "Nothing has ever existed like this disparity of power; nothing", he said of America's position today. "Charlemagne's empire was merely western European in its reach. The Roman empire stretched farther afield, but there was another great empire in Persia, and a larger one in China. There is, therefore, no comparison."[1] . . .

Where are we twelve years later? The two defining features of the new post-Cold War world remain: unipolarity and rogue states with weapons of mass destruction. Indeed, these characteristics have grown even more pronounced. Contrary to expectation, the United States has not regressed to the mean; rather, its dominance has dramatically increased. And during our holiday from history in the 1990s, the rogue state/WMD problem grew more acute. . . .

UNIPOLARITY AFTER SEPTEMBER 11, 2001

There is little need to rehearse the acceleration of unipolarity in the 1990s. Japan, whose claim to power rested exclusively on economics, went into economic decline. Germany stagnated. The Soviet Union ceased to exist, contracting into a smaller, radically weakened Russia. The European Union turned inward toward

Excerpted from "The Unipolar Moment Revisited" by Charles Krauthammer from *The National Interest*, No. 70 (Winter 2002-03), pp.5-17. Reprinted by permission of Charles Krauthammer Associates.

the great project of integration and built a strong social infrastructure at the expense of military capacity. Only China grew in strength, but coming from so far behind it will be decades before it can challenge American primacy—and that assumes that its current growth continues unabated.

The result is the dominance of a single power unlike anything ever seen. Even at its height Britain could always be seriously challenged by the next greatest powers. Britain had a smaller army than the land powers of Europe and its navy was equaled by the next two navies combined. Today, American military spending exceeds that of the next *twenty* countries combined. Its navy, air force and space power are unrivaled. Its technology is irresistible. It is dominant by every measure: military, economic, technological, diplomatic, cultural, even linguistic, with a myriad of countries trying to fend off the inexorable march of Internet-fueled MTV English.

American dominance has not gone unnoticed. During the 1990s, it was mainly China and Russia that denounced unipolarity in their occasional joint communiqués. As the new century dawned it was on everyone's lips. A French foreign minister dubbed the United States not a superpower but a hyperpower. The dominant concern of foreign policy establishments everywhere became understanding and living with the 800-pound American gorilla.

And then September 11 *heightened* the asymmetry. It did so in three ways. First, and most obviously, it led to a demonstration of heretofore latent American military power. Kosovo, the first war ever fought and won exclusively from the air, had given a hint of America's quantum leap in military power (and the enormous gap that had developed between American and European military capabilities). But it took September 11 for the United States to unleash with concentrated fury a fuller display of its power in Afghanistan. Being a relatively pacific, commercial republic, the United States does not go around looking for demonstration wars. This one was thrust upon it. In response, America showed that at a range of 7,000 miles and with but a handful of losses, it could destroy within weeks a hardened, fanatical regime favored by geography and climate in the "graveyard of empires.". . .

Second, September 11 demonstrated a new form of American strength. The center of its economy was struck, its aviation shut down, Congress brought to a halt, the government sent underground, the country paralyzed and fearful. Yet within days the markets reopened, the economy began its recovery, the president mobilized the nation, and a united Congress immediately underwrote a huge new worldwide campaign against terror. The Pentagon started planning the U.S. military response even as its demolished western façade still smoldered.

America had long been perceived as invulnerable. That illusion was shattered on September 11, 2001. But with a demonstration of its recuperative powers—an economy and political system so deeply rooted and fundamentally sound that it could spring back to life within days—that sense of invulnerability assumed a new character. It was transmuted from impermeability to resilience, the product of unrivaled human, technological and political reserves.

The third effect of September 11 was to accelerate the realignment of the current great powers, such as they are, behind the United States. In 1990, America's principal ally was NATO. A decade later, its alliance base had grown to include former members of the Warsaw Pact. Some of the major powers, however, remained uncommitted. Russia and China flirted with the idea of an "anti-hegemonic alliance." Russian leaders made ostentatious visits to pieces of the old Soviet empire such as Cuba and North Korea. India and Pakistan, frozen out by the United States because of their nuclear testing, remained focused mainly on one another. But after September 11, the bystanders came calling. Pakistan made an immediate strategic decision to join the American camp. India enlisted with equal alacrity, offering the United States basing, overflight rights and a level of cooperation unheard of during its half century of Nehruist genuflection to anti-American non-alignment. Russia's Putin, seeing both a coincidence of interests in the fight against Islamic radicalism and an opportunity to gain acceptance in the Western camp, dramatically realigned Russian foreign policy toward the United States. (Russia has already been rewarded with a larger role in NATO and tacit American recognition of Russia's interests in its "near abroad.") China remains more distant but, also having a coincidence of interests with the United States in fighting Islamic radicalism, it has cooperated with the war on terror and muted its competition with America in the Pacific.

The realignment of the fence-sitters simply accentuates the historical anomaly of American unipolarity. Our experience with hegemony historically is that it inevitably creates a counterbalancing coalition of weaker powers, most recently against Napoleonic France and Germany (twice) in the 20th century. Nature abhors a vacuum; history abhors hegemony. Yet during the first decade of American unipolarity no such counterbalancing occurred. On the contrary, the great powers lined up behind the United States, all the more so after September 11.

The American hegemon has no great power enemies, an historical oddity of the first order. Yet it does face a serious threat to its dominance, indeed to its essential security. It comes from a source even more historically odd: an archipelago of rogue states (some connected with transnational terrorists) wielding weapons of mass destruction.

The threat is not trivial. It is the single greatest danger to the United States because, for all of America's dominance, and for all of its recently demonstrated resilience, there is one thing it might not survive: decapitation. The detonation of a dozen nuclear weapons in major American cities, or the spreading of smallpox or anthrax throughout the general population, is an existential threat. It is perhaps the only realistic threat to America as a functioning hegemon, perhaps even to America as a functioning modern society.

Like unipolarity, this is historically unique. WMD are not new, nor are rogue states. Their conjunction is. We have had fifty years of experience with nuclear weapons—but in the context of bipolarity, which gave the system a predictable, if perilous, stability. We have just now entered an era in which the capacity for inflicting mass death, and thus posing a threat both to world peace and to the dominant power, resides in small, peripheral states.

What does this conjunction of unique circumstances—unipolarity and the proliferation of terrible weapons—mean for American foreign policy? That the first and most urgent task is protection from these weapons. The catalyst for this realization was again September 11. Throughout the 1990s, it had been assumed that WMD posed no emergency because traditional concepts of deterrence would hold. September 11 revealed the possibility of future WMD-armed enemies both undeterrable and potentially undetectable. The 9/11 suicide bombers were undeterrable; the author of the subsequent anthrax attacks has proven undetectable. The possible alliance of rogue states with such undeterrables and undetectables—and the possible transfer to them of weapons of mass destruction—presents a new strategic situation that demands a new strategic doctrine.

THE CRISIS OF UNIPOLARITY

Accordingly, not one but a host of new doctrines have come tumbling out since September 11. First came the with-us-or-against-us ultimatum to any state aiding, abetting or harboring terrorists. Then, pre-emptive attack on any enemy state developing weapons of mass destruction. And now, regime change in any such state.

The boldness of these policies—or, as much of the world contends, their arrogance—is breathtaking. The American anti-terrorism ultimatum, it is said, is high-handed and permits the arbitrary application of American power everywhere. Pre-emption is said to violate traditional doctrines of just war. And regime change, as Henry Kissinger has argued, threatens 350 years of post-Westphalian international practice. Taken together, they amount to an unprecedented assertion of American freedom of action and a definitive statement of a new American unilateralism.

To be sure, these are not the first instances of American unilateralism. Before September 11, the Bush Administration had acted unilaterally, but on more minor matters, such as the Kyoto Protocol and the Biological Weapons Convention, and with less bluntness, as in its protracted negotiations with Russia over the ABM treaty. The "axis of evil" speech of January 29, however, took unilateralism to a new level. Latent resentments about American willfulness are latent no more. American dominance, which had been tolerated if not welcomed, is now producing such irritation and hostility in once friendly quarters, such as Europe, that some suggest we have arrived at the end of the opposition-free grace period that America had enjoyed during the unipolar moment.

In short, post-9/11 U.S. unilateralism has produced the first crisis of unipolarity. It revolves around the central question of the unipolar age: Who will define the hegemon's ends?

The issue is not one of style but of purpose. Secretary of Defense Donald Rumsfeld gave the classic formulation of unilateralism when he said (regarding the Afghan war and the war on terrorism, but the principle is universal), "the mission determines the coalition." We take our friends where we find them, but only in order to help us in accomplishing the mission. The mission comes first, and we decide it.

Contrast this with the classic case study of multilateralism at work: the U.S. decision in February 1991 to conclude the Gulf War. As the Iraqi army was fleeing, the first Bush Administration had to decide its final goal: the liberation of Kuwait or regime change in Iraq. It stopped at Kuwait. Why? Because, as Brent Scowcroft has explained, going further would have fractured the coalition, gone against our promises to allies and violated the UN resolutions under which we were acting. "Had we added occupation of Iraq and removal of Saddam Hussein to those objectives", wrote Scowcroft in the *Washington Post* on October 16, 2001, ". . . our Arab allies, refusing to countenance an invasion of an Arab colleague, would have deserted us." The coalition defined the mission.

Who should define American ends today? This is a question of agency but it leads directly to a fundamental question of policy. If the coalition—whether NATO, the wider Western alliance, *ad hoc* outfits such as the Gulf War alliance, the UN, or the "international community"—defines America's mission, we have one vision of America's role in the world. If, on the other hand, the mission defines the coalition, we have an entirely different vision.

LIBERAL INTERNATIONALISM

For many Americans, multilateralism is no pretense. On the contrary: It has become the very core of the liberal internationalist school of American foreign policy. In the October 2002 debate authorizing the use of force in Iraq, the Democratic chairman of the Senate Armed Services Committee, Carl Levin, proposed authorizing the president to act only with prior approval from the UN Security Council. Senator Edward Kennedy put it succinctly while addressing the Johns Hopkins School of Advanced International Studies on September 27: "I'm waiting for the final recommendation of the Security Council before I'm going to say how I'm going to vote."

This logic is deeply puzzling. How exactly does the Security Council confer moral authority on American action? The Security Council is a committee of great powers, heirs to the victors in the Second World War. They manage the world in their own interest. The Security Council is, on the very rare occasions when it actually works, realpolitik by committee. But by what logic is it a repository of international morality? How does the approval of France and Russia, acting clearly and rationally in pursuit of their own interests in Iraq (largely oil and investment), confer legitimacy on an invasion?

That question was beyond me twelve years ago. It remains beyond me now. Yet this kind of logic utterly dominated the intervening Clinton years. The 1990s were marked by an obsession with "international legality" as expressed by this or that Security Council resolution. . . .

Early in the Clinton years, Madeleine Albright formulated the vision of the liberal internationalist school then in power as "assertive multilateralism." Its principal diplomatic activity was the pursuit of a dizzying array of universal treaties on chemical weapons, biological weapons, nuclear testing, global environment, land mines and the like. Its trademark was consultation: Clinton was famous for sending Secretary of State Warren Christopher on long trips (for example, through Europe on Balkan policy) or endless shuttles (uncountable pilgrimages to Damascus) to consult; he invariably returned home empty-handed and diminished. And its principal objective was good international citizenship: It was argued on myriad foreign policy issues that we could not do X because it would leave us "isolated." Thus in 1997 the Senate passed a chemical weapons convention that even some of its proponents admitted was unenforceable, largely because of the argument that everyone else had signed it and that failure to ratify would leave us isolated. Isolation, in and of itself, was seen as a diminished and even morally suspect condition. . . .

Multilateralism is the liberal internationalist's means of saving us from this shameful condition. But the point of the multilateralist imperative is not merely psychological. It has a clear and coherent geopolitical objective. It is a means that defines the ends. Its means—internationalism (the moral, legal and strategic primacy of international institutions over national interests) and legalism (the belief that the sinews of stability are laws, treaties and binding international contracts)—are in service to a larger vision: remaking the international system in the image of domestic civil society. The multilateralist imperative seeks to establish an international order based not on sovereignty and power but on interdependence—a new order that, as Secretary of State Cordell Hull said upon returning from the Moscow Conference of 1943, abolishes the "need for spheres of influence, for alliances, for balance of power."

Liberal internationalism seeks through multilateralism to transcend power politics, narrow national interest and, ultimately, the nation-state itself. The nation-state is seen as some kind of archaic residue of an anarchic past, an affront to the vision of a domesticated international arena. This is why liberal thinkers embrace the erosion of sovereignty promised by the new information technologies and the easy movement of capital across borders. They welcome the decline of sovereignty as the road to the new globalism of a norm-driven, legally-bound international system broken to the mold of domestic society.

The greatest sovereign, of course, is the American superpower, which is why liberal internationalists feel such acute discomfort with American dominance. To achieve their vision, America too—America especially—must be domesticated. Their project is thus to restrain America by building an entangling web of interdependence, tying down Gulliver with myriad strings that diminish his overweening power. Who, after all, was the ABM treaty or a land mine treaty going to restrain? North Korea?

This liberal internationalist vision—the multilateral handcuffing of American power—is, as Robert Kagan has pointed out, the dominant view in Europe.[2] That is to be expected, given Europe's weakness and America's power. But it is a mistake to see this as only a European view. The idea of a new international community with self-governing institutions and self-enforcing norms—the vision that requires the domestication of American power—is the view of the Democratic Party in the United States and of a large part of the American foreign policy establishment. They spent the last decade in power fashioning precisely those multilateral ties to restrain the American Gulliver and remake him into a tame international citizen. The multilateralist project is to use—indeed, to use up—current American dominance to create a new international system in which new norms of legalism and interdependence rule in America's place—in short, a system that is no longer unipolar.

REALISM AND THE NEW UNILATERALISM

The basic division between the two major foreign policy schools in America centers on the question of what is, and what should be, the fundamental basis of international relations: paper or power. Liberal internationalism envisions a world order that, like domestic society, is governed by laws and not men. Realists see this vision as hopelessly utopian. The history of paper treaties—from the prewar Kellogg-Briand Pact and Munich to the post-Cold War Oslo accords and the 1994 Agreed Framework with North Korea—is a history of naiveté and cynicism, a combination both toxic and volatile that invariably ends badly. Trade agreements with Canada are one thing. Pieces of parchment to which existential enemies affix a signature are quite another. They are worse than worthless because they give a false sense of security and breed complacency. For the realist, the ultimate determinant of the most basic elements of international life—security, stability and peace—is power.

Which is why a realist would hardly forfeit the current unipolarity for the vain promise of goo-goo one-worldism. Nor, however, should a realist want to forfeit unipolarity for the familiarity of traditional multipolarity. Multipolarity is inherently fluid and unpredictable. Europe practiced multipolarity for centuries and found it so unstable and bloody, culminating in 1914 in the catastrophic collapse of delicately balanced alliance systems, that Europe sought its permanent abolition in political and economic union. Having abjured multipolarity for the region, it is odd in the extreme to then prefer multipolarity for the world.

Less can be said about the destiny of unipolarity. It is too new. Yet we do have the history of the last decade, our only modern experience with unipolarity, and it was a decade of unusual stability among all major powers. It would be foolish to project from just a ten-year experience, but that experience does call into question the basis for the claims that unipolarity is intrinsically unstable or impossible to sustain in a mass democracy.

I would argue that unipolarity, managed benignly, is far more likely to keep the peace. Benignity is, of course, in the eye of the beholder. But the American claim to benignity is not mere self-congratulation. We have a track record. Consider one of history's rare controlled experiments. In the 1940s, lines were drawn through three peoples—Germans, Koreans and Chinese—one side closely bound to the United States, the other to its adversary. It turned into a controlled experiment because both states in the divided lands shared a common culture. Fifty years later the results are in. Does anyone doubt the superiority, both moral and material, of West Germany vs. East Germany, South Korea vs. North Korea and Taiwan vs. China?[3]

Benignity is also manifest in the way others welcome our power. It is the reason, for example, that the Pacific Rim countries are loath to see our military presence diminished: They know that the United States is not an imperial power with a desire to rule other countries—which is why they so readily accept it as a balancer. It is the reason, too, why Europe, so seized with complaints about American high-handedness, nonetheless reacts with alarm to the occasional suggestion that America might withdraw its military presence. America came, but it did not come to rule. Unlike other hegemons and would-be hegemons, it does not entertain a grand vision of a new world. No Thousand Year Reich. No New Soviet Man. It has no great desire to remake human nature, to conquer for the extraction of natural resources, or to rule for the simple pleasure of dominion. Indeed, America is the first hegemonic power in history to be obsessed with "exit strategies." It could not wait to get out of Haiti and Somalia; it would get out of Kosovo and Bosnia today if it could. Its principal aim is to maintain the stability and relative tranquility of the current international system by enforcing, maintaining and extending the current peace.

The form of realism that I am arguing for—call it the new unilateralism—is clear in its determination to self-consciously and confidently deploy American power in pursuit of those global ends. Note: global ends. There is a form of unilateralism that is devoted only to narrow American self-interest and it has a name, too: It is called isolationism. Critics of the new unilateralism often confuse it with isolationism because both are prepared to unashamedly exercise American power. But isolationists *oppose* America acting as a unipolar power not because they disagree with the unilateral means, but because they deem the ends far too broad. Isolationists would abandon the larger world and use American power exclusively for the narrowest of American interests: manning Fortress America by defending the American homeland and putting up barriers to trade and immigration.

The new unilateralism defines American interests far beyond narrow self-defense. In particular, it identifies two other major interests, both global: extending the peace by advancing democracy and preserving the peace by acting as balancer of last resort. Britain was the balancer in Europe, joining the weaker coalition against the stronger to create equilibrium. America's unique global power allows it to be the balancer in every region. We balanced Iraq by supporting its weaker neighbors in the Gulf War. We balance China by supporting the ring of smaller states at its periphery (from South Korea to Taiwan, even to Vietnam). Our role in the Balkans was essentially to create a microbalance: to support the weaker Bosnian Muslims against their more dominant neighbors, and subsequently to support the weaker Albanian Kosovars against the Serbs.

Of course, both of these tasks often advance American national interests as well. The promotion of democracy multiplies the number of nations likely to be friendly to the United States, and regional equilibria produce stability that benefits a commercial republic like the United States. America's (intended) exertions on behalf of pre-emptive non-proliferation, too, are clearly in the interest of both the United States and the international system as a whole.

Critics find this paradoxical: acting unilaterally but for global ends. Why paradoxical? One can hardly argue that depriving Saddam (and potentially, terrorists) of WMD is not a global end. Unilateralism may be required to pursue this end. We may be left isolated in so doing, but we would be acting nevertheless in the name of global interests—larger than narrow American self-interest and larger, too, than the narrowly perceived self-interest of smaller, weaker powers (even great powers) that dare not confront the rising danger.

What is the essence of that larger interest? Most broadly defined, it is maintaining a stable, open and functioning unipolar system. Liberal internationalists disdain that goal as too selfish, as it makes paramount the preservation of both American power and independence. Isolationists reject the goal as too selfless, for defining American interests too globally and thus too generously.

A third critique comes from what might be called pragmatic realists, who see the new unilateralism I have outlined as hubristic, and whose objections are practical. They are prepared to engage in a pragmatic multilateralism. They value great power concert. They seek Security Council support not because it confers any moral authority, but because it spreads risk. In their view, a single hegemon risks far more violent resentment than would a power that consistently acts as *primus inter pares,* sharing rule-making functions with others.

I have my doubts. The United States made an extraordinary effort in the Gulf War to get UN support, share decision-making, assemble a coalition and, as we have seen, deny itself the fruits of victory in order to honor coalition goals. Did that diminish the anti-American feeling in the region? Did it garner support for subsequent Iraq policy dictated by the original acquiescence to the coalition?

The attacks of September 11 were planned during the Clinton Administration, an administration that made a fetish of consultation and did its utmost to subordinate American hegemony and smother unipolarity. The resentments were hardly assuaged. Why? Because the extremist rage against the United States is engendered by the very structure of the international system, not by the details of our management of it.

Pragmatic realists also value international support in the interest of sharing burdens, on the theory that sharing decision-making enlists others in our own hegemonic enterprise and makes things less costly. If you are too vigorous in asserting yourself in the short-term, they argue, you are likely to injure yourself in the long-term when you encounter problems that require the full cooperation of other partners, such as counter-terrorism. . . .

If the concern about the new unilateralism is that American assertiveness be judiciously rationed, and that one needs to think long-term, it is hard to disagree. One does not go it alone or dictate terms on every issue. On some issues such as membership in and support of the WTO, where the long-term benefit both to the American national interest and global interests is demonstrable, one willingly constricts sovereignty. Trade agreements are easy calls, however, free trade being perhaps the only mathematically provable political good. Others require great skepticism. The Kyoto Protocol, for example, would have harmed the American economy while doing nothing for the global environment. (Increased emissions from China, India and Third World countries exempt from its provisions would have more than made up for American cuts.) Kyoto failed on its merits, but was nonetheless pushed because the rest of the world supported it. The same case was made for the chemical and biological weapons treaties—sure, they are useless or worse, but why not give in there in order to build good will for future needs? But appeasing multilateralism does not assuage it; appeasement merely legitimizes it. Repeated acquiescence to provisions that America deems injurious reinforces the notion that legitimacy derives from international consensus, thus undermining America's future freedom of action—and thus contradicting the pragmatic realists' own goals.

America must be guided by its independent judgment, both about its own interest and about the global interest. Especially on matters of national security, war-making and the deployment of power, America should neither defer nor contract out decision-making, particularly when the concessions involve permanent structural constrictions such as those imposed by an International Criminal Court. Prudence, yes. No need to act the superpower in East Timor or Bosnia. But there is a need to do so in Afghanistan and in Iraq. No need to act the superpower on steel tariffs. But there is a need to do so on missile defense.

The prudent exercise of power allows, indeed calls for, occasional concessions on non-vital issues if only to maintain psychological good will. Arrogance and gratuitous high-handedness are counterproductive. But we should not delude ourselves as to what psychological good will buys. Countries will cooperate with us, first, out of their own self-interest and, second, out of the need and desire to cultivate good relations with the world's superpower. Warm and fuzzy feelings are a distant third. Take counterterrorism. After the attack on the U.S.S. *Cole,* Yemen did everything it could to stymie the American investigation. It lifted not a finger to suppress terrorism. This was under an American administration that was obsessively accommodating and multilateralist. Today, under the most unilateralist of administrations, Yemen has decided to assist in the war on terrorism. This was not a result of a sudden attack of good will toward America. It was a result of the war in Afghanistan, which concentrated the mind of heretofore recalcitrant states like Yemen on the costs of non-cooperation with the United States. Coalitions are not made by superpowers going begging hat in hand. They are made by asserting a position and inviting others to join. What "pragmatic" realists often fail to realize is that unilateralism is the high road to multilateralism. When George Bush senior said of the Iraqi invasion of Kuwait, "this will not stand", and made it clear that he was prepared to act alone if necessary, that declaration—and the credibility of American determination to act unilaterally—in and of itself created a coalition. Hafez al-Asad did not join out of feelings of good will. He joined because no one wants to be left at the dock when the hegemon is sailing.

Unilateralism does not mean *seeking* to act alone. One acts in concert with others if possible. Unilateralism simply means that one does not allow oneself to be hostage to others. No unilateralist would, say, reject Security Council support for an attack on Iraq. The nontrivial question that separates unilateralism from multilateralism—and that tests the "pragmatic realists"—is this: What do you do if, at the end of the day, the Security Council refuses to back you? Do you allow yourself to be dictated to on issues of vital national—and international—security?

When I first proposed the unipolar model in 1990, I suggested that we should accept both its burdens and opportunities and that, if America did not wreck its economy, unipolarity could last thirty or forty years. That seemed bold at the time.

Today, it seems rather modest. The unipolar moment has become the unipolar era. It remains true, however, that its durability will be decided at home. It will depend largely on whether it is welcomed by Americans or seen as a burden to be shed—either because we are too good for the world (the isolationist critique) or because we are not worthy of it (the liberal internationalist critique).

The new unilateralism argues explicitly and unashamedly for maintaining unipolarity, for sustaining America's unrivaled dominance for the foreseeable future. It could be a long future, assuming we successfully manage the single greatest threat, namely, weapons of mass destruction in the hands of rogue states. This in itself will require the aggressive and confident application of unipolar power rather than falling back, as we did in the 1990s, on paralyzing multilateralism. The future of the unipolar era hinges on whether America is governed by those who wish to retain, augment and use unipolarity to advance not just American but global ends, or whether America is governed by those who wish to give it up—either by allowing unipolarity to decay as they retreat to Fortress America, or by passing on the burden by gradually transferring power to multilateral institutions as heirs to American hegemony. The challenge to unipolarity is not from the outside but from the inside. The choice is ours. To impiously paraphrase Benjamin Franklin: History has given you an empire, if you will keep it.

NOTES

1. Kennedy, "The Eagle has Landed", *Financial Times,* February 2, 2002.
2. Kagan, "Power and Weakness", *Policy Review* (June 2002).
3. This is not to claim, by any means, a perfect record of benignity. America has often made and continues to make alliances with unpleasant authoritarian regimes. As I argued recently in *Time* ("Dictatorships and Double Standards", September 23, 2002), such alliances are nonetheless justified so long as they are instrumental (meant to defeat the larger evil) and temporary (expire with the emergency). When Hitler was defeated, we stopped coddling Stalin. Forty years later, as the Soviet threat receded, the United States was instrumental in easing Pinochet out of power and overthrowing Marcos. We withdrew our support for these dictators once the two conditions that justified such alliances had disappeared: The global threat of Soviet communism had receded, and truly democratic domestic alternatives to these dictators had emerged.

The Battle Between Unilateralists and Multilateralists

■ JOSEPH S. NYE, JR.

How should we engage with other countries? There are three main approaches: isolation, unilateralism, and multilateralism. Isolationism persists in public opinion, but it is not a major strategic option for American foreign policy today. While some people responded to the September 2001 terrorist attacks by suggesting that we cut back on foreign involvements, the majority realized that such a policy would not curtail our vulnerability and could even exacerbate it. The main battle lines are drawn among internationalists, between those who advocate unilateralism and those who prefer multilateral tactics. In William Safire's phrase, "Uni- is not iso-. In our reluctance to appear imperious, we could all too quickly abdicate leadership by catering to the envious crowd."[1] Of course, the differences are a matter of degree, and there are few pure unilateralists or multilateralists. When the early actions of the Bush administration led to cries of outrage about unilateralism, the president disclaimed the label and State Department officials described the administration's posture as selective multilateralism. But the two ends of the spectrum anchor different views of the degree of choice that grows out of America's position in the world today. I will suggest below some rules for the middle ground.

Some unilateralists advocate an assertive damn-the-torpedoes approach to promoting American values. They see the danger as a flagging of our internal will and confusion of our goals, which should be to turn a unipolar moment "into a unipolar era." In this view, a principal aim of American foreign policy should be to bring about a change of regime in undemocratic countries such as Iraq, North Korea, and China. Unilateralists believe that our intentions are good, American hegemony is benevolent, and that should end the discussion. Multilateralism would mean "submerging American will in a mush of collective decision-making— you have sentenced yourself to reacting to events or passing the buck to multilingual committees with fancy acronyms.[2] They argue that "the main issue of contention between the United States and those who express opposition to its hegemony is not American 'arrogance.' It is the inescapable reality of American power in its many forms. Those who suggest that these international resentments could somehow be eliminated by a more restrained American foreign policy are engaging in pleasant delusions."[3]

But Americans are not immune from hubris, nor do we have all the answers. Even if it happened to be true, it would be dangerous to act according to such an idea. "For if we were truly acting in the interests of others as well as our own, we would presumably accord to others a substantive role and, by doing so, end up embracing some form of multilateralism. Others, after all, must be supposed to know their interests better than we can know them."[4] As one sympathetic European correctly observed, "From the law of the seas to the Kyoto Protocol, from the biodiversity convention, from the extraterritorial application of the trade embargo against Cuba or Iran, from the brusk calls for reform of the World Bank and the International Monetary Fund to the International Criminal Court: American unilateralism appears as an omnipresent syndrome pervading world politics."[5] When Congress legislated heavy penalties on foreign companies that did business with countries that the United States did not like, the Canadian foreign minister complained, "This is bullying, but in America, you call it 'global leadership.'"[6]

Other unilateralists (sometimes called sovereigntists) focus less on the promotion of American values than on their protection, and they sometimes gain support from the significant minority of isolationist opinion that still exists in this country. As one put it, the strongest and richest country in the world can afford to safeguard its sovereignty. "An America that stands aloof from various international undertakings will not find that it is thereby shut out from the rest of the world. On the contrary, we have every reason to expect that other nations, eager for access to American markets and eager for other cooperative arrangements with the United States, will often adapt themselves to American preferences."[7] In this view, Americans should resist the encroachment of international law, especially claims of universal jurisdiction. Instead, "the United States should strongly espouse national sovereignty, the bedrock upon which democracy and self-government are built, as the fundamental organizing principle of the international system."[8] Or as Senator Jesse Helms warned, the United Nations can be a useful instrument for America's world role, but if it "aspires to establish itself as the central moral authority of a new international order . . . then it begs for confrontation and, more important, eventual U.S. withdrawal."[9]

This battle between multilateralists and unilateralists, often played out in a struggle between the president and Congress, has led to a somewhat schizophrenic American foreign policy. The United States played a prominent role in promoting such multilateral projects as the Law of the Seas Treaty, the Comprehensive Test Ban Treaty, the Land Mines Treaty, the International Criminal Court, the Kyoto Protocol on climate change, and others, but it has failed to follow through with congressional ratification. In some instances, the result has been what *The Economist* calls "parallel unilateralism—a willingness to go along with international accords, but only so far as they suit America, which is prepared to conduct policy outside their constraints.[10] For instance, the United States asserts the jurisdictional limits of the unratified Law of the Seas Treaty. It has pledged not to resume testing nuclear weapons, but because of the unilateral nature of the decision, it does not gain the benefits of verification and the ability to bind others. In other instances, such as antipersonnel land mines, the United States has argued that it needs them to defend against tanks in Korea, but it has undertaken research on a new type of mine that might allow it to join by 2006. In the case of the Kyoto Protocol, President Bush refused to negotiate and peremptorily pronounced it "dead." The result was a foreign reaction of frustration and anger that undermined our soft power.

During the 2000 political campaign, George W. Bush aptly described the situation: "Our nation stands alone right now in the world in terms of power. And that's why we've got to be humble and yet project strength in a way that promotes freedom. . . . If we are an arrogant nation, they'll view us that way, but if we're a humble nation, they'll respect us."[11] Yet our allies and other foreign nations considered the early actions of his administration arrogantly unilateral. Within a few months, America's European allies joined other countries in refusing for the first time to reelect the United States to the UN Human Rights Commission. The secretary of defense, Donald Rumsfeld, said that "gratitude is gone,"[12] and the secretary of state, Colin Powell, explained that "the 'sole superpower' charge is always out there and that may have influenced some."[13] In the less temperate words of television commentator Morton Kondracke, "We're the most powerful country in the world by far, and a lot of pipsqueak wannabes like France resent the hell out of it. . . . When they have a chance to stick it to us, they try."[14] The House of Representatives responded by voting to withhold funds from the UN. But the situation was more complicated than such responses acknowledged.

At the beginning of the last century, as America rose to world power, Teddy Roosevelt advised that we should speak softly but carry a big stick. Now that we have the stick, we need to pay more attention to the first part of his admonition. And we need not just to speak more softly but to listen more carefully. As Chris Patten, the EU commissioner for external affairs and former British Conservative leader, explained a year earlier, the United States is a staunch friend with much to admire, "but there are also many areas in which I think they have got it wrong, the UN, for example, environmental policy, and a pursuit of extraterritorial powers combined with a neuralgic hostility to any external authority over their own affairs."[15] In the words of one observer, at the start of his administration President Bush "contrived to prove his own theory that arrogance provokes resentment for a country that, long before his arrival, was already the world's most conspicuous and convenient target."[16]

The United States should aim to work with other nations on global problems in a multilateral manner whenever possible. I agree with the recent bipartisan commission on our national security, chaired by former senators Gary Hart and Warren Rudman, which concluded that "emerging powers—either singly or in coalition—will increasingly constrain U.S. options regionally and limit its strategic influence. As a result we will remain limited in our ability to impose our will, and we will be vulnerable to an increasing range of threats." Borders will become more porous, rapid advances in information and biotechnologies will create new vulnerabilities, the United States will become "increasingly vulnerable to hostile attack on the American homeland, and the U.S. military superiority will not entirely protect us."[17] This means we must develop multilateral laws and institutions that constrain others and provide a framework for cooperation. In the words of the Hart-Rudman Commission, "America cannot secure and advance its own interests in isolation."[18] As the terrorist attacks of September 11 showed, even a superpower needs friends.

Granted, multilateralism can be used as a strategy by smaller states to tie the United States down like Gulliver among the Lilliputians. It is no wonder that France prefers a multipolar and multilateral world, and less developed countries see multilateralism as in their interests, because it gives them some leverage on the United States. But this does not mean multilateralism is not generally in American interests as well. "By resting our actions on a legal basis (and accepting the correlative constraints), we can make the continued exercise of our disproportionate power easier for others to accept."[19]

Multilateralism involves costs, but in the larger picture, they are outweighed by the benefits. International rules bind the United States and limit our freedom at action in the short term, but they also serve our interest by binding others as well. Americans should use our power now to shape institutions that will serve our long-term national interest in promoting international order. "Since there is little reason for believing that the means of policy will be increased, we are left to rely on the greater cooperation of others. But the greater cooperation of others will mean that our freedom of action is narrowed."[20] It is not just that excessive unilateralism can hurt us; multilateralism is often the best way to achieve our long-run objectives.

Action to shape multilateralism now is a good investment for our future. Today, as we have seen, "worried states are making small adjustments, creating alternatives to alliance with the United States. These small steps may not look important today, but eventually the ground will shift and the U.S.-led postwar order will fragment and disappear."[21] These tendencies are countered by the very openness of the American system. The pluralistic and regularized way in which foreign policy is made reduces surprises. Opportunities for foreigners to raise their voice and influence the American political and governmental system not only are plentiful but constitute an important incentive for alliance. Ever since Athens transformed the Delian League into an empire, smaller allies have been torn between anxieties over abandonment or entrapment. The fact that American allies are able to voice their concerns helps to explain why American alliances have persisted so long after Cold War threats receded.

The other element of the American order that reduces worry about power asymmetries is our membership in a web of multilateral institutions ranging from the UN to NATO. Some call it an institutional bargain. The price for the United States was reduction in Washington's policy autonomy, in that institutional rules and joint decision making reduced U.S. unilateralist capacities. But what Washington got in return was worth the price. America's partners also had their autonomy constrained, but they were able to operate in a world where U.S. power was more restrained and reliable. Seen in the light of a constitutional bargain, the multilateralism of American preeminence is a key to its longevity, because it reduces the incentives for constructing alliances against us. And to the extent that the EU is the major potential challenger in terms of capacity, the idea of a loose constitutional framework between the United States and the societies with which we share the most values makes sense.

Of course, not all multilateral arrangements are good or in our interests, and the United States should occasionally use unilateral tactics in certain situations. . . . The presumption in favor of multilateralism that I recommend need not be a straitjacket. Richard Haass, the State Department's director of policy planning, says, "What you're going to get from this administration is 'à la carte multilateralism.' We'll look at each agreement and make a decision, rather than come out with a broad-based approach."[22] So how should Americans choose between unilateral and multilateral tactics? Here are seven tests to consider.

First, in cases that involve vital survival interests, we should not rule out unilateral action, though when possible we should seek international support for these actions. The starkest case in the last half century was the 1962 Cuban missile crisis. American leaders felt obliged to consider unilateral use of force, though it is important to note that President Kennedy also sought the legitimacy of opinion expressed in multilateral forums such as the United Nations and the Organization of American States. Strikes against terrorist camps and safe havens are a current example, but again, unilateral actions are best when buttressed by multilateral support.

Second, we should be cautious about multilateral arrangements that interfere with our ability to produce stable peace in volatile areas. Because of our global military role, the United States sometimes has interests and vulnerabilities that are different from those of smaller states with more limited interests—witness the role of land mines in preventing North Korean tanks crossing the demilitarized zone into South Korea. Thus the multilateral treaty banning land mines was easier for other countries to sign. As noted previously, the United States announced that it would work to develop new mines that might allow it to sign by 2006. Similarly, given the global role of American military forces, if the procedures of the International Criminal Court cannot be clarified to ensure protection of American troops from unjustified charges of war crimes, they might deter the United States from contributing to the public good of peacekeeping. The ICC procedures currently proposed give primary jurisdiction over alleged war crimes by American servicemen to the United States, but there is still a danger of overzealous prosecutors egged on by hostile NGOs in instances where the United States finds no case. We should seek further assurances such as clarifying declarations by the UN Security Council. While the ICC has problems, helping to shape its procedures would be a better policy than abetting the current trend toward national claims of universal legal jurisdiction that are evolving in ad hoc fashion beyond our control.

Third, unilateral tactics sometimes help lead others to compromises that advance multilateral interests. The multilateralism of free trade and the international gold standard in the nineteenth century were achieved not by multilateral means but by Britain's unilateral moves of opening its markets and maintaining the stability of its currency. America's relative openness after 1945 and, more recently, trade legislation that threatened unilateral sanctions if others did not negotiate helped create conditions that prodded other countries to move forward with the WTO dispute settlement mechanism. Sometimes the United States is big enough to set high standards and get away with it—witness our more stringent regulations for financial markets. Such actions can lead to the creation of higher international standards. The key is whether the unilateral action was designed to promote a global public good.

The Kyoto Protocol, which caused President Bush such trouble at the beginning of his presidency, could have been another case in point had it been handled differently. Many who accept the reality of global warming and support the Framework Convention on Climate Change (the Rio agreement signed by President George H. Bush and ratified by the Senate in 1992) believed that the Kyoto agreement was badly flawed because it did not include developing countries and because its target for emission cuts, according to *The Economist*, "could not be done except at ruinous cost, and perhaps not even then." A longer-term plan based on milder reductions at the start followed by more demanding targets farther out would provide time for capital stocks to adjust and market-based instruments such as tradable permits to lower the costs of emissions reductions. It would also reduce the trade-off with economic growth, which benefits a wide range of nations, including the poor. If, instead of resisting the science and abruptly pronouncing the protocol dead on grounds of domestic interest, the Bush administration had said, "We will work on a domestic energy policy that cuts emissions and at the same time negotiate with you for a better treaty," his initial unilateralism would arguably have advanced multilateral interests.

Fourth, the United States should reject multilateral initiatives that are recipes for inaction, promote others' self-interest, or are contrary to our values. The New International Information Order proposed by the UN Educational, Scientific and Cultural Organization (UNESCO) in the 1970s would have helped authoritarian governments to restrict freedom of the press. Similarly, the New International Economic Order fostered by the General Assembly at the same time would have interfered with the public good of open markets. Sometimes multilateral procedures are obstructive—for example, Russia's and China's efforts to prevent Security Council authorization of intervention to stop the human rights violations in Kosovo in 1999. Ultimately the United States decided to go ahead without Security Council approval, but even then the American intervention was not purely unilateral but taken with strong support of our allies in NATO.

Fifth, multilateralism is essential on intrinsically cooperative issues that cannot be managed by the United States without the help of other countries. Climate change is a perfect example. Global warming will be costly to us, but it cannot be prevented by the United States alone cutting emissions of carbon dioxide, methane, and particulates. The United States is the largest source of such warming agents, but three-quarters of the sources originate outside our borders. Without cooperation, the problem is beyond our control. The same is true of a long list of items: the spread of infectious diseases, the stability of global financial markets, the international trade system, the proliferation of weapons of mass destruction, narcotics trafficking, international crime syndicates, transnational terrorism. All these problems have major effects on Americans, and their control ranks as an important national interest—but one that cannot be achieved except by multilateral means.

Sixth, multilateralism should be sought as a means to get others to share the burden and buy into the idea of providing public goods. Sharing helps foster commitment to common values. Even militarily, the United States should rarely intervene alone. Not only does this comport with the preferences of the American public, but it has practical implications. The United States pays a minority share of the cost of UN and NATO peacekeeping operations, and the legitimacy of a multilateral umbrella reduces collateral political costs to our soft power.

Seventh, in choosing between multilateral and unilateral tactics, we must consider the effects of the decision on our soft power. If we continue to define our power too heavily in military terms, we may fail to understand the need to invest in other instruments. As we have seen, soft power is becoming increasingly important, but soft power is fragile and can be destroyed by excessive unilateralism and arrogance. In balancing whether to use multilateral or unilateral tactics, or to adhere to or refuse to go along with particular multilateral initiatives, we have to consider how we explain it to others and what the effects will be on our soft power.

In short, American foreign policy in a global information age should have a general preference for multilateralism, but not all multilateralism. At times we will have to go it alone. When we do so in pursuit of public goods, the nature of our ends may substitute for the means in legitimizing our power in the eyes of others. If, on the other hand, the new unilateralists try to elevate unilateralism from an occasional temporary tactic to a full-fledged strategy, they are likely to fail for three reasons: (1) the intrinsically multilateral nature of a number of important transnational issues in a global age, (2) the costly effects on our soft power, and (3) the changing nature of sovereignty.

NOTES

1. William Safire, "The Purloined Treaty," *New York Times,* April 9, 2001, A21.
2. Charles Krauthammer, "The New Unilateralism," *Washington Post,* June 8, 2001, A29.
3. Robert Kagan and William Kristol, "The Present Danger," *The National Interest,* spring 2000, 67.
4. Robert W. Tucker in "American Power—For What? A Symposium," *Commentary,* January 2000, 46.
5. Harald Muller quoted in Franz Nuscheler, "Multilateralism vs. Unilateralism," Development and Peace Foundation, Bonn, 2001, 5.
6. Lloyd Axworthy quoted in Stewart Patrick, "Lead, Follow, or Get Out of the Way: America's Retreat from Multilateralism," *Current History,* December 2000, 433.
7. Quoted in Peter Spiro, "The New Sovereigntist," *Foreign Affairs,* November-December 2000, 12–13.
8. David B. Rivkin Jr. and Lee A. Casey, "The Rocky Shoals of International Law," *The National Interest,* winter 2000–1, 42.
9. Jesse Helms, "American Sovereignty and the UN," *The National Interest,* winter 2000–1, 34.
10. "Working Out the World," *The Economist,* March 31, 2001, 24.
11. "2nd Presidential Debate Between Gov. Bush and Vice President Gore," *New York Times,* October 12, 2000, A20.
12. Brian Knowlton, "Bush Aide Calls UN Vote an Outrage," *International Herald Tribune,* May 7, 2001 (http://www.iht.com/articles/19081.html).

13. David Sanger, "House Threatens to Hold U.N. Dues in Loss of a Seat," *New York Times,* May 9, 2001, A1.
14. Quoted in *The Hotline: National Journal's Daily Briefing on Politics,* May 8, 2001, 4.
15. Barry James, "The EU Counterweight to American Influence," *International Herald Tribune,* June 16, 2000, 4.
16. Roger Cohen, "Arrogant or Humble? Bush Encounters Europeans' Hostility," *International Herald Tribune,* May 8, 2001, 1.
17. United States Commission on National Security in the Twenty-first Century, *New World Coming: American Security in the 21st Century* (Washington, D.C., 1999), 4.
18. United States Commission on National Security in the Twenty-first Century, *Roadmap for National Security: Imperative for Change, Phase III Report* (Washington, D.C., 2001), 2, 5.
19. Joshua Muravchik in "American Power—For What? A Symposium," *Commentary,* January 2000, 41.
20. Robert W. Tucker in "American Power—For What? A Symposium," *Commentary,* January 2000, 46.
21. G. John Ikenberry, "Getting Hegemony Right," *The National Interest,* spring 2001, 19.
22. Shanker, "White House Says the US Is Not a Loner, Just Choosy."

FAILED STATES, CIVIL WARS, AND ■ NATION-BUILDING

Failed States, Collapsed States, Weak States: Causes and Indicators

■ ROBERT I. ROTBERG

This decade's failed states are Afghanistan, Angola, Burundi, the Congo, Liberia, Sierra Leone, and the Sudan. . . . Somalia is a collapsed state. Together they are the contemporary classical failed and collapsed states, but others were once collapsed or failed and many other modern nation-states now approach the brink of failure, some much more ominously than others. Another group of states drifts disastrously downward from weak to failing to failed. What is of particular interest is why and how states slip from weakness toward failure, or not. The list of weak states is long, but only a few of those weak and poorly governed states need necessarily edge into failure. Why? Even the categorization of a state as failing—Colombia and Indonesia, among others—need not doom it irretrievably to full failure. What does it take to drive a failing state over the edge into failure or collapse? . . .

How [could] Somalia, a nation-state of about 9 million people with a strongly cohesive cultural tradition, a common language, a common religion, and a shared history of nationalism . . . fail, and then collapse? Perhaps . . . it never constituted a single coherent territory, having been part of the colonial empires of two suzerains, with other Somalis living outside the boundaries of the two colonies. Then, as was often the experience elsewhere in Africa and Asia, the first elected, proto-democratic, post-independence civilian governments proved to be "experimental, inefficient, corrupt, and incapable of creating any kind of national political

Reprinted by permission of the Brookings Institution Press.

culture."[1] General Mohammed Siad Barre, commander of the army, decided that the politicians were ruining the country, so he usurped power in 1969, suspending the constitution, banning political parties, and promising an end to corruption. Twenty years and many misadventures later, Siad Barre had succeeded in destroying any semblance of national governmental legitimacy. Backed first by the Soviet Union and then by the United States, Siad Barre destroyed institutions of government and democracy, abused his citizens' human rights, channeled as many of the resources of the state as possible into his own and his subclan's hands, and deprived everyone else at the end of the Cold War of what was left of the spoils of Somali supreme rule. All of the major clans and subclans, other than Siad Barre's own, became alienated. His shock troops perpetrated one outrage after another against fellow Somalis. By the onset of civil war in 1991, the Somali state had long since failed. The civil war destroyed what was left, and Somalia collapsed onto itself. . . .

President Stevens (1968–1985) systematically reduced human security within Sierra Leone so as to maximize his own personal power, and . . . that increase in personal power permitted a quantum leap in his control over the country's rents and riches. Stevens "sold chances to profit from disorder to those who could pay for it through providing services."[2] He created a private military force to terrorize his own people and to aggrandize, especially in the diamond fields. As the official rule of law receded, the law of the jungle, presided over by Stevens, took its place. Institutions of government were broken or corrupted. The state became illegitimate, and a civil war over spoils, encouraged and assisted from outside, turned failure into a collapse. In 2002, after hideous atrocities, a brutal intervention by a West African peace enforcement contingent, much more war, and the arrival of British paratroopers and a large UN peacekeeping force, Sierra Leone recovered sufficiently to be considered failed rather than collapsed. It even held effective elections.

Mobutu used analogous tactics in the patrimony of Zaire. As his people's self-proclaimed *guide,* or as the personalist embodiment of national leadership during the Cold War, he deployed the largesse of his American and other Western patrons to enhance his personal wealth, to heighten his stature over his countrymen, and to weave a tightly manipulated web of loyalties across the army and into all aspects of Zairese society. Every proper political and democratic institution was an obstacle to the edifice that he created. So was civil society, politics itself in the broad sense, and economic development. Letting the country's Belgian-built infrastructure rot, maintaining a colonial type of resource extraction (of copper, other metals, and diamonds), rebuffing the rise of a real bourgeoisie, and feeding his people false glories instead of real substance and per capita growth accentuated his own power, wealth, and importance. As with Stevens and Siad Barre, the modernizing state was the enemy. Mobutu had no sense of noblesse oblige. René Lemarchand says that for Mobutu's state, patronage was the indispensable lubricant. Ultimately, however, "the lubricant ran out and the Mobutist machine was brought to a . . . standstill. . . . The inability of the Mobutist state to generate a volume of rewards consistent with its clientelistic ambitions is the key . . . [to] . . . its rapid loss of legitimacy."[3]

The warring divisions of the failed Sudanese state, north and south, reflect fundamental ethnic, religious, and linguistic differences; Egyptian and British conquest and colonial administrative flaws and patterns; post-independence disparities and discriminations (the north dominating the south); and the discovery of oil in the south. A weak state in the north, providing political goods at minimal levels for its mostly Muslim constituents, became the nucleus of a truly failed state when its long war with the south (from 1955 to 1972 and from 1983 through 2002) entered the equation. The Sudanese war has the dubious distinction of having inflicted the largest number of civilian casualties (over 2 million) in any intrastate war, coupled with the largest internally displaced and refugee population in the world (about 4 million). Slavery (north against south) flourishes, as well. Moreover, in the south, the central government's writ rarely runs. It provides no political goods to its southern citizens, bombs them, raids them, and regards black southerners as enemy. As a result, the Sudan has long been failed. Yet, northerners still regard their state as legitimate, even though the southern insurgents do not and have sought either secession or autonomy for decades. . . . However, so long as oil revenues shore up the north, the Sudan is unlikely to collapse entirely. . . .

The paradigm of failure . . . holds equally well, with similar but differently detailed material, in Afghanistan, Angola, Burundi, and Liberia. . . . Indeed, Angola's killing fields and internally displaced circumstances are almost as intense and certainly as destructive as the Sudan's. The wars in Afghanistan, Angola, Burundi, and Liberia have been equally traumatic for ordinary combatants and hapless civilians unwittingly caught up in a vicious and (until 2002 in Angola) interminable battle for resources and power between determined opponents. Burundi's majority-minority war has produced fewer deaths in recent decades, but it continues an enduring contest for primacy that antedates the modern nation-state itself. From birth economically weak and geographically limited, Burundi's capacity to perform has for a decade been fatally crippled by majority-backed insurgencies against autocratic minority-led governments.

WEAKNESS AND THE POSSIBILITY OF FAILURE

Collapsed and failed designate the consequences of a process of decay at the nation-state level. The capacity of those nation-states to perform positively for their citizens has atrophied. But, as the Lebanese and Tajikistani cases show, that atrophy is neither inevitable nor the result of happenstance. For a state to fail is not that easy. Crossing from weakness into failure takes will as well as neglect. Thus, weak nation-states need not tip into failure. . . .

There are several interesting cases that indeed test the precision of the distinction between weakness and failure:

Sri Lanka has been embroiled in a bitter and destructive civil war for nineteen years. As much as 15 percent of its total land mass has at times in the last decade been controlled by the rebel Liberation Tigers of Tamil Eeelam (LTTE), a Tamil separatist insurgency. Additionally, the LTTE with relative impunity has been able to assassinate prime ministers, bomb presidents, kill off rival Tamils, and in 2001, even destroy the nation's civil air terminal and main air force base. But, as incapable as the Sinhala-dominated governments of the island have been of putting down the LTTE rebellion, so the nation-state has remained merely weak . . . , never close to tipping over into failure. For 80 percent of Sri Lankans, the government performs reasonably well. The roads are maintained and schools and hospitals function, to some limited extent even in the war-torn north and east. Since the early 1990s, too, Sri Lanka has exhibited robust levels of economic growth. The authority of successive governments extends securely to the Sinhala-speaking 80 percent of the country, and into the recaptured Tamil areas. For these reasons, despite a consuming internal conflict founded on intense majority-minority discrimination and deprivation and on pronounced ethnic and religious differences, Sri Lanka projects authority throughout much of the country, has suffered no loss of legitimacy among Sinhala, and has successfully escaped failure.

Indonesia is another case of weakness avoiding failure despite widespread insecurity. As the world's largest Muslim nation, its far-flung archipelago harbors separatist wars in Aceh in the west and in Papua (formerly Irian Jaya) in the east, plus large pockets of Muslim-Christian conflict in Ambon and the Maluku islands, Muslim-Christian hostility in northern Sulawesi, and ethnic xenophobic outbursts in Kalimantan. Given all of these conflictual situations, none of which has become less bitter since the end of the Soeharto dictatorship, it would be easy to conclude that Indonesia was approaching failure. Yet . . . only the insurgents in Aceh and Papua want to secede and are contesting the state. The several other battles take place within the state, not against it. They do not threaten the integrity and resources of the state in the way that the enduring, but low-level, war in Aceh does. In Aceh and Papua, the government retains the upper hand. Overall, most of Indonesia is still secure. In most of the country the government projects power and authority. It manages to provide most other necessary political goods to most of Indonesia despite dangerous economic and other developments in the post-Soeharto era.

What about Colombia? An otherwise well-endowed, prosperous, and ostensibly stable state controls only two-thirds of its territory, a clear hint of failure. Three private armies project their own power across large zones carved out of the very body of the state. The official defense and political establishment has renounced or lost authority in those zones to insurgent groups and drug traffickers. Moreover, Colombia is tense and disturbed. It boasts the second highest annual per capita murder rate in the world. Its politicians and businessmen routinely wear armored vests and travel with well-armed guards, a clear indicator of the state's inability to ensure personal security. Even so . . . the rest of Colombia as a state still delivers schooling and medical care, organizes a physical and communications infrastructure, provides economic opportunity, and remains legitimate. Colombia is weak because of its multiple insurgencies, but is comparatively strong and well-performing in the areas over which it maintains control. When and if the government of Colombia can re-insert itself into the disputed zones and further reduce the power of drug traffickers, the state's reach will expand. Then, a weak, endangered state will be able to move farther away from possible failure toward strength.

Zimbabwe is an example of a once unquestionably strong African state that has fallen rapidly through weakness to the very edge of the abyss of failure. All Zimbabwe lacks in order to join the ranks of failed states is a widespread internal insurgent movement directed against the government. That could come, particularly if the political and economic deterioration of the country continues unchecked. In 2000 and 2001, GDP per capita slid backward by 10 percent a year. Inflation galloped from 30 percent to 116 percent. The local currency fell against the U.S. dollar from 38:1 to 500:1. Foreign and domestic investment ceased. Unemployment rose to 60 percent in a country of 12 million. Health and educational services vanished. HIV infection rates climbed to 30 percent, with about 2000 Zimbabweans dying every week. Respect for the rule of law was badly battered and then subverted. Political institutions ceased to function fully. Agents of the state preyed on its real and its supposed opponents, chilling free expression and shamelessly stealing a presidential election. The government's legitimacy vanished. Corruption, meanwhile, flourished, with the ruling elite pocketing their local and Congolese war gains and letting most Zimbabweans go hungry. Real starvation appeared in mid-2002, despite food aid from abroad. All of this misery, and the tendency to fail, resulted (as it had earlier in the Congo and Sierra Leone) from the ruthless designs and vengeance of an omnipotent ruler. . . .

A number of other nation-states belong in the category of weak states that show a high potential to fail. Nepal has been a clear case since its Maoist insurgency began again roiling the mountains and plains of the monarchist country. Already hindered by geography and poverty, Nepal has never been a robust provider of political goods to its inhabitants. The palace massacre of 2001 undermined the legitimacy of the monarchy, and thus of the ruling government. With the flare-up of a determined rural rebellion in 2002, and Nepal's demonstrated inability to cope effectively, security of persons and of regions became harder and harder to achieve, absent military assistance from India. Under these circumstances, Nepal can hardly project power or credibility. Failure becomes a distinct possibility. . . .

A third variety of weak state includes the enduringly weak. . . . Haiti has always been on the edge of failure, particularly during the nineteenth and twentieth centuries. But its entrenched weaknesses include no ethnic, religious, or other communal cleavages. There are no insurgent movements. Nor has Haiti experienced radical or rapid deflation in standards of living and national expectations, like Argentina in 2002 and Russia in the 1990s. Haiti has always been the poorest polity in the Western hemisphere.

Haiti's national capacity to provide political goods has always been compromised by autocratic and corrupt leadership, weak institutions, an intimidated civil society, high levels of crime, low GDP levels per capita, high rates of infant mortality, suspicion or outright hostility from its neighbors, and many other deficiencies. Narcotics trafficking has been a serious problem since the 1980s. The Haitian government has been unable or unwilling to interdict smugglers in general, and drugs transshippers in particular. Haiti, even under President Jean-Bertrand Aristide (1990–1991, 1994–1995, 2000–), is gripped in a vise of weakness. Yet, given very limited organized internal dissidence, almost no internal ethnic, religious, or linguistic cleavages within Haitian society except a deep distrust by the majority of the upper classes, and of mulattos because of their historic class affiliations, the ingredients of major civil strife are absent. Failure demands communal differences capable of being transformed into consuming cross-group violence. Haiti seems condemned to remain weak, but without failing.

Nation-states that, given their geographical and physical legacy (and future peril, in several cases, because of global warming and cataclysmic climatic change), can be considered inherently weak include (not a full list) Burkina Faso, Chad, Ghana, Guinea, and Niger, in Africa; Georgia and Moldova in the former Soviet Union, and Cambodia, East Timor, and Laos in Asia. Each has its own distinguishing features, and Georgia and Moldova battle their own so far successful separatist movements. Chad at one time harbored a vicious civil war, and Burkina Faso, Niger, Cambodia, and Laos are all ruled by autocrats unfriendly to civil society and to participatory governance. East Timor is a very new state, having been rescued and resuscitated by the United Nations after two bitter and unrewarding colonial interludes and a brutal final Indonesian spree of destruction and death. East Timor, even with UN help, enters its full majority without a cadre of experienced professionals and bureaucrats and without much in the way of physical resources. The willingness of these weak states to provide political goods in quantity and quality is severely limited at the best of times. Almost any external shock or internal emergency could push them over the brink.

INDICATORS OF FAILURE

As this chapter has suggested earlier, the road to nation-state failure is littered with serious mistakes of omission and commission. Even in the modern states with inherited weaknesses, failure is not preordained. Poor, arbitrary, absent-minded creations predisposed to failure need not fail. Indeed, Botswana, dirt poor at independence and a forlorn excuse for a state, under determined and visionary leadership created a state strong enough to take full advantage of a subsequent, and much unexpected, resource bonanza. Similarly, a sugar monoculture like Mauritius was transformed by determined visionary leadership into a thriving plural society based on manufacturing for export. In contrast, Malawi and Mali (two examples among many) remain weak and very poor, albeit democratic, having both been unable, in their different circumstances, to overcome the arbitrary configuration of their borders, a common absence of easily exploitable resources, geographical hindrances, and decades of despotism. Climatic change may hit both Malawi and Mali particularly hard, too.

Nation-states are blessed or cursed by the discovery or absence of natural resources, like oil or diamonds, within received borders. But it is not the accidental quality of their borders that is the original flaw; it is what has been made of the challenges and opportunities of a given outline that determines whether a state remains weak, becomes stronger, or slides toward failure and collapse. The colonial errors were many, especially the freeing of Africa south of the Sahara as forty-eight administrative territories instead of six or seven larger ones, and the abysmal failure to transfer the reins of authority much earlier and much more thoroughly to an indigenat. But it is not possible to predict this century's candidates for failure solely or even largely on the basis of colonial mistreatment. . . .

Three kinds of signals of impending failure—economic, political, and deaths in combat—provide clearer, more timely, and more actionable warnings. On the economic front, Indonesia in 1997–1999, Nigeria in 1993–1999, Lebanon in 1972–1979, and Zimbabwe in 2001–2002, each provide instances of how rapid reductions in incomes and living standards indicated the possibility of failure early enough to be noted and for preventive measures to have been attempted. Once the downward spiral starts in earnest, only a concerted, determined effort can slow its momentum; corrupt autocrats and their equally corrupt associates usually have few incentives to arrest their state's slide, since they find clever ways to benefit from impoverishment and misery. As foreign and domestic investment dries up, jobs vanish, and per capita incomes fall, the mass of citizens in an imperiled state see their health, educational, and logistical entitlements melt away. Food and fuel shortages occur. Privation and hunger follow, especially if a climatic catastrophe intervenes. Thanks to foreign exchange scarcities, there is less and less of everything that matters. Meanwhile, in the typical failing state, ruling families and cadres arrogate to themselves increasing portions of the available pie. They systematically skim the state treasury, take advantage of official versus street costs of foreign exchange, partake of smuggling and the rents of smuggling, and gather what little is available into their own sticky palms. If it were possible reliably to calibrate the flow of illicit funds into overseas accounts, nation by nation, robust early warnings would be available. Absent detailed reports of such theft, the descriptors in this paragraph become very suggestive indicators that can be watched, in real time, and can forecast serious trouble, if not an end state of failure.

Politically, the available indicators are equally clear, if somewhat less quantifiably precise. A leader and his associates begin by subverting democratic norms, greatly restricting participatory processes, and coercing a legislature and the bureaucracy into subservience. They end judicial independence, block civil society, and suborn the security forces. Political goods become scarce or are supplied to the leading class only. The rulers demonstrate more and more contempt for their peoples, surround themselves with family, clan, or ethnic allies, and distance themselves from their subjects. The state becomes equated in the eyes of most citizens with the particular drives and desires of a leader and a smallish group. Many of these leaders drive grandly down their boulevards in motorcades, commandeer commercial aircraft for foreign excursions, and put their faces prominently on the local currency, on airports and ships, and on oversize photographs in public places.

The third indicator is the level of violence. If it rises precipitously because of skirmishes, hostilities, or outright civil war, the state can be considered crumbling. As national human security rates fall, the probability of failure rises. Not every civil conflict precipitates failure, but each offers a warning sign. Absolute or relative crime rates and civilian combat death counts above a certain number cannot prescribe failure. But they show that a society is deteriorating and that the glue that binds a new (or an old) state together is becoming fatally thin.

No single indicator provides certain evidence that a strong state is becoming weak or a weak state is heading pell-mell into failure. But a judicious assessment of the several available indicators discussed in this section, taken together, should provide both quantifiable and qualitative warnings. Then avoidance maneuvers can occur and efforts at prevention can be mounted. . . .

THE HAND OF MAN

State failure is largely man made, not accidental. Institutional fragilities and structural flaws contribute to failure, but those deficiencies usually hark back to decisions or actions of men (rarely women). So it is that leadership errors across history have destroyed states for personal gain; in the contemporary era, leadership mistakes continue to erode fragile polities in Africa, Asia, and Oceania that already operate on the cusp of failure. . . .

Wherever there has been state failure or collapse, human agency has engineered the slide from strength or weakness and willfully presided over profound and destabilizing resource shifts from the state to the ruling few. As those resource transfers accelerated and human rights abuses mounted, countervailing violence signified the extent to which states in question had broken fundamental social contracts and become hollow receptacles of personalist privilege, personalist rule, and national impoverishment. Inhabitants of failed states understand what it means for life to be brutish and short.

In earlier, less interconnected eras, state weakness and failure could be isolated and kept distant from the developed world. Failure once held fewer implications for the surrounding regions and for the peace and security of the globe. Now, however, as much as their citizens suffer, the failings of states also pose enormous dangers beyond their own borders. Preventing nation-states from failing, and resuscitating those that have failed and will fail, have thus become the critical, all-consuming, strategic and moral imperatives of our terrorized time. The chapters in this book demonstrate how and why states have failed and will fail, and how weak states have in several cases been spared the descent into despair and destruction.

NOTES

1. Walter Clarke and Robert Gosende, "Somalia: Can a Collapsed State Reconstitute Itself," in Robert Rotberg, ed., *State Failure and State Weakness in a Time of Terror* (Washington, D.C.: Brookings Institution, 2003), 129–158.
2. William Reno, "Sierra Leone: Warfare in a Post-State Society," in Rotberg, ed., 75.
3. René Lemarchand, "The Democratic Republic of the Congo: From Failure to Potential Reconstruction," in Rotberg, ed., 37.

The Market for Civil War

■ PAUL COLLIER

Every time a civil war breaks out, some historian traces its origin to the 14th century and some anthropologist expounds on its ethnic roots. Don't buy into such explanations too quickly. Certain countries are more prone to civil war than others, but distant history and ethnic tensions are rarely the best explanations for a conflict. Look instead at a nation's recent past and, most important, its economic conditions.

Once a country has reached a per capita income rivaling that of the world's richest nations, its risk of civil war is negligible. Today, about 900 million people live in such societies. Four billion more live in countries that are either already middle income or on track to becoming so, thanks to rapidly growing and diversifying economies. This group, which includes the economic success stories of the post–World War II era, faces fairly low risk of civil war. The potential for conflict is concentrated among the countries inhabited by the world's remaining 1.1 billion people. These countries typically have poor and declining economies and rely on natural resources—such as diamonds or oil—for a large proportion of national income. As the British, French, Portuguese, and Soviet empires successively dissolved during the last century, the number of such countries increased in waves.

Such at-risk countries are engaged in a sort of Russian roulette. Every year that their dismal economic conditions persist increases the odds that their societies will fall into armed conflict. Whether by luck or prudence, many such nations have so far escaped civil war. Others have not. And once civil war has started, the decline in income and the accumulation of arms, fighting skills, and military capabilities greatly increase the risks of further conflict.

To date, academics and policymakers alike have misdiagnosed the nature of the problem; little surprise, then, that their efforts to prevent civil wars have been ineffective. When the world's leaders can identify the real factors most likely to drive such conflicts, they will have a better chance of preventing future wars.

THE MYTH OF ETHNIC STRIFE

Between 1960 and 1999, there were 52 major civil wars for which comprehensive data is available on social, political, historical, economic, and geographic circumstances. Such wars spanned the developing regions, with the typical conflict lasting around seven years and leaving a legacy of persistent poverty and disease in its wake. To understand the causes of these conflicts, economist Anke Hoeffler and I studied each five-year period from 1960 to 1999 and identified preexisting conditions that helped predict the outbreak of war.

For example, income inequality and ethnic-religious diversity are frequently cited as causes for conflict. Yet surprisingly, inequality—either of household incomes or of land ownership—does not appear to increase systematically the risk of civil war. Brazil got away with its high inequality; Colombia didn't. And, in fact, ethnic and religious diversity actually reduces the risk of civil conflict. One important exception: Where the largest ethnic group constitutes a majority but lives alongside a substantial minority, such as in Sri Lanka and Rwanda, the risk of civil war roughly doubles. Once wars start, they also tend to last much longer if the nation in question displays two or three dominant ethnic groups.

Conflicts in ethnically diverse countries may be ethnically patterned without being ethnically caused. International media coverage of civil wars often focuses on history and ethnicity because rebel leaders adopt this sort of discourse. Grievances are to a rebel organization what image is to a business. The rebel group needs to stimulate a sense of collective grievance to build cohesion in its army and to attract funding from its diaspora living in rich countries.

Much to the dismay of democratization activists, democracy fails to reduce the risk of civil war, at least in low-income countries. Indeed, politically repressive societies have no greater risk of civil war than full-fledged democracies. Countries falling between the extremes of autocracy and full democracy—where citizens enjoy some limited political rights—are at a greater risk of war. Low-income societies with new democratic institutions are often at enhanced risk: Just consider the current catastrophe in Ivory Coast, where uncertainty over who could stand for the presidential election in 2000 triggered violent clashes and ongoing political instability.

Wherever a civil war occurs, observers will invariably find some deep history of conflict. But overwhelmingly, conflicts in the distant past are not generating civil wars in the present. The history that matters is recent history, not that of the 14th century. If a country recently experienced a civil war, it is much more likely to have another one. This risk fades the longer peace endures.

Civil war is self-perpetuating, partly because it changes the balance of interests within countries. Groups engaged in conflict invest in armaments, skills, and infrastructure that are only good for violence. These groups' leaders, and indeed all those who gain from lawlessness, prosper during war, even though society as a whole suffers. The part of the elite that prefers peace will have shifted much of its wealth outside the country. Hence, as a result of the conflict, the balance of elite interests shifts toward further conflict.

Geography matters, too. If a country is mountainous and has a large, lightly populated hinterland, it faces an enhanced risk of rebellion. Presumably, rebels are harder to find and defeat in such terrain. Nepal is therefore more at risk of civil war, geographically speaking, than Singapore.

DIAMONDS, A REBEL'S BEST FRIEND

All these factors notwithstanding, economic conditions remain paramount in explaining civil wars. For the average country in our study, the risk of a civil war in each five-year period was around 6 percent, but the risks increased alarmingly if the economy was poor, declining, and dependent on natural resource exports. For a country with conditions like those in the Democratic Republic of the Congo (formerly Zaire) in the late 1990s—with deep poverty, a collapsing economy, and huge mineral exploitation—the risk reaches nearly 80 percent.

Once started, wars last longer in low-income countries, which are prone to rebellion for many reasons: Recruits have less of a stake in the status quo, and central governments are typically weak. Each additional percentage point in the growth rate of per capita income shaves off about 1 percentage point of conflict risk; conversely, wars are more likely to follow periods of economic collapse—such as the conflicts that have surged in Indonesia since the East Asian economic crisis of the late 1990s. If a country's per capita income doubles, its risk of conflict drops by roughly half. Simply put, economic growth matters because opportunities for youth depend upon a robust economy.

Conflict is also more likely in countries that depend heavily on natural resources for their export earnings, in part because rebel groups can extort the gains from this trade to finance their operations. Diamonds funded the National Union for the Total Independence of Angola (UNITA) rebel group during Angola's long civil war, as well as the Revolutionary United Front (RUF) in Sierra Leone; timber funded the Khmer Rouge in Cambodia. Indeed, methods of extortion abound. For example, multinational corporations that extract natural resources must often pay huge sums to ransom kidnapped workers and to protect infrastructure from sabotage at the hands of rebel groups. Laughably, such payments are sometimes charged to the companies' "corporate social responsibility" budgets.

Natural resources also fuel war because they make secession more likely. When valuable natural resources are discovered in a particular region of a country, the people living in such localities suddenly have an economic incentive to secede, violently if necessary. Since most countries are ethnically diverse, the lucky, resource-rich locality is likely to be ethnically distinct as well. Often, the weak political force of ethnic romanticism latches on to the stronger force of economic self-interest so that secessionist movements voice ethnic grievances—Biafra (Nigeria), Cabinda (Angola), and Aceh (Indonesia) come to mind. The incentive to secede is probably compounded by the corrupt, incompetent way in which governments commonly use natural resource wealth: The greed of a resource-rich locality can seem ethically less ugly if a corrupt national elite is already hijacking the resources.

THE WAR DIVIDEND

One striking lesson from these patterns is that the motivations for rebellion generally matter less than the conditions that make a rebellion financially and militarily viable. Civil wars only occur if a rebel organization can build and sustain a private army. These organizations are unlike traditional opposition groups such as political parties or protest movements. They are hierarchical, authoritarian, expensive, and usually small. Where such organizations are financially and militarily feasible, rebellions are likely to emerge, promoting whatever political agenda their leaders happen to support.

Global efforts to curb civil war should therefore focus on reducing the viability—rather than just the rationale—of rebellion. Of course, policies should address legitimate grievances, not because addressing them paves a royal road to peace but because they are legitimate.

Those nations currently at war and those that have recently emerged from civil war constitute the core of the problem. Many countries have fallen into a conflict trap: a damaging war that sharply increases the risk of further conflict, followed by a fragile peace, and then back to war. The expected duration of a civil war is currently about eight years—double what it was before the 1980s. Wars therefore do more damage now and thus more powerfully provoke further conflict.

No one knows why wars last longer now. Perhaps global markets in both natural resources and arms make rebellion easier to finance and equip. Rebel groups can now sell the future rights to mineral extraction (conditional on rebel victory) to raise funds for weapons purchases. . . .

So, what specific measures can countries take to reduce the occurrence and likelihood of civil war?

For developing countries already growing rapidly, the most significant risk may be episodes of economic crisis, such as that experienced by Indonesia in the late 1990s. The opportunity to prevent war in such cases only strengthens the justification for international efforts to avert economic crises. In this light, initiatives to reform and rethink the workings of the global financial system are not merely an academic debate or an effort to ease investors' concerns, but rather a much more serious matter with immediate life-and-death consequences.

Poor countries that are not developing but have so far escaped civil war, such as Zambia and Malawi, are also racing against time. If they do not find ways to accelerate their economic growth and development, they will likely stumble into conflict. Recent casualties include Ivory Coast and Nepal. Nations in these conditions should get the message that change is urgent. Often, the remedy should go beyond the standard package of market access, debt relief, and aid programs from the developed countries to include credible policy reform and honest governance within vulnerable countries.

Due to their heavy dependence on natural resource revenues, the governments in many at-risk nations face acute problems of corruption and exposure to international price shocks. But natural resources need not be a curse. Twenty-five years ago, Botswana and Sierra Leone were similarly poor countries, both sitting on vast diamond deposits. Over the ensuing quarter century, Botswana harnessed this opportunity, becoming the fastest-growing economy in the world. Sierra Leone used the same resources to impoverish itself, experiencing the most rapid sustained decline of any country; it now ranks at the bottom of the Human Development Index put out by the United Nations Development Programme. These contrasting examples show that good policy and governance are especially vital where natural resources are discovered.

So far, the record has been dismal: There are many more Sierra Leones than Botswanas. But some encouraging signs are emerging. The "Fowler Report" to the U.N. Security Council in 2000 detailed how UNITA evaded U.N. sanctions against arms smuggling and diamond-based financing; as a result, scrutiny of the international diamond trade increased. Such attention may well have contributed to the demise of UNITA in Angola and the RUF in Sierra Leone, two highly durable, diamond-dependent rebel organizations. Moreover, diamonds are now being tracked through the new Kimberley Process certification scheme, making it harder for rebel groups to obtain financing from these goods. Transparency is the first step toward effective national scrutiny . . . A new compact could emerge: Rich nations take action to cut rebel financing and cushion adverse shocks, while low-income nations adopt better governance of their revenues from natural resources.

ESCAPING THE CONFLICT TRAP

From 1960 to 1999, international interventions—whether economic or military—intended to shorten civil wars were disappointing. Some strategies may have succeeded in individual cases (as in the recent destruction of the Taliban regime in Afghanistan), but no type of intervention has worked regularly.

More effective interventions could target the systems that finance and equip rebel organizations, beyond solely focusing on the trade in diamonds and other commodities. Many rebel movements also receive illicit support from neighboring governments. Such support can be exposed and penalized, and the penalties should outweigh the benefits of rebel alliances. Moreover, governments can discourage huge ransom payments by corporations—such as the $20 million reputedly paid in 1984 by the German engineering company Mannesmann-Anlagenbau AG to the Colombian rebel group ELN, or National Liberation Army, for the release of three of the company's staff. Should such payments be tax deductible and so, in effect, subsidized? Governments could ban the insurance arrangements that facilitate and inevitably inflate such payments. National authorities have started to improve scrutiny of national and international banking systems. . . . National and multilateral policymakers should also look again at drug policy. Wouldn't it be easier and more effective to curb the demand for criminally supplied drugs? And certainly, the flow of arms can be curtailed, especially if efforts are made earlier to catch the big operators, like suspected gunrunner Victor Bout, who is thought to have supplied arms to rebel groups in several African nations, including Angola.

The best way to break out of the conflict trap is to ensure that countries that have just ended one conflict do not quickly become enmeshed in another. In some nations, the risks of renewed conflicts are so high that an external military peacekeeping force is normally necessary. The operative word is "external" because high military spending by a post-conflict government actually increases the risk of another war. That external military presence must be credible. In Sierra Leone, the RUF took hostage a large U.N. force that it sensed would not fight, yet when confronted by a smaller British force, the rebel group collapsed.

Unfortunately, peacekeeping missions normally do not last long enough to allow economic recovery to take hold and help keep the peace. The peak time for economic recovery is usually during the middle of the first post-conflict decade. That is also when aid is most effective in promoting economic growth. Unfortunately, international aid is frequently mistimed. It pours in during the first year of peace, when the country's institutions are too weak for the money to be used effectively, then tapers out just when it would be most useful.

Governments in countries recovering from civil war also must give greater priority to economic reform: The post-conflict period is a good time to reform because vested interests are loosened up. For example, after the end of civil conflict in Uganda in 1986, the country's economic policies moved from among the worst in Africa to among the best in the following decade.

Finally, diasporas in rich countries pose a particular danger in post-conflict situations. They tend to be more extreme than the populations they leave behind, and they finance extremist and violent organizations. For example, the Tamil and Irish diasporas in North America have both been gullible financiers of murder in the past. Diaspora organizations can play an important role in economic recovery; their networks of skills and businesses are potentially valuable. Afghanistan is now trying constructively to deploy its diaspora, for example. But governments of rich nations should help keep the behavior of diaspora organizations in their borders within legitimate bounds.

LOCAL WARS, GLOBAL CASUALTIES

Civil war is not just disastrous for the countries directly affected; it hurts the surrounding regions and often poses risks for even remote, seemingly unaffected nations. Within the country at war, combat-related deaths represent just a small if gruesome part of the costs: War-related economic ruin also intensifies poverty and disease. Throughout the region, economic growth declines and investment flows dry up. Disease spreads across borders through the flow of refugees. And higher military spending induced by real or potential civil war can fuel pointless regional arms races.

Finally, civil war creates territories beyond the control of recognized governments. These no-go areas can be damaging to the international community. Around 95 percent of the global production of hard drugs is located in civil war countries. Witness how sources of supply shift in response to the changing pattern of conflict: As the Shining Path guerrillas were defeated in Peru in the early 1990s, drug production shifted to territory held by the FARC, or the Revolutionary Armed Forces of Colombia. These lawless areas also provide safe havens and training for international terrorists.

Over the last several decades, national, regional, and global organizations seeking to end or prevent civil wars have often focused on the wrong challenges, or on the right challenges but at the wrong time. Certainly, no single, magic policy will fix the problem; a range of initiatives is urgently required across a broad front. But if governments and multilateral organizations can help curb rebel financing and armament, accelerate the economic development of the countries most at risk, and provide an effective military presence in post-conflict settings, the global incidence of civil war will decline dramatically. These are viable objectives, and they are likely much cheaper than the long-term consequences of continued conflict and neglect.

Possible and Impossible Solutions to Ethnic Civil Wars

◼◼◼ CHAIM KAUFMANN

. . . This paper offers a theory of how ethnic wars end, and proposes an intervention strategy based on it.[1] The theory rests on two insights: First, in ethnic wars both hypernationalist mobilization rhetoric and real atrocities harden ethnic identities to the point that cross-ethnic political appeals are unlikely to be made and even less likely to be heard. Second, intermingled population settlement patterns create real security dilemmas that intensify violence, motivate ethnic "cleansing," and prevent de-escalation unless the groups are separated. As a result, restoring civil politics in multi-ethnic states shattered by war is impossible because the war itself destroys the possibilities for ethnic cooperation.

Stable resolutions of ethnic civil wars are possible, but only when the opposing groups are demographically separated into defensible enclaves. Separation reduces both incentives and opportunity for further combat, and largely eliminates both reasons and chances for ethnic cleansing of civilians. While ethnic fighting can be stopped by other means, such as peace enforcement by international forces or by a conquering empire, such peaces last only as long as the enforcers remain.

This means that to save lives threatened by genocide, the international community must abandon attempts to restore war-torn multi-ethnic states. Instead, it must facilitate and protect population movements to create true national homelands. Sovereignty is secondary: Defensible ethnic enclaves reduce violence with or without independent sovereignty, while partition without separation does nothing to stop mass killing. Once massacres have taken place, ethnic cleansing will occur. The alternative is to let the *interahamwe* and the Chetniks "cleanse" their enemies in their own way.

The remainder of this paper has three parts. The next part develops a theory of how ethnic wars end. Then, I present a strategy for international military intervention to stop ethnic wars and dampen future violence and rebut possible objections to this strategy. The conclusion addresses the moral and political stakes in humanitarian intervention in ethnic conflicts.

From Chaim Kaufmann, "Possible and Impossible Solutions to Ethnic Civil Wars," *International Security,* 20; 4 (Spring 1996), pp. 136–175. Copyright © 1996 by the President and Fellows of Harvard College and the Massachusetts Institute of Technology.

HOW ETHNIC CIVIL WARS END

Civil wars are not all alike. Ethnic conflicts are disputes between communities which see themselves as having distinct heritages over the power relationship between the communities, while ideological civil wars are contests between factions within the same community over how that community should be governed.[2] The key difference is the flexibility of individual loyalties, which are quite fluid in ideological conflicts, but almost completely rigid in ethnic wars.[3]

The possible and impossible solutions to ethnic civil wars follow from this fact. War hardens ethnic identities to the point that cross-ethnic political appeals become futile, which means that victory can be assured only by physical control over the territory in dispute. Ethnic wars also generate intense security dilemmas, both because the escalation of each side's mobilization rhetoric presents a real threat to the other, and even more because intermingled population settlement patterns create defensive vulnerabilities and offensive opportunities.

Once this occurs, the war cannot end until the security dilemma is reduced by physical separation of the rival groups. Solutions that aim at restoring multi-ethnic civil politics and at avoiding population transfers—such as power-sharing, state rebuilding, or identity reconstruction—cannot work because they do nothing to dampen the security dilemma, and because ethnic fears and hatreds hardened by war are extremely resistant to change.

The result is that ethnic wars can end in only three ways: with complete victory of one side; by temporary suppression of the conflict by third party military occupation; or by self-governance of separate communities. The record of the ethnic wars of the last half century bears this out.

The Dynamics of Ethnic War

It is useful to compare characteristics of ethnic conflicts with those of ideological conflicts. The latter are competitions between the government and the rebels for the loyalties of the people. The critical features of these conflicts are that ideological loyalties are changeable and difficult to assess, and the same population serves as the shared mobilization base for both sides. As a result, winning the "hearts and minds" of the population is both possible and necessary for victory. The most important instruments are political, economic, and social reforms that redress popular grievances such as poverty, inequality, corruption, and physical insecurity. Control of access to population is also important, both to allow recruitment and implementation of reform promises, and to block the enemy from these tasks. Population control, however, cannot be guaranteed solely by physical control over territory, but depends on careful intelligence, persuasion, and coercion. Purely military successes are often indecisive as long as the enemy's base of political support is undamaged.

Ethnic wars, however, have nearly the opposite properties. Individual loyalties are both rigid and transparent, while each side's mobilization base is limited to members of its own group in friendly-controlled territory. The result is that ethnic conflicts are primarily military struggles in which victory depends on physical control over the disputed territory, not on appeals to members of the other group.

Identity in Ethnic Wars

Competition to sway individual loyalties does not play an important role in ethnic civil wars, because ethnic identities are fixed by birth. While not everyone may be mobilized as an active fighter for his or her own group, hardly anyone ever fights for the opposing ethnic group.

Different identity categories imply their own membership rules. Ideological identity is relatively soft, as it is a matter of individual belief, or sometimes of political behavior. Religious identities are harder, because while they also depend on belief, change generally requires formal acceptance by the new faith, which may be denied. Ethnic identities are hardest, since they depend on language, culture, and religion, which are hard to change, as well as parentage, which no one can change.

Ethnic identities are hardened further by intense conflict, so that leaders cannot broaden their appeals to include members of opposing groups. As ethnic conflicts escalate, populations come increasingly to hold enemy images of the other group, either because of deliberate efforts by elites to create such images or because of increasing real threats. . . .

Once the conflict reaches the level of large-scale violence, tales of atrocities—true or invented—perpetuated or planned against members of the group by the ethnic enemy provide hard-liners with an unanswerable argument. In March 1992 a Serb woman in Foca in Eastern Bosnia was convinced that "there were lists of Serbs who were marked for death. My two sons were down on the list to be slaughtered like pigs. I was listed under rape." The fact that neither she nor other townspeople had seen any such lists did not prevent them from believing such tales without question.[4] The Croatian Ustasha in World War II went further, terrorizing Serbs in order to provoke a backlash that could then be used to mobilize Croats for defense against Serb retaliation.

In this environment, cross-ethnic appeals are not likely to attract members of the other group. The Yugoslav Partisans in World War II are often credited with transcending the ethnic conflict between the Croatian Ustasha and the Serbian Chetniks with an anti-German, pan-Yugoslav program. In fact it did not work. Tito was a Croat, but Partisan officers as well as the rank and file were virtually all Serbs and Montenegrins. Only in 1944, when German withdrawal made Partisan victory certain, did Croats begin to join the Partisans in numbers, not because they preferred a multi-ethnic Yugoslavia to a Greater Croatia, but because they preferred a multi-ethnic Yugoslavia to a Yugoslavia cleansed of Croatians. . . .

Ethnic war also shrinks scope for individual identity choice. Even those who put little value on their ethnic identity are pressed towards ethnic mobilization for two reasons. First, extremists within each community are likely to impose sanctions on those who do not contribute to the cause. In 1992 the leader of the Croatian Democratic Union in Bosnia was dismissed on the ground that he "was too much Bosnian, too little Croat." Conciliation is easy to denounce as dangerous to group security or as actually traitorous. Such arguments drove nationalist extremists to overthrow President Makarios of Cyprus in 1974, to assassinate Mahatma Gandhi in 1948, to massacre nearly the whole government of Rwanda in 1994, and to kill Yitzhak Rabin in 1995.

Second and more important, identity is often imposed by the opposing group, specifically by its most murderous members. Assimilation or political passivity did no good for German Jews, Rwandan Tutsis, or Azerbaijanis in Nagorno-Karabakh. A Bosnian Muslim schoolteacher recently lamented:

> We never, until the war, thought of ourselves as Muslims. We were Yugoslavs. But when we began to be murdered, because we are Muslims, things changed. The definition of who we are today has been determined by our killers.[5]

Choice contracts further the longer the conflict continues. Multi-ethnic towns as yet untouched by war are swamped by radicalized refugees, undermining moderate leaders who preach tolerance. For example, while a portion of the pre-war Serb population remained in Bosnian government-controlled Sarajevo when the fighting started, their numbers have declined as the government has taken on a more narrowly Muslim religious character over years of war, and pressure on Serbs has increased. Where 80,000 remained in July 1993, only 30,000 were left in August 1995. The Tutsi Rwandan Patriotic Front (RPF) showed remarkable restraint during the 1994 civil war, but since then the RPF has imprisoned tens of thousands of genocide suspects in appalling conditions, failed to prevent massacres of thousands of Hutu civilians in several incidents, and allowed Tutsi squatters to seize the property of many absent Hutus.

What can finally eliminate identity choice altogether is fear of genocide. The hypernationalist rhetoric used for group mobilization often includes images of the enemy group as a threat to the physical existence of the nation, in turn justifying unlimited violence against the ethnic enemy; this threatening discourse can usually be observed by members of the target group. Even worse are actual massacres of civilians, especially when condoned by leaders of the perpetrating group, which are virtually certain to convince the members of the targeted group that group defense is their only option. . . .

Identifying Loyalties

A consequence of the hardness of ethnic identities is that in ethnic wars assessing individual loyalties is much easier than in ideological conflicts. Even if some members of both groups remain unmobilized, as long as virtually none actively support the other group, each side can treat all co-ethnics as friends without risk of coddling an enemy agent and can treat all members of the other group as enemies without risk of losing a recruit.

Although it often requires effort, each side can almost always identify members of its own and the other group in any territory it controls. Ethnicity can be identified by outward appearance, public or private records, and local social knowledge. In societies where ethnicity is important, it is often officially recorded in personal identity documents or in censuses. In 1994 Rwandan death squads used neighborhood target lists prepared in advance, as well as roadblocks that checked identity cards. In 1983 riots in Sri Lanka, Sinhalese mobs went through mixed neighborhoods selecting Tamil dwellings for destruction with the help of Buddhist monks carrying electoral lists. While it might not have been possible to predict the Yugoslav civil war thirty years in advance, one could have identified the members of each of the warring groups from the 1961 census, which identified the nationality of all but 1.8 percent of the population.

Where public records are not adequate, private ones can be used instead. Pre–World War II Yugoslav censuses relied on church records. Absent any records at all, reliable demographic intelligence can often be obtained from local co-ethnics. . . .

Finally, in unprepared encounters ethnicity can often be gauged by outward appearance: Tutsis are generally tall and thin, while Hutus are relatively short and stocky; Russians are generally fairer than Kazakhs. When physiognomy is ambiguous, other signs such as language or accent, surname, dress, posture, ritual mutilation, diet, habits, occupation, region or neighborhood within urban areas, or certain possessions may give clues. Residents of Zagreb, for example, are marked as Serbs by certain names, attendance at an Orthodox church, or possession of books printed in Cyrillic.

Perhaps the strongest evidence of intelligence reliability in ethnic conflicts is that—in dramatic contrast to ideological insurgencies—history records almost no instances of mistaken "cleansing" of co-ethnics.

The Decisiveness of Territory

Another consequence of the hardness of ethnic identities is that population control depends wholly on territorial control. Since each side can recruit only from its own community and only in friendly-controlled territory, incentives to seize areas populated by co-ethnics are strong, as is the pressure to cleanse friendly-controlled territory of enemy ethnics by relocation to *de facto* concentration camps, expulsion, or massacre.

Because of the decisiveness of territorial control, military strategy in ethnic wars is very different than in ideological conflicts. Unlike ideological insurgents, who often evade rather than risk battle, or a counter-insurgent government, which might forbear to attack rather than risk bombarding civilians, ethnic combatants must fight for every piece of land. By contrast, combatants in ethnic wars are much less free to decline unfavorable battles because they cannot afford to abandon any settlement to an enemy who is likely to "cleanse" it by massacre, expulsion, destruction of homes, and possibly colonization. By the time a town can be retaken, its value will have been lost.

In ethnic civil wars, military operations are decisive. Attrition matters because the side's mobilization pools are separate and can be depleted. Most important, since each side's mobilization base is limited to members of its own community in friendly-controlled territory, conquering the enemy's population centers reduces its mobilization base, while loss of friendly settlements reduces one's own. Military control of the entire territory at issue is tantamount to total victory.

Security Dilemmas in Ethnic Wars

The second problem that must be overcome by any remedy for severe ethnic conflict is the security dilemma. Regardless of the origins of ethnic strife, once violence (or abuse of state power by one group that controls it) reaches the point that ethnic communities cannot rely on the state to protect them, each community must mobilize to take responsibility for its own security.

Under conditions of anarchy, each group's mobilization constitutes a real threat to the security of others for two reasons. First, the nationalist rhetoric that accompanies mobilization often seems to and often does indicate offensive intent. Under these conditions, group identity itself can be seen by other groups as a threat to their safety.

Second, military capability acquired for defense can usually also be used for offense. Further, offense often has an advantage over defense in inter-community conflict, especially when settlement patterns are inter-mingled, because isolated pockets are harder to hold than to take.

The reality of the mutual security threats means that solutions to ethnic conflicts must do more than undo the causes; until or unless the security dilemma can be reduced or eliminated, neither side can afford to demobilize.

Demography and Security Dilemmas

The severity of ethnic security dilemmas is greatest when demography is most intermixed, weakest when community settlements are most separate. The more mixed the opposing groups, the stronger the offense in relation to the defense; the more separated they are, the stronger the defense in relation to offense.[6] When settlement patterns are extremely mixed, both sides are vulnerable to attack not only by organized military forces but also by local militias or gangs from adjacent towns or neighborhoods. Since well-defined fronts are impossible, there is no effective means of defense against such raids. Accordingly, each side has a strong incentive—at both national and local levels—to kill or drive out enemy populations before the enemy does the same to it, as well as to create homogeneous enclaves more practical to defend.

Better, but still bad, are well-defined enclaves with islands of one or both sides' populations behind the other's front. Each side then has an incentive to attack to rescue its surrounded co-ethnics before they are destroyed by the enemy, as well as incentives to wipe out enemy islands behind its own lines, both to pre-empt rescue attempts and to eliminate possible bases for fifth columnists or guerrillas.

The safest pattern is a well-defined demographic front that separates nearly homogeneous regions. Such a front can be defended by organized military forces, so populations are not at risk unless defenses are breached. At the same time the strongest motive for attack disappears, since there are few or no endangered co-ethnics behind enemy lines.

Further, offensive and defensive mobilization measures are more distinguishable when populations are separated than when they are mixed. Although hypernationalist political rhetoric, as well as conventional military forces, have both offensive and defensive uses regardless of population settlement patterns, some other forms of ethnic mobilization do not. Local militias and ethnically based local self-governing authorities have both offensive and defensive capabilities when populations are mixed: Ethnic militias can become death squads, while local governments dominated by one group can disenfranchise minorities. When populations are separated, however, such local organizations have defensive value only.

War and Ethnic Unmixing

Because of the security dilemma, ethnic war causes ethnic unmixing. The war between Greece and Turkey, the partition of India, the 1948–49 Arab-Israeli war, and the recent war between Armenia and Azerbaijan were all followed by emigration or expulsion of most of the minority populations on each side. More than one million Ibo left northern Nigeria during the Nigerian Civil War. Following 1983 pogroms, three-fourths of the Tamil population of Colombo fled to the predominantly Tamil north and east of the island. By the end of 1994, only about 70,000 non-Serbs remained in Serb-controlled areas of Bosnia, with less than 40,000 Serbs still in Muslim- and Croat-controlled regions. Of 600,000 Serbs in pre-war Croatia, probably no more than 100,000 remain outside of Serb-controlled eastern Slavonia.

Collapse of multi-ethnic states often causes some ethnic unmixing even without war. The retreat of the Ottoman Empire from the Balkans sparked movement of Muslims southward and eastward as well as some unmixing of different Christian peoples in the southern Balkans. Twelve million Germans left Eastern Europe after World War II, one and a half million between 1950 and 1987, and another one and a half million since 1989, essentially dissolving the German diaspora. Of 25 million Russians outside Russia in 1989, as many as three to four million had gone to Russia by the end of 1992. From 1990 to 1993, 200,000 Hungarians left Vojvodina, replaced by 400,000 Serb refugees from other parts of ex-Yugoslavia.

Ethnic Separation and Peace

Once ethnic groups are mobilized for war, the war cannot end until the populations are separated into defensible, mostly homogeneous regions. Even if an international force or an imperial conqueror were to impose peace, the conflict would resume as soon as it left. Even if a national government were somehow re-created despite mutual suspicions, neither group could safely entrust its security to it. Continuing mutual threat also ensures perpetuation of hypernationalist propaganda, both for mobilization and because the plausibility of the threat posed by the enemy gives radical nationalists an unanswerable advantage over moderates in intra-group debates.

Ethnic separation does not guarantee peace, but it allows it. Once populations are separated, both cleansing and rescue imperatives disappear; war is no longer mandatory. At the same time, any attempt to seize more territory requires a major conventional military offensive. Thus the conflict changes from one of mutual preemptive ethnic cleansing to something approaching conventional interstate war in which normal deterrence dynamics apply. Mutual deterrence does not guarantee that there will be no further violence, but it reduces the probability of outbreaks, as well as the likely aims and intensity of those that do occur.

There have been no wars among Bulgaria, Greece, and Turkey since their population exchanges of the 1920s. Ethnic violence on Cyprus, which reached crisis on several occasions between 1960 and 1974, has been zero since the partition and population exchange which followed Turkish invasion. The Armenian-Azeri ethnic conflict, sparked by independence demands of the mostly Armenian Nagorno-Karabakh Autonomous Oblast, escalated to full-scale war by 1992. Armenian conquest of all of Karabakh together with the land which formerly separated it from Armenia proper, along with displacement of nearly all members of each group from enemy-controlled territories, created a defensible separation with no minorities to fight over, leading to a cease-fire in April 1994.

THEORIES OF ETHNIC PEACE

Those considering humanitarian intervention to end ethnic civil wars should set as their goal lasting safety, rather than perfect peace. Given the persistence of ethnic rivalries, "safety" is best defined as freedom from threats of ethnic murder, expropriation, or expulsion for the overwhelming majority of civilians of all groups. Absence of formal peace, even occasional terrorism or border skirmishes, would not undermine this, provided that the great majority of civilians are not at risk. "Lasting" must mean that the situation remains stable indefinitely after the intervention forces leave. Truces of weeks, months, or even years do not qualify as lasting safety if ethnic cleansing eventually resumes with full force.

Alternatives to Separation

Besides demographic separation, the literature on possible solutions to ethnic conflicts contains four main alternatives: suppression, reconstruction of ethnic identities, power-sharing, and state-building.

Suppression
Many ethnic civil wars lead to the complete victory of one side and the forcible suppression of the other. This may reduce violence in some cases, but will never be an aim of outsiders considering humanitarian intervention. Further, remission of violence may be only temporary, as the defeated group usually rebels again at any opportunity. Even the fact that certain conquerors, such as the English in Scotland or the Dutch in Friesland, eventually permitted genuine political assimilation after decades of suppression, does not recommend this as a remedy for endangered peoples today.

Reconstruction of Ethnic Identities
The most ambitious program to end ethnic violence would be to reconstruct ethnic identities according to the "Constructivist Model" of nationalism. Constructivists argue that individual and group identities are fluid, continually being made and re-made in social discourse. Further, these identities are manipulable by

political entrepreneurs. Violent ethnic conflicts are the result of pernicious group identities created by hypernationalist myth-making; many inter-group conflicts are quite recent, as are the ethnic identities themselves.

The key is elite rivalries within communities, in which aggressive leaders use hypernationalist propaganda to gain and hold power. History does not matter; whether past inter-community relations have in fact been peaceful or conflictual, leaders can redefine, reinterpret, and invent facts to suit their arguments, including alleged atrocities and exaggerated or imagined threats. This process can feed on itself, as nationalists use the self-fulfilling nature of their arguments both to escalate the conflict and to justify their own power, so that intra-community politics becomes a competition in hypernationalist extremism, and inter-community relations enter a descending spiral of violence.

It follows that ethnic conflicts generated by the promotion of pernicious, exclusive identities should be reversible by encouraging individuals and groups to adopt more benign, inclusive identities. Leaders can choose to mobilize support on the basis of broader identities that transcend the ethnic division, such as ideology, class, or civic loyalty to the nation-state. If members of the opposing groups can be persuaded to adopt a larger identity, ethnic antagonisms should fade away. . . .

However, even if ethnic hostility can be "constructed," there are strong reasons to believe that violent conflicts cannot be "reconstructed" back to ethnic harmony. Identity reconstruction under conditions of intense conflict is probably impossible because once ethnic groups are mobilized for war, they will have already produced, and will continue reproducing, social institutions and discourses that reinforce their group identity and shut out or shout down competing identities.

Replacement of ethnicity by some other basis for political identification requires that political parties have cross-ethnic appeal, but examples of this in the midst of ethnic violence are virtually impossible to find. . . . In fact, even ethnic tension far short of war often undermines not just political appeals across ethnic lines but also appeals within a single group for cooperation with other groups. In Yugoslavia in the 1920s, Malaya in the 1940s, Ceylon in the 1950s, and in Nigeria in the 1950s and 1960, parties that advocated cooperation across ethnic lines proved unable to compete with strictly nationalist parties.

Even if constructivists are right that the ancient past does not matter, recent history does. Intense violence creates personal experiences of fear, misery, and loss which lock people into their group identity and their enemy relationship with the other group. Elite as well as mass opinions are affected; more than 5,000 deaths in the 1946 Calcutta riots convinced many previously optimistic Hindu and Muslim leaders that the groups could not live together. The Tutsi-controlled government of Burundi, which had witnessed the partial genocide against Tutsis in Rwanda in 1962–63 and survived Hutu-led coup attempts in 1965 and 1969, regarded the 1972 rebellion as another attempt at genocide, and responded by murdering between 100,000 and 200,000 Hutus. Fresh rounds of violence in 1988 and 1993–94 have reinforced the apocalyptic fears of both sides.

Finally, literacy preserves atrocity memories and enhances their use for political mobilization.[7] The result is that atrocity histories cannot be reconstructed;

victims can sometimes be persuaded to accept exaggerated atrocity tales, but cannot be talked out of real ones. The result is that the bounds of debate are permanently altered; the leaders who used World War II Croatian atrocities to whip up Serbian nationalism in the 1980s were making use of a resource which, since then, remains always available in Serbian political discourse.

If direct action to transform exclusive ethnic identities into inclusive civic ones is infeasible, outside powers or international institutions could enforce peace temporarily in the hope that reduced security threats would permit moderate leaders within each group to promote the reconstruction of more benign identities. While persuading ethnic war survivors to adopt an overarching identity may be impossible, a sufficiently prolonged period of guaranteed safety might allow moderate leaders to temper some of the most extreme hypernationalism back towards more benign, albeit still separate nationalisms. However, this still leaves both sides vulnerable to later revival of hypernationalism by radical political entrepreneurs, especially after the peacekeepers have left and security threats once again appear more realistic.

Power-Sharing

The best-developed blueprint for civic peace in multi-ethnic states is power-sharing or "consociational democracy," proposed by Arend Lijphart. This approach assumes that ethnicity is somewhat manipulable, but not so freely as constructivists say. Ethnic division, however, need not result in conflict; even if political mobilization is organized on ethnic lines, civil politics can be maintained if ethnic elites adhere to a power-sharing bargain that equitably protects all groups. The key components are: 1) joint exercise of governmental power; 2) proportional distribution of government funds and jobs; 3) autonomy on ethnic issues (which, if groups are concentrated territorially, may be achieved by regional federation); and 4) a minority veto on issues of vital importance to each group. Even if power-sharing can avert potential ethnic conflicts or dampen mild ones, our concern here is whether it can bring peace under the conditions of intense violence and extreme ethnic mobilization that are likely to motivate intervention.

The answer is no. The indispensable component of any power-sharing deal is a plausible minority veto, one which the strongest side will accept and which the weaker side believes that the stronger will respect. Traditions of stronger loyalties to the state than to parochial groups and histories of inter-ethnic compromise could provide reason for confidence, but in a civil war these will have been destroyed, if they were ever present, by the fighting itself and accompanying ethnic mobilization.

Only a balance of power among the competing groups can provide a "hard" veto—one which the majority must respect. Regional concentration of populations could partially substitute for balanced power if the minority group can credibly threaten to secede if its veto is overridden. In any situation where humanitarian intervention might be considered, however, these conditions too are unlikely to be met. Interventions are likely to be aimed at saving a weak group that cannot defend itself; balanced sides do not need defense. Demographic separation is also unlikely, because if the populations were already separated, the ethnic cleansing and related atrocities which are most likely to provoke intervention would not be occurring.

The core reason why power-sharing cannot resolve ethnic civil wars is that it is inherently voluntaristic; it requires conscious decisions by elites to cooperate to avoid ethnic strife. Under conditions of hypernationalist mobilization and real security threats, group leaders are unlikely to be receptive to compromise, and even if they are, they cannot act without being discredited and replaced by harder-line rivals.

Could outside intervention make power-sharing work? One approach would be to adjust the balance of power between the warring sides to a "hurting stalemate" by arming the weaker side, blockading the stronger, or partially disarming the stronger by direct military intervention. When both sides realize that further fighting will bring them costs but no profit, they will negotiate an agreement. This can balance power, although if populations are still intermingled it may actually worsen security dilemmas and increase violence—especially against civilians—as both sides eliminate the threats posed by pockets of the opposing group in their midst.

Further, once there has been heavy fighting, the sides are likely to distrust each other far too much to entrust any authority to a central government that could potentially be used against them. . . .

The final approach is international imposition of power-sharing, which requires occupying the country to coerce both sides into accepting the agreement and to prevent inter-ethnic violence until it can be implemented. The interveners, however, cannot bind the stronger side to uphold the agreement after the intervention forces leave. . . . The British did impose power-sharing as a condition for Cypriot independence, but it broke down almost immediately. The Greek Cypriots, incensed by what they saw as Turkish Cypriot abuse of their minority veto, simply overrode the veto and operated the government in violation of the constitution. Similarly, while at independence in 1948 the Sri Lankan constitution banned religious or communal discrimination, the Sinhalese majority promptly disenfranchised half of the Tamils on the grounds that they were actually Indians, and increasingly discriminated against Tamils in education, government employment, and other areas.

State-Building

Gerald Helman and Steven Ratner argue that states in which government breakdown, economic failure, and internal violence imperil their own citizens and threaten neighboring states can be rescued by international "conservatorship" to administer critical government functions until the country can govern itself following a free and fair election. Ideally, the failed state would voluntarily delegate specified functions to an international executor, although in extreme cases involving massive violations of human rights or the prospect of large-scale warfare, the international community could act even without an invitation.

As with imposing power-sharing, this requires occupying the country (and may require conquering it), coercing all sides to accept a democratic constitution, enforcing peace until elections can be held, and administering the economy and the elections. Conservatorship thus requires even more finesse than enforced power-sharing, and probably more military risks.

Helman and Ratner cite the UN intervention in Cambodia in 1992–93 to create a safe environment for free elections as conservatorship's best success. However, this was an ideological war over the governance of Cambodia, not an ethnic conflict over disempowering minorities or dismembering the country. By contrast, the growth of the U.S.-UN mission in Somalia from famine relief to state-rebuilding was a failure, and no one has been so bold as to propose conservatorship for Bosnia or Rwanda.

Even if conservatorship could rapidly, effectively, and cheaply stop an ethnic civil war, rebuild institutions, and ensure free elections, nothing would be gained unless the electoral outcome protected all parties' interests and safety; that is, power-sharing would still be necessary. Thus, in serious ethnic conflicts, conservatorship would only be a more expensive way to reach the same impasse.

Ethnic Separation

Regardless of the causes of a particular conflict, once communities are mobilized for violence, the reality of mutual security threats prevents both demobilization and de-escalation of hypernationalist discourse. Thus, lasting peace requires removal of the security dilemma. The most effective and in many cases the only way to do this is to separate the ethnic groups. The more intense the violence, the more likely it is that separation will be the only option.

The exact threshold remains an open question. The deductive logic of the problem suggests that the critical variable is fear for survival. Once a majority of either group comes to believe that the killing of noncombatants of their own group is not considered a crime by the other, they cannot accept any governing arrangement that could be captured by the enemy group and used against them.

The most persuasive source of such beliefs is the massacre of civilians, but it is not clear that there is a specific number of incidents or total deaths beyond which ethnic reconciliation becomes impossible. More important is the extent to which wide sections of the attacking group seem to condone the killings, and can be observed doing so by members of the target group. In this situation the attacks are likely to be seen as reflecting not just the bloodthirstiness of a particular regime or terrorist faction, but the preference of the opposing group as a whole, which means that no promise of non-repetition can be believed.

Testing this proposition directly requires better data on the attitudes of threatened populations during and after ethnic wars than we now have. Next best is aggregate analysis of the patterns of ends of ethnic wars, supplemented by investigation of individual cases as deeply as the data permits. I make a start at such an analysis below.

How Ethnic Wars Have Ended

At least 46 significant ethnic civil wars have ended since 1944.[8] Of the total, nineteen were ended by the military victory of one side, sixteen by *de jure* or *de facto* partition, and two have been suppressed by military occupation by a third party. Only nine ethnic civil wars have been ended by a negotiated agreement that did not partition the country. (See Table 1.)

TABLE 1 ■ ETHNIC CIVIL WARS RESOLVED 1944–1997

Combatants	Dates	Deaths (000s)	Outcome
A. Military victory (19):			
Kurds vs. Iran	45–80s	40	Suppressed
Karens, others vs. Myanmar	45–	.400	Largely suppressed; sporadic violence
Chinese vs. Malaya	48–60	15	Suppressed
Tibetans vs. China	51–89	100	Suppressed
Hmong vs. Laos	59–72	50	Suppressed
Katangans vs. Congo	60–64	.100	Suppressed
Papuans vs. Indonesia	64–86	19	Suppressed
Blacks vs. Rhodesia	65–80	50	Rebels victorious
Ibos vs. Nigeria	67–70	2000	Suppressed
Hmong vs. Thailand	67–80	.30	Suppressed
Palestinians vs. Jordan	70	15	Suppressed
Timorese vs. Indonesia	74–82	200	Suppressed
Aceh vs. Indonesia	75–80s	15	Suppressed
Tigreans, others vs. Ethiopia	75–91	.600	Rebels victorious
Uighurs etc. vs. China	80	2	Suppressed
Sikhs vs. India	84	25	Suppressed
Bouganvilleans vs. Papua	88	1	Suppressed
Tutsis vs. Rwanda	90–94	750	Rebels victorious
Shiites vs. Iraq	91	35	Suppressed
B. *De facto* or *de jure* partition (16):			
Ukrainians vs. USSR	44–50s	150	Suppressed; later independent 1991
Lithuanians vs. USSR	45–52	40	Suppressed; later independent 1991
Muslims vs. Sikhs, Hindus (India)	46–47	.500	Partition 1947
Jews vs. Arabs (Palestine)	47–49	20	Partition 1948
Eritreans vs. Ethiopia	61–91	250	Independent 1993
Turks vs. Cyprus	63–74	.10	*De facto* partition
Bengalis vs. Pakistan	71	1000	Independent 1971
Armenians vs. Azerbaijan	88–	15	*De facto* partition
Somali clans	88–	350	*De facto* partition in N.; ongoing in S.
South Ossetians	90–92	1	*De facto* partition
Russians vs. Moldova	92–	2	*De facto* partition
Slovenia vs. Yugoslavia	91	1	Independent 1991
Croatia vs. Yugoslavia	91–95	30	Independent 1991
Serbs vs. Bosnia	92–95	150	*De facto* partition
Abkhazians vs. Georgia	92–	15	*De facto* partition; sporadic violence
Chechnyans vs. Russia	94–97	.20	*De facto* partition

(continued)

TABLE 1 ■ (Continued)

Combatants	Dates	Deaths (000s)	Outcome
C. Conflict suppressed by ongoing 3rd party military occupation (2):			
Kurds vs. Iraq	60–	215	*De facto* partition
Lebanese Civil War	75–90	120	Nominal power sharing; *de facto* partition
D. Regional Autonomy Agreements (8):			
Nagas vs. India	52–75	13	Autonomy 1972
Basques vs. Spain	59–80s	1	Autonomy 1980
Tripuras vs. India	67–89	13	Autonomy 1972
Moros vs. Philippines	72–87	50	Limited autonomy 1990
Baluchis vs. Pakistan	73–77	.5	Limited autonomy
Chittagong hill peoples vs. Bangladesh	75–89	24	Limited autonomy 1989
Miskitos vs. Nicaragua	81–88	1	Autonomy 1990
Mayas vs. Guatemala	61–97	166	Limited autonomy 1997
E. Power-sharing Agreements (1):			
Blacks vs. South Africa	60s–93	20	Modified majority rule

The data support the argument that separation of groups is the key to ending ethnic civil wars. Every case in which the state was preserved by agreement involved a regionally concentrated minority, and in every case but one the solution reinforced the ethnic role in politics by allowing regionally concentrated minorities to control their own destinies through autonomy for the regions where they form a majority of the population. South Africa is a partial exception, since the main element of the agreement was majority rule, although even in this case the powers reserved to the provinces offer some autonomy to whites, coloreds, and Zulus. There is not a single case where non-ethnic civil politics were created or restored by reconstruction of ethnic identities, power-sharing coalitions, or state-building.

Further, deaths in these cases average roughly five times lower than in the wars which ended in either suppression or partition: slightly more than 30,000, compared to about 175,000. This lends support to the proposition that the more extreme the violence, the less the chances for any form of reconciliation. Finally, it should be noted that all eight of the cases resolved through autonomy involve groups that were largely demographically separated even at the beginning of the conflict, which may help explain why there were fewer deaths.

INTERVENTION TO RESOLVE ETHNIC CIVIL WARS

International interventions that seek to ensure lasting safety for populations endangered by ethnic war—whether by the United Nations, by major powers with global reach, or by regional powers—must be guided by two principles. First, settlements must aim at physically separating the warring communities and establishing a balance of relative strength that makes it unprofitable for either side to attempt to revise the territorial settlement. Second, although economic or military assistance may suffice in some cases, direct military intervention will be necessary when aid to the weaker side would create a window of opportunity for the stronger, or when there is an immediate need to stop ongoing genocide.

Designing Settlements

Unless outsiders are willing to provide permanent security guarantees, stable resolution of an ethnic civil war requires separation of the groups into defensible regions. The critical variable is demography, not sovereignty. Political partition without ethnic separation leaves incentives for ethnic cleansing unchanged; it actually increases them if it creates new minorities. Conversely, demographic separation dampens ethnic conflicts even without separate sovereignty, although the more intense the previous fighting, the smaller the prospects for preserving a single state, even if loosely federated.

Partition without ethnic separation increases conflict because, while boundaries of sovereign successor states may provide defensible fronts that reduce the vulnerability of the majority group in each state, stay-behind minorities are completely exposed. Significant irredenta are both a call to their ethnic homeland and a danger to their hosts. They create incentives to mount rescue or ethnic cleansing operations before the situation solidifies. Greece's 1920 invasion of Turkey was justified in this way, while the 1947 decision to partition Palestine generated a civil war in advance of implementation, and the inclusion of Muslim-majority Kashmir within India has helped cause three wars. International recognition of Croatian and Bosnian independence did more to cause than to stop Serbian invasion. The war between Armenia and Azerbaijan has the same source, as do concerns over the international security risks of the several Russian diasporas.

Inter-ethnic security dilemmas can be nearly or wholly eliminated without partition if three conditions are met: First, there must be enough demographic separation that ethnic regions do not themselves contain militarily significant minorities. Second, there must be enough regional self-defense capability that abrogating the autonomy of any region would be more costly than any possible motive for doing so. Third, local autonomy must be so complete that minority groups can protect their key interests even lacking any influence at the national level. Even after an ethnic war, a single state could offer some advantages, not least of which are the economic benefits of a common market. However, potential interveners should recognize that groups that control distinct territories can insist on the *de facto* partition, and often will.

While peace requires separation of groups into distinct regions, it does not require total ethnic purity. Rather, remaining minorities must be small enough that the host group does not fear them as either a potential military threat or a possible target for irredentist rescue operations. Before the Krajina offensive, for example, President Franjo Tudjman of Croatia is said to have thought that the 12 percent Serb minority in Croatia was too large, but that half as many would be tolerable. The 173,000 Arabs remaining in Israel by 1951 were too few and too disorganized to be seen as a serious threat.

Geographic distribution of minorities is also important; in particular, concentrations near disputed borders or astride strategic communications constitute both a military vulnerability and an irredentist opportunity, and so are likely to spark conflict. It is not surprising that India's portion of Kashmir, with its Muslim majority, has been at the center of three interstate wars and an ongoing insurgency which continues today, while there has been no international conflict over the hundred million Muslims who live dispersed throughout most of the rest of India, and relatively little violence.

Where possible, inter-group boundaries should be drawn along the best defensive terrain, such as rivers and mountain ranges. Lines should also be as short as possible, to allow the heaviest possible manning of defensive fronts. . . . Access to the sea or to a friendly neighbor is also important, both for trade and for possible military assistance. Successor state arsenals should be encouraged, by aid to the weaker or sanctions on the stronger, to focus on defensive armaments such as forward artillery and antiaircraft missiles and rockets, while avoiding instruments that could make blitzkrieg attacks possible, such as tanks, fighter-bombers, and mobile artillery. These conditions would make subsequent offensives exceedingly expensive and likely to fail.

Intervention Strategy

The level of international action required to resolve an ethnic war will depend on the military situation on the ground. If there is an existing stalemate along defensible lines, the international community should simply recognize and strengthen it, providing transportation, protection, and resettlement assistance for refugees. However, where one side has the capacity to go on the offensive against the other, intervention will be necessary.

Interventions should therefore almost always be on behalf of the weaker side; the stronger needs no defense. Moreover, unless the international community can agree on a clear aggressor and a clear victim, there is no moral or political case for intervention. If both sides have behaved so badly that there is little to choose between them, intervention should not and probably will not be undertaken.[9] Almost no one in the West, for instance, has advocated assisting either side in the Croatian-Serb conflict.[10] While the intervention itself could be carried out by any willing actors, UN sponsorship is highly desirable, most of all to head off possible external aid to the group identified as the aggressor.

The three available tools are sanctions, military aid, and direct military intervention. Economic sanctions have limited leverage against combatants in ethnic wars, who often see their territorial security requirements as absolute. . . .

Whether military aid to the client can achieve an acceptable territorial outcome depends on the population balance between the sides, the local geography, and the organizational cohesion of the client group. . . . The . . . problem with "arm's length" aid is that it cannot prevent ethnic aggressors from killing members of the client group in territories from which they expect to have to retreat. Aid also does not restrain possible atrocities by the client group if their military fortunes improve.

If the client is too weak to achieve a viable separation with material aid alone, or if either or both sides cannot be trusted to abide by promises of non-retribution against enemy civilians, the international community must designate a separation line and deploy an intervention force to take physical control of the territory on the client's side of the line. We might call this approach "conquer and divide."

The separation campaign is waged as a conventional military operation. The larger the forces committed the better, both to minimize intervenors' casualties and to shorten the campaign by threatening the opponent with overwhelming defeat. Although some argue that any intervention force would become mired in a Vietnam-like quagmire, the fundamentally different nature of ethnic conflict means that the main pitfalls to foreign military interventions in ideological insurgencies are either weaker or absent. Most important, the intervenors' intelligence problems are much simpler, since loyalty intelligence is both less important and easier: Outsiders can safely assume that members of the allied group are friends and those of the other are enemies. Even if outsiders cannot tell the groups apart, locals can, and the loyalty of guides provided by the local ally can be counted on. As a result, the main intelligence task shifts from assessing loyalties to locating enemy forces, a task of which major power militaries are very capable.

On the ground, the intervenors would begin at one end of the target region and gradually advance to capture the entire target territory, maintaining a continuous front the entire time. It is not necessary to conquer the whole country; indeed, friendly ground forces need never cross the designated line. After enemy forces are driven out of each locality, civilians of the enemy ethnic group who remain behind are interned, to be exchanged after the war. This removes the enemy's local support base, preventing counterinsurgency problems from arising. Enemy civilians should be protected by close supervision of client troops in action, as well as by foreign control of internees.

The final concern is possible massacres of civilians of the client group in territory not yet captured or beyond the planned separation line. Some of this must be expected, since ongoing atrocities are the most likely impetus for outside intervention; the question is whether intervention actually increases the risk of attacks on civilians. A major advantage of a powerful ground presence is that opponent behavior can be coerced by threatening to advance the separation line in retaliation for any atrocities.

Once the military campaign is complete and refugees have been resettled, further reconstruction and military aid may be needed to help the client achieve a viable economy and self-defense capability before the intervenors can depart. The ease of exit will depend on the regional geography and balance of power. Bosnia has sufficient population and skills to be made economically and militarily viable, provided that access to the outside world through Croatia is maintained. Although the weakness of the Turkish Republic of Northern Cyprus has required a permanent Turkish garrison, the almost equal weakness of the Greek Cypriots allows the garrison to be small, cheap, and inactive. U.S. Operation Provide Comfort helps secure the Kurdish enclave in northern Iraq by prohibiting Iraqi air operations as well as by threatening air strikes against an Iraqi ground invasion of the region. This intervention has no easy exit, however, since the Iraqi Kurds are landlocked and threatened by Turkey, which is waging a war against its own Kurdish minority. Real security for the Kurds might require partitioning Turkey as well as Iraq, a task no outside actor is willing to contemplate. . . .

OBJECTIONS TO ETHNIC SEPARATION AND PARTITION

There are five important objections to ethnic separation as policy for resolving ethnic conflicts: that it encourages splintering of states, that population exchanges cause human suffering, that it simply transforms civil wars into international ones, that rump states will not be viable, and that, in the end, it does nothing to resolve ethnic antagonisms.

Among most international organizations, western leaders, and scholars, population exchanges and partition are anathema. They contradict cherished western values of social integration, trample on the international legal norm of state sovereignty, and suggest particular policies that have been condemned by most of the world (e.g., Turkey's unilateral partition of Cyprus). The integrity of states and their borders is usually seen as a paramount principle, while self-determination takes second place. In ethnic wars, however, saving lives may require ignoring state-centered legal norms. The legal costs of ethnic separation must be compared to the human consequences, both immediate and long term, if the warring groups are not separated. To paraphrase Winston Churchill: separation is the worst solution, except for all the others.

Partition Encourages Splintering of States

If international interventions for ethnic separation encourage secession attempts elsewhere, they could increase rather than decrease global ethnic violence. However, this is unlikely, because government use of force to suppress them makes almost all secession attempts extremely costly; only groups that see no viable alternative try. What intervention can do is reduce loss of life where states are breaking up anyway. An expectation that the international community will never intervene, however, encourages repression of minorities, as in Turkey or the Sudan, and wars of ethnic conquest, as by Serbia.

Population Transfers Cause Suffering

Separation of intermingled ethnic groups necessarily involves significant refugee flows, usually in both directions. Population transfers during ethnic conflicts have often led to much suffering, so an obvious question is whether foreign intervention to relocate populations would only increase suffering. In fact, however, the biggest cause of suffering in population exchanges is spontaneous refugee movement. Planned population transfers are much safer. When ethnic conflicts turn violent, they generate spontaneous refugee movements as people flee from intense fighting or are kicked out by neighbors, marauding gangs, or a conquering army. Spontaneous refugees frequently suffer direct attack by hostile civilians or armed forces. They often leave precipitately, with inadequate money, transport, or food supplies, and before relief can be organized. They make vulnerable targets for banditry and plunder, and are often so needy as to be likely perpetrators also. Planned population exchanges can address all of these risks by preparing refugee relief and security operations in advance.

In the 1947 India-Pakistan exchange, nearly the entire movement of between 12 and 16 million people took place in a few months. The British were surprised by the speed with which this movement took place, and were not ready to control, support, and protect the refugees. Estimates of deaths go as high as one million. In the first stages of the population exchanges among Greece, Bulgaria, and Turkey in the 1920s, hundreds of thousands of refugees moved spontaneously and many died due to banditry and exposure. When after 1925 the League of Nations deployed capable relief services, the remaining transfers—one million, over 60 percent of the total—were carried out in an organized and planned way, with virtually no losses.

A related criticism is that transfers require the intervenors to operate *de facto* concentration camps for civilians of the opposing ethnic groups until transfers can be carried out. However, this is safer than the alternatives of administration by the local ally or allowing the war to run its course. As with transfers, the risks to the internees depend on planning and resources.

Separation Merely Substitutes International for Civil Wars

Post-separation wars are possible, motivated either by revanchism or by security fears if one side suspects the other of revisionist plans. The frequency and human cost of such wars, however, must be compared to the likely consequences of not separating. When the alternative is intercommunal slaughter, separation is the only defensible choice.

In fact the record of twentieth-century ethnic partitions is fairly good. The partition of Ireland has produced no interstate violence, although intercommunal violence continues in demographically mixed Northern Ireland. India and Pakistan have fought two wars since partition, one in 1965 over ethnically mixed Kashmir, while the second in 1971 resulted not from Indo-Pakistani state rivalry or Hindu-Muslim religious conflict but from ethnic conflict between (West) Pakistanis and Bengalis. Indian intervention resolved the conflict by enabling the independence of Bangladesh. These wars have been much less dangerous, especially to civilians, than the political and possible physical extinction that Muslims feared if the subcontinent were not divided. The worst post-partition history is probably that of the Arab-Israeli conflict. Even here, civilian deaths would almost certainly have been higher without partition. It is difficult even to imagine any alternative; the British could not and would not stay, and neither side would share power or submit to rule by the other.

Rump States Will Not Be Viable

Many analysts of ethnic conflict question the economic and military viability of partitioned states. History, however, records no examples of ethnic partitions which failed for economic reasons. In any case, intervenors have substantial influence over economic outcomes: They can determine partition lines, guarantee trade access and, if necessary, provide significant aid in relation to the economic sizes of likely candidates. Peace itself also enhances recovery prospects.

Thus the more important issue is military viability, particularly since interventions will most often be in favor of the weaker side. If the client has economic strength comparable to the opponent, it can provide for its own defense. If it does not, the intervenors will have to provide military aid and possibly a security guarantee.

Ensuring the client's security will be made easier by the opponent's scarcity of options for revision. First, any large-scale conventional attack is likely to fail because the intervenors will have drawn the borders for maximum defensibility and ensured that the client is better armed. If necessary, they can lend further assistance through air strikes. Breaking up conventional offensives is what high-technology air power does best.

Second, infiltration of small guerrilla parties, if successful over a period of time, could cause boundaries to become "fuzzy," and eventually to break down. This has been a major concern of some observers of Bosnia, but it should not be. Infiltration can only work where at least some civilians will support, house, feed, and hide the guerrillas. After ethnic separation, however, any infiltrators would be entering a completely hostile region where no one will help them; instead, all will inform on them and cooperate fully with authorities against them. The worst case is probably Israel, where terrorist infiltration has cost lives, but never comes close to threatening the state's territorial integrity. Retaliatory capabilities could also allow the client to dampen, even stop, such behavior.

Partition Does Not Resolve Ethnic Hatreds

It is not clear that it is in anyone's power to resolve ethnic hatreds once there has been large-scale violence, especially murders of civilians. In the long run, however, separation may help reduce inter-ethnic antagonism; once real security threats are reduced, the plausibility of hypernationalist appeals may eventually decline. Certainly ethnic hostility cannot be reduced without separation. As long as either side fears, even intermittently, that it will be attacked by the other, past atrocities and old hatreds can easily be aroused. If, however, it becomes and remains implausible that the other group could ever seriously endanger the nation, hypernationalist drum-beating may fall on deafer and deafer ears.

The only stronger measure would be to attempt a thorough re-engineering of the involved groups' political and social systems, comparable to the rehabilitation of Germany after World War II. The costs would be steep, since this would require conquering the country and occupying it for a long time, possibly for decades. The apparent benignification of Germany suggests that, if the international community is prepared to go this far, this approach could succeed.

CONCLUSION

Humanitarian intervention to establish lasting safety for peoples endangered by ethnic civil wars is feasible, but only if the international community is prepared to recognize that some shattered states cannot be restored, and that population transfers are sometimes necessary. . . .

Ultimately we have a responsibility to be honest with ourselves as well as with the victims of ethnic wars all over the world. The world's major powers must decide whether they will be willing to spend any of their own soldiers' lives to save strangers, or whether they will continue to offer false hopes to endangered peoples.

NOTES

1. Ethnic wars involve organized large-scale violence, whether by regular forces (Turkish or Iraqi operations against the Kurds) or highly mobilized civilian populations (the *interahamwe* in Rwanda or the Palestinian *intifada*). A frequent aspect is "ethnic cleansing": efforts by members of one ethnic group to eliminate the population of another from a certain area by means such as discrimination, expropriation, terror, expulsion, and massacre. For proposals on managing ethnic rivalries involving lower levels of ethnic mobilization and violence, see Stephen Van Evera, "Managing the Eastern Crisis: Preventing War in the Former Soviet Empire," *Security Studies* 3 (Spring 1992), 361–382; Ted Hopf, "Managing Soviet Disintegration: A Demand for Behavioral Regimes," *International Security* 17, 1 (Summer 1992), 44–75.

2. An ethnic group (or nation) is commonly defined as a body of individuals who purportedly share cultural or racial characteristics, especially common ancestry or territorial origin, which distinguish them from members of other groups. See Max Weber (Guenther Roth, and Claus Wittich, eds.), *Economy and Society: An Outline of Interpretive Sociology,* Vol. 1 (Berkeley, Calif.: University of California Press, 1968), pp. 389, 395; Anthony D. Smith, *National Identity* (Reno: University of Nevada Press, 1991), pp. 14, 21. Opposing communities in ethnic civil conflicts hold irreconcilable visions of the identity, borders, and citizenship of the state. They do not seek to control a state whose identity all sides accept, but rather to redefine or divide the state itself. By contrast, ideological conflicts may be defined as those in which all sides share a common vision of community membership, a common preference for political organization of the community as a single state, and a common sense of the legitimate boundaries of that state. The opposing sides seek control of the state, not its division or destruction. It follows that some religious conflicts—those between confessions which see themselves as separate communities, as between Catholics and Protestants in Northern Ireland—are best categorized with ethnic conflicts, while others—over interpretation of a shared religion, e.g., disputes over the social roles of Islam in Iran, Algeria, and Egypt—should be considered ideological contests. On religious differences as ethnic divisions, see Arend Lijphart, "The Power-Sharing Approach," in Joseph V. Montville, ed., *Conflict and Peacemaking in Multiethnic Societies* (Lexington, Mass.: Lexington Books, 1990), pp. 491–509, at 491.

3. While the discussion below delineates ideal types, mixed cases occur. The key distinction is the extent to which mobilization appeals are based on race or confession (ethnic)

rather than on political, economic, or social ideals (ideological). During the Cold War a number of Third World ethnic conflicts were misidentified by the superpowers as ideological struggles because local groups stressed ideology to gain outside support. In Angola the MPLA drew their support from the coastal Kimbundu tribe, the FNLA from the Bankongo in the north (and across the border in Zaire), and UNITA from Ovimbundu, Chokwe, and Ngangela in the interior of the south. The former were aided by the Soviets and the latter two, at various times, by both the United States and China. . . .

4. Reported by Andrej Gustinčić of *Reuters,* cited in Misha Glenny, *The Fall of Yugoslavia* (New York: Penguin, 1992), p. 166. Another tactic used by extremists to radicalize co-ethnics is to accuse the other side of crimes similar to their own. In July 1992, amidst large-scale rape of Bosnian Muslim women by Serb forces, Bosnian Serbs accused Muslims of impregnating kidnapped Serb women in order to create a new race of Janissary soldiers. Roy Gutman, *A Witness to Genocide* (New York: Macmillan, 1993), p. x.

5. Mikica Babić quoted in Chris Hedges, "War Turns Sarajevo Away from Europe," *New York Times* (July 28, 1995).

6. Increased geographic intermixing of ethnic groups often intensifies conflict, particularly if the state is too weak or too biased to assure the security of all groups. Increasing numbers of Jewish settlers in the West Bank had this effect on Israeli-Palestinian relations. A major reason for the failure of the negotiations that preceded the Nigerian civil war was the inability of northern leaders to guarantee the safety of Ibo living in the northern region. Harold D. Nelson, ed., *Nigeria: A Country Study* (Washington, D.C.: U.S. GPO, 1982), p. 55.

7. Ethnic combatants have noticed this. In World War II, the Croatian Ustasha refused to accept educated Serbs as converts because they were assumed to have a national consciousness independent of religion, whereas illiterate peasants were expected to forget their Serbian identity once converted. In 1992 Bosnian Serb ethnic cleansers annihilated the most educated Muslims. . . . Tutsi massacres of Hutus in Burundi in 1972 concentrated on educated people who were seen as potential ethnic leaders and afterwards the government restricted admission of Hutus to secondary schools. . . .

8. This total does not include civil wars which stopped temporarily but in which the same combatants later resumed fighting over the same issues (e.g., Burundi or Sudan) or cases in which peace agreements have been signed but not fully implemented as of this writing (e.g., Palestinians vs. Israel, Ovimbundu vs. Angola).

9. This is why the strongest advocates of intervention in Bosnia have emphasized Serb crimes, while those opposed to intervention insist on the moral equivalence of the two sides. Anthony Lewis, "Crimes of War," *New York Times* (April 25, 1994); Charles G. Boyd, "Making Peace with the Guilty," *Foreign Affairs,* 74, 5 (September/October 1995), pp. 22–38.

10. Further, attempts at even-handed intervention rarely achieve their goals, leading either to nearly complete passivity, as in the case of UNPROFOR In Bosnia, or eventually to open combat against one or all sides. At worst, peace-keeping efforts may actually prolong fighting. . . .

The United States and Nation-Building

FROM GERMANY TO AFGHANISTAN

The cases of Germany and Japan set a standard for postconflict nation-building that has not been matched since. Both were comprehensive efforts at social, political, and economic reconstruction. These successes demonstrated that democracy was transferable, that societies could be encouraged to transform themselves, and that major transformations could endure.

For the next 40 years, there were few attempts to replicate these early successes. During the cold war with the Soviet Union, America employed its military power to preserve the status quo, not to alter it; to manage crises, not to resolve the underlying problems; to overthrow unfriendly regimes and reinstall friendly ones, not to bring about fundamental societal change.

After 1989, a policy of global containment of the Soviet Union no longer impelled the United States to preserve the status quo. Washington was now free to overlook regional instability in places like Yugoslavia and Afghanistan as long as the instability did not directly threaten American interests. At the same time, though, the United States had the unprecedented opportunity of using its unrivaled power to resolve, not just to manage or to contain, international problems of strategic importance. In addition, the United States could secure broader international support for such efforts than ever before.

Throughout the 1990s, each successive post-cold war effort became wider in scope and more ambitious in intent than its predecessor had been. In Somalia, the original objective was purely humanitarian but was subsequently expanded to democratization. In Haiti, the objective was to reinstall a president and to conduct elections according to an existing constitution. In Bosnia, the objective was to create a multiethnic state out of a former Yugoslav republic. In Kosovo, the objective was to establish a democratic polity and market economy virtually from scratch.

From Somalia in 1992 to Kosovo in 1999, each nation-building effort was somewhat better managed than the previous one. Somalia was the nadir. Everything that could go wrong did. The operation culminated in the withdrawal of U.S. troops in 1994 after a sharp tactical setback that had resulted in 18 American deaths in October 1993. This reverse, which became memorialized in the book and

From "Nation Building: The Inescapable Responsibility of the World's Only Superpower" by James Dobbins. Copyright © 2003 by John Godges, editor of *Rand Review*, Vol. 27, No. 2, Summer 2003, pp. 17-27.

film "Black Hawk Down," was largely the result of an unnecessarily complicated U.S. and United Nations command structure that had three distinct forces operating with three distinct chains of command. Despite its failure, the Somalia mission taught America crucial lessons for the future. One was the importance of unity of command in peace operations as well as in war. Second was the need to scale mission objectives to available resources in troops, money, and staying power. A third lesson was the importance of deploying significant numbers of international police alongside international military forces to places where the local law enforcement institutions had disappeared or become illegitimate.

America applied these lessons to Haiti in the mid-1990s. We had unity of command throughout the operation. We did not have parallel American and allied forces. We had a single force under a single command with a clear hierarchy of decisionmaking. We deployed a large number of police within weeks of the military deployment, and the police were armed with both weapons and arrest authority. Unfortunately, we were obsessed with exit strategies and exit deadlines in the wake of the Somalia debacle. So we pulled out of Haiti with the job at best half done.

The Bosnia experience of the late 1990s was more successful. We set an exit deadline but wisely ignored it when the time came. On the negative side, there was a lack of coordination between the military stabilization efforts of NATO and those organizations responsible for civilian reconstruction. Consequently, the authority for implementing the civilian reconstruction projects became fragmented among numerous competing institutions. To complicate the situation further, the international police who had been deployed were armed with neither weapons nor arrest authority.

By the time of the Kosovo conflict in 1999, we and our allies had absorbed most of these lessons. We then made smarter choices in Kosovo. We achieved unity of command on both the civil and military sides. As in Bosnia, NATO was responsible for military operations. On the civil side, we established a clear hierarchical structure under a United Nations representative. Leadership was shared effectively between Europe and the United States. Working together, we deployed nearly 5,000 well-armed police alongside military peacekeepers. Although far from perfect, the arrangement was more successful than it had been in Bosnia. . . .

QUANTITATIVE COMPARISONS OF CASES

For each of the seven historical cases of nation-building, we at RAND compared quantitative data on the "inputs" (troops, money, and time) and "outputs." The outputs included casualties (or lack thereof), democratic elections, and increases in per capita gross domestic product (GDP).

Troop levels varied widely across the cases. The levels ranged from 1.6 million U.S. troops in the American sector in Germany at the end of World War II to 14,000 U.S. and international troops currently in Afghanistan. Gross numbers, however, are not the most useful numbers for comparison, because the size and populations of the nations being built have been so disparate. We chose instead to compare the numbers of U.S. and foreign soldiers *per thousand inhabitants* in

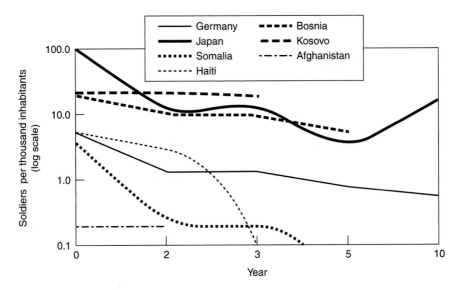

FIGURE 1 ■ HIGHER FORCE LEVELS FOR LONGER TIME PERIODS PROMOTE SUCCESSFUL NATION-BUILDING
Source: America's Role in Nation-Building, 2003.
Note: Year 0 represents the end of the conflict. The numbers for Germany include only those in the U.S. sector. The data for the other nations include all participants.

each occupied territory. We then compared the proportional force levels at specified times after the conflict ended (or after the U.S. rebuilding efforts began).

Figure 1 shows the number of international troops (or in the German and Japanese cases, U.S. troops) per thousand inhabitants in each territory at the outset of the intervention and at various intervals thereafter. As the data illustrate, even the proportional force levels vary immensely across the operations. (The levels vary so tremendously that they require a logarithmic, or exponential, scale for manageable illustration.)

Bosnia, Kosovo, and particularly the U.S.-occupied sector of Germany started with substantial proportions of military forces, whereas the initial levels in Japan, Somalia, Haiti, and especially Afghanistan were much more modest. The levels generally decreased over time. In Germany, the level then rose again for reasons having to do with the cold war. Overall, the differences in force levels across the cases had significant implications for other aspects of the operations.

Figure 2 compares the amount of foreign economic aid per capita (in constant 2001 U.S. dollars) provided to six of the territories during the first two years. Although Germany received the most aid in raw dollar terms ($12 billion), the country did not rank high on a per capita basis. Per capita assistance there ran a little over $200. Kosovo, which ranked fourth in terms of total assistance, received over $800 per resident. With the second-highest level of economic assistance per capita, Kosovo enjoyed the most rapid recovery in levels of per capita GDP. In contrast, Haiti, which received much less per capita than Kosovo, has experienced little growth in per capita GDP.

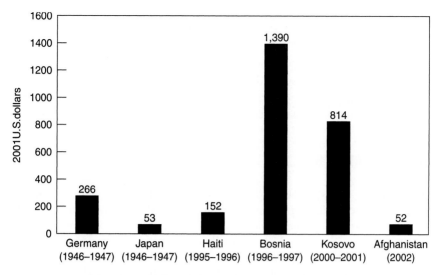

FIGURE 2 ■ FOREIGN AID PER CAPITA DURING THE FIRST TWO YEARS
Source: America's Role in Nation-Building, 2003.

Germany and Japan both stand out as unequaled success stories. One of the most important questions is why both operations fared so well compared with the others. The easiest answer is that Germany and Japan were already highly developed and economically advanced societies. This certainly explains why it was easier to reconstruct their economies than it was to reconstruct those in the other territories. But economics is not a sufficient answer to explain the transition to democracy. The spread of democracy to poor countries in Latin America, Asia, and parts of Africa suggests that this form of government is not unique to advanced industrial economies. Indeed, democracy can take root in countries where neither Western culture nor significant economic development exists. Nation-building is not principally about economic reconstruction, but rather about political transformation.

Because Germany and Japan were also ethnically homogeneous societies, some people might argue that homogeneity is the key to success. We believe that homogeneity helps greatly but that it is not essential, either. It is true that Somalia, Haiti, and Afghanistan are divided ethnically, socioeconomically, or tribally in ways that Germany and Japan were not. However, the kinds of communal hatred that mark Somalia, Haiti, and Afghanistan are even more pronounced in Bosnia and Kosovo, where the process of democratization has nevertheless made some progress.

What principally distinguishes Germany, Japan, Bosnia, and Kosovo from Somalia, Haiti, and Afghanistan is not their levels of Western culture, democratic history, economic development, or ethnic homogeneity, Rather, the principal distinction is the level of effort that the United States and the international community have put into the democratic transformations. Among the recent operations, the United States and its allies have put 25 times more money and 50 times more troops on a per capita basis into post-conflict Kosovo than into post-conflict

Afghanistan. These higher levels of input account in significant measure for the higher levels of output in terms of democratic institutionbuilding and economic growth. . . .

The seven historical cases have differed in terms of duration. The record suggests that although staying long does not guarantee success, leaving early assures failure. To date, no effort at enforced democratization has been brought to a successful conclusion in less than seven years.

UNITY OF COMMAND

Throughout the 1990s, the United States wrestled with the challenge of gaining wider participation in its nation-building endeavors while also preserving adequate unity of command. In Somalia and Haiti, the United States experimented with sequential arrangements in which it initially managed and funded the operations but then quickly turned responsibility over to the United Nations. In Bosnia, the United States succeeded in achieving both broad participation and unity of command on the military side of the operation through NATO. But in Bosnia the United States resisted the logic of achieving a comparable and cohesive arrangement on the civil side. In Kosovo, the United States achieved broad participation and unity of command on both the military and civil sides by working through NATO and the United Nations.

None of these models proved entirely satisfactory. However, the arrangements in Kosovo seem to have provided the best amalgam to date of American leadership, European and other participation, financial burdensharing, and unity of command. Every international official in Kosovo works ultimately for either the NATO commander or the Special Representative of the U.N. Secretary General. Neither of these is an American. But by virtue of America's credibility in the region and America's influence in NATO and on the U.N. Security Council, the United States has been able to maintain a satisfactory leadership role while fielding only 16 percent of the peacekeeping troops and paying only 16 percent of the reconstruction costs.

The efficacy of the Bosnia and Kosovo models has depended on the ability of the United States and its principal allies to attain a common vision of the objectives and then to coordinate the relevant institutions—principally NATO, the Organization for Security and Cooperation in Europe, the European Union, and the United Nations—to meet the objectives. These two models offer a viable fusion of burden-sharing and unity of command.

In Afghanistan, in contrast, the United States opted for parallel arrangements on the military side and even greater divergence on the civil side. An international force—with no U.S. participation—operates in the capital of Kabul, while a national and mostly U.S. force operates everywhere else. The United Nations has responsibility for promoting political transformation, while individual donors coordinate economic reconstruction—or, more often, fail to do so.

The arrangement in Afghanistan is a marginal improvement over that in Somalia, because the separate U.S. and international forces are at least not operating in the same physical space. But the arrangement represents a clear regression from what we achieved in Haiti, Bosnia, or, in particular, Kosovo. It is therefore not surprising that the overall results achieved to date in Afghanistan are better than in Somalia, not yet better than in Haiti, and not as good as in Bosnia or Kosovo. The operation in Afghanistan, though, is a good deal less expensive than those in Bosnia or Kosovo.

APPLYING THE LESSONS TO IRAQ

The challenges facing the United States in Iraq today are formidable. Still, it is possible to draw valuable lessons from America's previous experiences with nation-building. There are four main lessons to be learned for Iraq.

The first lesson is that democratic nation-building can work given sufficient inputs of resources. These inputs, however, can be very high. . . . For example, if Kosovo levels of troop commitments were deployed to Iraq, the number would be some 500,000 U.S. and coalition troops through 2005. (There are roughly 150,000 coalition troops stationed in Iraq today.) To provide troop coverage at Bosnia levels, the requisite troop figures would be 460,000 initially, falling to 258,000 by 2005 and 145,000 by 2008.

In addition to military forces, it is often important to deploy a significant number of international civil police. To achieve a level comparable to the nearly 5,000 police deployed in Kosovo, Iraq would need an infusion of 53,000 international civil police officers through 2005. . . .

It is too early to predict with accuracy the required levels of foreign aid, but we can draw comparisons with the previous historical cases. . . . If Bosnia levels of foreign aid per capita were provided to Iraq, the country would require some $36 billion in aid from now through 2005. Conversely, aid at the same level as Afghanistan would total $1 billion over the next two years.

According to the lessons learned, the ultimate consequences for Iraq of a failure to generate adequate international manpower and money are likely to be lower levels of security, higher casualties sustained and inflicted, lower economic growth rates, and slower, less thoroughgoing political transformation.

The second lesson for Iraq is that short departure deadlines are incompatible with nation-building. The United States will succeed only if it makes a long-term commitment to establishing strong democratic institutions and does not beat a hasty retreat tied to artificial deadlines. Moreover, setting premature dates for early national elections can be counterproductive.

Third, important hindrances to nation-building include both internal fragmentation (along political, ethnic, or sectarian lines) and a lack of external support from neighboring states. Germany and Japan had homogeneous societies. Bosnia and Kosovo had neighbors that, following the democratic transitions in Croatia and Serbia, collaborated with the international community. Iraq could combine the worst of both worlds, lacking both internal cohesion and regional support. The United States should consider putting a consultative mechanism in place, on the model of the Peace Implementation Council in the Balkans or the "Two Plus Six" group that involved Afghanistan's six neighbors plus Russia and the United States, as a means of consulting with the neighboring countries of Iraq.

Fourth, building a democracy, a strong economy, and long-term legitimacy depends in each case on striking the balance between international burden-sharing and unity of command. As noted above, the United States is unlikely to be able to generate adequate levels of troops, money, or endurance as long as it relies principally upon the limited coalition with which it fought the war. On the other hand, engaging a broader coalition, to include major countries that will expect to secure influence commensurate with their contributions, will require either new institutional arrangements or the extension of existing ones, such as NATO. . . .

In Somalia, Bosnia, Kosovo, and Afghanistan, extremist elements emerged to fill the resultant vacuum of power. In all five cases, organized crime quickly developed into a major challenge to the occupying authority. In Bosnia and Kosovo, the external stabilization forces ultimately proved adequate to surmount these challenges. In Somalia and Afghanistan, they did not or have not yet, respectively.

Throughout the 1990s, the management of each major stabilization and reconstruction mission represented a marginal advance over its predecessor, but in the past several years this modestly positive learning curve has not been sustained. The Afghan mission cannot yet be deemed more successful than the one in Haiti. It is certainly too early to evaluate the success of the Iraqi nation-building mission, but its first few months do not raise it above those in Bosnia and Kosovo at a similar stage.

Over the past decade, the United States has made major investments in the combat efficiency of its forces. The return on investment has been evident in the dramatic improvements demonstrated from one campaign to the next, from Desert Storm to the Kosovo air campaign to Operation Iraqi Freedom. But there has been no comparable increase in the capacity of U.S. armed forces, or of U.S. civilian agencies for that matter, to conduct post-combat stabilization and reconstruction operations. . . .

Post-conflict stabilization and reconstruction with the objective of promoting a transition to democracy appear to be the inescapable responsibility of the world's only superpower. Therefore, in addition to securing the major resources that will be needed to carry through the current operation in Iraq to success, the United States ought to make the smaller long-term investments in its own institutional capacity to conduct such operations. In this way, the ongoing improvements in combat performance of American forces could be matched by improvements in the postconflict performance of our government as a whole.

THE ENVIRONMENT AND ■ CLIMATE CHANGE

The Tragedy of the Commons

■ GARRETT HARDIN

We can make little progress in working toward optimum population size until we explicitly exorcize the spirit of Adam Smith in the field of practical demography. In economic affairs, *The Wealth of Nations* (1776) popularized the "invisible hand," the idea that an individual who "intends only his own gain," is, as it were, "led by an invisible hand to promote . . . the public interest."[1] Adam Smith did not assert that this was invariably true, and perhaps neither did any of his followers. But he contributed to a dominant tendency of thought that has ever since interfered with positive action based on rational analysis, namely, the tendency to assume that decisions reached individually will, in fact, be the best decisions for an entire society. If this assumption is correct it justifies the continuance of our present policy of laissez-faire in reproduction. If it is correct we can assume that men will control their individual fecundity so as to produce the optimum population. If the assumption is not correct, we need to reexamine our individual freedoms to see which ones are defensible.

TRAGEDY OF FREEDOM IN A COMMONS

The rebuttal to the invisible hand in population control is to be found in a scenario first sketched in a little-known pamphlet in 1833 by a mathematical amateur named William Foster Lloyd (1794–1852).[2] We may well call it "the tragedy of the commons," using the word "tragedy" as the philosopher Whitehead used it: "The essence of dramatic tragedy is not unhappiness. It resides in the solemnity of the remorseless working of things."[3] He then goes on to say, "This inevitableness of destiny can only be illustrated in terms of human life by incidents which in fact involve unhappiness. For it is only by them that the futility of escape can be made evident in the drama."

The tragedy of the commons develops in this way. Picture a pasture open to all. It is to be expected that each herdsman will try to keep as many cattle as possible on the commons. Such an arrangement may work reasonably satisfactorily for centuries because tribal wars, poaching, and disease keep the numbers of both man and beast well below the carrying capacity of the land. Finally, however, comes the day of reckoning, that is, the day when the long-desired goal of social stability becomes a reality. At this point, the inherent logic of the commons remorselessly generates tragedy.

As a rational being, each herdsman seeks to maximize his gain. Explicitly or implicitly, more or less consciously, he asks, "What is the utility *to me* of adding one more animal to my herd?" This utility has one negative and one positive component.

The positive component is a function of the increment of one animal. Since the herdsman receives all the proceeds from the sale of the additional animal, the positive utility is nearly +1.

The negative component is a function of the additional overgrazing created by one more animal. Since, however, the effects of overgrazing are shared by all the herdsmen, the negative utility for any particular decision-making herdsman is only a fraction of −1.

Adding together the component partial utilities, the rational herdsman concludes that the only sensible course for him to pursue is to add another animal to his herd. And another; and another. . . . But this is the conclusion reached by each and every rational herdsman sharing a commons. Therein is the tragedy. Each man is locked into a system that compels him to increase his herd without limit—in a world that is limited. Ruin is the destination toward which all men rush, each pursuing his own best interest in a society that believes in the freedom of the commons. Freedom in a commons brings ruin to all. . . .

In an approximate way, the logic of the commons has been understood for a long time, perhaps since the discovery of agriculture or the invention of private property in real estate. But it is understood mostly only in special cases which are not sufficiently generalized. Even at this late date, cattlemen leasing national land on the western ranges demonstrate no more than an ambivalent understanding, in constantly pressuring federal authorities to increase the head count to the point where overgrazing produces erosion and weed-dominance. Likewise, the oceans of the world continue to suffer from the survival of the philosophy of the commons. Maritime nations will respond automatically to the shibboleth of the "freedom of the seas." Professing to believe in the "inexhaustible resources of the oceans," they bring species after species of fish and whales closer to extinction. . . .

POLLUTION

In a reverse way, the tragedy of the commons reappears in problems of pollution. Here it is not a question of taking something out of the commons, but of putting something in—sewage, or chemical, radioactive, and heat wastes into water;

noxious and dangerous fumes into the air; and distracting and unpleasant advertising signs into the line of sight. The calculations of utility are much the same as before. The rational man finds that his share of the cost of the wastes he discharges into the commons is less than the cost of purifying his wastes before releasing them. Since this is true for everyone, we are locked into a system of "fouling our own nest," so long as we behave only as independent, rational, free-enterprisers.

The tragedy of the commons as a food basket is averted by private property, or something formally like it. But the air and waters surrounding us cannot readily be fenced, and so the tragedy of the commons as a cesspool must be prevented by different means, by coercive laws or taxing devices that make it cheaper for the polluter to treat his pollutant than to discharge them untreated. We have not progressed as far with the solution of this problem as we have with the first. Indeed, our particular concept of private property, which deters us from exhausting the positive resources of the earth, favors pollution. The owner of a factory on the bank of a stream—whose property extends to the middle of the stream—often has difficulty seeing why it is not his natural right to muddy the waters flowing past his door. The law, always behind the times, requires elaborate stitching and fitting to adapt to it this newly perceived aspect of the commons.

The pollution problem is a consequence of populations. It did not much matter how a lonely American frontiersman disposed of his waste. "Flowing water purifies itself every 10 miles," my grandfather used to say, and the myth was near enough to the truth when he was a boy, for there were not too many people. But as population became denser, the natural chemical and biological recycling processes became overloaded, calling for a redefinition of property rights.

HOW TO LEGISLATE TEMPERANCE?

Analysis of the pollution problem as a function of population density uncovers a not generally recognized principle of morality, namely: *The morality of an act is a function of the state of the system at the time it is performed.*[4] Using the commons as a cesspool does not harm the general public under frontier conditions, because there is no public; the same behavior in a metropolis is unbearable. A hundred and fifty years ago a plainsman could kill an American bison, cut out only the tongue for his dinner, and discard the rest of the animal. He was not in any important sense being wasteful. Today, with only a few thousand bison left, we would be appalled at such behavior. . . .

That morality is system-sensitive escaped the attention of most codifiers of ethics in the past. "Thou shalt not . . . " is the form of traditional ethical directives which make no allowance for particular circumstances. The laws of our society follow the pattern of ancient ethics, and therefore are poorly suited to governing a complex, crowded, changeable world. Our epicyclic solution is to augment statutory law with administrative law. Since it is practically impossible to spell out all the conditions under which it is safe to burn trash in the backyard or to run an automobile without smog-control, by law we delegate the details to bureaus. The result is administrative law, which is rightly feared for an ancient reason—*Quis custodiet ipsos custodes?*—"Who shall watch the watchers themselves?" John Adams said that we must have "a government of laws and not men." Bureau administrators, trying to evaluate the morality of acts in the total system, are singularly liable to corruption, producing a government by men, not laws.

Prohibition is easy to legislate (though not necessarily to enforce); but how do we legislate temperance? Experience indicates that it can be accomplished best through the mediation of administrative law. We limit possibilities unnecessarily if we suppose that the sentiment of *Quis custodiet* denies us the use of administrative law. We should rather retain the phrase as a perpetual reminder of fearful dangers we cannot avoid. The great challenge facing us now is to invent the corrective feedbacks that are needed to keep custodians honest. We must find ways to legitimate the needed authority of both the custodians and the corrective feedbacks.

FREEDOM TO BREED IS INTOLERABLE

The tragedy of the commons is involved in population problems in another way. In a world governed solely by the principle of "dog eat dog"—if indeed there ever was such a world—how many children a family had would not be a matter of public concern. Parents who bred too exuberantly would leave fewer descendants, not more, because they would be unable to care adequately for their children. . . .

If each human family were dependent only on its own resources; *if* the children of improvident parents starved to death; *if*, thus, overbreeding brought its own "punishment" to the germ line—*then* there would be no public interest in controlling the breeding of families. But our society is deeply committed to the welfare state and hence is confronted with another aspect of the tragedy of the commons.

In a welfare state, how shall we deal with the family, the religion, the race, or the class (or indeed any distinguishable and cohesive group) that adopts overbreeding as a policy to secure its own aggrandizement? To couple the concept of freedom to breed with the belief that everyone born has an equal right to the commons is to lock the world into a tragic course of action. . . .

CONSCIENCE IS SELF-ELIMINATING

It is a mistake to think that we can control the breeding of mankind in the long run by an appeal to conscience. Charles Galton Darwin made this point when he spoke on the centennial of the publication of his grandfather's great book. The argument is straightforward and Darwinian.

People vary. Confronted with appeals to limit breeding, some people will undoubtedly respond to the plea more than others. Those who have more children will produce a larger fraction of the next generation than those with more susceptible consciences. The difference will be accentuated, generation by generation.

In C. G. Darwin's words: "It may well be that it would take hundreds of generations for the progenitive instinct to develop in this way, but if it should do so, nature would have taken her revenge, and the variety *Homo contracipiens* would become extinct and would be replaced by the variety *Homo progenitivus*."[5]

The argument assumes that conscience or the desire for children (no matter which) is hereditary—but hereditary only in the most general formal sense. The result will be the same whether the attitude is transmitted through germ cells, or exosomatically. . . . The argument has here been stated in the context of the population problem, but it applies equally well to any instance in which society appeals to an individual exploiting a commons to restrain himself for the general good—by means of his conscience. To make such an appeal is to set up a selective system that works toward the elimination of conscience from the race. . . .

MUTUAL COERCION MUTUALLY AGREED UPON

The social arrangements that produce responsibility are arrangements that create coercion, of some sort. Consider bank-robbing. The man who takes money from a bank acts as if the bank were a commons. How do we prevent such action? Certainly not by trying to control his behavior solely by a verbal appeal to his sense of responsibility. Rather than rely on propaganda we follow Frankel's lead and insist that a bank is not a commons; we seek the definite social arrangements that will keep it from becoming a commons. That we thereby infringe on the freedom of would-be robbers we neither deny nor regret.

The morality of bank-robbing is particularly easy to understand because we accept complete prohibition of this activity. We are willing to say "Thou shalt not rob banks," without providing for exceptions. But temperance also can be created by coercion. Taxing is a good coercive device. To keep downtown shoppers temperate in their use of parking space we introduce parking meters for short periods, and traffic fines for longer ones. We need not actually forbid a citizen to park as long as he wants to; we need merely make it increasingly expensive for him to do so. Not prohibition, but carefully biased options are what we offer him. A Madison Avenue man might call this persuasion; I prefer the greater candor of the word coercion. . . .

To many, the word coercion implies arbitrary decisions of distant and irresponsible bureaucrats; but this is not a necessary part of its meaning. The only kind of coercion I recommend is mutual coercion, mutually agreed upon by the majority of the people affected.

To say that we mutually agree to coercion is not to say that we are required to enjoy it, or even to pretend we enjoy it. Who enjoys taxes? We all grumble about them. But we accept compulsory taxes because we recognize that voluntary taxes would favor the conscienceless. We institute and (grumblingly) support taxes and other coercive devices to escape the horror of the commons. . . .

RECOGNITION OF NECESSITY

Perhaps the simplest summary of this analysis of man's population problems is this: The commons, if justifiable at all, is justifiable only under conditions of low population density. As the human population has increased, the commons has had to be abandoned in one aspect after another.

First we abandoned the commons in food gathering, enclosing farm land and restricting pastures and hunting and fishing areas. These restrictions are still not complete throughout the world.

Somewhat later we saw that the commons as a place for waste disposal would also have to be abandoned. Restrictions on the disposal of domestic sewage are widely accepted in the Western world; we are still struggling to close the commons to pollution by automobiles, factories, insecticide sprayers, fertilizing operations, and atomic energy installations. . . .

Every new enclosure of the commons involves the infringement of some-body's personal liberty. Infringements made in the distant past are accepted because no contemporary complains of a loss. It is the newly proposed infringe-ments that we vigorously oppose; cries of "rights" and "freedom" fill the air. But what does "freedom" mean? When men mutually agreed to pass laws against rob-bing, mankind became more free, not less so. Individuals locked into the logic of the commons are free only to bring on universal ruin; once they see the necessity of mutual coercion, they become free to pursue other goals. I believe it was Hegel who said, "Freedom is the recognition of necessity."

The most important aspect of necessity that we must now recognize is the necessity of abandoning the commons in breeding. No technical solution can res-cue us from the misery of overpopulation. Freedom to breed will bring ruin to all. At the moment, to avoid hard decisions many of us are tempted to propagandize for conscience and responsible parenthood. The temptation must be resisted, because an appeal to independently acting consciences selects for the disappear-ance of all conscience in the long run, and an increase in anxiety in the short.

The only way we can preserve and nurture other and more precious freedoms is by relinquishing the freedom to breed, and that very soon. "Freedom is the recognition of necessity"—and it is the role of education to reveal to all the neces-sity of abandoning the freedom to breed. Only so can we put an end to this aspect of the tragedy of the commons.

NOTES

1. Adam Smith, *The Wealth of Nations* (New York: Modern Library, 1937), p. 423.
2. William Foster Lloyd, *Two Lectures on the Checks to Population* (Oxford: Oxford Uni-versity Press, 1853), reprinted in part in *Population, Evolution, and Birth Control*, A. Harding, ed. (San Francisco: Freeman, 1964), p. 37.
3. A. N. Whitehead, *Science and the Modern World* (New York: Mentor, 1948), p. 17.
4. J. Fletcher, *Situation Ethics* (Philadelphia: Westminster, 1966).
5. S. Tax, ed., *Evolution after Darwin*, vol. 2 (Chicago: University of Chicago Press, 1960), p. 469.

The Infinite Supply
of Natural Resources

████████ JULIAN L. SIMON

Natural resources are not finite. Yes, you read correctly. This chapter shows that the supply of natural resources is not finite in any economic sense, which is why their cost can continue to fall in the future.

On the face of it, even to inquire whether natural resources are finite seems like nonsense. Everyone "knows" that resources are finite, from C.P. Snow to Isaac Asimov to as many other persons as you have time to read about in the newspaper. And this belief has led many persons to draw far-reaching conclusions about the future of our world economy and civilization. A prominent example is the *Limits to Growth* group, who open the preface to their 1974 book, a sequel to the *Limits,* as follows:

> Most people acknowledge that the earth is finite. . . . Policy makers generally assume that growth will provide them tomorrow with the resources required to deal with today's problems. . . . Recently, however, concern about the consequences of population growth, increased environmental pollution, and the depletion of fossil fuels has cast doubt upon the belief that continuous growth is either possible or a panacea.[1]

(Note the rhetorical device embedded in the term "acknowledge" in the first sentence of the quotation. That word suggests that the statement is a fact, and that anyone who does not "acknowledge" it is simply refusing to accept or admit it.)

The idea that resources are finite in supply is so pervasive and influential that the President's 1972 Commission on Population Growth and the American Future based its policy recommendations squarely upon this assumption. Right at the beginning of its report the commission asked, "What does this nation stand for and where is it going? At some point in the future, the finite earth will not satisfactorily accommodate more human beings—nor will the United States. . . . It is both proper and in our best interest to participate fully in the worldwide search for the good life, which must include the eventual stabilization of our numbers."[2]

The assumption of finiteness is responsible for misleading many scientific forecasters because their conclusions follow inexorably from that assumption. From the *Limits to Growth* team again, this time on food: "The world model is based on the fundamental assumption that there is an upper limit to the total amount of food that can be produced annually by the world's agricultural system."[3]

THE THEORY OF DECREASING NATURAL-RESOURCE SCARCITY

We shall begin with a far-out example to see what contrasting possibilities there are. (Such an analysis of far-out examples is a useful and favorite trick of economists and mathematicians.) If there is just one person, Alpha Crusoe, on an island, with a single copper mine on his island, it will be harder to get raw copper next year if Alpha makes a lot of copper pots and bronze tools this year. And if he continues to use his mine, his son Beta Crusoe will have a tougher time getting copper than did his daddy.

Recycling could change the outcome. If Alpha decides in the second year to make new tools to replace the old tools he made in the first year, it will be easier for him to get the necessary copper than it was the first year because he can reuse the copper from the old tools without much new mining. And if Alpha adds fewer new pots and tools from year to year, the proportion of copper that can come from recycling can rise year by year. This could mean a progressive decrease in the cost of obtaining copper with each successive year for this reason alone, even while the total amount of copper in pots and tools increases.

But let us be "conservative" for the moment and ignore the possibility of recycling. Another scenario: If there are two people on the island, Alpha Crusoe and Gamma Defoe, copper will be more scarce for each of them this year than if Alpha lived there alone, unless by cooperative efforts they can devise a more complex but more efficient mining operation—say, one man on the surface and one in the shaft. Or, if there are two fellows this year instead of one, and if copper is therefore harder to get and more scarce, both Alpha and Gamma may spend considerable time looking for new lodes of copper. And they are likely to be successful in their search. This discovery may lower the cost of copper to them somewhat, but on the average the cost will still be higher than if Alpha lived alone on the island.

Alpha and Gamma may follow still other courses of action. Perhaps they will invent better ways of obtaining copper from a given lode, say a better digging tool, or they may develop new materials to substitute for copper, perhaps iron.

The cause of these new discoveries, or the cause of applying ideas that were discovered earlier, is the "shortage" of copper—that is, the increased cost of getting copper. So a "shortage" of copper causes the creation of its own remedy. This has been the key process in the supply and use of natural resources throughout history.

Discovery of an improved mining method or of a substitute product differs, in a manner that affects future generations, from the discovery of a new lode. Even after the discovery of a new lode, on the average it will still be more costly to obtain copper, that is, more costly than if copper had never been used enough to lead to a "shortage." But discoveries of improved mining methods and of substitute products, caused by the shortage of copper, can lead to lower costs of the services people see from copper. Let's see how.

The key point is that a discovery of a substitute process or product by Alpha or Gamma can benefit innumerable future generations. Alpha and Gamma cannot themselves extract nearly the full benefit from their discovery of iron. (You and I still benefit from the discoveries of the uses of iron and methods of processing it that our ancestors made thousands of years ago.) This benefit to later generations is an example of what economists call an "externality" due to Alpha and Gamma's activities, that is, a result of their discovery that does not affect them directly.

So, if the cost of copper to Alpha and Gamma does not increase, they may not be impelled to develop improved methods and substitutes. If the cost of getting copper does rise for them, however, they may then bestir themselves to make a new discovery. The discovery may not immediately lower the cost of copper dramatically, and Alpha and Gamma may still not be as well off as if the cost had never risen. But subsequent generations may be better off because their ancestor suffered from increasing cost and "scarcity."

This sequence of events explains how it can be that people have been using cooking pots for thousands of years, as well as using copper for many other purposes, and yet the cost of a pot today is vastly cheaper by any measure than it was 100 or 1,000 or 10,000 years ago.

It is all-important to recognize that discoveries of improved methods and of substitute products are not just luck. They happen in response to "scarcity"—an increase in cost. Even after a discovery is made, there is a good chance that it will not be put into operation until there is need for it due to rising cost. This point is important: Scarcity and technological advance are not two unrelated competitors in a race; rather, each influences the other.

The last major U.S. governmental inquiry into raw materials was the 1952 President's Materials Policy Commission (Paley Commission), organized in response to fears of raw-material shortages during and just after World War II. The Paley Commission's report is distinguished by having some of the right logic, but exactly the wrong predictions, for its twenty-five-year forecast.

> There is no completely satisfactory way to measure the real costs of materials over the long sweep of our history. But clearly the manhours required per unit of output declined heavily from 1900 to 1940, thanks especially to improvements in production technology and the heavier use of energy and capital equipment per worker. This long-term decline in real costs is reflected in the downward drift of prices of various groups of materials in relation to the general level of prices in the economy.
>
> [But since 1940 the trend has been] soaring demands, shrinking resources, the consequences pressure toward rising real costs, the risk of wartime shortages, the strong possibility of an arrest or decline in the standard of living we cherish and hope to share.[4]

For the quarter century for which the commission predicted, however, costs declined rather than rose.

The two reasons why the Paley Commission's cost predictions were topsy-turvy should help keep us from making the same mistakes. First, the commission reasoned from the notion of finiteness and from a static technological analysis.

> A hundred years ago resources seemed limitless and the struggle upward from meager conditions of life was the struggle to create the means and methods of getting these

materials into use. In this struggle we have by now succeeded all too well. . . . The nature of the problem can perhaps be successfully over-simplified by saying that the consumption of almost all materials is expanding at compound rates and is thus pressing harder and harder against resources which whatever else they may be doing are not similarly expanding.[5]

The second reason the Paley Commission went wrong is that it looked at the wrong facts. Its report gave too much emphasis to the trends of costs over the short period from 1940 to 1950, which included World War II and therefore was almost inevitably a period of rising costs, instead of examining the longer period from 1900 to 1940, during which the commission knew that "the manhours required per unit of output declined heavily."[6]

We must not repeat the same mistakes. We should look at cost trends for the longest period, rather than focus on a historical blip; the OPEC-led price rise in all resources after 1973 is for us as the temporary 1940–50 wartime reversal for the Paley Commission. And the long-run trends make it very clear that the costs of materials, and their scarcity, continuously decline with the growth of income and technology.

RESOURCES AS SERVICES

As economists or as consumers, we are interested in the particular services that resources yield, not in the resources themselves. Examples of such services are an ability to conduct electricity, an ability to support weight, energy to fuel autos, energy to fuel electrical generators, and food calories.

The supply of a service will depend upon (a) which raw materials can supply that service with the present technology; (b) the availabilities of these materials at various qualities; (c) the costs of extracting and processing them; (d) the amounts needed at the present level of technology to supply the services that we want; (e) the extent to which the previously extracted materials can be recycled; (f) the cost of recycling; (g) the cost of transporting the raw materials and services; and (h) the social and institutional arrangements in force. What is relevant to us is not whether we can find any lead in existing lead mines but whether we can have the services of lead batteries at a reasonable price; it does not matter to us whether this is accomplished by recycling lead, by making batteries last forever, or by replacing lead batteries with another contraption. Similarly, we want intercontinental telephone and television communication, and, as long as we got it, we do not care whether this requires 100,000 tons of copper for cables or just a single quarter-ton communications satellite in space that uses no copper at all.[7]

Let us see how this concept of services is crucial to our understanding of natural resources and the economy. To return to Crusoe's cooking pot, we are interested in a utensil that we can put over the fire and cook with. After iron and aluminum were discovered, quite satisfactory cooking pots, perhaps even better than pots of copper, could be made of these materials. The cost that interests us is the cost of providing the cooking service rather than the cost of copper. If we suppose that copper is used only for pots and that iron is quite satisfactory for the same purpose, as long as we have cheap iron it does not matter if the cost of copper rises sky high. (But in fact that has not happened. As we have seen, the prices of the minerals themselves, as well as the prices of the services they perform, have fallen over the years.)

ARE NATURAL RESOURCES FINITE?

Incredible as it may seem at first, the term "finite" is not only inappropriate but is downright misleading when applied to natural resources, from both the practical and philosophical points of view. As with many of the important arguments in this world, the one about "finiteness" is "just semantic." Yet the semantics of resource scarcity muddle public discussion and bring about wrong-headed policy decisions.

The word "finite" originates in mathematics, in which context we all learn it as schoolchildren. But even in mathematics the word's meaning is far from unambiguous. It can have two principal meanings, sometimes with an apparent contradiction between them.[8] For example, the length of a one-inch line is finite in the sense that it is bounded at both ends. But the line within the endpoints contains an infinite number of points; these points cannot be counted, because they have no defined size. Therefore the number of points in that one-inch segment is not finite. Similarly, the quantity of copper that will even be available to us is not finite, because there is no method (even in principle) of making an appropriate count of it, given the problem of the economic definition of "copper," the possibility of creating copper or its economic equivalent from other materials, and thus the lack of boundaries to the sources from which copper might be drawn.

Consider this quote about potential oil and gas from Sheldon Lambert, an energy forecaster. He begins, "It's like trying to guess the number of beans in a jar without knowing how big the jar is." So far so good. But then he adds, "God is the only one who knows—and even He may not be sure."[9] Of course Lambert is speaking lightly. But the notion that some mind might know the "actual" size of the jar is misleading, because it implies that there is a fixed quantity of standard-sized beans. The quantity of a natural resource that might be available to us—and even more important the quantity of the services that can eventually be rendered to us by that natural resource—can never be known even in principle, just as the number of points in a one-inch line can never be counted even in principle. Even if the "jar" were fixed in size, it might yield ever more "beans." Hence resources are not "finite" in any meaningful sense.

To restate: A satisfactory *operational* definition of the quantity of a natural resource, or of the services we now get from it, is the only sort of definition that is of any use in policy decisions. The definition must tell us about the quantities of a resource (or of a particular service) that we can expect to receive in any particular year to come, at each particular price, conditional on other events that we might reasonably expect to know (such as use of the resource in prior years). And there is no reason to believe that at any given moment in the future the available quantity of any natural resource or service at present prices will be much smaller than it is now, or non-existent. Only such one-of-a-kind resources as an Arthur Rubenstein concert or a Julius Erving basketball game, for which there are no close replacements, will disappear in the future and hence are finite in quantity.

Why do we become hypnotized by the word "finite"? That is an interesting question in psychology, education, and philosophy. A first likely reason is that the word "finite" seems to have a precise and unambiguous meaning in any context, even though it does not. Second, we learn the word in the context of mathematics, where all propositions are tautologous definitions and hence can be shown logically to be true or false (at least in principle). But scientific subjects are empirical rather than definitional, as twentieth-century philosophers have been at great pains to emphasize. Mathematics is not a science in the ordinary sense because it does not deal with facts other than the stuff of mathematics itself, and hence such terms as "finite" do not have the same meaning elsewhere that they do in mathematics.

Third, much of our daily life about which we need to make decisions is countable and finite—our weekly or monthly salaries, the number of gallons of gas in a full tank, the width of the backyard, the number of greeting cards you sent out last year, or those you will send out next year. Since these quantities are finite, why shouldn't the world's total possible salary in the future, or the gasoline in the possible tanks in the future, or the number of cards you ought to send out, also be finite? Though the analogy is appealing, it is not sound. And it is in making this incorrect analogy that we go astray in using the term "finite."

A fourth reason that the term "finite" is not meaningful is that we cannot say with any practical surety where the bounds of a relevant resource system lie, or even if there are any bounds. The bounds for the Crusoes are the shores of their island, and so it was for early man. But then the Crusoes found other islands. Mankind traveled farther and farther in search of resources—finally to the bounds of continents, and then to other continents. When America was opened up, the world, which for Europeans had been bounded by Europe and perhaps by Asia too, was suddenly expanded. Each epoch has seen a shift in the bounds of the relevant resource system. Each time, the old ideas about "limits," and the calculations of "finite resources" within those bounds, were thereby falsified. Now we have begun to explore the sea, which contains amounts of metallic and other resources that dwarf any deposits we know about on land. And we have begun to explore the moon. Why shouldn't the boundaries of the system from which we derive resources continue to expand in such directions, just as they have expanded in the past? This is one more reason not to regard resources as "finite" in principle.

You may wonder, however, whether "non-renewable" energy resources such as oil, coal, and natural gas differ from the recyclable minerals in such a fashion that the foregoing arguments do not apply. Energy is particularly important because it is the "master resource"; energy is the key constraint on the availability of all other resources. Even so, our energy supply is non-finite, and oil is an important example. (1) The oil potential of a particular well may be measured, and hence is limited (though it is interesting and relevant that as we develop new ways of extracting hard-to-get oil, the economic capacity of a well increases). But the number of wells that will eventually produce oil, and in what quantities, is not known or measurable at present and probably never will be, and hence is not meaningfully finite. (2) Even if we make the unrealistic assumption that the number of potential wells in the earth might be surveyed completely and that we could arrive at a reasonable estimate of the oil that might be obtained with present technology (or even with technology that will be developed in the next 100 years), we still would have to reckon the future possibilities of shale oil and tar sands—a difficult task. (3) But let us assume that we could reckon the oil potential of shale and tar sands. We would then have to reckon the conversion of coal to oil. That, too, might be done; yet we still could not consider the resulting quantity to be "finite" and "limited." (4) Then there is the oil that we might produce not from fossils but from new crops—palm oil, soybean oil, and so on. Clearly, there is no meaningful limit to this source except the sun's energy. The notion of finiteness does not make sense here, either. (5) If we allow for the substitution of nuclear and solar power for oil, since what we really want are the services of oil, not necessarily oil itself, the notion of a limit makes even less sense. (6) Of course the sun may eventually run down. But even if our sun were not as vast as it is, there may well be other suns elsewhere.

About energy from the sun: The assertion that our resources are ultimately finite seems most relevant to energy but yet is actually more misleading with respect to energy than with respect to other resources. When people say that mineral resources are "finite" they are invariably referring to the earth as a boundary, the "spaceship earth," to which we are apparently confined just as astronauts are confined to their spaceship. But the main source of our energy even now is the sun, no matter how you think of the matter. This goes far beyond the fact that the sun was the prior source of the energy locked into the oil and coal we use. The sun is also the source of the energy in the food we eat, and in the trees that we use for many purposes. In coming years, solar energy may be used to heat homes and water in many parts of the world. (Much of Israel's hot water has been heated by solar devices for years, even when the price of oil was much lower than it is now.) And if the prices of conventional energy supplies were to rise considerably higher than they now are, solar energy could be called on for much more of our needs, though this price rise seems unlikely given present technology. And even if the earth were sometime to run out of sources of energy for nuclear processes—a prospect so distant that it is a waste of time to talk about it—there are energy sources on other planets. Hence the notion that the supply of energy is finite because the earth's fossil fuels even its nuclear fuels are limited is sheer nonsense.

Whether there is an "ultimate" end to all this—that is, whether the energy supply really is "finite" after the sun and all the other planets have been exhausted—is a question so hypothetical that it should be compared with other metaphysical entertainments such as calculating the number of angels that can dance on the head of a pin. As long as we continue to draw energy from the sun, any conclusion about whether energy is "ultimately finite" or not has no bearing upon present policy decisions. . . .

SUMMARY

A conceptual quantity is not finite or infinite in itself. Rather, it is finite or infinite if you make it so—by your own definitions. If you define the subject of discussion suitably, and sufficiently closely so that it can be counted, then it is finite—for example, the money in your wallet or the socks in your top drawer. But without sufficient definition the subject is not finite—for example, the thoughts in your head, the strength of your wish to go to Turkey, your dog's love for you, the number of points in a one-inch line. You can, of course, develop definitions that will make these quantities finite; but that makes it clear that the finiteness inheres in you and in your definitions rather than in the money, love, or one-inch line themselves. There is no necessity either in logic or in historical trends to suggest that the supply of any given resource is "finite."

NOTES

1. Meadows, Dennis L.; William W. Behrens, III; Donella H. Meadows; Roger F. Naill; Jorgen Randers; and Erich K. O. Zahn, *Dynamics of Growth in a Finite World* (Cambridge, Mass.: Wright-Allen, 1974), p. vii.
2. U.S. The White House, Population and the American Future, *The Report of the Commission on Population Growth and the American Future* (New York: Signet, 1972), pp. 2–3.
3. Meadows, Dennis L. et al., *op. cit.,* p. 265.
4. U.S. The White House, The President's Materials Policy Commission (The Paley Commission), *Resources for Freedom,* 4 vols. (Washington, D.C.: GPO, 1952), summary of vol. 1, pp. 12–13; *idem,* p. 1.
5. Ibid., p. 2.
6. Ibid., p. 1.
7. Fuller, Buckminster, *Utopia or Oblivion: The Prospect for Humanity* (New York: Bantam, 1969), p. 4, quoted by Weber, James A., *Grow or Die!* (New Rochelle, N.Y.: Arlington House, 1977), p. 45.
8. I appreciate a discussion of this point with Alvin Roth.
9. Sheldon Lambert, quoted in *Newsweek,* June 27, 1977, p. 71.

Cornucopians and Neo-Malthusians

THOMAS HOMER-DIXON

Experts in environmental studies now commonly use the labels "cornucopian" for optimists like [Julian] Simon and "neo-Malthusian" for pessimists like Paul and Anne Ehrlich. Cornucopians do not worry much about protecting the stock of any single resource, because of their faith that market-driven human ingenuity can always be tapped to allow the substitution of more abundant resources to produce the same end-use service. . . .

Historically, cornucopians have been right to criticize the idea that resource scarcity places fixed limits on human activity. Time and time again, human beings have circumvented scarcities, and neo-Malthusians have often been justly accused of "crying wolf." But in assuming that this experience pertains to the future, cornucopians overlook seven factors.

First, whereas serious scarcities of critical resources in the past usually appeared singly, now we face multiple scarcities that exhibit powerful interactive, feedback, and threshold effects. An agricultural region may, for example, be simultaneously affected by degraded water and soil, greenhouse-induced precipitation changes, and increased ultraviolet radiation. This makes the future highly uncertain for policymakers and economic actors; tomorrow will be full of extreme events and surprises. Furthermore, as numerous resources become scarce simultaneously, it will be harder to identify substitution possibilities that produce the same end-use services at costs that prevailed when scarcity was less severe. Second, in the past the scarcity of a given resource usually increased slowly, allowing time for social, economic, and technological adjustment. But human populations are much larger and activities of individuals are, on a global average, much more resource-intensive than before. This means that debilitating scarcities often develop much more quickly: whole countries may be deforested in a few decades; most of a region's topsoil can disappear in a generation; and critical ozone depletion may occur in as little as twenty years. Third, today's consumption has far greater momentum than in the past, because of the size of the consuming population, the sheer quantity of material consumed by this population, and the density of its interwoven fabric of consumption activities. The countless individual and corporate economic actors making up human society are heavily committed to certain

From "On the Threshold: Environmental Change as Causes of Acute Conflict," by Thomas Homer-Dixon from *International Security*, Vol. 16 (Fall 1991), pp. 99–104. Copyright 1991 by MIT Press. Reprinted by permission. Portions of the text and some footnotes have been omitted.

patterns of resource use; and the ability of our markets to adapt may be sharply constrained by these entrenched interests.

These first three factors may soon combine to produce a daunting syndrome of environmentally induced scarcity: humankind will face multiple resource shortages that are interacting and unpredictable, that grow to crisis proportions rapidly, and that will be hard to address because of powerful commitments to certain consumption patterns.

The fourth reason that cornucopian arguments may not apply in the future is that the free-market price mechanism is a bad gauge of scarcity, especially for resources held in common, such as a benign climate and productive seas. In the past, many such resources seemed endlessly abundant; now they are being degraded and depleted, and we are learning that their increased scarcity often has tremendous bearing on a society's well-being. Yet this scarcity is at best reflected only indirectly in market prices. In addition, people often cannot participate in market transactions in which they have an interest, either because they lack the resources or because they are distant from the transaction process in time or space; in these cases the true scarcity of the resource is not reflected by its price.

The fifth reason is an extension of a point made earlier: market-driven adaptation to resource scarcity is most likely to succeed in wealthy societies, where abundant reserves of capital, knowledge, and talent help economic actors invent new technologies, identify conservation possibilities, and make the transition to new production and consumption patterns. Yet many of the societies facing the most serious environmental problems in the coming decades will be poor; even if they have efficient markets, lack of capital and know-how will hinder their response to these problems.

Sixth, cornucopians have an anachronistic faith in humankind's ability to unravel and manage the myriad processes of nature. There is no *a priori* reason to expect that human scientific and technical ingenuity can always surmount all types of scarcity. Human beings may not have the mental capacity to understand adequately the complexities of environmental-social systems. Or it may simply be impossible, given the physical, biological, and social laws governing these systems, to reduce all scarcity or repair all environmental damage. Moreover, the chaotic nature of these systems may keep us from fully anticipating the consequences of various adaptation and intervention strategies. Perhaps most important, scientific and technical knowledge must be built incrementally—layer upon layer—and its diffusion to the broader society often takes decades. Any technical solutions to environmental scarcity may arrive too late to prevent catastrophe.

Seventh and finally, future environmental problems, rather than inspiring the wave of ingenuity predicted by cornucopians, may instead reduce the supply of ingenuity available in a society. The success of market mechanisms depends on an intricate and stable system of institutions, social relations, and shared understandings. Cornucopians often overlook the role of *social* ingenuity in producing the complex legal and economic climate in which *technical* ingenuity can flourish. Policymakers must be clever "social engineers" to design and implement effective market mechanisms. Unfortunately, however, the syndrome of multiple, interacting, unpredictable, and rapidly changing environmental problems will increase the complexity and pressure of the policymaking setting. It will also generate increased "social friction" as elites and interest groups struggle to protect their prerogatives. The ability of policymakers to be good social engineers is likely to go *down*, not up, as these stresses increase.

Population size and growth are key variables producing the syndrome of environmental scarcity I have described. While sometimes population growth does not damage the environment, often this growth—in combination with prevailing social structures, technologies, and consumption patterns—makes environmental degradation worse. During the 1970s and early 1980s, family size dropped dramatically in many countries from six or seven children to three or four. But family planners have discovered that it is much more difficult to convince parents to forgo a further one or two children to bring family size down to replacement rate. . . . These developments have recently led the United Nations to increase its mid-range estimate of the globe's population when it stabilizes (predicted to occur towards the end of the twenty-first century) from 10.2 to 11 billion, which is over twice the size of the planet's current population.

Consequently, many countries will have to keep boosting their agricultural production by 2 to 4 percent per year well into the next century to avoid huge food imports. But, for the seven reasons discussed above, the social and technical engineers in these countries might not be able to supply the ever-increasing ingenuity required over this extended period. In particular, in many developing countries the effects of land scarcity and degradation are likely to become much more evident as the potential gains from green revolution technologies are fully realized. Unfortunately, there is no new generation of agricultural technologies waiting in the wings to keep productivity rising. Genetic engineering may eventually help scientists develop nitrogen-fixing, salinity-resistant, and drought-resistant grains, but their widespread use in the developing world is undoubtedly decades in the future.

Although we must be careful not to slip into environmental determinism, when it comes to the poorest countries on this planet we should not invest too much faith in the potential of human ingenuity to respond to multiple, interacting, and rapidly changing environmental problems once they have become severe. The most important of the seven factors above is the last: growing population, consumption, and environmental stresses will increase social friction. This will reduce the capacity of policymakers in developing countries to intervene as good social engineers in order to chart a sustainable development path and prevent further social disruption. Neo-Malthusians may underestimate human adaptability in *today's* environmental-social system, but as time passes their analysis may become ever more compelling.

What Makes Greenhouse Sense?

▅▅▅▅ THOMAS C. SCHELLING

The Kyoto Protocol should not be a partisan issue. The percentage reduction of greenhouse-gas emissions to which the United States committed itself by signing the 1997 Protocol to the 1992 UN Framework Convention on Climate Change was probably unachievable when the protocol was adopted. The protocol then languished in Washington for the final three years of the Clinton administration, which chose not to present it to the Senate for ratification. In accordance with a Senate resolution calling for the full participation of the main developing countries in the protocol's emissions-cutting requirements, that pause was supposed to allow time for negotiation to bring those countries on board. But nobody thought any such negotiation could produce results, and no negotiation was ever attempted. George W. Bush, succeeding to the presidency three years after the protocol's signing, had some choices and may not have made the best choice when he rejected the plan outright last year. But the one option he did not have was to submit the protocol to the Senate for ratification.

The U.S. "commitment" to the protocol meant cutting emissions significantly below their 1990 level by 2010—which required a 25 or 30 percent reduction in projected emissions levels. Such a cut was almost certainly infeasible when the Clinton administration signed the protocol in 1997. Three years later, with no action toward reducing emissions, no evidence of any planning on how to reduce emissions, and no attempt to inform the public or Congress about what might be required to meet that commitment, what might barely have been possible to achieve over 15 years—1997 to 2012—had become unreasonable. The Senate will not confirm a treaty unless it knows what actions the "commitment" entails, and no president could answer that question without a year's preparation. No such preparation appears to have been done in the Clinton administration. Bush, in stating that he would not submit the treaty to the Senate, at least avoided hypocrisy.

In declining to support the Kyoto Protocol, Bush outlined three concerns regarding any future greenhouse-gas agreement. First, the main developing countries need to adhere as full participants, as the Senate had earlier resolved; so far, developing countries have made clear they have no intention of doing so. Second, he cited the immense uncertainty about the likely extent of climate change and its impact on society. Third, he expressed a preference for "voluntarism" over

Reprinted by permission of *Foreign Affairs*, (Vol. 81, No. 3, May/June 2002). Copyright © 2002 by the Council on Foreign Relations, Inc.

enforceable regulation, even though he did not make clear whether his "volun-tarism" referred to domestic or international commitments.

A FAIR DEAL?

There is no likelihood that China, India, Indonesia, Brazil, or Nigeria will fully participate in any greenhouse-gas regime for the next few decades. They have done their best to make that point clear, and it serves no purpose to disbelieve them. Although their spokespersons regularly allege that rich countries are the most worried about climate change, developing nations have the most to lose from climate change. They are much more dependent on agriculture and will therefore suffer much more from global warming. Constrained by poverty and technological backwardness, their ability to adapt to climate change is limited. The best way for developing countries to mitigate global warming, therefore, is through economic growth.

There are undoubtedly opportunities in those countries for improved energy efficiencies that may simultaneously cut carbon dioxide emissions and improve public health; China, for example, could easily reduce its dependence on coal. But any major reductions in worldwide carbon dioxide emissions over the next few decades will have to be at the expense of the rich countries. Calling for the immediate participation of the big developing nations is futile. Once the developed countries have demonstrated that they can cooperate in reducing greenhouse gases, they can undertake arrangements to include developing countries in a greenhouse-gas regime, aiding them with economic incentives.

THE UNCERTAINTY PRINCIPLE

As Bush has emphasized, there are many uncertainties in the greenhouse-gas debate. But what is least uncertain is that climate change is real and likely to be serious. In any case, residual ambiguity about this question should not delay essential research and development in nonfossil energy sources, energy conservation, and policies to exploit the most cost-effective ways to reduce emissions.

A huge uncertainty that will make any lasting regime impossible for many decades to come, however, is how much carbon dioxide can safely be emitted over the coming century. A reading of the evidence—including climate sensitivity, regional climate changes, likely severity of impact, and the effectiveness of adaptation—suggests that the highest ceiling for carbon dioxide concentration, beyond which damage would be unacceptable, is probably between 600 and 1,200 parts per million. (It is currently about 370 ppm.) Further uncertainty exists about how much carbon dioxide can be absorbed into various natural sinks—oceans and forests—or sequestered underground or deep in the ocean. Thus any estimate of the level at which total carbon dioxide emissions worldwide over the coming hundred years should be capped is wide-ranging, falling between 500 billion tons and 2 trillion tons. (Worldwide emissions are currently approaching

7 billion tons, half of which stays in the atmosphere). In any event, what is ultimately unacceptable depends on the costs of moderating emissions, and these costs are also uncertain.

As a result, any "rationing scheme" would necessarily be subject to repeated revision and renegotiation. It is noteworthy that the Intergovernmental Panel on Climate Change—the international body, comprising more than a thousand scientists from scores of countries, that is the acknowledged (if controversial) authority on the subject—has never proposed what concentration of greenhouse gases would constitute unacceptable damage. Nor has any other representative body yet dared to hazard an estimate.

IN THE LONG RUN

The Kyoto Protocol had a short-term focus. It assumed correctly that developed countries could achieve significant reductions in emissions fairly promptly. As the National Academy of Sciences emphasized ten years ago, there are a number of opportunities to reduce emissions at little or no cost. They are mostly one-time measures that are not indefinitely exploitable. Had they been promptly attempted, they might have made the Kyoto approach feasible. Postponing these steps merely loses time.

But the protocol was embedded in the 1992 Convention on Climate Change, which was oriented toward the long term. So it has been interpreted as heralding the beginning (for developed countries) of a long-term decline in carbon dioxide emissions. But any reasonable trajectory of emissions in the future ought to show a rise for some decades and a rapid decline later in the century.

There are several reasons for such a trajectory. First, the technologies needed to drastically reduce fossil-fuel consumption through alternative energy sources, greater energy efficiency, and sequestration of carbon dioxide or its removal from fuel are not developed. Decades of investment are needed. The necessary investments will not happen by themselves; government action and support, especially in arranging market incentives, will be essential.

Second, it is economical to use durable equipment until it is due for replacement; early scrapping is wasteful. Much capital, such as electric power plants, is very long-lived. Auto fleets can turn over in 15 or 20 years, but most industrial plants cannot. Furthermore, deferring expenses saves interest on loans for capital investment. Finally, the richer countries will almost certainly have higher incomes in the future and be better able to afford drastic changes in energy use.

The economical trajectory for emissions over the coming century will differ substantially among the developed countries. Thus any reasonable rationing scheme should contemplate a timeline of at least a century, not a few decades. But no possible consensus exists on how much total emissions should be allowed for the coming century. That confusion makes any scheme of fixed quotas, including "emissions trading," out of the question.

In short, the Kyoto Protocol's exclusive focus on the short term neglected the crucial importance of expanding worldwide research and development of technologies to make severe reductions feasible later in the century. It also adopted a format incompatible with the most economical trajectory of emissions over time: a rise for some decades followed by a sharp decline.

FREE TO CHOOSE?

The Bush administration has favored "voluntary" measures over "mandatory" ones. But it is not clear whether these terms referred mainly to domestic or to international measures. Domestically, a voluntary approach would make the greenhouse question unique among issues of environment and health, which fall under government jurisdiction. The research of the National Institutes of Health, for example, is universally acknowledged to be essential; leaving such research to the market or to voluntary industrial altruism would not appeal to anyone. The same approach should apply to research on new low-carbon or non-carbon energies or carbon sequestration. Major replacement of fossil fuels or reductions in energy demand, carbon dioxide "containment" efforts, or investment in new technologies to bring them about will not occur without serious market incentives. Domestically, "voluntarism" is an ineffectual approach that would put blame only on firms that have no market support for what they may be asked to do.

An international regime, in contrast, can be only voluntary. Commitments will not be "enforceable." At best they may be honored, because respectable governments prefer to keep commitments. The U.S. government has a strong aversion to any commitments it does not think it will keep. And neither the United States nor the other major developed countries will likely accept serious sanctions for missing emissions targets. There is talk of "binding commitments," as if "commitment" itself was not binding, but there is no expectation of penalties for shortfall.

HOT AIR

Emissions trading is popular, especially with economists. Trading means that any nation that underuses its emissions quota (commitment) may transfer its unused quota (the excess of its allowed emissions over actual emissions) to any country that offers financial compensation. The "purchasing" nation then uses its bought allotment to increase its own emissions quota. The idea is to permit emissions to be reduced wherever their reduction is most economical. Countries that have the greatest difficulty (highest costs) in reducing emissions can purchase relief from countries that are comparatively most able to effect emissions reductions.

When 2,000 economists, including some Nobel laureates, circulated a recommendation a few years ago that nations should adopt enforceable quotas for carbon dioxide emissions and allow the purchase and sale of unused quotas, the concept was aesthetically pleasing but politically unconvincing. Although emissions should be reduced in those countries where they can be cut most economically, the economists' proposed trading system was perfectionist and impractical. The problem with trading regimes is that initial quotas are negotiated to reflect what each nation can reasonably be expected to reduce. Any country that is tempted to sell part of an emissions quota will realize that the regime is continually subject to renegotiation, so selling any "excess" is tantamount to admitting it got a generous allotment the last time around. It then sets itself up for stiffer negotiation next time.

Still, the latest version of the Kyoto Protocol, negotiated in November 2001, does contemplate trading and even anticipates who the sellers will be. It conceded carbon dioxide emissions quotas to Russia and Ukraine—countries that, because of their depressed economies, will keep their emissions relatively low during the Kyoto time period. They will have what is called "hot air" to sell to any Kyoto participant willing to pay to remain within its own commitment. This arrangement may have been an essential inducement to get Russia to ratify the Kyoto Protocol, and countries that were not sure they would meet their commitments on their own saw it as a cheap safety valve.

It requires a sense of humor to appreciate this latest modification of the Kyoto Protocol: respectable governments being willing to pay money, or make their domestic industries pay money, to an ailing former enemy in the guise of a sophisticated emissions-trading scheme. The purpose is to bribe the recipient into ratifying a treaty and providing governments a cheap way to buy out of emissions commitments, with the pretense that it serves to reduce emissions in accordance with the principle of comparative advantage.

PAST AS PROLOGUE

There is remarkable consensus among economists that nations will not make sacrifices in the interest of global objectives unless they are bound by a regime that can impose penalties if they do not comply. Despite this consensus, however, there is no historical example of any regime that could impose effective penalties, at least with something of the magnitude of global warming. But there are historical precedents of regimes that lacked coercive authority but were still able to divide benefits and burdens of a magnitude perhaps comparable to the demands of a global-warming regime. (In this case, cutting emissions is the burden; allowing emissions is the benefit.) There are two interesting precedents outside wartime. Both hold promise.

One is the division of Marshall Plan aid, which began in 1948. The magnitude of the aid, as a percentage of the national income of the recipient countries, is not easy to determine today, because most European currencies were grossly overvalued after the war. But a reasonable estimate places the aid's value anywhere from 5 percent to 20 percent of national income, depending on the recipient country.

For the first two years of the Marshall Plan, the United States divided the money itself. For the third year, it insisted that the recipient countries divide the aid among themselves. Government representatives therefore went through a process of "reciprocal multilateral scrutiny." Each government prepared extensive documentation of all aspects of its economy: its projected private and public investments, consumption, imports, exports, what it was doing about railroads and livestock herds, how it was rationing gasoline or butter, and how its living standard compared to prewar conditions. Each government team was examined and cross-examined by other government teams; it then defended itself, revised its proposals, and cross-examined other teams. More aid for one country meant less for the rest.

There was no formula. Rather, each country developed "relevant criteria." The parties did not quite reach agreement, but they were close enough that two respected people—the secretary-general of the Organization for European Economic Cooperation and the representative of Belgium (which was not requesting any aid)—offered a proposed division that was promptly accepted. Of course, the United States was demanding the countries reach agreement on aid. Today, there is no such "angel" behind greenhouse negotiations. Still, the Marshall Plan represents something of a precedent.

NATO went through the same process a year later (1951–52) in its "burden-sharing exercise." This time, it involved U.S. aid and included targets for national military participation, conscription of soldiers, investments in equipment, contributions to military infrastructure and real estate, and so on. Again, the process was one of reciprocal scrutiny and cross-examination, with high-level officials spending months negotiating. Again, they did not quite reach final agreement. But this time, three officials fashioned a proposal that was accepted. After one more year, NATO proceeded without U.S. aid—except for the contribution of U.S. military forces to NATO itself.

With the possible exception of the reciprocal-trade negotiations that ultimately created the World Trade Organization (WTO), the Marshall Plan and NATO experiences are the only non-wartime precedents in which so many countries cooperated over such high economic stakes. They were not aesthetically satisfying processes: no formulae were developed, just a civilized procedure of argument. Those examples are a model for what might succeed the Kyoto Protocol if it fails or evolves into something else. Their procedure is one that the main developed nations might pursue prior to any attempt to include developing nations. NATO has been an enormous success; member nations made large contributions in money, troops, and real estate. They did it all voluntarily; there were no penalties for shortfalls in performance. And, without explicit trading, they practiced the theory of comparative advantage (in geographical location, for instance, or demographics, or industrial structure). It was an example of highly motivated partnership, involving resources on a scale commensurate with what a greenhouse regime might eventually require.

The WTO experience is also instructive. It involves a much broader array of nations than NATO does, and it has its own system of sanctions: the enforcement of commitments. Because it is essentially a system of detailed reciprocal undertakings, and because most infractions tend to be bilateral and specific as to commodities, offended parties can undertake retaliation and make the penalty fit the crime (thus exercising the principle of reciprocity). A judicial system can evaluate offenses on their merits to authorize or approve the retaliatory measure. Fulfilling or failing WTO commitments is piecemeal, not holistic. There is no overall "target" to which a WTO member is committed. In contrast, if a greenhouse-regime nation fails to meet its target, there is no particular offended partner to take the initiative and penalize the offender—and if there were, it might be difficult to identify an appropriate "reciprocal" retaliatory measure.

PROMISES, PROMISES

One striking contrast between NATO and the Kyoto Protocol deserves emphasis: the difference between "inputs" and "outputs," or actions and results. NATO nations argued about what they should do, and commitments were made to actions. What countries actually did—raise and train troops; procure equipment, ammunition, and supplies; and deploy these assets geographically—could be observed, estimated, and compared. But results—such as how much each NATO nation's actions contributed to deterring the Warsaw Pact—could not be remotely approximated.

Like NATO, commitments under the WTO's auspices are also made to what nations will do, or will abstain from doing; there are no commitments to specific consequences. No nation is committed to imports of any sort from anywhere; it is committed only to its actions—such as tariffs and other restrictions, subsidies, and tax preferences.

With the Kyoto Protocol, commitments were made not to actions but to results that were to be measured after a decade or more. This approach has disadvantages. An obvious one is that no one can tell, until close to the target date, which nations are on course to meet their goals. More important, nations undertaking result-based commitments are unlikely to have any reliable way of knowing what actions will be required—that is, what quantitative results will occur on what timetable for various policies. The Kyoto approach implied without evident justification that governments actually knew how to reach 10- or 15-year emissions goals. (The energy crisis of the 1970s did not last long enough to reveal, for example, the long-run elasticity of demand for motor fuel, electricity, industrial heat, and so on.) A government that commits to actions at least knows what it is committed to, and its partners also know and can observe compliance. In contrast, a government that commits to the consequences of various actions on emissions can only hope that its estimates, or guesses, are on target, and so can its partners.

SPREADING THE WEALTH

Eventually, to bring in the developing nations and achieve emissions reductions most economically, the proper approach is not a trading system but financial contributions from the rich countries to an institution that would help finance energy-efficient and decarbonized technologies in the developing world. Examples might be funding a pipeline to bring Siberian natural gas to northern China to help replace carbon-intensive coal, or financing the imported components of nuclear-power reactors, which emit no greenhouse gases.

Such a regime will suffer the appearance of "foreign aid." But that is the form it will necessarily take. The recipients will benefit and should be required to assume commitments to emissions-reducing actions. Meanwhile, the burden on the rich countries will undoubtedly be more political than economic. Large-scale aid for reducing carbon dioxide emissions in China is economically bearable but enormously difficult to justify to the American public, or to agree on with Japan and the European Union.

While European countries are lamenting the U.S. defection from the Kyoto Protocol, a major U.S. unilateral initiative in research and development oriented toward phasing out fossil fuels over the next century would both produce welcome returns and display American seriousness about global warming.

The greenhouse gas issue will persist through the entire century and beyond. Even though the developed nations have not succeeded in finding a collaborative way to approach the issue, it is still early. We have been at it for only a decade. But time should not be wasted getting started. Global climate change may become what nuclear arms control was for the past half century. It took more than a decade to develop a concept of arms control. It is not surprising that it is taking that long to find a way to come to consensus on an approach to the greenhouse problem.

NEW ACTORS
AND NEW FORCES

Transnational Activist Networks

MARGARET E. KECK AND KATHRYN SIKKINK

Networks are forms of organization characterized by voluntary, reciprocal, and horizontal patterns of communication and exchange. . . . Major actors in advocacy networks may include the following: (1) international and domestic nongovernmental research and advocacy organizations; (2) local social movements; (3) foundations; (4) the media; (5) churches, trade unions, consumer organizations, and intellectuals; (6) parts of regional and international intergovernmental organizations; and (7) parts of the executive and/or parliamentary branches of governments. Not all these will be present in each advocacy network. Initial research suggests, however, that international and domestic NGOs [non-governmental organizations] play a central role in all advocacy networks, usually initiating actions and pressuring more powerful actors to take positions. NGOs introduce new ideas, provide information, and lobby for policy changes.

Groups in a network share values and frequently exchange information and services. The flow of information among actors in the network reveals a dense web of connections among these groups, both formal and informal. The movement of funds and services is especially notable between foundations and NGOs, and some NGOs provide services such as training for other NGOs in the same and sometimes other advocacy networks. Personnel also circulate within and among networks, as relevant players move from one to another in a version of the "revolving door.". . .

Advocacy networks are not new. We can find examples as far back as the nineteenth-century campaign for the abolition of slavery. But their number, size, and professionalism, and the speed, density, and complexity of international linkages among them has grown dramatically in the last three decades. . . .

Transnational advocacy networks appear most likely to emerge around those issues where (1) channels between domestic groups and their governments are blocked or hampered or where such channels are ineffective for resolving a conflict, setting into motion the "boomerang" pattern of influence characteristic of these networks; (2) activists or "political entrepreneurs" believe that networking will further their missions and campaigns, and actively promote networks; and (3) conferences and other forms of international contact create arenas for forming and strengthening networks. Where channels of participation are blocked, the international arena may be the only means that domestic activists have to gain attention to their issues. Boomerang strategies are most common in campaigns where the target is a state's domestic policies or behavior; where a campaign seeks broad procedural change involving dispersed actors, strategies are more diffuse.

It is no accident that so many advocacy networks address claims about rights in their campaigns. Governments are the primary "guarantors" of rights, but also their primary violators. When a government violates or refuses to recognize rights, individuals and domestic groups often have no recourse within domestic political or judicial arenas. They may seek international connections finally to express their concerns and even to protect their lives.

When channels between the state and its domestic actors are blocked, the boomerang pattern of influence characteristic of transnational networks may occur: Domestic NGOs bypass their state and directly search out international allies to try to bring pressure on their states from outside. This is most obviously the case in human rights campaigns. Similarly, indigenous rights campaigns and environmental campaigns that support the demands of local peoples for participation in development projects that would affect them frequently involve this kind of triangulation. Linkages are important for both sides: For the less powerful Third World actors, networks provide access, leverage, and information (and often money) they could not expect to have on their own; for northern groups, they make credible the assertion that they are struggling with, and not only for, their southern partners. Not surprisingly, such relationships can produce considerable tensions. . . .

Just as oppression and injustice do not themselves produce movements or revolutions, claims around issues amenable to international action do not produce transnational networks. Activists—"people who care enough about some issue that they are prepared to incur significant costs and act to achieve their goals"[1]—do. They create them when they believe that transnational networking will further their organizational missions—by sharing information, attaining greater visibility, gaining access to wider publics, multiplying channels of institutional access, and so forth. For example, in the campaign to stop the promotion of infant formula to poor women in developing countries, organizers settled on a boycott of Nestlé, the largest producer, as its main tactic. Because Nestlé was a transnational actor, activists believed a transnational network was necessary to bring pressure on corporations and governments.[2] Over time, in such issue areas, participation in transnational networks has become an essential component of the collective identities of the activists involved, and networking a part of their common repertoire.

The political entrepreneurs who become the core networkers for a new campaign have often gained experience in earlier ones.

Opportunities for network activities have increased over the last two decades. In addition to the efforts of pioneers, a proliferation of international organizations and conferences has provided foci for connections. Cheaper air travel and new electronic communication technologies speed information flows and simplify personal contact among activists. Underlying these trends is a broader cultural shift. The new networks have depended on the creation of a new kind of global public (or civil society), which grew as a cultural legacy of the 1960s. . . .

HOW DO TRANSNATIONAL ADVOCACY NETWORKS WORK?

Transnational advocacy networks seek influence in many of the same ways that other political groups or social movements do. Since they are not powerful in a traditional sense of the word, they must use the power of their information, ideas, and strategies to alter the information and value contexts within which states make policies. The bulk of what networks do might be termed persuasion or socialization, but neither process is devoid of conflict. Persuasion and socialization often involve not just reasoning with opponents, but also bringing pressure, arm-twisting, encouraging sanctions, and shaming. . . .

Our typology of tactics that networks use in their efforts at persuasion, socialization, and pressure includes (1) *information politics,* or the ability to quickly and credibly generate politically usable information and move it to where it will have the most impact; (2) *symbolic politics,* or the ability to call upon symbols, actions, or stories that make sense of a situation for an audience that is frequently far away; (3) *leverage politics,* or the ability to call upon powerful actors to affect a situation where weaker members of a network are unlikely to have influence; and (4) *accountability politics,* or the effort to hold powerful actors to their previously stated policies or principles. . . .

Network members actively seek ways to bring issues to the public agenda by framing them in innovative ways and by seeking hospitable venues. Sometimes they create issues by framing old problems in new ways; occasionally they help transform other actors' understanding of their identities and their interests. Land use rights in the Amazon, for example, took on an entirely different character and gained quite different allies viewed in a deforestation frame than they did in either social justice or regional development frames. In the 1970s and 1980s many states decided for the first time that promotion of human rights in other countries was a legitimate foreign policy goal and an authentic expression of national interest. This decision came in part from interaction with an emerging global human rights network. We argue that this represents not the victory of morality over self-interest, but a transformed understanding of national interest, possible in part because of structured interactions between state components and networks. This changed understanding cannot be derived solely from changing global and economic conditions, although these are relevant. . . .

Information Politics

Information binds network members together and is essential for network effectiveness. Many information exchanges are informal—telephone calls, e-mail and fax communications, and the circulation of newsletters, pamphlets, and bulletins. They provide information that would not otherwise be available, from sources that might not otherwise be heard, and they must make this information comprehensible and useful to activists and publics who may be geographically and/or socially distant.

Nonstate actors gain influence by serving as alternate sources of information. Information flows in advocacy networks provide not only facts but testimony—stories told by people whose lives have been affected. Moreover, activists interpret facts and testimony, usually framing issues simply, in terms of right and wrong, because their purpose is to persuade people and stimulate them to act. How does this process of persuasion occur? An effective frame must show that a given state of affairs is neither natural nor accidental, identify the responsible party or parties, and propose credible solutions. These aims require clear, powerful messages that appeal to shared principles, which often have more impact on state policy than advice of technical experts. An important part of the political struggle over information is precisely whether an issue is defined primarily as technical—and thus subject to consideration by "qualified" experts—or as something that concerns a broader global constituency. . . .

Networks strive to uncover and investigate problems, and alert the press and policymakers. One activist described this as the "human rights methodology"—"promoting change by reporting facts."[3] To be credible, the information produced by networks must be reliable and well documented. To gain attention, the information must be timely and dramatic. Sometimes these multiple goals of information politics conflict, but both credibility and drama seem to be essential components of a strategy aimed at persuading publics and policymakers to change their minds.

The notion of "reporting facts" does not fully express the way networks strategically use information to frame issues. Networks call attention to issues, or even create issues by using language that dramatizes and draws attention to their concerns. A good example is the recent campaign against the practice of female genital mutilation. Before 1976 the widespread practice of female circumcision in many African and a few Asian and Middle Eastern countries was known outside these regions mainly among medical experts and anthropologists.[4] A controversial campaign, initiated in 1974 by a network of women's and human rights organizations, began to draw wider attention to the issues by renaming the problem. Previously the practice was referred to by technically "neutral" terms such as female circumcision, clitoridectomy, or infibulation. The campaign around female genital "mutilation" raised its salience, literally creating the issue as a matter of public international concern. By renaming the practice the network broke the linkage with male circumcision (seen as a personal medical or cultural decision), implied a linkage with the more feared procedure of castration, and reframed the issue as one of violence against women. It thus resituated the practice as a human rights violation. . . .

Human rights activists, baby food campaigners, and women's groups . . . dramatize the situations of the victims and turn the cold facts into human stories, intended to move people to action. The baby food campaign, for example, relied heavily on public health studies that proved that improper bottle feeding contributed to infant malnutrition and mortality, and that corporate sales promotion was leading to a decline in breast feeding. Network activists repackaged and interpreted this information in dramatic ways designed to promote action: The British development organization War on Want published a pamphlet entitled "The Baby Killers," which the Swiss Third World Action Group translated into German and retitled "Nestlé Kills Babies." Nestlé inadvertently gave activists a prominent public forum when it sued the Third World Action Group for defamation and libel. . . .

A dense web of north-south exchange, aided by computer and fax communication, means that governments can no longer monopolize information flows as they could a mere half-decade ago. These technologies have had an enormous impact on moving information to and from Third World countries, where mail service has often been slow and precarious; they also give special advantages of course, to organizations that have access to them. A good example of the new informational role of networks occurred when U.S. environmentalists pressured President George Bush to raise the issue of gold miners' ongoing invasions of the Yanomami indigenous reserve when Brazilian president Fernando Collor de Mello was in Washington in 1991. Collor believed that he had squelched protest over the Yanomami question by creating major media events out of the dynamiting of airstrips used by gold miners, but network members had current information faxed from Brazil, and they countered his claims with evidence that miners had rebuilt the airstrips and were still invading the Yanomami area. . . .

The media is an essential partner in network information politics. To reach a broader audience, networks strive to attract press attention. Sympathetic journalists may become part of the network, but more often network activists cultivate a reputation for credibility with the press, and package their information in a timely and dramatic way to draw press attention.

Symbolic Politics

Activists frame issues by identifying and providing convincing explanations for powerful symbolic events, which in turn become catalysts for the growth of networks. Symbolic interpretation is part of the process of persuasion by which networks create awareness and expand their constituencies. Awarding the 1992 Nobel Peace Prize to Maya activist Rigoberta Menchú and the UN's designation of 1993 as the Year of Indigenous Peoples heightened public awareness of the situation of indigenous peoples in the Americas. Indigenous peoples' use of 1992, the 500th anniversary of the voyage of Columbus to the Americas, to raise a host of issues well illustrates the use of symbolic events to reshape understandings. . . .

Leverage Politics

Activists in advocacy networks are concerned with political effectiveness. Their definition of effectiveness often includes some policy change by "target actors" such as governments, international financial institutions like the World Bank, or private actors like transnational corporations. In order to bring about policy change, networks need to pressure and persuade more powerful actors. To gain influence the networks seek leverage (the word appears often in the discourse of advocacy organizations) over more powerful actors. By leveraging more powerful institutions, weak groups gain influence far beyond their ability to influence state practices directly. The identification of material or moral leverage is a crucial strategic step in network campaigns.

Material leverage usually links the issue to money or goods (but potentially also to votes in international organizations, prestigious offices, or other benefits). The human rights issue became negotiable because governments or financial institutions connected human rights practices to military and economic aid, or to bilateral diplomatic relations. In the United States, human rights groups got leverage by providing policy-makers with information that convinced them to cut off military and economic aid. To make the issue negotiable, NGOs first had to raise its profile or salience, using information and symbolic politics. Then more powerful members of the network had to link cooperation to something else of value: money, trade, or prestige. Similarly, in the environmentalists' multilateral development bank campaign, linkage of environmental protection with access to loans was very powerful.

Although NGO influence often depends on securing powerful allies, their credibility still depends in part on their ability to mobilize their own members and affect public opinion via the media. In democracies the potential to influence votes gives large membership organizations an advantage over nonmembership organizations in lobbying for policy change; environmental organizations, several of whose memberships number in the millions, are more likely to have this added clout than are human rights organizations.

Moral leverage involves what some commentators have called the *"mobilization of shame,"* where the behavior of target actors is held up to the light of international scrutiny. Network activists exert moral leverage on the assumption that governments value the good opinion of others; insofar as networks can demonstrate that a state is violating international obligations or is not living up to its own claims, they hope to jeopardize its credit enough to motivate a change in policy or behavior. The degree to which states are vulnerable to this kind of pressure varies, and will be discussed further below.

Accountability Politics

Networks devote considerable energy to convincing governments and other actors to publicly change their positions on issues. This is often dismissed as inconsequential change, since talk is cheap and governments sometimes change discursive positions hoping to divert network and public attention. Network activists, however, try to make such statements into opportunities for accountability politics. Once a government has publicly committed itself to a principle—for example, in favor of human rights or democracy—networks can use those positions, and their command of information, to expose the distance between discourse and practice. This is embarrassing to many governments, which may try to save face by closing that distance.

Perhaps the best example of network accountability politics was the ability of the human rights network to use the human rights provisions of the 1975 Helsinki Accords to pressure the Soviet Union and the governments of Eastern Europe for change. The Helsinki Accords helped revive the human rights movement in the Soviet Union, spawned new organizations like the Moscow Helsinki Group and the Helsinki Watch Committee in the United States, and helped protect activists from repression.[5] The human rights network referred to Moscow's obligations under the Helsinki Final Act and juxtaposed these with examples of abuses. . . .

NOTES

1. Pamela E. Oliver and Gerald Marwell, "Mobilizing Technologies for Collective Action," in *Frontiers in Social Movement Theory*, ed. Aldon D. Morris and Carol McClurg Mueller (New Haven: Yale University Press, 1992), p. 252.
2. See Kathryn Sikkink, "Codes of Conduct for Transnational Corporations: The Case of the WHO/UNICEF Code," *International Organization* 40 (Autumn 1986): 815–40.
3. Dorothy Q. Thomas, "Holding Governments Accountable by Public Pressure," in *Ours by Right: Women's Rights as Human Rights*, ed. Joanna Kerr (London: Zed Books, 1993), p. 83.
4. Female genital mutilation is most widely practiced in Africa, where it is reported to occur in at least twenty-six countries. Between 85 and 114 million women in the world today are estimated to have experienced genital mutilation. *World Bank Development Report 1993: Investing in Health* (New York: Oxford University Press, 1993), p. 50.
5. Discussion of the Helsinki Accords is based on Daniel Thomas, "Norms and Change in World Politics: Human Rights, the Helsinki Accords, and the Demise of Communism, 1975–1990," Ph.D. diss., Cornell University, 1997.

Human Rights in World Politics

RHODA E. HOWARD AND JACK DONNELLY

The International Human Rights Covenants[1] note that human rights "derive from the inherent dignity of the human person." But while the struggle to assure a life of dignity is probably as old as human society itself, reliance on human rights as a mechanism to realize that dignity is a relatively recent development.

Human rights are, by definition, the rights one has simply because one is a human being. This simple and relatively uncontroversial definition, though, is more complicated than it may appear on the surface. It identifies human rights as *rights*, in the strict and strong sense of that term, and it establishes that they are held simply by virtue of being human. . . .

WHAT RIGHTS DO WE HAVE?

The definition of human or natural rights as the rights of each person simply as a human being specifies their character; they are rights. The definition also specifies their source: (human) nature. . . .

What is it in human nature that gives rise to human rights? There are two basic answers to this question. On the one hand, many people argue that human rights arise from human needs, from the naturally given requisites for physical and mental health and well-being. On the other hand, many argue that human rights reflect the minimum requirements for human dignity or *moral* personality. These latter arguments derive from essentially philosophical theories of human "nature," dignity, or moral personality.

Needs theories of human rights run into the problem of empirical confirmations; the simple fact is that there is sound scientific evidence only for a very narrow list of human needs. But if we use "needs" in a broader, in part nonscientific, sense, then the two theories overlap. We can thus say that people have human rights to those things "needed" for a life of dignity, for the full development of their moral personality. The "nature" that gives rise to human rights is thus *moral* nature.

This moral nature is, in part, a social creation. Human nature, in the relevant sense, is an amalgam consisting both of psycho-biological facts (constraints and possibilities) and of the social structures and experiences that are no less a part of the essential nature of men and women. Human beings are not isolated individuals, but rather individuals who are essentially social creatures, in part even social creations. Therefore, a theory of human rights must recognize both the essential universality of human nature and the no less essential particularity arising from cultural and socioeconomic traditions and institutions.

Human rights are, by their nature, universal; it is not coincidental that we have a *Universal* Declaration of Human Rights, for human rights are the rights of all men and women. Therefore, in its basic outlines a list of human rights must apply at least more or less "across the board." But the nature of human beings is also shaped by the particular societies in which they live. Thus the universality of human rights must be qualified in at least two important ways.

First, the forms in which universal rights are institutionalized are subject to some legitimate cultural and political variation. For example, what counts as popular participation in government may vary, within a certain range, from society to society. Both multiparty and single-party regimes may reflect legitimate notions of political participation. Although the ruling party cannot be removed from power, in some one-party states individual representatives can be changed and electoral pressure may result in significant policy changes.

Second, and no less important, the universality (in principle) of human rights is qualified by the obvious fact that any particular list, no matter how broad its cross-cultural and international acceptance, reflects the necessarily contingent understandings of a particular era. For example, in the seventeenth and eighteenth centuries, the rights of man were indeed the rights of men, not women, and social and economic rights (other than the right to private property) were unheard of. Thus we must expect a gradual evolution of even a consensual list of human rights, as collective understandings of the essential elements of human dignity, the conditions of moral personality, evolve in response to changing ideas and material circumstances.

In other words, human rights are by their essential nature universal in form. They are, by definition, the rights held by each (and every) person simply as a human being. But any universal list of human rights is subject to a variety of justifiable implementations.

In our time, the Universal Declaration of Human Rights (1948) is a minimum list that is nearly universally accepted, although additional rights have been added (e.g., self-determination) and further new rights (e.g., the right to nondiscrimination on the grounds of sexual orientation or the right to peace) may be added in the future. We are in no position to offer a philosophical defense of the list of rights in the Universal Declaration. To do so would require an account of the source of human rights—human nature—that would certainly exceed the space available to us. Nonetheless, the Universal Declaration is nearly universally accepted by states. For practical political purposes we can treat it as authoritative. . . .

INTERNATIONAL HUMAN RIGHTS INSTITUTIONS

The international context of national practices deserves some attention. There are, as we have already noted, international human rights standards that are widely accepted—in principle at least—by states. Thus the discussion and evaluation of national practices take place within an overarching set of international standards to which virtually all states have explicitly committed themselves. Whatever the force of claims of national sovereignty, with its attendant legal immunity from international action, the evaluation of national human rights practices from the perspective of the international standards of the Universal Declaration thus is certainly appropriate, even if one is uncomfortable with the moral claim sketched above that such universalistic scrutiny is demanded by the very idea of human rights.

In the literature on international relations it has recently become fashionable to talk of "international regimes," that is, norms and decision-making procedures accepted by states in a given issue area. National human rights practices do take place within the broader context of an international human rights regime centered on the United Nations.

We have already sketched the principal norms of this regime—the list of rights in the Universal Declaration. These norms/rights are further elaborated in two major treaties, the International Covenant on Economic, Social and Cultural Rights and the International Covenant on Civil and Political Rights, which were opened for signature and ratification in 1966 and came into force in 1976. Almost all of the countries studied in this volume have ratified (become a party to) both the Covenant on Civil and Political Rights and the Covenant on Economic, Social and Cultural Rights. . . . Even the countries that are not parties to the Covenants often accept the principles of the Universal Declaration. In addition, there are a variety of single-issue treaties that have been formulated under UN auspices on topics such as racial discrimination, the rights of women, and torture. These later Covenants and Conventions go into much greater detail than the Universal Declaration and include a few important changes. For example, the Covenants prominently include a right to national self-determination, which is absent in the Universal Declaration, but do not include a right to private property. Nevertheless, for the most part they can be seen simply as elaborations on the Universal Declaration, which remains the central normative document in the international human rights regime.

What is the legal and political force of these norms? The Universal Declaration of Human Rights was proclaimed in 1948 by the United Nations General Assembly. As such, it has no force of law. Resolutions of the General Assembly, even solemn declarations, are merely recommendations to states; the General Assembly has no international legislative powers. Over the years, however, the Universal Declaration has come to be something more than a mere recommendation.

There are two principal sources of international law, namely, treaty and custom. Although today we tend to think first of treaty, historically custom is at least as important. A rule or principle attains the force of customary international law when it can meet two tests. First, the principle or rule must reflect the general practice of the overwhelming majority of states. Second, what lawyers call *opinio juris*, the sense of obligation, must be taken into account. Is the customary practice seen by states as an obligation, rather than a mere convenience or courtesy? Today it is a common view of international lawyers that the Universal Declaration has attained something of the status of customary international law, so that the rights it contains are in some important sense binding on states.

Furthermore, the International Human Rights Covenants are treaties and as such do have the force of international law, but only for the parties to the treaties, that is, those states that have (voluntarily) ratified or acceded to the treaties. The same is true of the single-issue treaties that round out the regime's norms. It is perhaps possible that the norms of the Covenants are coming to acquire the force of customary international law even for states that are not parties. But in either case, the fundamental weakness of international law is underscored: Virtually all international legal obligations are voluntarily accepted.

This is obviously the case for treaties: states are free to become parties or not entirely as they choose. It is no less true, though, of custom, where the tests of state practice and *opinio juris* likewise assure that international legal obligation is only voluntarily acquired. In fact, a state that explicitly rejects a practice during the process of custom formation is exempt even from customary international legal obligations. For example, Saudi Arabia's objection to the provisions on the equal rights of women during the drafting of the Universal Declaration might be held to exempt it from such a norm, even if the norm is accepted internationally as customarily binding. Such considerations are particularly important when we ask what force there is to international law and what mechanisms exist to implement and enforce the rights specified in the Universal Declaration and the Covenants.

Acceptance of an obligation by states does not carry with it acceptance of any method of international enforcement. Quite the contrary. Unless there is an explicit enforcement mechanism attached to the obligation, its enforcement rests simply on the good faith of the parties. The Universal Declaration contains no enforcement mechanisms of any sort. Even if we accept it as having the force of international law, its implementation is left entirely in the hands of individual states. The Covenants do have some implementation machinery, but the machinery's practical weakness is perhaps its most striking feature. . . .

The one other major locus of activity in the international human rights regime is the UN Commission on Human Rights. In addition to being the body that played the principal role in the formulation of the Universal Declaration, the Covenants, and most of the major single-issue human rights treaties, it has some weak implementation powers. Its public discussion of human rights situations in various countries can help to mobilize international public opinion, which is not always utterly useless in helping to reform national practice. For example, in the 1970s the Commission played a major role in publicizing the human rights conditions in Chile, Israel, and South Africa. Furthermore, it is empowered by ECOSOC resolution 1503 (1970) to investigate communications (complaints) from individuals and groups that "appear to reveal a consistent pattern of gross and reliably attested violations of human rights."

The 1503 procedure, however, is at least as thoroughly hemmed in by constraints as are the other enforcement mechanisms that we have considered.[2] Although individuals may communicate grievances, the 1503 procedure deals only with "*situations*" of gross and systematic violations, not the particular cases of individuals. Individuals cannot even obtain an international judgment in their particular case, let alone international enforcement of the human rights obligations of their government. Furthermore, the entire procedure remains confidential until a case is concluded, although the Commission does publicly announce a "blacklist" of countries being studied. In only four cases (Equatorial Guinea, Haiti, Malawi, and Uruguay) has the Commission gone public with a 1503 case. Its most forceful conclusion was a 1980 resolution provoked by the plight of Jehovah's Witnesses in Malawi, which merely expressed the hope that all human rights were being respected in Malawi.

In addition to this global human rights regime, there are regional regimes. The 1981 African Charter of Human and Peoples' Rights, drawn up by the Organization of African Unity, provides for a Human Rights Commission, but it is not yet functioning. In Europe and the Americas there are highly developed systems involving both commissions with very strong investigatory powers and regional human rights courts with the authority to make legally binding decisions on complaints by individuals (although only eight states have accepted the jurisdiction of the Inter-American Court of Human Rights).

Even in Europe and the Americas, however, implementation and enforcement remain primarily national. In nearly thirty years the European Commission of Human Rights has considered only about 350 cases, while the European Court of Human Rights has handled only one-fifth that number. Such regional powers certainly should not be ignored or denigrated. They provide authoritative interpretations in cases of genuine disagreements and a powerful check on backsliding and occasional deviations by states. But the real force of even the European regime lies in the voluntary acceptance of human rights by the states in question, which has infinitely more to do with domestic politics than with international procedures.

In sum, at the international level there are comprehensive, authoritative human rights norms that are widely accepted as binding on all states. Implementation and enforcement of these norms, however, both in theory and in practice, are left to states. The international context of national human rights practices certainly cannot be ignored. Furthermore, international norms may have an important socializing effect on national leaders and be useful to national advocates of improved domestic human rights practices. But the real work of implementing and enforcing human rights takes place at the national level. . . . Before the level of the nation-state is discussed, however, one final element of the international context needs to be considered, namely, human rights as an issue in national foreign policies.

HUMAN RIGHTS AND FOREIGN POLICY

Beyond the human rights related activities of states in international institutions such as those discussed in the preceding section, many states have chosen to make human rights a concern in their bilateral foreign relations.[3] in fact, much of the surge of interest in human rights in the last decade can be traced to the catalyzing effect of President Jimmy Carter's (1977–1981) efforts to make international human rights an objective of U.S. foreign policy.

In a discussion of human rights as an issue in national foreign policy, at least three problems need to be considered. First, a nation must select a particular set of rights to pursue. Second, the legal and moral issues raised by intervention on behalf of human rights abroad need to be explored. Third, human rights concerns must be integrated into the nation's broader foreign policy, since human rights are at best only one of several foreign policy objectives.

The international normative consensus on human rights noted above largely solves the problem of the choice of a set of rights to pursue, for unless a state chooses a list very similar to that of the Universal Declaration, its efforts are almost certain to be dismissed as fatally flawed by partisan or ideological bias. Thus, for example, claims by officials of the Reagan administration that economic and social rights are not really true human rights are almost universally denounced. By the same token, the Carter administration's serious attention to economic and social rights, even if it was ultimately subordinate to a concern for civil and political rights, greatly contributed to the international perception of its policy as genuinely concerned with human rights, not just a new rhetoric for the Cold War or neo-colonialism. Such an international perception is almost a necessary condition—although by no means a sufficient condition—for an effective international human rights policy.

A state is, of course, free to pursue any objectives it wishes in its foreign policy. If it wishes its human rights policy to be taken seriously, however, the policy must at least be enunciated in terms consistent with the international consensus that has been forged around the Universal Declaration. In practice, some rights must be given particular prominence in a nation's foreign policy, given the limited material resources and international political capital of even the most powerful state, but the basic contours of policy must be set by the Universal Declaration.

After the rights to be pursued have been selected, the second problem, that of intervention on behalf of human rights, arises. When state A pursues human rights in its relations with state B, A usually will be seeking to alter the way that B treats its own citizens. This is, by definition, a matter essentially within the domestic jurisdiction of B and thus outside the legitimate jurisdiction of A. A's action, therefore, is vulnerable to the charge of intervention, a charge that carries considerable legal, moral, and political force in a world, such as ours, that is structured at the international level around sovereign nation-states.

The legal problems raised by foreign policy action on behalf of human rights abroad are probably the most troubling. Sovereignty entails the principle of nonintervention; to say that A has sovereign jurisdiction over X is essentially equivalent to saying that no one else may intervene in A with respect to X. Because sovereignty is the foundation of international law, any foreign policy action that amounts to intervention is prohibited by international law. On the face of it at least, this prohibition applies to action on behalf of human rights as much as any other activity.

It might be suggested that we can circumvent the legal proscription of intervention in the case of human rights by reference to particular treaties or even the general international normative consensus discussed above. International norms per se, however, do not authorize even international organizations, let alone individual states acting independently, to enforce those norms. Even if all states are legally bound to implement the rights enumerated in the Universal Declaration, it simply does not follow, in logic or in law, that any particular state or group of states is entitled to enforce that obligation. States are perfectly free to accept international legal obligations that have no enforcement mechanisms attached.

Scrupulously avoiding intervention (coercive interference) thus still leaves considerable room for international action at improving the human rights performance of a foreign country. Quiet diplomacy, public protests or condemnations, downgrading or breaking diplomatic relations, reducing or halting foreign aid, and selective or comprehensive restrictions of trade and other forms of interation are all actions that fall short of intervention. Thus in most circumstances they will be legally permissible actions on behalf of human rights abroad.

An international legal perspective on humanitarian intervention, however, does not exhaust the subject. Recently, several authors have argued, strongly and we believe convincingly, that moral considerations in at least some circumstances justify humanitarian intervention on behalf of human rights.[4] Michael Walzer, whose book *Just and Unjust Wars* has provoked much of the recent moral discussion of humanitarian intervention, can be taken as illustrative of such arguments.

Walzer presents a strong defense of the morality of the general international principle of nonintervention, arguing that it gives force to the basic right of peoples to self-determination, which in turn rests on the rights of individuals, acting in concert as a community, to choose their own government. Walzer has been criticized for interpreting this principle in a way that is excessively favorable to states by arguing that the presumption of legitimacy (and thus against intervention) should hold in all but the most extreme circumstances. Nonetheless, even Walzer allows that intervention must be permitted "when the violation of human rights is so terrible that it makes talk of community or self-determination . . . seem cynical and irrelevant,"[5] when gross, persistent, and systematic violations of human rights shock the moral conscience of mankind.

The idea underlying such arguments is that human rights are of such paramount moral importance that gross and systematic violations present a moral justification for remedial international action. If the international community as a whole cannot or will not act—and above we have shown that an effective collective international response will usually be impossible—then one or more states may be morally justified in acting ad hoc on behalf of the international community.

International law and morality thus lead to different and conflicting conclusions in at least some cases. One of the functions of international politics is to help to resolve such a conflict; political considerations will play a substantial role in determining how a state will respond in its foreign policy to the competing moral and legal demands placed on it. But the political dimensions of such decisions point to the practical dangers by moral arguments in favor of humanitarian intervention. . . .

Human rights may be moral concerns, but often they are not *merely* moral concerns. Morality and realism are not necessarily incompatible, and to treat them as if they always were can harm not only a state's human rights policy but its broader foreign policy as well.

Sometimes a country can afford to act on its human rights concerns; other times it cannot. Politics involves compromise, as a result of multiple and not always compatible goals that are pursued and the resistance of a world that more often than not is unsupportive of the particular objectives being sought. Human rights, like other goals of foreign policy, must at times be compromised. In some instances there is little that a country can afford to do even in the face of major human rights violations. . . .

If such variations in the treatment of human rights violators are to be part of a consistent policy, human rights concerns need to be explicitly and coherently integrated into the broader framework of foreign policy. A human rights policy must be an integral part of, not just something tacked on to, a country's overall foreign policy.

Difficult decisions have to be made about the relative weights to be given to human rights, as well as other foreign policy goals, and at least rough rules for making trade-offs need to be formulated. Furthermore, such decisions need to be made early in the process of working out a policy, and as a matter of principle. Ad hoc responses to immediate problems and crises, which have been the rule in the human rights policies of countries such as Canada and the United States, are almost sure to lead to inconsistencies and incoherence, both in appearance and in fact. Without such efforts to integrate human rights into the structure of national foreign policy, any trade-offs that are made will remain, literally, unprincipled.

Standards will be undeniably difficult to formulate, and their application will raise no less severe problems. Hard cases and exceptions are unavoidable. So are gray areas and fuzzy boundaries. Unless such efforts are seriously undertaken, however, the resulting policy is likely to appear baseless or inconsistent, and probably will be so in fact as well.

There are many opportunities for foreign policy action on behalf of human rights in foreign countries, but effective action requires the same sort of care and attention required for success in any area of foreign policy. . . .

CULTURE AND HUMAN RIGHTS

This view of the creation of the individual, with individual needs for human rights, is criticized by many advocates of the "cultural relativist" school of human rights. They present the argument that human rights are a "Western construct with limited [universal] applicability."[6] But cultural relativism, as applied to human rights, fails to grasp the nature of culture. A number of erroneous assumptions underlie this viewpoint.

Criticism of the universality of human rights often stems from erroneous perceptions of the persistence of traditional societies, societies in which principles of social justice are based not on rights but on status and on the intermixture of privilege and responsibility. Often anthropologically anachronistic pictures are presented of premodern societies, taking no account whatsoever of the social changes we have described above. It is assumed that culture is a static entity. But culture— like the individual—is adaptive. One can accept the principle that customs, values, and norms do indeed glue society together, and that they will endure, without assuming cultural stasis. Even though elements of culture have a strong hold on people's individual psyches, cultures can and do change. Individuals are actors who can influence their own fate, even if their range of choice is circumscribed by the prevalent social structure, culture, or ideology.

Cultural relativist arguments also often assume that culture is a unitary and unique whole; that is, that one is born into, and will always be, a part of a distinctive, comprehensive, and integrated set of cultural values and institutions that cannot be changed incrementally or only in part. Since in each culture the social norms and roles vary, so, it is argued, human rights must vary. The norms of each society are held to be both valuable in and of their own right, and so firmly rooted as to be impervious to challenge. Therefore, such arguments are applicable only to certain Western societies; to impose them on other societies from which they did not originally arise would do serious and irreparable damage to those cultures. In fact, though, people are quite adept cultural accommodationists; they are able to choose which aspects of a "new" culture they wish to adopt and which aspects of the "old" they wish to retain. For example, the marabouts (priests), who lead Senegal's traditional Muslim brotherhoods, have become leading political figures and have acquired considerable wealth and power through the peanut trade.

Still another assumption of the cultural relativism school is that culture is unaffected by social structure. But structure does affect culture. To a significant extent cultures and values reflect the basic economic and political organization of a society. For example, a society such as Tokugawa Japan that moves from a feudal structure to an organized bureaucratic state is bound to experience changes in values. Or the amalgamation of many different ethnic groups into one nation-state inevitably changes the way that individuals view themselves: For example, state-sponsored retention of ethnic customs, as under Canada's multicultural policy of preserving ethnic communities, cannot mask the fact that most of those communities are merging into the larger Canadian society.

A final assumption of the cultural relativist view of human rights is that cultural practices are neutral in their impact on different individuals and groups. Yet very few social practices, whether cultural or otherwise, distribute the same benefits to each member of a group. In considering any cultural practice it is useful to ask, who benefits from its retention? Those who speak for the group are usually those most capable of articulating the group's values to the outside world. But such spokesmen are likely to stress, in their articulation of "group" values, those particular values that are most to their own advantage. Both those who choose to adopt "new" ideals, such as political democracy or atheism, and those who choose to retain "old" ideals, such as a God-fearing political consensus, may be doing so in their own interests. Culture is both influenced by, and an instrument of, conflict among individuals or social groups. Just as those who attempt to modify or change customs may have personal interests in so doing, so also do those who attempt to preserve them. Quite often, relativist arguments are adopted principally to protect the interests of those in power.

Thus the notion that human rights cannot be applied across cultures violates both the principle of human rights and its practice. Human rights mean precisely that: rights held by virtue of being human. Human rights do not mean human dignity, nor do they represent the sum of personal resources (material, moral, or spiritual) that an individual might hold. Cultural variances that do not violate basic human rights undoubtedly enrich the world. But to permit the interests of the powerful to masquerade behind spurious defenses of cultural relativity is merely to lessen the chance that the victims of their policies will be able to complain. In the modern world, concepts such as cultural relativity, which deny to individuals the moral right to make comparisons and to insist on universal standards of right and wrong, are happily adopted by those who control the state.

THIRD WORLD CRITICISMS

In recent years a number of commentators from the Third World have criticized the concept of universal human rights. Frequently, the intention of the criticisms appears to be to exempt some Third World governments from the standard of judgment generated by the concept of universal human rights. Much of the criticism in fact serves to cover abuses of human rights by state corporatist, developmental dictatorship, or allegedly "socialist" regimes.

A common criticism of the concept of universal human rights is that since it is Western in origin, it must be limited in its applicability to the Western world. Both logically and empirically, this criticism is invalid. Knowledge is not limited in its applicability to its place or people of origin—one does not assume, for example, that medicines discovered in the developed Western world will cure only people of European origin. Nor is it reasonable to state that knowledge or thought of a certain kind—about social arrangements instead of about human biology or natural science—is limited to its place of origin. Those same Third World critics who reject universal concepts of human rights often happily accept Marxist socialism, which also originated in the Western world, in the mind of a German Jew.

The fact that human rights is originally a liberal notion, rooted in the rise of a class of bourgeois citizens in Europe who demanded individual rights against the power of kings and nobility, does not make human rights inapplicable to the rest of the world. As we argue above, all over the world there are now formal states, whose citizens are increasingly individualized. All over the world, therefore, there are people who need protections against the depradations of class-ruled governments.

Moreover, whatever the liberal origins of human rights, the list now accepted as universal includes a wide range of economic and social rights that were first advocated by socialist and social-democratic critics of liberalism. Although eighteenth-century liberals stressed the right to private property, the 1966 International Human Rights Covenants do not mention it, substituting instead the right to sovereignty over national resources. . . . To attribute the idea of universal human rights to an outdated liberalism, unaffected by later notions of welfare democracy and uninfluenced by socialist concerns with economic rights, is simply incorrect.

The absence of a right to private property in the Covenants indicates a sensitivity to the legitimate preoccupations of socialist and postcolonial Third World governments. Conservative critics of recent trends in international human rights in fact deplore the right to national sovereignty over resources, as some of them also deplore any attention to the economic rights of the individual. We certainly do not share this view of rights; we believe that the economic rights of the individual are as important as civil and political rights. But it is the individual we are concerned with. We would like to see a world in which *every individual* has enough to eat, not merely a world in which every *state* has the right to economic sovereignty.

We are skeptical, therefore, of the radical Third Worldist assertion that "group" rights ought to be more important than individual rights. Too often, the "group" in question proves to be the state. Why allocate rights to a social institution that is already the chief violator of individuals' rights? Similarly, we fear the expression "peoples' rights." The communal rights of individuals to practice their own religion, speak their own language, and indulge in their own ancestral customs are protected in the Covenant on Civil and Political Rights. Individuals are free to come together in groups to engage in those cultural practices which are meaningful to them. On the other hand, often a "group" right can simply mean that the individual is subordinate to the group—for example, that the individual Christian fundamentalist in the Soviet Union risks arrest because of the desire of the larger "group" to enforce official atheism.

The one compelling use that we can envisage for the term "group rights" is in protection of native peoples, usually hunter-gatherers, pastoralists, or subsistence agriculturalists, whose property rights as collectivities are being violated by the larger state societies that encroach upon them. Such groups are fighting a battle against the forces of modernization and the state's accumulative tendencies. For example, native peoples in Canada began in the 1970s to object to state development projects, such as the James Bay Hydroelectric project in Quebec, which deprived them of their traditional lands. At the moment, there is no international human rights protection for such groups or their "way of life."

One way to protect such group rights would be to incorporate the group as a legal entity in order to preserve their land claims. However, even if the law protects such group rights, individual members of the group may prefer to move into the larger society in response to the processes of modernization discussed above. Both opinions must be protected.

If the purpose of group rights is to protect large, established groups of people who share the same territory, customs, language, religion, and ancestry, then such protection could only occur at the expense of states' rights. These groups, under international human rights law, do not have the right to withdraw from the states that enfold them. Moreover, it is clearly not the intention of Third World defenders of group rights to allow such a right to secession. A first principle of the Organization of African Unity, for example, is to preserve the sovereignty of all its member states not only against outside attack but also against internal attempts at secession. Group rights appear to mean, in practice, states' rights. But the rights of states are the rights of the individuals and classes who control the state.

Many Third World and socialist regimes also argue that rights ought to be tied to duties. A citizen's rights, it is argued, ought to be contingent upon his duties toward the society at large—privilege is contingent on responsibility. Such a view of rights made sense in nonstate societies in which each "person" fulfilled his roles along with others, all of the roles together creating a close-knit, tradition-bound group. But in modern state societies, to tie rights to duties is to risk the former's complete disappearance. All duties will be aimed toward the preservation of the state and of the interests of those who control it.

It is true that no human rights are absolute; even in societies that adhere in principle to the liberal ethos, individuals are frequently deprived of rights, especially in wartime or if they are convicted of criminal acts. However, such deprivations can legitimately be made only after the most scrupulous protection of civil and political rights under the rule of law. The difficulty with tying rights to duties without the intermediate step of scrutiny by a genuinely independent judiciary is the likelihood of wholesale cancellation of rights by the ruling class. But if one has rights merely because one is human, and for no other reason, then it is much more difficult, in principle, for the state to cancel them. It cannot legitimate the denial of rights by saying that only certain types of human beings, exhibiting certain kinds of behavior, are entitled to them.

One final criticism of the view of universal human rights embedded in the International Covenants is that an undue stress is laid on civil and political rights, whereas the overriding rights priority in the Third World is economic rights. In this view, the state as the agent of economic development—and hence, presumably, of eventual distribution of economic goods or "rights" to the masses—should not be bothered with problems of guaranteeing political participation in decision making, or of protecting people's basic civil rights. These rights, it is argued, come "after" development is completed. The empirical basis for this argument is weak. . . . Economic development per se will not guarantee future human rights, whether of an economic or any other kind. Often, development means economic growth, but without equitable distributive measures. Moreover, development strategies often fail because of insufficient attention to citizens' needs and views. Finally, development plans are often a cover for the continued violations of citizens' rights by the ruling class.

Thus we return to where we started: the rights of all men and women against all governments to treatment as free, equal, materially and physically secure persons. This is what human dignity means and requires in our era. And the individual human rights of the Universal Declaration and the Covenants are the means by which individuals today carry out the struggle to achieve their dignity. . . .

NOTES

1. The International Bill of Human Rights includes the Universal Declaration of Human Rights (1948), the International Covenant on Economic, Social and Cultural Rights (1966), the International Covenant on Civil and Political Rights (1966), and the Optional Protocol to the latter Covenant.
2. Howard Tolley, "The Concealed Crack in the Citadel: The United Nations Commission on Human Rights' Response to Confidential Communications," *Human Rights Quarterly* 6 (November 1984): 420–62.
3. This section draws heavily on Jack Donnelly, "Human Rights and Foreign Policy," *World Politics* 34 (July 1982): 574–95, and "Human Rights, Humanitarian Intervention and American Foreign Policy: Law, Morality and Politics," *Journal of International Affairs* 37 (Winter 1984): 311–28.

4. See, for example, Jerome Slater and Terry Nardin, "Nonintervention and Human Rights," *Journal of Politics* 48 (February 1986): 86–96; Charles R. Beitz, "Nonintervention and Communal Integrity," *Philosophy and Public Affairs* 9 (Summer 1980): 385–91; and Robert Matthews and Cranford Pratt, "Human Rights and Foreign Policy: Principles and Canadian Practice," *Human Rights Quarterly* 7 (May 1985): 159–88.

5. Michael Walzer, *Just and Unjust Wars* (New York: Basic Books, 1977), p. 90. For criticisms of Walzer see Slater and Nardin, "Nonintervention"; Beitz, "Nonintervention"; and David Luban, "The Romance of the Nation State," *Philosophy and Public Affairs* 9 (Summer 1980): 392–97.

6. Adamantia Pollis and Peter Schwab, "Human Rights: A Western Concept with Limited Applicability," in *Human Rights: Cultural and Ideological Perspectives,* Pollis and Schwab, ed. (New York: Praeger, 1979), pp. 1–18.

The Five Wars of Globalization

MOISÉS NAÍM

The persistence of al Qaeda underscores how hard it is for governments to stamp out stateless, decentralized networks that move freely, quickly, and stealthily across national borders to engage in terror. The intense media coverage devoted to the war on terrorism, however, obscures five other similar global wars that pit governments against agile, well-financed networks of highly dedicated individuals. These are the fights against the illegal international trade in drugs, arms, intellectual property, people, and money. Religious zeal or political goals drive terrorists, but the promise of enormous financial gain motivates those who battle governments in these five wars. Tragically, profit is no less a motivator for murder, mayhem, and global insecurity than religious fanaticism.

In one form or another, governments have been fighting these five wars for centuries. And losing them. Indeed, thanks to the changes spurred by globalization over the last decade, their losing streak has become even more pronounced. To be sure, nation-states have benefited from the information revolution, stronger political and economic linkages, and the shrinking importance of geographic distance. Unfortunately, criminal networks have benefited even more. Never fettered by the niceties of sovereignty, they are now increasingly free of geographic constraints. Moreover, globalization has not only expanded illegal markets and boosted the size and the resources of criminal networks, it has also imposed more burdens on governments: Tighter public budgets, decentralization, privatization, deregulation, and a more open environment for international trade and investment all make the task of fighting global criminals more difficult. Governments are made up of cumbersome bureaucracies that generally cooperate with difficulty, but drug traffickers, arms dealers, alien smugglers, counterfeiters, and money launderers have refined networking to a high science, entering into complex and improbable strategic alliances that span cultures and continents.

Defeating these foes may prove impossible. But the first steps to reversing their recent dramatic gains must be to recognize the fundamental similarities among the five wars and to treat these conflicts not as law enforcement problems but as a new global trend that shapes the world as much as confrontations between nation-states did in the past. Customs officials, police officers, lawyers, and judges alone will never win these wars. Governments must recruit and deploy more spies, soldiers, diplomats, and economists who understand how to use incentives and regulations to steer markets away from bad social outcomes. But changing the skill set of government combatants alone will not end these wars. Their doctrines and institutions also need a major overhaul.

THE FIVE WARS

Pick up any newspaper anywhere in the world, any day, and you will find news about illegal migrants, drug busts, smuggled weapons, laundered money, or counterfeit goods. The global nature of these five wars was unimaginable just a decade ago. The resources—financial, human, institutional, technological—deployed by the combatants have reached unfathomable orders of magnitude. So have the numbers of victims. The tactics and tricks of both sides boggle the mind. Yet if you cut through the fog of daily headlines and orchestrated photo ops, one inescapable truth emerges: The world's governments are fighting a qualitatively new phenomenon with obsolete tools, inadequate laws, inefficient bureaucratic arrangements, and ineffective strategies. Not surprisingly, the evidence shows that governments are losing.

Drugs

The best known of the five wars is, of course, the war on drugs. In 1999, the United Nations' "Human Development Report" calculated the annual trade in illicit drugs at $400 billion, roughly the size of the Spanish economy and about 8 percent of world trade. Many countries are reporting an increase in drug use. Feeding this habit is a global supply chain that uses everything from passenger jets that can carry shipments of cocaine worth $500 million in a single trip to custom-built submarines that ply the waters between Colombia and Puerto Rico. To foil eavesdroppers, drug smugglers use "cloned" cell phones and broadband radio receivers while also relying on complex financial structures that blend legitimate and illegitimate enterprises with elaborate fronts and structures of cross-ownership.

The United States spends between $35 billion and $40 billion each year on the war on drugs; most of this money is spent on interdiction and intelligence. But the creativity and boldness of drug cartels has routinely outstripped steady increases in government resources. Responding to tighter security at the U.S.-Mexican border, drug smugglers built a tunnel to move tons of drugs and billions of dollars in cash until authorities discovered it in March 2002. Over the last decade, the success of the Bolivian and Peruvian governments in eradicating coca plantations has shifted production to Colombia. Now, the U.S.-supported Plan Colombia is displacing coca production and processing labs back to other Andean countries. Despite the heroic efforts of these Andean countries and the massive financial and technical support of the United States, the total acreage of coca plantations in Peru, Colombia, and Bolivia has increased in the last decade from 206,200 hectares in 1991 to 210,939 in 2001. Between 1990 and 2000, according to economist Jeff DeSimone, the median price of a gram of cocaine in the United States fell from $152 to $112. . . .

Arms Trafficking

Drugs and arms often go together. In 1999, the Peruvian military parachuted 10,000 AK-47s to the Revolutionary Armed Forces of Colombia, a guerrilla group closely allied to drug growers and traffickers. The group purchased the weapons in Jordan. Most of the roughly 80 million AK-47s in circulation today are in the wrong hands. According to the United Nations, only 18 million (or about 3 percent) of the 550 million small arms and light weapons in circulation today are used by government, military, or police forces. Illict trade accounts for almost 20 percent of the total small arms trade and generates more than $1 billion a year. Small arms helped fuel 46 of the 49 largest conflicts of the last decade and in 2001 were estimated to be responsible for 1,000 deaths a day; more than 80 percent of those victims were women and children.

Small arms are just a small part of the problem. The illegal market for munitions encompasses top-of-the-line tanks, radar systems that detect Stealth aircraft, and the makings of the deadliest weapons of mass destruction. The International Atomic Energy Agency has confirmed more than a dozen cases of smuggled nuclear-weapons-usable material, and hundreds more cases have been reported and investigated over the last decade. The actual supply of stolen nuclear-, biological-, or chemical-weapons materials and technology may still be small. But the potential demand is strong and growing from both would-be nuclear powers and terrorists. Constrained supply and increasing demand cause prices to rise and create enormous incentives for illegal activities. More than one fifth of the 120,000 workers in Russia's former "nuclear cities"—where more than half of all employees earn less than $50 a month—say they would be willing to work in the military complex of another country.

Governments have been largely ineffective in curbing either supply or demand. . . . Multilateral efforts to curb the manufacture and distribution of weapons are faltering, not least because some powers are unwilling to accept curbs on their own activities. In 2001, for example, the United States blocked a legally binding global treaty to control small arms in part because it worried about restrictions on its own citizens' rights to own guns. In the absence of effective international legislation and enforcement, the laws of economics dictate the sale of more weapons at cheaper prices: In 1986, an AK-47 in Kolowa, Kenya, cost 15 cows. Today, it costs just four.

Intellectual Property

In 2001, two days after recording the voice track of a movie in Hollywood, actor Dennis Hopper was in Shanghai where a street vendor sold him an excellent pirated copy of the movie with his voice already on it. "I don't know how they got my voice into the country before I got here," he wondered. Hopper's experience is one tiny slice of an illicit trade that cost the United States an estimated $9.4 billion in 2001. The piracy rate of business software in Japan and France is 40 percent, in Greece and South Korea it is about 60 percent, and in Germany and Britain it hovers around 30 percent. Forty percent of Procter & Gamble shampoos and 60 percent of Honda motorbikes sold in China in 2001 were pirated. Up to 50 percent of medical drugs in Nigeria and Thailand are bootleg copies. This problem is not limited to consumer products: Italian makers of industrial valves worry that their $2 billion a year export market is eroded by counterfeit Chinese valves sold in world markets at prices that are 40 percent cheaper.

The drivers of this bootlegging boom are complex. Technology is obviously boosting both the demand and the supply of illegally copied products. Users of Napster, the now defunct Internet company that allowed anyone, anywhere to download and reproduce copyrighted music for free, grew from zero to 20 million in just one year. Some 500,000 film files are traded daily through file-sharing services such as Kazaa and Morpheus; and in late 2002, some 900 million music files could be downloaded for free on the Internet—that is, almost two and a half times more files than those available when Napster reached its peak in February 2001.

Global marketing and branding are also playing a part, as more people are attracted to products bearing a well-known brand like Prada or Cartier. And thanks to the rapid growth and integration into the global economy of countries, such as China, with weak central governments and ineffective laws, producing and exporting near perfect knockoffs are both less expensive and less risky. In the words of the CEO of one of the best known Swiss watchmakers: "We now compete with a product manufactured by Chinese prisoners. The business is run by the Chinese military, their families and friends, using roughly the same machines we have, which they purchased at the same industrial fairs we go to." . . .

Governments have attempted to protect intellectual property rights through various means, most notably the World Trade Organization's Agreement on Trade-Related Aspects of Intellectual Property Rights (TRIPS). Several other organizations such as the World Intellectual Property Organization, the World Customs Union, and Interpol are also involved. Yet the large and growing volume of this trade, or a simple stroll in the streets of Manhattan or Madrid, show that governments are far from winning this fight.

Alien Smuggling

The man or woman who sells a bogus Hermes scarf or a Rolex watch in the streets of Milan is likely to be an illegal alien. Just as likely, he or she was transported across several continents by a trafficking network allied with another network that specializes in the illegal copying, manufacturing, and distributing of high-end, brand-name products.

Alien smuggling is a $7 billion a year enterprise and according to the United Nations is the fastest growing business of organized crime. Roughly 500,000 people enter the United States illegally each year—about the same number as illegally enter the European Union, and part of the approximately 150 million who live outside their countries of origin. Many of these backdoor travelers are voluntary migrants who pay smugglers up to $35,000, the top-dollar fee for passage from China to New York. Others, instead, are trafficked—that is, bought and sold internationally—as commodities. The U.S. Congressional Research Service reckons that each year between 1 million and 2 million people are trafficked across borders, the majority of whom are women and children. A woman can be "bought" in

Timisoara, Romania, for between $50 and $200 and "resold" in Western Europe for 10 times that price. The United Nations Children's Fund estimates that cross-border smugglers in Central and Western Africa enslave 200,000 children a year. Traffickers initially tempt victims with job offers or, in the case of children, with offers of adoption in wealthier countries, and then keep the victims in subservience through physical violence, debt bondage, passport confiscation, and threats of arrest, deportation, or violence against their families back home.

Governments everywhere are enacting tougher immigration laws and devoting more time, money, and technology to fight the flow of illegal aliens. But the plight of the United Kingdom's government illustrates how tough that fight is. The British government throws money at the problem, plans to use the Royal Navy and Royal Air Force to intercept illegal immigrants, and imposes large fines on truck drivers who (generally unwittingly) transport stowaways. Still, 42,000 of the 50,000 refugees who have passed through the Sangatte camp (a main entry point for illegal immigration to the United Kingdom) over the last three years have made it to Britain. At current rates, it will take 43 years for Britain to clear its asylum backlog. And that country is an island. Continental nations such as Spain, Italy, or the United States face an even greater challenge as immigration pressures overwhelm their ability to control the inflow of illegal aliens.

Money Laundering

The Cayman Islands has a population of 36,000. It also has more than 2,200 mutual funds, 500 insurance companies, 60,000 businesses, and 600 banks and trust companies with almost $800 billion in assets. Not surprisingly, it figures prominently in any discussion of money laundering. So does the United States, several of whose major banks have been caught up in investigations of money laundering, tax evasion, and fraud. Few, if any, countries can claim to be free of the practice of helping individuals and companies hide funds from governments, creditors, business partners, or even family members, including the proceeds of tax evasion, gambling, and other crimes. Estimates of the volume of global money laundering range between 2 and 5 percent of the world's annual gross national product, or between $800 billion and $2 trillion.

Smuggling money, gold coins, and other valuables is an ancient trade. Yet in the last two decades, new political and economic trends coincided with technological changes to make this ancient trade easier, cheaper, and less risky. Political changes led to the deregulation of financial markets that now facilitate cross-border money transfers, and technological changes made distance less of a factor and money less "physical." Suitcases full of banknotes are still a key tool for money launderers, but computers, the Internet, and complex financial schemes that combine legal and illegal practices and institutions are more common. The sophistication of technology, the complex web of financial institutions that crisscross the globe, and the ease with which "dirty" funds can be electronically morphed into legitimate assets make the regulation of international flows of money a daunting task. In Russia, for example, it is estimated that by the mid-1990s organized crime groups had set up 700 legal and financial institutions to launder their money.

Faced with this growing tide, governments have stepped up their efforts to clamp down on rogue international banking, tax havens, and money laundering. The imminent, large-scale introduction of e-money—cards with microchips that can store large amounts of money and thus can be easily transported outside regular channels or simply exchanged among individuals—will only magnify this challenge.

WHY GOVERNMENTS CAN'T WIN

The fundamental changes that have given the five wars new intensity over the last decade are likely to persist. Technology will continue to spread widely; criminal networks will be able to exploit these technologies more quickly than governments that must cope with tight budgets, bureaucracies, media scrutiny, and electorates. International trade will continue to grow, providing more cover for the expansion of illicit trade. International migration will likewise grow, with much the same effect, offering ethnically based gangs an ever growing supply of recruits and victims. The spread of democracy may also help criminal cartels, which can manipulate weak public institutions by corrupting police officers or tempting politicians with offers of cash for their increasingly expensive election campaigns. And ironically, even the spread of international law—with its growing web of embargoes, sanctions, and conventions—will offer criminals new opportunities for providing forbidden goods to those on the wrong side of the international community.

These changes may affect each of the five wars in different ways, but these conflicts will continue to share four common characteristics:

They are not bound by geography.   Some forms of crime have always had an international component: The Mafia was born in Sicily and exported to the United States, and smuggling has always been by definition international. But the five wars are truly global. Where is the theater or front line of the war on drugs? Is it Colombia or Miami? Myanmar (Burma) or Milan? Where are the battles against money launderers being fought? In Nauru or in London? Is China the main theater in the war against the infringement of intellectual property, or are the trenches of that war on the Internet?

They defy traditional notions of sovereignty.   Al Qaeda's members have passports and nationalities—and often more than one—but they are truly stateless. Their allegiance is to their cause, not to any nation. The same is also true of the criminal networks engaged in the five wars. The same, however, is patently *not* true of government employees—police officers, customs agents, and judges—who fight them. This asymmetry is a crippling disadvantage for governments waging these wars. Highly paid, hypermotivated, and resource-rich combatants on one side of the wars (the criminal gangs) can seek refuge in and take advantage of national borders, but combatants of the other side (the governments) have fewer resources and are hampered by traditional notions of sovereignty. A former senior CIA official reported that international criminal gangs are able to move people, money, and weapons globally faster than he can move resources inside his own agency, let alone worldwide. Coordination and information sharing among government agencies in different countries has certainly improved, especially after September 11. Yet these tactics fall short of what is needed to combat agile organizations that can exploit every nook and cranny of an evolving but imperfect body of international law and multilateral treaties.

They pit governments against market forces.   In each of the five wars, one or more government bureaucracies fight to contain the disparate, uncoordinated actions of thousands of independent, stateless organizations. These groups are motivated by large profits obtained by exploiting international price differentials, an unsatisfied demand, or the cost advantages produced by theft. Hourly wages for a Chinese cook are far higher in Manhattan than in Fujian. A gram of cocaine in Kansas City is 17,000 percent more expensive than in Bogotá. Fake Italian valves are 40 percent cheaper because counterfeiters don't have to cover the costs of developing the product. A well-funded guerrilla group will pay anything to get the weapons it needs. In each of these five wars, the incentives to successfully overcome government-imposed limits to trade are simply enormous.

They pit bureaucracies against networks.   The same network that smuggles East European women to Berlin may be involved in distributing opium there. The proceeds of the latter fund the purchase of counterfeit Bulgari watches made in China and often sold on the streets of Manhattan by illegal African immigrants. Colombian drug cartels make deals with Ukrainian arms traffickers, while Wall Street brokers controlled by the U.S.-based Mafia have been known to front for Russian money launderers. These highly decentralized groups and individuals are bound by strong ties of loyalty and common purpose and organized around semi-autonomous clusters or "nodes" capable of operating swiftly and flexibly. John Arquilla and David Ronfeldt, two of the best known experts on these types of organizations, observe that networks often lack central leadership, command, or headquarters, thus "no precise heart or head that can be targeted. The network as a whole (but not necessarily each node) has little to no hierarchy; there may be multiple leaders. . . . Thus the [organization's] design may sometimes appear acephalous (headless), and at other times polycephalous (Hydra-headed)." Typically, governments respond to these challenges by forming interagency task forces or creating new bureaucracies. Consider the creation of the new Department of Homeland Security in the United States, which encompasses 22 former federal agencies and their 170,000 employees and is responsible for, among other things, fighting the war on drugs.

RETHINKING THE PROBLEM

Governments may never be able to completely eradicate the kind of international trade involved in the five wars. But they can and should do better. There are at least four areas where efforts can yield better ideas on how to tackle the problems posed by these wars:

Develop more flexible notions of sovereignty.   Governments need to recognize that restricting the scope of multilateral action for the sake of protecting their sovereignty is often a moot point. Their sovereignty is compromised daily, not by nation-states but by stateless networks that break laws and cross borders in pursuit of trade. In May 1999, for example, the Venezuelan government denied U.S. planes authorization to fly over Venezuelan territory to monitor air routes commonly used by narcotraffickers. Venezuelan authorities placed more importance on the symbolic value of asserting sovereignty over air space than on the fact that drug traffickers' planes regularly violate Venezuelan territory. Without new forms of codifying and "managing" sovereignty, governments will continue to face a large disadvantage while fighting the five wars.

Strengthen existing multilateral institutions.   The global nature of these wars means no government, regardless of its economic, political, or military power, will make much progress acting alone. If this seems obvious, then why does Interpol, the multilateral agency in charge of fighting international crime, have a staff of 384, only 112 of whom are police officers, and an annual budget of $28 million, less than the price of some boats or planes used by drug traffickers? Similarly, Europol, Europe's Interpol equivalent, has a staff of 240 and a budget of $51 million.

One reason Interpol is poorly funded and staffed is because its 181 member governments don't trust each other. Many assume, and perhaps rightly so, that the criminal networks they are fighting have penetrated the police departments of other countries and that sharing information with such compromised officials would not be prudent. Others fear today's allies will become tomorrow's enemies. Still others face legal impediments to sharing intelligence with fellow nation-states or have intelligence services and law enforcement agencies with organizational cultures that make effective collaboration almost impossible. Progress will only be made if the world's governments unite behind stronger, more effective multilateral organizations.

Devise new mechanisms and institutions.   These five wars stretch and even render obsolete many of the existing institutions, legal frameworks, military doctrines, weapons systems, and law enforcement techniques on which governments have relied for years. Analysts need to rethink the concept of war "fronts" defined by geography and the definition of "combatants" according to the Geneva Convention. The functions of intelligence agents, soldiers, police officers, customs agents, or immigration officers need rethinking and adaptation to the new realities. Policymakers also need to reconsider the notion that ownership is essentially a physical reality and not a "virtual" one or that only sovereign nations can issue money when thinking about ways to fight the five wars.

Move from repression to regulation.   Beating market forces is next to impossible. In some cases, this reality may force governments to move from repressing the market to regulating it. In others, creating market incentives may be better than using bureaucracies to curb the excesses of these markets. Technology can often accomplish more than government policies can. For example, powerful encryption techniques can better protect software or CDs from being copied in Ukraine than would making the country enforce patents and copyrights and trademarks.

In all of the five wars, government agencies fight against networks motivated by the enormous profit opportunities created by other government agencies. In all cases, these profits can be traced to some form of government intervention that creates a major imbalance between demand and supply and makes prices and profit margins skyrocket. In some cases, these government interventions are often justified and it would be imprudent to eliminate them—governments can't simply walk away from the fight against trafficking in heroin, human beings, or weapons of mass destruction. But society can better deal with other segments of these kinds of illegal trade through regulation, not prohibition. Policymakers must focus on opportunities where market regulation can ameliorate problems that have defied approaches based on prohibition and armed interdiction of international trade.

Ultimately, governments, politicians, and voters need to realize that the way in which the world is conducting these five wars is doomed to fail—not for lack of effort, resources, or political will but because the collective thinking that guides government strategies in the five wars is rooted in wrong ideas, false assumptions, and obsolete institutions. Recognizing that governments have no chance of winning unless they change the ways they wage these wars is an indispensable first step in the search for solutions.

Europe's Floundering Fathers

JACK RAKOVE

Americans can perhaps be pardoned for remaining ignorant of the proposed constitution for the expanding European Union (EU) unveiled to its member governments on June 20, 2003. . . . It was perhaps to pique American interest that the convention's president, former French president Valéry Giscard d'Estaing, periodically compared his convention with the Philadelphia convention of 1787. . . .

Both by American standards and those of contemporary constitutionalism, the nature of the current European project remains ambiguous and arguably deficient. *"La Convention propose une Constitution à 450 millions d'Européens,"* read a headline in *Le Monde* the weekend after Giscard and his colleagues adjourned. It would have been more accurate to say that the constitution was being proposed *for* 450 million Europeans and *to* the 15 states of the current EU and the 10 new states preparing to join. A constitutional treaty, as the new charter is sometimes called, is still more a treaty among nation-states than a constitution for a common people. In theory, it allows individual members of the EU either to block the adoption of the constitution or to truck and bargain for points they deem particularly important. And even though the constitution may weaken the legislative and regulatory powers of the member governments, it may not deprive them of a residual sovereign authority to opt out of the union should they so wish.

To an American eye, the proposed constitution falls somewhere between the Articles of Confederation drafted between 1776 and 1777 and the federal U.S. Constitution framed a decade later. Like the Continental Congress under the Articles, the EU lacks the authority to tax. The economic and social authority of the EU, however, still goes well beyond anything Americans contemplated in the 1770s or arguably even after the U.S. Constitution was ratified. Under the Articles, the American states retained full authority over their internal police. Well into the 19th century, the only federal activity that Americans ordinarily noticed was the delivery of the mail.

Yet the Continental Congress did have real authority over war and diplomacy, those classic markers of true sovereignty. Europe's proposed constitution, by contrast, goes no further than to create a new position of foreign minister without reducing the capacity of member states to maintain their individual and independent foreign policies. Much of the movement to reform the Articles in the mid-

1780s was predicated on the inability of Congress to carry out the national security functions it clearly possessed. It remains difficult to imagine the nation-states of the EU rallying around a movement to centralize authority in the EU because the peoples of Europe want to cut a bolder figure on the world stage.

By any standard, then, the proposed constitution still falls well short of the ambitions released at Philadelphia two and a quarter centuries ago, and the ultimate course and character of constitutional change in Europe remain among what James Madison called "the arcana of futurity." Nor is the convoluted and protracted process of drafting, renegotiating, and finally approving the finished constitution likely to produce anything like the clear and unequivocal decision that emerged from the American deliberations of 1787 to 1791. Those debates laid to rest the idea that sovereignty could only be vested in government. They showed that all legitimate governments, state and national, actually derived their authority from the consent of the people. Whatever else the European constitution may accomplish, it is not about to strike a blow for the cause of popular sovereignty.

Beyond these and other points of historical comparison, how does the European constitutional project illuminate the state of European and American relations at this vexed moment in the transatlantic relationship? More than three decades ago, when the late R.R. Palmer memorably titled his sweeping history of the era of the American and French revolutions *The Age of the Democratic Revolution,* the first movements toward the European Economic Community were seen as portents of a united European entity that would emulate its savior-ally across the Atlantic. Today, faced with the aftermath of the Iraq war, the chilling of U.S. relations with the Franco-German entente, and the unilateralism of the Bush administration, we might ask whether the process of constitution-making across the Atlantic is evidence of how much Americans and Europeans share or how widely and persistently we differ. As the brothers Peter and Nicholas Onuf have suggested, Americans once saw their federal union as a solution to the rivalries that Europeans tried to manage through the diplomacy and warfare of balance of power. It would be a nice historical irony for Europeans to contrive a constitutional union that some of them hope would counterbalance the greatest hegemon of them all.

WE THE PEOPLES

From an American perspective, the proposed constitution is easy to disparage. It contains, for example, one of those shopping lists of social rights that conservatives love to lampoon, rights that emphasize entitlements to education, employment, healthcare, and even job training, rather than restrictions on the authority of the state designed to foster the individual liberty and autonomy Americans hold dear. Its affirmation of the principle of "subsidiarity," which calls for decisions to be made at the lowest level of governance possible, seems like a weak barrier against the centralizing tendencies that Euroskeptics routinely ascribe to Brussels. Nor does the constitution do much to promote the political accountability of

EU institutions to the European people (or peoples) who are its constituents. Its principal institutional innovation appears to be the creation of a full-time president of the Council of Ministers, the body that represents the governments of the member states. But this gives the EU two presidents: one for the Council of Ministers and one for the European Commission at Brussels, the executive arm of the EU proper.

On the other hand, the proposed constitution does seem to represent a significant step toward the centralization of public policy. Euroskeptics already profess disappointment and alarm over the continued federalization of economic and social "competences"—the term that the EU uses to describe who has authority over an area. To an American who likes the specificity of the enumerated powers of the U.S. Congress set out in Article I, Section 8, of the Constitution, the notion of vaguely defined "competences" may seem incredibly, and therefore dangerously, vague. But Eurofederalists can rightly claim that the proposed constitution sharply reduces the uncertainty about EU authority evident in the existing cluster of treaties. Moreover, the constitution increases the areas in which both the commission and the council can make decisions by a form of majority voting while reducing the capacity of individual states to veto action. Yet that great badge of sovereignty—the power to tax—remains the reserve of the member states, as does the responsibility for administering the relentless flow of regulations from Brussels. In this sense, the proposed constitution again seems closer to the Articles of Confederation than the Constitution of 1787.

THAT WAS THEN, THIS IS EUROPE

The task of consolidating European governance today is far more daunting than the one the American framers faced at Philadelphia. To admit this point takes nothing away from the achievements of 1787. Anyone who studies the formation of the Constitution has to be impressed not only by the high seriousness with which its framers discharged their duties but also by the remarkably inventive and critical way in which they combined a deep knowledge of history and political philosophy with the lessons of their own experience. That they were, at bottom, a collection of provincial rustics living at the far periphery of the European world makes their achievements all the more striking.

Yet they also enjoyed certain advantages that made designing a federal constitution less difficult. Most important, the member states of the union had never been truly sovereign in the full or accurate sense of the term. Neither in 1776 nor in 1787 were the separate American states independent sovereignties in the same way as the nation-states of modern Europe. Though they exercised certain essential powers of sovereignty, notably the authority to enact legislation and taxation, they never pretended to be sovereign in an international sense. As Rufus King of Massachusetts reminded the delegates at Philadelphia, when it came to interacting with other nations, the states "were dumb." From its inception in the revolutionary crisis of 1774, the Continental Congress monopolized the basic functions of diplomacy and war.

Nor did the American states ever command the popular sources of affection and attachment commonly associated with the romantic and rapacious nationalism of 19th- and 20th-century Europe. Not that provincial Americans were unaware of the history of their individual communities. In Puritan New England, and among the ruling gentry elsewhere, place did matter. But much of the American population consisted of immigrants and their first offspring, families more attached to their farms than their provinces. And much of this population was already mobile, willing to cross boundaries in pursuit of opportunity without regard to political loyalties.

The contrast with Europe could not be more profound. All EU members are nation-states possessing full political sovereignty and a self-conscious sense of their historical peoplehood. For many of these nations, the relative novelty of their status as self-governing entities (compared with the United States) may deepen, rather than weaken, their reluctance to relinquish national sovereignty to the faceless bureaucrats of Brussels and to obscure parliamentarians at Strasbourg. Each European nation-state has conducted its own foreign relations, and each is aware of the consequences of losing its capacity to assert its national interests. And their peoples are heirs to a history that has generated passions and memories that dwarf the closest counterpart one can find in the United States: the celebration of Southern heritage typically expressed by Confederate flags and decals and a willful denial that the Civil War really was about the ownership of human property. In particular, the new, intensely nationalistic members entering the EU from the old Soviet bloc are loath to see their stature as sovereign nation-states, capable of acting on the world stage, so soon submerged to an amorphous entity.

This stubborn sense of national interest and identity is manifest in two significant elements of the proposed European constitution.

First, notwithstanding the establishment of a foreign minister who will also serve as a vice president of the commission, member states are unlikely to cede their right to conduct their own foreign policy to the EU. The constitution is far from clear on this point, but any revision to it made by an intergovernmental conference representing the member states is unlikely to enhance the prospects for conducting a genuinely European foreign policy. Perhaps such a revision might have happened had the Iraq war not punctuated the work of the convention. But that episode was a painful reminder of how distant the ideal of a common European foreign policy remains. The notion that Britain, Italy, Spain, or Poland will happily acquiesce in a foreign policy likely to reflect the Franco-German entente is difficult to credit.

In the second place, consider the dilemma of the constitution-making process itself. It remains, in essence, a negotiation among nation-states and their governments, with a formal requirement for unanimity that, in theory, places the entire project in jeopardy. The European convention, by itself, satisfied one of the basic American criteria for making a constitution fully constitutional. It met and deliberated as an independent body, with no other responsibilities or obligations, theoretically free to determine what was best for the future polity without considering narrow political loyalties. But the process as it goes forward from this point remains subject to the manipulation of the member governments, and the role of the European peoples in its approval remains uncertain.

Here a contrast with the American experience is most instructive. The starting position for the constitutional reformers of the 1780s was similar to the European case today. Amendment of the Articles of Confederation required the unanimous approval of all 13 state legislatures, and this imposed two insuperable obstacles. One was the requirement for unanimity, which enabled a small state like Rhode Island to thwart a reform desired by all the others. The other was the improbability that the state legislatures would endorse any project that would radically reduce their own authority.

The framers' solution to this dilemma was both politically expedient and theoretically potent. The unanimity rule of the Articles of Confederation clearly had to go. The rogue state of Rhode Island had refused even to send a delegation to Philadelphia; leaving the entire movement for reform subject to its veto seemed absurd. Abandoning the rule of unanimity made it easier to dispense with the requirement that the new constitution be submitted to the state legislatures for approval. Instead, the convention asked the legislatures only to arrange for the election of ratification conventions, distinct bodies that, it was claimed, would represent the people more directly than their legislatures, grounding the U.S. Constitution on an expression of popular sovereignty. And to make the decision of these bodies completely unambiguous, they were allowed only to vote on the Constitution in its entirety, not article by article or clause by clause. True, they could also recommend amendments. But federalists struggled long and successfully to make sure that the approval of individual states was not made contingent upon the prior adoption of these amendments.

Two great advantages flowed from this process. First, it produced a completely unambiguous decision, bestowing upon the constitution-making process a deep legitimacy that was conceded even by the two states, Rhode Island and North Carolina, that initially rejected the Constitution and thereby briefly left the union. Second, the direct appeal to popular sovereignty powerfully affirmed that the Constitution would indeed be "the supreme Law of the Land" in a way that mere approval by Congress and the state legislatures could not.

The entire process took less than two years, from the meeting of the Annapolis Convention in September 1786 to the ratification by New York, the 11th state, in July 1788. A critic could object that the adoption of the first 10 amendments lengthened the process by another three years, but in reality the Bill of Rights (as these amendments came to be known) was more of a denouement than an essential component of the process. All in all, the clarity, economy, and efficiency of this pioneering venture in constitution making remain impressive.

Contrast this, again, with the more diffuse, protracted, negotiated, and public nature of the European deliberations. Allowances must, of course, be made for the greater difficulty of coordinating the interests and concerns of so many independent jurisdictions, representing nearly 500 million people. But other differences are no less salient. The American convention met secretly behind closed doors and remained leak free even after the early departure of a handful of dissident delegates who could have exposed the constitutional coup under way. The European convention has not only enjoyed regular press coverage and a Web site publishing the various drafts and protocols; it has also actively collaborated with a wide variety of nongovernmental organizations, highly mobilized interest groups reflecting a modern pluralism that James Madison, in his most expansive moments, never envisioned. Their inputs are all too well represented in the litany of social rights and nobly vacuous statements of ideals that the proposed constitution endorses. And then there is the ongoing debate as to whether a Europe that is far more secular than the United States and that is uneasily absorbing significant numbers of Muslim immigrants should constitutionally acknowledge its Christian heritage.

Of course, were the United States lucky enough to hold another constitutional convention today—say to eliminate a zany institution like the Electoral College or to redress the injustice of giving an equal number of senators to California and Idaho or to limit justices of the Supreme Court to 12-year terms (sensible reforms all)—its procedures and politics might well be similar. But the deeper difference between the elegant American process of the 1780s and the diffuse European labors of today ultimately rests on the fundamental ambiguity of the nature of the proposed constitution and of contemporary European constitutionalism more generally.

TREATY OR CONSTITUTION?

The Convention on the Future of Europe was conceived both as a means of rationalizing, redacting, and (to some extent) superceding the past treaties that have been the instruments of European integration, and of further defining and refining the "competences" and the institutions of the EU. Though the ambition of promoting a genuine constitution for Europe has a laudable ring to it, the reality still seems far more prosaic. Can a set of institutional arrangements that ultimately depends on negotiations among member states ever form a constitution in the robust sense? Can a constitutional treaty ever become more constitution than treaty?

For what remains most difficult to conjure is the political identity of the new entity that Eurofederalists contemplate creating. Critics charge that this new community's political vision is indelibly elitist, bureaucratic, and technocratic and that the new Europe being fashioned will never mobilize the patriotic affections of the citizens whose lives it will regulate. There is little in the draft constitution to alter this view.

Perhaps it would be otherwise if the member states could acquire the confidence to submit the final version of the constitution to a general referendum, rather than resort to a potpourri of procedures in which some states will act legislatively while others allow the people to vote. Admittedly, a 1787-style exercise in popular sovereignty presents real problem (even though most European countries have significantly more experience in this regard than the Americans had). Referenda are, in fact, proscribed in Germany, which is to the EU what Virginia was to the early American union. And in Britain it is the Europhobic Tories who clamor for a referendum, confident that a visceral Anglo-nationalism will send the constitution to defeat with the same esprit with which *Sun* readers roared "Up Yours Delors" at Jacques Delors, the then President of the European Commission.

Nor is Britain the only nation where one can imagine a populist reaction rejecting the federalist vision. In Ireland, a referendum is legally required, but it took the Irish two tries to approve the last major exercise of this kind, the Treaty of Nice, and even then with surprisingly low turnouts both times. In Denmark, where it also took two referenda to ratify the Treaty of Maastricht a decade ago, a popular vote will also be held. For Eurofederalists, there is a cautionary lesson to be found here, one that suggests the discretion of continued intergovernmental negotiations might be preferable to the valor of popular approval. Yet as the German daily *Frankfurter Allgemeine Zeitung* editorialized last October, "As long as the leading politicians fail to bring Europe closer to its people, Irish and Danish referendums will be almost indispensable."

If there is indeed a lesson for today from the experience of 1787, it is that political ambitions of this magnitude require risk taking. If a genuine constitution of peoples as well as nations is what is desired, as Giscard has promised, a continual series of negotiated treaties will never suffice. Popular interest in the European Parliament remains tepid, as measured either by participation in elections or coverage in the media. The creation of a permanent presidency for the council as well as a foreign minister will doubtless have important implications for policymaking and coordination among the council, commission, and parliament, but the political ramifications of these new positions remain similarly problematic. This is a president for the governments who are linked through the council, not for the peoples they represent.

One could have said something similar about the presidency that the American framers designed at Philadelphia in 1787. By and large, they lacked any coherent conception of its political potentiality. Most of them assumed that the Electoral College system they cobbled together at the last moment would rarely work and that the House of Representatives would typically elect presidents. They had high hopes for the presidency's first likely occupant, George Washington, but few if any plausible expectations for his successors. Yet as soon as the first contested election for the presidency occurred in 1796, competition to control this one office became the principal mechanism for integrating Americans into a single coordinated polity. The new presidency of the council simply cannot serve the same function— unless, that is, its first incumbents discover some means to give their position genuine political stature within Europe.

Absent that sort of political transformation, European constitutionalism seems destined to develop along decidedly non-American lines, not by constitutional *coups de main,* but incrementally, as the product of arrangements and accommodations evolving within the complex institutional structure the convention inherited and only ramified. As the Italian political theorist Pasquale Pasquino likes to suggest, the real constitution Europe is developing is closer to a British model, not in form or structure, of course, but as the product of experience, precedent setting, and the development of new habits of doing business. The changes proposed by Giscard's convention and the revisions to emanate from the intergovernmental conference by next spring will push the process forward, but not in the dramatic and bold way that Madison, Hamilton, and their coadjutors seized the main chance in 1787.

A TRANS-ATLANTIC MIXED BLESSING

Does this difference in character make the European project somehow inferior to its American counterpart, or does it expose yet another fault line in the much-remarked divergence between Europe and the United States?

The underlying differences between the revolutionary condition of the Americans in the 1780s and the situation of contemporary Europe work against any serious effort to answer the first question. American constitutionalism was thoroughly revolutionary in its origins and ambitions: revolutionary in its rejection of British authority in 1776, revolutionary in its willingness to establish republican governments in the individual states, and still self-consciously revolutionary when the framers tried to apply the lessons learned since independence to the problem of national government. European enthusiasm for revolution ended conclusively in 1989, exactly two centuries after its Parisian birth. Moreover, the project of European integration has always been more an exercise in improving coordination than in achieving genuine political integration. The rhetorical appeal of calling this latest step in the process a constitution has only modified, not altered, its essential gradualist character.

Will this difference in constitutional development affect the potential divergence of Europe and the United States? At least one noteworthy feature of Europe's proposed constitution does favor greater convergence. The European Charter of Fundamental Rights, previously a freestanding document, is now incorporated within the constitutional text. Its inclusion will greatly facilitate its enforcement by European judges, a process already under way. Europeans may still have a hard time grasping the nuances of the American separation of powers, but the one aspect of the American constitutional system they probably understand best is the practice of judicial review. There would be some irony in seeing European judicial power deployed as a force for integration at a moment when the "new federalism" of the Supreme Court is nudging American doctrine in the opposite direction. Even so, the idea of judicial power as a centralizing mechanism is one Americans can readily appreciate.

But in the American case, the judiciary eventually came to play this role because quarrels over the proper meaning and interpretation of the Constitution almost immediately began to accompany every major political dispute and decision the new government faced. For Americans, the flourishing of rival modes and canons of constitutional interpretation simply became (to borrow a dictum from Karl von Clausewitz) the continuation of politics by other means. A full 21 decades after Hamilton and Madison first laid out the cases for and against an expansive interpretation of presidential authority in foreign affairs in their "Pacificus" and "Helvidius" letters of 1793, it is still possible to replay their arguments and see how well each applies to the brave new world we have inhabited these past two years.

Hamilton and Madison could have that argument because the consolidation of national authority over foreign relations had been both a principal inspiration and undisputed outcome of the constitutional deliberations of 1787. No such consolidation is proposed in the European constitution or about to be conceded by the majority of the EU member states. The designation of a new foreign minister may be a glimmer in the eye of a future genuinely European foreign policy, but at this point it is only that, nothing more. Absent any genuine consensus on the possibility of a truly European foreign policy, it is difficult to see how the current constitutionalist project will make any material difference, for good or ill, in the current strained state of European-American relations. Next to the other sources of tension between Europe and the United States—over foreign policy and military interventions, attitudes toward work and leisure even the appropriate hour when a latte or cappuccino may be taken—the notion that differences in constitutional philosophy will deepen the current estrangement seems far-fetched.

International Law: The Trials of Global Norms

■ STEVEN R. RATNER

The move from describing the world to prescribing for it forms the core of international law. Can those committing human rights atrocities—war criminals from Bosnia or political leaders from Cambodia—be tried in foreign courts or before international tribunals? How can members of the United Nations ensure respect for the decisions of its Security Council? What is the best way to regulate transnational environmental hazards such as greenhouse gas emissions or ocean dumping? Can the United States allow its citizens to sue European companies for their use of land and factories confiscated by the Cuban government from Americans more than a generation ago?

All these questions turn on political decisions by states—but what international lawyers see and seek in such scenarios is a process whose actions are informed and influenced by principles of law, not just raw power. For international lawyers, devising and enforcing universal rules of conduct for states means overcoming two cardinal challenges: how to make such precepts legitimate in a diverse community of nations; and how to make them stick in the absence of any one sovereign authority or supranational enforcement mechanism. . . .

Today, the end of the Cold War has loosened many of the blockages to international lawmaking and implementation. Although legal scholars still ask what states can do on their own—pass extraterritorial laws, use force, or prosecute war criminals—they do so assuming that coordinated action is now more feasible than in the past. Global and regional treaties such as the Chemical Weapons Convention, the Convention on the Prohibition of Anti-Personnel Mines, the Maastricht Treaty, and the North American Free Trade Agreement now serve as the starting point for scrutinizing state behavior according to some objective standard.

The ground seems ready then for an acceleration of this century's great trend in international law: the increasing international regulation of more and more issues once typically seen as part of state domestic jurisdiction. But any attempt to create the lofty, supranational legal edifice idealized by some of the field's practitioners and scholars promises to be problematic at best. Once paralyzed by the deadlock between East and West, and between North and South, the international legal system must now contend not just with the challenge of persuading new states such as Belarus or Croatia to comply with established norms but of coping with Somalia and other failed states, whose circumstances make a mockery of international rules. International law must seek to embrace a growing range of forms, topics, and technologies, as well as a host of new actors. And as it moves further away from strictly "foreign" concerns—the treatment of diplomats or ships on the seas—to traditionally domestic areas—environmental or labor standards—its proponents must increasingly confront new obstacles head-on.

NEW REALITIES, NEW IDEAS

This new global context surrounding the field has led to at least four fundamental shifts in the kinds of issues that legal scholars now talk about and study.

New Forms, New Players

Traditionally, most rules of international law could be found in one of two places: treaties—binding, written agreements between states; or customary law—uncodified, but equally binding rules based on longstanding behavior that states accept as compulsory. The strategic arms reduction treaties requiring the United States and Russia to cut their nuclear weapons arsenals offer examples of the former; the rule that governments cannot be sued in the courts of another state for most of their public acts provides an example of the latter. Historically, treaties have gradually displaced much customary law, as international rules have become increasingly codified.

But as new domains from the environment to the Internet come to be seen as appropriate for international regulation, states are sometimes reluctant to embrace any sort of binding rule. In the past, many legal scholars and international courts simply accepted the notion that no law governed a particular subject until a new treaty was concluded or states signaled their consent to a new customary-law rule (witness the reluctance with which human rights norms were considered law prior to the UN's two key treaties in 1966) or, alternatively, struggled to find customary law where none existed. However, today all but the most doctrinaire of scholars see a role for so-called soft law—precepts emanating from international bodies that conform in some sense to expectations of required behavior but that are not binding on states.

For example, in 1992 the World Bank completed a set of Guidelines on the Treatment of Foreign Direct Investment. Though these are not binding on any bank member, states and corporations invoke them as the standard for how developing nations should treat foreign capital to encourage investment. This soft law enables states to adjust to the regulation of many new areas of international concern without fearing a violation (and possible legal countermeasures) if they fail to comply. Normative expectations are built more quickly than they would through the evolution of a customary-law rule, and more gently than if a new treaty rule were foisted on states. Soft law principles also represent a starting point for new hard law, which attaches a penalty to noncompliance. In this case, the bank's guidelines have served as the basis for the negotiation of a new treaty—the Multilateral Agreement on Investment (MAI)—by the Organization for Economic Cooperation and Development (OECD). The MAI gives foreign investors the right to take any government to international arbitration for compensation when a law or state practice limits their freedom to invest or divest.

Whether in the case of hard or soft law, new participants are making increased demands for representation in international bodies, conferences, and other legal groupings and processes. They include substate entities, both those recognized in some way by the international community (Chechnya, Hong Kong) and those not (Tibet, Kashmir); nongovernmental organizations (NGOs); and corporations. Claiming that the states to which they belong do not always adequately represent their interests, these nonstate actors demand a say in the content of new norms. Some have faced staunch opposition to their participation in decision making: In 1995, China's government relegated NGOs to a distant venue during the UN's Fourth World Conference on Women in Beijing.

But other groups may succeed even as far as effectively taking over an official delegation. For example, U.S. telecommunications companies such as Motorola have seemed almost to dictate U.S. positions in the International Telecommunication Union (ITU), the UN agency responsible for setting global telecommunications standards. At the ITU's 1992 conference on allocating the radio spectrum for new technologies, Motorola's stake in protecting its plans for new satellites became a paramount U.S. interest, resulting in a sizeable Motorola team attending as part of the U.S. delegation. Other corporations have acted outside government channels entirely by promulgating private codes: In response to public pressure, Nike issued a set of self-imposed rules to protect worker rights in the developing world. It is not that states are no longer the primary makers of international law. But . . . these other actors have independent views—and the resources to push them—that do not fit neatly into traditional theories of how law is made and enforced.

New Enforcement Strategies

Most states comply with much, even most, international law almost continually—whether the law of the sea, diplomatic immunity, or civil aviation rules. But without mechanisms to bring transgressors into line, international law will be "law" in name only. This state of affairs, when it occurs, is ignored by too many lawyers, who delight in large bodies of rules but often discount patterns of noncompliance. For example, Western governments, and many scholars, insisted throughout the 1960s and 1970s that when nationalizing foreign property, developing states were legally bound to compensate former owners for the full economic value, despite those states' repeated refusals to pay such huge sums.

The traditional toolbox to secure compliance with the law of nations consists of negotiations, mediation, countermeasures (reciprocal action against the violator), or, in rare cases, recourse to supranational judicial bodies such as the International Court of Justice. (The last of these was the linchpin of the world of law that Americans such as Andrew Carnegie and Elihu Root sought to bring into being.) For many years, these tools have been supplemented by the work of international institutions, whose reports and resolutions often help "mobilize shame" against violators. But today, states, NGOs, and private entities, aided by their lawyers, have striven for sanctions with more teeth. They have galvanized the UN Security Council to issue economic sanctions against Iraq, Haiti, Libya, Serbia, Sudan, and other nations refusing to comply with UN resolutions.

On the free-trade front, the dispute settlement panels in the World Trade Organization (WTO) now have the legal authority to issue binding rulings that allow the victor in a trade dispute to impose specific tariffs on the loser. . . . And the UN's ad hoc criminal tribunals for the former Yugoslavia and Rwanda show that it is at least possible to devise institutions to punish individuals for human rights atrocities. Nonetheless, as the impunity to date of former Bosnian Serb president Radovan Karadzic and General Ratko Mladic reveals, the success of these enforcement mechanisms depends on the willingness of states to support them: legalism meets realism. . . .

Increasingly, domestic courts provide an additional venue to enforce international law. In Spain, for example, Judge Manuel García Castellóni of the National Court has agreed to hear a controversial human rights case involving charges against Chile's former dictator, General Augusto Pinochet. Meanwhile, Castellóni's colleague, Judge Baltasar Garzón, hears testimony against those responsible for the "Dirty War" of the 1970s in Argentina. (Spain is asserting jurisdiction in both cases because its nationals were among the thousands of victims tortured and killed.) And though Karadzic remains at large, he has been sued in U.S. federal court under the Alien Tort Claims Act, which allows foreign nationals recovery against Karadzic for the rape and torture of civilians during his "ethnic cleansing" campaign in the former Yugoslavia. At a minimum, this provides a symbolic measure of solace for his victims.

The Legitimacy Problem

Even as scholars seek to devise better enforcement mechanisms, a serious debate is brewing about the legitimacy of such measures. As international organizations are freed up to take more actions by the end of the East-West conflict and the tempering of North-South tensions, the United States and its like-minded allies seem well positioned to impose their agenda on all. Legal scholars question whether Western dominance of the Organization for Security and Cooperation in Europe, UN, WTO, and other international institutions is not merely raw power asserting its muscle again, albeit through multilateral bodies, to the detriment of a genuine rule of law. That this debate is more than academic can be seen vividly in the ongoing discussion about reforming the Security Council. Many Americans may laud the council's new muscle—during the last five years, it has slapped a debilitating embargo and weapons inspection regime on Iraq, prohibited air traffic with Libya due to its sanctuary for those accused of the Pan Am 103 bombing, and approved a U.S.-led occupation of Haiti. But smaller states feel threatened by a Security Council in which the West is often able to convince enough states to approve such council actions, and only a Chinese veto (which was used only once in the last 25 years) seems to protect them. . . .

Focusing on enforcement and legitimacy also provides a useful lens through which to evaluate U.S. reactions to international norms: Even as the United States seeks to strengthen the enforcement of international law for its own ends, it has often recoiled at the prospect that these norms might be enforced against it. In the WTO, the very dispute resolution panels that the United States hopes to use to force open closed markets could order it to choose between environmental protection laws (such as those banning imports of tuna caught in nets that kill dolphins) and the prospects of retaliatory sanctions if those laws have incidental discriminatory effects on trade. In such a scenario, international law, as interpreted by the WTO, becomes the friend of business and bugaboo of environmentalists. But when the UN seeks to promulgate environmental law, as it has with the proposed greenhouse gas convention just concluded at Kyoto, then the tables are turned.

Similarly, the United States wants to use the Security Council to keep in place a comprehensive sanctions regime on Iraq that has the diplomatic appeal of being "international" rather than "U.S.-imposed," all the while holding back on paying its dues because not all UN programs conform to Washington's wishes. As the world's sole superpower, the United States can defy international standards with little fear of immediate sanction; but other states will begin to question its motives in trying to strengthen important legal regimes such as those covering nuclear and chemical nonproliferation.

New Linkages

The notion of hermetically sealed areas of international law—each a nice chapter in a treatise—is increasingly anachronistic. Environmental and trade law can no longer be discussed separately as the tuna-dolphin example shows; and when private investors have to reckon with serious abuses by local governments, foreign investment law cannot be examined without some consideration of human rights and labor law. The result is a new breed of scholarship linking previously distinct subjects and the realization among some practitioners that overspecialization leads to myopic lawyering.

Moreover, beyond the legal field, international lawyers must address the two-way interaction between international law and broader sociological and cultural trends in society. In one notable example, the debate on a clash of cultures involving so-called Asian values has forced students of human rights to stand back and consider whether rights granted in human rights treaties mean the same thing in all states. Can Singapore suppress free speech for the goal of national unity and development, especially if it claims that its culture sees uninhibited political speech as less than a birthright? Of course, cultural assertions tend to be overly broad, and many human rights activists interpret these claims as excuses for authoritarianism; the arguments, however, can no longer be ignored, and black and white rules of treaty interpretation will not help much.

In the other direction, the proliferation of new norms has direct effects on debates over globalization—the "Jihad versus McWorld" controversy. A global treaty on ozone or greenhouse gases, for instance, will clearly accommodate different perspectives on the priority of environmental protection versus development, but once adopted it cannot tolerate violations in the name of "diversity." Indeed, almost by definition, the decision by states to subject a once strictly domestic concern to international regulation means that cultural, value-based, or "sovereignty" arguments no longer enjoy the upper hand. If a state elects not to sign a major treaty, or ignores one it has assigned—as with the United States and the agreement on the elimination of landmines or Iraq and the one on nuclear nonproliferation—it is more likely to be condemned as a pariah than admired for its rugged individualism.